WITHDRAWN

(Continued on Inside Back Cover)

SEVENTH EDITION

42.00
75D

Introduction to the Foundations of American Education

James A. Johnson
Northern Illinois University

Harold W. Collins
Northern Illinois University

Victor L. Dupuis
Pennsylvania State University

John H. Johansen
Northern Illinois University

ALLYN AND BACON, INC.
Boston   London   Sydney   Toronto

Photo Credits
Part I, Read D. Brugger/The Picture Cube; Part II, Larry C. Morris/NYT Pictures; Part III, Fredrik D.
Bodin/Stock, Boston; Part IV, P. Price/The Picture Cube; Part V, David S. Strickler/The Picture Cube;
Part VI, Stuart Spates; Part VII, Janice Fullman/The Picture Cube. Chapter 17: "A Day in the Life of
A Teacher," Gordon Means/Northern Illinois University.

Managing Editor: Mylan Jaixen
Series Editor: Susanne F. Canavan
Associate Developmental Editor: Elizabeth Brooks
Production Coordinator: Annette Joseph
Editorial-Production Service: Woodstock Publishers' Services
Cover Administrator: Linda K. Dickinson
Cover Designer: Movidea Studio

Library of Congress Cataloging-in-Publication Data

Introduction to the foundations of American education.

   Includes bibliographies and indexes.
   1. Education—United States. 2. Educational
sociology—United States. I. Johnson, James Allen.
LA212.I57 1988   370'.973   87–19303
ISBN 0–205–11079–7

Printed in the United States of America

10 9 8 7 6 5 4 3   92 91 90 89 88

Brief Contents

Contents

Preface

The basis of professional education for prospective teachers is resident in the careful study of the foundations of education. From such study future teachers will learn to appreciate the proud heritage of the teaching profession and will be able to develop their personal philosophies of education to guide their classroom practices. Future teachers will also be enlightened about the school's responsibilities to society and will be able to form an understanding of school administration and curricula.

The seventh edition of this text is a detailed overview of the foundations of American education. Information in the book is extensive, current, and given in response to the opinions solicited from several users in the academic communities. This edition is organized into seven parts:

Professional aspects of teaching
School and society
Control, organization, and support of American education
Historical foundations of education
Philosophical concepts, educational views, and teaching styles
Program design, experiences, and instructional practices
American education and the future

In our efforts to ensure that this text remain a benchmark for the foundations course, we were guided by extensive reviews provided by practicing field professionals, our students, and the consultants and editorial staff of Allyn and Bacon. The research and information base for the content of this revision of the text was drawn from these references.

New features include an added chapter on the status of educational reform, with special attention devoted to clinical experiences and other national report recommendations. Extended coverage is given to students' and teachers' rights and responsibilities to include recent controversial matters such as child abuse and neglect, AIDS, book banning, and discrimination. A different conceptual approach is taken in the chapter dealing with social problems affecting the school. Focus is directed toward the aspects of alienated youths and their problems and the demographic dimensions of society. In the discussion of control and organization, chapter summary statements are used to clarify governance of education, use of public funds for parochial education, and affirmative action. Emphasis is placed on teacher evaluation and leadership with regard to the administration of our schools. The possible effects of educational reform on school financing are introduced.

Treatment of recent developments in education is extended to include new emphasis in education and analysis of teaching. The entire philosophy section has been reordered and revised to illustrate the evolvement of preferred teaching styles from the classical philosophies translated to current educational views. An analytical tool for the analysis of teaching styles is presented to provide prospective teachers with a practical means of relating philosophical systems of thought to classroom management and discipline maintenance. State-of-the-art uses of technology for the delivery of instruction in the classroom is well developed in the curriculum presentation. This edition is closed with a consolidated chapter on futurism and selected societal trends. The chapter on futurism and future society and the chapter on schools and the future in the previous edition were combined and reconstructed to emphasize and illustrate the applications of futurism to six societal issues: changing family, children in poverty, diversity of population, school clinics, technology, and business-education partnerships.

In addition to the continued presentation of the educational issues which are discussed and indexed throughout the text, each chapter has new professional perspective statements intended to guide prospective teachers in their application of the content presented. Other chapter support questions and activities of the previous edition are retained. The text glossary has been edited and expanded to correspond with this edition.

The companion Instructor's manual, *Resource Booklet and Overhead Transparency Masters,* serves as a teaching aid for the instructor of foundations courses. The IM is composed of materials which are correlated with the text content and format. Included are overhead transparencies, student assignment sheets, enrichment handouts (new in this edition), and test items with answer keys which are page-referenced to the text.

The active professional experiences of the authors lend to the interpretations and extrapolations of the data in relation to the real worlds of both private and public education in the United States. In addition to the teaching and administrative assignments at their respective universities, the authors serve on state and national educational policy boards; serve as consultants to many school districts and universities; write and speak at local, state, and national meetings; work with school board associations and local boards in selecting personnel; advise and counsel several American Indian tribes; and serve as references for educators at all levels. We are indebted to the many people throughout the United States who have used previous editions and who provided suggestions and materials for this edition. In particular, we are grateful to the following persons:

Don Barnes
Ball State University

Paul Burden
Kansas State University

Lloyd Duck
George Mason University

Dwight Hare
Northeast Louisiana University

H.C. Hudgins
*The University of North
Carolina—Greensboro*

Dorothy Huenecke
Georgia State University

Robert Kinderman
Kutztown University

Mary Beth Lake
Normandale Community College

William Matthias
Southern Illinois University

Randy Steinheimer
*Aurora West School District #129
Aurora, Ill.*

Jack Stirton
San Joaquin Delta College

Eugene Sullivan
The University of Michigan—Flint

James Thorne
Grove City College

PART I

Professional Aspects of Teaching

Increasing numbers of talented college students are selecting teaching as a career throughout the United States. As the job market and salaries continue to improve for prospective teachers in the late 1980s, the number of college students selecting teacher preparation programs is expected to rise even more. In choosing a career, the thoughtful undergraduate must consider all aspects of the working conditions associated with a particular area of employment. Students weighing careers in teaching should seek information about what the average teacher is like, criticisms and expectations about teachers, teacher supply and demand, teacher salaries, legal aspects of teaching, teacher and student rights, professional liability, and teacher organizations. The first part of the book discusses many of these important professional questions.

We do not suggest that teaching is an appropriate career for everyone. For those who possess the prerequisite commitment to education, adequate personal and social skills, and the basic ability to develop the technical skills, a teaching career is an excellent choice. Teaching provides an opportunity to work with other college-educated persons, each committed to educating young people.

While elementary and secondary public school enrollments have dropped considerably in the past decade, the whole of education represents one of the largest enterprises in the United States. According to estimates provided by the Department of Education's National Center for Education Statistics, education is now the primary activity of about 61 million Americans. Included in that total are approximately 58 million students estimated to be enrolled in classes from kindergarten through graduate school.

The entire field of education continues to be one of the largest employment fields in the United States. In addition to the 3.3 million classroom teachers, about 300,000 other educators serve as superintendents, principals, supervisors, and other instructional staff members. When the noncertified support staff of secretaries, custodians, bus drivers, cafeteria employees, maintenance personnel, and others employed directly by the school are included, the total number of employees rises considerably.

Teachers represent the foundation of the educational system. While prospects for employment are excellent, considerations related to salary and fringe benefits, the legal aspects of teaching, and membership in teacher organizations should also be reviewed carefully when one considers teaching as a profession. For example, the impact of inflation—particularly in the cost of such necessities as fuel, food, housing, and medical care—should be carefully weighed against salary.

A host of recent reports and studies produced by various agencies, commissions, and foundations focus on the status of education in America. Several reports suggest that not enough academically able students are being attracted to teaching and that teacher preparation programs need substantial improvement. The impact of these reports will also be reviewed in this section of the book.

Classroom teachers are affected in varying degrees by the interest and controversy sparked by court decisions. Some teacher-related issues involve the personal lifestyles of teachers, pupil rights, and community issues. In some situations the emotions associated with such court decisions relate directly back to classroom practices and beliefs utilized by teachers.

Teachers continue to improve their benefits through membership in national, state, and local teacher unions. Since the views expressed by the Holmes Group and the Carnegie Report call for increased attention to more rigorous academic programs, classroom teachers also depend on memberships in other professional organizations which are identified with their respective teaching assignments for current views and practices to incorporate into their teaching styles.

We believe that this first part of the book will provide college students with an excellent introduction to the professional aspects of teaching. This information should answer most questions about the advantages and disadvantages of a teaching career. Most importantly, these first five chapters should help you decide whether you want to be a teacher. ■

1

Teaching as a Career

Focus Questions

- Why do you want to be a teacher?
- What do you think the average citizen thinks about our schools today?
- How important do you believe teachers are in our society? Why?
- What are the characteristics of the best teachers you ever had?
- How would you rate American teachers as a group?

Key Terms and Concepts

Teaching career
Educated citizenry
Information age
National economy
Public school teacher

Public confidence
Job opportunities
Teacher salaries
Teacher self-concept
Class size

What Would You Do?

A friend of yours states that American schools and American teachers are generally lousy. What is your opinion?

As you begin your first year of teaching, you find that parents and educators in your community expect increased discipline, higher standards for students, and more homework. At the same time, your school is an open school. Many of the parents have few years of formal schooling, and the school philosophy has been to assign homework that can be completed during the day at school. How would you plan your teaching assignments to cope with these conflicting views?

This chapter attempts to help you learn more about a career in teaching. It has been written with the assumption that some of you are not yet sure you wish to be a teacher, and others have firmly decided on a teaching career. This chapter, as well as the entire book, should be useful to both types of readers.

The Importance of Teachers in a Democracy

Teaching is one of the most important careers in any democratic society. In fact, a democracy is totally dependent upon an educated citizenry that is well informed about the many political issues which must be resolved by a democratic society. Furthermore, people in a democracy must feel that voting and participating in other ways in the democratic process are important—an attitude that must somehow be learned. Our nation looks to our teachers to provide the education essential to sustaining our democratic society.

To Our Children

It has often been said that our nation's most important natural resource is our children. Also, nearly all parents feel that a good education is essential for their children. Children must learn the basics, but they also must be cultured, nurtured, and inspired. Each must be allowed to learn at her or his own pace, but all must be challenged—and accomplishing both tasks is extremely difficult because no two children are alike.

Parents, legislators, and our society in general feel that education is essential for our nation's children. Teachers are asked to carry most of the responsibility for providing this high-quality education. Perhaps the following letter (p. 5) from a parent to her child's teacher best explains how very important teachers are to our children.

In the Information Age

Each year our society becomes more complex. In fact, we now live in what is often called an "information age" where knowledge has been expanded to the point at which managing the huge amount of available information is one of our largest problems. Almost all fields of human endeavor have progressed so that knowledge in each field of study is expanding geometrically.

This rapid expansion of knowledge has required that citizens become "information managers." And who does our society expect to provide the education needed by our youth to function as "information managers"? If your answer is "teachers," you are absolutely correct.

AN OPEN LETTER TO MY CHILD'S TEACHER

When I found out that my child would be in your room this year, I "checked you out" with parents of your previous students. I wanted to know if you were a "good teacher"; if you were fair; if you were fun to be with in class; if you challenged the students but not so as to frustrate them. Then I began to wonder if you had checked out my child with his previous teachers. Was he a "good student"? Was he fair? Was he fun to have in class? Was he a challenge yet not a frustration?

I guess the best thing to do is to let my child and you develop your own kind of working, sharing relationship. You are not perfect, nor is my child.

I realize that the ultimate responsibility of raising this child is mine, but I wonder if you will share this responsibility with me. You are a major factor in stimulating my child's desire to learn and encouraging him to develop his intellectual capacities to their fullest.

I also realize that my child has a responsibility to you, to me, and to himself to make the most of the opportunities and challenges this school year will represent.

My child is very special to me. And because you are my child's teacher— you are very special too.

Linda Kispert
Valrico, Florida

Source: This letter was reprinted in *Today's Education 1986–87* by the National Education Association. Linda Kispert is a PTA board member at Buckhorn Elementary in Valrico, a Tampa suburb. Used by permission.

To Our Nation's Economy

Teachers play an extremely important role in our nation's economy in at least two major ways. It is well established that better-educated people earn more money during their lifetime. Figure 1.1 illustrates this phenomenon, showing annual family income by education level of the household head. The average income for a family headed by an elementary school–educated person is only $15,000, for a family headed by a high school graduate, $27,000, for a family headed by a college graduate the figure jumps to $43,000. So teachers help our nation's economy by providing the education that enables individuals to earn much higher salaries.

Teachers also contribute to the economy by providing the educated workers for our nation's businesses. Needless to say, the American industrial complex simply could not function without a constant supply of workers who possess good basic skills. Interestingly, some states have recently increased their financial support of schools as a catalyst for the development of high-tech industry.

Every day, in many ways, we see evidence that teachers serve an extremely important function in our society.

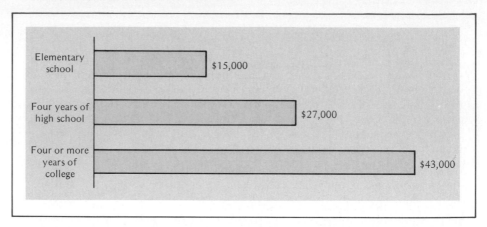

FIGURE 1.1   *Annual Family Income by Education Level* (*Source:* Census Bureau)

Profile of the Public School Teacher

There are over 2 million public school teachers in the United States. Slightly over one-half of them teach at the elementary school level. Besides our large number of public school teachers, there are an additional 350,000 private school teachers and about 750,000 college and university teachers in the United States. Added to this total are over 800,000 other administrative and professional staff. It is also estimated that there are over a million education-related jobs in the United States; including such positions as education specialists in industry, instructional technologists in the military, museum educators, and training consultants in the business world.

Thus altogether, we have roughly 5 million educators in the country. Education is one of the largest professions in the United States. It is estimated, however, that about 6 percent of our teachers leave the classroom each year for various reasons (retirement, resignations, poor health, etc.). So roughly 300,000 new educators are needed just to replace those leaving the profession each year.

The Typical American Teacher

A recent national educator opinion poll conducted by the Educational Research Service helps to paint a composite picture of American teachers. They found that the majority of teachers are female.

The average age of all teachers is 39.7 years. The typical teacher has worked in the same school district for 11.9 years and has been a teacher for an average of 14.3 years. Most teachers belong to the National Education Association and to state and local teacher organizations. Most are covered by collective bargaining agreements.

For working an average of 184 days a year and spending about 8 hours each day at school, teachers earn an average of $23,325. Most believe that, taking into consideration academic preparation, teaching experience, and responsibilities,

The typical American teacher is female, with an average age of 39.7 years. She has been a teacher for an average of 14.3 years, and earns an average salary of $23,325. (*Source:* Rick Friedman/The Picture Cube)

the salary level is not appropriate and that teachers should earn an average of $30,000 per year. Most did not anticipate earning any merit pay.

Paperwork, concern about salary, and lack of concern or support from parents rank among the biggest problems facing teachers. From a more positive standpoint, most agree that the recognition of student achievements, the willingness of the principal to discuss problems with teachers, and the clear communication of school rules to students are characteristic of their schools. They are less likely to view their students as being interested in academics and learning or parents as either supportive of school rules or involved in the educational process.

The teachers support basic goals of education such as the command of basic skills that were developed over sixty-five years ago and reaffirmed by another group of teachers in 1966. Most of them have mixed feelings about the quality of professional development opportunities available in their school districts and specify the "use of computers" as the area in which they feel the greatest need

15

for professional development. About half of them *used* computers in their teaching at least a few times. Most teachers report that they do not have a major problem with such discipline infractions as extreme verbal abuse, physical attacks, theft, or damage to personal property in their classrooms.

The average class size reported by teachers is 24 students. When teachers were asked about the class size in which they could do the best possible job of teaching, the average was 20 students. Most teachers do not have a teacher aide available to them on a regular basis. Most are evaluated by their principals and consider the evaluations to be helpful. They view the current evaluation system as an administrative function in which teachers are not formally involved. Although they prefer that it remain an administrative responsibility, the teachers would like to see increased peer involvement.

Most teachers would recommend teaching as a profession (although with major reservations) to young persons who expressed interest. Most teachers consider teaching their career and intend to teach as long as they can.

Portraits of typical teachers at different grade levels also emerge from this survey. The majority of elementary school teachers are female. The average age of all elementary school teachers is 40.2 years, and the average teacher has 14.2 years total teaching experience. The average salary is $22,656. The average class size for these teachers is 24 pupils, although they would prefer a class size of 20. These elementary school teachers are working in schools with an average enrollment of 505 students. They are likely to use computers in relation to their teaching responsibilities, primarily to provide supplemental instruction for all their students. Too much paperwork, insufficient time for class preparation, and inadequate salary are their three most serious problems.

The majority of intermediate-level teachers are also female. The average age is 38.7 years, and they have an average of 13.7 years teaching experience. The average salary is $23,096. These teachers are working in schools with an average enrollment of 753 students. Intermediate-level teachers consider inadequate salary, lack of concern and support from parents, and too much paperwork as the major obstacles to their teaching performance.

The majority of high school teachers are male. The average age is 39.9 years, with 14.9 years teaching experience. The average salary is $24,203. These teachers are working in schools with an average enrollment of 1,282 students. They are working in a departmentalized setting and have an average class size of 24 students. These teachers feel that they could do their best job teaching with an average class size of 20. They are likely to work without the assistance of teacher aides. Inadequate salary, too much paperwork, and inadequate preparation of students for grade-level work are ranked highest among the problems of senior high school teachers.

Teachers' Pet Peeves

Like any professionals, teachers have a number of complaints about their work. These complaints vary from teacher to teacher and from job to job; however, a composite list of teacher complaints should help a college student understand

**Professional
Perspectives**

Don't become a teacher unless you enjoy working with young people, like academic endeavors, and honestly believe you have the basic skills needed to be an excellent teacher.

the potential frustrations of a teaching career. A recent survey by the Educational Research Service revealed the following list of teacher complaints:

Too much paperwork	47.4%
Lack of concern or support from parents	40.8%
Low salary level	38.3%
Too many students per class	38.1%
Inadequate preparation of students for grade level	36.3%
Insufficient time for class	34.2%
Classroom discipline problems	31%
Mix of student abilities too broad	29%
Lack of leadership or support from school board	26.3%
Lack of community support	25.3%

12

In this same study only about 2 percent of the teachers were concerned about violence in the schools (a topic that much has been written about), and only 6.2 percent were concerned about losing their jobs.

The Improving Status of American Teachers

It is difficult to generalize about the status of American teachers. Everyone can remember teachers they had who were not effective. And nearly every parent has been unhappy with certain teachers their children have had. Even so, teachers have generally been respected in our society.

Increased Public Confidence

There is evidence that the American public has a good deal of confidence in their public schools and in teachers. The 1986 Gallup Poll of the Public's Attitudes Toward the Public Schools shows that people generally think highly of their local schools. This information, presented in Table 1.1, also shows that people generally grade our nation's schools lower than they do their own local schools. This result may be due to the tendency of the media to dwell on the problems of schools more than the successes, which may cause the public to feel that schools generally must be worse than the local schools with which they are familiar. So generally speaking, the public has considerable confidence in our public schools and in our teachers. It is also worth noting that the public's

2

TABLE 1.1   *Public's Grading of Schools, 1986*

School Description	A and B	A	B	C	D	F	Don't Know
				Grade Assigned			
Public schools nationally	28%	3%	25%	41%	10%	5%	16%
My oldest child's school	65%	28%	37%	26%	4%	2%	3%

Source: Alec M. Gallup, "The 18th Annual Gallup Poll of the Public's Attitude Toward the Public Schools," *Phi Delta Kappan,* September 1986, 43–59.

attitude toward our schools has steadily been improving over the past ten years. These facts should be encouraging to young people contemplating teaching careers.

Improving Job Opportunities and Teacher Salaries

An entire chapter is devoted to teacher supply and demand and salaries later in this part of the book; however, some information on these topics will be presented at this time to support a contention. The "contention" is that job opportunities and salaries for teachers have improved significantly in recent years. So much so, in fact, that this phenomenon has improved the status of American teachers.

The United States is in the grips of a mounting teacher shortage. The National Center for Education Statistics estimates that by 1993 we will need 1.65 million new teachers, but our colleges will produce only 1.25 million, resulting in a shortage of about 80,000 teachers. Although this shortage is a worrisome national problem, it is nevertheless good news for new teachers, who will have excellent job opportunities.

There is more good news for new graduates of teacher education programs. Teachers' salaries are improving and will likely continue to do so for some time into the future. For example, teacher salaries nationwide have risen 25 percent over the past three years, according to a survey conducted by the American Federation of Teachers. Even when corrected for inflation, this figure amounts to a significant increase. We do not mean to say that teachers are currently overpaid—or for that matter, even adequately paid. Salary and its adequacy will very likely be debated as long as schools exist. The point is, however, that teachers' salaries have risen substantially in recent years. Furthermore, given the growing shortage of teachers, the laws of supply and demand will very likely continue to improve teachers' salaries for some time into the future—a phenomenon that will help to improve the status of American teachers.

Professional Perspectives   Remember that though teaching has many rewards, it also has many frustrations.

More Student Respect for Teachers

The extent to which students respect teachers is a very difficult thing to deter-mine and to make valid generalizations about. Obviously, most students respect some teachers. Also, it is clear that some teachers are respected by more students than other teachers. Likewise, the degree to which a given teacher is respected by students is dependent upon many variables such as the given school, the nature of the students in each class, the personality and skills of the teachers, likely even the nature of the subject being taught.

A recent survey by the *Weekly Reader* of 90,000 students in grades 2 through 9 found that 55 percent of the students liked their teachers, but only 35 percent liked their school "a lot." They also found that younger students are generally more positive than older students.

Insight into what students like about teachers can be gleaned from a survey conducted by *Learning* magazine, which asked eighth graders in Michigan for tips for teachers. Students gave the following advice to teachers:

Don't assign extra work to students who finish their work early.

Don't be mean.

Don't be overconfident.

Correct papers with appropriate comments.

Be versatile.

Don't yell.

Teaching is a rewarding career, especially when students like and respect their teachers. On the last day of school, this 4th grader and her classmates decorated the chalkboard with messages for their teacher. (*Source:* AP/Wide World Photos)

Be patient.
Don't give up on students.
Let students go to the bathroom.
Be supportive and reassuring.
Have a sense of humor.
Don't leave the classroom.
Check on students while they work.

Be qualified in your subject area.
Don't be too intelligent.
Use textbooks.
Don't have class favorites.
Don't complain.
Dress neatly and stay young.

In summary, there is considerable evidence to suggest that, generally speaking, most students like and respect the majority of their teachers. This compliment should be good news to teacher education students in colleges and universities throughout America.

Teachers Feeling Better About Themselves and Their Profession

In spite of the fact that teaching is a very demanding profession, and even though educators are not paid as much as they should be, teachers generally feel good about themselves and their profession. This contention is supported by a recent study conducted by the National Education Association, in which they asked teachers about their level of satisfaction concerning a number of job variables. As Table 1.2 shows, teachers were most satisfied with their contribution to society and least satisfied with the prestige of their profession.

On the subject of prestige, it is interesting to note the results of yet another 1985 survey conducted by the Gallup organization for the NEA. As shown in Figure 1.2, the public rated teachers below many other professions in "prestige" but rated teaching as very demanding (second only to medical doctors).

TABLE 1.2   *Teacher Satisfaction*

Area	Percent Satisfied
Contribution to society	85
Job security	84
Level of responsibility	82
Challenge	81
Appreciation by parents	68
Respect from students	67
Relaxed environment	59
Recognition from administrators	55
Prestige	38

Source: Survey of NEA K–12 Teacher Members 1985 (Washington, D.C.: National Education Association), p. 11. Used by permission.

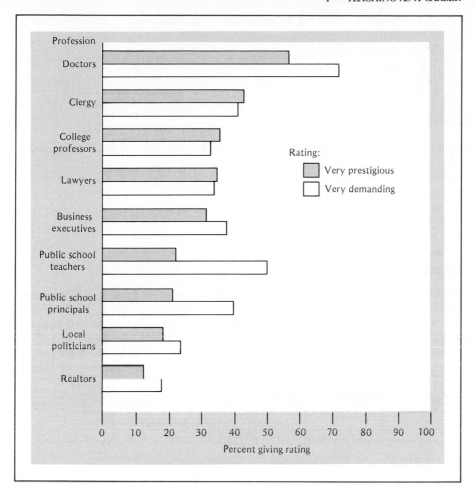

FIGURE 1.2 *Public Ratings of the Professions* [*Source: Survey of NEA K–12 Teacher Members 1985* (Washington, D.C.: National Educational Association), p. 12. Used by permission.]

Summary and Implications

This chapter has briefly introduced you to the world of the teacher. We hope it has convinced you that teaching is an extremely important profession—to the future success of our democracy, to the happiness and welfare of our children, and to our nation's economy. It has also reminded you that teaching is one of the largest professions in America, and that despite some understandable frustrations, teachers generally feel their careers are fulfilling and satisfactory. Another contention of this chapter is that society, parents, and students as a rule value and respect teachers. Some of the implications of this chapter for those who are contemplating a career in teaching include the following:

- You would be entering a time-honored profession
- That serves an extremely important function in our society
- In which most of your colleagues find fulfillment
- At a time when jobs are available and salaries are improving

Discussion Questions

1. How important do you think teachers are in our society?
2. What qualities distinguish a good teacher? A poor teacher?
3. To what extent do you believe teachers have job security? How important is job security to you?
4. How do you think the "typical" student feels about teachers in general?
5. What are some of the advantages and disadvantages of a career in teaching?

Supplemental Activities

1. Visit with several public school teachers and solicit their views concerning the topics discussed in this chapter.
2. Interview some of your college friends about their views concerning the advantages and disadvantages of teaching as a career.
3. Make a list of ways that teachers have been "fair" to you. Make another list of ways teachers have been "unfair" to you.
4. Watch for articles about teachers in the newspaper over the next several months. Try to develop a general feeling about what seems to be "newsworthy" about education.
5. Visit with a retired teacher and ask about the changes that have accrued in education over the past fifty years.
6. Volunteer to help a teacher in a nearby school.

Bibliography

Ballantine, J. H. *The Sociology of Education*. Englewood Cliffs, N.J.: Prentice-Hall, 1983.

Boyer, Ernest L. *High School*. New York: Harper & Row, 1983.

Goodlad, J. I. *A Place Called School*. New York: McGraw-Hill, 1984.

Hessong, Robert F., and Weeks, Thomas H. *Introduction to Education*. New York: Macmillan, 1987.

Ornstein, A. C., and Levine, D. U. *An Introduction to the Foundations of Education*. Boston: Houghton Mifflin, 1984.

Today's Education. Annual Editions. Washington, D.C.: Journal of the National Education Association, 1987.

Woodring, Paul. *The Persistent Problems of Education*. Bloomington, Ind.: Phi Delta Kappan, 1983.

2

Employment Opportunities
for Teachers

Focus Questions

- Since teachers have been considered poorly paid for their efforts in relation to the college preparation required for certification, what other aspects of teaching attract new teachers?
- Why are teachers reluctant to follow the general population shifts in the country? Shouldn't teachers move to where they are most needed?
- Illustrate the ways in which lower pupil-teacher ratios would aid classroom teachers. Are there some classes that would function just as well with larger numbers of students?
- How do you account for critical teacher shortages in chemistry, mathematics, physics, and data processing?
- Why is it that the beginning salary for teachers continues to be lower than the salary paid the beginner in business and industry? What needs to be done to correct this difference?

Key Terms and Concepts

Pupil-teacher ratio
Supply and demand
Differential pay
Salary schedules
Job-hunting hints

Cost of living
Retirement incentives
Fringe benefits
Annual increments
Moonlighting

What Would You Do?

A professor of one of your classes claims that although starting salaries for teachers are low in some schools, the salary for experienced teachers with master's degrees is excellent in many schools. What do you think?

After your first year of teaching, your supervisor informs you that your yearly evaluation was highly satisfactory.

At this time you are offered a position in private business at a modest raise in monthly salary. You then learn that your school will adopt a merit pay plan within the next two years. Your thoughts?

$\boxed{4}$ **W**e are facing a growing shortage of teachers in America. This shortage has become critical in certain parts of the country, particularly for some types of teachers. Since 1970 the percentage of new-teacher graduates among bachelor's degree recipients dropped from 37 percent to only 12 percent in 1981. As a result, the supply of new-teacher graduates has decreased from 284,000 to 159,000 over the same period.[1] The projections of new-teacher graduates show an increase to 238,000 in 1990–1991, representing about 26 percent of bachelor's degrees that year. This projection is based on the assumption that as the demand for additional teachers increases and as teachers' salaries improve during the 1980s, the proportion of college students preparing to teach will also increase.

The total demand for additional teachers includes those needed to allow for enrollment changes, for changes in pupil-teacher ratios, and for replacement of teachers leaving the profession. In the late 1980s, as enrollments begin to increase, the demand for additional teachers will rise, resulting in the expected hiring of 983,000 teachers during 1986–1990. This demand represents an increase from 138,000 additional teachers hired each year (from 1981 to 1985) to 197,000 additional teachers each year (in the 1986–1990 period).

The supply of additional teachers consists of new-teacher graduates and former-teacher graduates who were not employed as teachers in the previous year. New-teacher graduates are those graduates of institutions of higher education in a given year who are prepared to teach for the first time. Former-teacher graduates are those who graduated in preceding years and are prepared to teach but who did not hold teaching positions in the previous year. Some of these former-teacher graduates are former teachers; the remainder have never been employed as teachers.

For many years teachers have been considered to be poorly paid for their efforts in relation to the college preparation required for certification. Such intangible rewards as the opportunity to work with students at every age level and professional status in the community were assumed to be attractive fringe benefits. As teacher organizations became increasingly powerful and militant, particularly during the 1960s, teachers began to demand increased salaries and other fringe benefits. Consequently, boards of education have since approved substantial increases in salaries and benefits.

The Limited Supply of New Teachers

There are a number of factors that determine job availability for teachers. These factors include the total number of children enrolled in our schools, the number of new teachers graduating from colleges each year, and the number of students taught by each teacher. We will briefly explore several of these variables in this section.

Enrollment Projections

During the next decade, enrollment declines in elementary and secondary schools will end, and a gradual increase will begin as the 5- to 17-year-old population begins to increase. The enrollment increase is expected to continue into the 1990s, resulting in an enrollment boom that will create new demands for teachers.

The enrollment rates for most of the school-age population (5- to 17-year-olds) are all close to 100 percent. Since school is compulsory to age 16 in most states, elementary enrollment closely reflects the 5- to 13-year-old population, and secondary enrollment tends to reflect the 14- to 17-year-old population. Enrollment in our educational institutions is expected to grow to 57,762,000 by 1990, as shown in Table 2.1.

The character of education is shaped to a large extent by the size of the population it serves. During the late 1980s American population is expected to increase, and the age composition will be significantly different from that of the previous decade. By 1990 the median age is expected to be 32.8 years, almost five years older than the median age in 1970. This aging of the population is the result of several social trends that have had and will have a strong influence on the educational system in the United States.

All indications point to the fact that we will experience a severe shortage of teachers in the United States in the near future. This assurance of job availability should help encourage talented young people to enter the teaching profession.

Supply of New Teachers

Each year approximately 140,000 new teachers are graduated from the more than 1,200 teacher-training programs in America. However, the supply of new teachers is a combination of the graduates who have recently received a degree qualifying them to teach plus previous teachers who left the classroom and decided to return to the profession, as well as others previously prepared to teach who never started a classroom career. Although there will likely be a steady increase into the 1980s in the total number of graduates with bachelor's

TABLE 2.1 *Estimated Enrollment in Educational Institutions, Fall 1985–Fall 1990*

Level	Fall 1985	Fall 1990
Preprimary	3,898,000	4,159,000
Grades 1–8	27,322,000	29,366,000
Grades 9–12	13,830,000	12,144,000
Higher education	12,150,000	12,093,000
Total	57,200,000	57,762,000

Source: Digest of Education Statistics 1985–86 (Washington, D.C.: U.S. Department of Education), p. 7.

The outlook for college graduates seeking a career in teaching is promising: the projected demand for additional teachers in the late 1980s will result in better employment prospects and higher teacher salaries. (*Source:* Janice Fullman/The Picture Cube)

degrees, the number of degrees granted in education will likely continue to decline until the late 1980s. The number of education degrees decreased from approximately 37 percent of all those graduating from college in 1970 to about 14 percent in 1983.

There are, however, some brighter possibilities. The projected demand for additional teachers in the late 1980s will result in better employment prospects and higher teacher salaries. Just as students reacted to the drop in demand by moving out of teacher preparation, so too are students projected to enter teacher training as the job market improves. Table 2.2 provides estimates of new-teacher graduates compared with estimated demand for additional teachers from 1970 to 1990. This table shows the dramatic twenty-year change from an oversupply of teachers to a serious shortage of teachers. It should also be noted that 15–20 percent of new-teacher graduates do not apply for teaching positions at all. That factor is not subtracted from the supply numbers in the table.

TABLE 2.2 *Estimated Supply of New-Teacher Graduates Compared with Total Demand for Additional Teachers*

Year	Estimated Supply of New-Teacher Graduates	Estimated Demand for Additional Teachers	Supply as a Percent of Demand
1970	284,000	208,000	136
1975	238,000	186,000	128
1980	144,000	127,000	113
1985	142,000	170,000	92
1990	139,000	183,000	76

Source: Projections of Education Statistics to 1992–93 (Washington, D.C.: U.S. Department of Education), p. 79.

Pupil-Teacher Ratios

The number of pupils taught by each teacher has a profound influence on the demand for new teachers. Nearly all schools would hire more teachers to reduce the pupil-teacher ratio if they could afford to do so. As school budgets become "tighter," the pupil-teacher ratio typically rises, resulting in larger classes and fewer new teachers being hired.

Pupil-teacher ratios vary considerably from school to school and from state to state. In fact, the pupil-teacher ratio will vary from teacher to teacher within a school district, depending upon the type of students and/or subjects taught. A special education teacher working with severely and profoundly handicapped students must have a smaller class than, for instance, a physical education teacher working with large activity classes.

Recent data shows considerable variation in pupil-teacher ratios from state to state. For example, Utah, with the highest pupil-teacher ratio of 25 pupils per teacher in its public schools, had 10 more pupils per teacher than Vermont, which had the lowest ratio. It should be noted that pupil-teacher ratios are usually computed by dividing the number of pupils in the school by the number of certified teachers on the entire staff, some of whom are not assigned to a classroom. Therefore the actual number of pupils per classroom is usually more than the pupil-teacher ratio for the school.

The Growing Teacher Shortage

The demand for new teachers is increasing rapidly in the United States. In fact, there is a severe teacher shortage in some states, particularly in certain subjects and at certain levels.

An Increasing Teacher Demand

One cause of this growing demand for new teachers is explained in Figure 2.1, which shows the dramatically increased preprimary enrollment. This figure points out that enrollments of very young children have increased from approximately 4.3 million in 1970 to a projected 7 million by 1993. This large

2

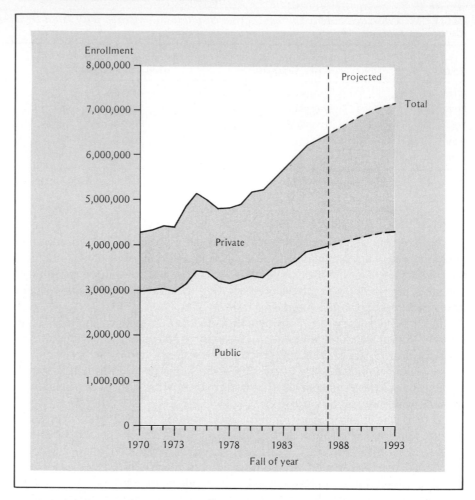

FIGURE 2.1 *Preprimary Enrollment Trends, by Control of School* [*Source: The Condition of Education,* 1985 ed. (Washington, D.C.: National Center for Education Statistics), p. 23.]

increase in the number of children entering our schools will greatly increase the demand for teachers as these students move up through the school system.

This increasing demand for teachers is shown in Figure 2.2. Demand for additional elementary school teachers is expected to peak in 1990, but the demand for additional secondary teachers will likely continue to increase through 1995. The good news for people planning teaching careers is that there will continue to be a growing demand for teachers for at least the next decade.

Shortage by Geographical and Subject Areas

As mentioned earlier, the demand for new teachers varies from place to place, from grade to grade, and from subject to subject. Even within one metropolitan area one school district may be growing rapidly, building new schools, and

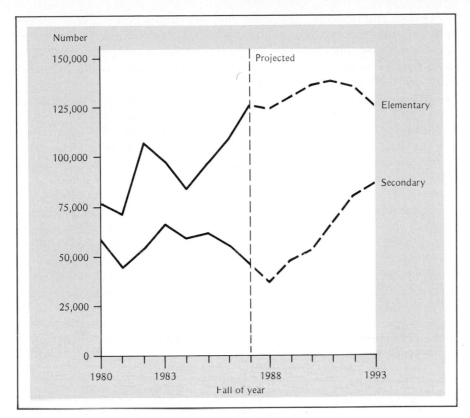

FIGURE 2.2 *Estimated Demand for Additional Teachers, by Level of School*
[*Source: The Condition of Education*, 1985 ed. (Washington, D.C.: National Center for
Education Statistics), p. 145.]

hiring new teachers because of new housing developments, while the school
district next door may be closing schools and reducing its number of teachers.

Therefore, it is difficult to generalize about the nature of the teacher short
age. Generally, however, the greatest shortage of teachers exists in our larger
cities (New York, Chicago, Los Angeles, for instance) and in the southern and
southwestern parts of the country.

Unfortunately, many teachers seem to prefer not to teach in large metropolitan schools, presumably for a variety of reasons including heavy city traffic
on the freeways, longer commuting time to and from work, more difficult student
problems, and higher costs of living. Higher teacher turnover also contributes
to the staffing problems of large-city schools. Fortunately, many teachers feel
that teaching in a large city is challenging and fulfilling, with many advantages.

The general teacher shortage that exists in the southern and southwestern
parts of the United States has come about as a result of the population shift that
has occurred over the past twenty years. Many Americans have moved to these
sun belt states largely because industrial development has made jobs available
there. This migration has increased school enrollment, which, in turn, has created a considerable demand for teachers.

College and university placement directors suggest that students planning to become teachers should be apprised of the fact that opportunity exists in any field for the top-quality graduate. For example, even in times of a good supply of teachers, far more graduates are employed in elementary education, English, and social studies than in subject areas which need relatively few teachers (such as Russian language, for instance). Thus high-quality candidates in some teaching areas having less demand are still likely to find a teaching position.

Also, the U.S. Department of Defense operates a school system for the children of American men and women in the armed services abroad. This school system, the United States Dependents School, is one of our nation's largest school systems, enrolling about 130,000 students in over 260 schools in 23 countries. The approximately 7,500 teachers in this system come from every state in the union. Although not officially organized as an international education program, these U.S. Dependents Schools widen the chance for citizens of the United States and citizens of other nations to exchange cultural experiences.

Opportunities for Americans to teach abroad are increasing. Teacher demands in other nations, especially for English teachers, have heightened foreign employment. Recruiters from foreign countries have visited many college and university campuses hoping to hire teachers from the United States.

A concise summary of opportunities for studying or teaching abroad can be found in *Educational and Cultural Exchange Opportunities,* a booklet published by the U.S. Department of State.[2]

The Misassignment of Teachers

An alarming number of teachers in American classrooms are not well prepared for their current teaching assignments. This unfortunate situation comes about in a variety of ways. Sometimes, a school cannot find a qualified teacher for a vacancy and resorts to hiring a minimally qualified teacher out of necessity. Smaller schools often have their teachers teach a variety of subjects out of necessity. Yet other schools, when enrollments decrease and they must let some teachers go, end up with older, tenured teachers who are less qualified than the younger teachers they replace.

A recent report entitled *Making Do in the Classroom: A Report on the Misassignment of Teachers*[3] suggests that misassignment is a much larger problem than most people realize. Many states, in fact, do not know the extent of the problem and have little control over the situation. A survey of out-of-field teaching assignments in Utah, for example, showed that 82 percent of earth science classes, 28 percent of mathematics classes, and 25 percent of biology classes were the major assignments of teachers who did not have a major or a minor in that subject. This same general picture is reflected in other state surveys, even for subjects such as English where there is not a drastic shortage of teachers. This problem may well be the most serious at the middle and junior high school level, where many states lack specific teaching certificates.

This problem simply must be solved if we are to improve the quality of education in our country. Teachers who are not prepared in the subjects they are assigned to teach are not likely to do a very good job. Furthermore, parents should not tolerate this practice. They and their students deserve and should demand well-qualified teachers. Albert Shanker, president of the American Federation of Teachers, suggests that this "dirty little secret" of our educational system should "shame us all." $\boxed{17}$

The misassignment of teachers should be of particular concern to people such as the readers of this book who are currently enrolled in rigorous teacher education programs. These unqualified teachers are occupying potential job slots for well-qualified new teachers. But new teachers should likewise not accept an assignment for which they are not well trained. Educators who do accept such assignments should ask themselves whether they would allow a physician who was not qualified to prescribe medicine for their child.

Improving Salaries and Fringe Benefits

There is good news and bad news about salaries and fringe benefits. The good news is that salaries have improved considerably in recent years and are projected to improve even more in the near future. The bad news is that teachers are still not paid as well as they should be. $\boxed{1}$

Teacher Salaries in Public Schools

The average teacher salary in the United States rose to $25,257 per year in 1985–1986. This figure represents a 36 percent increase since 1981, just before the deluge of national reports launched the school reform movement. Table 2.3 shows the average 1985–1986 teacher salary for each state, as well as the percentage increase from the previous year.

TABLE 2.3 *Teachers' Salaries, 1985–1986*

State	1985–1986 Average Pay	One-Year Change
Mississippi	$18,443	+15.8%
Nevada	$25,620	+13.8%
New Jersey	$28,216	+13.6%
Alabama	$22,934	+13.0%
Oklahoma	$21,419	+12.6%
Virginia	$23,382	+ 9.9%
California	$29,750	+ 9.0%
Wisconsin	$26,800	+ 9.0%
Connecticut	$26,610	+ 8.8%
New Hampshire	$20,148	+ 8.5%
North Carolina	$22,476	+ 8.0%
Texas	$24,419	+ 8.0%
Kansas	$22,768	+ 7.8%
Pennsylvania	$26,009	+ 7.5%
Delaware	$24,625	+ 7.4%

TABLE 2.3   *(Continued)*

State	1985–1986 Average Pay	One-Year Change
U.S. Average	**$25,257**	**+ 7.3%**
Georgia	$22,080	+ 7.1%
Ohio	$24,500	+ 7.1%
Florida	$22,296	+ 7.0%
Missouri	$21,884	+ 7.0%
New York	$30,200	+ 7.0%
Vermont	$20,325	+ 7.0%
Maine	$19,583	+ 6.8%
Illinois	$27,190	+ 6.7%
Indiana	$24,333	+ 6.5%
Tennessee	$21,800	+ 6.5%
Rhode Island	$29,470	+ 6.4%
South Carolina	$21,428	+ 6.4%
Dist. of Columbia	$33,990	+ 6.0%
Minnesota	$26,970	+ 6.0%
Colorado	$25,900	+ 5.9%
Oregon	$25,788	+ 5.8%
Arizona	$24,680	+ 5.6%
Wyoming	$27,876	+ 5.6%
Michigan	$30,168	+ 5.5%
Nebraska	$20,939	+ 5.5%
Utah	$22,341	+ 5.5%
West Virginia	$20,625	+ 5.4%
Maryland	$27,186	+ 5.1%
Louisiana	$20,460	+ 5.0%
Massachusetts	$25,849	+ 5.0%
Hawaii	$25,845	+ 4.9%
Idaho	$20,969	+ 4.7%
Arkansas	$19,538	+ 4.5%
Alaska	$41,480	+ 4.3%
South Dakota	$18,095	+ 4.3%
Iowa	$21,690	+ 3.6%
Montana	$22,492	+ 3.6%
North Dakota	$20,816	+ 3.6%
Kentucky	$20,940	+ 3.5%
New Mexico	$22,526	+ 3.3%
Washington	$26,015	+ 2.0%

Source: U.S. Department of Education (Washington, D.C., 1986).

One of the more encouraging trends for new teachers is that beginning salaries are improving, especially in larger school districts where teacher shortages exist. A 1986 study[4] showed average beginning teachers' salaries at the bachelor's degree level as high as $20,617 for elementary and secondary teachers and $22,000 for special education teachers. This study also reported average beginning salaries at the master's degree level as high as $27,000. If we keep in mind that these beginning salaries are for nine months' work, they represent very competitive beginning salaries with most other professions. Unfortunately, many school districts offer beginning teachers much lower salaries.

Remember that some classroom teachers (who have a master's degree and fifteen years of teaching experience) have a salary in the range of $50,000 for nine months' work.

Private School Teacher Demand and Salaries

The need for private school teachers, preprimary through grade 12, is projected to reach 400,000 by 1993. Thus approximately one out of every seven teachers in America at the preprimary through twelfth-grade level will be teaching in a private school in the early 1990s. Also, many teachers each year are hired to teach in private schools throughout the country.

[2]

While private schools are not usually required by law to hire fully certified teachers, increasingly they are attempting to do so. In fact, a recent survey[5] found that nearly 85 percent of all private school teachers were fully certified.

Teachers' salaries in private schools are generally somewhat lower than those in public schools. This lower salary level is largely due to the fact that a high percentage of the private schools are religious and, of course, are not tax-supported. A recent study[6] of private schools in Illinois found that starting salaries range from $8,000 to $14,000 for nine months.

Students who are now enrolled in teacher education programs should keep in mind that private schools represent another career option and should become familiar with these important educational institutions.

Merit Pay—Differential Pay

School systems in a number of states are considering various forms of incentive plans as the means to reward the best teachers for teaching excellence and to address shortages in certain disciplines. The teacher unions have historically been against incentive plans, claiming that they are often subject to the opinions of administrators, include questionable criteria for judging teaching excellence, and cause morale problems among teachers. However, many of the best teachers realize that the typical salary schedule rewards all teachers in the same way whether they are good or bad in the classroom. These teachers support the merit concept as a possible way to provide a differential for exceptional teaching above the provisions of the salary schedule. Previous limited attempts to utilize merit pay plans have not proved worthwhile; but ideally, basing teachers' salaries on some form of evaluation seems plausible. Consequently, it is expected that many merit plans will be developed and implemented in the future.

[5]

At least the need for schools to provide additional incentive pay to attract top-notch teachers to the critical shortage areas seems without question. In the marketplace of private industry additional pay is always used as a mechanism for attracting employees to fill critical needs. For example, though the computer science field is relatively new, the demand is very strong. Consequently, beginning salaries for graduates with a bachelor's degree in computer science have

Many people believe that in order to attract top-notch teachers to critical shortage areas, schools will need to provide additional incentive pay, just as private industry rewards its valuable employees. (*Source:* Rick Friedman/The Picture Cube)

been high. If the need for computer science graduates declines, so will the amounts paid to attract those employees.

Salary Schedules and Yearly Increments

Each board of education is an agent of the state and therefore empowered to set salary levels for employees of the school district it governs. Each school system usually has a salary schedule that outlines the minimum and maximum salary for several levels of study beyond the bachelor's degree and for each year of teaching experience. A beginning teacher with a bachelor's degree may be paid $20,000, one with a master's degree may be paid $25,000, and a beginning teacher with a master's degree and 30 additional semester hours of graduate study may be paid $30,000.

Teachers with less than a master's degree may be granted year-to-year increases for ten years; teachers with preparation beyond a master's degree may be granted increments for up to seventeen years. Therefore teachers are rewarded for both a maximum number of years of experience and for additional education beyond the bachelor's degree. Teachers who have reached the maximum experience level for their particular education do not receive additional raises except when all the salaries listed in the salary schedule are revised upward.

Retirement Incentives

School districts around the country are faced with the problem of aging teacher staffs. The increased proportion of older teachers has prompted many districts to offer early-retirement incentives to speed up attrition.

Early-retirement (ages 55–59) incentives typically offer a substantial salary increase in the last year of teaching, which results in increased pension benefits. In addition, free medical and life insurance is provided by the school district until age 65, when Medicare benefits are available. Though most administrators stress that a school needs young teachers, they also acknowledge that money is a key consideration. Younger teachers cost school districts a lot less. Many high school teachers at the typical retirement age (65) are earning $30,000 a year or more; a beginning teacher with a bachelor's degree starts at much less. The ideal situation for the school district occurs when young teachers are kept while salary money is saved by offering early-retirement incentives to older faculty members.

The early-retirement push has not met with favor among all teachers. Some instructors believe that they are being pushed out and resent the pressure put upon them to retire. Some of the older teachers are excellent teachers who prefer to continue in the classroom. The opportunity to enjoy other careers during the later years of their planned working life has no appeal. Perhaps for this reason, the growing emphasis on early retirement has not resulted in a mass exodus of older teachers. In Illinois, for example, original estimates that retirements might actually double with the early-retirement plans have not proved true. Nonetheless, more and more school districts will likely offer early-retirement incentives as a means of keeping young teachers while saving much-needed salary dollars.

Fringe Benefits and Extra Pay

Fringe benefits for teachers vary from school district to school district and from state to state. Certain fringe benefits are required by law; other benefits result from negotiations between the teachers and boards of education. School districts are required by law to provide teacher retirement plans and to pay for workmen's compensation, unemployment insurance coverage, and some form of sick leave provisions. Through teacher–school board negotiations, some districts provide extended health and dental insurance plans for the spouse and children of teachers, leave-of-absence provisions, extended sick leave, and payment of tuition fees for advanced study. A small proportion of school systems provide plans for sabbatical leaves, cooperative purchase programs, and extended contracts for summer employment.

9

Most school systems pay teachers an amount beyond their scheduled salary for extra time given to coaching athletic teams and speech teams, producing musicals and plays, doing yearbook and newspaper assignments, sponsoring clubs, and other extra duties of various kinds. In a few cases teachers are paid for teaching an extra class beyond the regular teaching load.

When considering employment in a school district, prospective teachers should carefully examine the fringe benefits and extra-pay provisions, as well as retirement benefits, in concert with the salary schedule.

Moonlighting

Many American teachers work at a second job, particularly in the summer. A recent study[7] showed that over half of all public school teachers supplement their income by moonlighting on other jobs. This same study reported that over half of our teachers also have a spouse who works.

Job-Hunting Hints

3

It is never too early for a teacher education student to start thinking about job hunting—not even in the first year of college. The most important job-hunting hint that can be given to any teacher education student is to study hard throughout college and get the best possible grades in all college classes. Also, majors and minors should be selected which give the most employment options. By careful planning, college students can graduate qualified to teach in a variety of fields and with more than one certificate.

All teacher education students should also seize every opportunity to gain on-the-job experience by working with children. There are many volunteer programs available in most geographical areas through schools, churches, and various agencies that involve working with children. There are also many paid-job opportunities such as summer recreation programs, youth camps, and teacher aids that provide opportunities to work with youths. The point is that the more experience teacher education students have in working with youths, the more they will learn about young people.

As teacher education students approach graduation, they also need to receive job-hunting hints about developing job placement files, writing letters of application, and developing good interview techniques. Fortunately, most teacher education programs and college job placement offices automatically provide such job-hunting hints.

Professional Perspectives

The person with the best credentials gets the job. So study diligently during your college career, and work very hard during your clinical experiences in the schools.

Summary and Implications

Only a few aspects of teacher supply, demand, and salaries were examined in this chapter. Job prospects for new teacher graduates should improve markedly in the late 1980s.

School enrollment is projected to increase into the 1990s, which could result in an enrollment boom that may surpass the peak levels of the early 1970s. Consequently, a teacher shortage is a distinct possibility in the late 1980s unless college students respond to the improved market by increasing their enrollments in teacher preparation programs.

The total number of elementary and secondary teachers in the United States increased from 1970 through 1980. During this period additional teachers were readily available, and many were hired in order to decrease the pupil-teacher ratios from those in previously overcrowded classrooms. As school budgets became more restricted, the local districts did not have the means to sustain such hiring practices; in fact, the rapid enrollment declines resulted in many teachers being released. Consequently, the number of elementary teachers is now on the rise. The number of secondary teachers will continue to decrease into the 1990s as the enrollment declines further affect the secondary student population. At the same time, shortages in selected discipline areas will become more pronounced according to the emphasis on given areas of the secondary curriculum.

New academic achievement tests that compare children in the United States with children of other countries show the United States lagging behind in all academic areas, especially in math and science. Such results, coupled with reports such as the one from the National Commission on Excellence in Education, bring pressure on the schools to raise standards of study. Consequently, severe teacher shortages are predicted in certain academic areas. The most critical shortages are in chemistry, mathematics, physics, and data processing. Areas of surplus will continue to be art, physical education, social science, home economics, and foreign languages.

Opportunities for Americans to teach abroad are increasing. The U.S. Department of Defense operates a school system for the children of American men and women in the services abroad. Teacher shortages in other nations also heighten opportunities for foreign employment.

Teachers' salaries continue to be less than those of comparably prepared employees in business and industries. Even though teachers' salaries have increased considerably in recent years, teachers' buying power in actual dollars has not kept up with the cost of living. As local districts struggle to meet rising costs, teachers will find gains in salary hard to achieve unless there are new sources of income.

Several school districts are attempting to devise salary incentive plans that reward the best teachers with additional merit pay. Another incentive would provide higher salaries for teachers in areas of short supply, such as the math and science disciplines. Even though teachers' unions generally oppose such incentive plans, teachers realize that salary schedules reward all teachers equally whether or not they are good in the classroom. The general public and school boards favor merit pay for the best teachers and extra stipends to attract well-qualified teachers in critical shortage areas. The late 1980s will see more use of salary incentive plans than ever before.

Retirement incentives are being used to reduce the number of higher-salaried older teachers while keeping younger, less well-paid teachers. These retirement incentive plans have been only moderately successful to date, however. Consequently, fewer young teachers have been retained in our schools than was originally projected.

The implications of these variables for prospective teachers are straightforward. More teachers will be needed in the late 1980s than during the previous decade. In order to satisfy the clamor for improving the quality of education, more and better-prepared teachers will be needed. Furthermore, teachers' salaries will be reviewed to determine ways to upgrade salaries for those prepared to teach in the critical shortage disciplines and for those determined to be most effective in the classroom. Teacher organizations and teacher preparation schools are challenged to upgrade the competency levels of certified teachers now on the job and of students entering teacher preparation programs. Teacher tenure laws and union seniority rules are under more rigorous attack than ever before for protecting incompetent teachers. The question of how to identify and how to remove incompetent teachers are open to much debate. The opportunity to revitalize the teaching profession is at hand. The degree to which all educators work to gain renewed faith and dignity in the profession will determine the benefits to future generations of American youth.

Discussion Questions

1. How can colleges and departments of education better prepare beginning teachers so that their chances of employment in a tight job market will be enhanced?
2. Teacher shortages are reported in the subject areas of chemistry, mathematics, and physics. Are these disciplines too difficult to attract prospective teachers? What should teacher-training institutions do to meet demands for teachers in the sciences?
3. Discuss the pros and cons of the early-retirement incentive plans offered by some school districts. In your response, explain your beliefs about the values of young teachers to a school and of older teachers to a school.
4. Many people believe that teachers are overpaid. As a prospective teacher, how would you respond to this charge?
5. Many young teachers work at a second job to increase their yearly income. How do you feel about teachers holding additional jobs?

Supplemental Activities

1. Invite a member of your school's placement office to class to discuss application procedures, credentials, and teacher supply and demand.
2. Invite hiring officials from nearby school districts to your class to discuss teacher supply and demand. Compare this discussion with the presentation by the placement officer.
3. Review a big-city newspaper for at least one week to obtain a selection of current discussions about education-related topics. Report your findings. Also, assess trends indicated by your findings.
4. Identify several school districts that have had teacher strikes recently. Write to the teacher organizations in these districts and ask for information on the strike issues. Summarize the data obtained.

5. Invite to your class members of your graduating class who are going to work in business or industry. Why did these students choose their fields of employment? Why did they not choose teaching as a career?

Notes

1. William S. Graybeal, *Teacher Supply and Demand in Public Schools, 1980–81* (Washington, D.C.: National Education Association, 1981).
2. *Educational and Cultural Exchange Opportunities* (Washington, D.C.: U.S. Department of State, Bureau of Cultural Affairs, 1986).
3. *Making Do in the Classroom: A Report on the Misassignment of Teachers* (Washington, D.C.: Council for Basic Education, 1985).
4. James N. Akin, *Tenth Annual Teacher Supply/Demand Report* (Madison, Wis.: Association for School, College, and University Staffing, 1986). Based on a survey of teacher placement officers.
5. *The Condition of Education, 1985 Edition* (Washington, D.C.: U.S. Department of Education), p. 158.
6. George Kubat, Richard Mueller, and Homer Sherman, "A Study of Employment Practices in Nonpublic Schools (K–12) in Illinois" (unpublished, 1986).
7. *The Condition of Education,* 142.

Bibliography

The American Federation of Teachers collects and distributes data on salaries and demand for educators throughout each year.

Educational Research Service, Inc. *Fringe Benefits for Teachers in Public Schools, 1985.* Washington, D.C.
———. *Scheduled Salaries for Professional Personnel in Public Schools, 1985.* Washington, D.C.

A Job Search Handbook for Educators. Published annually by the Association for School, College, and University Staffing (ASCUS), Madison, Wis.

Johansen, John J., Collins, Harold W., and Johnson, James A. *American Education: An Introduction to Teaching.* Dubuque, Iowa: Brown, 1986.

The National Education Association periodically publishes and reports on teacher supply, demand, and salaries.

"Revitalizing Teacher Education." *Educational Horizons,* 65(2) (Winter 1987). Entire issue is devoted to teacher education.

Teacher Supply/Demand. Annual reports of the Association of School, College, and University Staffing (ASCUS), Madison, Wis.

3

Education Reform: A Status Report

Focus Questions

- Which of the many recent national reports on education are attracting the most attention?
- What are the main criticisms being leveled at American education in the current calls for reform?
- What will it take to really improve education in America?
- To what extent is educational reform taking place in the United States?

Key Terms and Concepts

Education reform
A Nation at Risk
National Commission on Excellence in Education
Carnegie Foundation for the Advancement of Teaching

Clinical experiences
Teacher certifications
Teacher induction
The Holmes Group
The Carnegie Report

What Would You Do?

Knowing that you are preparing to be a teacher, a friend asks your opinion about the current state of public schools in America. What would you tell your friend?

What are some of the things that you would probably try to do in your first few years of teaching to help reform education?

Much has been written about educational reform in the United States in recent years. In 1983 the first major national report calling for educational reform was published by the National Commission on Excellence in Education, under the title *A Nation at Risk: The Imperative for Educational Reform.* Here is the introductory paragraph of the report:

> Our Nation is at risk. Our once unchallenged preeminence in commerce, industry, science, and technological innovation is being overtaken by competitors throughout the world. This report is concerned with only one of the many causes and dimensions of the problem, but it is the one that undergirds American prosperity, security, and civility. We report to the American people that while we can take justifiable pride in what our schools and colleges have historically accomplished and contributed to the United States and the well-being of its people, the educational foundations of our society are presently being eroded by a rising tide of mediocrity that threatens our very future as a Nation and a people. What was unimaginable a generation ago has begun to occur—others are matching and surpassing our educational attainments.

Findings and recommendations were presented regarding content (curriculum), expectations (knowledge, abilities, and skills), time (in classroom and on homework), and teaching. Here is the text of the findings and recommendations:

> The Commission found that not enough of the academically able students are being attracted to teaching, that teacher preparation programs need substantial improvement; that the professional working life of teachers is on the whole unacceptable; and that a serious shortage of teachers exists in key fields.
>
> - Too many teachers are being drawn from the bottom quarter of graduating high school and college students.
> - The teacher preparation curriculum is weighted heavily with courses in "educational methods" at the expense of courses in subjects to be taught. A survey of 1,350 institutions training teachers indicated that 41 percent of the time of elementary school teacher candidates is spent in education courses, which reduces the amount of time available for subject matter courses.
> - The average salary after 12 years of teaching is only $17,000 per year, and many teachers are required to supplement their income with part-time and summer employment. In addition, individual teachers have little influence in such critical professional decisions as, for example, textbook selection.
> - Despite widespread publicity about an overpopulation of teachers, severe shortages of certain kinds of teachers exist: in the fields of mathematics, science, and foreign languages; and among specialists in education for gifted and talented, language minority, and handicapped students.

The recommendation regarding teaching consists of seven parts. Each is intended to improve the preparation of teachers or to make teaching a more rewarding and respected profession. Each of the seven stands on its own and should not be considered solely as an implementing recommendation.

1. Persons preparing to teach should be required to meet high educational standards, to demonstrate an aptitude for teaching, and to demonstrate competence in an academic discipline. Colleges and universities offering teacher preparation programs should be judged by how well their graduates meet these criteria.
2. Salaries for the teaching profession should be increased and should be professionally competitive, market-sensitive, and performance-based. Salary, promotion, tenure, and retention decisions should be tied to an effective evaluation system that includes peer review so that superior teachers can be rewarded, average ones encouraged, and poor ones either improved or terminated.
3. School boards should adopt an 11-month contract for teachers. This would ensure time for curriculum and professional development, programs for students with special needs, and a more adequate level of teacher compensation.
4. School boards, administrators, and teachers should cooperate to develop career ladders for teachers that distinguish among the beginning instructor, the experienced teacher, and the master teacher.
5. Substantial nonschool personnel resources should be employed to help solve the immediate problem of the shortage of mathematics and science teachers. Qualified individuals including recent graduates with mathematics and science degrees, graduate students, and industrial and retired scientists could, with appropriate preparation, immediately begin teaching in these fields. A number of our leading science centers have the capacity to begin educating and retraining teachers immediately. Other areas of critical teacher need, such as English, must be addressed.
6. Incentives, such as grants and loans, should be made available to attract outstanding students to the teaching profession, particularly in those areas of critical shortage.
7. Master teachers should be involved in designing teacher preparation programs and in supervising teachers during their probationary years.

In addition to the *Nation at Risk* report, there were many other reports about our schools. In May 1983 the College Board Report—*Academic Preparation for College: What Students Need to Know and Be Able to Do*—asserted that high school students who intend to go to college should master a comprehensive body of knowledge that includes six basic academic subjects: English, mathematics, science, social studies, foreign language, and the arts. This report was prepared as part of the Educational Equality Project, a ten-year effort to develop and implement a national standard for achievement in secondary education.

In August 1983 a report by the Carnegie Foundation for the Advancement of Teaching, entitled *High School: A Report on Secondary Education in America,* was published. In an introduction to the study Ernest Boyer, president of the foundation, said that better teaching is essential if the current proposals for improving schools are to succeed. He also suggested that whatever is wrong

Professional Perspectives

The first few years of one's teaching career can be particularly difficult. We recommend you participate in a well-designed teacher induction program if one is available to you.

with American public schools cannot be fixed without the help of those teachers already in the nation's classrooms, since most of them will be there for years to come.

Depending upon who was doing the counting, there were approximately twenty or thirty reports about various aspects of American schools during the next several years. Never before had our schools received so much attention in the media, thanks to these many reports.

This chapter takes stock of the current status of the educational reforms recommended by these reports. A review of some additional new reports that call for school reform is also provided. Lastly, the effects these reform movements are having on our classroom teachers are examined.

The Reform of Teacher Education

Most of the national reports published in recent years have called for changes in the way we prepare teachers in the United States. One of the inevitable recommendations to solve any school problem is to prepare better teachers. [10] There seems to be a prevalent belief that if we only had better teachers, we would eliminate, or at least partially solve, whatever school problem is being discussed at the moment. Let's look at some of the ways the reform movement is bringing about changes in teacher education programs.

Raising of Standards

It is becoming more difficult to get into, through, and graduate from most teacher education programs. For instance, many colleges now require students to successfully pass basic-skills tests dealing with reading, writing, and mathematics before they can begin the teacher education program. Some states have even gone so far as to mandate such entrance-level testing. Such tests have predictably been controversial, resulting in heated debate and even some court action. Nevertheless, entrance-level testing for admission to teacher education programs is increasingly advocated and supported as part of the reform movement.

As is the case with all reform activity, there is good news and bad news about entrance-level testing as it applies to teacher education programs. Included in the good news are such things as preventing students with extremely low basic skills from wasting a lot of time preparing for a job in which they may not ultimately have the skills to succeed. Weeding out such students also allows the colleges to concentrate their limited resources on students more likely to succeed. In addition, ensuring that new teachers have good basic skills avoids the possibility of teachers with poor basic skills passing these weaknesses on to their students. Among the bad news that has come out of entrance testing is the fact that the failure rate for minority students is often as high as 60 to 70 percent. This fact is particularly distressing at a time when minority enrollment in our public elementary and secondary schools is rapidly increasing and our country especially needs more minority educators. Some educators also question

Much has been written about education reform recently, and most reports have called for changes in the way we train students for the teaching profession. (*Source:* Janice Fullman/The Picture Cube)

the fairness of such testing when it is not required in other professions, such as law, medicine, and engineering.

Perhaps the best single indication of rising standards in teacher education programs is found in the new National Council for the Accreditation of Teacher Education (NCATE) standards for accrediting teacher education programs. These new standards demand that teacher education programs use higher entrance requirements and generally present more rigorous teacher education programs.

More Clinical Experiences

7   Various kinds of on-the-job training have always been important components of most teacher education programs; however, in the past decade states have mandated a significant increase in this practical training for future teachers.

Although the format and details vary from state to state and college to college, it is not unusual for teacher education students to devote at least one-fourth of their time to clinical work in the field.

This clinical work serves many important functions. It helps the college students see what teaching is really like on a day-by-day basis so that they can decide if they really want to enter the teaching profession. By the same token, it allows students to test their skills to see whether they are well suited to teaching. As students progress through the program, clinical experiences allow them to see and practice the application in the classroom of the theory they are learning on the college campus. Near the end of the teacher education program when most students do extended clinical work (student teaching or internship), they have an opportunity to use all of the combined knowledge and skills they have learned, still under the supervision and with the help of an experienced teacher. Studies show that graduates typically rate their clinical experiences as the single most valuable part of the teacher education programs.

Various levels of clinical experiences will be classified as follows:

1. *Observation:* Watching youth and/or the teaching-learning process
2. *Participation:* Assisting in the teaching-learning process
3. *Simulation:* Participating in activity that is similar to parts of the teaching act
4. *Microteaching:* Teaching short lessons to small groups, often while being videotaped   33
5. *Student teaching:* A final extensive clinical experience, just before graduation, during which the student gradually assumes nearly the entire role of the teacher
6. *Internship:* A clinical experience that is often the equivalent of the first year of teaching, during which the intern is often paid and receives close supervision and assistance

Although colleges and universities develop their own unique clinical programs, there is general agreement that on-the-job experiences are extremely valuable in teacher education programs.

Rigorous Certification Requirements

Each state determines its own requirements for the various teaching certificates issued in that state. In recent years, due at least in part to recommendations from various reform reports, states have developed more rigorous certification requirements.   8

An increasing number of states now administer some type of competency examination prior to issuing a teaching certificate. Such examinations often include tests of basic skills (such as reading, writing, and mathematics), knowledge in the subjects to be taught (e.g., biology or history for high school certificates; mathematics or language arts for elementary school certificates), and topics dealing with pedagogy (such as educational psychology or teaching methodology).

The Teacher Induction Concept

Educational leaders have struggled for many years with a problem experienced by nearly every first-year teacher. This problem deals with the transition from the life as a college student to life as a classroom teacher. First-year teachers typically need a considerable amount of help from other professionals during their "induction" into the teaching profession. This problem has received renewed attention in recent years, resulting in the evolution of what is now commonly called the teacher induction concept.

A growing number of colleges and universities are creating teacher induction programs. While the details of these programs vary from school to school, they are all designed to provide more help for first-year teachers. Some of the common features of these induction programs include the following:

- A hot line whereby recent graduates or their employers (schools) can call the college for help with some problem the alumnus is having on the job
- On-site visitation by a college faculty member in an attempt to help the first-year teacher remediate any problems and to become more effective
- Conferences sponsored by the college for its recent graduates structured around the common problems of first-year teachers
- A free course(s) for first-year teachers designed to help alumni better succeed in their first year on the job
- A "guarantee" of the college's product (the new teacher) whereby the college provides the graduate and the employer with whatever help might be necessary to ensure effective performance in the classroom

These are but a few of the ways the current education reform movements are bringing about change in teacher education programs throughout the country. Most authorities believe we will likely see more reform measures take place in teacher education as our nation searches for ways to provide better beginning teachers for our classrooms.

New Reports Calling for More Reform

There have been even more national reports dealing with various aspects of education. Several of these major reports will be briefly highlighted at this point.

The Holmes Group Report

A relatively small group of college of education deans from major research universities published a set of recommendations for improving teacher education in the United States. These recommendations were published under the title *Tomorrow's Teachers: A Report of the Holmes Group.* The changes proposed by the Holmes Group are proving to be very controversial and received much attention throughout the teacher education community.

The basic reform goals of the Holmes Group are presented in Figure 3.1. These goals and the ways to achieve them will probably be the subject of discussion for some time to come.

The Carnegie Report

Another report receiving wide national attention is published under the title *A Nation Prepared: Teachers for the 21st Century.* This report, prepared by the Carnegie Task Force on Teaching as a Profession,[1] calls for the following reforms in teacher education:

1. Make teachers' salaries and career opportunities competitive with those in other professions.
2. Require a bachelor's degree in the arts and sciences as a prerequisite for the professional study of teaching.
3. Relate incentives for teachers to schoolwide student performance, and provide schools with technology, services, and staff essential to teacher productivity.
4. Develop a new professional curriculum in graduate schools of education leading to a Master in Teaching degree, based on systematic knowledge of teaching and including internships and residencies in the schools.
5. Create a National Board for Professional Teaching Standards, organized with a regional and state membership structure, to establish high standards for what teachers need to know and be able to do, and to certify teachers who meet those standards.
6. Restructure schools to provide a professional environment for teaching, freeing them to decide how best to meet state and local goals for children while holding them accountable for student progress.
7. Restructure the teaching force and introduce a new category of lead teachers with the proven ability to provide active leadership in redesigning the schools and in helping their colleagues to uphold high standards of learning and teaching.
8. Mobilize the nation's resources to prepare minority youngsters for teaching careers.

Governors' Report on Education

The National Governors' Association has also recently published a report on education which, given the power that governors have in their respective states to influence public education, may become one of the more important educational reports published in recent years. This report, entitled *Time for Results: The Governors' 1991 Report on Education,* advocates that states should act as follows:

1. Provide early-childhood education for all disadvantaged 3- and 4-year-olds, kindergarten for all 5-year-olds, and extra help for students who

The Institutional Environment for Teacher Education

1. The university honors its commitment to the nation's elementary and secondary schools through multiple investments in teachers and teaching.

2. The university works with selected school districts to create exemplary school sites for student and faculty learning about teaching excellence.

3. The university fosters an interdisciplinary climate in teacher education that reflects the importance of disciplinary diversity, depth, and relatedness to teaching.

4. The university expects an ethos of inquiry to permeate its teacher education programs at the university.

5. The university creates significant opportunities for teacher education students to develop collegial and professional norms.

6. The university assures equitable rights and responsibilities to the academic unit accountable for teacher education.

7. The university supports regular improvement of teacher education and participation in a national consortium for ongoing research, development, and program improvement.

Faculty in Teacher Education

1. The faculty responsible for preparing teachers is drawn from competent and committed teachers.

2. The faculty responsible for educating teachers includes both university-based and school-based faculty members.

3. The academic faculty members responsible for teacher education contribute regularly to better knowledge and understanding of teaching and schooling.

4. The teacher education faculty members who demonstrate competence as strong teacher-scholars are recognized for this unique and important combination of abilities.

Students in Teacher Education

1. Students passing through the various phases of study required for career professionals are academically talented and committed to teaching.

2. Students recruited and accepted into teacher education reflect our nation's obligation to a multicultural society.

3. Students evidence mastery of requisite content knowledge through written examination at various stages of their development.

4. Students, as judged by professionals, evidence appropriate ethical commitments and teaching capabilities prior to successful completion of their internship.

Curriculum in Teacher Education

1. The curriculum for prospective career teachers does not permit a major in education during the baccalaureate years—instead, undergraduates pursue more serious general/liberal study and a standard academic subject normally taught in schools.

2. The curriculum for prospective career teachers requires a master's degree in education and a successful year of well-supervised internship.

3. The curriculum for elementary career teachers requires study in multiple areas of concentration (each equivalent to a minor) in the subject fields for which teachers assume general teaching authority and responsibility.

4. The curriculum for secondary career teachers includes significant graduate study in their major teaching field and area concentrations in all other subjects they would teach.

5. The curriculum for all prospective career teachers includes substantial knowledge and work designed to develop skill regarding appropriate policy and practice in teaching students with special needs—advanced graduate study would be required for career professional roles in special education.

6. The curriculum required for teacher attainment of career professional status requires advanced study appropriate for specialized work in education with other adult professionals.

are falling behind. The report also recommends reducing class sizes in kindergarten through third grade and setting up alternative programs for high school dropouts who want to obtain a degree.

2. Establish day care and after-school care in schools, possibly allowing parents to transfer their child to a school near their work. The report suggested that in-school day care would encourage former teachers to return to the classroom and help teenage mothers to stay in school.

3. Set up home programs to teach first-time, low-income parents how to play with and care for their infants. All interested parents of preschool children also would be provided with information on successful parenting techniques.

4. Allow parents to choose the elementary and high school their child will attend, even if the school is in another district. The state would provide transportation, and state and local tax money would follow the students to their new districts.

5. Pass laws to permit a state to declare school districts "educationally bankrupt" if they fail to educate students to acceptable standards. The districts would be placed under state direction until they improve.

6. Publish "report cards" on each school in the state to inform the public how well the schools are doing and what resources they have.

7. Place pressure on schools to share facilities with other community organizations and to convert to year-round calendars in order to make more efficient use of their facilities.

8. Eliminate the emergency licensing used to alleviate teacher shortages and develop new ways to attract qualified college graduates to teaching without requiring them to take undergraduate courses in education.

9. Develop fair, affordable career ladder salaries that recognize differences in teachers' functions, competencies, and performance.

10. Support the creation of a national teacher certification board.

11. Train new teachers to use technology, such as computers and robotics, as classroom tools.

12. Tie principals' salaries and promotions to the results they obtain in their schools, and fire those who show repeated failures.

Report on Elementary Education in America

The U.S. secretary of education published a report entitled *First Lessons: A Report on Elementary Education in America* which contains many recommendations for improving the education of young children. Here is the introduction of this report:

◀ FIGURE 3.1 *Holmes Group Goals* [*Source:* Charles W. Case, Judith E. Lanier, and Cecil G. Miskel, "The Holmes Group Report: Impetus for Gaining Professional Status for Teachers," *Journal of Teacher Education* (American Association of Colleges for Teacher Education), July–August 1986, 41. Used by permission.]

Within the next decade, almost 50 million children will pass through the doors of America's elementary schools. This year alone, in 80,000 elementary schools across the United States, 31 million boys and girls will be taught by 1.45 million teachers. By the middle of the 1990s, enrollments will nearly equal those of the "baby boom" years following World War II.

Elementary education is an enterprise of vast proportions in this nation; and for each child it is an experience of unsurpassed importance. After the family, elementary school is the most influential institution in children's lives; helping to shape first and lasting views of themselves, molding aspirations and skills, introducing them to their country, their culture, to the universe itself.

Yet since 1953, no major national report has examined the condition of elementary education. The "excellence movement" of recent years has looked closely at our high schools and, to a lesser extent, our colleges. But it has not yet paid sustained attention to the condition of elementary education. The time has come to do so—not because elementary schools are in deep trouble, but because they are so deeply important.

After studying elementary schools, visiting them, discussing them, and consulting with some of the country's leading educators, I conclude that American elementary education is not menaced by a "rising tide of mediocrity." It is, overall, in pretty good shape. By some measures, elementary schools are doing better now than they have in years. Yet elementary education in the United States could be better still. Indeed, it will need to be better in the years ahead because we depend so much on it, because not all schools are yet as good as they ought to be—and because it is not in our nature as a society to settle for less than excellence for all.

In the remainder of this report I go into some detail about the condition and direction of elementary education in America. Let me here set forth certain general observations and recommendations:

1. The principal goals of elementary education are to build for every child a strong foundation for further education, for democratic citizenship, and for eventual entry into responsible adulthood.
2. Parents have the central role in children's education and must be empowered to play it successfully.
3. Children do not just "grow up." They must be raised by the community of adults— all adults. The community should accept as its solemn responsibilty—as a covenant—the nurture, care, and education of the coming generation.
4. Teachers should be enabled to become professionals. Certification should depend on demonstrated knowledge and skills, not on paper credentials.
5. The principalship should be deregulated so that accomplished people from many fields may become elementary school principals.
6. In order to provide for more teaching and more learning, elementary schools will need more learning time.
7. The chronological lockstep by which children ordinarily enter and progress through school should be loosened to provide for differences in children's abilities.
8. In specific curriculum areas:

■ Every elementary school can and must teach all its students to read.
■ Children should learn that writing is more than filling in blanks. Writing must be part of the whole curriculum, not just language arts.
■ Elementary schools need to teach science, and their science programs should include "hands-on," experimental activities in addition to texts and lectures.
■ Mathematics should extend beyond simple computation and should emphasize problem solving.
■ The social studies curriculum should be transformed. Schools should teach children not only the basic lessons and habits of life in democratic societies, but also

impart to them substantial instruction in history, geography, and civics, beginning at the earliest ages.
- The arts and instruction in the arts should be integral parts of every elementary school.
- Children should gain a basic grasp of the uses and limitations of computers.
- Elementary curricula should include health and physical education.
- Every school should have a library, and every child should have and use a public library card.[2]

In conclusion, as shown by these few examples, we continue to see a stream of new reports calling for more reform in our nation's educational programs. Since schools serve such an important function in our society, it is likely that they will continue to be the focus of considerable scrutiny.

What School Reform Means to Classroom Teachers

Reform measures that are initiated in our schools impact teachers—sometimes positively and sometimes negatively. Let's examine some of the ways current educational reform is affecting the day-by-day work of teachers in the classroom.

More Money, but Still Not Enough

Nearly all of the reform reports recommend that more must be spent on education to bring about improvements—teachers should be better paid, class sizes should be smaller, schools should be better equipped, and so on.

A modest increase in school funding has occurred throughout the nation as a result of the many reform reports that have been published in recent years. One of the more visible signs of this increase is in the form of higher beginning teacher salaries. Some additional money has also been made available to improve very specific parts of education such as programs for special student populations, to improve in-service teacher education, and to redesign educational goals and objectives. Unfortunately, these additional funds have been inadequate. Education is such a massive financial enterprise that even relatively modest improvements require large additional funds. Many authorities are unsure that our society is willing to provide massive new funds to fuel the reform movement.

Pressure for Higher Quality

A consistent theme running throughout all of the nearly one hundred educational reports published over the past decade, including those most recently released, is that we must find ways to improve the quality of the education our children receive. These recommendations have put extreme pressure on our schools in general, and especially on our teachers, to provide higher-quality education. Ironically, informed observers realize that such demands for higher-quality education will only be possible if significantly more funds are provided for our

The pressure for education reform is a volatile issue and—fairly or unfairly—much of the focus has centered on the quality of teachers. (*Source:* Stuart Spates)

schools. The old adage "You get what you pay for" also applies to education. Although some modest improvements in education can be achieved without many additional funds, if our society wants to significantly improve education, it must also be willing to spend more money on our schools.

Teachers' Comments on School Reform

The National Education Association recently asked a number of teachers across America how the current educational reform movement had affected their life in the classroom. Following are some of these teachers' comments:

> From a seventh grade English teacher in Idaho—
>
> "Two years ago, our state legislature passed an education reform act that required increased funding for programs and teacher salaries, but the legislature hasn't lived up to its promise. We need more teachers to enforce our new stringent high school graduation requirements, but there's no money appropriated for them. Teachers haven't gotten the promised raise. In this election year, legislators won't ask for a tax increase to fund education reform. In fact, they're looking at a $9 million cut in education."

8

Educational reform is only possible in each teacher's classroom. The ultimate goal of all educational reform should be to improve student learning.

Professional Perspectives

From a reading specialist in California—

"California's education reform package, passed in 1983, includes a mentor teacher program that allows teachers to share skills, methods, and curriculum ideas with other teachers. The program is working well in my district. We're looking at curriculum development, standardized tests, and gifted and talented programs, among other things. I serve on a curriculum committee that includes both mentors and other key people from schools. We get valuable feedback from our colleagues at school. I'm planning activities for the extended day program that will help kids enjoy school and encourage them to stay in school."

From an attendance officer and director of adult basic education in Texas—

"We have lots of disgruntled teachers here. Before March all we heard about was the teacher and administrator competency test. Newspapers predicted that 10 percent would fail. How's that for building morale? The career ladder plan has caused a lot of disagreement within school districts. I've taught for 29 years, and I know what we really need to improve schools: more work on classroom discipline, school attendance, and parental cooperation."

From a first grade teacher in Indiana—

"The state legislature enacted a 'Prime Time' program in 1984 to reduce class size in first through third grades. My class size has gone from thirty-one first graders to twenty. That means I have more one-on-one and small group instruction, less noise, and fewer discipline problems. But fourth through sixth grade teachers now have larger classes. The kids we send them are used to more time and attention. Our local Association is studying just how Prime Time affects classrooms through high school."

From an English teacher in Minnesota—

"Minnesota's Post-secondary Option Plan allows high school students to take college courses at the state's expense. This may be good for individual students, but the results for the school system are disastrous. The money spent on these students is school aid lost to the district and reduces programs for those who remain in high school. The major consideration is often the financial advantage to a family, not a student's emotional readiness for college."

From an industrial arts and math teacher in Tennessee—

" 'We pay better teachers more' is easy to say but difficult to carry out. Tennessee's career ladder plan, enacted in 1984, has led to an enormous bureaucracy and a high degree of teacher mistrust in the system. Secrecy and manipulation of data in order to maintain a quota make the evaluations unworkable and unfair. Merit pay brought success to some politicians, but the $14,000 starting salary won't attract the best and the brightest into the teaching profession. It's driving them away."

From a ninth grade science teacher and teacher of the gifted in Arkansas—

"We're happy about the new state regulations that require administrators to evaluate teachers. This is what we've advocated—and worked for through AEA— all along. If classroom observations had been standard procedure, there would have been no possible justification for the competency test all teachers in our state were forced to take last spring. Observations are a much better measure of a teacher's performance. Teachers want to know both their strengths and their weaknesses and to show the community that they're good teachers."

From an English and French teacher in South Carolina—

"I worked on the Governor's Blue Ribbon Task Force that developed the South Carolina Education Improvement Act. As a classroom teacher, I can now see that it's working. In my school, attendance is up, test scores are up, and teacher morale is up. One of the plan's best provisions is the money it appropriates for remedial classes. There are some problems—such as too much paperwork—but overall, I am very pleased. What's most important is that we know our reform package is just a beginning."

From a history teacher in New Jersey—

"New Jersey's $18,000 minimum salary bill is a step in the right direction for keeping teachers in the classroom and encouraging the best students to come into the profession. We're leading the nation on that. And I'm happy that NJEA successfully fought for a teacher recognition plan rather than merit pay. Every school will recognize a teacher who will determine how the $1,000 award will be used in his or her school. Teachers will have tremendous input on who that person will be."

From a teacher of trainable children aged 9–11 in Florida—

"I got a $3,000 bonus under the master teacher program implemented last year. The test I took to qualify for the bonus had very little to do with what I do in the classroom. The money for bonuses would be better spent for increased salaries and classroom improvements. For any politician to feel that a businessperson or another politician knows more about education reform than an educator is absurd. If I could talk to Governor Graham and his cabinet, I would tell them to drop merit pay. Absolutely!"[3]

As shown by these teacher comments, the ideas of school reform will require many changes in the working conditions within the classroom if they are to become reality and to bring about significant improvements in education.

Summary and Implications

Several national reports dealing with various aspects of education have been published by different groups in recent years. The first of these, commonly referred to as *A Nation at Risk,* sets the tone for those that followed. For the most part, these reports have been critical of our public schools in general and of teacher education programs in particular. Most of the reports call for many educational reforms, such as a more basic and rigorous public school curriculum and for higher standards in teacher-training programs.

This chapter has pointed out that the publication of national reports on various aspects of education continues right up to the present time. These reports undoubtedly serve a useful purpose in reminding Americans that our schools and educators serve an extremely important function in our society and are deserving of generous public support.

This message implies that teachers work in the public spotlight and will continue to receive considerable scrutiny by society through a variety of ways, including national reports. In the long run, such scrutiny and attention is necessary to bring about improvements in our educational system.

Discussion Questions

1. In your opinion, which of the reform reports discussed in this chapter is the most important?

2. What conditions will be necessary for the *Nation at Risk* report recommendations to be implemented?

3. What are the main barriers to educational reform in America?

4. What purposes do reform reports such as those discussed in this chapter serve?

5. What good, if any, has come from the many school reform reports that have been published in the past decade?

Supplemental Activities

1. Read several recent professional articles that call for some type of reform in the schools.

2. Visit with a number of teachers and solicit their ideas on needed school reform.

3. Do a critique of one of the school reform reports that has been published in recent years.

4. Write your own school reform recommendations.

5. Discuss with other teacher education students ways to improve American public education.

Notes

1. *A Nation Prepared: Teachers for the 21st Century,* The Report of the Task Force on Teaching as a Profession (New York: Carnegie Forum on Education and the Economy, 1986).

2. William J. Bennett, U.S. Secretary of Education, *First Lessons: A Report on Elementary Education in America* (Washington, D.C.: U.S. Government Printing Office, 1986)

3. National Education Association, *NEA Today* (Washington, D.C.: National Education Association, April 1986), pp. 12–13. Used by permission.

Bibliography

Garcia, Peter A. *A Study on Teacher Competency Testing and Test Validity with Implications for Minorities and the Results and Implications of the Use of the Pre-Professional Skills Test (PPST) as a Screening Device for Entrance into Teacher Education Programs in Texas.* Edinburg, Tex.: Pan American University, 1986

Haberman, Martin. "Licensing Teachers: Lessons from Other Professions." *Phi Delta Kappan,* LXVII (June 1986): 719–722.

Hessong, Robert F., and Weeks, Thomas H. *Introduction to Education.* New York: Macmillan, 1987.

Housam, Robert B., et al. *Educating a Profession.* Washington, D.C.: American Association of Colleges for Teacher Education, 1976.

Magrath, C. Peter, Chair, National Commission for Excellence in Teacher Education. *A Call for Change in Teacher Education.* Washington, D.C.: American Association of Colleges for Teacher Education, 1985.

Mehlinger, Howard D. "Simple but Radical Reform of Teacher Education." *Educational Horizons,* 65(2) (Winter 1987): 58–61.

Nathan, Joe. "Implications for Educators of Time for Results. A report of the National Governor's Association Report on Education." *Phi Delta Kappan,* 68 (4) (November 1986): 197–201.

National Commission on Excellence in Education. *A Nation at Risk: The Imperative for Educational Reform.* Washington, D.C.: U.S. Department of Education, 1983.

A Nation Prepared: Teachers for the 21st Century. The Report of the Task Force on Teaching as a Profession. New York: Carnegie Forum on Education and the Economy, 1986.

NCATE Redesign. Washington, D.C.: National Council for Accreditation of Teacher Education, 1985.

NEA Leadership Briefing Paper on the Report of the Task Force on Teaching as a Profession. New York: Carnegie Forum on Education and the Economy, 1986.

Pipho, Chris. "States Move Reform Closer to Reality." *Phi Delta Kappan,* 68(4) (December 1986): K1–K8.

Presseisen, Barbara Z. *Unlearned Lessons: Current and Past Reforms for School Improvement.* Philadelphia: International Publishers, 1985.

"Teacher Unions Give Qualified Backing to Carnegie Proposals on School Reform." *Chronicle of Higher Education,* XXXII (July 16, 1986): 1,22.

Tomorrow's Teachers, A Report of the Holmes Group. East Lansing, Mich.: The Holmes Group, 1986.

Visions of Reform: Implications for the Education Profession. Washington, D.C.: Association of Teacher Education, 1986.

4

Legal Aspects
of Teaching

Focus Questions

- One of the top issues for the late 1980s will be increased demands that the nation's schools act as parents. Would this issue imply that teachers need not be threatened by being sued by parents?
- Judges rarely have any training for needs of the handicapped, yet courts are increasingly ordering expensive individualized programs for handicapped students. In what way do such court orders provide for students' rights, on the one hand, and take away from students' rights, on the other hand?
- A group of students brought suit in a state court seek-

ing to block the testing of urine samples for the presence of drugs. The state court sided with the students. Do such court decisions go too far in protecting students' rights in our schools? How?

- Affirmative action and reverse discrimination will continue to be vexing issues in the courts. How do these kinds of cases relate to the teaching profession?
- Does the fact that teachers are increasingly being sued by students and parents for violations of student rights and teacher misconduct bother you? How? Why?

Key Terms and Concepts

Book banning
Student rights
Due process
Corporal punishment
Sex discrimination
Educational malpractice

Teacher certification
Teacher contracts
Academic freedom
Collective bargaining
Liability
In loco parentis

What Would You Do?

A teacher at a privately endowed high school was dismissed for several alleged infractions, and she requested a hearing before the board of trustees. The board members refused to give her a hearing. If this situation happened to you, how would you respond?

You notice that a girl in one of your classes often appears to have bruise marks on her face sufficient to suggest physical abuse. Another classmate of the girl confides in you and tells you that the girl is being physically and sexually abused by her father. How would you deal with the problem of this girl?

Beginning with the 1954 U.S. Supreme Court decision in *Brown* v. *Board of Education of Topeka,* which repudiated the separate-but-equal doctrine, hundreds of education-related court cases have been decided at all levels identifying and enforcing individual rights. Cases involving racially motivated practices related to attendance and curriculum, nondisruptive free expression inside the schools, dress codes, locker searches, student records, and religion created individual student and teacher rights that reduced the discretion of local school officials. Since 1975 the Supreme Court has tended to refuse the creation of new individual rights and in some instances has curtailed rights established earlier. This tendency has resulted in claims that the past ten years may be viewed as a swing back toward an emphasis on the rights of school officials to run schools to best serve their districts. The legalistic age in which we live suggests a continuance of large numbers of education-related court decisions. Affected are not only the professional classroom practices of teachers when dealing with students but also the personal lifestyles of teachers. Although actions and decisions of school boards and lower courts are of considerable local importance and provide the bases for appeal to supreme courts (state and national), the Supreme Court decisions have a much broader range of influence. Therefore this chapter, for the most part, uses Supreme Court decisions as references regarding the topics discussed.

14

Teachers are subject to the U.S. Constitution, state constitutions, statutory law, and school board policy and are protected by them when interacting with pupils, colleagues, and employers. Although the federal courts have abandoned their traditional hands-off policy in cases involving local school boards, disputes involving special education, sex discrimination, school libraries, student rights, desegregation, and education for alien children all provoke dissension among the justices. Nonetheless, the leadership of the U.S. Supreme Court is vital in resolving some of the primary legal issues in education.

Selected school-related court cases dealing with student rights and responsibilities are discussed in this chapter. Topics include rights to an education, pupil conduct, *in loco parentis,* due process, corporal punishment, dress codes and grooming, sex discrimination, marriage and pregnancy, child abuse and neglect, AIDS, school records, student and locker searches, and educational malpractice. Teacher rights and responsibilities discussed include teacher certification, teacher employment contracts, discrimination, teacher tenure, academic freedom, right to bargain collectively, right to strike, and liability for negligence.

Student Rights and Responsibilities

In the middle and late 1960s student protests were common across the campuses of American colleges and universities. Student protests increased during the last half of the decade, spreading to the junior and senior high school levels from coast to coast. In 1969 a national survey of over a thousand principals conducted by the National Association of Secondary School Principals found that 56 percent of those in junior high schools and 59 percent of those in senior high schools had experienced some kind of protest. Many educators and lay citizens bemoan [14] this progress toward a clear definition of student rights and responsibilities as legal trespass on educators' power over and control of students in the school. Some claim that the dimensions of student responsibility have never been determined.

Although student protests became less frequent, the decade of the 1970s saw a substantial increase in student violence and vandalism. Large school systems were particularly hard hit with significant increases in drug and alcohol offenses on school property, assaults on teachers, school building burglaries, number of weapons confiscated by school authorities, assaults on students, and other acts of violence.

Many of the recommendations for school reform offered by state and national study groups in the 1980s were based on views of students that were shaped by the protests of the 1960s and 1970s.[1] Similarly, the courts have also become active in matters dealing with student rights and responsibilities.

Many court decisions are against students whose nonconformism seems to go beyond a reasonable norm. Often the courts support the right of the local school authority to exercise considerable control over matters that affect students. What often happens is that there is so much emotionalism that the original question of student rights and responsibilities becomes obscured.

Specific court cases are discussed here briefly to illustrate some of the issues and decisions related to aspects of student rights and responsibilities. Note that the cases selected do not necessarily constitute the last word regarding student rights but, rather, are used to provide an overview of some of the issues that have been decided in our courts. Table 4.1 summarizes the issues and decisions of the selected cases about student rights and responsibilities. This summary table is not intended to provide a complete understanding of the court decisions cited. You should read the textual narrative for a more complete understanding.

TABLE 4.1 *Summary of Selected Student Rights and Responsibility Cases*

Case	Issue	Decision
Plyler v. *Doe* (1982)	Right to education of children of illegal aliens	Struck down Texas law denying a free public education to these children
Goss v. *Lopez* (1975)	Suspension of high school students without a hearing	Court ruled that students cannot be suspended without a hearing
Wood v. *Strickland* (1975)	Can school board members be sued for depriving students of their constitutional rights (suspended)?	Students could seek damages from individual school board members but not from the school district
Carey v. *Piphus* (1978)	Clarified *Wood* case above; what conditions for damages to be awarded students and what amount?	Student must clearly establish that an injury has occurred before damages can be collected from board members

TABLE 4.1 *(Continued)*

Case	Issue	Decision
Tinker v. *Des Moines Independent Community School District* (1969)	*In loco parentis* doctrine questioned; school denied students right to wear black armbands to protest Vietnam	Court ruled against school district—established constitutional rights of pupils
Board of Education, Inland Trees Union Free School District No. 26 v. *Pico* (1982)	Challenged school board's decision to remove books from the school library	U.S. Supreme Court issued decision that under certain circumstances children may challenge board's decision to remove books
Ingraham v. *Wright* (1977)	May states authorize corporal punishment without consent of student's parent?	Yes, states may constitutionally authorize corporal punishment
Long v. *Zopp* (1973)	School's right to invoke dress code and hair length regulations	Divided opinions among courts on this issue; this case ruled the school must prove that the hair or dress interfered with students' ability to play the sport or perform the activity
Scoville v. *Board of Education* (1970)	Students were expelled for distributing a newspaper that criticized school officials and used vulgar language	Court ruled against school and said that students were entitled to the declaratory judgment and damage relief sought
Peter W. v. *San Francisco Unified School District* (1976) and *Donahue* v. *Copiague Union Free School District* (1978)	Former students sued for not receiving an adequate education	Courts dismissed suits by students—no way to assess the school's negligence
Hunter v. *Board of Education of Montgomery County* (1981)	Court was asked to recognize educational malpractice as tort liability of the school district	Court rejected the request, saying that suit for educational malpractice might arise every time a child failed a grade
Board of Education of Hendrick Hudson Central School District v. *Rowley* (1982)	What constitutes "related services" under Public Law 94–142?	A school district is not required to provide a hearing interpreter for a deaf student
Bethel School District No. 403 v. *Fraser* (1986)	May school officials restrain student speech?	School officials may discipline a student for making lewd and indecent speech in a school assembly attended by other students

Student Rights to an Education

American children have a right to an education; this right is assured in many state constitutions. It has been further defined by court decisions and is now interpreted to mean that each child shall have an equal opportunity to pursue education.

The right to an education, however, is not without certain prerequisites. Citizenship alone does not guarantee a free education. Statutes that establish public school systems also generally establish how operating costs will be met.

Real estate taxes are the usual source of funds, so the residence requirement is necessary for school attendance without tuition. *Residence* does not mean that the student, parent, or guardian must pay real estate taxes; it means that the student must live in the school district in which he or she wants to attend school. Residence then is a prerequisite to the right of a free public education within a specific school district.

In June 1982 the U.S. Supreme Court extended this right to include the children of undocumented illegal aliens. In *Plyler* v. *Doe* (1982) the controversial five-to-four majority decision struck down a Texas law denying a free public education to these children. The majority opinion held that the Texas law "imposes a lifetime of hardship on a discrete class of children not accountable for their disabling status and promotes the creation and perpetuation of a sub-class of illiterates within our boundaries, surely adding to the problems and costs of unemployment, welfare, and crime."

Pupil Conduct

The right, or privilege, of children to attend school also depends on their compliance with the rules and regulations of the school. To ensure the day-to-day orderly operation of schools, boards of education have been given the right to establish reasonable rules and regulations controlling pupils and their conduct. In a number of instances the boards' actions have been challenged, however. Most challenges have concerned corporal punishment, rights of married students to an education, dress codes, and freedom of expression.

Goss v. *Lopez* (U.S. Supreme Court, 1975) dealt with the suspension of high school students in Columbus, Ohio. In that case the named plaintiffs alleged that they had been suspended from public high school for up to ten days without a hearing. The action was brought for deprivation of constitutional rights. Two students who were suspended for a semester brought suit charging that their due process rights were denied—because they were not present at the board meeting when the suspensions were handed out. In ruling that students cannot be suspended without some kind of hearing, the Court said:

> The prospect of imposing elaborate hearing requirements in every suspension case is viewed with great concern, and many school authorities may well prefer the untrammeled power to act unilaterally, unhampered by rules about notice and hearing. But it would be a strange disciplinary system in an educational institution if no communication was sought by the disciplinarian with the student in an effort to inform him of his defalcation and to let him tell his side of the story in order to make sure that an injustice is not done. Fairness can rarely be obtained by secret, one-sided determination of the facts decisive of rights. . . . Secrecy is not congenial to truth-seeking and self-righteousness gives too slender an assurance of rightness. No better instrument has been devised for arriving at truth than to give a person in jeopardy of serious loss notice of the case against him and opportunity to meet it.

Just a month after the *Goss* v. *Lopez* decision, the U.S. Supreme Court handed down a more significant decision, which affirmed that students may sue school

To ensure the efficient, day-to-day operation of schools, boards of education have been given the right to establish reasonable rules and regulations. (*Source:* Mike Penney)

board members who are guilty of intentionally depriving students of their constitutional rights. In *Wood* v. *Strickland* (1975) the Supreme Court held that school officials who discipline students unfairly cannot defend themselves against civil rights suits by claiming ignorance of pupils' basic constitutional rights. As a result of this decision, Judge Paul Williams, a federal judge in Arkansas, ordered that the girls who had been suspended could seek damages from individual school board members—though not from the school district as a corporate body. The judge also ruled that the school records of the pupils must be cleared of the suspension incident. From these decisions it is apparent that the U.S. Supreme Court is taking into account the rights of students.

The Supreme Court extended and clarified its ruling in *Wood* three years later when it considered the rights of students to collect damages for having been suspended without a hearing. The case, *Carey* v. *Piphus* (1978), treated two issues: under what conditions damages may be awarded to students who have been deprived of their constitutional rights and the amount of damages they can receive. The Court held that a student must first clearly establish that an injury has occurred before damages can be collected. Since that condition had not been established, the Court ruled that the students were entitled only to symbolic damages of $1.00.

In *Bethel School District No. 403* v. *Fraser* (1986), the Court upheld the suspension of a senior high school student for making a nominating speech which contained sexual comments which caused disruptive behavior among students at a school assembly. The student's rights were judged not to have been violated by the suspension.

Efforts have been made to define student rights. One such effort, *A Bill of Rights for High School Students,* was developed by the American Civil Liberties Union of Maryland. It is based partly on court decisions and illustrates current thinking about student rights. It addresses, for example, freedom of expression, religion, and privacy and rights of equality of opportunity and due process. (The complete text is given in Appendix A.) Many school systems also have established their own bill of rights.

In Loco Parentis

Historically, schools have functioned under the doctrine of *in loco parentis* (in place of a parent). This doctrine means that schools may exercise almost complete control over students because they act as parent substitutes. Under the doctrine of *in loco parentis* the courts usually upheld the rules and regulations of local boards of education, particularly about pupil conduct. Recently, there has been a change toward more regard for the constitutional rights of pupils: the *Tinker* case (*Tinker* v. *Des Moines Independent Community School District,* 1969) was significant. It involved a school board's attempt to keep students from wearing black armbands in a protest against hostilities in Vietnam. In 1969 the U.S. Supreme Court ruled against the Des Moines school board. The majority opinion of the Court was that

> the wearing of armbands in the circumstances of this case was entirely divorced from actually or potentially disruptive conduct by those participating in it. It was closely akin to "pure speech" which, we have repeatedly held, is entitled to comprehensive protection, under the First Amendment. . . .
>
> First Amendment rights, applied in the light of the special characteristics of the school environment, are available to teachers and students. It can hardly be argued that either students or teachers shed their constitutional rights to freedom at the schoolhouse gate.

In the *Tinker* opinion the Court clearly designated that the decision "does not concern aggressive, disruptive action or even group demonstrations." The decision did make it clear that whatever their age, students have constitutional rights; and the decision has had widespread effect on the operation of schools in the United States. Schools have had to pay attention to school law. Educators as well as lawyers have been guided by the principles set forth in the decision regarding the constitutional relationship between public school students and school officials.

A recent U.S. Supreme Court decision appears to at least have narrowed the breadth of application of the *Tinker* ruling. The case involved Matthew Fraser, a high school senior in a school outside Tacoma, Washington. In the spring of 1983 Fraser was suspended from school for two days after he gave a short speech at a school assembly nominating a friend for a position in student government. School officials argued that Fraser's speech contained sexual innuendos which provoked other students to engage in disruptive behaviors unfavorable to the school setting. The U.S. District Court for the Western District of Washington held that Fraser's punishment violated his rights to free speech under the First Amendment and awarded him damages. The U.S. Court of Appeals for the Ninth Circuit affirmed the decision, holding that Fraser's speech was not disruptive under the standards of *Tinker*.[2] In the majority opinion in *Bethel School District No. 403* v. *Fraser* (1986), Chief Justice Warren Burger wrote: "The determination of what manner of speech in the classroom or in school assembly is inappropriate properly rests with the school board."

Attorney Thomas J. Flygare suggests that the major unanswered question appears to be whether *Fraser* will be interpreted to permit school officials to place an outright ban on political speech as "inappropriate" or whether it will be interpreted only to permit punishment for "indecent" and similar forms of speech.[3]

Due Process

Much of the recent involvement of the courts with student rights has concerned due process of law for pupils. Due process has two connotations—procedural and substantive. Procedural due process has to do with whether or not the procedures used in disciplinary cases are fair; substantive due process is concerned with whether or not the school authorities have deprived a student of basic substantive constitutional rights like freedom of speech or personal liberty.[4]

Procedural due process is frequently scrutinized in cases of suspension and expulsion. These cases most often result from disciplinary action taken by the school, which may or may not have violated a pupil's substantive constitutional right. In the *Tinker* case, in which students were suspended, the decision was made primarily on the violation of the substantive right of freedom of speech or expression.

Procedural due process cases usually involve alleged violations of the Fourteenth Amendment, which provides for the protection of specified privileges of citizens, including due process of law. They may also involve alleged violations of state constitutions or statutory law that call for specific procedures. Many states have procedures for expulsion or suspension. Expulsion usually involves notifying parents or guardians in a specific way, perhaps by registered mail, and giving students the opportunity for a hearing before the board of education or a designated hearing officer. Suspension procedures are usually detailed as well, designating who has the authority to suspend and the length of time for suspension. Teachers and administrators should know due process regulations, including the specific regulations of the state where they are employed.

Corporal Punishment

In 1977 the U.S. Supreme Court ruled on and finally resolved many of the issues related to corporal punishment (*Ingraham* v. *Wright,* 1977). The opinion established that states may *constitutionally* authorize corporal punishment without prior hearing or notice and without consent by the student's parents and may as a matter of policy elect to prohibit or limit the use of corporal punishment. It also held that corporal punishment is not in violation of the Eighth Amendment.

In response to the greater sensitivity to student rights, many school districts have adopted administrative rules and regulations to restrict the occasions, nature, and manner of administering corporal punishment. In some instances school districts specify that corporal punishment may be administered only under the direction of the principal and in the presence of another adult.

For the most part, courts have been consistent over the years in upholding school personnel in administering *reasonable* corporal punishment. Reasonableness frequently reflects local attitudes; its definition will therefore vary from region to region. In determining whether or not to administer corporal punishment, school personnel should consider these factors: age, sex, and size of pupil; size and suitability of the instrument and force employed; and the degree of the punishment in respect to the nature of the infraction. It should be noted that the lower courts across the country do vary in their judgments regarding the reasonableness of corporal punishment. Of nineteen cases reviewed by the *1986 Deskbook Encyclopedia of American School Law,* in eight cases the corporal punishment was judged reasonable and in the eleven other cases the punishment was judged to be unreasonable. In those unreasonable corporal punishment cases, school personnel were either fined or dismissed from their jobs. Teachers are cautioned to be very careful in the use of corporal punishment.

Dress Codes and Grooming

Lower-court cases dealing with grooming have been decided in some instances in favor of the board of education—in support of their rules and regulations—and in other instances in favor of the student. A general principle seems to be that if the dress and grooming do not incite or cause disruptive behavior or pose a health or safety problem, the court ruling is likely to support the student. Dress codes, once very much in vogue, are much less evident today. Although the U.S. Supreme Court has yet to consider a so-called long-hair case, federal courts in every circuit have issued rulings in such cases; half of them found such regulations unconstitutional, and half upheld them. In all, over a two-decade period, more than three hundred cases on this subject were decided by federal and state courts.

The courts have usually refused to uphold dress and hair length regulations for athletic teams or extracurricular activities unless the school proves that the hair or dress interfered with a student's ability to play the sport or perform the activity, as in *Long* v. *Zopp* (1973).

In the late 1970s and continuing into the 1980s, courts began to entertain fewer challenges to grooming regulations. The later decisions have continued to be consistent, however, with earlier court rulings. Courts have supported school officials who attempted to regulate student appearance if the regulation could be based on disruption, health, or safety. Presumably, the controversy over the length of a student's hair or one's grooming in general is no longer critical because officials and students have a more common ground of agreement about what is acceptable.

Sex Discrimination

Until recently, educational institutions could discriminate against females—whether they were students, staff, or faculty. In 1972 the Ninety-second Congress enacted Title IX of the Education Amendments Act to remove sex discrimination against students and employees in federally assisted programs. The key provision in Title IX states: "No person in the United States shall, on the basis of sex, be excluded from participation in, be denied the benefits of, or be subjected to discrimination under any education program or activity receiving federal financial assistance." Title IX is enforced by the Office of Civil Rights of the Department of Health, Education, and Welfare (HEW), now the Department of Education. An individual or organization can allege any policy or practice as discriminatory by writing a letter of complaint to the secretary of the Department of Education. An administrative hearing is the next step in the process.

Schools at all levels are required to comply with Title IX. The statute does exempt military school, some religious institutions, and private undergraduate schools. After admitting students of both sexes, however, these schools cannot alter admission policy to discriminate purposely on the basis of sex.

Marriage and Pregnancy

In the past it was not unusual for school officials to expel students who married. Some educators reasoned that marriage brought on additional responsibilities such as the establishment of a household and relating as a member of the local community. Courts tended to uphold school officials in these positions. Both courts and school officials acted consistently in not rigidly enforcing compulsory attendance statutes for underage students. However, school officials today cannot prohibit a student from attending school merely because he or she is married. This position is based on the notion that every child has a right to attend school.

Public policy currently encourages students to acquire as much education as they can. Not only are married students encouraged to remain in school, but

Professional Perspectives

Periodically discuss students' rights and responsibilities with your students. Share the outcomes of selected court cases in these discussions to illustrate responsibilities which accompany rights.

they are also entitled to the same rights and privileges as unmarried students. Thus they have the right to take any course the school offers and to participate in extracurricular activities open to other students. That is, participation in extracurricular activities cannot be denied a student solely on the basis of married status. A student's attendance and participation rights may be removed when his or her behavior is deleterious to other students.

Today's schools also enroll more pregnant students than ever before. Current legal opinion holds that pregnancy in and of itself is no reason to exclude a student from school or from participation in extracurricular activities. A number of school systems have reorganized their school programs so that courses can be offered during after-school hours or in the evenings to accommodate married and pregnant students. This arrangement makes it easier for students to work during the day and complete their education at a time convenient to them. Included in such programs are courses and topics aimed for the specific audience and a counseling program to assist students with their adjustment to marriage and family life.

Child Abuse and Neglect

Our system of government has the right of exercising police power, which means that government is entrusted with the responsibility of looking after the health, safety, and welfare of all its citizens. In effect, a state acts as a guardian over all its people, exercising that role specifically over individuals not able to look after themselves. This guardianship extends to care for children who have been either abused or neglected by their parents. To date, all 50 states have statutes dealing with this issue. These statutes generally protect children under age eighteen, but the scope of protection and definitions of abuse and neglect vary considerably among the states. In 1974 the federal Congress passed the Child Abuse Prevention and Treatment Act. This act provides financial assistance to states that have developed and implemented programs for identifying, preventing, and treating instances of child abuse and neglect.

The severity of this problem has been highlighted by the requirement of mandatory reporting of suspected abuse and neglect. Formerly, this reporting was limited mainly to physicians, but today educators are also required to report instances of suspected abuse and neglect. Some teachers are reluctant to do so because they fear a breakdown in student-teacher-parent relationships and the possibility of a law suit based on an invasion of privacy, assault, or slander. Their fear should be diminished, however, by statutes which grant them immunity for acting in good faith.

AIDS

One of the most recent controversies to face the schools has been the presence of children with AIDS (acquired immune deficiency syndrome). The disease itself has been identified in this country for less than a decade. According to *Education Week* (September 11, 1985), as of late August that year, there were

12,599 reported cases of AIDS in this country, with 183 of them being children under age eighteen. The Center for Disease Control predicted that the number would double within a year. The disease attacks the body's defense system, gradually rendering it incapable of fighting diseases. To date, there is no known cure.

Even though current evidence indicates that AIDS is not transmitted through casual person-to-person contact, many people have reacted to it by avoiding its victims. Since the disease is transmitted through exchange of blood or contact with body fluids, many people prefer to avoid a risk of the disease by avoiding completely an AIDS victim.

When the 1985–1986 school year began, New Jersey had reported a total of 22 children with AIDS. The issue of children with AIDS attending school received considerable publicity when in Kokomo, Indiana, an early-teenage boy acquired AIDS as a result of a blood transfusion. When his disease was discovered, he was at first not allowed to return to the public schools. The school district later reversed itself, at which time a number of parents refused to send their children to school. Later, a court order permitted the boy to enroll in school in the fall of 1986. Public school personnel, including board members, administrators, and teachers, need to give considerable thought to policies regulating the rights of AIDS victims as well as the protection of other persons. Surely, the courts will be increasingly called upon to rule on the school rights of students who are AIDS victims.

School Records

Before November 19, 1974, the effective date of the Buckley Amendment, the law regarding the privacy of student records was extremely unclear. Many school administrators—and most parents—do not yet realize that parents now have the right to view their children's educational records. Students over the age of eighteen also have the right to see their school records for themselves. Many teachers are not yet aware that their written comments, which they submit as part of a student's record, must be shown at a parent's request, or at a student's request if the student is eighteen.

The new law (Public Law 93–380 as amended by Public Law 93–568) requires that schools receiving federal funds must comply with the privacy requirements or face loss of those funds. What must a school district do to comply? According to a 1976 clarification by HEW, the Buckley Amendment sets forth these main requirements that the school district must follow:

> Allow all parents, even those not having custody of their children, access to each educational record that a school district keeps on their child.
>
> Establish a district policy on how parents can go about seeing specific records.
>
> Inform all parents what rights they have under the Amendment, how they can act on these rights according to school policy, and where they can see a copy of the policy.
>
> Seek parental permission in writing before disclosing any personally identifiable record on a child to individuals other than professional personnel employed in the district (and others who meet certain specific requirements).[5]

Since the loss of federal funds could present serious problems to some school districts, the responsibility for procedures to meet the requirements of the Buckley Amendment are self-evident. Many school districts have carefully formulated procedures; others are striving to clarify such procedures in order to prevent conflicts.

Student Publications

A significant decision for student newspapers was made in *Scoville* v. *Board of Education* (1970), originating in Illinois. Students were expelled for distributing a newspaper named *Grass High,* which criticized school officials and used vulgar language. The students were expelled under an Illinois statute that empowered boards of education to expel pupils guilty of gross disobedience or misconduct. The board of education was supported by a federal court in Illinois, but on appeal the Court of Appeals for the Seventh Circuit reversed the decision. The court concluded:

> . . . absent an evidentiary showing, and an appropriate balancing of the evidence by the district court to determine whether the Board was justified in a "forecast" of the disruption and interference, as required under *Tinker,* plaintiffs are entitled to the declaratory judgment, injunctive and damage relief sought.

In 1975 the Second Circuit Court of Appeals affirmed a lower-court decision that school newspaper editors had a constitutional right to publish a sex supplement that included articles on contraception and abortion.[6] Furthermore, the court ruled that school authorities, on the basis of their opinion that the material was not fit for high school students, could not seize or ban its distribution. The same court in 1977 ruled that high school administrators could ban school newspaper editors from conducting and publishing a student poll that sought personal and frank information about students' sexual experiences and attitudes.[7] The court found that the state's interest in preventing psychological harm to immature students was enough to override the students' claims for license.

The issue of institutional control over publications has not yet been fully resolved. On the basis of the decisions of courts to date, a school official must be very careful in restricting the content of a school-sponsored publication unless it is clearly obscene. If the newspaper leads to disruption, school officials have a much better chance of being upheld in restricting the publication. School officials have also been protected where there is reasonable expectation of disruption or interference.

Student and Locker Searches

Most lower courts have refused to subject public school searches to the same strict Fourth Amendment standards that govern warrantless searches of criminal suspects by police and prosecutors. In general, the Fourth Amendment protects individuals from search without a warrant (court order). Many lower courts have decided in favor of a lenient interpretation of the Fourth Amendment in school searches. The rationale is that school authorities are obligated to maintain discipline and a sound educational environment and that responsibility, along with their *in loco parentis* powers, gives them the right to conduct searches and seize contraband upon reasonable suspicion without a judicial warrant.

School authorities do not need a warrant to search a student's locker or a student vehicle on campus. For searches of a student's person, however, courts apply a higher standard. Where reasonable suspicion exists, a school official will likely be upheld. Reasonable suspicion exists when one has information that a student is in possession of something harmful, illegal, or dangerous. The second consideration is the way in which the search of a student's person is conducted. School officials are advised to have students remove contents from their clothing rather than have a teacher or administrator do it. A further caution is not to force students to remove all their clothing or undress to their underwear. To date, courts have not upheld school officials in strip searches. These cases evoke the greatest judicial sympathy toward student damages for illegal searches.[8]

Considerable support for administrators' search of students has resulted from an early 1985 decision by the U.S. Supreme Court (1985). In this case the justices answered two questions. The Court ruled unanimously that school officials are subject to the Fourth Amendment protection against unreasonable searches when they engage in searches of students. In the second question the justices ruled that school officials are not bound by the probable cause of the standard amendment but rather by a reasonable-cause standard when engaged in searches. In exploring the application of reasonable cause for conducting a search, Justice White stated that a search is justified when an administrator has
reasonable grounds to suspect that a search will turn up evidence that the student is in violation of the law or of school rules. Also, a search will be upheld when it is reasonably related to the objectives of the search and is not excessively obtrusive in terms of the student's age and sex and the nature of the infraction. What the Court held was that the rules governing search of students are not as strict as those that apply to law enforcement officials because the rules should not interfere "with the maintenance of the swift and informal disciplinary procedures needed in the schools." Since this decision, a number of cases have been handed down by lower courts (state courts in Illinois, Michigan, Wisconsin, Florida, and California; and U.S. appeals courts in Cincinnati, New Orleans, and San Francisco) that are in agreement with the Supreme Court holding.

The following grounds have been held to justify a search: information from student informers, police tips, anonymous callers, unusual conduct by the searched student (secretive movements), fleeing an instructor when called, and tips from outside callers and personnel.[9] A recent question involving searches of students concerns the use of dogs in sniffing out narcotics. The first such case was decided in 1980, and the few cases handed down since then reveal a lack of unanimity among the courts. On the one hand, some courts have held that the use of a dog is merely preliminary to a search; on the other hand, some courts have viewed such a search as being highly invasive. Further court decisions are required to clarify this issue.

Educational Malpractice

The courts of California (*Peter W.* v. *San Francisco Unified School District,* 1976) and New York (*Donahue* v. *Copiague Union Free School District,* 1978) dismissed suits by former students alleging indirect injury. That is, they did not achieve an adequate education, and that they did not was the fault of the school district. In the California case the student, after graduating from high school, could barely read and write. The judge in his opinion stated:

> The science of pedagogy itself is fraught with different and conflicting theories . . . and any layman might—and commonly does—have his own emphatic viewpoints on the subject. . . . The achievement of literacy in the schools, or its failure, is influenced by a host of factors from outside the formal teaching process, and beyond the course of its ministries.

In essence, the judge stated that there is no way to assess the school's [16] negligence. In the New York case the judge said, "The failure to learn does not bespeak a failure to teach."

The *Hunter* decision of 1981 followed previous rulings, although the plaintiffs had asked the court specifically to reject the notion that public policy considerations forbade such a suit (*Hunter* v. *Board of Education,* 1981). The court also rejected the suggestion that it recognize a new tort, that of educational malpractice. It saw a number of problems arising from such a tort:

> It is conceivable that, if allowed, suits for educational malpractice might arise every time a child failed a grade, subject, or test, with the result that teachers could possibly spend more time in lawyers' offices and courtrooms than in the classroom. That happening could give rise to claims of educational malpractice predicted on the teacher's failure to devote sufficient time to teaching. The opposite side of the matter is that if, to avoid suits arising from a student's failing a grade, subject or test, the teacher "passed" the child, the teacher would likely find himself or herself defending a malpractice suit because the child was promoted when promotion was not warranted.

As a summary of the discussion of this section, Table 4.2 lists brief statements related to the rights and responsibilities of students.

Teacher Rights and Responsibilities

Teachers have the same rights as other citizens. The Fourteenth Amendment provides for substantive due process (e.g., protection against the deprivation of constitutional rights such as freedom of expression) and procedural due process (procedural protection against unjustified deprivation of substantive rights). Most court cases related to teachers evolve from either liberty or property interests. Liberty interests are created by the Constitution itself; property interests are found in some form of legal entitlement such as tenure or certification.

TABLE 4.2 *Summary Statements on Students' Rights and Responsibilities*

State constitutions provide that a child has the right to an education; to date, students have been unsuccessful in suing school board members on the grounds that they have not learned anything

The due process clause provides that a child is entitled to notice of charges and the opportunity for a hearing prior to being suspended from school for misbehavior

Students enjoy freedom of speech at school unless that speech is indecent or leads to disruption; courts are not in agreement about the extent to which school officials can regulate the content of student newspapers

Students may be awarded damages from school board members for a violation of their constitutional rights if they can establish that they were actually injured by the deprivation

The use of corporal punishment is not prohibited by the federal constitution

Students may be restricted in their dress when there are problems of disruption, health, or safety

Assignment of students to activities or classes on the basis of sex is not consistent with Title IX

Restricting student activities on the basis of marriage or pregnancy is inconsistent with the equal-protection clause; state laws and local school board policies determine the rights of AIDS victims in the schools

Teachers are required to report to proper authorities suspected instances of child abuse and neglect

Parents have the right to examine their children's educational records; children age eighteen and older have the right to examine their records; school officials may search students, lockers, and student property without a search warrant

Teachers also have the same responsibilities as other citizens. They must abide by federal, state, and local laws and by the provisions of contracts. As professionals, they must also assume the heavy responsibility of educating young people. Specific court cases are discussed briefly to illustrate some of the issues and decisions related to aspects of teacher rights and responsibilities. Note that the cases selected do not necessarily constitute the last word regarding teacher rights but, rather, are used to provide an overview of some of the issues that have been decided in our courts. Table 4.3 summarizes the issues and decisions in selected cases involving teacher rights and responsibilities. This summary table is not intended to provide a complete understanding of the court decisions cited. You should read the textual narrative for a more complete understanding.

Teacher Certification

The primary purpose of teacher certification is to make sure there are qualified and competent teachers in the public schools. All states have established requirements for teacher certification. Carrying out the policies of certification is usually a function of a state certification board. The board first has to make certain that applicants meet legal requirements; it then issues the appropriate certificates. Certifying agencies may not arbitrarily refuse to issue a certificate to a qualified candidate. The courts have ruled that local boards of education

TABLE 4.3 *Summary of Selected Teacher Rights and Responsibility Cases*

Case	Issue	Decision
North Haven Board of Education v. *Bell* (1982)	Former women faculty members alleged sex discrimination	U.S. Supreme Court ruled that school employees as well as students are protected under Title IX
Burkey v. *Marshall County Board of Education* (1981)	Pay equity for female coach and male coach	Ruled that board's policy of paying female coach less than male coach violated the Equal Pay Act
Turk v. *Franklin Special School District* (1982)	School board dismissed tenured teacher after she was arrested for driving under the influence of alcohol	Tennessee Supreme Court ruled that before a tenured teacher can be dismissed, charges shall be made in writing specifically stating the offenses
Lucia v. *Duggan* (1969)	Is it necessary for a school district to follow due process procedures in dismissing nontenured teachers?	Court ruled that the rights of procedural due process are applicable to nontenured as well as tenured faculty
Cooper v. *Ross* (1979)	University teacher contract not renewed because he taught classes from a Marxist view	Court ordered teacher reinstated for university's failure to advance convincing reasons related to academic freedom issue
Hillis v. *Stephen F. Austin University* (1982)	Is awarding a course grade a right of academic freedom?	Since the university gave reasons for the nonrenewal of the instructor's contract, court ruled in favor of the university
Kingsville Independent School District v. *Cooper* (1980)	High school teacher's contract not renewed because simulation of rural life evoked controversy in the school and community	Court ruled that the school erred, and the teacher was ordered reinstated
Pickering v. *Board of Education* (1968)	Illinois teacher dismissed for criticizing school board and superintendent in a letter published by a local newspaper	Court upheld teacher's claim that his First and Fourteenth Amendment rights were denied
Norwalk Teachers' Association v. *Board of Education* (1951) and *City of Manchester* v. *Manchester Teachers' Guild* (1957)	Do teachers have the right to strike?	Supreme courts in these two states ruled that teachers may not strike
Board of Education of City of Minneapolis v. *Public School Employees Union* (1951)	Do teachers have the right to strike?	Court upheld teachers' right to strike except when denied by clear language in state law; shortly thereafter, Minnesota legislature passed an antistrike law
Hortonville Joint School District No. 1 v. *Hortonville Education Association* (1976)	May boards of education dismiss teachers who are striking illegally?	Court said the law gave the board power to employ and dismiss teachers as a part of the municipal labor relations balance

TABLE 4.3   *(Continued)*

Case	Issue	Decision
Mastrangelo v. *West Side Union High School District* (1935)	Are a teacher and the board liable for injuries suffered in a classroom accident?	Even though the teacher was in the room and had instructed pupils regarding dangers of chemistry experiment, court held the teacher and the board of education liable
Morris v. *Douglas County School District* (1966)	Teacher and school liability for student injury at school	Court declared the teacher negligent for not foreseeing the possibility of injury to the students

may prescribe additional or higher qualifications beyond the state requirements, provided such requirements are not irrelevant, unreasonable, or arbitrary. A teaching certificate is a license or a privilege granted to practice a profession— it is not a right. Teacher certification is a property interest that cannot be revoked without constitutional due process. Certification laws usually require, in addition, that the candidate show evidence of citizenship, good moral character, and good physical health. A minimum age is frequently specified.

Teacher Employment Contracts

Usually, boards of education have the statutory authority to employ teachers. This authority includes the power to enter into contracts and to fix terms of employment and compensation. In some states only specific members of the school board may sign teacher contracts. When statutes confer the employing authority to boards of education, the authority cannot be delegated. It is usually the responsibility of the superintendent to screen and nominate candidates to the board. The board, meeting in official session, then acts officially as a group to enter into contractual agreement. Employment procedures vary from state to state, but the process is fundamentally prescribed by the legislature and must be strictly followed by local boards.

A contract usually contains elements like the following: the identification of the teacher and the board of education, a statement of the legal capacity of each party to enter into contract, a definition of the assignment specified, a statement of the salary and how it is to be paid, and a provision for signature by the teacher and by the legally authorized agents of the board. In some states contract forms are provided by state departments of education, and these forms must be used; in others, forms are optional.

A teacher may not enter into legal contract without having a valid teaching certificate issued by the state. Funds may not be legally expended under a contract with a teacher who is not legally certified. The requirement of certification for the contract to be valid is intended to protect the public from incompetent teachers.

Often a new teacher will enter into a contract before receiving state certification, with certification scheduled before teaching duties begin. The question
may be raised about whether or not such a contract is valid. The answer depends
on the specific wording and interpretation of the state statute. In some states
this practice is legally sanctioned. In general, "the weight of authority is that a
certificate must be had at the time of making the contract unless the statutory
language clearly indicates that is was the legislative intention that possession of
a certificate at the time of beginning of teaching is sufficient."[10]

Teachers are responsible for making certain that they are legally qualified
to enter into contractual agreements. Furthermore, they are responsible for
carrying out the terms of the contract and abiding by them. In turn, under the
contract they can legally expect proper treatment from an employer.

Discrimination

School districts are prohibited from use of discriminatory practices in the hiring,
dismissal, promotion, and demotion of school personnel. Most discrimination
cases against the school are brought on charges of discrimination on the basis
of sex, race, religion, age, and/or a handicap. The burden falls on the defendant
(schools) to show that a legitimate nondiscriminatory reason existed for the
personnel decision.

In *North Haven Board of Education* v. *Bell* (1982) the U.S. Supreme Court
ruled that school employees as well as students are protected under Title IX.
The North Haven decision involved former women faculty members who alleged
sex discrimination in employment. In upholding Title IX regulations, the decision not only allows the U.S. Department of Education to investigate complaints
from school employees but also permits the department to cut off federal aid
to institutions that discriminate.

Burkey v. *Marshall County Board of Education* (1981) was a landmark
decision regarding pay equity. It ruled that the Marshall County school board's
policy of paying the female coach of the girls' basketball team half the salary of
the male coach of the boys' basketball team violated the Equal Pay Act, Title VII
of the Civil Rights Act of 1964, and the Constitution. The Court also ruled that
the board's policy of hiring only male teachers as coaches of boys' sports constituted illegal sex discrimination.

Courts will not intervene where the school board can prove that its decision
not to hire or promote a minority was based on legitimate criteria, such as
academic qualifications, work experience, licensing, attitude, or job performance. For example, an untenured black school teacher in Missouri was laid
off because of declining enrollment. When she was not recalled to fill a subsequent teaching vacancy, she sued the school board. The U.S. Court of Appeals,
Eighth Circuit, denied her claim of racial discrimination, saying that the board
had based its decision on the fact that she lacked permanent state licensing.[11]

As another example, an Iowa man, employed by his school board to perform
both teaching and administrative duties, charged his employer with religious
discrimination after he was denied paid time off to observe Rosh Hashanah and

Yom Kippur. After a lower court failed to find any basis for his claim, he appealed to the Iowa Supreme Court. Evidence showed that the board had allowed the teacher to take off work without pay for the days requested. The court concluded that this action constituted a reasonable accommodation of the teacher's beliefs. The accommodations were ruled not to be merely a pretext under which intentional religious discrimination was veiled. The lower court's decision was therefore affirmed.[12]

As a final example, a legally blind librarian in Arkansas brought suit against a local school board claiming that she was unlawfully discriminated against in not being hired for a librarian position. The librarian then brought suit in a U.S. district court in Arkansas which held that although she was an "otherwise qualified handicapped individual" under Section 504 of the Rehabilitation Act, the school board had articulated genuine nondiscriminatory reasons for the failure to hire her. The court concluded, therefore, that the librarian was not denied employment by the school board because of her handicap and that the board had a rational basis for hiring the other applicant. Thus there was no violation of the Rehabilitation Act, and the board's decision was upheld.[13]

Teacher Tenure

Teacher tenure legislation exists in most states. In many, tenure or fair dismissal laws are mandatory and apply to all school districts without exception. In other states they do not. The various tenure laws differ not only in extent of coverage but also in provision for coverage.

Tenure laws are intended to provide security for teachers in their positions and to prevent removal of capable teachers by capricious action or political motive. Tenure statutes generally include detailed specifications necessary for attaining tenure and for dismissing teachers who have tenure. These statutes have been upheld when attacked on constitutional grounds. The courts reason that since state legislatures create school districts, they have the right to limit their power.

A teacher becomes tenured by serving satisfactorily for a stated time. This period is referred to as the probationary period and varies in length from state to state. The actual process of acquiring tenure after serving the probationary period depends on the applicable statute. In some states the process is automatic at the satisfactory completion of the probationary period; in other states, official action by the school board is necessary.

In *Turk* v. *Franklin Special School District* (1982), the school board dismissed Jane Turk from her teaching position after she was arrested for driving under the influence of alcohol (DUI). Turk's appeal was upheld by the lower-court judge, since there was no evidence of an adverse effect on her capacity and fitness as a teacher. The school board appealed to the Tennessee Supreme Court, which found that the school board "acted in flagrant disregard of the statutory requirement and fundamental fairness in considering matters that should have been specifically charged in writing." Tennessee law requires that before a tenured teacher can be dismissed, "the charges shall be made in writing specifically stating the offenses which are charged." Thus teacher tenure may be affected by teacher conduct outside school as well as inside. This issue, in a sense, deals with the personal freedom of teachers; freedom to behave as other citizens do, freedom to engage in political activities, and academic freedom in the classroom.

Tenure laws are frequently attacked by those who claim that they protect the incompetent teacher. There is undoubtedly some truth in the assertion, but it must be stated clearly and unequivocally that they also protect the competent and most able teachers. Teachers who accept the challenge of their profession and dare to use new methods, who inspire curiosity in their students, and who discuss controversial issues in their classrooms need protection from dismissal through political or capricious methods. Incompetent teachers, whether tenured or not, can be dismissed under the law by capable administrators and careful school boards who allow due process while evaluating teacher performance.

Although due process has been applicable for years to tenured teachers, nontenured teachers do not, for the most part, enjoy the same rights. Tenured teachers enjoy two key rights—protection from dismissal except for cause as provided in state statutes and the right to prescribed procedures, also spelled out in the statutes. Nontenured teachers may also have due process rights if spelled out in state statutes, or they may be nonrenewed without any reason being given in those states not providing for due process. If a nontenured teacher is dismissed (as distinguished from nonrenewed) before the expiration of the contract, the teacher is then entitled to due process. In most states, however, provisions are only perfunctory, providing calendar dates for nonrenewal of contracts. Cases in Massachusetts (*Lucia* v. *Duggan,* 1969) and Wisconsin (*Gouge* v. *Joint School District No. 1,* 1970) point to the necessity of following due process in dismissing nontenured teachers. In the *Lucia* case the court said: "The particular circumstances of a dismissal of a public school teacher provide compelling reasons for application of a doctrine of procedural due process."[14] In the *Gouge* case the court said:

> A teacher in a public elementary or secondary school is protected by the due process clause of the Fourteenth Amendment against a nonrenewal decision which is wholly without basis in fact and also against a decision which is wholly unreasoned, as well as a decision which is impermissibly based.

In 1972 the Supreme Court helped to clarify the difference in the rights of tenured and nontenured teachers. In one case in Wisconsin (*Board of Regents* v. *Roth,* 1972), it held that nontenured teachers were assured of no rights that were not specified in state statutes. In this instance the only right that probationary teachers had was the one to be notified of nonrenewal by a specified date. In a second case the Court ruled that a nontenured teacher in the Texas system of community colleges was entitled to due process, for the language of the institution's policy manual was such that an unofficial tenure system was in effect. Guidelines in the policy manual provided that a faculty member with seven years of employment in the system acquired tenure and could be dismissed only for cause (*Perry* v. *Sindermann,* 1972).

Whether a teacher is tenured or not, that person cannot be dismissed for exercise of a right guaranteed by the federal Constitution. A school board cannot dismiss a teacher, for example, for engaging in civil rights activities outside school, speaking on matters of public concern, belonging to a given church, or running for public office. These rights are guaranteed to all citizens, including teachers.

Academic Freedom

A sensitive and vital concern to the educator is academic freedom—freedom to control what one will teach and to teach the truth as one discovers it, without fear of penalty. Academic freedom is thus essentially a pedagogical philosophy that has been applied to a variety of professional activities. A philosophical position, however, is *not necessarily* a legal right.[15] Federal judges have generally recognized certain academic protections in the college classroom while exhibiting reluctance to recognize rights for elementary and secondary school teachers.

The contract of a history teacher at the University of Arkansas–Little Rock was not renewed after he announced that he taught his classes from a Marxist point of view, since he was a communist (*Cooper* v. *Ross,* 1979). The court ordered Cooper reinstated in light of the university's failure to advance convincing reasons related to the academic freedom issue to warrant his nonrenewal. In another case (*Hillis* v. *Stephen F. Austin University,* 1982) the instructor claimed that he was denied tenure because he refused to change a student's grade. He argued that awarding a course grade was the instructor's right of academic freedom. Since the university had given several reasons for the nonrenewal of the instructor's contract, the court did not order Hillis's reinstatement. These examples illustrate the reluctance of judges to interfere in the internal affairs of colleges and universities. The scope of a professor's right to teach is thus determined more by the institution's own policies than by the federal courts.[16]

Although federal courts generally have not recognized academic freedom for elementary and secondary school teachers, the most supportive ruling was in *Kingsville Independent School District* v. *Cooper* (1980), which involved a high school history teacher who used a simulation game to introduce her students to the characteristics of rural life during the post–Civil War Reconstruction era. While the role playing evoked controversy in the school and community, there was no evidence that the teacher's usefulness had been impaired. Thus the school erred in not renewing the teacher's contract, and she was ordered reinstated.

In *Pickering* v. *Board of Education* (1968), the U.S. Supreme Court dealt with academic freedom at the public school level. Pickering was a teacher in Illinois who, in a letter published by a local newspaper, was critical of the school board and the superintendent for the way they handled past proposals to raise and use new revenues for the schools. After a full hearing, the board of education terminated Pickering's employment, whereupon he brought suit under the First and Fourteenth Amendments. The Illinois courts rejected his claim. The U.S. Supreme Court, however, upheld Pickering's claim and, in its opinion, stated:

> To the extent that the Illinois Supreme Court's opinion may be read to suggest that teachers may constitutionally be compelled to relinquish the First Amendment rights they would otherwise enjoy as citizens to comment on matters of public interest in connection with the operation of the public schools in which they work, it proceeds on a premise that has been unequivocally rejected in numerous prior decisions of this Court.

The Court then addressed the problem of dealing with cases involving academic freedom. It held that the problem was how to arrive at a balance between the interests of the teacher, who as citizen comments on matters of public concern, and the interests of the state, which as employer promotes the efficiency of its public services through its employees. It is difficult to define precisely the limits of academic freedom. In general, the courts strongly support it yet recognize that teachers must be professionally responsible when interacting with pupils.

Because the law regarding academic freedom is considerably unsettled, teachers should be cautious in asserting a claim to engage in classroom discussion or to choose a teaching methodology unless they are aware of supportive law in their region or are acting according to school board policy. School authorities should devote attention to developing legally sound school curriculum policies which would help avoid many potential disputes.

Generally, teachers have been supported in their rights to dress in their preferred manner, criticize the policies of their local school boards, wear symbols representing stated causes, participate in unpopular movements, and live unconventional lifestyles. But where the exercise of these rights can be shown to have a direct bearing on the teacher's effectiveness, respect, or discipline, these rights may have to be curtailed. For example, a teacher may have the right to wear a "punk" outfit to class, but if the wearing of the outfit leads to disruption and an inability to manage students, the teacher may be ordered to wear more traditional clothes.

Book Banning

Each state has almost complete power in determining the curriculum of its schools. Legislators can enact laws requiring or forbidding certain subjects or topics to be taught. They can also delegate considerable authority to state boards of education and state departments of education for determining curriculum. This ability to delegate authority accounts for the variety within curriculums among the various states.

Many curriculum decisions are also made at the local level. These decisions may involve a policy on teaching a specific topic, the determination of a given method, or the adoption of a given text. The choice of supplementary teaching materials is also often made at the local school level.

Ever since we have had public schools, there have been people who have taken issue with what has been taught, how it has been taught, and the materials used. The number of people challenging these issues and the intensity of their feeling have escalated over the past decade and a half. A number of well-organized and well-financed pressure groups have opposed the teaching of a number of topics, including political, economic, scientific, and religious theories; the teaching of values grounded in religion, morality, or ethnicity; and the portrayal of stereotypes based on gender, race, or ethnicity. Some of these complaints have involved differences of opinion over the central role of the school—whether it is to transmit traditional values, indoctrinate students, or teach students to do their own thinking.

A number of court cases in the 1970s and 1980s involved the legality of removal of books from the school curriculum and school libraries. The courts have given some guidance but have not fully resolved the issue. In 1972 a court of appeals held that a book does not acquire tenure, so a school board was upheld in the removal of *Down These Mean Streets*. Four years later a suburban Cleveland school board was also upheld in removing *Cat's Cradle* and *Catch 22*. The court ruled that a school board is not required to provide a library nor books for it; thus no constitutional rights of students were violated. Similarly, the seventh circuit court in 1980 upheld the removal of the book *Values Clarification,* ruling that local boards have considerable authority in selecting materials for schools. Removal of books on the basis of the vulgar language they contain has also been upheld.

The U.S. Supreme Court treated this issue in *Pico* (1982). The decision disappointed people who had hoped that the justices would issue a definitive ruling on banning of books. Instead, Justice Brennan ruled that students may sue school boards for a denial of their rights, including the right to receive information. The Court indicated that removal of a book because one disagrees with its content cannot be upheld. The net effect of this decision was that the school board decided to return the questionable books to the library.

Controversy over the curriculum continues to rage. It is well for a teacher to recognize that where a state requires a course, the rights of parents are less evident than where a school board itself decides to require a course. We can expect that school boards, administrators, and teachers will continue to receive complaints about ideas, materials, and methods used in the curriculum.

Right to Bargain Collectively

What are the rights of teachers to bargain collectively? This issue has been an active one in recent years. In the past teacher groups met informally with boards of education to discuss salaries and other teacher welfare provisions. Sometimes, the superintendent even was the spokesperson for such teacher groups. In recent years formal collective procedures have evolved. These procedures have been labeled collective bargaining, professional negotiation, cooperative determination, and collective negotiation. They represent a growing desire of teachers to participate officially and directly in formulating policy, particularly matters about their welfare. Teachers are demanding that the procedures of employer-employee relations be made formal by official written procedural agreements.

Collective bargaining has been defined as a way of winning improved goals and not the goal itself. A contract means that salaries, working conditions, and other matters within the scope of the collective bargaining agreement can no longer be decided unilaterally by the school administration and board of education. Instead, the contract outlines effective participation by the teachers' union and its members in formulating the school policies and programs under which they work.

The first teachers' group to bargain collectively with its local board of education was the Maywood, Illinois, Proviso Council of West Suburban Teachers, Union Local 571, in 1938. In 1957 a second local, the East St. Louis, Illinois, Federation of Teachers, was successful in negotiating a written contract. The breakthrough, however, came in December 1961, when the United Federation of Teachers, Local 2 of the American Federation of Teachers (AFT), won the right to bargain for New York City's teachers. Since then, collective bargaining agreements between boards of education and teachers' groups have grown phenomenally. Both the AFT and the NEA have been active in promoting collective bargaining. Today, approximately 75 percent of the nation's teachers are covered by collective bargaining agreements.

Both the NEA and the AFT have actively proposed bargaining legislation. Many states already have collective bargaining agreements; undoubtedly, more statutes will be enacted. The details of the statutes and the proposed bills vary, but generally they include the right of public employees to organize and to bargain collectively, to determine the bargaining agent (in the case of teachers, usually either an AFT or an NEA affiliate, or a combination), to describe the scope of negotiation, and to provide an impasse procedure. In many negotiation statutes strikes are prohibited. In some instances, when the statutes called for a single organization to represent all employees exclusively, election campaigns to select the bargaining organization have been bitterly waged. In the future we can expect that the courts and legislatures frequently will have to determine the rights of teachers and the rights of boards of education in collective bargaining.

When through unified action teachers finally get the right to help make educational policy, they must assume commensurate responsibility. Teachers share responsibility for deciding policy with boards of education and administrators who recognize a democratic principle: Those affected by policy should have a voice in its determination. This participation should commit teachers to abide by these policies. Teachers, as professional educators and frontline workers dealing daily with pupils, have valuable knowledge for deciding educational policy. As specialists, they have expertise that board members often do not have and are not expected to have. Cooperative participation will benefit the schoolchildren both directly and indirectly.

Right to Strike

Courts have ruled on the legality of teacher strikes. The Supreme Court of Connecticut (*Norwalk Teachers' Association* v. *Board of Education,* 1951) and the Supreme Court of New Hampshire (*City of Manchester* v. *Manchester Teachers' Guild,* 1957) ruled that teachers may not strike. The court opinion in Connecticut stated:

> Under our system, the government is established by and run for all of the people, not for the benefit of any person or group. The profit motive, inherent in the principle of free enterprise, is absent. It should be the aim of every employee of the government to do his or her part to make it function as efficiently and economically as possible. The drastic remedy or the organized strike to enforce the demands of unions of government employees is in direct contravention of this principle.

Judges have generally held that public employees do not have the right to strike. A state district court in Minnesota deviated from this view when it said that to hold that a public employee has no right to strike is a personal belief

Many teachers believe that strikes are a justifiable means of protesting intolerable working conditions, when all other means have failed. Do you agree or disagree? (*Source:* Owen Franken/Stock, Boston)

that looks for legality on some tenuous theory of sovereignty or supremacy of government. The court upheld the right to strike as rooted in the freedom of men and women and was not to be denied except by clear, unequivocal language in a constitution, statute, ordinance, rule, or contract.

The decision was upheld by the Supreme Court of Minnesota (*Board of Education of City of Minneapolis* v. *Public School Employees Union,* 1951). Shortly thereafter, the Minnesota legislature passed an antistrike law applicable to public employees. At least seven states—Alaska, Hawaii, Montana, New Hampshire, Oregon, Pennsylvania, and Vermont—permit strikes in their collective bargaining statutes. At least twenty states have statutes that prohibit strikes. Whether or not there are specific statutes prohibiting strikes, boards of education threatened by strikes usually can get a court injunction forestalling them. Both the NEA and the AFT view the strike as a last-resort technique, although justifiable in some circumstances.

In the 1960s there was a large increase in the number of teacher strikes. There were over five hundred strikes during the decade, with more than half a million teachers participating. The New York City teachers' strike was perhaps the most significant in that punitive action was taken against the union. The strike took place in September 1967 and lasted for eighteen days. The strike violated the state of New York's Taylor Law, which bars strikes by public employees. The United Federation of Teachers was fined $150,000, and its president was sentenced to fifteen days in jail and fined $250 for contempt of court. The board of education had obtained an injunction against the strike. The Taylor Law in this case did not prevent a strike, but it did provide the means for punitive action against the union for violating the court injunction.

Schools continued to be plagued with strikes in the 1970s at about the same level as in the 1960s. There were a number of factors interacting in the early 1980s that had decided effects on bargaining and strikes in that period. These factors include the retrenchment of public education, public support for retrenchment, an oversupply of teachers except in certain fields, and increased sophistication in collective bargaining. For the next few years, public school enrollments will continue to decline. At the same time, efforts are being made in many parts of the nation to limit local property taxes and curtail government spending. There will be increased competition for public money, resulting in tension and controversy. Many school board members are inclined to believe that the public will be squarely behind them as they fend off employee demands for wage increases. While the sophistication of both management and labor in the bargaining process has increased, citizens continue to press for involvement in public school bargaining. Parents and taxpayers feel a sense of helplessness over critical decisions being made in which they do not feel represented by their elected school board members. Taking these facts into consideration, we cannot predict how prominent strikes will be in the future, but we can say quite clearly that there will be tension, controversy, competition for resources, and strife.

Recently, the U.S. Supreme Court, by a six-to-three vote, ruled that boards of education can discharge teachers who are striking illegally. Ramifications of this decision, involving a Wisconsin public school, are potentially far-reaching. The Court viewed discharge as a policy matter rather than an issue for adjudication: "What choice among the alternative responses to the teachers' strike will best serve the interests of the school system, the interests of the parents and children who depend on the system, and the interests of the citizens whose taxes support it?" The Court said that the state law in question gave the board the power to employ and dismiss teachers as a part of the balance it had struck in municipal labor relations (*Hortonville Joint School District No. 1* v. *Hortonville Education Association,* 1976).

One can argue that strikes are unlawful when a statute is violated, that the courts in their decisions have questioned the right of public employees to strike, and that some teachers and teacher organizations consider strikes unprofessional. The question before teachers seems to be whether the strike is a justifiable and responsible means—after all other ways have been exhausted—of declaring abominable educational and working conditions and trying to remedy them.

Liability for Negligence

With nearly 50 million students enrolled in elementary and secondary schools, it is almost inevitable that some will be injured in educational activities. Each year, some injuries will occasion lawsuits in which plaintiffs seek damages. Such suits are often brought against both the school districts and their employees. Actions seeking monetary damages for injuries are referred to as *actions in tort*. Technically, a tort is a legal wrong—an act or the omission of an act that violates the private rights of an individual. Actions in tort are generally based on alleged negligence; the basis of tort liability or legal responsibility is negligence. Understanding the concept of negligence is essential to understanding liability.

Legally, negligence is the result of a failure to exercise or practice due care. It includes a factor of foreseeability of harm. Court cases on record involving negligence are numerous and varied.

In a California high school chemistry class, pupils were injured while experimenting in the manufacture of gunpowder (*Mastrangelo* v. *West Side Union High School District,* 1935). The teacher was in the room and had supplemented the laboratory manual instructions with his own directions. Nevertheless, an explosion occurred, allegedly caused by failure of pupils to follow directions. A court held the teacher and the board of education liable. Negligence in this case meant the lack of supervision of laboratory work, a potentially dangerous activity requiring a high level of due care.

In Oregon a child was injured while on a field trip (*Morris* v. *Douglas County School District,* 1966). Children were playing on a large log in a relatively

Professional Perspectives

Try to analyze ahead of time whether or not your actions might violate the private rights of an individual (a student). Negligence, for which a teacher may be held liable, is the result of a failure to exercise or practice due care.

dry space on a beach. A large wave surged up onto the beach dislodging the log, which began to roll. One of the children fell seaward off the log, and the receding wave pulled the log over the child, injuring him. In the subsequent court action the teacher was declared negligent for not foreseeing the possibility of such an occurrence. The court said:

> The first proposition asks this court to hold, as a matter of fact, that unusual wave action on the shore of the Pacific Ocean is a hazard so unforeseeable that there is no duty to guard against it. On the contrary, we agree with the trial judge, who observed that it is common knowledge that accidents substantially like the one that occurred in this case have occurred at beaches along the Oregon coast. Foreseeability of such harm is not so remote as to be ruled out as a matter of law.

Although negligence is a vague concept involving due care and foreseeability, it is defined more specifically each time a court decides such a case. In each instance, somewhat reflecting past decisions, courts decide what constitutes reasonable due care and adequate foresight.

Historically, when there are no statutes imposing liability, school districts have generally been held liable for torts resulting from the negligence of their officers, agents, or employees while the school districts are acting in their governmental capacity. That concept was based on the doctrine that the state is sovereign and cannot be sued without consent. A school district, as an arm of state government, would therefore be immune from tort liability. Unlike school districts, employees of school districts have not been protected by the immunity school districts enjoy; teachers may be held liable for their actions. Teachers must act as reasonable and prudent people, foreseeing dangerous situations. The degree of care that is required increases with the immaturity of the pupil. Lack of supervision and foresight forms the basis of negligence charges.

There has been a trend away from governmental immunity from tort liability. As of 1986, over half of the states had abrogated governmental immunity either judicially, statutorily, or through some form of legal modification; in 1985 only two states had abrogated such immunity, and nineteen had maintained it.[17] There has also been an increase in the number of lawsuits.

Many states authorize school districts to purchase insurance to protect teachers, school districts, administrators, and school board members against suits. It is important that school districts and their employees and board members be thus protected, through either school district insurance or their own personal policies. The costs of school district liability insurance have increased so dramatically in the past few years that many school districts are contemplating the elimination of extracurricular activities. Consequently, state legislatures are being pressured to fix liability insurance rates for school districts, as well as passing laws to limit maximum liability amounts for school-related cases. For teachers, membership in the state affiliates of the NEA and membership in the AFT permit teachers to participate in liability insurance programs sponsored by those organizations.

As a summary of the discussion of this section, Table 4.4 lists brief statements related to the rights and responsibilities of teachers.

TABLE 4.4 *Summary Statements on Teachers' Rights and Responsibilities*

Prospective teachers must fulfill the requirements of laws and policies regarding certification prior to being employed as teachers

Boards of education have the authority to employ teachers, including the authority to enter into contracts and to fix terms of employment and compensation

School districts are prohibited from use of discriminatory practices; discrimination in employment and salary of teachers on the basis of sex is in violation of Title IX

Most states have tenure laws which provide protection for teachers against their arbitrary dismissal; rights of nontenured teachers are found in state laws

Teachers may speak out on matters of public concern, even in criticism of their school board

Boards of education may remove books from library shelves under their authority to select materials for schools; however, the removal of a book merely because someone disagrees with its content was not upheld by the U.S. Supreme Court

Many states provide for school boards and teacher unions to bargain collectively on wages, hours, and terms and conditions of employment

Teacher strikes are unlawful when a statute is violated; in some states, it is legal for teachers to strike

Teachers are expected to exercise due care in foreseeing possible accidents and in working to prevent their occurrence; teachers may be sued for their negligence which led to pupil injury

Teachers who administer corporal punishment must act in a way consistent with state laws, local board policies, and reasonable practices

Summary and Implications

Court cases that deal with issues related to the rights and responsibilities of students and teachers provide the basis for more and more discussions in newsletters, newspapers, professional journals, magazines, radio, and television across our country. The range and scope of the education-related court decisions have become so broad that concentration in school law is a recognized field of preparation in the legal profession. These specialized school lawyers are in great demand to serve increasing numbers of student and teacher clients who seek court relief from what they consider abuses to their rights.

Although student rights and responsibilities are being more clearly defined by court decisions, many court decisions are against students whose nonconformism seems to go beyond a reasonable norm. American children have a right to an education but not, however, without certain prerequisites. Boards of education have the right to establish reasonable rules and regulations providing that the *in loco parentis* doctrine of the schools is reasonable, rather than arbitrary, regarding student rights. Courts are faced with determining the reasonableness of either the student behavior and/or the reasonableness of board rules and regulations. Most student challenges have been related to corporal punishment, rights of married students, dress codes, and freedom of expression. Particularly in cases of suspension and expulsion, corporal punishment, dress codes, and sex discrimination, actions of school administrators and teachers may be examined regarding the due process dimensions of fairness and constitutionality. Procedures for dealing with school records, student publications,

student searches, child abuse, AIDS victims, and locker searches are being studied more thoroughly to avoid conflicts, which often end up in the courts.

Educational malpractice charges by students against the schools will be
closely observed during the late 1980s in light of the increased call for excellence
in education. Recent controversies to face the schools are instances related to
the suspected abuse and neglect of students and the rights of attendance for
students with AIDS. Although several states mandate the reporting of suspected
abuse and neglect, teachers are reluctant to report it because of the possibility
of a lawsuit based on invasion of privacy or slander. With regard to AIDS, even
though evidence indicates that it is not transmitted through casual person-to-
person contact, the issue of children with AIDS attending school is the basis for
emotional parental reactions to court decisions permitting attendance privileges
to AIDS-inflicted students.

Teachers have the same rights and responsibilities as other citizens. With
the assistance of support organizations such as the American Civil Liberties Union
(ACLU) and the teacher unions, more and more teachers are airing their grievances in court. The courts have said that a teaching certificate is a license to
practice a profession and that it cannot be revoked without constitutional due
process. At the same time, the courts have ruled that boards of education may
prescribe requirements beyond the state requirements for certification. Teachers
are responsible for making certain that they are legally certified to enter into
contracts. The grounds and procedures for dismissing teachers are usually spelled
out as part of the tenure statute of the respective states. Teacher dismissals by
capricious actions of boards of education are often taken to court for consideration of due process. School districts are prohibited from use of discriminatory
practices in the hiring, dismissal, promotion and demotion of school personnel.
The law regarding academic freedom is unsettled, especially for elementary and
secondary teachers, since federal judges have been reluctant to recognize academic freedom rights at this level. Controversy over the curriculum continues.
It is expected that school boards, administrators, and teachers will continue to
receive complaints about what has been taught, how it has been taught, and the
materials used. The courts have clarified teachers' rights to bargain collectively
and to strike (where state law permits). Court cases brought against both the
school districts and their employees involving negligence are numerous and
varied. Teachers should be fully aware that negligence is the result of failure to
exercise or practice due care

The implications of the actions of the courts are highly significant to the
teaching profession. From the many court decisions relating to education a
framework has evolved for acceptable conduct of teachers within the school
setting. Today's teacher no longer can assume that personal ignorance of acceptable standards of conduct will be overlooked by the courts in adjudicating
a suit brought against the teacher. (Nor should the teacher be intimidated by
the courts when reasonable rules of conduct are now being evolved for the
practice of pedagogy.) Courts do not start hearings on their own efforts; school
boards, school employees, and teachers must be sued before a court case can
develop. However, prospective teachers need to be deliberately sensitive to the

legal boundaries in teaching. Although beginning teachers need not have the knowledge and expertise of a lawyer, knowing the law well as it relates to education can contribute more than incidentally to becoming a successful teacher.

Discussion Questions

1. How do the rights of students today compare with their rights a decade ago?

2. Have the rights of teachers today compared with their rights a decade ago changed in the same way as students' rights? Discuss.

3. How are the expanding legal decisions related to students' rights and responsibilities infringing on teachers' rights and responsibilities, and vice versa?

4. What position would you take regarding the right of a student with AIDS to attend school? How do you feel about drug- and alcohol-related problems with regard to school attendance?

5. Increasing numbers of classroom teachers are becoming school board members in districts other than where they are employed. What legal, ethical, and professional problems could arise from this practice?

Supplemental Activities

1. Prepare a presentation you would give to a parent-community meeting on your rights as a teacher to use whatever materials you choose in teaching your classes.

2. Interview your superintendent regarding the needs of the district related to legal services. Interview the school attorney to determine how he or she serves the school district. Report your findings to your class.

3. Determine how your local teachers' union uses legal services for teachers. Invite a teachers' union attor-

ney to class to discuss his or her role in serving member teachers.

4. Accompany a truant officer to a court hearing of a school truancy case; report the specific findings of your trip to class. Discuss the relation of the courts to the schools.

5. Invite to your class individuals or groups who have filed legal suits against the schools. (Staff members of the American Civil Liberties Union may respond to such a request.)

Notes

1. Ronald F. Campbell, Luvern L. Cunningham, Raphael O. Nystrand, and Michael D. Usdan, *The Organization and Control of American Schools,* 5th ed. (Columbus, Ohio: Merrill, 1985), p. 286.

2. Thomas J. Flygare, "De Jure," *Phi Delta Kappan,* 68 (October 1986): 165–166.

3. Ibid., 165.

4. Lee O. Garber and Reynolds C. Seitz, *The Yearbook of School Law, 1971* (Danville, Ill.: Interstate, 1971), p. 253.

5. Lucy Knight, "Facts About Mr. Buckley's Amendment," *American Education,* 13 (June 1977): 7.

6. *Bayler* v. *Kinzler* (N.Y., 1974) (affirmed Second Circuit Court, 1975).

7. *Trachtmann* v. *Anker* (Second Circuit Court, 1977).

8. William D. Valente, *Law in the Schools* (Columbus, Ohio: Merrill, 1980), p. 282.

9. Ibid.

10. Robert R. Hamilton and Paul R. Mort, *The Law and Public Education* (St. Paul, Minn.: Foundation Press, 1969), p. 359.

11. *1986 Deskbook Encyclopedia of American School Law* (Rosemount, Minn.: Data Research), p. 55.

12. Ibid., p. 59.

13. Ibid., p. 61.

14. Haskell C. Freedman, "The Legal Rights of Untenured Teachers," *Nolpe School Law Journal,* 1 (Fall 1970): 100.

15. Frank W. Kemerer, "Classroom Academic Freedom: Is It a Right?," *Kappa Delta Pi Record,* 19 (Summer 1983): 101.

16. Ibid., p. 102.

17. Wayne R. Fetter and Don C. Patton, "Liability Protection for Professional School Personnel," *Phi Delta Kappan,* 60 (March 1979): 525.

Bibliography

Ackerly, Robert T. *The Reasonable Exercise of Authority.* Washington, D.C.: National Association of Secondary School Principals (1201 Sixteenth Street, N.W.), 1969.

Appenzeller, Herb. *The Right to Participate.* Charlottesville, Va.: Michie, 1983.

The Equal Access Act, Public Law No. 98–377 (Implications for Secondary School Policies). Oak Park, Ill.: Christian Legal Society (P.O. Box 2069), 1984.

Flygare, Thomas J. "De Jure." *Phi Delta Kappan,* November 1985, 229–230.

———. *"Schools and the Law." Phi Delta Kappan.* (A regular feature in each issue of the *Phi Delta Kappan,* providing timely and pertinent information.)

Hudgins, H. C., Jr. "The Perspective of the Courts: Their Effect on Educational Policy." *Thresholds in Education,* 12 (May 1986): 9–12.

———, and Vacca, Richard S. *Law and Education: Contemporary Issues and Court Decisions.* Rev. ed. Charlottesville, Va.: Michie, 1985.

Kemerer, Frank, and Deutsch, Kenneth. *Constitutional Rights and Student Life.* St. Paul, Minn.: West, 1979.

McCarthy, Martha M., and Cambron, Nelda H. *Public School Law: Teachers' and Students' Rights.* Boston: Allyn and Bacon, 1981.

Mirga, Tom. "Justices Decline to Review Cases on Desegregation." *Education Week,* November 12, 1986, 1 and 9.

Moran, K. D., and McGhehey, M. A. *The Legal Aspects of School Communications.* Topeka, Kans.: National Organization on Legal Problems of Education, 1980.

1986 Deskbook Encyclopedia of American School Law. Rosemount, Minn.: Data Research (P.O. Box 409).

Reutter, E. Edmund, Jr. *The Supreme Court's Impact on Public Education.* Bloomington, Ind.: Phi Delta Kappa and the National Organization on Legal Problems of Education, 1982.

Stelzer, Leigh, and Banthin, Joanna. *Teachers Have Rights, Too. What Educators Should Know about School Law.* Boulder, Colo.: Social Science Education Consortium, 1980.

5

Professional Organizations

Focus Questions

- Many educators talk to prospective teachers about the teaching profession. On the job, most teachers are members of organized labor unions. What are the assumptions about a profession versus the assumptions of labor unions?
- The National Education Association (NEA) refuses to consider merging with the American Federation of Teachers (AFT) because the AFT is affiliated with organized labor. Does this position make sense to you? Why or why not?
- Local teacher power is manifested through the designated teachers' union of the school district. How will you weigh the pros and cons of joining a teachers' organization?

- Various polls indicate that the largest portion of teachers identify themselves as Democrats. Does this affiliation pose problems when a teachers' organization supports political candidates and/or political causes? What is your opinion of teachers' organizations developing political action committees?
- Some people argue that membership in organizations identified with teaching areas (English, vocational education, etc.) would be extremely valuable to beginning teachers. Would you join such an organization before joining the local teachers' union? What factors would influence your decision?

Key Terms and Concepts

Professionalism versus unionism
Teacher power
Unified dues
National Education Association (NEA)
American Federation of Teachers (AFT)

Teaching area organizations
Religious education organizations
Political action committees
World Confederation of Organizations of the
    Teaching Profession (WCOTP)

What Would You Do?

Teacher strikes sometimes provoke considerable animosity in the community toward teachers. Do you consider such a possibility as a factor when you seek employment? If animosity exists in a district of your choice, what could you do to help smooth over such community feelings?

Teachers' organizations defend the rights, materials, and moral interests of the teaching profession. What could you do in regard to such matters if your employing community and board of education was actively engaged in restricting your professional judgments about use of certain materials in your teaching?

Teacher unionism and professionalism are not necessarily mutually exclusive. In many school districts, boards of education and school administrators resent the strength of teacher organizations, but they also realize the need to cope with teacher unionism. Before the 1960s little attention was given to the activities of the various organizations; teachers' organizations had not yet become the powerful groups they are today. Teachers, like other professionals, have always belonged to groups organized to serve common needs and to solve problems. Teachers usually consider the voice provided at the national level regarding teacher rights, legislation favoring education, and the development of ethical codes of teacher conduct to be of value. Similarly, political involvement, promotion of education, and lobbying the legislature are valuable at the state level. Probably the strongest factor for an individual teacher in joining a teachers' union is the support of the organization for the efforts at the local level. Local teachers' organizations provide teachers with representation to the school board on matters related to working conditions such as class size, salaries, and fringe benefits. Assistance to each teacher with grievance procedures and the provision of legal services with due process rights give teachers assurances against unwarranted reprisals.

Teachers will always be actively involved in the activities of teachers' organizations (unions) which continue to deal with matters related to working conditions. However, the current clamor for upgrading standards for admission to teacher preparation programs and for certification requirements lends to increased teacher interest in membership in many other professional organizations which serve common needs identified with their respective academic disciplines, improving classroom instruction, and providing leadership in curriculum, administration, guidance and counseling, the principalship, and other related roles. Reports from the Carnegie Task Force on Teaching as a Profession, the National Governor's Association, and others, which were discussed in Chapter 3, hint that teachers would be well served by following the models offered by those professions whose organizations deal with upgrading and improving their professional activities. Thus elementary classroom teachers would profit from membership in organizations whose primary purpose is directed toward upgrading their expertise and improving their classroom practices; secondary teachers in academic-related groups; department chairs in curriculum groups; administrators in administration groups. Attention will be given in this chapter to other professional education organizations as well as to the National Education Association (NEA) and the American Federation of Teachers (AFT).

18

Classroom Teacher Organizations

The National Education Association (NEA) is by far the largest teachers' organization, with over 1.8 million members, including teachers, administrators, clerical and custodial employees, and other school personnel. The American Federation of Teachers (AFT), affiliated with the AFL–CIO, has over 600,000 members but does not offer membership to school administrators.

In other large and small districts throughout the United States, teachers are members of strong local organizations that are not affiliated with national or state organizations. In New York the Federation of Catholic Teachers represents the 3000 lay teachers employed in 300 Catholic schools. Other religious teachers' organizations represent teachers in other areas. At the higher-education level the American Association of Colleges of Teacher Education (AACTE) is another group that has begun to acknowledge that powerful teacher unionism and professionalism are not mutually exclusive. The result has been a continuous attempt on the part of the AACTE to consult with teacher organizations and take their recommendations seriously. On many community college, college, and university campuses, faculties are represented by chapters of the American Association of University Professors (AAUP), as well as by units affiliated with the NEA and AFT.

Teacher Power

For many years the large membership in teachers' organizations remained a latent force; this force emerged as "teacher power" during the 1960s. As teacher power became even stronger during the 1970s, teachers' organizations became more and more militant about salary issues and other concerns of teachers. As teachers worked together to identify themselves clearly as a homogeneous professional group, their most common conscious group goals were also iden-

The two major teacher organizations are the National Education Association (NEA) and the American Federation of Teachers (AFT). (*Source:* David Powers/Stock, Boston)

tified. The concept of teacher power developed when the teacher groups worked to organize activities and to carry out common goals.

The main organizations that have competed for membership throughout the United States are the NEA and the AFT. Before the teacher militancy of the 1960s, the NEA espoused nonstriking professionalism and deplored the unionistic stance of the AFT, an affiliate of the AFL–CIO. Over the years the NEA has refused to join the AFL–CIO, which the AFT refuses to leave. At the same time, the AFT leaders oppose a union that admits principals and other supervisors, as some NEA locals do. The AFT has also stressed the need for collective bargaining contracts like those gained in Maywood, Illinois (1948); Pawtucket, Rhode Island (1951); and Butte, Montana (1953). These early contracts, as well as today's contracts, spell out the working conditions and the expectations related to each teacher's assignments. During the 1950s the rivalry between the NEA and the AFT intensified. In some school systems the NEA began to associate strongly with the union views. The first collective bargaining election between the NEA and the AFT, which took place in East St. Louis, Illinois, in 1957, was won by the AFT.

In the fall of 1961 the teachers in New York City conducted an election to determine which organization was to be the sole bargaining agent in their behalf with the board of education. The United Federation of Teachers (UFT), affiliated with the AFL–CIO, won the election over the Teachers' Bargaining Organization (TBO), which was supported by the NEA. This election was the first to determine a sole bargaining agent with a board of education. For this reason the 1961 New York City election is regarded as the springboard for the growth of organized power for teachers. Although such bargaining elections continued to be scarce in the early 1960s, teachers' organizations have since directed much of their resources to organizing members and concentrating their combined influence for desired goals. Today, the power of teachers' unions is permanently established; most school districts operate with contracts negotiated between the boards of education and the representative teachers' unions. |18|

State and Local Teachers' Organizations

While state and local units that are affiliated with a national organization operate under the umbrella of the parent national offices, these units are the power base of the organizations. The local association of teachers has the highest priority in the whole organization; however, the strength of any single local union lies in the solidarity in numbers, in resource personnel, and in services the state organization provides. In the early 1960s teachers generally became more militant regarding salary and working conditions. Classroom teachers' associations at the local level became more active in seeking assistance from state and national associations. As competition between the larger national associations grew in intensity, and continues to be intense, elections at the local level have become the procedure for gaining the bargaining representation for each district. Local elections for the role of bargaining agent among competitive teacher groups remain the most important steps in the process for organizing teachers in any district, whether or not the local classroom teacher association (CTA) is affiliated with a state or national organization.

For the most part, teachers participate directly in the affairs of local organizations. Solutions to the problems at hand are therefore primarily the concerns of local teachers' groups. The influence of these groups obviously would be weakened without the support and resources of strong state and national parent organizations. At the same time, local organizations sometimes become restive about their national and state affiliation. However, leadership at the national level views the problems and differences in beliefs among the local organizations as a viable part of the democratic process rather than as divisive to the groups. From the many geographic locations, grass roots views of local teachers' organizations may surface through the state associations to the national level or from the local organizations directly to the national level. Decisions related to national policy are then made by majority vote with attention allowed for input from all levels—local, state, and national. There have been instances in which local organizations have severed relations with their state and national affiliates when the members felt their particular needs were not well met. Since the power of the state and national organizations is reduced somewhat each time a local organization withdraws state and national affiliation, state organizations especially are compelled to pay careful attention to the express needs of local teachers' association affiliates.

National Education Association (NEA)

The NEA, with national headquarters located at 1201 Sixteenth Street, N.W., Washington, D.C., is headed by an executive director. The NEA is a highly developed organization with many departments, divisions, and commissions. The basic purpose of the NEA, as stated in Section 2 of the charter, is to elevate the character and advance the interests of the profession of teaching and to promote education in the United States. Figure 5.1 traces the organizational chronology of the NEA from its founding in 1857 as the National Teachers' Association (NTA). In 1870 the NTA united with the National Association of School Superintendents, organized in 1865, and the American Normal School Association, organized in 1858, to form the National Education Association. The organization was incorporated in 1886 in the District of Columbia as the National Education Association and in 1906 was chartered by act of Congress. The charter was officially adopted at the association's annual meeting of 1907, with the name "National Education Association of the United States." The original statement of purpose of the NTA remains unchanged in the present NEA charter.

The NEA organization comprises several units, including the representative assembly, board of directors, executive committee, standing committees, and special committees. Figure 5.2, the organizational chart, shows the subdivisions. The councils conduct investigations, recommend standards, build supporting programs for better programs of education, and work for freedom of teaching and learning. Through the special committees the NEA cooperates with other organizations having common interests in specific problems.

National Education Association
1857-1870

The National Teachers' Association
    Organized August 26, 1857, in Philadelphia, Pennsylvania.
    Purpose—*To elevate the character and advance the interests of the profession of teaching and to promote the cause of popular education in the United States.* [The word "popular" was dropped in the 1907 Act of Incorporation.]
    The name of the Association was changed at Cleveland, Ohio, on August 15, 1870, to the "National Educational Association."

1870-1907

National Educational Association
    Incorporated under the laws of the District of Columbia, February 24, 1886, under the name "National Education Association," which was changed to "National Educational Association," by certificate filed November 6, 1886.

1907-

National Education Association of the United States
    Incorporated under a special Act of Congress, approved June 30, 1906, to succeed the "National Educational Association." The Charter was accepted and Bylaws were adopted at the Fiftieth Anniversary Convention held July 10, 1907, at Los Angeles, California.

FIGURE 5.1 *Organizational Chronology of the National Education Association (NEA)* [Source: *NEA Handbook, 1983–84* (Washington, D.C.: National Education Association, 1984), p. 138. Reprinted by permission.]

Many special needs of teachers are met through the departments, national affiliates, and associated organizations. Some of these special interest groups were originally organized as national organizations separate from the NEA, and they continue to choose their own officers and plan their own programs. Departments serve general interests such as the Association of Classroom Teachers (ACT); national affiliates represent separate disciplines like music educators; and associated organizations represent groups like the school administrators.

NEA membership reached an all-time high of almost 1.9 million in 1976, stabilized at over 1.6 million in the early 1980s, and has grown to 1.8 million as of April 1986.

American Federation of Teachers (AFT)

The AFT, with national headquarters located in Washington, D.C., is headed by a president. The AFT was organized on April 15, 1916, and became affiliated with the American Federation of Labor in May 1916. John Dewey held the first membership card in the AFT. Teachers' unions had existed earlier than 1916; for example, the Chicago Teachers' Federation was formed in 1897 and became affiliated with the American Federation of Labor in 1902. AFT membership grew steadily from 110,522 members in 1965 to 205,323 members in 1970—almost doubling. Membership exceeded 415,854 by 1974 and reached 624,406 in May

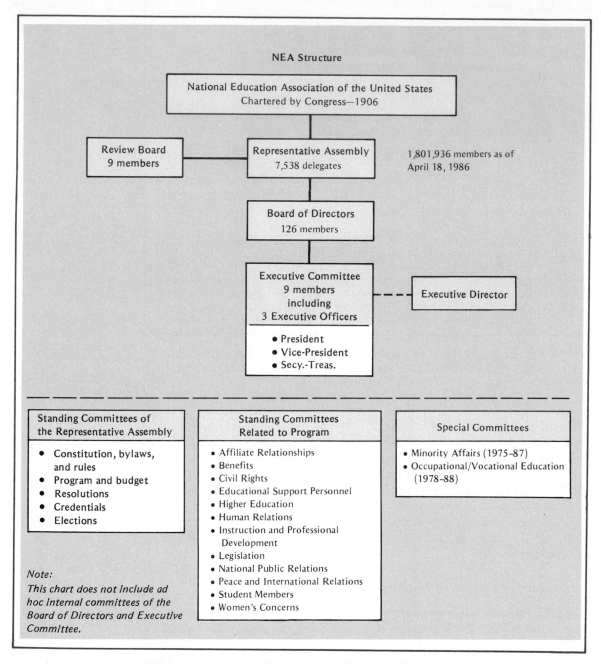

FIGURE 5.2 *Organization Chart of the National Education Association* [*Source: NEA Handbook, 1986–87* (Washington, D.C.: National Education Association, 1987), p. 10. Reprinted by permission. Membership data for 1986: News release (Mary Hatwood Futrell, President, National Education Association, April 23, 1986).]

1986. The AFT has local unions in the United States, Canal Zone, Guam, and the armed forces overseas schools for the dependents of military personnel. Besides the national federations, there are state federations of teachers in most states. In an effort to stabilize costs and provide better services to members, the AFT built a new building to house the national office at 555 New Jersey Avenue, N.W., Washington, D.C.

Figure 5.3 shows the organization of the AFT, which includes the president, 30 vice-presidents, the secretary-treasurer, an administrative staff, and eleven departments as listed in the figure. The Committee of Political Education (COPE) is becoming more active as the AFT participates increasingly in political discussions related to education.

The AFT has boasted of its affiliation since inception with the AFL–CIO. It has stressed that organized labor was an important force in establishing our system of free public schools and has actively supported school improvement programs at local, state, and national levels. Affiliation with organized labor gives the AFT the support of more than 15 million members of the AFL–CIO. This support by local labor unions has often worked to the advantage of local AFT unions in gaining better salaries and improved fringe benefits from local boards of education.

NEA and AFT Compared

In the early 1960s the NEA appealed to teachers by drawing a distinction between professionalism and unionism. As a "professional association," it claimed, only the NEA could truly represent teachers. A union like the AFT, on the other hand, was seen as beneath professionalism by the NEA leadership because of its alliance with other workers within the American Federation of Labor and Congress of Industrial Organizations (AFL–CIO). The NEA has since identified itself as a union and no longer draws lines between professionalism and unionism.

To the AFT, professionalism is not possible without unionism. A degree of self-control, the ability to help set professional standards, mastery of a specific body of knowledge, and the authority to define conditions of work are essential elements in the AFT's definition of professionalism. Since none of these can be gained without the kind of collective assertion of power that unionism makes possible, the AFT maintains that without unionism teaching can never become truly professional.

During the 1960s the AFT was generally viewed as a collection of teachers' unions that would willingly, though illegally in most states, close the schools by striking to gain their demands. Many educators, NEA members especially, looked upon the strike as a labor union technique that should not be used by "professional" teachers. At that time the NEA used a procedure termed *sanctions*. When sanctions were imposed against a school, the professional association advertised the school district as being an unacceptable place to work and discouraged association members from taking employment in the district. Teachers completed existing contractual agreements without closing the schools. Gen-

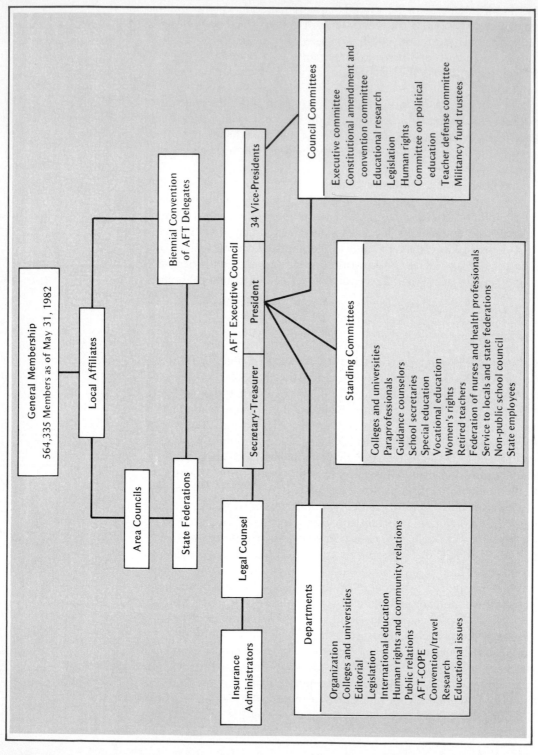

FIGURE 5.3 *Table of Organization of the American Federation of Teachers*
[*Source: Constitution of the AFT* (Washington, D.C.: American Federation of Teachers, AFL–CIO, 1986), p. 23. Reprinted by permission.]

erally, several months' notice was given before sanctions were invoked. Sanctions were applied by the NEA to local districts and also to entire states (Oklahoma and Utah). Technically, the NEA did not have a no-strike policy at that time, but such was strongly implied.

The strong competition between the AFT and the NEA for memberships and bargaining rights during the late 1960s was vocally volatile and highly intense. Teacher militancy among members of both the NEA and the AFT grew considerably. The strike tactic used by the AFT seemed to be more quickly effective than NEA sanctions. As a consequence, the NEA began to embrace the strike as a last resort rather than sanctions. The NEA also came to embrace collective bargaining, which the AFT had initiated. Thus the influences of the AFT and the NEA on each other have produced a growing convergence of philosophy and purpose. Today, most teachers, administrators, and board members consider both organizations to be teachers' unions using those tactics that the trade unions of organized labor have found most successful.

Political Action

An area of rapid development within teachers' organizations are the political action committees. The AFT has an active Committee on Political Education (COPE). A similar NEA committee is called the Political Action Committee for Education (NEA-PAC). The NEA political action budget of over $1 million makes it the fifth largest such committee in the United States, behind committees of the National Association of Realtors, American Medical Association, United Auto Workers, and International Association of Machinists.

One reason for this move toward the political arena is the success other unions and organizations have had through effective political action. In the past many organizations used moral persuasion, whereby delegates presented themselves to legislators or legislative committees to ask for legislation to meet organizational needs. The lessons of history show that this procedure does not work very well. Other organizations, including teachers' organizations, have found a much more effective method—helping elect political candidates who are sympathetic to their particular needs. Thus the political action committees monitor elected officials' voting records on education bills and analyze the platforms of new candidates. Teachers' organizations plan to support actively those candidates who will perform according to the organizations' views.

The state and national political action committees of the NEA and AFT have a common aim—to promote education by encouraging teachers to participate in the political life of their local, state, and national communities. These committees throughout the states are responsible for recommending political endorsements to their respective boards of directors. Interestingly, the NEA and [38] AFT political action committees usually agree on which candidates to endorse during national elections. Both organizations have been strongly supportive of the Democratic party candidates, feeling that they would be more supportive of education at the national level.

National teachers' union leaders continue to suggest that their political clout pays off for education. Regarding support of future political candidates, teachers' unions remain consistent in their claims that they support those candidates who seem to favor public education. Teachers' unions monitor the federal administration's actions that affect public education and have been vehement in their opposition to funding cuts in public education programs.

17

Assignment-Related, Religious Education, and Worldwide Organizations

An excellent listing of about six thousand national trade associations, labor unions, professional, scientific, or technical societies, and other national organizations composed of groups united for a common purpose, is given in the annual edition of *National Trade and Professional Associations of the United States* (published by Columbia Books Inc., 1350 New York Avenue, N.W., Suite 207, Washington, D.C. 20005). The subject index of the 1985 edition listed 540 organizations under the "Education" heading, including those identified with specific academic disciplines, religions, and other education-related categories. Prospective teachers are encouraged to locate the most recent annual edition of this publication in their college or university library and peruse it to gain a broader perspective of the organizations which exist to serve their individual needs and purposes.

Assignment-Related Organizations

As one would think, teachers' organizations have been formed for each of the academic disciplines, as well as for each of the other curriculum areas such as vocational-technical, business, health, home economics, physical education, and driver education. We cannot attempt to list all of these organizations here. For purposes of illustration only, a few of the teaching assignment-related organizations given in the 1985 annual edition of the *National Trade and Professional Associations of the United States* are listed next.

English

American Comparative Literature Association
Conference on English Education
National Conference of Teachers of English

Professional Perspectives

Examine the similarities among the many professional teachers' organizations prior to pledging your membership. Such examinations will illustrate the underlying values and concepts of the organization which may or may not be in agreement with your beliefs.

Mathematics
American Mathematical Society
Association for Women in Mathematics
National Council of Teachers of Mathematics

Sciences
American Association of Physics Teachers
National Association of Biology Teachers
National Association for Research in Science Teaching

In addition to union membership, many teachers also profit from professional organizations related to their specific disciplines, for example, the National Conference of Teachers of English (NCTE) and the National Council of Teachers of Mathematics (NCTM). (*Source:* Ellis Herwig/The Picture Cube)

Vocational-technical

Technology Transfer Society
International Council for Computers in Education
American Association for Vocational Instructional Materials

Religious Education Associations

There are many religious education associations of various denominations. These national and regional religious education associations are under denominational or interdenominational control and do one or more of the following: operate sectarian schools attended by students who prefer them to public or private schools, supplement the public or private school program by offering educational activities for youth and adults, operate adult educational programs open to the public, and formally promote scholarships among their members in sciences and liberal arts. A partial listing of religious education associations is given next.

[32]

> Association of Seventh-day Adventists Educators
> Catholic Biblical Association of America
> Council for Jewish Education
> National Association of Episcopal Schools
> Association of Christian Schools International
> Religious Education Association

World Confederation of Organizations of the Teaching Profession (WCOTP)

The aims of the WCOTP foster a conception of education directed toward the promotion of international understanding and goodwill, with a view to safeguarding peace, freedom, and respect for human dignity. WCOTP supports efforts to improve teaching methods, educational organizations, and the academic and professional training of teachers so as to equip them better to serve the interests of youth; to defend the rights, materials, and moral interests of the teaching profession; and to promote closer relationships between teachers in the different countries.

Members of the WCOTP are from approximately a hundred nations. The AFT, the American Teacher Association, and the NEA of the United States are members. In a study based on questionnaire data gathered by WCOTP, many educational problems common to all nations were identified, including lack of funds, shortage of excellent teachers, need for school buildings, and need for compulsory and free education. The WCOTP, facing these problems with determination, holds an assembly of delegates once each year. Resolutions of the assembly have ranged widely, from intensive literary programs to free education at all levels, from increased availability and status of technical education to special and adequate provision for the educational and medical needs of the physically and mentally handicapped. WCOTP also sponsors regional conferences. In the

Teacher power is especially reflected in national elections in support of candidates who pledge to place education in a high priority. Study platforms, speeches, news releases, and the like in order to search out those who regard education highly.

past these conferences have dealt with such topics as the status of the teaching profession in Niamey, Niger; teaching science in elementary schools in Asia; and the teacher's part in nation building. WCOTP's bulletin *Echo*, designed to promote international understanding, is published in thirteen languages. *Educational Panorama*, another WCOTP publication, is published in English, French, Spanish, Japanese, and Arabic.

Summary and Implications

This chapter presented the concept of teacher power as a viable force in the formulation of education-related decisions. Discussion of teacher power was followed by information about teachers' organizations (local, state, and national), which are the vehicles through which teacher power is expressed. The National Education Association (NEA) with 1,801,936 members and the American Federation of Teachers (AFT) with 624,406 members are the largest of the teachers' organizations (unions). Therefore detailed attention was given to the organizational structure of both agencies and to comparisons of the two. Perhaps the ultimate manifestation of teacher power comes from the rapidly increasing development of the respective NEA and AFT political action committees, NEA–PAC and COPE.

Attention was also given to assignment-related, religious education, and worldwide organizations. From the annual edition of the *National Trade and Professional Associations of the United States*, associations related to teaching assignments in English, mathematics, the sciences, and vocational-technical education were listed. Similarly, several associations related to religious education were listed. Finally, a brief description of the aims and memberships of the World Confederation of Organizations of the Teaching Profession (WCOTP) was presented.

The implications are straightforward. Prospective teachers will find concerted pressure placed on them to affiliate with the recognized teachers' organizations. Each teacher must decide the advantages and disadvantages of such paid memberships. In some districts the climate of the working environment of teachers is very similar to that of trade unions. In other districts teachers try to keep a more scholarly, professional climate analogous to that of traditional professions like law, dentistry, and medicine. How each teacher will contribute to the organizational climate associated with a particular membership must be a personal decision.

Similarly, the extent to which each teacher utilizes the professional and personal programs of teachers' organizations will vary. Many teachers feel that their organizations should not engage in partisan politics, but other teachers will eagerly participate in the work of political action committees at local, state, and national levels. Beginning teachers typically, and rightfully, place the highest priority on organizing and managing their classrooms for instruction. Yet as concerns related to working conditions, salaries, teaching assignments, insurance benefits, and others are defined, teachers find that their voices are best heard through the teachers' organization of the district.

Discussion Questions

1. What is your opinion of efforts by teachers' organizations which support higher standards for teachers to be certified? Also, should teachers have a larger role in removing poor teachers from the classroom?

2. How would you react to a school district policy stating that all grades must be based on subject matter examinations and other teacher information? To what extent should teachers' organizations be involved in the development of grading policies? How?

3. During a teachers' strike members of a factory union from a neighboring city joined the teachers' picket line to support the teachers' demands. Do you agree or disagree with the factory union action? Discuss.

4. Teachers' organizations defend the rights, materials, and moral interests of the teaching profession. To what extent should the organization defend a teacher's choice of reading material for classroom use? To defend the rights of gay teachers?

5. Most public school teachers know little about religious education associations and/or the World Confederation of Organizations of the Teaching Profession. What should the public schools do (if anything) to provide their teachers with knowledge about these organizations? Discuss your rationale.

Supplemental Activities

1. Write or telephone several education organizations (other than the NEA and AFT) which are teaching area–related. Ask questions about jobs in your teaching discipline other than classroom teaching. Report and discuss your findings.

2. Examine a copy of a negotiated teacher contract between a teacher organization and a school district. Interview a tenured teacher and a building principal regarding the pros and cons of negotiated teacher contracts. Report the interview results to your class.

3. Unions have lost popularity in many sectors of the industrial segment in the United States with management claims that these unions have forced jobs outside the United States. In some quarters education managers suggest that teachers' unions are taking away from quality education in our schools. Organize a class debate of the pros and cons about teachers' unions as related to quality education.

4. Attend a board of education meeting for at least two different school districts. Compare the differences and similarities of the proceedings. What was discussed? Who conducted the meetings? Did the audience take part in any of the discussions? Report your findings to your class.

5. Invite a superintendent to class to discuss teaching opportunities, teacher-administrator relationships, teachers' unions, and teachers' strikes. Prepare a paper outlining the way in which you will seek your first position.

Bibliography

AFT/NEA: The Crucial Differences. Washington, D.C.: American Federation of Teachers, AFL–CIO, 1984.

Constitution of the AFT, 1986. Washington, D.C.: American Federation of Teachers, AFL–CIO, 1986.

Feistritzer, C. Emily. *The Conditions of Teaching.* Princeton, N.J.: Carnegie Foundation for the Advancement of Teaching, 1983.

First, Patricia F., and Carr, David. "Removing Barriers to Communications Between Principals and Teachers." *Catalyst for Change,* Spring 1986, 5–7.

Justiz, Manuel J., and Kameen, Marilyn C. "Business Offers a Hand to Education." *Phi Delta Kappan,* January 1987, 379–383.

NEA Handbook 1986–87. Washington, D.C.: National Education Association, 1986.

Nielsen, Robert M., and Polishook, Irwin H. *Academic Unions, Values, and Democracy,* Pamphlet series. Washington, D.C.: American Federation of Teachers.

Shannon, Thomas A. "Shanker Is Dead Wrong About School Boards." *Illinois School Board Journal,* July–August 1986, 25–26.

Soltis, Jonas F. "Teaching Professional Ethics." *Journal of Teacher Education,* May–June 1986, 2–4.

Wiggins, Sam P. "Revolution in the Teaching Profession: A Comparative Review of Two Reform Reports." *Educational Leadership,* October 1986, 56–59.

PART II

School and Society

All cultures are identified by their common customs, attitudes, and beliefs. Within the American culture, however, there is a maze of diversity associated with these cultural elements. This diversity can be seen in religious organizations, political affiliation and practices, social and economic practices, and educational expectations and practices. It is this unique cultural diversity that creates a special challenge for the school.

The American school is an integral part of the American culture and has the special task of transmitting America's diversity to its students. In performing this special task, the school has had to coexist with other institutions in the American society. Among these other institutions are the home, church, government, private enterprise, and the like. All of these institutions have special expectations of the school as it attempts to carry out its special mission of transmitting the diverse American culture to its students.

The school, as an institution in society, has its own culture, customs, attitudes, and beliefs. Recognizing and fostering these attributes, the school must still deal with a constantly changing school population, a continuing exploration in knowledge and technology, and an expanding parental and institutional diversity as the nation embraces cultural pluralism. Of particular importance is that the beginning teacher have a firm grasp of the institutional character of the school, the impact of societal problems, the intent and operation of the school, and the types of special school programs that have been created to respond to different needs among the nation's diversity.

In Part II we examine society, the school, and the diverse elements in the culture. As a means of understanding the milieu of the school, we first look at some of the basic elements of a culture and then examine the school from that perspective. The school is presented as a basic cultural institution that attempts to orchestrate cultural diversity in meeting an individual learner's needs. However, at the same time, the school gives attention to the societal expectations for the institution. The school is viewed as a contemporary vehicle that faces radically shifting customs and values of its students and parents. Some of these differences are easily seen as a result of population diversity, extensive mobility, and types of schools by setting—rural, urban, and suburban.

Few societies, if any, escape societal problems and pressures. The more heterogeneous a society, the more problems it encounters. The teacher in the school needs to recognize these problems and appreciate the school's inability to exist in a vacuum free from problems. We identify and examine a variety of societal problems that have a very direct effect on the task of the school. As is evident from past and present history, the school alone cannot cure the ills of society. The curing of these ills requires the cooperative efforts of all societal institutions. The school can, however, be ever alert to the problems and recognize their shifting intensity of importance. The school can alter its program to contribute to a societal effort in solving these problems.

There have been and continue to be nationwide efforts to solve social problems. Some of these efforts are undertaken solely by the school, and others are undertaken by the general society with the school as an active participant. Many of these efforts have been initiated by the federal government, and others have been mounted by state government, foundations, and local agencies. There is little doubt that the severity of the problem directs the intensity of the effort to address the problem. For the school, sifting through the variety of social problems inherent in the society becomes a special challenge. Then the school can identify those special problems that it can effect positively through school programs. ∎

6

Culture, People,
and the School

Focus Questions

- In what way is the teacher unique when the role of the teacher in society is examined?
- What makes the school an open institution in society?
- How does an examination of sociological concepts help the teacher to understand the institutional status of the school?
- Are there differences in rural, suburban, and urban schools?
- Can the school have a value structure of its own?

Key Terms and Concepts

Culture
Anthropology
Sociology
Cultural tools
Acculturation
Socioeconomic status
Social class
Mores and folkways

Mobility
Standard metropolitan statistical area
Values
Purposes of education
Community schools
Pressure groups
Teacher roles
Peer influences

What Would You Do?

While reading the local newspaper from the community in which you teach, you come across a news article that reports on the establishment of a new school achievement award to be presented to a senior student each year. The award will be given to the student that "best models" the Christian ethic. As a new teacher, you have become sensitive to the diverse ethic and religious makeup of the student body in your school. You also have some strong feelings about the institutional and constitutional tradition of separation of church and state. What are three types of action you could take concerning the establishment of this new award?

With a 200-year history the American school has become a recognized social institution. From a meager beginning in the original 13 colonies, our 50-state educational program ranks as one of the best in the world. Fostering both free and private systems of education, the formal institution of school, in its many forms, has become the primary agent for cultural preservation. Educational responsibilities formerly provided by the home and church have become programs of the schools. Examples are programs that deal with values, chemical education, and human sexuality. At the same time that the school has become a permanent social institution in its own right, it has been increasingly subjected to the conflicting pressures from society. It has not had the privilege of exclusive status, as have home and church, which are relatively free to do what they want in their interactions with people, provided that they do not overtly violate constitutional or legal expectations.

American schools tend to mirror society. Although many elements of society tolerate and promote change, most Americans still resist structural or programatic change for the schools. The societal norms for the school are traditional. Schools educate for twelve years, are open during nine months for five days a week, and emphasize the traditional subjects of the dominant culture.

Home living and general family structure have changed rapidly since World War II. However, society has permitted only limited change in schooling. If the school attempts change and that change threatens what is perceived to be the customs, traditions, and values of the home, the school will eventually adjust its program to the perceived norm. Since school is a reflection of societal norms, an examination and discussion of culture in general and the culture of the school in particular are pertinent.

Elements of Culture

If we want to examine the school as an institution of society, we must examine the elements of society. As a social concept, the elements of society are borrowed from an assortment of disciplines and the various tenets of those disciplines. Many of those elements are presented here but only to the degree necessary for the teacher to understand the school's place in society.

Anthropology

Much of the knowledge about culture that concerns human development of relations between races and subgroups of races, social customs, human ways of worshiping, and human pursuits, constraints, and fears comes from the scientific study of humankind called anthropology. Anthropologists study and examine the culture of people present and past. Four specialized branches of anthropology that have significance to the school and society are physical anthropology, archaeology, cultural anthropology, and linguistics. Although each branch may require a different method of examination, the anthropological findings are shared so that an understanding of humankind can develop. Charles Darwin's theory of evolution (1857) helped motivate a flourishing study of anthropology. As research techniques have continued to advance and as more anthropologists have been trained, a vast storehouse of findings has contributed to the current understanding of schooling as a social need.

Sociology

Sociology is the behavioral science that deals with the many aspects of a person's behavior while the person is living as a member of a group. A culture—a sociological concern—is defined as the sum of the aspects of life of a group of people who live together or have done so in the past. Specialized areas of study in sociology are general sociology, social psychology, demography, the community, social organization, and social change. Important to educators is general sociology, which studies how people behave while members of all sorts of groups. The school is one such group.

Sociology was named by the French philosopher Auguste Comte (1798–1857). From his time on, interest in sociology has spread rapidly, and it continues to thrive today. It provides teachers and school personnel with knowledge about the individual and personality, about the home environment and its effect on students, and about social class structure in the American culture. Furthermore, the study of sociology helps the teacher understand how class structure affects the school's efforts, how different value structures affect school programs, and how the attitudes of teachers can be affected.

Institutions, Tools, and Arts

All cultures have generic elements in common: institutions, tools, and arts of the culture. They deal with material needs of people, such as clothing, food, and shelter, or with nonmaterial activities, such as social behaviors, mores, and religion. Every culture develops its own unique elements, such as the use of tools to meet daily living needs, a system of communication (language), the systems or organized group activities called institutions, and a system of expressing the desire for beauty, usually called the arts. No culture has been discovered that did not use tools for catching, growing, preparing, cooking, and eating food and for constructing houses, making clothing, and altering the physical surroundings in many ways. Every culture maintains a system of language that provides communication within the culture. Languages grow and change as needs arise within the culture or as different cultures come in contact with each other. In every culture there is a desire for beauty, expressed through a system of arts, including music, dancing, painting, sculpture, and rituals. In every culture institutions have considerable stability, since each centers around a cultural need. An institution unites a group of people who share a common need that is satisfied through that institution. The school is one of the cultural institutions.

Although different cultures have many of the same general characteristics, they also differ greatly. All cultures use tools, but the kinds of tools and how they are used vary considerably. Languages are very different from one another, as are institutions and art forms. A culture that does not touch more advanced cultures may exist for hundreds of years with very little change, as have some of the more remote cultures of the world. For example, the study of Malayan tribes, isolated from much of the modern world, has revealed little change in their customs and practices for hundreds of years.

One of the ways in which cultures grow and change is by borrowing from other cultures. Another way is by invention. While invention and borrowing induce cultural change, within every culture there is some inherent resistance to change. The fixed customs within a culture represent the desire to do things in the same manner and enforce conformity. For a culture to remain strong, the forces of conformity and change must balance. A reasonable amount of conformity is needed to keep groups of people working together, but growth and change are also needed for progress.

Acculturation

As a result of improved communication and rapid travel, the people of most cultures can now easily meet people of other cultures. When cultures meet, an exchange of ideas and materials results. Frequently, the people of a simple culture try to adopt a more complex culture, a process called *acculturation*. The acculturation process takes place piecemeal, and humans tend to adapt or adopt human experiences that are beneficial to them as persons or favorable to their social processes. Typically, people tend to resist learning about or adapting to a new culture; acculturation is therefore very slow. The Western world has influenced the acculturation of many non-Western peoples who have tried to learn Western culture. This influence has extended from the immediate past and still exists. With the advance of technology and increased interdependent economic systems, a new sense of worldly consciousness has surfaced in the Western world; Western people are studying Eastern social, economic, political, and art forms. For example, in the United States interest in the study of Japanese theory has introduced new management and economic considerations for public and private institutions. Acculturation is worldwide.

A new type of acculturation within the United States began during the 1960s and 1970s. Seen as a new social consciousness, it has affected a growing number of minority groups. This social consciousness has fostered a different kind of acculturation, which challenges the American "melting pot" notion; this new type of acculturation is called cultural pluralism. It attempts to preserve the cultural differences of blacks, American Indians, Spanish-speaking Americans, and others who have made unique contributions to American civilization. This movement carries with it extensive program implications for the schools. That is, we need to provide the necessary common elements of schooling yet also provide for the special needs of the diverse groups.

When different cultures meet, an exchange of ideas and materials results. This six-year-old Chinese boy plays the violin for his classmates as his mother watches. (*Source:* AP/Wide World Photos)

Class Structure

One feature of American society directly related to the school is the social class structure. Although our society does not have a rigid caste system in which no one can rise above the position he or she is born in or is placed in by religious laws, the United States is still a class society. Sociologists usually refer to five or six class divisions in the American social system: the upper-upper, the lower-upper, the upper middle, the lower-middle, the upper-lower, and the lower-lower. A five-class division combines the two upper classes into one. The criteria usually determining social class in the United States are occupation, values, wealth, income, prestige, social contacts, birth, and such intangibles as control over the action of others. These criteria usually constitute what is called socioeconomic status (SES) and are used as common referents for studies of schooling.

In the United States extreme variations exist from community to community in the proportion of people within the different classes. Examples of the different types of communities that exhibit different proportions of social classes within them are metropolitan areas and small communities that are not satellites of

19

large cities. All contain elements from the six class divisions, but the distributions are different.

The upper-upper and lower-upper classes consist of wealthy and socially prominent families. The distinguishing feature about these classes is that they are made up of Social Register families of long standing. Their SES is of long duration, usually inherited, and carries an air of aristocratic values. Members of the upper-middle class are professional workers and business people who tend to be associated with the upper classes but are not as wealthy or prominent. Their SES, although sometimes comparable to the upper classes, is relatively new. In part it can be attributed to hard work, education, and the strong economic and technological growth of the United States since World War II. The lower-middle class consists of some professional workers, small business people, and white collar workers. The upper-lower class is the largest group in the American class system and consists of skilled and unskilled workers. Ironically, professional teachers, because of their SES, tend to be classified in the upper-lower class but have the practices and values of the lower-middle and upper-middle classes. The lower-lower class, often looked down on by the other classes, consists of manual laborers, migrant workers, the unemployed, and many others who have existed for two or more generations on public welfare.

Social Stratification

Studies have been conducted that examine social stratification, the general term that includes characteristics like hierarchy and rank within the social class structure. Although social classes may be examined as distinct groups, the various classes in American society are interrelated in a hierarchical structure. You can locate your own position in the structure by comparing your characteristics and the characteristics of your group with what the community has ascribed to the specific classes. In doing so, you identify your class rank as an individual or the class rank of your group in the community class structure. Identification of rank aids in understanding the power and prestige hierarchy of the community. Interrelation among social class groups exists with other individuals or groups having more or less influence within the same community. Studies of social stratification try to measure specific aspects of the class structure such as prestige, occupation, wealth, social interaction, class consciousness, values, and power.

Figure 6.1 shows how there can be both upward and downward social mobility in the social structure of American society. It also depicts the approximate distribution of classes in the United States. The dark, heavier arrow in the figure signifies more upward than downward mobility. Such mobility is seldom possible in a caste system. Although possible, movement from the lower-lower class to one of the upper classes is rarely, if ever, attained in one generation. After several generations some families have moved to that extreme, however.

Although the several social classes are all a part of the larger American culture, each class is a subculture, and each has characteristics somewhat different from those of the other classes. Anyone moving from one class to another—either up or down—must learn to adopt the characteristics of the

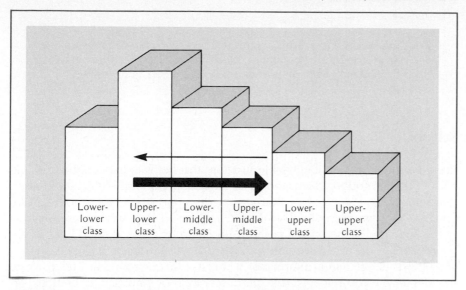

FIGURE 6.1   *Social Mobility and Classes. People move freely within the social structure of the United States, and that movement tends to be upward.*

subculture in order to adjust easily to and function in the new environment. Almost every school district in this nation has elements of all classes in it. Teachers who understand the characteristics of the social classes will be better able to work with students from each of the groups.

Mores and Folkways

Within each of the elements of social class structure, one can distinguish the mores and folkways of a class. *Mores* have generally been defined as rules that govern behavior. They are the morally binding customs of a particular group and tend to be classified as "good" or "bad." They are assumed to be laws of the culture, and to counter them or to violate their tenents is taboo. An example of a middle class taboo is openly promiscuous social behavior.

Whereas mores tend to connote good or bad, *folkways* tend to connote "correct" or "incorrect" conduct, etiquette, or dress. It is not taboo to violate a folkway, but social censure may follow the challenging of a folkway. An example of such a violation is a teacher's dressing in a way that does not conform to the image of a professional in that school district. As society and the various classes within the social structure have continued to change, identifying and examining mores and folkways has become very difficult. In addition, ethnic groups have their own mores and folkways, and these may, at times, conflict with the mainstream culture. The rapid rate of change during the past two decades has created a cultural lag that has thoroughly shaken the confidence and comfort of the many social and ethnic groups.

Consider the social effect that class structure has on learners in the school.
Think about the unique contributions that the school acquires from the culture.
Respect the notion of cultural differences among learners in the school.

Structure of the School

Every institution has an identifiable structure that helps to explain the how and
what of the institution. The school is no exception. Although difficult to understand and often criticized as being rudderless, the American school can be
understood if its institutional structure is examined. A graphic representation
of the structure of the school is shown in Figure 6.2. The dashed lines in the
figure outline the structure and indicate that the school is an open system,
[2]   accepting and exchanging information within its own environment. The structure
has identifiable components: role, purposes, areas of emphasis, operations, organization, human and material resources, and outcomes. Besides various external social forces that affect the school, such conditions within the educational
system as curricular trends and changing pupil attitudes strongly affect the school
as an institution. Successful performance of the institution depends wholly on
how successfully all the components interact.

Role and Purposes of the School

The perceived role of the school is based on philosophical beliefs about it. A
philosophical position usually encompasses national expectations, but it tends
to reflect more strongly the desires of a local community. How a local school
district envisions its role has significant implications for the program the school
offers. Although a role for a school can be distinctly of one type, most schools
tend to combine the philosophical viewpoints of three different roles: reproduction, readjustment, and reconstruction.

A role of *reproduction* suggests that the school act to preserve traditions
and heritage; emphasis is on the past, and decisions on what to teach are based
on the customs and traditions of the past. A role of *readjustment* suggests that
the school alter its program as society indicates. Whereas change in the past
was measured in periods, ages, or centuries, today—for educational purposes—
it is measured in decades and years. This role requires continuous change in
the school program. Emphasis on a readjustment role is judged to be utilitarian
and reflects the current survival for change in society. The role of *reconstruction*
suggests that the school is an agent for change in society. The school is expected
to assume the major responsibility for guiding the future. In this view of the
role of the school, the moral and social ills of the past and present must be
remedied; therefore the school tries to reconstruct society for the future.

As today's school tries to do its job, it should attend to three especially
significant purposes: commitments to universal education, equality of oppor-

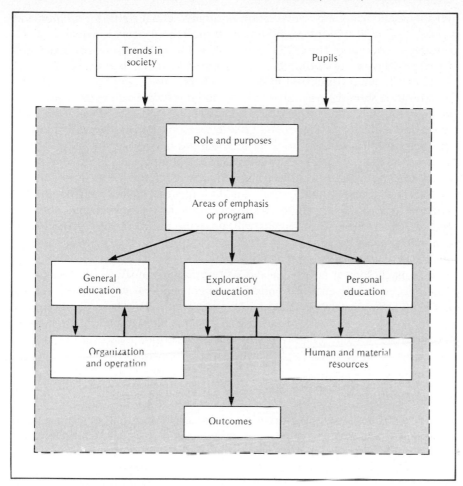

FIGURE 6.2   *The Institutional Structure of School*

tunity, and provision for meeting basic academic and psychological needs of learners. Compulsory attendance laws, child labor laws, and other state and national social legislation have guided this nation in its efforts toward providing universal education. The United States provides a comprehensive educational system for all of its young citizens. Despite certain critics who claim that schools no longer emphasize basics, the school has been able to provide most people with the basic tools necessary to communicate and earn a living. In other words, the school meets a commitment to universal education. However, if the school is to keep pace with the present rate of technological change, universal education may have to be extended to include lifelong learning programs for adults.

Schools should provide programs that are worthwhile, that are as extensive as people want, and that give equal opportunity. But equality of opportunity has not always had the same meaning to all people. A turning point in education came with the *Brown* v. *Board of Education* decision (1954). Continued civil rights legislation and affirmative action programs (equal rights for women and members of racial minorities) have helped the school provide equality of opportunity in education. The 1975 Public Law 94–142 addresses the national trend toward equality of opportunity for handicapped learners, as do other national efforts in education (discussed in detail in Chapter 8).

Education should satisfy the *academic* and *psychological* needs of students. The fundamental academic needs are knowledge, understanding of choices, values, and ability to produce. The great increase in knowledge over the past forty years emphasizes how tools of learning are needed in the different disciplines. The nuclear age, both exciting and foreboding, calls for a keen sense of how to choose the tools of learning properly for shaping the future. And as our society changes, so do the mores and folkways that traditionally have aided us in developing values. As these traditional mores and folkways change, students need to perceive how the changes will affect the future. Every person needs economic productivity; one of the purposes of the school is to provide students with the proper tools for earning a living.

The psychological needs that the school tries to satisfy involve status, security, affection, independence, and achievement. Students whose needs are not satisfied become frustrated. If the teacher can help satisfy these psychological needs, the student will be more successful in concentrating on academic goals. Of course, psychological needs are seldom fully satisfied; however, if the level of frustration can be minimized, learning will be spurred.

Areas of Emphasis

Education encompasses three broad areas: general education, exploratory education, and personal education. General education is usually considered the foundation, or core, of formal learning. Although this kind of education is present at all levels of learning from kindergarten through college, it is primarily associated with the elementary school. Exploratory education is usually a special function of the junior high school or middle school. At this level the student is exposed, at an individual rate of acceptance, to the many areas of specialization he or she may want to explore in senior high school or later. Exploratory education may be the student's last formal education, or it may be preparatory work for higher education. Personal education provides special learning for students and is generally a function of the high school. It may prepare students for college entrance, post–high school vocational-technical learning, or the world of work.

Operations

Schools have certain formal patterns and legal obligations to meet. There are also the regular operations, including the *methodology* of teachers and the *working relation* of the four levels of rank within the institution. These four levels are the school board or the public, the administration, the teachers, and the pupils. Methodology is concerned with matters such as how mathematics or English can best be taught and what environment is conducive to the best learning. These issues are not the only ones involved, but they are typical concerns. Operational matters are important for establishing a productive theory of learning that accommodates the individual differences of all students.

Organization

The typical vertical structure of the educational system is line and staff, as in the military. A line-and-staff organization uses the chain-of-command principle. Teachers answer to principals, principals to superintendents, and superintendents to school boards. As teachers have become well educated and professionally competent, a definite trend has developed toward horizontal organization, in which the staff assumes wider responsibility for program development. Strong professional teacher organizations have also speeded up teacher participation in program development. Thus teachers should understand the organization of school systems in general and how organization may differ among the many local systems. (See Part III.)

Human and Material Resources

Education would not exist without students and teachers; specialists, supervisors, administrators, and the school board are their backup. As society has become more specialized, the school staff has tried to respond to a demand for similar specialization in education. Because each member of the system is becoming more specialized, all members have to understand one another's function and cooperate to achieve school goals.

Besides the human resources, the school also needs material resources, including the physical plant, educational hardware (machines, projectors), and software (books, papers). School staffs must cooperate in planning and designing new facilities or in adapting old school buildings for maximum learning. Well-planned school buildings give teachers a chance to create a receptive learning atmosphere.

Program Pressures on Schools

The school as a social institution does not exist in a vacuum. Since education is still primarily a function of each state, there are 50 separate school systems in the United States. Within each of the states the schools are an integral part of each community and subject to the likes and dislikes of the community's residents. Thus no two schools are completely alike, and the beginning teacher must understand the various forces acting on what is taught in the classroom. These forces can be classified as *legal forces* and *quasi-legal forces,* and they exist at the local, state, regional, and national levels.

The legal forces derive from state constitutions, statutes, legal opinions, court cases, and common law. The quasi-legal forces have no legal origin but behave as pressure points much the same as legal forces. They mirror the society in general and constitute social pressure. Both the legal and quasi-legal forces directly and indirectly influence classroom instruction. At the local level the direct legal force in public education is the school board. Indirectly, the people [15] represent the legal forces in that they elect the members of the school board. An example of a quasi-legal force operating directly at the local level is the Parent-Teacher Association (PTA). Figure 6.3 shows the direct and indirect influences at all levels of government. This interplay of influence between the school system and society establishes the educational policy affecting students and teachers.

Socioeconomic Influences

In addition to the legal and quasi-legal forces, local social and economic factors [20] influence the school system. Two such factors are the wealth of the community and the availability of this wealth for education. Wealth is related to SES and the diversity of the business and industrial makeup of a community. Wealth

	Legal		Quasi-legal	
	Direct	Indirect	Direct	Indirect
Local	Local board of education ——— Local teachers' association	Superintendent of local school ——— People	PTA/PTO	Local Chamber of Commerce ——— Churches ——— DAR ACLU
State	Legislature ——— State school board	State courts ——— Attorney general	State PTA ——— State teachers' association	State Chamber of Commerce ——— American Legion
Regional	None	None	College and university accrediting agencies	
National	None	Departments: HEW Agriculture Treasury Defense	PTA NEA AFT	U.S. Chamber of Commerce and NAM

FIGURE 6.3 *Legal and Quasi-legal Influences on the School* [*Source:* Norbert J. Nelson, *The Logical Structure Theory* (West Lafayette, Ind.: Purdue University).]

involves not only financial ability but also, more importantly, financial effort—the effort made through local taxes to support the schools.

In large metropolitan areas the taxes on business and industry provide considerable revenue. But since these areas must also provide other municipal services for their residents and for commuters who do not live in the area, the funds available for education are not automatically large. There is intense municipal and school government competition for the tax dollar.

In middle class suburban communities with limited industry to support the tax burden, homeowners have traditionally allowed themselves to be taxed heavily to support the schools. As inflation escalated in the early 1980s while the general growth of the economy became stagnant, a demand arose for substantial increases in public taxes for continued public services. Almost uncontrolled spiraling inflation hit schools, government, and the private sector of the national economy. The problem was not unique to the United States but was worldwide. Shrinking school enrollments, national and international comparisons of learner performance in schools, and a general public reluctance to pay higher local, state, and federal taxes led to extreme taxpayer revolts. The California tax revision Proposition 13 and the Massachusetts' Proposition $2\frac{1}{2}$ had immediate impact on local financial support of public schools. These laws were aimed at property taxes, the chief tax for school board budgets. In an attempt to respond to these local tax pressures, school boards began furloughing teachers, supervisors, and specialists as enrollments declined. Ironically, the fixed costs of school operations—fringe benefits for staff, heat, light, transportation, materials, and the like—have continued to escalate, and the schools have even greater competition for their share of the local tax dollar. With enrollment increases now taking place in the latter half of this decade, the pressures for financial support of schools will become even greater.

Another factor affecting local influence is the social and racial composition of the community. Upper-middle class groups have traditionally been more supportive of education and more active in developing educational policy. Lower socioeconomic groups, feeling inferior in their financial and policy efforts, have typically not taken this same interest in education. Recently, though, blacks, Spanish-speaking Americans, and other minorities have increased their interest and participation in school concerns. However, these groups do not have the financial ability to support their desires. Trapped in a Catch-22 situation, they seek financial redress from other sources, chiefly the federal government. A national discrepancy remains: Even though the low-socioeconomic groups may be in the majority, the upper-middle class still may control the school program and the school board.

A third factor is the family makeup of the community. If the community is dominated by families with preschool or school-age children, there is usually active and enthusiastic interest in the educational program. But if the community consists mostly of people without school-age children, the educational program may lack local support. Examples are retirement areas of Florida and Arizona with older people, suburbs adjacent to large cities, and rural areas where young families have moved out.

Value Influences

Regional beliefs and attitudes also influence local school systems. The varied ways integration has been handled reflect this influence; many areas of the South, for example, have experienced more integration than areas of the North. In the Midwest conservative and traditional views have dominated education. Regional beliefs have also influenced what reading materials are to be used in the classroom. Textbook selection for courses, library materials for supplemental use, and other software such as films, videodisks, and computer software remain subject to local and regional value systems. The moral majority has exerted significant influence on what will be taught and what texts will be used. Condemnation of public schools by Fundamentalist religious leaders aided the movement toward greater numbers of private schools in the early eighties. The impact of the movement has been felt differently in different parts of the country. As enrollments and private school costs increase, that impact will lessen. Public schools will feel a greater impact from the baby boomlet enrollment increases and private school students whose parents cannot afford increased tuition.

The school as a social institution is thus pushed this way and that. To maintain its viability as an institution, it must learn to accommodate these influences, guiding them purposefully. In 1980 a ten-year history of national public opinion by the Gallup poll identified the six chief problems facing public schools (see Figure 6.4). Examination of these problems indicates lack of discipline to be the major problem as perceived by the public in 1980. Note that discipline was [20] reported as the number-one problem from 1970 to 1985. During this same period the use of drugs as a problem increased and in 1986 became the number-one problem in the eyes of the public. If the alcohol problem, another problem of chemical use, is added to the drug problem, the two are currently viewed by 33% of the public as the number-one problem for schools. Discipline remains a strong number-two problem (24%), but the other problems of the past decade have ceased to assume national significance.

As an open structure in society, the school cannot afford to resist or neglect prevailing public opinion about the school; school and society are interdependent. The school wholly depends on society for its livelihood; society likewise depends on the school to maintain and develop the culture. The school is challenged to address the growing chemical problem in the school.

Subculture of the School

Most educators agree that one of the school's functions is to transmit the pre-[21] vailing culture to the child. In 1975 Havighurst and Neugarten, describing the school as a social system, wrote on the culture of the school; and their conclusions are still valid:

> The school has a subculture of its own—a complex set of beliefs, values and traditions, ways of thinking and behaving—that differentiate it from other social in-

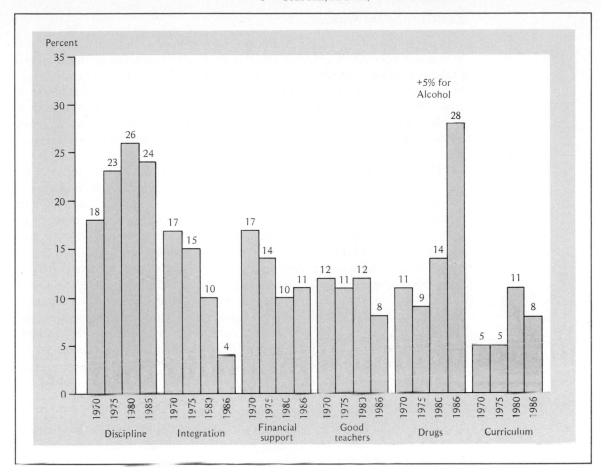

FIGURE 6.4   *Changes in Public Opinion About Problems Facing the Schools,*
1970–1986 (*Source.* Report of the Gallup poll.)

stitutions. Education in the school, as compared with that in the family or in the
peer group, goes on in relatively formal ways; and even those activities that are least
formal (as in children's play at recess) are evaluated in terms of their contribution
to the learning situation. Groupings are formed, not on the basis of voluntary choice,
but in terms of aptitudes for learning and teaching.

Differentiation develops gradually according to achievement. In the elementary
school, achievement proceeds along two lines; the first is the "cognitive," or the
learning of information and skills; the second is what Parsons calls "moral" or
social—learning respect for the teacher, consideration of fellow-pupils, good work
habits, initiative, and responsibility. In the secondary school, the emphasis is upon
types, rather than levels of achievement. With its variety of subject matter, personnel,
and activities, the high school offers the students a wider range of choices along
both the cognitive and the social axes of achievement.[1]

Elements of the Subculture

The subculture of the school comprises many elements. In most instances the mores and folkways of the school have long persisted and directly affect school plant, personnel, students, curriculum, laws, and values. For example, although most recently built physical plants have open learning areas, the majority of school plants are still of the egg crate variety, with single and double corridors of classrooms. Furthermore, teachers and other educational specialists must meet changing but long-established certification regulations that govern by credential examination persons who teach or work in the schools.

Despite individual differences in ability, rate of learning, and personal interest, most students are subjected to the same type of information retrieval and processing, as determined by state curriculum regulations. The Carnegie unit (a required time period of 200 minutes per week for 36 weeks devoted to learning) persists despite its questionable validity. Special school laws regulate fiscal practice and structure, transportation, curriculum, and social and moral behavior. The school's own system of common law regulates classroom behavior, dress code, speech behavior, and other local school board policies. Common rituals for school practice are found in athletics, clubs, promotion exercises, and a host of special events, usually referred to as routine school activities. The signs and emblems of the school's own culture are displayed by school songs, colors, and cheers. The culture is essentially middle class, and general values reflect that part of the society.

Formal Practices

The school operation itself embraces varied formal practices. Children are assigned to grade levels for learning on the basis of age instead of readiness, ability, or interest. Almost all children start the first grade at age six. This age standard may vary by a year or so from state to state, but in general, the practice is traditional rather than based on educational or special findings.

Time modules of learning are another school formality. Classes meet for certain periods each day, and all learning is concentrated in these specified time blocks. Authority is adult-centered, and the learner has little or nothing to say about the lesson. Boys and girls are grouped for learning despite many findings that suggest very different maturation rates related to age and gender differences.

The whole reporting system of educational achievements is still another example of school formality. Traditional letter grades are awarded to students in a comparative grading with other learners who have received the same type of learning stimuli. This grading system is a norm-referenced reporting system.

Only recently have significant attempts been made to reduce the formalism in education by creating open-space learning centers, nongraded programs, and individualized-learning packages based on readiness and interest. With increased use of computers more attention is being given to the individualization of instruction. New grading systems judge how a child has learned by comparing individual beginning performance with what the child can do at the end of a unit. Accomplishment is referred to an established criterion, and we thus have criterion-referenced reporting systems.

Traditions

To be sure, the culture of the school is not uniform. Variations may be associated with regional influences, school location (rural, urban, suburban), length of operation of the school, or social structure of the community. Regional interests may deeply influence certain athletic programs. In some regions of the Midwest, for example, basketball is generally thought to be the state sport. In one particular midwestern state it even carries a hysteria label. In other parts of the country this kind of fierce athletic competition is evident with football, swimming, wrestling, and gymnastics. The great high school marching bands of many schools are a feature of the local school curriculum. Rural schools may emphasize Future Farmers of America clubs, agricultural programs, and 4-H clubs, whereas urban schools seldom sponsor such activities. A region's special interests often show in the school program.

    Older schools have stronger traditions than newer schools, of course, and thus variations exist even within large, growing communities. These variations can be found in feelings of pupil pride or of resignation to mediocrity. Such feelings can be carried to the adult part of the community and can affect the school positively or negatively. Local traditions can also show up in emphasis on sports or academic programs, upsetting a balance in the school program.

    Undoubtedly, the culture of the school must be taken into account if its contribution to the total culture of society is to be studied. Values of students, teachers, and parents interact significantly, thereby affecting the total operation of the school and its contribution to social development.

Values

From the beginning of civilization, scholars have studied the values associated with human beings as individuals and as members of groups. One's personal preferences—values—influence personal behavior. Some personal frustration may arise from such a premise, since individual behavior is also influenced by the value structure of one's group as well as by a personal value system. We must each focus on our own values so that we can know what we hold foremost and act accordingly.

    Personality and individual values are formed and affected by social class position. American schools are, in turn, influenced by the values of those who manage the schools and teach the pupils. Since most school board members are from the middle classes and since most American teachers have middle class backgrounds, the public schools are predominately influenced by middle class values. This kind of influence presents no problem when the students are of middle class origin. The biggest problem facing city schools is the clash of values in institutions dominated by middle class people and attended by minority pupils, many of whom represent a different class. For success in the classroom the beginning teacher must not only learn the values of the several social and racial classes but also be able to teach the individual pupils who hold differing values. All too often in our schools the only attention given to value systems is in disciplining and managing pupils and guiding parents, while the school concentrates on passing along skills and knowledge.

Professional
Perspectives

Remember that the school, as an institution, exists openly in the society.
Think of how you, the teacher, can react to the variety of pressures you will
encounter as a teacher.
Respect the notion that each school is unique and has a subculture of its own.

Peer Influence

Although the school-age peer group reflects adult society, it has a personality of its own that rubs off on its members; it also influences adults. A school peer group is a collection of school-age children who have certain characteristics in [21] common. These characteristics tend to guide the attitudes and actions of the group. Personality determinants such as role, values, behavior, socialization concepts, status, and experiences of all kinds are learned by the child from his or her peers.

The school provides prolonged contact with the peer group away from the parents. When children first make acquaintances at school, they usually respond according to the patterns they have learned at home. While early home influences are being carried along within the child as he or she develops, influences from the peer group also increasingly affect the child's personality. The satisfaction of social needs contributes to a positive personality, and strong associations with peers tend to satisfy strong social needs such as approval from others, desire for success, and yielding to the feelings of others.

The Teacher

Teachers may assume many roles in the community: spouse, parent, member of a religious group, club member, and participating citizen. Teachers also have subroles in their professional capacity that are related to their behavior in the [3] community and with their students. The beginning teacher who wants to succeed professionally must understand his or her position. Specifically, teachers should have predetermined perceptions of what their roles in society should be and should recognize that society expects certain standards from a teacher. A potential danger for the beginning teacher is a conflict in role identity. If community expectations are different from what the teacher expects to give, tension and conflict are likely. The possibility for misunderstanding is increased when teach- [21] ers live outside the community where they are employed, as is often the case in both urban and suburban areas. Sometimes, for a teacher to understand and appreciate a community is extremely difficult when he or she does not live there. Teachers who live outside their school district must make a special effort to understand the composition of the community where their learners live.

The teacher is a well-educated individual, possessing many skills that the community can use profitably. At one time a primary community expectation for teachers was involvement in Sunday school activities, choir singing, or service organizations. At present teachers commonly are active in welfare or social

Parents often expect teachers to be a special kind of model for their children.
(*Source:* Stuart Spates)

organizations, local government, and occasionally partisan politics; teachers serve
on school boards, city councils, and state and national legislatures. Some communities still try to keep teachers from participating in community government.
Generally, however, the trend is toward teacher participation in an ever-wid-
ening range of community activities. One reason for this growth is the increasing
number of people from all social levels entering the teaching profession.

One of the teacher's many expected subroles is protector of morality. The
level of community feeling about this role depends on the particular community.
On the whole, however, parents expect the teacher to be a special kind of model
for their children. Although the parents' habits may be unethical and at times
illegal, they do not want the teacher to exhibit such behavior. Since teacher
behavior is held up for public display, teachers must use discretion in their
personal lives. Exemplary behavior is vital for the young teacher, since most
students tend to hold their teachers in high esteem and to emulate their behavior,
as they do their parents'. Other subroles that the teacher may be expected to
fulfill in the community are those of a cultured individual who is widely read
and traveled, an explorer of knowledge who works for the continual improvement of society, a preserver of tradition and the status quo, and an expert in
child growth and development. Needless to say, some of these roles conflict.

The teacher, besides being an employee of the school board, a subordinate
of the principal and other superiors, and a colleague to fellow teachers, also
has many roles in the classroom. Teachers transmit knowledge and direct learn-

ing. They enter the classroom to teach; and if there is any role they can perform best, it should be teaching. They should have acquired a thorough understanding of their subject and have received special training through professional work in teaching methods, curriculum, philosophy, and psychology. The teacher has been specially trained to teach for maximum learning. Teacher success is usually gauged by how successfully pupils master subject matter.

Teachers also discipline; they strive to guide children toward appropriate behavior. This guidance may be carried out in various ways. Some teachers become strict disciplinarians; some try to get students to cooperate voluntarily; still others let students be free to act as they want. Many teachers never learn to manage classrooms successfully, and discipline problems plague many beginning teachers. Learning the techniques of disciplining students is difficult, since these techniques cannot be specifically taught in teacher preparation programs. However, teachers who have a firm background in their subjects, in educational philosophy, and in psychology of learning have the best chance for handling classroom discipline well.

The teacher is an evaluator. Like discipline, evaluation is a difficult task for a teacher. Children receive grades and are passed or held back by the decision of a teacher. Also, the teacher determines what is appropriate moral and ethical behavior of students. In many respects teachers are entrusted with the authority of judge and jury; they need all their personal resources to evaluate each child fairly.

Often the teacher acts as a substitute for the parent. In most states the teacher stands *in loco parentis* while the child is in school. Teachers are expected not only to discipline a child as the parent might, and at the same time teach, but also to help the child manage personal problems. The teacher performs a multitude of duties, ranging from helping little children with their clothing to helping older students adjust to the anxieties of adolescence. Occasionally, the teacher becomes the special confidant of students—when, for example, students find it hard to tell their parents about particular personal problems.

The foregoing discussion does not imply that the teacher must be everything to all persons to be successful. Situations will dictate appropriate teacher response. Teachers must perceive their proper role, and they must understand the expectations and limitations that accompany that role.

Community Schools

The community is the dominant resource in the education of its children. In most states the local community provides the major amount of financial support for local schools. Although regulatory responsibility resides with state legislatures and federal laws promulgated for the general welfare of citizens, local communities create the kinds of schools they have. The community school concept—local control of the school program—has been carefully preserved.

There are three types of community schools, which are easily identifiable with sociological patterns of population densities: rural, suburban, and urban.

While many features of the three are similar, each has unique features peculiar to its sociological setting. It is not fair to generalize that all rural schools are the same, nor is such a generalization appropriate for the suburban or urban schools. There are differences between and among schools, and there are features that are unique to different communities.

Rural Schools

Science, technology, and economics have helped to bring an end to the one-room schoolhouse of rural America. Where one-room schoolhouses exist today, they exist either because of nostalgia or because some rural areas have too few children for the large geographical areas they serve. Developments in transportation and communication have helped to consolidate small rural schools into large regional rural schools. Many rural school plants in the 1980s do not appear to be any different from many urban or suburban school plants. Rural schools have been tastefully designed and reflect current thinking in the functional planning of educational facilities, but their programs are often different. As a type of community school, they reflect the value structures of the rural populations they serve.

The rural sections of America have changed considerably in the past 40 years. The small operating farms that existed in great numbers through World War II have almost disappeared. In their place are large-scale mechanized farms, many of which are owned by nonresidents. While technology and science have produced modern farm machinery, crop fertilizers, land-use management procedures, and increased productivity, they have created for many rural youth career options other than farming. It is not uncommon today for a single North [22] Dakotan farm owner, with minimum help, to operate a 5,000- to 10,000-acre farm. Since many rural communities have remained principally agricultural, however, many rural youth have migrated to the cities for employment. All this change has effaced rural America as it was known before World War II. The rural school, to be effective for rural students, has had to adjust its educational program to prepare youth for work other than farming. Many consolidated schools have taken this direction and progressed rapidly.

Despite all the change that has taken place, rural America still retains its distinctive patterns. Many rural schools are the center of rural life; values tend to be conservative; and the immediate rural family tends to remain a cohesive unit. The extended family, however, has begun to disappear. Schoolchildren travel long distances to school, and social contacts at school are vital. By urban and suburban standards, rural families live long distances from one another. To the rural family, however, the distances are not great, and there is a feeling of neighborliness. This close community feeling is strongest in the rural area. The social structure is less stratified than in most populous geographical areas, and everyone tends to know everyone else.

Since the early 1970s increasing numbers of people have escaped the cities to enjoy a rural type of living. Although employment in rural areas is scarce, increasing numbers of urban and suburban people are choosing to live in the country and commute to their jobs in the more populous geographical areas. Those who have returned to the rural areas are generally young and well educated. They are fleeing the complexities of metropolitan life to acquire self-reliance and self-confidence and to return to a physically healthier environment. In some instances, however, this exodus to the country has caused problems for the rural schools, because the values of the newcomers have clashed with those of the rural community. Family living habits and expectations for school programs differ, and some newcomers demand increased social services. In many rural communities, however, it takes a considerable length of time for newcomers to be accepted into the social structure, and those "new" rural people are not easily assimilated into the mainstream of rural life.

Expectations for rural teachers are different from those in urban and suburban areas. In general, rural teachers are an integral part of the rural community and are expected to behave accordingly. Patterns of dress, values, and community school participation are expected to conform to those of the community. Rural school boards reflect these expectations. School programs are for general education, and unless specialized programs have been mandated by law, these schools tend to neglect the less able or academically talented learner. Vocational programs, with the exception of agricultural education, are often inadequate in number and type. Traveling distances and the required cooperation among school districts tend to limit vocational-technical offerings. The rural curriculum, much like the urban and suburban curriculum, still relies on the use of a single textbook for each course offering.

There are many exceptions to this general description of rural schools. With the increase in state and federal mandates for school improvement, more teacher organization activities, and greater education consciousness on the part of parents, many rural schools have developed fine educational programs. Thus many rural school systems of the 1980s have come a long way since 1900.

Suburban Schools

Suburban educational systems burgeoned after World War II. To escape the so-called evils of the big city, the large middle class moved to the fringe areas. They left the cities for a variety of reasons, such as to escape school integration and the financial problems of the large-city school system. In suburbia they sought the unobstructed view of a blue sky, yet they wanted ready access to the service area of the city. In effect, the city dweller was transplanted to a semirural setting.

The biggest growth in suburbia has been concentrated around the nation's largest cities—New York, Boston, Chicago, Washington, Atlanta, and Los Angeles. This growth has brought about what demographers call the *megalopolis.* That is, a person traveling between Washington, D.C., and Boston observes very little countryside. The same can be said for the traveler from Michigan City, Indiana, to Milwaukee, Wisconsin. California and the sun belt states have experienced similar kinds of growth.

The key to the social pattern in suburbia has been the housing development.

The city dweller has tended to be segregated by religion, nationality, or race, and the suburban dweller by income. The row houses of the city exist in kind in suburbia—but with larger building lots and lawns.

What was once the retreat of the rich welcomed the middle class leaving the city. But many of the city's problems have also moved to suburbia. Vandalism, drug and alcohol use, and teenage pregnancy are not unique to the urban setting; they exist in suburbia in increasing numbers, although the causes of these problems may be different there. The suburban family has in many ways turned to matriarchal supervision if the family unit is intact, since the father spends little time at home. The hours saved by the reduced workweek are used in commuting to and from the city. And when the commuting suburban mother or father is home, neither has much time for family life. In addition to weekly catch-up activities such as maintenance of the home, shopping, and laundry, civic activities, clubs, and recreation compete for time. Suburban parents are highly organized socially and attempt to keep their children that way also.

Psychologists suggest that many of the problems children bring with them to school can be traced to this changing pattern of family life. Also, suburban school districts are experiencing more single-parent families. In some school districts 50 percent of the student body comes from single-parent families. The single parent is forced to work, and the parent's absence in the home can have an effect on the child's performance in school. When these school problems occur, they are manifested by a need for psychological and social attention, which the child seeks because he or she is apparently not receiving it at home.

The suburban school is not a community school like the rural school, and recreation and social activities emanate from a variety of sources. Thus young people of the suburbs are dependent on the car and the telephone. Most suburban families have two cars and either an extension phone or a private phone for the children. Teenagers like to be on the move, and a car is considered a necessity.

Suburbs continue to grow in number and size, but the pattern for schooling has changed. The suburban schools close to the city that once enjoyed community support are now experiencing a shift to an older population with fewer children and new middle class minorities migrating from the cities. These areas continue to experience declining enrollments despite the baby boomlet affecting other schools. The boomlet is felt further out in the newer suburbs, where property values are not as high and young parents with families can afford housing.

The education programs, however, still reflect what the middle class family believes is necessary education for its children's success in life. We mentioned that special programs are not found in rural America, but they are found in suburbia. Suburban schools try to provide all services for all students; one need only examine the activity program of a modern suburban high school to see this. Suburban education emphasizes college preparation, and parents have a keen interest in how the school operates. Because of the greater pressure of college entrance requirements, the suburban school has been subjected to excessive parental influence. Parents often demand more homework for their children and insist that they be continually challenged. Parental pressure for a return to the basics is greatest here.

With all this attention to education, suburban children appear to develop in a passive and sheltered atmosphere. Everybody wants to be like everybody else. Preparation for a secure life is the by-product of the suburban school. An inherent weakness in this kind of education is the hidden emphasis on conformity and social isolation. There are many social problems in America, and suburbanites cannot isolate themselves from these problems. Social contact is needed among all strata of society if social problems are to be solved. In our mobile society interdependence among immediate family members (father, mother, and children) and other relatives (grandparents, aunts, uncles, cousins) has lessened. Thus the school is forced to assume greater responsibility for transmitting the culture of all social levels of the vast middle class of suburbia.

Big-City Schools

The move to suburbia hastened the decay of the city. City stores and recreational establishments found it profitable to locate elaborate branches in spacious and beautifully designed shopping centers in suburbia. To shop near home became more convenient than to travel to the center of the city. Since wealth, or at least "credit" wealth, was centered in the suburbs, business had to cater more to the people of suburbia and less to the people of the inner city.

As white city dwellers have moved to the suburbs, many people of the black, brown, and yellow races have moved into the city. These immigrants are primarily black, Puerto Rican, Mexican-American, and American Indian. Lately, many Korean, Southeast Asian, and Cuban families have moved to the cities, too. Where the city was once a temporary domicile for the white migrant, it has become a trap for its more recent occupants. Grouped together in certain areas of the
22 city, these new migrants find it almost impossible to move elsewhere, even if they do manage to get good jobs. The typical big-city child lives in a multifamily unit surrounded by thousands of people. The more deteriorated the slum, the more inhabitants there are. The child who lives in the center of the slum is restricted by it and has few contacts outside the area. Problems of the big city are more acute toward the city center. Here there are too few and poorly kept parks, inadequate police protection, and old, poorly maintained schools.

The multiple problems of the big city have brought about increased problems for many of our large, urban school systems. The problems lie not in a clash of value structures associated with education but in different ways of providing for the needs of learners. City children need just as many skills and as much knowledge as do their suburban and rural peers, but minority customs and language barriers too often hamper efforts to provide the sound educational programs that city children need. Previously funded federal and state programs have provided day care, bilingual education, reading programs, and adult education as compensatory efforts for inner-city residents. If funds for these programs continue to be cut, the problems involved may increase substantially.

To hire and hold high-caliber teachers in big-city schools is difficult despite the high salaries that teacher organizations have secured for all big-city teachers.

Discipline problems, social class prejudice, low economic status, increased use of drugs, and deplorable living conditions all contribute to what appear to be insurmountable problems of urban education. The financial plight of the large urban areas has caused many people to declare the cities potential disaster areas. School superintendents find their jobs next to impossible and continually request federal government aid for a massive overhaul of urban education.

Summary and Implications

Schools and society are interdependent. The diversity of our social classes, society's expectation for schooling, and the social setting of the schools add to the complexity of the school as a social institution. Cultural transmission is best protected by the school, since religious institutions and the home have continued to abandon these educative roles. School practices, programs, and traditions have not markedly changed, perhaps mirroring what little value change has occurred in the majority of society. The teacher remains society's model for the learner.

These observations imply that the prospective teacher must understand and appreciate the cultural diversity in which the school functions. They suggest that how well a school responds to the demands of the society may determine the future existence of the school. Teachers must continue to respond to societal expectations.

Discussion Questions

1. How can the school continue to mirror the expectations of society and still respond to a need be on the cutting edge of change?
2. How can equal opportunity for students be achieved when communities have different expectations for their schools?
3. Is the expectation for the teacher to be a model realistic when society has a set of expectations for the teacher that are not mirrors of societal practices?

4. How can the schools counter a two-decade public image history of ineffective discipline?
5. Urban schools need help. Is there a need for greater state and national control over schooling if the urban problems are to be addressed to the benefit of the urban students? Why and how?

Supplemental Activities

1. Visit a local high school and interview a group of students about the school subculture. How are their responses similar to or different from your expectations?
2. Attend a PTA meeting and report on your observations to your class.
3. Compare a community's expectations for an elementary teacher and for a secondary school teacher. Should they be different?

4. Interview a Chamber of Commerce member and detail his or her expectations for the community school.
5. Meet with a school administrator and find out how the administrator responds to community pressures. Discuss your findings in class.

Note

1. Robert J. Havighurst and Bernice L. Neugarten, *Society and Education,* 4th ed. (Boston: Allyn and Bacon, 1975), p. 139.

Bibliography

A Curricular Response to Critical Realities. Washington, D.C.: Association for Supervision and Curriculum Development, 1978.

Fullan, Michael. *The Meaning of Educational Change.* New York: Teachers College Press, 1982.

Havighurst, Robert J., and Levine, Daniel. *Society and Education.* 5th ed. Boston: Allyn and Bacon, 1979.

Naisbitt, John. *Megatrends: Ten New Directions Transforming Our Lives.* New York: Warner Books, 1982.

Noll, James William, ed. *Taking Sides: Clashing Views on Controversial Educational Issues.* Guilford, Conn.: Dushkin Publishing Group, 1980.

Partners: Parents and Schools. Alexandria, Va.: Association for Supervision and Curriculum Development, 1979.

Patterson, Jerry L., Purkey, Stewart C., and Parker, Jackson V. *Productive School Systems for a Nonrational World.* Alexandria, Va.: Association for Supervision and Curriculum Development, 1986.

Postman, Neil. *The Disappearing Child.* New York: Delacorte Press, 1982.

Pritchard, Keith W., and Buxton, Thomas H. *Concepts and Theories in Sociology of Education.* Lincoln, Nebr.: Professional Educators Publications, 1973.

Roberts, Arthur D., and Cawelti, Gordon. *Redefining General Education in the American High School.* Alexandria, Va.: Association for Supervision and Curriculum Development, 1984.

Social Problems
Affecting the School

Focus Questions

- How can the school begin to combat some of the major social problems facing students?
- What is the relationship between the social problems of youth and youth's performance in school?
- Should our schools help solve social problems? Why?
- What is the relationship between poverty and school completion?
- What kinds of stress do the schools face because of the changing diversity of the school population?

Key Terms and Concepts

Chemical dependency
Suicide
Dropouts
Youth sexuality
Crime
Delinquency
Child abuse
Poverty

Unemployment
Welfare
Minority groups
Blacks
Spanish-speaking Americans
American Indians
Refugees
Sex discrimination

What Would You Do?

Following graduation, you have begun teaching in a small suburban community which has a homogeneous social makeup. You are in the middle of a lesson when there is a knock on your classroom door. You open the door to find your principal with a new student for your classroom. The new student is a recent immigrant who speaks no English. As a beginning teacher, where would you turn for help with this student? How would you work with your class to help ease the new student into the group?

There is a considerable amount of debate over how far the schools can and should go to help solve our country's social problems. Some people believe that the schools should be concerned only with the academic development of students. Others believe that the schools are in a unique position to help solve many of the nation's pressing social problems—and should do so. While this debate continues, social problems persist and noticeably affect students and schools. In this chapter we identify a wide variety of social problems that have a direct effect upon students. That the severity of the problem causes varying amounts of stress for learners as they move through the school program should become apparent to the teacher in training.

Problems of the Youth Culture

Young people today face a complexity of problems as they mature to adulthood. Changing family structures, alteration of what was once considered to be a societal set of expected values, and increased pressures to grow up quickly and be adult all have contributed to the social problems of alienated youth. These young people, reacting to the pressures of the time, have found their own ways of countering what appears to them to be circumstances with which they cannot cope. As learners in the schools, they need special attention relating to their needs.

Chemical Dependency

One of the most tragic social problems in America today is the misuse of drugs by young people. As reported by a recent Gallup poll, the number-one problem facing the school, in the eyes of the public, is the overuse of drugs. Alarmingly, the U.S. Public Health Service reports that about two-thirds of all high school seniors have experienced use of illicit drugs, and over 90 percent of those seniors have used alcohol. Chemical dependency, whether it be drugs, alcohol, or tobacco, is one of the leading causes of other social and academic problems of youth. Figure 7.1 provides information on the extent of this chemical problem in our society.

To counter the drug problem, schools have embarked on a variety of programs. Many of these programs are funded by state and national governments, and they are intended to be preventative. The problem is acute and is affecting all age groups. Since the drug problem is viewed as a national concern, the White House, under the direction of Nancy Reagan, has sponsored a nationwide effort to educate the public in an attempt to curb the use of drugs. Many of the state and national programs provide students with information about drugs so that they realize the dangers of drug abuse. The major objective of these programs is that students, as informed persons, will decide they are better off not

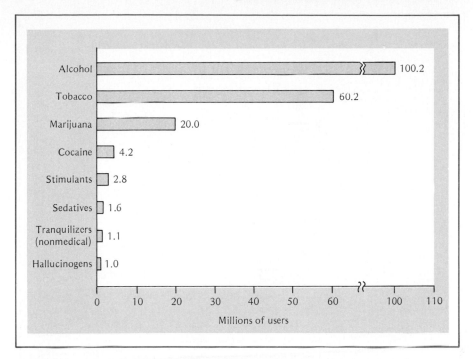

FIGURE 7.1 *Chemical Use in the United States* (*Source:* Data for the graph compiled from various U.S. government bureaus.)

using illicit drugs. Generally, the drug education programs that have been adequately funded, that involve parents and students, that are taught by well-trained teachers, and that avoid preaching and moralizing have been the most successful.

Student use of alcohol has risen sharply in recent years. Figure 7.2 shows the results of a recent survey that asked high school seniors to estimate the percentage of their friends who used various drugs and the degree of use. The survey found that alcohol was the most commonly used drug and that sizable percentages of students got drunk at least once a week. In many schools students consume alcohol in school buildings during the day. Furthermore, medical authorities report a rapid rise in "polydrug" use—combining drugs and alcohol—among students. Polydrug use is extremely dangerous; for instance, alcohol used with barbiturates, sedatives, or tranquilizers gives a heightened effect for each substance but can cause death. Thus alcohol and drugs have become the foremost chemical problem for young people in America.

Millions of American students regularly smoke cigarettes. The growing evidence that smoking is a serious health hazard has prompted educators to search for ways to combat this problem. National educational efforts directed toward the physical hazards of smoking have been successful in reducing the total number of Americans who smoke. However, young people, particularly young women, continue to smoke. This increased use of tobacco by young women has led to increased rates of lung cancer among women, making the rates among the female and the male populations about equal.

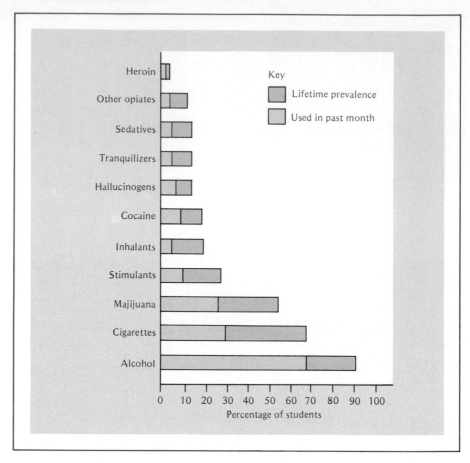

FIGURE 7.2 *Prevalence of Drug Use Among High School Seniors, 1985* (*Source:* National Institute on Drug Abuse.)

Most people believe that the school is the only agency that has a chance to significantly reduce teenage smoking, and more and more schools are accepting the challenge. Some schools include a systematic study of the effects of smoking as part of their curriculum. The most promising approach to smoking education is one in which the youngsters themselves run antismoking campaigns. Some schools have joined parent groups, the American Cancer Society, the American Heart Association, and the National Tuberculosis and Respiratory Diseases Association to fight teenage smoking.

Suicide

Suicide rates among young people are on the rise. In fact, during the past 30 years the rate of teen suicide has tripled. At the same time, suicide rates for the rest of the U.S. population have remained relatively stable. Although suicide is thought to be highest among lower-socioeconomic groups and many of the minorities, it is not. The highest-risk group for teen suicide is white, Protestant, and above-average in school performance. Most of these same students appear to be performing normally, and many hold part-time jobs. Although many more teen girls than teen boys attempt suicide, the boys are more successful in their attempts.

The usual cause of adolescent suicide is extreme depression. It usually appears during early adolescence when normal physical and social development directs teenagers away from family ties. During this period teens begin to look beyond the home for friendships and assistance in making value decisions. Chief causes that become specific contributors to attempted teen suicide are conflict with one or both parents, the breakup of boy- or girlfriend relationships, parental divorce, moving to a new school or area, and trouble with a teacher.

There is a high incidence rate between adolescent suicide and some form of chemical dependency. Alcohol and/or drugs are used to counter depression; and when these drugs fail to deliver the desired effects, the teen is ripe for a suicide attempt. Teachers need to be especially sensitive to the early signs of growing depression among students. Student withdrawal behaviors, irritability, and sudden changes in work, sleep, and eating habits are all early signs of a teen going through some stage of depression and in need of professional help. The best aid that a teacher can give is to encourage the student to talk about the problem and seek medical help. Although teen suicide is growing at an alarming rate, it can be prevented if sensitive parents and professionals seek help for the adolescent when the early signs of depression are observed.

Dropouts

Although high school students and college students drop out of school for different reasons, both represent a substantial loss to our society. In most states students must attend school until they are sixteen. Thus they cannot drop out of school during the early years of high school. However, once they are past the compulsory attendance age, a disturbing number drop out of school. Approximately 25 percent of the eighteen-year-olds in the United States have not completed high school. This rate has not decreased in over two decades, and it is considerably higher among the minority groups. Current estimates from the Bureau of the Census are that 35 percent of Hispanics and 25 percent of blacks, ages eighteen to twenty-one, are dropouts. Other minority groups have even greater rates. Urban native Americans and Puerto Ricans have dropout rates of 70 to 80 percent. The rate of school dropouts is disturbing for many reasons. Most of these students cannot get jobs, many get into trouble with the law, and many do not qualify for military service. Most of them are not yet prepared to be productive citizens, and a large number are destined to become social liabilities.

Table 7.1 shows the percentage of seventeen-year-olds graduating from high school in the period 1870–1984. Although considerable progress has been made over this period, there are still many American youths who drop out and do

TABLE 7.1 *High School Seventeen-Year-Olds Graduating*

Year	Percent
1870	2
1900	6
1940	51
1950	59
1960	65
1970	76
1980	74
1984	70

Source: U.S. Education Department, February 1986.

not finish high school. Figure 7.3 shows the breakdown of various dropout groups in the 1980s.

These data point to the desperate need for the school and society to find ways to keep children in school and to teach them at least basic life skills—not only for their own good but for the good of society. The economic cost of ignoring the problem is staggering. In other words, the money spent to keep

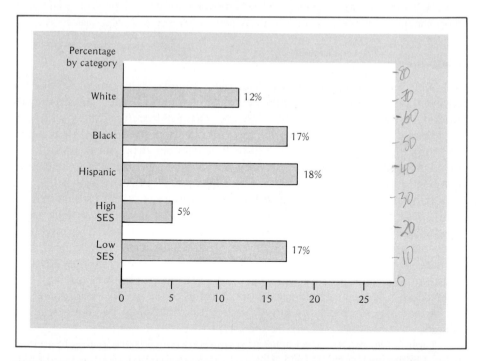

FIGURE 7.3 *Comparisons of High School Sophomore Dropouts in the 1980s by Race/Ethnicity and SES.* (*Source:* Education Commission of the States.)

our children in school and prevent dropouts is not really an expense but an excellent long-term investment that returns handsome dividends for society.

The gifted high school graduate who does not go to college represents still another kind of school dropout. Furthermore, half of the students who enter college never graduate. Although some of these students leave college for academic reasons, many of them have exceptional academic ability. The underdeveloped talent of these gifted students represents a substantial loss to society. Needless to say, our society and our schools have a long way to go before they solve the school dropout problem.

Delinquency and Crime

There is a definite relationship between juvenile delinquency and school dropouts. Various studies of delinquency have shown that many delinquents did failing work while in school and often were less able than nondelinquents. The alarming point is that many of today's dropouts will be tomorrow's criminals. And statistics on crime in the United States are staggering. Figure 7.4 shows the dramatic increase in serious crime in recent years. To make matters worse, fewer than one in four serious crimes leads to arrest; in other words, three-fourths of the people who commit serious crimes do not get caught.

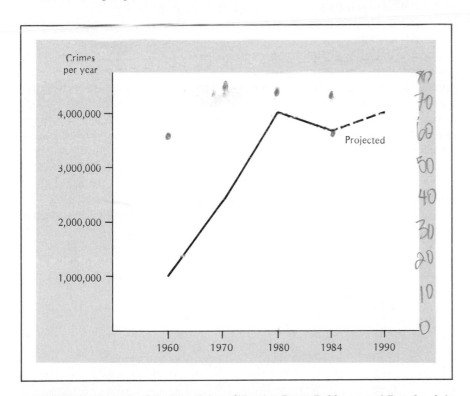

FIGURE 7.4 *Growth of Serious Crime (Murder, Rape, Robbery, and Burglary) in the United States* (*Source:* U.S. Bureau of Justice Statistics.)

The president's commission on law enforcement and administration of justice recently reported that organized crime has become so great and sophisticated that it now involves narcotics, prostitution, murder, gambling, protection rackets, real estate, confidence games, politics, and the stock market—touching every American. All of this crime costs our society an unbelievable amount of money. Table 7.2 shows the escalating cost of law enforcement. Law enforcement alone now costs every American man, woman, and child over $100 a year.

As the world has witnessed increasing violence, so have the schools. Violence and vandalism have now become very serious problems in many schools. The U.S. Senate Committee on Delinquency has estimated that school vandalism costs our nation over $600 million each year. The National Association of School Security Directors estimates that each year there are 12,000 armed robberies, 270,000 burglaries, 204,000 aggravated assaults, and 9,000 rapes in our schools. Furthermore, an estimated 70,000 serious physical assaults are made on teachers each year.

These statistics suggest the size of the problems of vandalism and violence faced by the schools. Unfortunately, very few solutions to these problems have been found. Some schools have hired police officers, adopted strict rules, expelled troublesome students, and taken a determined stance. Other schools have solicited the help of students and parents, have tried to change the curriculum to make it more appealing to students, have gone to great lengths to keep all students in school, and have generally adopted a democratic, humanistic, and sympathetic attitude.

Unfortunately, few schools have been successful in combating violence, for two reasons: First, few schools have the financial resources to make a serious, concerted attack on the problem. Second, violence has become so prevalent in American society that some social scientists believe there is simply no way to keep it out of the schools. Violence, crime, and a general disregard and disrespect for the rights and welfare of others have become commonplace. The size and diversity of the violence problem can be understood by considering a list of related problems: child abuse and neglect, wife beating, juvenile delinquency, television and movie violence, illegitimate births, divorce rates, tax fraud, governmental corruption, welfare cheating, price fixing, stock manipulation, organized crime, business crime, and employee theft. Crime and violence have indeed pervaded both American life and the schools.

TABLE 7.2   *Cost of Law Enforcement, 1960–1985*

Year	Cost (Dollars)
1960	3,349,000,000
1970	8,571,000,000
1975	17,249,000,000
1980	27,026,000,000
1985	32,801,000,000

Source: Bureau of the Census, 1985 projections.

Sexuality

The youth culture of the American society is experiencing a sexual revolution. Teenage pregnancy, venereal disease, and sex-related psychological problems are on the increase. The National Center for Health Statistics reports that teenage pregnancy is at an epidemic rate. For fifteen- to nineteen-year-olds, it has risen almost 100% in the past fifteen years. Despite national efforts by right-to-life groups opposing abortions, teenage girls, like their older counterparts, resort to abortion to terminate unwanted pregnancies. Although nonwhite teenage illegitimate birth rates have begun to decline, white illegitimate birth rates have increased during the same period. This social phenomenon is a response to the changing sexual values of the teen culture. However, this change in values is little different from the change in values of the general society.

     Annual reports issued jointly by the American Public Health Association, the American Social Health Association, and the Venereal Disease Association continue to show increases of venereal diseases among teenagers. Gonorrhea and syphilis head the list of venereal infections. Syphilis, a medically serious venereal disease, touches the lives of many young victims. If left untreated, it can cause

According to the National Center for Health Statistics, teenage pregnancy has reached epidemic proportions. Many schools are now implementing special educational programs to assist young mothers. (*Source:* Mike Penney)

serious health problems such as sterility, paralysis, blindness, heart disease, insanity, and death. Often babies of infected mothers are born with mental and physical defects.

Increased sexual activity among teens and adults has led to a national health problem with the spread of AIDS (acquired immune deficiency syndrome). At first it was considered to be a disease associated only with homosexuality, but the surgeon general of the United States reports the spread of this virus among all ages and classes of people. Figure 7.5 shows the estimated growth of this disease at the current time.

Some 70 percent of the AIDS virus cases are attributed to sexual transmission and are found in heterosexual as well as homosexual practices. Some 25 percent of the cases are linked to the practice of sharing needles when using drugs. The expected sharp increase in the national death rate is due to the current lack of an effective vaccine. Because no vaccine is available, the surgeon general has urged the schools to offer educational programs. Educational program efforts are underway in major cities such as New York, Philadelphia, San Antonio, and Seattle.

Problems associated with sexual values will continue to challenge the school. Even though the mounting evidence suggests that these problems are often related to ignorance or misinformation, well-designed and well-taught sex education programs in the schools have not been universally supported by the public. Lacking program efforts, teachers need to be knowledgeable on the

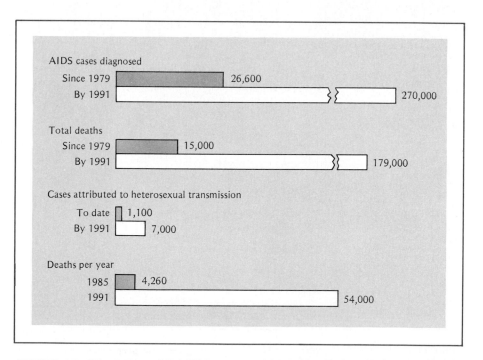

FIGURE 7.5 *The Status of the AIDS Virus and Its Projected Growth* (*Source:* The Surgeon General's Report on AIDS.)

Remember to look for personal problems if students are experiencing learning problems.

Be prepared to work closely with trained guidance counselors when you are suspicious of a student's chemical use.

Try to keep communication lines open with learners who appear to be experiencing some type of social problem.

sexuality issues of youth and recognize symptoms of behavior that can be referred to professionals for help.

Child Abuse

Closeted until recent years, child abuse has become a major problem for the schools. The latest national reports estimate that almost 2 million school-age children will suffer some form of physical or mental abuse each year. This abuse includes child molestation and abduction. Over one-half of the abused children are female, and the majority of abusers are parents.

The U.S. Department of Justice reports that a child is abused every 2 minutes in the United States. Over two thousand children die each year from some form of child abuse. At least one girl in four and one boy in ten will be sexually abused before they are eighteen years old, and the principal abuser will be a parent. The child abuser is not a dangerous stranger but generally is a trusted friend of the child. Table 7.3 identifies the myths associated with sexual abuse of children.

Teachers need to be watchful for potential child abuse victims in their classrooms. The telltale signs of child abuse are the following behaviors:

TABLE 7.3   *Myths and Facts About Sexual Abuse of Children*

Myths	Facts
Children are sexually abused by strangers	About 80% of children are sexually abused by family members or someone known to the child
Sexual abuse of children is a violent act	Only 5% of cases are acts of violence
Persons who abuse children are mentally ill	Not all persons who abuse children are mentally ill, but many have difficulty with appropriate child-adult relationships
Sexual abuse of children only happens in poor families, certain ethnic groups, or uneducated families	Child abuse takes place in all economic, ethnic, and educational levels of society
Sexual abuse does not occur in foster care	About 25% of abuse complaints in foster care are sex-related
Only men sexually abuse children, and the victims are female	Both sexes abuse children, and both male and female children are victims

Source: The National Center of Child Abuse and Neglect.

- A sudden change of behavior in school learning
- No visible sign of medical attention to physical or medical problems of the child after the parents have been alerted
- Overly watchful behavior, as though the child thought something dangerous were about to happen
- Overly compliant behavior, where the child tries to please everyone
- Behavior indicating a lack of adult supervision
- Exhibition of learning problems that are foreign to expected normal behavior
- Continual early arrival at school, desire to stay late, and little desire to go home

Teachers should not be reluctant to report these types of abnormal behavior to the proper authorities. National statistics tell the story on child abuse, and the teacher is protected from civil and criminal liability if the report is rendered honestly from suspicion and is considered valid.

Demographic Implications for Schools

The size, diversity, and ethnicity of the U.S. population continues to have a profound effect on the operation of the school. Although the general birth rate is not as high as it once was, it remains high among the nonwhite groups in our society. Additionally, the economic structure of society affects subgroups of the American culture differently. Family structures have changed, and poverty touches all elements of society. Thus the school must attend to a diversity of students it has not seen before. The school population for the 21st century presents challenges for teachers that they have to date not experienced.

The Changing Family

American families have changed dramatically during the past three decades. As reported in 1980, only about 11 percent of American families fit the traditional description of a working father, a mother at home with the children, and two or more school-aged children. In the late 1980s that percentage has dropped to 4 percent. Family lifestyles have changed; and where married couples with children fit the societal norm, that lifestyle is now the exception. The following data sketches a profile of the American family in 1987:

- There are over 80 million households in the United States.
- Twenty-six million married couples have no children.
- Seven out of ten women with children are active members of the work force.
- The divorce rate has quadrupled in the past twenty years, and the number of single-parent families is estimated at 25 percent. There are 14 million children being raised in single-parent families.

The Role of Education in Society

"A good education is that which gives to the body and to the soul all the beauty and all the perfection of which they are capable."

Plato

One view of the role of schools is that they should strive to discover and develop the intellectual, physical, and creative abilities of each individual.

The Picture Cube/Betsy Cole

The Picture Cube/E. Williamson

FPG International

Historically, education has functioned to promote citizenship and to instill a sense of patriotism in children. Thomas Jefferson believed that education is fundamental to the preservation of a free society, and that it is vital to the success of democracy.

Schools have the special task of helping to assimilate immigrants into American society by passing on the knowledge, values, and customs of our culture.

In recent years many schools have begun to sponsor programs aimed at preventing some of the social problems facing youth, such as drug abuse, drunk driving, suicide prevention, sex education, and AIDS awareness. In addition, some schools provide their students with birth control clinics and special courses for teenage mothers.

According to the U.S. Census Bureau, the number of young children enrolled in daycare has increased by 400 percent since 1965. In the future, public schools may be expected to provide educational services for preschool children.

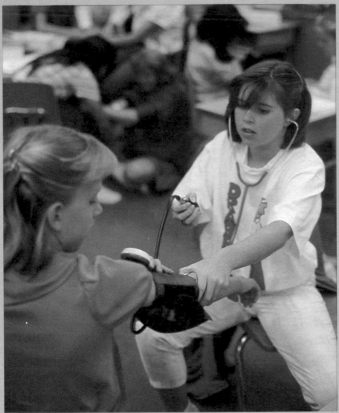

The success of the United States economy is closely tied to the success of the educational system. As society becomes increasingly complex, the need for a literate, well-educated workforce becomes vital.

Schools can play a role in helping students develop areas of interest and make career decisions.

The future will be guided by new generations of teachers, scientists, inventors, explorers, and dreamers. . . . Progress depends on the quality of education that our children receive.

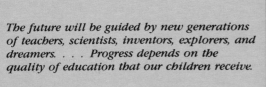

- Sixteen percent of these single-parent children have mothers under the age of 25, and 4 percent of the total of these children have teenage mothers.
- Sixty-two percent of the children who come from single-parent families fall below the poverty level.
- Twenty-four percent of the children from single-parent families were born out of wedlock.
- Teenage pregnancy, with children born out of wedlock, is greatest among some of the minority populations, but the percentage for white teenagers is increasing.   [69]
- The range of socioeconomic status for families without children is markedly different, with only 23 percent in the high-socioeconomic bracket. (The largest percentage of these family members, 50 percent, however, are in the 55-years-and-over age group.)

The American family of the past may be described as a young couple living in a home, with children, with room for grandparents, with a male-dominated relationship and with the expectation of the couple living out their years together side by side. There has been a rapid decline in such an extended family. The 1980s family, sometimes described as the nuclear family, is the same as the family of the past for some Americans but vastly different for many others. Today's family may be two people who have never married, a man and woman who have had other marriages, a man and woman without children, a man and woman without extended family ties, a man and woman with a less male-dominated relationship, or a single parent raising children after a divorce or the death of a partner.

Families are smaller today, the average size, as projected from census reports for 1986 by the Bureau of the Census, being 2.63 members. It does not include the traditions of the extended family. Although the divorce rate among couples continues to escalate, four out of five divorced persons remarry. The divorce rate for these people is higher than the regular rate. There is an increase in commune living, and a growing number of children are being born from these relationships.

All of these family changes have affected children. The family now has considerably less influence on family members' religious practices, education, and value structures and on the general socialization of the child. Although the school has assumed many of these responsibilities, other institutions also contribute to the socialization of the child. These institutions include peer groups; organized groups such as scouts, 4-H, and Little League; and TV, radio, newspapers, and magazines. Because of increased female influence in the family, the   [24] family is no longer patriarchal but rather has become increasingly egalitarian.

This continuing change in family structure and living has created a new social label for children in families where both parents work or in single-parent families where the parent works: They are called latchkey children, and they now number some 5.2 million elementary school children. Latchkey children, because of working parents, are left to take care of themselves when they come home from school. This practice has led to the development of school programs for children who must fend for themselves after school. The programs work with the children on such issues as first aid, nutrition and health, baby-sitting, and being on their own at home. Nationally, however, the public does not seem to be willing to fund programs for these children. Since the number of latchkey children is growing, teachers must be sensitive to the fact that these children become frightened and bored and suffer from being denied normal social interaction with their peers after school.

Poverty

Poverty has existed since the human race appeared on earth and probably will be around as long as humans are. Poverty in the United States is complex; determining what factors contribute to poverty is difficult, if not impossible. Notions about what constitutes poverty are continually changing. One person may define poverty as physical hunger or even starvation; another may define it as a lack of luxuries. In other words, poverty is relative. Thus poverty in the United States includes people who are literally starving to death as well as people who have relatively little compared with those who have very much.

Most people would agree that there is less poverty today in the United States than in the past. The government's definition of poverty is based on changing economic conditions, further adjusted by such factors as family size, sex of family head, number of children, and farm or nonfarm residence. Table 7.4 presents information about the percentage of families below the poverty level in the United States. This table illustrates that poverty is greater for minority families. Table 7.5 shows the percentage of children, by race, that live in poverty.

Slightly over 10 percent of our American families live in poverty. Although there is a higher *percentage* of nonwhite families living in poverty, *numerically* there are many more impoverished white families. For instance, many Appalachian white families earn very little each year. Their per capita income is far less than that of the rest of the country. Many Appalachian adults are unemployed, and many have very little formal schooling. The Appalachian subculture has created a way of life that keeps these mountain people impoverished. Farming and mining have traditionally furnished their livelihood; however, the mountain farms are no longer productive enough to provide a good living, and automation has largely replaced humans in the coal mines. Those who have left the mountains to go to the cities have found that their education and skills do not qualify

TABLE 7.4 *Percentage of Families Below the Poverty Level*

White	9.1
Black	29.3
Hispanic	24.1
Total U.S.	10.6

Source: U.S. Department of Commerce, 1986.

TABLE 7.5   *Percentage of Children by Race and Ethnicity That Live in Poverty*

Age	White	Black	Hispanic and Others
Total (all ages)	12.1	35.7	28.4
Under 15	18.1	47.6	39.0
15–17	13.9	42.6	34.0
18–21	13.7	39.6	28.0

Source: U.S. Bureau of the Census, 1986.

them for desirable jobs. Many people believe that education alone cannot solve the problem. There are immediate needs such as employment, housing, medical care, and legal advice that must be met. Although immediate assistance in these areas is essential to the war on poverty, it cannot solve the long-range problem in the way that better education can.

Fortunately, our nation is concerned about poverty. Moreover, tax money spent to eradicate poverty is a profitable investment. In other words, it costs less in the long run to help people lift themselves out of poverty than to pay the consequences of allowing them to remain impoverished. One need only check the cost of welfare programs and crime fighting to be convinced of this statement.

The nation's current war on poverty is being waged partly through education. One of the many federal education efforts directed toward reducing poverty is the Elementary and Secondary Education Act (Public Law 89–10), passed in 1965. Chapters I and II of this act have provided several billion additional dollars a year for the American school system. The purpose of the act is "to strengthen and improve educational quality and educational opportunities in the nation's elementary and secondary schools." This and other federal efforts to improve education are discussed in Chapter 8 of this book.

We must realize that if we are to eradicate poverty, we must treat the disease itself and not just the symptoms. Indeed, we must try to prevent the disease in the first place, and the most effective "vaccine" at our disposal is education. It is incongruous that a nation that has amassed far more material wealth than any other nation in history can still contain pockets of severe poverty. Poverty prevents people from being productive citizens, from pursuing excellence, and from developing a sense of dignity. If we are committed to the importance of these ideals, then we must continue to work toward eliminating poverty in the United States. Fortunately, we have begun to realize the democratic, human, and economic necessity for reducing poverty, and we have iniated many immediate and long-range programs—some of which involve education—aimed at eradicating it.

Unemployment rates in the United States are directly affected by the general economic condition of the country. However, many other factors also influence the unemployment picture. The additional women entering the labor force, the decreased number of young people in military service, and changing trends in college enrollments all contribute to the country's unemployment rates.

Certain groups within our society are more affected by unemployment than others, as Figure 7.6 points out. Although actual employment rates change from year to year, the relative unemployment picture for the various groups has remained essentially the same in recent history. Generally, nonwhites and teenagers have the highest unemployment rates.

There is a growing change in the job market of the future, and this change has serious implications for the school if poverty is to be reduced. Table 7.6 identifies where the largest number of new jobs will be and the fastest-growing occupations. Examination of this projection readily shows the influence of technology for future occupations. If the schools are to contribute to the efforts to correct poverty, computer training must receive increased emphasis. As the majority population in the country becomes nonwhite, and if the school has given greater attention to meaningful job preparation, the minority unemployment figures of the eighties should decrease significantly.

Diversity of Population

Demographers report that over the next 30 years the U.S. population will change significantly. By the year 2020 the population will have swelled to 265 million people, but the ethnicity will be different. The current fertility rate for white women, 1.7 children, is not high enough to replace the current white population (see Table 7.7). However, the increased fertility rates of blacks and Hispanics are as high as or higher than the white rates during the baby boom of the forties and fifties. So in coming years the minority population of the United States will be larger than ever before. Additionally, the average white American is six to eight years older than his or her average American minority counterpart. The nonwhite student population is increasing at a significantly greater rate than the

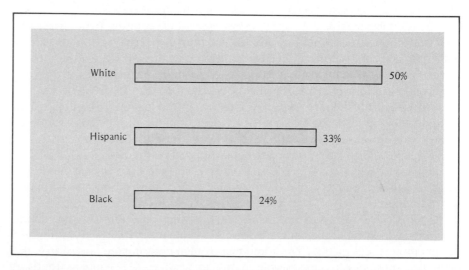

FIGURE 7.6 *Teenage Employment by Race/Ethnicity, 1985* (*Source:* Education Commission of the States.)

TABLE 7.6 *Projected New Jobs and Growth of New Jobs by 1990*

New Jobs	Growth, 1978–1990 (Thousands)
Janitors	671.2
Nurses aides	594.0
Salesclerks	590.7
Cashiers	545.5
Waitresses	531.9
Clerks	529.8
Nurses	515.8
Secretaries	487.8

Occupations	Number of New Jobs by 1990
All occupations	21,980,000
Data processing	96,572
Computer systems analysts	203,357
Computer operators	151,100
Computer programmers	153,051
Food preparation and service workers	491,900

Source: Monthly Labor Review.

white student population. The majority of students in elementary schools are now nonwhite. The large-growth states for nonwhite children are California, Texas, New Mexico, Mississippi, Alabama, Georgia, and South Carolina. The baby boomlet is greatest in these states, and the needs for schoolteachers are also greatest here. In the nation's 26 largest cities the majority of students are nonwhite.

Immigrants continue to enter the United States legally and illegally. The current rate of legal immigration, 500,000, is equal to the peak years of the 1920s. Additionally, some 300,000 to 500,000 immigrants enter the country illegally on a yearly basis. Most of these new immigrants are of Asian or Hispanic backgrounds. Most of these new immigrants are settling in western and southern

TABLE 7.7 *Fertility Rates of American Women*

Race/Ethnicity	1957	1986
White	2.9	1.7[1]
Black	—	2.4
Mexican-American	—	2.9
Total	3.7	1.8

Source: Education Week, May 14, 1986.
[1]A 2.1 fertility rate is necessary for one generation to replace itself with another of equal size.

states. Estimates suggest that by the year 2010 California, like Hawaii, will have a population that has a nonwhite majority.

Implications for the schools are many. Most minorities view their native language as their most precious cultural heritage, and they wish to see it retained. The pressures for increased bilingual programs in the schools and communities will continue despite the California passage of a law declaring English as the language of the state. A major question of concern for communities and schools will be, "How tolerant will the white population be of the new racial and ethnic diversity of the country?" With minority school enrollments growing, teacher-training institutions will be forced to address these issues.

The changing distribution of ages in the population provides another demographic change in the United States. The United States is becoming a nation of older people. Today, there are more people over the age of 65 than there are teenagers. This change has come about because of the slowdown in the national birth rate in the past fifteen years and an increase in the years of life expectancy. The latter has occurred because of improved medical science and the continued control and elimination of some fatal diseases. People are living longer, as shown by the change in the mortality tables of insurance companies. The median age of the U.S. population is 30 and is estimated to reach 36 by the turn of the century.

Ethnicity

There are numerous minority groups in American society today, including blacks, Spanish-speaking Americans, American Indians, and Asian-Americans. In fact, within our society there are countless groups—economic, social, religious, political, agrarian, educational, and nationality groups. The challenge to our schools

[25] presented by this rising tide of minority students is staggering. Minority students often have special learning problems, often come from single-parent homes, are likely to be poor, may have trouble with the standard form of the English language, and often are truant and/or involved in suspensions or expulsions from school.

Approximately 12 percent of all the people in the United States are blacks. Black Americans suffer considerably from many of the nation's social problems—

[70] racial discrimination, violence, school dropout, drugs, alcohol, unemployment, substandard housing, housing discrimination, and unequal educational opportunities.

The 1954 Supreme Court decision (*Brown* v. *Board of Education of Topeka*) made it illegal for schools to practice de jure segregation—segregation which is deliberate. However, nearly all school systems built neighborhood schools that serve only the children living in a particular neighborhood. Since blacks generally live together in certain neighborhoods, black children usually attend black schools. This type of segregation is called de facto segregation—segregation which is not necessarily deliberate but a consequence of conditions. In 1961 a federal district court ruled that the attendance lines drawn by a school board are illegal if these lines promote de facto segregation (*Taylor* v. *Board of Education,* New Rochelle, N.Y.). This decision has prompted integrationists to work toward the abolishment of de facto segregation, particularly in large northern cities. Some school systems have transported children to other neighborhood schools to try to minimize de facto segregation. Some large-city school districts such as Louisville, Kentucky, reorganized with nearby suburban school districts to integrate races in their schools.

The 1980 census revealed that 14.5 million (6.5 percent) people of the U.S. population is Spanish speaking. Estimates are that as many as 5 million additional migrants and illegal aliens in this country speak Spanish. In addition, birth rates are climbing within this group, and some three to five hundred thousand new Hispanic immigrants are entering the country each year. Some demographers predict that Spanish-speaking Americans will surpass blacks as the largest minority group by 1990.

There are many different types of Spanish-speaking Americans, each with a different set of problems. For example, the 1980 census reported that over 1.6 million people of Spanish origin live in the state of New York alone. Many are Puerto Ricans, who generally pride themselves in being self-sufficient. Unfortunately, handicaps such as language barriers, poor job skills, and lack of education keep most Puerto Ricans poor. Children from these families frequently do poorly in school because of language difficulties, impoverished cultural backgrounds, and a highly transient lifestyle.

There are also numerous Mexican-Americans who live in poverty. Many have recently moved to the United States in hopes of finding a better life. The immigrants usually come from the poor sections of Mexico, and most have had little formal education or special job training. Their cultural background makes it hard for them to succeed economically in a highly technical society. Numerous Mexican-Americans live in the southwestern part of the United States; many others travel throughout the country as seasonal workers.

Migrant workers constitute a particularly difficult social problem. About a million workers and their families move about constantly, following the growing season as it progresses northward each year. Historically, the pay and the living conditions for these migrant workers have been poor. Because of the constant moving, the migrant worker's child has difficulty attending school and receiving an adequate education. Some tangible improvements in the form of better pay and more healthful living conditions have been made for migrant workers; however, most still face an uncertain future. The migrant child moving from school to school as the parents follow their work still has serious school problems.

American Indians constitute still another impoverished minority of the U.S. population. Since losing the vast majority of their lands to the white people, and having lost additional lands through broken treaty rights with the U.S. government, they have suffered the additional loss of their native heritage and have been forced to live largely on government subsidies. American Indians still suffer from a lack of education and special skills that would permit them to get ahead in a technological society. Dropout rates for American Indian students are the highest in the nation. Indian children have more than their

**Professional
Perspectives**

> Be sure you understand the different types of families that are represented in your classes.
> Be attentive to the special needs of children of poverty, and know the kinds of assistance available for them.
> Strive to be a model of equality when teaching minority students.

share of educational problems. Many Indian children start school unable to speak English. Most educational programs reflect the dominant white culture, and continued attempts at assimilation have created an American Indian generation that is unsure of its cultural heritage.

The Indian Education Act of 1972 and its 1974 amendments are designed to help native Americans help themselves. Each year over a quarter of a million Indian schoolchildren in over a thousand school districts now receive some benefits from the Indian Education Act. These grants are aimed at providing bilingual and bicultural enrichment activities. They also attempt to improve reading programs, guidance services, and transportation. Unfortunately, most of these programs are not sensitive to the cultural needs of these children, and consequently, many of the children drop out of school. Other grants try to involve Indian parents and Indian communities in educational activities; still other parts of the act are aimed at training teachers for Indian schools, providing financial aid for Indian college students, instituting adult Indian education, and establishing tribal improvement projects.

Although these recent steps are viewed by the majority population as encouraging, American Indian citizens are still beset with many serious social problems. Alcohol and suicide rates are extremely high and can be correlated with the extreme rates of poverty on the reservations and in the Indian communities of the large cities. There continues to be a drastic shortage of trained Indian teachers for the growing number of reservation Indian schools. Unfortunately, all American Indians tend to be viewed as the same—when, in reality, there are as many differences as there are numbers of bands and tribes.

Indian children are often caught between old traditions and new educational efforts. As contributing members of the U.S. society, they are forced to live and work in two societies. The Indian way has its roots in the culture and is dominant on the reservation. But off the reservation the Indians must conform and rid themselves of "Indianness" if they are to be successful in society. Teachers seeking positions in American Indian schools should become immersed in the Indian culture if they wish to be responsive to the special needs of Indian learners.

Recent Refugees

Relatively new minority groups that constitute a social problem in the United States are the recent refugees. Growing numbers of displaced persons are immigrating, particularly from Southeast Asia, Cuba, and most recently from Poland.

Schools throughout the country are creating meaningful educational programs to serve the needs of recent immigrants, many of whom do not speak English. (*Source:* Mike Penney)

A high percentage of these persons do not speak English, bring few employable skills, and know very little about the American culture. Nearly one-half of these refugees are school-age children, and 15 percent are illiterate in their own native language. Estimates are that by the mid 1980s the number of such recent refugees will have grown to 15 million.

Schools throughout the country are struggling to create meaningful programs to serve the needs of these unique immigrant students. Congress provides some financial help to the schools in these efforts through the Indochina Migration and Refugee Assistance Act (Public law 94–23).

American Women

In 1972 Title IX of the Education Amendments was enacted, stating: "No person in the United States shall, on the basis of sex, be excluded from participation in, be denied the benefits of, or be subjected to discrimination in education, job placement, individual rights, and general status within the social structure of the nation."

Many women work out of economic necessity, others for self-fulfillment (see Figure 7.7 for the percentage of the U.S. labor force that is female). Over 50 percent of the U.S. labor force is now women. This significant rise of women in the labor force is expected to continue into the 1990s (see Figure 7.8). Of this labor force, 60 percent are mothers who work outside the home. In all likelihood, the escalating divorce rate contributes to the large number of women in the labor force. Between 1970 and 1980 the number of one-parent families increased by 2.6 million, and the number of two-parent families decreased by 1 million. Estimates suggest that one out of every five students now comes from a home with divorced parents. These children may require special understanding and skill from the teacher.

Although women may be well educated and highly qualified, they often do not enjoy equal job status with men and earn considerably less money for comparable or identical jobs. Except for teaching, nursing, library service, and social work, the professional and technical fields are dominated by males; discrimination against women persists in white collar and sales positions. Women tend to be concentrated in the low-skilled, poorly paying jobs of the labor market.

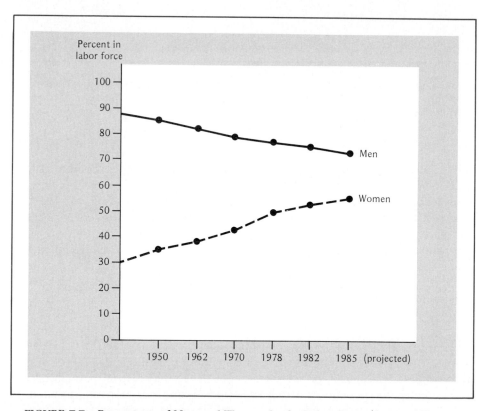

FIGURE 7.7 *Percentage of Men and Women in the Labor Force* (*Source:* U.S. Department of Labor, Labor Statistics.)

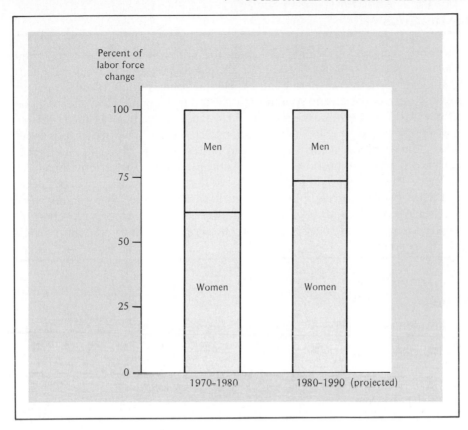

FIGURE 7.8 *Percentage of Change in Women's and Men's Share of the Labor Force*
(*Source:* U.S. Department of Labor, Labor Statistics.)

Even when women are well represented in any given profession, they do not always receive the same pay as men.

The National Organization for Women (NOW) and the Women's Equity Action League (WEAL) have pressed American society for an awakening to sex discrimination. This movement has had an influence on American society. In addition, the feminist movement has gained national recognition with the support of a feminist press. The KNOW Press, the ERIC (Educational Research Information Clearinghouse) women's studies reports, and Betty Friedan's *Feminine Mystique* have all raised issue with the male-dominated societal expectations for women.

Although the Civil Rights Act of 1964, Title VII, prohibited discrimination, it was not until the 1970s that women began to receive equal treatment under the law. New federal guidelines from the Departments of Labor, Health and Human Services, and Education—and federal court cases—have helped women combat sex discrimination within all levels of society. The nation's schools are beginning to focus some attention on nonsexist education. All these steps are essential and encouraging to the cause of equal rights for women.

|26|

Summary and Implications

There are many serious social problems in the United States that have important effects on our schools. Schools cannot adequately meet the educational needs of students without considering the society the young people come from. Our schools and our society are so intimately related that any problem affecting one affects the other; therefore the schools alone cannot solve many of the problems confronting young people. The implication here is clear. If we are serious about solving the problems facing young people, both society at large and our schools must work together purposefully—probably in a way not yet envisioned by planners. This effort would undoubtedly require that more money be spent on education than is currently being spent. It would require that parents work much more closely with educators than they do now. It would ask American society to make a much deeper and broader commitment to education than it has up to now.

Discussion Questions

1. How can the school help in combating the chemical problems of youth?
2. How is learning performance affected when the learner is an abused child?
3. How does poverty continue to disenfranchise the educational development of children from poverty homes?
4. How will the growing population diversity alter the program of the school?
5. Should the United States impose rigid quotas on incoming refugees? How does the continued refugee growth affect the schools?

Supplemental Activities

1. Invite a law enforcement officer to your class to talk about the cost of policing criminal activity.
2. Gather different SES data from two different school districts, and compare the class status of two groups of students.
3. Invite a drug and alcohol center counselor to the class to discuss rehabilitation programs used with youth.
4. Compare and contrast the traditions and practices of two different minority groups.
5. Invite a school dropout to class to discuss his or her problems in getting employment.

Bibliography

Bianchi, Suzanne M., and Spain, Daphine. *American Women: Three Decades of Change.* Washington, D.C.: U.S. Department of Commerce, 1984.

Chesler, Mark A., and Cave, William M. *A Sociology of Education.* New York: Macmillan, 1980.

Christiansen, James. *Educational and Psychological Problems of Abused Children.* Saratoga, Calif.: Century Twenty One, 1980.

Ianni, F. A. J., and Reuss-Ianni, E. "Crime and Social Order in Schools." *Educational Digest,* 45 (May 1980): 2–5.

Musgrove, Frank. *School and the Social Order.* New York: Wiley, 1980.

National Strategy for Prevention of Drug Abuse and Drug Trafficking. Washington, D.C.: U.S. Government Printing Office, 1984.

Ornstein, Allan C., and Levin, Daniel U. *An Introduction to the Foundations of Education.* 3rd ed. Boston: Houghton Mifflin, 1985.

Postman, Neil. "Engaging Students in the Great Conversation." *Phi Delta Kappan,* 64 (January 1983): 310–316.

Wagnchal, Peter H., and Johnson, Lynell. "Children's Views of the Future: Innocence Almost Lost." *Kappan,* 67 (9) (May 1986): 666.

Women at Work: A Chartbook. Washington, D.C.: U.S. Department of Labor, Bureau of Labor Statistics, April 1983.

8

A Nation's Response
to Social Problems

Focus Questions

- What role can the federal government provide in assisting educational efforts in solving social problems?
- Should the school be responsible for providing compensatory programs?
- How does Public Law 94–142 affect the regular classroom teacher?

- What are the implications for bilingual-bicultural education programs in the future with population diversity increasing?
- Can minorities be assimilated and still keep their individual identities?

Key Terms and Concepts

Education and Improvement Act
Compensatory programs
Block grants
Direct grants
Chapter 1 funds
Chapter 2 funds

Public Law 94–142
Due process of students
Individualized Education Program (IEP)
Bilingual-bicultural
Adult literacy
Reading programs

What Would You Do?

You have observed some of your students coming to school with an identifiable odor of alcohol. There is a school policy which forbids drinking at the school, but you also know that if you report the students, they will probably be suspended. However, the students' behavior is having a negative effect on their performance in class. The school does not have any chemical education program or counselors for students with chemical dependence problems. You can probably rid yourself of the problem by reporting these students to the principal. However, as a teacher, there are additional things you could do to help these students. How would you handle this problem, and where would you seek help?

Following the passage of the National Defense Education Acts, the Elementary and Secondary Education Acts, and the War on Poverty Program in the late 1950s and 1960s, the federal government liberally pumped money into a variety of programs aimed at improving school efforts and social differences in the society. Different catagories of title funds abounded for a twenty-year period, and a new cabinet-level Department of Education was created in 1979. The creation of department-level status for education appeared to signal renewed federal support of education. However, federal policies took a more conservative turn with the change in the national administration in 1980, and the New Federalism stressed a return to greater control, participation, and financial effort for the states rather than the federal government. Although the dollar amounts have continued to increase for programs that the federal government continues to support, the real dollar values have declined. In the main, federal financial efforts in real dollars have declined as the government has wrestled with balancing an increasing budget deficit and addressing other program priorities. The federal government of the 1980s has assumed a stronger posture of rhetorical leadership with a variety of supported commission reports addressing social and educational issues.

Compensatory Programs

During the two decades preceding the 1980s, the federal government sponsored a variety of educational and social programs aimed at correcting or altering problems suffered by the less fortunate in our society. Many of these programs were aimed at youth because young people have no control over their conditions. Since the programs were intended to provide some very basic needs which these children did not have, the programs came to be labeled "compensatory programs." Some of the programs have survived into the 1980s and continue to receive federal government financial support. These federal programs are typical of a national response to social problems.

Education and Improvement Act

Before 1981 all federal support programs were administered by the federal government through a variety of agencies that had been created during the 1960s and 1970s as various educational public laws and acts were adopted. These public laws and acts were administered through a series of title regulations for each act and governed by regulatory agencies housed within and outside the Office of Education. The new cabinet-level department centralized this operation, with the exception of special programs allied with other cabinet-level departments (e.g., Commerce, Interior, Agriculture).

The Department of Education is organized into six major offices which direct federal efforts: the offices of Elementary and Secondary Education, Postsecondary Education, Research and Improvement, Special Education and Rehabilitation Services, Vocational and Adult Education, and Bilingual Education and Minority Languages Affairs. In addition to responding to national problems that affect the whole country, these offices administer programs of financial support. The programs span compensatory education, state and local special assistance, Indian education, migrant education, college student loans and grants, international fellowships and consultantships, higher-education support programs, research and dissemination, handicapped programs, rehabilitation and vocational development, and bilingual programs. For the total expenditures on all levels of education, preprimary through graduate school, the federal government provides approximately 10 percent of the funding.

In 1981 the Education and Improvement Act was passed, becoming effective in 1982. Two major changes to federal support were introduced with this act. First, Chapter 1 of the act superseded Title I of the Elementary and Secondary Education Act and extended to the states and local education agencies (LEAs) the prime responsibility for conducting the federal education program designed to meet the educational needs of disadvantaged children. Second, Chapter 2 of the act consolidated 42 other elementary and secondary education programs into block grants for three broad purposes: basic skills improvement, improvement of support services, and special projects. In addition, state agencies administer Chapter 2 programs.

The granting of federal money for the various programs may be accomplished by the awarding of direct grants or entitlement (block) grants. The direct grants are monies awarded from Washington and are used for projects having national priority. The secretary of education establishes different priorities each year and controls the discretionary use of the funds, which he then allocates for the special national projects. Recipients of these grants, public and private, must meet federal agency criteria, which are published regularly in the Federal Register. Entitlement grants are made to the states and are based upon numbers of children or students to be served and the amounts of federal money available. Each state determines how these monies are to be distributed in keeping with intended federal priorities. These funds have been reduced yearly since 1981. Although the percentage of reduction has been small and varies by category of support, inflation and increased numbers of people in need of support have caused the decline in the real dollar value of support to be substantial. Declining value has been particularly acute in the areas of higher education and research. Continued increases in higher-education tuition rates have lessened the real value of federally supported loans and grants. The state-administered grants may be awarded with or without criteria or formulas. The intent of the 1981 Improvement Act was to shift greater financial and administrative responsibility for compensatory educational efforts to the states.

Assisting the Handicapped

In 1967 Congress created the Bureau of Education for the Handicapped (BEH) and began providing the states with funds to create, improve, and operate compensatory programs for the millions of handicapped children in the United States. For over eleven years (1969–1980) the federal government allocated over $200 million each year to train or retrain special education teachers and to establish research and development. All this effort was directed toward helping children handicapped by mental retardation, speech problems, emotional disorders, deafness, blindness, and other health-related disabilities. The BEH programs undoubtedly improved the condition of the handicapped in the United States. Despite this national effort, substantial differences existed among the various state programs because the BEH-sponsored programs remained vol-

Public Law 94-142, passed by Congress in 1975, mandated that all handicapped learners have the right to a public education. (*Source:* Mike Penney)

untary rather than mandatory. The mainstreaming laws of many states during the late 1970s helped to equalize compensatory efforts within individual states, but the national differences remained acute. Handicapped children in some states received better help than the handicapped in other states.

Perhaps the single piece of legislation most significant for education during the 1970s was Public Law 94–142, the Education for the Handicapped Act. Congress, having ascertained that 8 million handicapped children existed in the United States, passed the act in 1975 and mandated partial operation for 1978. September 1, 1980, was established as the date for full compliance with the law. Although the bill was conceived and passed in a desire to improve school programs for the handicapped children alone, because of its due process implications, it has paved the way for individualized programs for all potential learners. In fact, this bill may have helped speed development of early-childhood programs because it requires early identification of youngsters needing help.

The main features of the act follow.

- All handicapped learners between the ages of three and twenty-one are to be provided with a free public education.
- Each handicapped child is to have an individualized education program (IEP), developed jointly by a school official, a teacher, the parents or guardian, and, if possible, the learner.
- Handicapped children are not to be grouped separately unless they are severely handicapped, in which case separate facilities and programs would be deemed more appropriate. (The stress is on creation of a least restrictive environment.)
- Tests for identification and placement are to be free of racial and cultural bias.
- School districts are to maintain continuous efforts in identifying handicapped children.
- School districts are to establish priorities for providing educational programs in compliance with the law.
- Placement of the handicapped must require parental approval.
- Private schools are to comply with the act.
- Retraining or in-service training of all workers with the handicapped is required.
- Special federal grants are available for modifying school buildings.
- State departments of education are to be designated as the responsible state agencies for all programs for the handicapped.

Handicapped children are defined in the act as those evaluated as mentally retarded, hard of hearing, deaf, speech-impaired, visually handicapped, seriously emotionally disturbed, orthopedically impaired, other health-impaired, deaf-blind, multihandicapped, or having specific learning disabilities. Furthermore, the law clearly explains least restrictive environment placement, individualized education programs, due process protection, and teacher education. Here are some of the most important specifics of this law:

1. The least restrictive environment placement ensures that handicapped children are educated with nonhandicapped children to the maximum extent possible and that the placement of a handicapped child outside the regular classroom occurs only when the nature or the severity of the handicap is such that education in regular classes with the use of supplementary aids and services cannot be achieved satisfactorily.

2. An individualized education program must comprise written statements developed by the public agency, the child's teacher, one or both of the child's parents, and the child, when appropriate. Other specialists may be involved if the parents or public agency so desire. Each written IEP must include the following:

    a. The child's present level of educational performance.

    b. Annual goals, including short-term instructional objectives.

    c. Specific special education and related services to be provided to the child, and the extent to which the child will be able to participate in regular educational programs.

    d. Projected dates for initiation and anticipated duration of special services.

    e. Objective criteria, evaluation procedures, and schedules for determining on at least an annual basis whether or not the short-term instructional objectives are being met.

3. The law requires a proper due process procedure be followed with the diagnosis and identified placement of each child. Parents of handicapped children must be notified in writing before a public agency initiates, changes, or refuses to initiate or change the identification, evaluation, or placement of the child or the provision of a free appropriate public education to the child. This notification in the parents' native language or other mode of communication (e.g., braille, oral communication, sign language) must include the following:

    a. A full explanation of parents' due process rights.

    b. A description of the action proposed or refused by the agency, why the agency proposes or refuses to take the action, and a description of any options considered by the agency and reasons why they were rejected.

    c. A description of each evaluation procedure—that is, a test, record, or report the agency uses as a basis for the proposal or refusal.

    d. Any other factors relevant to the agency's proposal or refusal.

The due process concerns of this act go to the core of programs for modifying education in the United States. Successful mass education has significantly raised the mean level of achievement, literacy, and grade completion for all U.S. citizens. At the same time, however, the schools have had to resort to teaching and learning practices directed at group goals. Despite their awareness of the benefits of individualized programs for all children, the schools have been unable to develop them because of money constraints and the sheer numbers of school-age children.

A substantive due process question for educators naturally arises. If handicapped children are required to have individually tailored programs to meet their needs and interests, why not all learners? No two children are alike, and

Professional Perspectives

Be sure you know the important elements of Public Law 94–142.

Practice putting together the essential elements of an IEP.

Be prepared to create different teaching materials for different ability levels of learners.

therefore each child should have his or her own program. As the constitutionality of Public Law 94–142 continues to be upheld and strengthened, the rights of all learners to have individual programs will have to be considered by the schools. Since the law was conceived under the due process clause and since that law requires individualized programs for special learners, we may safely project that in the future parents may request similar treatment for their nonspecial children under the guise of due process.

Public Law 94–142 does not specify any requirement for mainstreaming. The law speaks strictly of the need to provide for a least restrictive environment for learning. Since the 1960s the Council for Exceptional Children (CEC) has directed its efforts for special education toward the provision of mainstreaming services as organized under the Cascade model for intervention. This model projected placement of those in need of special education either in regular classrooms with special itinerant staff or in residential settings where the learner was isolated from the mainstream. Variations from those two extremes could be special classes in a regular school building or special classes in a daytime special education center. The idea was to move learners to more restrictive environments only as necessary and return them to less restrictive, mainstreamed environments as soon as feasible. Public Law 94–142 has given the CEC opportunity for a least restrictive interpretation of the cascade of services.

Many special education services are dictated by the type of physical environment provided for the learner. Typically, regular classrooms and schools are not physically fit for many special education students; they are built for the mainstream but not the exceptional child. The "new perspective," as CEC calls it, makes regular learning areas more powerful and diverse. It allows for a broadened interpretation of the instructional cascade (see Figure 8.1).

The regular classroom environment in this plan is a model of individualized instruction for all learners. Physically, learning spaces are treated better acoustically, with amplication devices and alternative treatments of illumination. Greater use of learning centers with a multiplicity of equipment and materials is provided for special needs and preferences. Collaborative teaching is expected, with special educators, other professionals, and aides working with regular teachers. Instruction is individualized for all learners. Special education students are moved out of the regular environment for minimal periods and only for complex individual needs. The CEC views the least restrictive environment as the new mainstream.

Reading

One of the most ambitious attacks in the war on poverty has been associated with Title I of the Elementary and Secondary Education Act (ESEA), the Title I

29

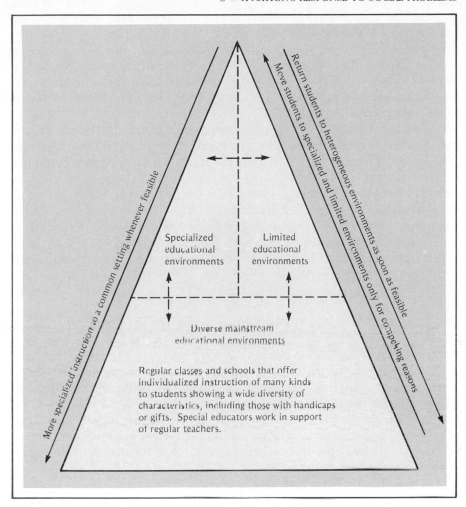

Specialized educational environments

Limited educational environments

Move students to specialized and limited environments only for compelling reasons

Return students to heterogeneous environments as soon as feasible

More specialized instruction to a common setting whenever feasible

Diverse mainstream educational environments

Regular classes and schools that offer individualized instruction of many kinds to students showing a wide diversity of characteristics, including those with handicaps or gifts. Special educators work in support of regular teachers.

FIGURE 8.1   *The Instructional Cascade* (*Source:* Jack W. Birch and Maynard C. Reynolds, *Teaching Exceptional Children in All America's Schools,* p. 47. Copyright 1982 by The Council for Exceptional Children. Reprinted with permission.)

Reading Program for economically disadvantaged children. Nationally supported reading programs began during the 1960s, and the funding for these programs increased substantially during the 1970s. As we began the decade of the 1980s, federal funds for economically disadvantaged students constituted almost 25 percent of the total federal budget in education. Only higher education received a larger share (40 percent), and over half of this amount was higher-education student assistance and educational opportunity grants.

Under the Reagan administration, much of the effort in reading programs was shifted to state departments with Chapter 2 funds and additional supportive funds from the states. These programs are still tied to socioeconomic conditions within the states, and thus the programs remain a type of compensatory effort toward poverty. Because the national economy has suffered with continued inflation and greater unemployment numbers in some of the older states, the number of children eligible for Chapter 2 funds has increased. Each year in which the poverty level has risen because of inflation, more compensatory reading programs have been provided, including additional reading specialists, more materials, and in many cases increased use of teacher aides. Although the national inflation rate has slowed considerably, the poverty-level cutoff continues to rise moderately.

Reading programs aim at "continuous progress learning." This aim means that the child is diagnosed at a given performance level and then moved individually through the program. This special treatment can be done within the regular program in the classroom or in special facilities for reading instruction. After a child begins to read at a given grade level, she or he is then placed in the regular reading program of the classroom. These special reading programs are meant to take care of those with the greatest need. Early intervention, researchers have found, leads to fewer dropouts, positive school attitudes, and reading performance that allows the child to progress normally within the regular school environment.

Programs for Special Needs

Many fine attempts at solving educational and social problems are being made at all levels of government and by private foundations. In addition to Chapter 2 funds being passed from the federal government to the states for distribution [70] to address state needs, the states have increased their financial efforts to solve problems of literacy and chemical dependence; and states have initiated programmatic improvements to address many of the various commission reports. Some representative examples of programs that are intended to address educational needs follow.

Bilingual-Bicultural Education

The Bilingual Education Act—Title VII of the Elementary and Secondary Education Act—was enacted into law in 1968. This act and its various amendments were enacted to help with the special needs of growing numbers of American [29] children whose first language is not English. Originally, the act was intended to focus on low-income learners, early-childhood education, adult education, dropouts, and vocational students. Funds were also provided for preservice and inservice training of teachers for these programs.

Bilingual-bicultural education is formal instruction for learners, using their native language for learning all subjects until second-language (English) skills have been developed. This approach increases the equal educational opportunity of minority children. The 1980 census reports that the size of the non-English-language background population in the United States is 30 million people. This number is expected to increase to 39.5 million by the year 2000. People of Spanish, German, and Italian descent make up the majority of this group, with the Spanish-speaking people who have migrated from Latin America and Puerto Rico by far the largest portion. The Spanish-speaking portion will continue to grow. As we discussed in Chapter 7, the minority populations are soon to be the majority in an increasing number of border and coastal states. The recently passed California bill declaring English to be the primary language of that state will face serious legal challenge as the minority numbers continue to grow in that state.

Since the fall of Saigon in 1975, over 500,000 Southeast Asian refugees have entered the United States. In 1980 alone the federal government allowed 170,000 such refugees to settle in the United States. Through 1987 about 100,000 have entered the United States each year since 1980. Almost one-half of these refugees are school-age children and are in need of bilingual education. About 75 percent are illiterate in their native language. The 1980 influx of Cuban refugees has added immensely to the growing number of Spanish-speaking groups. Many of these Spanish-speaking and Asian refugees are concentrated in California, Texas, Pennsylvania, Colorado, Louisiana, Iowa, Wisconsin, Florida, and New York. In addition to these refugees are the native American citizens, whose number has swelled as their tribal population has increased. Over 30 percent of American Indians speak a tribal tongue as their first language.

English monolingual schools have helped to deny to non-English speakers equal access to education and job opportunities. Hindered by language barriers in schooling, these minority Americans have suffered from illiteracy problems. The much publicized Coleman report (1966) showed that non-English-speaking learners were desperately behind the national achievement norms in reading, mathematics, and verbal ability. Language difficulties were cited as the source of the problem and were used to support the need for bilingual-bicultural legislation.

Three types of bilingual programs have been supported by the federal government:

1. *Bilingual-bicultural maintenance programs:* These programs are designed to teach skills needed for English that emphasize instruction in the learner's native tongue. The culture of the ethnic group receiving instruction is stressed through history, literature, and art offerings. The native language of the learner is considered an asset to society; retention of that language is a significant goal of this program.

2. *Bilingual-translational programs:* These programs are designed to provide intensive instruction in English yet retain support for instruction in the native language. Learners are integrated into the regular classroom as soon as they acquire sufficient skills in English. Critical in these programs is that the learner not be disadvantaged in expected achievement areas of the curriculum.

3. *English as a second language (ESL):* These programs provide intense study of English skills necessary to study the other subjects in the curriculum. The stress is on mastery of English grammar and phonology. One of the major goals is to help non-English speakers acquire skills that will help them communicate with their teachers.

Bilingual-bicultural education helps learners strengthen their identities by including their own historical, literary, and cultural traditions in the regular curriculum. Children are made to feel good about themselves and their backgrounds; their successes are stressed, and they are able to adjust more readily to the new culture. Special preservice and in-service training of teachers stresses the need for positive teacher-student interaction during learning. Early studies of results of bilingual-bicultural programs report that positive self-concepts and active participation have helped non-English-speaking pupils toward better learning.

The need for bilingual-bicultural programs will continue to grow. How that need will be addressed by the federal government in the future remains a question. As social leglislation continues to suffer financial cutbacks and the efforts to establish English as the national language continue, the education efforts for non-English-speaking people will surely diminish.

Adult Education

Education of adults includes any course or activity taken regularly or part-time by adults seventeen years or older. This definition is used by the federal government in identifying the increasing numbers of adults taking part in programs since the early 1980s. The total number of adult participants is approaching 25 million in 1988. The U.S. Department of Education estimates that about 11 percent of these adult students are attempting to complete elementary requirements or high school graduation requirements. Some 17 percent are completing requirements for a vocational certificate, and the remaining adults are pursuing

29

In 1986, the Department of Education estimated that 13 percent of all adults were illiterate. Many adult education programs have been created to assist these special learners. (*Source:* Eric Roth/The Picture Cube)

two-year, four-year, or postgraduate degree programs. Although these data seem to be impressive, they do not yet fully address the literacy problems of the adult population. Eighty percent of the participants are from the white majority population who have at least a high school education. Most are already gainfully employed and have annual family incomes of $13,000 or better.

Despite what appears to be a healthy situation among adults, the Department of Education issued a report in 1986 which estimated that 13 percent of all adults, between 17 and 21 million people, were illiterate. Most of these people belong to the minorities in the country. These data have spurred national efforts aimed at adult literacy programs administered by state agencies, public schools, and institutions of higher education. In addition, the national media has joined the national effort to reduce adult illiteracy.

The American Broadcasting Company and the Public Broadcasting Service have organized a national campaign called Project Literacy U.S. The programs will air literacy-related news broadcasts, entertainment programs, and public service announcements, all directed toward improving the literacy level of the adult population. Other national foundations have joined the efforts to curb adult illiteracy. The Scripps Howard Foundation provides a significant monetary award each year to the newspaper or broadcasting station that best promotes literacy programs in its community. The foundation also awards monetary community grants for the same purpose. The Gannett Foundation and *U.S.A. Today* have established a yearly financial program for the promotion of adult literacy. The intent of this program is to establish statewide efforts which provide adult literacy leadership, community-based tutoring programs, and the use of computers and videodisk programs for improving adult literacy efforts.

Chemical Education

The federal war on drugs has received increased emphasis under the current administration. The federal government, recognizing the national waste of human talent as a result of chemical dependency, has supported various efforts to curb drug abuse. At the federal, state, and local levels public and private funds are being employed to prohibit the use of drugs in the workplace. Mandatory drug-testing programs for job employment have begun in earnest at all levels of society. Special programs touch the schools, government activities, and even the sports world.

From the Department of Education has come the school team approach,

| 29 |

Professional Perspectives

Prepare yourself to work with learners whose first language is not English.
Remember to use due process procedures when you encounter students who are chemically dependent.
Be confident of your basic-skills competencies if you want to be certified as a teacher.

developed under the Alcohol and Drug Abuse Education Program. Designed to help local schools prevent and reduce drug and alcohol abuse, this program has established five regional centers that provide training and technical assistance to local schools. Some other representative national efforts are being provided by the following agencies:

- *The American Council on Drug Education:* This council organizes conferences and develops national media campaigns concerning drug education. It also provides films, books, and education kits for libraries and schools.
- *Narcotics Education, Inc.:* This organization provides pamphlets, books, teaching aids, posters, audiovisual aids, and prevention magazines that can be used with preteen and teens.
- *National Federation of Parents for Drug-Free Youth:* This national organization helps parent groups get started and provides current literature on drug legislation and resource lists for schools and libraries.
- *Target:* This national Federation of State High School Associations, an arm of the organization of interscholastic activities associations, offers workshops, seminars, and current information on chemical abuse and prevention.
- *Toughlove:* This national self-help group is for parents, children, and communities; it stresses cooperation, personal initiative, avoidance of blame, and suggested action for abusers.

These organizations and others have been assisting communities and schools in their efforts at combating the chemical problem. One such effort is Project DARE in Los Angeles, California. This project is operated by the school district in cooperation with the local police department. The program uses specially trained police officers to teach students how to say no to drugs. Other parts of the program include building self-esteem, managing stress, and developing personal skills to help resist drugs. The police teachers work in the schools with students and also conduct parent seminars in the evening. The success of this program has begun to spread to other California communities and other states.

Indian Education Programs

The American Indian Education Acts which began in the 1970s continue today but with reduced federal support; these programs are now controlled by the elementary and secondary departments of the Department of Education. Primary efforts of assistance for Indian tribes have been directed at education, community development, strengthening of tribal governance procedures and economic development, and curbing of alcohol and other chemical dependence.

During the 1970s and 1980s tribal communities assumed greater control over their educational programs. Increasing numbers of tribes were released from the Bureau of Indian Affairs school programs and were allowed to form their own contract schools with elected Indian school boards. These schools still receive federal financial support but have greater control over the education program and the hiring and firing processes as well as continued independence from the state-directed mandates for public schools. At the same time, the federally directed number of Indian boarding schools has been reduced drastically, as have the horrible conditions of those schools. In the wake of this new freedom and the enlightenment of Indian educators, there has emerged an increased emphasis has on higher education for Indian students. This emphasis has led to the creation of new Indian community colleges and junior colleges. As accredited schools, Indian students can complete at least two years of college work at an Indian school before transferring to a four-year institution for completion of the college baccalaureate degree.

There still are too few trained Indian teachers for the Indian schools, but some small progress has been achieved. Federal monies halp support Indian aides for the classrooms so that the non-Indian teachers can benefit from the cultural richness of the community by attending the same school program that is presented to the students. National programs supported by the federal government provide for educational leadership training so that increasing numbers of Indian schools are administered by university-trained personnel. The various district Indian offices also are staffed by trained itinerant Indian personnel.

Many of the western Indian reservations were located in areas deemed least desirable for the white majority population. Since that period of reservation demarcation in the 1880s, the "worthless" lands of the Indian reservations have been found to contain valuable deposits of needed minerals and also to be supportive of newer, more advanced programs of agriculture. Although there continues to be efforts directed at securing Indian lands for development purposes, many tribes have begun their own economic development programs aimed at creating economic independence. Trained Indian leaders in all areas of economic and social development are assisting tribes in their new development ventures. Unfortunately, however, not all tribes have large holdings of land which can be developed economically, and thus the less fortunate tribes remain dependent upon the federal government for community development.

Chemical dependence among Indian people remains as one of the most serious social problems in this nation. The myth of the Indian's weakness for alcohol has not been totally eliminated because of this problem, but it has been more aptly recognized as an economics-related issue. Nationally, there is a significantly higher rate of alcohol use among the downtrodden and economically deprived. The greater the poverty level, the greater is the use of debilitating chemicals in order to derive psychological comfort with poverty. Recognizing that chemical use among Indian people is no greater than the use by non-Indian people at the same levels of poverty, the federal government has begun to provide economic development grants which will assist in raising the economic level of the tribal people and help reduce poverty conditions. At the same time, educational programs of prevention and treatment for chemical abuse are being provided.

Although this group of minority Americans has the highest infant mortality rate in the United States, the total Indian population continues to grow. Since the Indian reservations continue to be recognized as territories of the United

States and not part of the various states where the reservations are located, the federal government will continue to be the chief source of economic support for the tribes.

Vocational Education

Vocational education has grown tremendously during the past twenty years. Although general enrollments in education have dropped dramatically during the past decade, the shift in enrollments to vocational education has been tremendous. These enrollment gains have increased by over 200 percent in the past fifteen years.

Gene Bottoms and Patricia Copa list five types of general vocational programs and four types of occupationally specific programs.[1] The general programs are as follows:

> Consumer/homemaking, focusing on family life
> Prevocational as introductory or exploratory
> Prevocational basic skills
> Related instruction in occupational service, mathematics, and communication skills needed for specific jobs
> Employability skills for cooperative work programs

The occupationally specific programs include the following:

> Occupational cluster programs of comprehensive high schools. These programs provide for a broader curricular approach, such as the study of electronics.
> Occupation-specific programs for one particular occupation. An example of this type of program is computer technology.
> Job-specific programs for an individual job within a broader cluster of occupations.
> Employer-specific programs as needed or requested by particular employers.

The latter three specific programs are usually found in a community college or vocational-technical school.

Vocational education has traditionally been highly dependent upon federal funding since the early part of this century, and that dependence has been supported. However, the Reagan administration, in keeping with its general policy toward education, has tended to shift the emphasis of financial support to state and local funding agencies. The change in philosophy for national financial support has had a serious impact on the quality and quantity of vocational programs. Federal mandates for vocational education continue to require program improvement and addition of new technological programs, but federal financial support continues to decline. In addition to the vocational-training needs of the school-age population, there is a growing need for initial training and retraining of an older adult population. If the United States is to take any steps toward reversing the growing shortages of technically skilled workers, the federal financial role in vocational education must be bolstered.

School Performance and Achievement Programs

One of the major impacts of the *Nation at Risk* report and the additional reports that followed was the national move to increase the graduation expectations for high school. Although not directed by the federal government, this movement has taken on a national flavor, with a few common elements in most state programs. Emerging from this movement are a stronger graduation requirement in mathematics and science and an increased expected competency in the basic-skills areas of reading, writing, and numerical reasoning. In the area of basic-skills development many states have now instituted minimum-skill competencies required for high school graduation. Statewide tests for these minimum competencies are given periodically during the elementary and secondary school years. Students found to be deficient are required to participate in remedial instruction and pass the tests successfully if they are to receive a high school diploma.

30

Whereas in the past most high schools required a minimum of one year of a laboratory science and one and a half years of mathematics, increasing numbers of states have raised graduation requirements to include a mandatory three years of mathematics and three years of science. The programmatic implications for these increased requirements have not yet been felt, but many students graduating in 1990 will have met these new requirements. The competency movement of the 1970s has been given added emphasis with increased numbers of statewide testing programs, all geared to improve upon what is considered a national priority to reduce adult illiteracy.

Concern has arisen for the quality of basic-skills development among the professional ranks in the public schools. Although most of the newly revised teacher education programs are addressing basic-skills development for professionals, there are still many practicing educators who did not have to meet basic-skills competencies to be certified to teach. Thus increasing numbers of states are now requiring experienced, licensed professionals to be tested for these competencies. In addition to teachers, administrators and other professional staff are also being tested. Those found deficient are required to take additional training if they wish to retain their professional certification. All of these efforts will aid in answering the many criticisms brought about by the commission reports of this decade.

Summary and Implications

The federal government's activities and influence can be readily seen in education, and its participation has increased significantly during the past two decades. Many of the federal programs that were begun during the 1960s were expanded significantly and supported by increased amounts of funding during the 1970s and the beginning of the 1980s. Although this financial support has lessened somewhat during the Reagan administration, the states and many local communities have continued the programs. Spawned by the need for social and welfare changes, many of these efforts in education have been compensatory.

Although the federal government has demonstrated its ability to respond more quickly to national needs in education than have states and local school systems, federal dollars still remain a very small amount of the total dollars now spent on education. Even though many national commissions and studies imply that a crisis in education still exists, the federal government has generally taken the position that the individual states must address this need. The states have begun to respond. National social and educational problems are receiving increased emphasis as a result of federal, state, and local financial initiatives. Furthermore, we can assume that due process and equal opportunity pressures will continue to expand during the remainder of the 1980s. The national response to these problems seems clear. There will be a united effort, federal-state-local, required if the problems associated with growth and economic development are to be addressed.

Discussion Questions

1. Discuss the different elements that are needed in preparing an IEP.
2. How does the recent California law declaring English to be the official language of the state affect the bilingual-bicultural education effort?
3. Discuss the cultural protection efforts associated with Indian education programs.
4. Should the federal government assume a stronger fiscal role in correcting educational problems?
5. How can teachers assist in developing school district chemical education programs?

Supplemental Activities

1. Visit a school and secure several examples of IEPs that can be used for discussion in class.
2. Invite an American Indian to visit your class and describe educational efforts among the Indian people.
3. Visit a school district that operates a bilingual program and observe the manner in which the teacher engages students in learning.
4. Have a reading specialist discuss reading programs in light of adult literacy needs.
5. Prepare a list of different state requirements for high school students that have resulted from the release of national commission studies and reports.

Note

1. Gene Bottoms and Patricia Copa, "A Perspective on Vocational Education Today," *Phi Delta Kappan,* 64 (5) (January 1983): 349–350.

Bibliography

Council for Exceptional Children. *Teaching Exceptional Children in All America's Schools.* Reston, Va., 1982.

Deno, Evelyn N. *Educating Children with Emotional, Learning, and Behavior Problems.* Minneapolis, Minn.: National Support Systems Project, 1978.

Down, A. Graham. "Excellence and Equity: The Unfinished Agenda of the 1990's." *Educational Horizons,* 63, (special issue, 1985): 1–53.

Fullan, Michael. *The Meaning of Educational Change.* Toronto, Ontario: OISE Press, 1982.

Full Educational Opportunity Under the Law. Washington, D.C.: U.S. Department of Health, Education, and Welfare, 1975.

McClure, Larry, ed. *Inside Experience-Based Career Education.* Washington, D.C.: National Institute of Education, 1979.

National Commission on Excellence in Education. *A Nation At Risk: The Imperative for Educational Reform.* Washington, D.C.: U.S. Department of Education, 1983.

Rauth, Marilyn. *A Guide to Understanding the Education for All Handicapped Children Act: P.L. 94–142.* Washington, D.C.: American Federation of Teachers, AFL–CIO, 1980.

Santiago, Ramon L. "Understanding Bilingual Education—Or the Sheep in Wolf's Clothing." *Educational Leadership,* 43 (1) (September 1985): 79.

Witherow, Frank B., Witherow, Margaret S., and Witherow, David F. "Technology and the Handicapped." *Technological Horizons in Education Journal,* 13 (6) (February 1986): 65.

PART III

Control, Organization, and Support of American Education

The control of education in the the United States involves the federal, state, and local levels of government. Control at the federal level is authorized by the United States Constitution and specific federal laws relating to education. Control at the state level derives from state constitutions and laws; local boards of education, as agents of the states, function under delegated authority from the states—with some discretionary power.

Legally, under the Tenth Amendment of the U.S. Constitution, education is a function of the states, yet the schools are operated by local governments. The federal government has a strong interest in education, particularly as it relates to national security, national domestic problems, and the rights of citizens as guaranteed by the Constitution and federal laws.

The organization of education in the United States is decentralized. Local boards of education in approximately 15,500 local school districts have the responsibility, delegated to them by the states, of providing education for the citizens of the districts. The local boards must abide by the federal and state constitutions and laws, but they may with their discretionary power decide policy uniquely appropriate to their own districts. As the nation has matured from colonial days to the present, centralized control has increased proportionally. Local boards of education are generally seen as having less and less control over education. This decrease in local control is a result of federal and state legislation, court decisions, the complexities of our society, and the quest for equality of opportunity in education.

Educational activities delegated to the local, state, and federal governments have changed over the years, and it is quite likely that they will continue to change and that new patterns of governmental interrelations will be established for education.

In Part III we consider the function of each level of government in education. For each there are legal, organizational, and financial aspects. Legal, administrative, and financial decisions made at any of the three levels are likely to stimulate further interactive decisions. For example, legal issues brought to the courts can emanate from federal, state, or local actions. The effects of those actions may result in a court decision by a federal or state court. That court decision may well have effects at all three levels of educational governance. By the same token, organizational or financial actions at the federal or state level may affect each of those levels and, in turn, affect local school districts. No matter what the decision, all citizens must be assured their inalienable rights as Americans.

The three chapters of Part III consider the legal basis for and control of education at the federal, state, and local levels. In Chapter 9 attention is directed toward the current interpretations of the Constitution as they apply to the separation of church and state, to school desegregation, and to affirmative action.

The organization of education in the United States is examined in Chapter 10. The legislative governance body at the federal level is the Congress of the United States; at the state level it is the state legislatures; and at the local level the corresponding group is the local school board, although it does not have a function precisely the same as the Congress or state legislatures. Local school boards are policymakers, as are state boards of education, both of which, however, lobby the state legislatures to influence them to provide the kinds of laws they desire. The U.S. Department of Education provides the executive dimension of federal governance. State departments or offices of education provide the executive dimension at the state level. At the local levels the school board provides that dimension in an indirect way. The secretary of education is the chief executive of the Department of Education. At the state level such executives are most often referred to as chief state school officers, and at the local level they are called superintendents of schools.

Chapter 11 deals with the financial aspects of public elementary and secondary schools. It presents information about the taxes that provide the revenue for school districts and how state funding is used in an effort to provide equal opportunity for education within a state. Chapter 11 also gives information about the relative levels of funding provided by federal, state, and local school districts to operate local elementary and secondary schools in the various states. Two major goals in the financing of schools are equitable taxation and equality of opportunity, both of which are discussed in Chapter 11.■

9

The Law
and American Education

Focus Questions

- Why should you as a future teacher know about the role of law in education?
- What value is there in a teacher's knowing how policies and laws are formulated and changed?
- Why should a teacher know about the rights assured under the First and Fourteenth Amendments of the U. S. Constitution and the interpretations of legal cases that affect these rights, as they relate to public and private education?

- Why should teachers have knowledge about such issues as compulsory education and home instruction?
- Why should teachers be concerned about equality of opportunity?
- Why should teachers have knowledge about affirmative action?

Key Terms and Concepts

Church and state in education
Public funds and parochial education
Tuition tax credits
Child benefit theory
Equal opportunity

School prayer
Compulsory education
Discrimination
Segregation and desegregation
Affirmative action

What Would You Do?

You have completed approximately six months in your teaching position. The school board has indicated that because of declining enrollments and fiscal constraints, it intends to release a number of teachers, without reference to seniority. The local teachers' association has called a meeting to discuss the matter. You are expected to attend the meeting and express your opinions. What will you say at the meeting?

A tenth-grade student in one of your classes insists on praying aloud at the beginning of your class. Reactions from other students include ridiculing the student, listening attentively to the student, and ignoring the student and visiting with nearby classmates. The general atmosphere is disruptive. In a conversation with the student you were informed that his parents feel strongly that he should pray aloud in school. What can you do to resolve this issue?

This chapter deals with the legal basis for and control of education at the federal, state, and local levels. Attention is directed toward the current interpretations of the Constitution, particularly as they relate to the separation of church and state, desegregation, and affirmative action. Each of those topics include a discussion of relevant and important rulings by the U.S. Supreme Court.

Constitutional Provisions for Education

The educational systems of the United States, both public and nonpublic, are governed by law. The U.S. Constitution provides the law for the nation, and state constitutions provide the law for each state. Since the U.S. Constitution was created by the people, a state legislature has no right to change that Constitution. State legislatures make laws that apply to education; these laws must be in accordance with both the U.S. Constitution and the applicable state constitution. The enabling and legislative agents of education are illustrated in the top portion of Figure 9.1 The lower portion of Figure 9.1 shows interpretive and administrative agents. Conflicts in this system of governance are not unusual. In such instances state and federal court systems make legal interpretations that form a body of case, or common, law.

38

The initial part of our examination of legal foundations considers how and to what extent the federal government, state legislatures, and local boards of education are legally empowered to govern public education. Note, however, that nonpublic schools, both sectarian and secular, are also under governmental control. The rights assured to citizens of the United States by the U.S. Constitution are valid and enforceable in nonpublic and public schools. Furthermore, nonpublic schools that accept public money must abide by the requirements that accompany that acceptance. For example, they may not have racially discriminatory practices. The power of government in educational matters was made quite clear by the U.S. Supreme Court as a part of its opinion in *Pierce* v. *Society of Sisters* (1925), discussed later in this chapter. The opinion stated:

> No question is raised concerning the power of the State reasonably to regulate all schools, to inspect, supervise, and examine them, their teachers and pupils; to require that all children of proper age attend some school, that teachers shall be of good moral character and patriotic disposition, that certain studies plainly essential to good citizenship must be taught, and nothing be taught which is manifestly inimical to the public welfare.

The following subsections explain how the Tenth, First, and Fourteenth Amendments of the U.S. Constitution relate to the governance of education, public and private, in the United States.

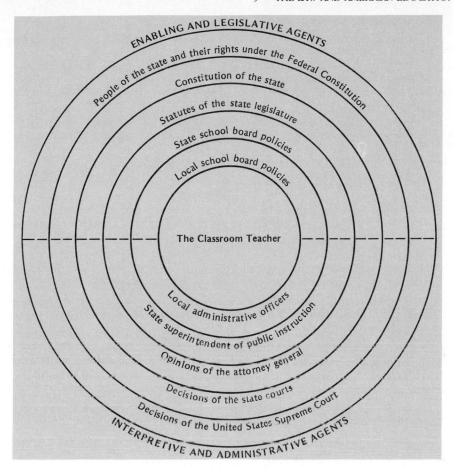

FIGURE 9.1   *Sources of Legal Control in American Education as They Affect the Classroom Teacher* (*Source:* Jefferson N. Eastmond, *The Teacher and School Administration,* p. 97. Copyright © 1959 by Houghton Mifflin Company. Reprinted by permission.)

Tenth Amendment

The U.S. Constitution does not specifically provide for public education; however, the *Tenth Amendment* has been interpreted as granting this power to the states. The amendment specifies that "the powers not delegated to the United States by the Constitution, nor prohibited by it to the states, are reserved to the states or to the people." Therefore education is legally the responsibility and the function of each of the 50 states. Education in the United States is not nationalized as it is in many other nations of the world.

Each state, reflecting its responsibility for education in its state, has provided for education either in its constitution or its basic statutory law. For example, Article X of the Illinois Constitution reads:

Section 1. Goal—free schools

A fundamental goal of the People of the State is the educational development of all persons to the limits of their capabilities.

The State shall provide for an efficient system of high quality educational institutions and services. Education in public schools through the secondary level shall be free. There may be such other free education as the General Assembly provides by law.

The State has the primary responsibility for financing the system of public education.

The current Michigan Constitution states in Section 2, Article VIII:

The Legislature shall maintain and support a system of free public elementary and secondary schools as defined by law. Each school district shall provide for the education of its pupils without discrimination as to religion, creed, race, color, or national origin.

The Utah Constitution, Section 1, Article X reads:

The Legislature shall provide for the establishment and maintenance of a uniform system of public schools, which shall be open to all children of the State, and be free from sectarian control.

Through such statements the people of the various states commit themselves to a responsibility for education. The state legislatures are obliged to fulfill this commitment.

First Amendment

The First Amendment ensures freedom of speech, of religion, of the press, and the right to petition. It specifies:

Congress shall make no law respecting an establishment of religion or prohibiting the free exercise thereof; or abridge the freedom of speech or of the press; or the right of the people peaceably to assemble and to petition the government for redress of grievances.

The application of the First Amendment to public education as considered in this chapter deals primarily with the establishment clause: "Congress shall make no law respecting an establishment of religion or prohibiting the free exercise thereof." While the interpretation of the Tenth Amendment places the responsibility for education on the states, the rights of citizens of the United States are protected by the Constitution and cannot be violated by any state. The First Amendment, in addition to ensuring other freedoms, assures the privilege of free practice of religion.

Fourteenth Amendment

The Fourteenth Amendment protects specified privileges of citizens. It reads in part:

No state shall make or enforce any law which shall abrogate the privileges or immunities of citizens of the United States; nor shall any state deprive any person of life, liberty or property without due process of law; nor deny to any person within its jurisdiction the equal protection of the laws.

The application of the Fourteenth Amendment to public education as considered in this chapter deals primarily with the protection clause: "nor shall any state . . . deny to any person within its jurisdiction the equal protection of the laws." Equal educational opportunity is protected under the Fourteenth Amendment. In effect, the rights of citizens of the United States are assured by the Constitution and cannot be violated by state laws or action. As has been indicated, state legislatures and local boards of education also have important roles in the legal governance of education.

State and Local Governance

State and local agencies also play a role in the governance of education. States have constitutions, with provisions for education as granted to them by the Tenth Amendment. State legislatures provide the laws which govern education within their respective states. Local school districts have boards of education whose major function is to develop policy for the local school district—policy that must be in harmony with both state and federal law.

State Legislatures

State legislatures are generally responsible for creating, operating, managing, and maintaining the state school systems. The legislators are the state policymakers for education. State departments of education are created by legislatures to serve as professional advisors and to execute state policy. State legislatures, though powerful agencies, also operate under controls. The governors of many states can veto school legislation as they can other legislation; and the attorney general and the state judiciary system, when called on, will rule on the constitutionality of educational legislation.

38

State legislatures make various decisions. These decisions generally concern how education is organized in the state; the certification standards and tenure rights of teachers; programs of studies; standards of building construction for health and safety; financing of schools, including tax structure and distribution; and pupil conduct and control, including compulsory attendance laws.

State legislatures, in their legislative deliberations about the schools, are continually importuned by special interest groups. These groups, realizing that the legislature is the focus of legal control of education, exert considerable influence on individual legislators. Some of the representative influential groups, as illustrated in Figure 9.2, include state school board associations, school adminstrators' associations, teachers' unions, taxpayers' federations, religious groups, labor unions, agricultural associations, civil rights groups, colleges and universities, chambers of commerce, business associations, and manufacturers' associations.

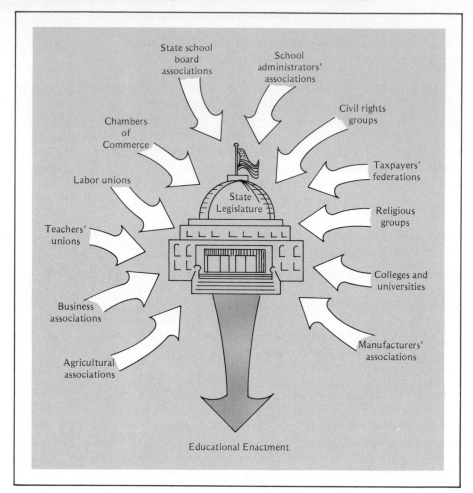

FIGURE 9.2   *Legislative Decision Making*

In general, organized special interest groups—that is, formal associations and coalitions of groups—are more effective than individuals in lobbying. Nevertheless, individuals can have an impact on legislation through aggressive and persistent political lobbying. Individuals can also be the catalyst in the formation of coalitions; or they can, if they are so inclined and have the time and energy, form their own special group.

It is not uncommon for over a thousand educational bills to be introduced each year in a state legislative session. Many of these bills originate with special interest groups. Throughout the nation in the past few years, state legislatures have dealt with educational proposals on a wide range of topics. These topics include the following:

Accountability of the school	Legal holidays
State aid	Aid to parochial schools
Textbooks	Daily meditation
Adult basic education	Certification of teachers
Negotiations	Teacher competency tests
Strikes	Teacher tenure regulations
Merit pay	Scholarships
Consumer education	Sex education
Lotteries	Fire drills
Education of the gifted	Civil and criminal liability

Many important decisions affecting education are hammered out in the political arena of state legislatures.

Local Boards of Education

Local school boards are governmental units of the state, are created by the state, and are responsible to it for educating pupils within specified local school districts. Their major function is the development of policy for the local school district—policy that must be in harmony with both federal and state law. They have only those powers granted or implied by statute that are necessary to carry out their responsibilities. Powers usually granted or implied to local school boards include the power to act as follows:

- Obtain revenue
- Maintain schools
- Purchase sites and build buildings
- Purchase materials and supplies
- Organize and provide programs of studies
- Employ necessary workers and regulate their services
- Admit and assign pupils to schools and to control their conduct

The legal structure just outlined, under which American education functions, underlies the federal-state-local interrelationship. (See Table 9.1 for summary statements related to the governance of education.) The local operation of schools under the law must abide by the constitutional and statutory provisions of the state and at the same time assure the rights of individuals as stated in the Constitution of the United States. Conflicts arise when state constitutional and statutory provisions for education are not in accord with the U.S. Constitution, or when individuals feel that their rights as citizens are being infringed on or are not being fully granted. From these conflicts court cases arise; the decisions resulting from the cases produce a body of case law that further interprets constitutions and statutes. Numerous conflicts and the resultant cases have centered around the separation of church and state. A number of these conflicts are treated in the sections that follow.

TABLE 9.1   *Summary Statements on Governance*

Each state has its own constitutional and statutory provisions for education

Local school boards enact policies for their respective school districts; these policies supplement and complement state laws

The rights of citizens of the United States are assured by the U.S. Constitution and cannot be violated by state laws or local school district policies or practices

Parents are permitted to have their children educated in private schools, and the state may reasonably regulate all schools, public and private

Compulsory attendance laws do not require that a child attend a public school only

Some states allow parents to educate their children at home

The assignment of a child to a specified public school is the function of a local board of education

---

Church and State

Traditionally, the United States has strongly supported separation of church and state. This basic principle, expressed in the First Amendment, was designed by our forefathers to assure each citizen freedom to practice the religion of his or her choice. Education, a governmental function necessary if an effective democracy is to survive, must be carried on so as to preserve this basic right of religious freedom.

Our nation also has a strong religious heritage. In colonial times education was primarily a religious matter; furthermore, much of this education was conducted in private religious schools. Many private schools today are still under religious sponsorship, and many students receive their education in private religiously sponsored schools. Approximately 12 percent of the total school population is now enrolled in nonpublic parochial and secular schools.

Court cases concerned with separation of church and state most frequently involve both the First and Fourteenth Amendments of the U.S. Constitution. The First Amendment is applicable to the states by the Fourteenth Amendment. For example, a state law requiring a daily prayer to be read in classrooms throughout the state could be interpreted as establishing a religion, or at least "prohibiting the free exercise thereof." Such a law would violate the Fourteenth Amendment, since states are not permitted to make laws that abridge the privileges of citizens of the United States. The First Amendment assures the privilege of free practice of religion.

Court cases related to the separation of church and state can be classified in three categories: those dealing with the use of public funds to support religious education, those dealing with the practice of religion in public schools, and those dealing with the rights of parents to provide private education for their children. In the late 1960s, 1970s, and into the last half of the 1980s, renewed attention was given to the use of public funds for parochial education. Other topics directly related to the use of public funds for parochial education include tuition tax credits and child benefit theory.

Public Funds and Parochial Education

The use of public funds to support parochial schools has been questioned on many occasions. Typically, state constitutions deny public funds to sectarian institutions or schools. However, public funds have been used to provide transportation for students to church schools and to provide textbooks for students in parochial schools. The use of funds for these purposes has been challenged in many instances.

The landmark case on the use of public funds to provide transportation for students to church schools was *Everson* v. *Board of Education,* ruled upon by the U.S. Supreme Court in 1947. The Court held that in using tax-raised funds to reimburse parents for bus fares expended to transport their children to church schools, a New Jersey school district did not violate the establishment clause of the First Amendment. The majority of the members of the Court viewed the New Jersey statute permitting free bus transportation to parochial school children as "public welfare legislation" to help get the children to and from school safely and expeditiously. Since the *Everson* decision, the highest courts in a number of states, under provisions in their own constitutions, have struck down enactments authorizing public funds to bus children attending denominational

32

The use of public funds to support parochial schools is a volatile issue which has been debated in the courts for years. (*Source:* David S. Strickler/The Picture Cube)

schools; others have upheld such enactments. Thus a law may be in harmony with the federal Constitution but not with the state constitution.

In 1975 the U.S. Supreme Court affirmed a federal district court decision in Missouri *(Luetkemeyer* v. *Kaufman)* that although a state may provide free transportation to parochial school students *(Everson* v. *Board of Education),* principles of equal protection do not require a state to do so merely because such services are provided to public school pupils. Apparent from the court decisions and legislation in the various states is that distinctly different opinions exist regarding the proper and valid use of public funds for private school transportation.

A similar question exists concerning the use of public funds to provide textbooks for private schools. The landmark case originated in Louisiana where a statute provided for textbooks to be supplied to nonpublic school children free of charge. The statute had been upheld by a state court on the theory that the children, and not the nonpublic schools, were the beneficiaries.

In *Cochran* v. *Louisiana State Board of Education* (1930) the U.S. Supreme Court held the Louisiana textbook statute valid under the Fourteenth Amendment. The Court discounted the taxpayers' contention that tax-raised funds for furnishing textbooks to private school pupils constituted a tax for a private rather than a public purpose and a deprivation of taxpayers' money without due process of law. This decision did not rest on the First Amendment, having been rendered before the Supreme Court ruled that under the Fourteenth Amendment the First Amendment applies to the states.

In a later case (*Board of Education of Central School District No. 1, Towns of Greenbush et al.* v. *Allen,* U.S. Supreme Court, 1968) the Court upheld the constitutionality of a New York textbook statute. The New York law required boards of education, on individual request, to lend textbooks free to children in grades 7 through 12 in private schools if these schools complied with the state compulsory attendance law. The majority opinion of the Court held:

> The express purpose of Sec. 701 was stated by the New York Legislature to be furtherance of the educational opportunities available to the young. Appellants have shown us nothing about the necessary effects of the statute that is contrary to its stated purpose. The law merely makes available to all children the benefits of a general program to lend school books free of charge. Books are furnished at the request of the pupil and ownership remains, at least technically, in the State. Thus no funds or books are furnished to parochial schools, and the financial benefit is to parents and children, not to schools. Perhaps free books make it more likely that some children choose to attend a sectarian school, but that was true of the state-paid bus fares in *Everson* and does not alone demonstrate an unconstitutional degree of support for a religious institution.

A recent case in Missouri introduced another perspective on this issue:

> In 1974, the Missouri Supreme Court held that it was a violation of the state constitution for the state to loan textbooks free of charge to parochial school students. The U.S. Supreme Court denied review of the case, thereby preserving the state court decision. "Thus, although a state *may* lend textbooks to parochial school

students, the Court declined to *compel* a state to do so if it is supplying free books to public school pupils."[1]

The Supreme Court, in its decision in the *Everson* case and again in the *Allen* case, made it clear that providing transportation or textbooks per se does not violate the First Amendment.

Recently, over twenty states have considered legislation providing for various forms of direct aid to nonpublic schools. In 1968 Pennsylvania enacted legislation to supply aid for the purchase of secular education services; these services were defined as consisting of courses in mathematics, modern foreign languages, physical science, and physical education. The aid embodied reimbursement for teachers' salaries, textbooks, and instructional materials. Provisions were made in the law for approval of textbooks and teachers by the superintendent of public instruction. Payments were to be made directly to the school, and school accounts were subject to audit.

In 1969 Rhode Island enacted legislation providing for salary supplements to eligible teachers in nonpublic schools. A teacher requesting supplementary salary had to satisfy certain eligibility requirements: certification, teaching only those subjects taught in public schools, and using only materials used in public schools.

Both the Pennsylvania and the Rhode Island laws were challenged, and the cases were eventually heard by the U.S. Supreme Court. The Court ruled in both the Pennsylvania case *(Lemon* v *Kurtzman,* 1971) and the Rhode Island case *(DiCenso* v. *Robinson,* 1971) that the respective laws were unconstitutional. It envisioned excessive entanglement between government and religion in accomplishing the necessary state supervision to ensure that the state aid would support only secular education. The Court pointed out another defect of the Pennsylvania statute — it provided for the aid to be given directly to the school. In the *Everson* and *Allen* cases the aid was provided either to the student or to the student's parents, not to the church-related school.

After the Pennsylvania and the Rhode Island cases the U.S. Supreme Court also ruled against a Pennsylvania tuition payment proposal, a New York tax credit plan, and a New York state financing plan for record keeping and testing in parochial schools.

In 1975, in *Meek* v. *Pittenger,* the Supreme Court again struck down an effort by Pennsylvania to aid its numerous parochial schools. Pennsylvania had proposed three separate aid programs: (1) providing auxiliary services like counseling, psychological services, and speech and hearing therapy by public school employees to nonpublic school pupils; (2) directly lending instructional materials and equipment to nonpublic schools; and (3) lending textbooks without charge to nonpublic school pupils. The law was drafted by the Pennsylvania legislature to avoid the pitfalls of *Lemon* v. *Kurtzman.* The Court upheld the textbook provision, basing its opinion on the *Allen* case, but struck down the provision for auxiliary services on the basis of "excessive entanglement" and the provision for instructional materials, since the materials and equipment would become subsumed in the "religious mission" of the schools.

32

Most recently, the U.S. Supreme Court in *Wolman* v. *Walter* (1977), a case originating in Ohio, affirmed that providing nonpublic school pupils with books, standardized testing and scoring, diagnostic services, and therapeutic and remedial services is constitutional. The proposals for instructional materials and field trip services were ruled unconstitutional.

The Court cited *Allen* and *Meek* in approving the textbook provision. Numerous cases were cited for standardized testing and scoring, diagnostic services, and therapeutic and remedial services. The Ohio law proposed "to supply for use by pupils attending nonpublic schools within the district such standardized tests and scoring services as are in use in the public schools of the state." The Court noted that (1) the tests are used to measure the progress of students in secular subjects; (2) nonpublic school personnel are not involved in either the drafting or the scoring of the tests; and (3) the statute does not authorize any payment to nonpublic school personnel for costs of administering the tests. On diagnostic services the Court noted that (1) speech, hearing, and psychological services are to be provided within the nonpublic school; (2) personnel who perform the services (except for physicians) are employees of the local school system; (3) physicians may be hired on a contract basis; (4) the purpose of the services is to determine the pupils' deficiency or need for assistance; and (5) treatment of any defect would take place off the nonpublic school premises. The Court concluded that providing diagnostic services on nonpublic school premises would not create an impermissible risk of fostering ideological views. It foresaw no need for excessive surveillance and therefore no impermissible entanglement.

In considering therapeutic services and remedial reading, the Court noted that the Ohio proposal, in contrast to the *Meek* proposal, called for the services to be rendered in public schools, public centers, or mobile units located off nonpublic school premises. It concluded: "It can hardly be said that the supervision of public employees performing public functions on public property creates an excessive entanglement between church and state."

In reversing the Ohio district court on instructional materials, the U.S. Supreme Court referred to *Meek*. Although the Ohio proposal differed from that of *Meek* since it purported to provide the materials to the pupils rather than to the school, the Court reasoned: "In the view of the impossibility of separating the secular education function from the sectarian, the state aid inevitably flows, in part, in support of the religious role of the schools." Two important points were made by the Court in reversing the district court in the provision of field trips: (1) "Nonpublic schools control the timing of the trips, their frequency, and destination; therefore the schools rather than the children are the recipients of the service"; (2) "The field trips are an integral part of the educational experience, and where the teacher works within and for a sectarian institution, an unacceptable risk of fostering religion is an inevitable byproduct." In concluding, the Court said, "Moreover, the public school authorities will be unable adequately to insure secular use of the field trip funds without close supervision of the nonpublic teachers. This would create excessive entanglement."

In 1980 the U.S. Supreme Court, by a five-to-four vote, finally settled a ten-year dispute over a New York law that provided for reimbursement to private and parochial schools for record keeping and standardized testing, both required by state law. The Court envisioned no excessive entanglement and voted that testing and record keeping have neither a religious purpose nor a religious effect, nor do they violate the intent of the First Amendment.

The latest decisions by the Supreme Court of the United States followed precedent in striking down two programs, one in New York City and the other in Grand Rapids, Michigan. The New York program (*Agiluar* v. *Felton,* 1985) involved the use of federal funds for sending public school teachers into parochial school classrooms to provide remedial or enrichment instruction, aimed mainly at educationally deprived children from poor neighborhoods. Instruction took place during the regular school day in classrooms from which religious symbols had been temporarily removed. The Supreme Court held that excessive entanglement resulted from the need to ensure that classes were free of religious content "requiring a permanent and pervasive state presence in the sectarian schools receiving aid." The Court did not treat the legality of offering this same kind of instruction at the public schools after school hours.

The Grand Rapids plan was similar to that of New York. One program involved sending public school teachers into private schools to teach remedial enrichment courses; a second program involved parochial school teachers who worked part-time after school offering foreign language, art, and other courses to children and adults.

Justice Brennan, speaking for the Court in *Grand Rapids* v *Ball* (1985), could not uphold the plan for three reasons. First, teachers might be led to participate in religious indoctrination because of the sectarian nature of the religious schools. Second, the setting for this instruction could convey a message of state support for religion. Third, "the programs in effect subsidize the religious functions of the parochial schools by taking over a substantial portion of their responsibility for teaching secular subjects."

Closely related to the issue of public funds to support parochial education is the renewed interest in federal tuition tax credits, which we consider next.

Tuition Tax Credits

Federal tuition tax credits can be defined as tax rebates to parents who pay private school tuition for their children. In effect, the federal government indirectly reimburses parents for some of their private school expenses. Tuition tax credits have been the subject of much debate in Congress in recent years. Opponents of legislation for tuition tax credit argue that such credits represent a clear attempt to provide unconstitutional aid to parochial schools. In addition, opponents argue that tuition tax credit will slow progress toward desegregation (as more white persons will have easier access to private education), provide an indirect subsidy to private schools, and perhaps increase racial discrimination. Those favoring tuition tax credit legislation argue that such credit is only fair and need not involve entanglement of government with religion, advance religious causes, or disturb the First Amendment barrier between church and state. They further point out that tuition tax credit will strengthen both public and private education through competition. In addition, they predict that tuition tax credit will increase the private school enrollments of blacks and Hispanics more than that of whites, that racial discrimination will be prohibited, and that a shift of students to lower-cost private schools can save billions of dollars for society as a whole. The Reagan administration has pledged its support for a tuition tax credit program; but as this book went to press, no legislation had been approved by Congress.

In 1983 the U.S. Supreme Court gave proponents of tuition tax deductions hope by upholding a Minnesota statute in *Mueller* v. *Allen*. Unlike legislation from Pennsylvania and New York, which had been applied only to nonpublic schools, the Minnesota law covered deductions also to parents of children in public schools. Parents could deduct up to $500 per child in elementary school and $700 per child in secondary school for costs incurred for tuition, textbooks, and transportation. The Court ruled five to four that the statute was constitutional.

Justice Rehnquist's majority opinion found no conflict with the *Lemon* test. The statute had a secular legislative purpose in that parents were assisted in helping defray the costs of educating their children. The statute's effect neither advanced nor inhibited religion because the service was available to parents of children in both public and nonpublic schools. Rehnquist saw the statute as being one of many in the state that aids in some way religious interests. The statute did not foster excessive entanglement of church and state because the only involvement of the state was in screening texts to determine whether they qualified for a deduction.

Because of the narrowness of the decision, as well as the decision itself, this case will be studied very closely by legislators for its possible bearing on proposed statutes.

The issue of public aid to church-related schools (see Table 9.2 for a summary of U.S. Supreme Court cases in this area) is still in the process of being settled. Although it is clear that aid for certain secular services (such as transportation, textbooks, and—under prescribed circumstances—testing, diagnostic, therapeutic, and remedial services) can be provided, it is not yet absolutely clear what further aid will be approved. State legislatures are trying to find ways to provide aid to parochial schools without violating the First Amendment. Probably other laws will be developed on the basis of findings in the *Lemon* v. *Kurtzman, DiCenso* v. *Robinson, Meek* v. *Pittenger, Wolamn* v. *Walter,* and *Mueller* v. *Allen* cases. Also probable is that the laws developed will be challenged and that further rulings from the courts will be forthcoming.

Child Benefit Theory

The use of public funds to provide secular services has led to a concept referred to as "child benefit theory." Child benefit theory can be defined as providing benefits to children in parochial schools with no benefits to the schools or to a religion. The decisions supporting use of public funds for transportation and textbooks for students in private schools have generally been based on the child

TABLE 9.2   *Selected U.S. Supreme Court Cases Related to the Use of Public Funds for Private Education*

Case	Issue	Decision
Everson v. *Board of Education* (1947)	Use of tax-raised funds to reimburse parents for transportation of students to church schools	Court ruled that reimbursement did not violate the First Amendment
Board of Education of Central School District No. 1, Town of Greenbush, et al. v. *Allen* (1968)	Loan of public school textbooks to children in private schools	Court ruled that the loan of books did not alone demonstrate an unconstitutional degree of support for a religious institution
Lemon v. *Kurtzman* (1971)	Legislation to provide direct aid for secular services to nonpublic schools, including teacher salaries, textbooks, and instructional materials	Court ruled the legislation unconstitutional because of the excessive entanglement between government and religion
Wolman v. *Walter* (1977)	Providing nonpublic school pupils with books, standardized testing and scoring, diagnostic services, and therapeutic and remedial services	Court ruled that providing such materials and services to nonpublic school pupils was constitutional
	Provision of instructional materials and field trips to nonpublic school pupils	Court ruled that providing such materials and service to nonpublic school pupils was unconstitutional
Mueller v. *Allen* (1983)	Legislation providing income tax deductions for parents of children in public and nonpublic schools for costs incurred, up to a maximum amount, for tuition, textbooks, and transportation	Court ruled that such deductions for parents of children in *public and nonpublic* schools was constitutional

benefit theory; the Supreme Court reasoned that transportation and books provide benefit to the children and not to the school or to a religion. Those opposed to the child benefit theory argue that aid to children receiving sectarian education instruction is effectively aiding the institution providing instruction.

The child benefit theory, as supported by the U.S. Supreme Court, has penetrated federal legislation. The Elementary and Secondary Education Act of 1965 (ESEA) and its subsequent amendments provide for assistance to both public and nonpublic school children. Title I of ESEA, which dealt with assistance for the education of children from low-income families, stated that children from families attending private schools must be provided services in proportion to their numbers.

As a summary, Table 9.3 presents brief statements about the relationship of religion and public education, particularly the use of public funds for parochial education.

Another issue related to separation of church and state centers around religious activities in public schools which we take up in the next section.

TABLE 9.3 *Summary Statements on Church and State; on Public Funds and Parochial Education*

Laws and policies which have the effect of establishing religion in the schools will not be upheld by the courts

Public tax funds to pay for books and transportation of parochial schoolchildren have been upheld by the courts

Public tax funds to pay for salaries of teachers in parochial schools have not been upheld by the courts

Tuition payments for parents of parochial school children have not been upheld; they have been upheld for parents of children in public *and* private schools

Special support services for children in parochial schools have not been upheld

Parochial schools may be reimbursed for the costs of standardized tests, test scoring, and record keeping required by the state

Public tax funds may not be used in support of public school teachers offering remedial or enrichment instruction in parochial schools

Religion in the Public Schools

Four topics to be addressed with regard to religious activities in public schools are released time from regular classes for religious instruction, prayer and Bible reading in schools, the teaching of creationism or the biblical version of creation in public schools, and the use of school facilities for religious purposes. Three of these topics—prayer and Bible reading in the public schools, the teaching of creationism or the biblical version of creation in the public schools, and the use of public schools—have been in the forefront in the past few years.

Released Time

Providing released time for religious instruction in public schools has been challenged and acted on by the U.S. Supreme Court. In 1948 the Court held that the released-time program of the Champaign, Illinois, schools violated the principle of separation of church and state (*People of the State of Illinois ex rel. McCollum* v. *Board of Education of School District No. 71, Champaign, Illinois,* 1948). The program in Champaign was a cooperative effort among the schools and a voluntary association of members of Jewish, Roman Catholic, and Protestant faiths. Classes were held in the public school classrooms. Pupils were released from their regular classes to attend religious classes; those who did not elect to take religious instruction were not excused from regular class duties. In its decision the Court pointed out that not only were tax-supported public school buildings being used for sectarian instruction but also the compulsory education law was aiding religious instruction by providing pupils with released time during the school day to study religion.

A released-time program in New York was challenged a few years after the *McCollum* case; in *Zorach* v. *Clauson* (1952) the Supreme Court upheld a New York statute that provided also for released time. The chief difference between the Champaign and New York cases is that in New York students were released from school to go to religious centers to receive religious instruction, whereas in Champaign the instruction was given in public school classrooms. The Court indicated that the precise type of released-time program is significant; programs differ in the extent of school cooperation and in the degree of sectarianism. We can conclude that the concept of released time in and of itself does not necessarily violate the First Amendment.

Bible and Prayer Reading

The courts have also rendered opinions on Bible and prayer reading in the public schools. In 1962 the U.S. Supreme Court *(Engle* v. *Vitale)* held that a prayer composed by the New York State Board of Regents and used as part of the opening exercises of school violated the U.S. Constitution. The prayer read as follows: "Almighty God, we acknowledge our dependence upon Thee, and we beg Thy blessings on us, our parents, our teachers, and our country." Pupils who objected to the prayer could be excused. The Court based its decision on the establishment clause of the First Amendment: "Congress shall make no law respecting an establishment of religion, or prohibiting the free exercise thereof." Justice Hugo Black, who wrote the decision, stated:

> The constitutional prohibition against laws respecting an establishment of religion must at least mean that   it is no part of the business of government to impose official prayers for any group of American people to recite as a part of a religious program carried on by the government.

In June 1963 the U.S. Supreme Court rendered a very significant decision in which it outlawed reading the Bible and reciting the Lord's Prayer as religious exercises in public schools. The Court indicated that these are religious ceremonies and, as such, violate the First and Fourteenth Amendments of the Constitution. The opinion emphasized that government must remain neutral in matters of religion. The Supreme Court decision resulted from appeals on two lower-court decisions, one from Pennsylvania (*Schempp* v. *School District of Abington Township,* 1963) and the other from Maryland (*Murray* v. *Curlett,* 1963), which had held that reading the Bible and saying the Lord's Prayer were not illegal.

The most recent major ruling on prayer in the public schools occurred in 1985, given by the Supreme Court of the United States. The justices overturned Alabama legislation of 1982 authorizing teachers to lead willing students in a prescribed prayer. That statute had supplemented an act one year earlier in which the Alabama legislature authorized a period of silence for meditation or voluntary prayer.

The Supreme Court ruled six to three on overturning the 1982 Alabama legislation. The majority held that the statute had a religious purpose which endorsed religion (*Wallace* v. *Jaffree,* 1985). The Court referred to testimony in the legislature wherein the bill's sponsor intended that prayer be returned to the public schools. Had the Alabama legislature not altered its 1978 action which authorized one minute of silence for meditation, the 1978 Alabama legislation probably would have been upheld. But when it sought later to include prayers, the legislature had exceeded the bounds of the First Amendment.

The rulings of the U.S. Supreme Court that forbid obligatory prayer and Bible reading have prompted attempts to amend the Constitution to permit voluntary prayer. The late Senator Everett Dirksen (R., Ill.) tried unsuccessfully in 1966 and 1967 to secure congressional approval of a prayer amendment. In 1971 Representative Chalmers P. Wylie (R., Ohio) also introduced a prayer amendment that was subsequently defeated. Since then, there have been numerous attempts to legalize prayer and Bible reading in public schools, with a strong endorsement by President Reagan.

A recent article that essentially analyzes the opinions of the U.S. Supreme Court in *Schempp* v. *School District of Abington Township* (1963) notes that public schools have not delineated a clear role for religion in public education that is consistent with the *Schempp* decision. The author of the article makes the following recommendations:

> The public must insist that the public schools address the religious dimension of human existence, and public educators must come to grips with the issues of curriculum, instructional materials, and methods that would support appropriate study about religion at the elementary and secondary levels. The *Schempp* decision provided a context for public education to deal with religion, but public school educators have not fully used it. Study about religion is both an opportunity and, the *Schempp* decision would suggest, a responsibility that public school educators have for too long failed to assume.[2]

Religious Meetings in Public Schools

In July 1984 President Reagan signed legislation permitting religious meetings in public schools, with some controls. This law guarantees to students the right to meet for "religious, political, philosophical or other" discussions in any high school that allows other extracurricular activities. The law has not as yet been challenged with a lawsuit of significant magnitude to be heard by the U.S. Supreme Court. The law, however, does have potential to bring about such a challenge.

32

Teaching Creationism in the Public Schools

Another volatile church-state controversy pertains to teaching in public schools about the origin of humanity. The initial controversy involved the constitutionality of state prohibitions against instruction suggesting that human beings evolved through a process of natural selection from lower forms of animals. The Ten-

**Professional
Perspectives**

Respect the law with regard to religious practices in your teaching and teaching environment.
Make certain that due process is accorded to you and your students.
Seek assistance when in doubt about appropriate responses or actions.

nessee Supreme Court upheld such a state law in the famous 1927 Scopes monkey trial, but the Supreme Court reached an opposite conclusion in 1968. In *Epperson* the Court ruled that an Arkansas antievolution statute violated the First Amendment. It declared that "the state has no legitimate interest in protecting any or all religions from views distasteful to them." It stated further that the amendment does not "permit the state to require that teaching and learning be tailor-made to the principles or prohibitions of any religious sect or dogma." [15]

The more recent controversy has focused on the constitutionality of teaching the biblical version of creation in public schools. Creationists assert that this theory deserved equal treatment to that of the scientific theory of the evolution of life.

In 1980–1981 equal-time provisions were introduced in the legislatures of fifteen states, and two were enacted. These statutes have since been the focus of court suits. The Arkansas statute was struck down by a federal district court in 1982. The judge reviewed the legislative history of the statute and concluded that it failed to satisfy the three-pronged test under *Lemon*. The judge ruled that there was no evidence of secular purpose; rather it was an attempt to introduce the biblical version of creationism into the public schools. Reasoning that creation-science is religious dogma, the court concluded that the only real effect of the statute was to advance religion. The court also held that the act created excessive governmental entanglement with religion because the Genesis account cannot be taught in a secular fashion.

In 1983 a federal district judge struck down a similar law from Louisiana. Using different reasoning, the judge held that the law usurped the authority under the state constitution which granted to the State Board of Elementary and Secondary Education the power to mandate how a course shall be taught; the legislature is empowered to establish and maintain public schools. Thus, reasoned the court, the legislature went too far in requiring the teaching of the biblical version of creationism. The decision did not address the issue of the conflict of the statute with the First Amendment. The issue was then heard in both state and federal courts until in 1985 the Court of Appeals for the Fifth Circuit ruled that the statute had as its purpose the promotion of a religious belief and thus is in violation of the First Amendment. The case is currently on appeal to the Supreme Court of the United States.

In 1986 two legal cases with issues similar to creationism were heard by federal judges, one in Tennessee and one in Alabama. In Tennessee (*Mozert et al.* v. *Hawkins County Public Schools,* 1986) Judge Thomas Hull ruled that the Hawkins County Public Schools had violated the constitutional rights of certain Fundamentalist Christian schoolchildren and their parents by requiring the use of the 1983 edition of the Holt, Rinehart and Winston basic reading series in grades 1 through 8. In stating the complaint of the parents, he said: [32]

> The plaintiffs believe that, after reading the entire Holt series, a child might adopt the views of a feminist, a humanist, a pacifist, an anti-christian, a vegetarian, or an advocate of a "one-world government." Plaintiffs sincerely believe that the repetitive affirmation of these philosophical viewpoints is repulsive to the Christian faith—so repulsive that they must not allow their children to be exposed to the Holt series. This is their religious belief.

He found that the plaintiffs' religious beliefs were sincere; that those beliefs were offended by certain recurring themes in the Holt series; that suspending students who refused to read from the Holt series deprived them of a free public education for exercising their religious freedom; and that school officials could achieve their legitimate educational interests by less restrictive means than compelling the use of the Holt series.

Judge Hull ordered school officials to allow students whose religious beliefs are offended by the Holt series to opt out of reading instruction only. The option is conditioned specifically upon parents' assurance that they will supervise and monitor the students' progress. Judge Hull awarded the plaintiffs $50,521 in damages. The decision is likely to be appealed and may be heard by the U.S. Supreme Court.

In Alabama (*Smith* v. *Board of School Commissioners of Mobile County, Alabama,* 1986) a federal court concluded that the textbooks used in the Alabama schools violate the establishment clause of the First Amendment. The plaintiffs, many of whom are Fundamentalist Christians, alleged that humanism is a religion and is being advanced by the textbooks; and that as a religion, humanism should be excluded from textbooks, as were other religious beliefs.

Judge Brevard Hand in effect ordered that 44 textbooks be removed from the Alabama schools. In his opinion Judge Hand noted that humanism is a religion:

> It purports to establish a closed definition of reality; not closed in that its adherents know everything, but in that everything is knowable: can be reconciled by the human intellect aided only by the devices of that intellect's own creation or discovery. The most important belief of this religion is its denial of the transcendent and/or supernatural: there is no God, no creator, no divinity. By force of logic, the universe is thus self-existing, completely physical and hence, essentially knowable.
>
> Whenever a belief system deals with fundamental questions of the nature of reality and man's relationship to reality it deals with essentially religious questions. . . . A religion need not posit a belief in a deity. For First Amendment purposes secular humanism is a religious belief system, entitled to the protections of, and subject to the prohibitions of, the religious clauses of the First Amendment. It is not a mere scientific methodology that may be promoted and advanced in the public schools.

The decision is likely to be appealed to the U.S. Supreme Court.

A third issue related to the separation of church and state deals with the rights of parents to provide education for their children. This issue, which is discussed in the next section, is closely related to compulsory education.

Rights of Parents to Provide Private Education

The United States has a strong religious heritage. That heritage fostered the development of private religious schools and school systems dedicated to teaching religion along with secular subjects including reading, writing, and arithmetic. Some private schools are not religion-sponsored and essentially offer secular subjects. As our nation grew, sectarian private schools also grew, frequently associated with established traditional religions, such as the Catholic and Lutheran religions. In recent years many Fundamentalist religious schools have been established. The Fundamentalist schools have had steadily and dramatically increasing enrollments, in contrast to the public schools and schools sponsored by the historically traditional religions, both of which had decreasing enrollments up to the middle 1980s. The amount of instruction of students in their homes has also escalated. The increased enrollments in Fundamentalist schools and the increased amount of home instruction are attributed in part to the perceived, if not real, lack of instruction of morality in the public schools. Private schools have been, and will continue to be, an important alternative part of education in the United States.

Private Education: An Alternative

The court cases having to do with the right of parents to provide private education for their children are closely related to cases about compulsory education. Compulsory attendance laws generally require parents, or whoever has custody of a child between specific chronological ages, to cause the child to attend school. The constitutional objection raised regarding compulsory attendance laws is that they infringe on the individual liberty guaranteed by the Fourteenth Amendment. The constitutionality of compulsory education laws has been attacked in numerous cases, but the principle has been uniformly upheld. Courts have generally reasoned that education is so necessary to the welfare of our nation that compulsory school attendance laws are valid and desirable. Compulsory education does not mean compulsory public education, however.

34

Whether a state can compel children to attend a public school was settled in a case in Oregon. (See Table 9.4 for a summary of this case and other important Supreme Court cases related to the practice of religion in public schools and the right to a private education.) In 1922 the legislature of Oregon passed a law requiring all children to attend public schools. The U.S. Supreme Court ruled that such a law was unconstitutional in that it infringed on the rights of parents to control the education of their children (*Pierce v. Society of Sisters,* 1925). This ruling established a precedent, permitting parents to have their children educated in private schools. In this same case the Court also established beyond doubt that the state may reasonably regulate all schools, public and private, and require certain subjects to be taught. It established that private schools have a right to exist, that pupils may meet the compulsory attendance laws by attending private schools, and that private schools are subject to state regulation.

Home Instruction

The courts have also ruled that education in a child's home can meet the requirement of compulsory education. In an early case in Indiana (*State* v. *Peterman,* 1904) the court specified that a school is a place where education is imparted to the young; therefore a home can be a school if a qualified teacher

TABLE 9.4 *Selected U.S. Supreme Court Cases Related to the Practice of Religion in Public Schools and the Right to a Private Education*

Case	Issue	Decision
People of the State of Illinois ex rel. McCollum v. *Board of Education of School District No. 71, Champaign, Illinois* (1948)	Released-time program that released pupils from their regular classes to attend religious classes in public school classrooms	Court held that the program violated the principle of separation of church and state
Zorach v. *Clauson* (1952)	Released time to go to religious centers to receive religious instruction	Court upheld a New York law that provided for released time in religious centers for religious instruction
Engle v. *Vitale* (1962)	Prayer proposed by the New York State Board of Regents to be used as a part of the opening exercise of school	Court held that such a prayer violated the First Amendment
Schempp v. *School District of Abington Township* (1963) and *Murray* v. *Curlett* (1963)	Reading the Bible and reciting the Lord's Prayer in public schools	Court held that reading the Bible and reciting the Lord's Prayer in public schools are religious ceremonies and violate the First and Fourteenth Amendments
Epperson v. *State of Arkansas* (1968)	Arkansas antievolution statute	Court held that to forbid the teaching of evolution as a theory violated the First Amendment
Wallace v. *Jaffree* (1985)	Legislation authorizing prayer in public schools, led by teachers; and a period of silence for meditation or voluntary prayer	Court held that state legislation authorizing a minute of silence for meditation or prayer led by teachers was unconstitutional
Pierce v. *Society of Sisters* (1925)	Law to require *all* children to attend public schools	Court ruled that the law was unconstitutional in that it infringed on the rights of parents to control their children

is engaged in instruction as prescribed by the state. The state controls home instruction, and the instruction generally must be equivalent to what a school provides. Home instruction must be carried out in good faith and not practiced as a subterfuge to avoid sending children to school. In a court case in New Jersey (*Stephens* v. *Bongart,* 1937) regarding equivalent home instruction, the opinion was rendered that the home instruction in this instance was not equivalent to the public school instruction. Most compulsory education laws provide for children who are physically or mentally unable to attend school, although the application of these laws has changed since the passage of the Education for All Handicapped Children Act in 1975.

Although the courts have generally upheld compulsory education, a decision by the U.S. Supreme Court in 1972 altered the position slightly. In *Wisconsin*

v. *Yoder* the Court ruled that the Amish religious sect is exempt from state compulsory education laws that require children to attend school beyond the eighth grade. This decision of the Court was its first in holding a religious group immune from compulsory attendance requirements. The Court held that state laws requiring children to attend school until they are sixteen years of age violate the rights of the Amish to free exercise of religion. The Court stressed the 300-year resistance of the Amish to modern influences. Justice Burger wrote:

> It cannot be overemphasized that we are not dealing with a way of life and a mode of education by a group claiming to have recently discovered some "progressive" or more enlightened process for rearing children for modern life.

In the past few years there has been a decided increase in parental requests to provide instruction in their homes for their children. Cases have been reported originating in Minnesota, Massachusetts, Maine, Virginia, Iowa, North Carolina, Illinois, and Washington, D.C. Many of the cases represent discontent with the public schools, mentioning that public schools are full of "drugs, sex, and Godlessness"; others claim that public schools are ineffective in dealing with gifted or handicapped children. The rulings of the state courts are individualized to each case, the guideline being whether or not the home instruction is equivalent to the instruction provided in a public school. *Yoder* is the most recent ruling of the U.S. Supreme Court relevant to home instruction.

The interpretation of compulsory education laws indicates that a reasonable balance is sought between the rights of the individual and the rights of the state. Parents who want a religious education for their children may meet the requirement of compulsory education by enrolling their children in private or parochial schools or in approved home instruction programs. At the same time, the state reserves the right to reasonably regulate private education.

Much of our discussion in the previous pages has dealt with the issues associated with the separation of church and state (see Table 9.5 for a summary) and judicial decisions made by the Supreme Court related to those issues (see Table 9.4). Frequently, the decisions made by the Court were based on the First Amendment. The next few pages address the issues associated with segregation and desegregation directly related to the Fourteenth Amendment.

34

TABLE 9.5   *Summary Statements on Church and State; on Practice of Religion in Public Schools*

To teach the Bible as a religion course in the public schools is illegal

To dismiss children from public schools during the day for religious instruction at religious centers is legal

Reading of scripture and reciting prayers as religious exercises are in violation of the establishment clause

Public schools may teach the scientific theory of evolution as a theory; a state may not require that the biblical version of evolution be taught

Segregation and Desegregation

Segregation in the context of this chapter refers to the separation of people by race specifically in the public schools. A major concern in the United States has been the separation of black students from white students, resulting in segregated schools—schools that have predominately black students and schools that have predominately white students. Such segregation has occurred by state law or other official action (de jure) or by other causes such as neighborhood populations resulting in part from housing patterns (de facto). Closely related to segregation and desegregation are the issues of busing, white flight, and resegregation, which are also discussed here.

De Jure Segregation

Prior to 1954 many states had laws either requiring or permitting racial segregation in public schools. Until 1954 lower courts had adhered to the doctrine of "separate but equal" as announced by the Supreme Court in 1896 *(Plessy* v. *Ferguson).* In *Plessy* v. *Ferguson* the Court upheld a Louisiana law that required railway companies to provide equal accommodations for the black and white races. The Court indicated in its opinion that the Fourteenth Amendment implied political, not social, equality.

This separate-but-equal doctrine appeared to be the rule until May 17, 1954, when the Supreme Court repudiated it in *Brown* v. *Board of Education of Topeka.* The Court, in its deliberations, phrased the following question: "Does segregation of children in public schools solely on the basis of race, even though the physical facilities and other tangible factors may be equal, deprive the children of the minority group of equal educational opportunities? We believe that it does." The Court said that in education the separate-but-equal doctrine has no place and that separate facilities are inherently unequal. In 1955 the Court rendered the second *Brown* v. *Board of Education of Topeka* decision, requiring that the principles of the first decision be carried out with all deliberate speed.

From 1954, the time of the *Brown* decision, to 1964, little progress was made in eliminating segregated schools. On May 25, 1964, the Supreme Court, referring to a situation in Prince Edward County, Virginia, said: "There has been entirely too much deliberation and not enough speed in enforcing the constitutional rights which we held in *Brown* v. *Board of Education.*" The Civil Rights Act of 1964 added legislative power to the 1954 judicial pronouncement. The act not only authorized the federal government to initiate court suits against school districts that were laggard in desegregating schools but also denied federal funds for programs that discriminated by race, color, or national origin.

Many segregated school systems have tried to meet federal desegregation demands by adopting a "freedom-of-choice" or "open-enrollment" plan. Under such a plan pupils are permitted to choose the public schools they want to attend. In 1968 the U.S. Supreme Court in *Green* v. *County School Board,* a case originating in Virginia, held that a freedom-of-choice plan was not unconstitutional in and of itself but that in this case freedom of choice was not effective

With *Brown v. Board of Education of Topeka,* the Supreme Court ruled that separate but equal facilities were inherently *unequal,* paving the way for desegregation. (*Source:* Martha Stewart/The Picture Cube)

in desegregating. Under the freedom-of-choice plan—after three years of operation—no white child had chosen to attend the black school, and 85 percent of the black children still attended the black school. Specifically, the Court said:

> In other words, the school system remains a dual system. Rather than further dismantling of the dual system, the plan has operated simply to burden children and their parents with a responsibility which *Brown II* placed squarely on the School Board. The Board must be required to formulate a new plan, and in light of other courses which appear open to the Board, such as zoning, fashion steps which promise realistically to convert promptly to a system without a "white" school and a "Negro" school, but just schools.

A further ruling of the U.S. Supreme Court on de jure segregation resulted from a case (*Swann* v. *Charlotte-Mecklenburg Board of Education*) arising in Charlotte-Mecklenburg County, North Carolina, in April 1971. A U.S. district judge had ordered extensive busing of pupils to achieve integration. The goal, as expressed by the judge, was to achieve a ratio of 71 whites to 29 blacks in each school to approximate the racial ratio in the entire district. In its deliberations the Court cited four main legal questions:

1. To what extent racial balance or racial quotas may be used as a tool in a remedial order to correct a previously segregated system
2. Whether every school that is all-black or all-white must be eliminated unconditionally in remedying segregation
3. What the limits, if any, are on rearranging school districts and attendance zones as a remedial measure
4. What the limits, if any, are on transporting pupils in correcting state-enforced racial school segregation

The Court said in its ruling:

> The Constitutional command to desegregate schools does not mean that every school in every community must always reflect the racial composition of the school system as a whole. . . . The use made of mathematical ratios was no more than a starting point in the process of shaping a remedy, rather than an inflexible requirement.

The Court upheld "the very limited use made of mathematical ratios" to be within the equitable remedial discretion of the district court.

About one-race schools, the Court said: "In some circumstances certain schools may remain all or largely of one race until new schools can be provided or neighborhood patterns change." Furthermore, "the existence of some small number of one-race or virtually one-race schools within a district is not in and of itself the mark of a system which still practices segregation by law." The Court cautioned, however, that "the District judge or school authorities should make every effort to achieve the greatest possible degree of actual desegregation and will thus necessarily be concerned with the elimination of one-race schools."

About limits on the rearrangement of school districts and attendance zones, the Court emphasized that no rule by itself can adequately embrace all the difficulties. But, it noted, since there has been a history of segregation, schools of disproportionate racial composition are suspect. The Court recognized majority-to-minority optional transfers with the provision of free student transportation, remedial altering of attendance zones, and "clustering" as legitimate ways of desegregating schools. The Court stated:

> The remedy for such segregation may be administratively awkward, inconvenient, and even bizarre in some situations and may impose burdens on some; but all awkwardness and inconvenience cannot be avoided in the interim period when remedial adjustments are being made to eliminate the dual school systems.

The *Swann* case dealt with desegregation within a single school district. In January 1972, U.S. District Court Judge Robert R. Merhige, Jr., ordered the Richmond, Virginia, schools to be consolidated with the suburban Henrico and Chesterfield County systems. Richmond schools were approximately 70 percent black; the schools of Henrico and Chesterfield Counties were about 90 percent white. Judge Merhige concluded that the constitutional rights of equality overrode the rights of cities and counties to establish educational boundaries. He reasoned that consolidation was the most promising remedy to integrate effectively. In June 1972 the Fourth U.S. Circuit Court of Appeals reversed the order of Judge Merhige, stating that he had exceeded his authority in ordering a merger of city and county school systems to improve racial balance.

In 1973 the Richmond metropolitan desegregation case was heard by the U.S. Supreme Court. By a four-to-four tie vote, with Justice Powell disqualifying himself, the Court upheld the Fourth U.S. Circuit Court of Appeals reversal of the metropolitan plan.

Like Judge Merhige, U.S. District Judge Stephen J. Roth ordered schools in Detroit and its surrounding suburbs to be desegregated. This case *(Milliken* v. *Bradley)* eventually reached the U.S. Supreme Court. In July 1974 the Court, in a five-to-four vote, overturned lower-court orders requiring the cross-busing of children between the Detroit city school system and 53 suburban school districts. Chief Justice Warren Burger delivered the opinion of the Court:

> Before the boundaries of separate and autonomous school districts may be set aside . . . it must first be shown that there has been a constitutional violation within one district that produces a significant segregative effect in another district. Specifically, it must be shown that racially discriminatory acts of the state or local school districts of a single school district have been a substantial cause of inter-district segregation. . . . Without an inner-district violation and inter-district effect, there is no constitutional wrong calling for an inter-district remedy.

The dissenting justices (Douglas, White, Brennan, and Marshall) saw the decision as a "giant step backward." Justice Douglas wrote: "When we rule against the metropolitan area remedy, we take a step that will likely put the problems of the blacks and our society back to the period that antedated the 'separate but equal' regime of *Plessy* v. *Ferguson.* " Justice Marshall noted: "The rights at issue in this case are too fundamental to be abridged on grounds as superficial as those relied on by the majority today. . . . Unless our children begin to learn together, there is little hope that our people will ever learn to live together."

Since the Detroit decision numerous cases involving metropolitan desegregation have been heard in various courts. The most significant cases originated in Wilmington, Delaware, and Louisville, Kentucky. In the fall of 1975 the U.S. Supreme Court upheld an earlier federal court order calling for the urban-suburban desegregation of the schools in the Wilmington area. The main factor in this case, which produced a ruling that differed from that of the Detroit case, was that state school reorganization involved other school districts besides the Wilmington city district in actions that caused blacks in Wilmington itself to be segregated. Therefore, the Court reasoned, other districts should be involved in the solution of the problem.

In the Louisville case *(Newburg Area Council Incorporated* v. *Board of*

Education of Jefferson County, Kentucky, 1975) the U.S. Sixth Circuit Court of Appeals in effect required the Louisville city school system and the Jefferson County school districts to eliminate "all vestiges of state-enforced discrimination" through metropolitan integration. The appeals court determined that in Louisville interdistrict actions had had the effect of maintaining segregated schools. In the spring of 1975 the U.S. Supreme Court decided not to review the Louisville case. In July 1975 a federal district court ordered a metropolitan plan put into action; the court ordered the Louisville city and county school systems to desegregate their schools jointly by transporting students across the lines dividing the districts. Approximately one-sixth of the district's 121,000 students needed to be bused to achieve a black enrollment of 12–40 percent in every school. Although Louisville suffered considerable turmoil in desegregating the metropolitan schools, the task was accomplished. The segregation in both Wilmington and Louisville was viewed by the courts as *resulting from governmental actions* either by the state or by multiple school districts.

An important decision related to desegregation was made by the U.S. Supreme Court in *Milliken* v. *Bradley II* (1977). The Court held:

> As part of a desegregation decree, a district court can, if the record warrants, order compensatory or remedial educational programs for school children who have been subjected to past acts of *de jure* segregation. Here the District Court, acting on substantial evidence in the record, did not abuse its discretion in approving a remedial plan going beyond pupil assignments and adopting specific programs that had been proposed by local school authorities.

The remedial programs included remedial reading, an in-service program for teachers and administrators, the development of an unbiased testing program, and the provision of counseling and career guidance programs for students. The costs of these programs were to be borne by the Detroit School Board and the state. *Milliken* v. *Bradley II* was the first case in which the U.S. Supreme Court had directly determined whether or not federal courts could order remedial education programs as a part of a school desegregation decree.

In 1986 the Court of Appeals for the Fourth Circuit handed down a ruling that potentially has considerable impact on desegregation of schools within cities. The case involved the Norfolk, Virginia, school system, which had been found to operate a segregated system. A court order in 1971 required a mandatory crosstown busing program. In the meantime, the total population of the city declined, and public school enrollment had dropped in the 1970s by 37 percent. The decline forced the closing of seventeen elementary schools, most of them in predominantly black neighborhoods.

In 1983 the school board reverted to the neighborhood school plan. It gerrymandered attendance zones to provide for maximum integration. In junior high schools the maximum black/white ratio was 72/28, and the minimum was 56/44. With respect to the elementary schools, twelve would be 70 percent or more black compared with four under the previous plan. Six schools would be 70 percent or more white.

The new plan also provided for majority-minority transfer whereby any student assigned to a school where his or her race constituted 70 percent or more of the student body could transfer to a school where his or her race constituted less than 50 percent of the students. Students choosing such a plan were entitled to free transportation.

The federal district court upheld Norfolk's plan. It found that the city was no longer operating a de jure dual system. It found that the plaintiffs had not established that the plan was based on discriminatory intent. It recognized that white flight cannot be used as a reason for failure to dismantle a dual school system. The court of appeals affirmed the opinion (*Riddick* v. *School Board of City of Norfolk,* 1986). The effect of that ruling is twofold. It signals a return to the neighborhood school concept. Second, it holds that once a school district converts from a dual (segregated) school system to a unitary (integrated) system, there is no affirmative duty to desegregate further.

Somewhat related to de jure segregation is the issue of tax-exempt status for private schools. The U.S. Supreme Court ruled on this issue in its decision in *Goldsboro Christian Schools* v. *United States* (1983). (See Table 9.6 for a summary of this case and other important Supreme Court cases related to desegregation.) The Court upheld a policy of the Internal Revenue Service (IRS) that denies tax-exempt status to schools that have racially discriminatory practices. The institutions that challenged this policy were a college and a private elementary and secondary school. They claimed that their policies were derived from their religious beliefs. The college admits blacks but does not permit interracial dating and marriage. The lower school does not admit blacks.

In upholding the IRS, the Court indicated that since the *Brown* decision of 1954 racial discrimination in public education has been inconsistent with public policy. In order for an agency to qualify for the IRS exemption, the agency must serve a public purpose and must not act contrary to public policy. The two schools met the first criterion but did not meet the second one.

De Facto Segregation

The U.S. Supreme Court has yet to rule on de facto discrimination—that is, discrimination based on causes *other than* state law or official state actions such as neighborhood populations resulting in part from housing patterns. However, in the *Swann* decision it did allude to de facto segregation. The Court said:

> We do not reach in this case the question whether a showing that school segregation is a consequence of other types of state action, without any discriminatory action by the school authorities, is a constitutional violation requiring remedial action by a school-desegregation decree. This case does not present that question and we therefore do not decide it.
>
> Our objective in dealing with the issues presented by these cases is to see that school authorities exclude no pupil of a racial minority from any school, directly or indirectly, on account of race; it does not and cannot embrace all the problems of racial prejudice, even when those problems contribute to disproportionate racial concentrations in some schools.

40

TABLE 9.6   *Selected U.S. Supreme Court Cases Related to Desegregation*

Case	Issue	Decision
Brown v. *Board of Education of Topeka* (1954)	Separate-but-equal education	Court ruled that separate-but-equal education is a violation of the Fourteenth Amendment
Green v. *County School Board* (1964)	Under a freedom-of-choice plan, after three years of operation, no white child chose to attend a black school	Court ruled that a freedom-of-choice plan is acceptable only if it leads to desegregation of schools
Swann v. *Charlotte-Mecklenburg Board of Education* (1971)	Racial composition of desegregated schools	Court ruled that "the Constitutional command to desegregate schools does not mean that every school in every community must always reflect the racial composition of the school system as a whole"
Milliken v. *Bradley* (1974)	Metropolitan desegregation of schools of Detroit and its surrounding suburbs	Court overturned the lower-court orders requiring cross-district busing on the basis that "it must first be shown that there has been a constitutional violation within one district that produces a significant segregative effect in another school district"
Milliken v. *Bradley II* (1977)	Federal courts ordering remedial education as a part of a desegregation decree	Court ruled that "as a part of desegregation decree, a district court can, if the record warrants, order compensatory or remedial programs for school children who have been subjected to past acts of *de jure* segregation"
Goldsboro Christian Schools and Bob Jones University v. *United States* (1983)	IRS tax-exempt status of schools that have racially discriminatory practices	The IRS may prohibit federal tax exemptions for private schools that discriminate against blacks

Lower courts have dealt with and ruled on what has appeared to be de facto segregation. In practice, to differentiate clearly between de jure and de facto segregation is difficult. Probably both types of segregation are present in varying degrees in segregated schools. In June 1967 a lower court, considering de facto segregation, made an important ruling. Judge J. Skelly Wright of the U.S. Court of Appeals for the District of Columbia, sitting as a district judge, ruled in *Hobson* v. *Hansen* that the segregation of black pupils in the District of Columbia schools that resulted from population patterns was unconstitutional. The judge pointed out in his ruling that Washington was formerly a de jure segregated school district. In a four-to-three decision a court of appeals upheld many of Judge Wright's orders. The case was complicated by the time of the appeal; the method of selecting school board members for the District of Columbia had changed from appointment to election. The appeals court made it clear that it did not want to bind the new board to former plans; it preferred to leave it to the board to evolve new programs.

A later case heard by the U.S. Supreme Court that touched on de facto segregation was *Keys* v. *School District No. 1, Denver, Colorado*. The Court, announcing its decision in June 1973, sent the suit back to a district court; this court was to decide whether or not school authorities had intentionally segregated a substantial portion of the school system. If proof affirmed that the school district was operating a dual system (segregated) even though there had never been any de jure or legal provisions for school segregation, then the entire system would be required to desegregate. In the spring of 1974 Judge William E. Doyle of the Tenth U.S. Circuit Court of Appeals ordered integration of the city's 70,000 children. The Supreme Court, however, had not resolved the question of de jure/de facto segregation. Justice Powell, in a separate opinion, stated: "We should abandon a distinction which long since has outlived its time, and formulate constitutional principles of national rather than merely regional applications." The Supreme Court did, however, change the concept of de facto segregation by turning over to federal and state trial courts the discretion to determine, as an issue of fact and not as a question of law, whether or not a local school board presides over a de facto or a de jure segregated school district. In a sense, the Supreme Court broadened the concept of de jure segregation.

Although questions might be raised about whether segregated schools were created by law and perpetuated by state or school board actions (de jure) or were the result of residential population patterns (de facto), and about how far the judiciary can go in ordering the end of de facto segregation, it is clear that equality of educational opportunity is a basic right in the United States and must be attained. This right permits maximum intellectual growth and social mobility. All citizens of our democracy must have this opportunity. The Supreme Court has said basically that equality of educational opportunity cannot be provided in segregated facilities, even though the facilities appear to be equal in such tangible assets as buildings, curricula, and staffs. Boards of education must proceed with deliberation and determination to desegregate schools—a very difficult task because in many instances residential neighborhoods are segregated. The efforts by local boards of education to assure the constitutional right of equality of opportunity to all citizens of all races will need the strong support of local citizens. The goal will not be easily or quickly realized.

Busing

As mentioned earlier, busing has been mandated by federal district courts as a means to bring about school desegregation. Busing has also been used voluntarily to bring about desegregation. Busing is an extremely controversial issue. Many school districts—including those of Boston, Seattle, Tulsa, Oklahoma City, Louisville, Austin, Dallas, Dayton, San Francisco, Los Angeles, Pontiac, and Indianapolis—have been ordered to bus school children to end segregation.

Proponents view busing as a necessary way, and sometimes the only way, to give children of all races a chance for equality of opportunity in education. They further argue that an integrated society is essential and that if people are going to live in an integrated society, preparation must begin in school. In a book by Gary Orfield[3] the author stated that although busing is not a natural solution to segregation, it quite simply is the only solution available if there is to be substantial integration in this generation. Myths about busing must be dispelled before public support for it will occur. Orfield's research indicates that (1) busing does not adversely affect the education of white children, (2) it does not increase violence in the schools, and (3) it does not destroy the neighborhood school. It is the way in which desegregation is carried out, he says, not the act in itself, that makes the difference. He notes that neighborhoods are almost as segregated as they were 30 years ago and that school integration may have to precede neighborhood integration.

Opponents of busing claim that it does not improve the quality of education and that busing requires large expenditures that ought to go toward compensatory education. As indicated in the discussion of *Milliken II* (1977), the U.S. Supreme Court has recognized both compensatory education and pupil assignment (which may involve busing) programs as legitimate remedies for past acts of de jure segregation.

The *Swann* (1971) decision, which approved busing as a segregation remedy, has been the basis for subsequent busing decisions. The Louisville and Wilmington busing orders involved metropolitan desegregation and were based on the determination that a pattern of interdistrict action had effectively maintained segregated schools. In May 1980 the U.S. Supreme Court, unable to secure the four votes necessary to review, decided not to review the Wilmington desegregation plan.

More recently, the Supreme Court of the United States delivered an opinion on busing involving the public schools of Los Angeles (*Crawford* v. *Board of City of Los Angeles,* 1982). It upheld a referendum of the city that amended the state constitution to prohibit state courts from ordering mandatory pupil busing unless a federal court did so to remedy a federal constitutional violation. Earlier, the school board had been ordered by a state court to implement a plan that included substantial busing, an order consistent with an earlier state supreme court decision that had interpreted the state constitution as requiring correction of de facto as well as de jure segregation. In its decision the U.S. Supreme Court noted that nearly 69 percent of the electorate had voted for the amendment.

The same day that the Court ruled in *Crawford,* it handed down a second ruling involving busing; this time it invalidated a referendum of the city of Seattle. That law had provided that no school board could require a student to attend a school other than one of the two nearest his or her residence that offered a given course of study, nor could it employ any of seven methods of "indirect" student assignment, including redefining attendance zones and pairing of schools.

The Seattle school district had for several years attempted to achieve a better racial balance. However, the Court determined that the referendum had been proposed for racial purposes. Under its terms persons who sought to eliminate de facto segregation must seek relief at the state level rather than at the local level. Yet the Court recognized that it is at the local level where decisions involving pupil assignment are made (*Washington* v. *Seattle School District No. 1,* 1982).

At the opening of school in the fall of 1983 the metropolitan area of St. Louis began a unique school desegregation plan based on voluntary, not mandatory, student transfers. Under the agreement transfer students would make up at least 15 percent of the school populations in each outlying suburban school district within the next five years. The plan also permitted suburban students to attend 21 specialized magnet schools in St. Louis. The voluntary plan was adopted to counter the threat of a court-ordered, forced-busing scheme that could have included dismantling all the suburban school districts and incorporating them along with the St. Louis schools into one metropolitan school district. A major obstacle to the success of the program centered around the estimated $1 million cost of the program and whether the city, state, or federal government would pay the cost.

Three years later (1986) two of the elements of the St. Louis plan were showing signs of success. As a result of the voluntary-transfer plan, about 9,600 black students from the St. Louis City School District are now enrolled in suburban schools, and about 600 white students from the suburban schools are enrolled in city magnet schools. The voluntary-transfer program is funded jointly by the St. Louis School District and the state of Missouri, each contributing one-half of the funds. The second element of the plan showing signs of success is the increased student enrollments in the magnet schools in St. Louis. Enrollments in the magnet schools in 1983 were about 8,000 students. In 1986 enrollments were about 9,000 students. The operating costs of the magnet school program are provided by the state. Unfortunately, there has not been funding provided to improve the quality of the magnet school buildings.

The issue of busing is far from being resolved. Further research and experience may help put it in perspective. The Supreme Court did give some assistance on this issue in 1976 when it ruled that once a school district has adopted a unitary—that is, an integrated—school system, annual readjustment of attendance zones is not required (*Pasadena City Board of Education* v. *Spangler,* 1976). That question was put to the Court by the Pasadena public schools, which had taken action to ensure that no school in the district would have a majority of minority pupils enrolled in it. When this goal had been achieved, a number of people moved their residences so that resegregation actually occurred. This situation forced the school board to consider whether annual adjustment of attendance zones was required. The Supreme Court ruled that such adjustment was not required. Citing *Swann,* the justices recognized that there are limits to the actions that a court may take in ordering the dismantling of a dual school system.

It remains to be seen whether this ruling will have general application to all school systems. Pasadena was not subject to the original *Brown* finding, and the Court may have adopted a less stringent policy here than in a school system

37

that had at one time practiced de jure segregation. The decision of the federal district court in Norfolk (1986), referred to earlier, may have an effect in terms of mandatory busing decisions in the future.

Busing and desegregation have been cited as factors that have contributed to white flight. Two laws have recently been enacted to limit busing. One law states that federal agencies must try all alternative methods of desegregation before resorting to busing; the other prevents the Department of Education from ordering a plan that requires assigning children to schools other than those nearest their homes. Antibusing amendments to the Constitution have also been proposed by Congress.

White Flight

The term *white flight,* as commonly used, refers to the decline in the percentage of whites in the population of large cities or in the percentage of white enrollments in big-city school systems. There are undoubtedly many causes of white flight, and they are interrelated in complex ways; nevertheless, desegregation of schools is viewed by some authorities as being one of the major causes. The facts that white enrollment in the Boston schools declined from 60 percent in 1972 to 28 percent in 1984 after busing for desegregation and that the Los Angeles schools reported a 30 percent drop in white enrollment from 1977 to 1978 offer some support to the contention that desegregation associated with busing is an important factor in white flight. James Coleman reported as a finding of his research that between-district segregation increased between 1968 and 1973, particularly in metropolitan areas, as whites moved to districts with fewer blacks.[4] Coleman also reported that within-system segregation had decreased in the South and the Southeast, with the chief reduction in small districts; in effect, the remaining segregation had a profile like the northern pattern—that is, considerable segregation in large cities and little in small districts.[5]

However, there is also evidence and research to support the position that busing and desegregation are not major factors in white flight. Robert Green and Thomas Pettigrew reviewed the work of Coleman and other researchers. They found that white flight would have gone on, regardless of desegregation, as a response to factors such as changing neighborhoods and an eroding tax base.[6] White flight, however, may be a factor in resegregation, the next topic we consider.

Resegregation

Robert Wegmann, after reviewing research findings, offered some tentative conclusions about white withdrawal and resegregation. Resegregation generally means a situation wherein an integrated school population becomes an almost totally black school population. Sometimes, resegregation occurs within a school when the neighborhood from which the school's population is drawn changes from an integrated to a predominantly black neighborhood. If the population of a city becomes predominantly black, the schools in the city will become the same. Often the growth of the black population proceeds from the inner part of the city toward the outer fringe areas. Resegregation can also occur after a governmental desegregation order. In such instances white students may withdraw or simply not reenter when the next term begins. Furthermore, white families may also move to another area not affected by the desegregation order. Wegmann concluded:

> Whites do not necessarily withdraw from desegregated schools. Some schools maintain a high level of integration for years, some change slowly, and some resegregate rapidly. Others may experience some white withdrawal followed by stability or even by white reentrance.
>
> Racially mixed schools located in areas bordering the inner city present some patterns of resegregation markedly different from school districts that have experienced districtwide desegregation. It is important not to extrapolate from the one situation to the other.
>
> In situations where there has been no governmental action to bring about desegregation, white withdrawal seems to be linked more than anything else to the underlying demographic consequences of increased minority population growth. This growth takes place primarily in neighborhoods located on the edge of the inner city as area after area "turns" from white to black. The schools "turn" more quickly than the area generally and play a significant role in making this process relatively rapid and apparently irreversible. Stable school integration seems to be a necessary, if not sufficient, precondition for stable neighborhood integration.
>
> Decisions on where to purchase a home or where to send one's children to school are made not only on the basis of the present situation but also on estimates of what is likely to happen in the future. The belief that presently integrated schools and neighborhoods will shortly resegregate is a major barrier to attracting whites to integrated settings.
>
> Little formal research has been done on the motivations behind white withdrawal from desegregated schooling. Concerns about quality of education, student safety, and social status differences may be among the chief causes. To the extent that this is true, it could be expected that—other things being equal—school integration would more likely be stable and successful (1) when combined with programs of educational improvement in settings where concerns about safety are adequately met and (2) when programs parents can be proud of are featured.
>
> School desegregation ordinarily creates situations that have the potential for both racial and class conflict. The expected degree of white withdrawal, when there is governmental intervention to desegregate schools, may vary depending on the proportion of minority students being assigned to a given school and on the social-class gap between the minority and the white students.
>
> Cost of white withdrawal from desegregated schools varies widely according to the setting. Moving to a nearby segregated suburb, moving outside a county school district, attending a parochial school, attending a private school, transferring to a segregated public school within the same system, or leaving the state are examples of options that may or may not be present in a given situation. Each of these options, if available, will have different costs for different families, just as families will have different abilities to meet these costs. As long as school desegregation is feared (or experienced) as painful, threatening, or undesirable, it can be expected that the number of families fleeing the desegregated school will be proportionate to these costs and the families' ability to pay these costs.
>
> Although there is a certain degree of racial mixing in many public schools, there may also be a notable lack of cross-racial friendship, understanding, and acceptance. Superintendents in desegregated districts tend to describe racial relationships as "calm" or characterized by few "incidents." Few claim they have attained anything like genuine community, nor is there much indication that extensive efforts are being made toward this end.[7]

This section has dealt with segregation, de jure and de facto, and with desegregation. Busing, white flight, and resegregation were also discussed. (See Table 9.7 for a summary of these issues.) All of these issues have prejudice and discrimination at their core, as does the next major topic, affirmative action.

Affirmative Action

Affirmative action has its basis in the protection clause of the Fourteenth Amendment, in Titles VI and VII of the Civil Rights Act of 1964, and in Title IX of the Education Amendments of 1972. Title VI states:

No person in the United States shall, on the ground of race, color, or national origin, be excluded from participation in, be denied the benefits of, or be subjected to discrimination under any program or activity receiving federal financial assistance.

[35]   Title VII states:

It shall be an unlawful employment practice for an employer (1) to fail or refuse to hire or to discharge any individual, or otherwise to discriminate against any individual with respect to his compensation, terms, conditions, or privileges of employment, because of such individual's race, sex, or national origin; or (2) to limit, segregate, or classify his employees or applicants for employment in any way which would deprive or tend to deprive any individual of employment opportunities or otherwise adversely affect his status as an employee, because of such individual's race, color, religion, sex or national origin.

Title IX of the Education Amendments of 1972 states:

No person in the United States shall, on the basis of sex, be excluded from participation in, be denied the benefits of, or be subjected to discrimination under any education program or activity receiving federal financial assistance.

TABLE 9.7 *Summary Statements on Segregation and Desegregation*

The assignment of a child to a school on the basis of race is in violation of the equal-protection clause of the Fourteenth Amendment

Desegregation plans having the effect of delaying integration of the school have not been upheld by the courts

Busing may be required for the operation of a unitary school system

Once a school district has been fully desegregated, the school board does not need to draw up a new plan if resegregation occurs

The merger of school districts may be required where the involved districts helped create the segregated school systems

Church-related schools may lose their tax-exempt status for having segregative policies

The neighborhood school concept is not in conflict with the protection clause

Where school boards have indirectly contributed to segregated communities, the school district can be required to desegregate

Apply the concept of equality of opportunity in your teaching practices.
Be attentive to the different backgrounds and needs of your students in your
interaction with them and in your instructional practices.
Remember that in your role as a teacher you ultimately have a hand in shaping
the society of the future.

One aspect of affirmative action is the affirmation of the aforementioned
rights. A second aspect of affirmative action is the development of plans and
programs to make certain that said rights are not violated. A third aspect includes
positive efforts to recruit and employ persons and to recruit and admit students
that are underrepresented in the workplace or educational setting.

As indicated earlier, prohibiting discrimination is a major goal of affirmative
action. This section provides information about discrimination and reverse discrimination and goals and quotas in educational and corporate settings. Specific
attention is given to recent cases related to discrimination not only in hiring
but also in releasing employees.

Discrimination and Reverse Discrimination

Discrimination can be defined as a determination that an individual or a group
of individuals—for example, blacks, women, or handicapped persons—has been
denied constitutional rights. In common usage the term refers to various minorities or individual members of a minority who lack rights typically accorded   35
the majority. The term *reverse discrimination* implies that a majority or an
individual of a majority has not been accorded certain rights because of different
or preferential treatment provided to a minority or an individual of a minority.

Most recently, reverse discrimination has been cited in respect to admissions
to law schools and medical schools. It has also been cited in connection with
affirmative action—that is, positive efforts undertaken by society to integrate the
races and to assure equal opportunities. An early test case concerned Allan
Bakke, a white male, who claimed that he was discriminated against when denied
admission to the University of California Medical School at Davis. In the medical
school's class of 100 students, 16 spaces were set aside for minority applicants.
The Supreme Court of California upheld Bakke's claim and ordered him admitted. Regents of the university appealed to the U.S. Supreme Court to overturn
the state ruling.

In general, the arguments supporting the denial of Bakke's admission pointed
out that (1) special admissions programs based on race are not quotas but goals;
(2) color-sensitive admissions policies are necessary to bring minorities fully
into the mainstream of American society; (3) benefits accrue to society at large
from special admissions; (4) merit alone, determined by academic grades and
test scores, has not been the single criterion of selection for schools; and (5)
the denial did not violate the equal-protection clause of the U.S. Constitution.

The arguments supporting Bakke's admission emphasized that (1) the special admissions program was a racial quota and (2) quotas are harmful to society and are unconstitutional.

In June 1978 the U.S. Supreme Court ruled in the Bakke case. In effect, the Court ruled five to four that the University of California at Davis admissions program, which reserved sixteen places in each class for minorities, was illegal. At the same time, the Court accepted minority status as a factor in admissions along with grades, test scores, and personal skills. The decision has been referred to by many legal authorities as a precedent for interpreting affirmative action in the future.

One year later the Supreme Court ruled in another significant case involving reverse discrimination (*United Steel Workers* v. *Weber,* 1979). This case did not involve education directly, but it helped to clarify the Court's position on affirmative action programs. The justices upheld a plan by Kaiser Aluminum, which, under an agreement with its union, agreed to have an equal number of slots for blacks and whites in supervisory positions until racial imbalance was corrected in its work force. Although 39 percent of its labor pool was black, only 2 percent of the blacks were skilled craftsmen. The suit originated after a white worker was rejected for the supervisory program, although two blacks with less seniority were selected for it.

The Supreme Court upheld the plan, for it saw that this program involved a voluntary agreement between private parties not subject to the equal-protection clause of the Fourteenth Amendment.

Hiring and Releasing Employees

After *Weber* there was little significant court opinion on reverse discrimination until the latter part of the 1985–1986 term of the Supreme Court. In a three-month period three cases were decided which have an impact on affirmative action in the public schools. In one case (*Wygant* v. *Jackson Board of Education,* 1986) the Court ruled that a Michigan school board's policy of laying off white teachers before minority teachers with less seniority were laid off was unconstitutional. The justices saw that a school board might give preference to minorities in hiring practices but not in layoffs if the plans were designed to correct past discrimination. In two non-school cases the Court held that lower courts have broad discretion in approving the settlement of discrimination suits whereby employers agree to preferential hiring or promotion of minorities; it also held as legal a lower court order requiring a sheet metal worker's union in New York City to meet a 39 percent minority membership goal by 1987.

Between *Weber* and the 1986 decisions, the Court had ruled that a seniority system could not be abandoned to benefit individuals who were not proven victims of discrimination. It overturned a lower-federal-court order that allowed recently hired blacks to keep their jobs as firefighters while whites with more seniority were laid off.

These opinions reveal that the courts are more lenient in discrimination in hiring than in releasing employees. (See Table 9.8 for summary statements

TABLE 9.8 *Summary Statements on Affirmative Action*

Reverse discrimination is not legally permissible in laying off employees

Reverse discrimination may be legally permissible in hiring practices to correct vestiges of past discrimination

The use of quotas in admitting persons to graduate schools or in hiring individuals is not in harmony with the Fourteenth Amendment

related to affirmative action.) Minorities can be given preference in hiring to correct past discrimination, but they cannot be given preference over more senior employees in termination of employment.

Summary and Implications

The law is involved with American education, and each level of government has legal responsibilities. The U.S. Supreme Court has interpreted the Constitution in many cases related to education. Of special interest are the cases dealing with the First and Fourteenth Amendments. The First Amendment ensures freedom of speech, religion, and the press and the right to petition. Public financial support of nonpublic education and the practice of sectarian religion in public schools have persisted as issues in American education.

The Fourteenth Amendment protects specified privileges of citizens. Segregated schools existed in the United States for many years. Desegregation in the public schools began in 1954 with the U.S. Supreme Court ruling on *Brown* v. *Board of Education of Topeka*. These social issues have a decided effect on how schools operate.

The implications of court decisions based on the First and Fourteenth Amendments are many. Local boards of education must develop and adopt policies that harmonize with federal and state legislation and court decisions. The board policies guide administrators and teachers as they carry out their responsibilities. Deciding policy on sensitive subjects like religion and desegregation is often not easy, nor is the mandated fulfillment. In classrooms throughout the United States teachers will need to deal with the proper relationship between religion and public education and with the diversity, potential conflict, discontinuity, and change in desegregated schools.

As indicated earlier in this chapter, public schools have tended to avoid the topic of religion. One reason given by parents for withdrawing their children from public schools was that public schools were promulgating secular humanism and ignoring religion. Public schools cannot foster any particular religion or have religious ceremonies. They can, however, recognize the religious dimension of human existence and conduct appropriate study *about* religion. Public schools and their teachers must address rather than avoid this issue.

Hawley has observed that desegregated schools tend to be more heterogeneous academically than their racially segregated counterparts; that parents worry about the potential interracial conflict in desegregated schools; that students find themselves in environments in which the expectations they experience at home and in their neighborhoods are different from those they experience at school; and that changes brought about by desegregation often require that teachers take part in a broader range of educational programs that can greatly increase teacher work loads.[8] Teachers in desegregated schools face challenges of a greater magnitude than those in homogeneous settings. Desegregation requires changes in instruction and in professional behavior.

35   A third issue presented in this chapter is affirmative action. The legal basis of affirmative action is found in Titles VI and VII of the Civil Rights Act of 1964 and in Title IX of the Education Amendments of 1972. In essence, they deal with prohibiting discrimination in employment with respect to race, color, religion, sex, or national origin, particularly in educational programs or activities receiving federal financial assistance. Affirmative action also involves positive efforts to recruit and employ persons and admit students that are underrepresented in the workplace or educational setting. Furthermore, affirmative action is involved in releasing employees. Recent court cases indicate that the courts are more lenient in issues involving hiring than in issues involving releasing employees. Minorities can be given preference in hiring to correct past discrimination, but they cannot be given preference over more senior employees in termination of employment.

The rights of students as citizens must be protected; teachers should know about these rights and protect them. Teachers, because they are a primary influence in shaping the attitudes of students, ultimately have a hand in shaping society.

Discussion Questions

1. Why has the federal government become more involved in education in recent years?
2. What function should the private school have in America?
3. What has been the rationale for using public money to supply transportation and textbooks to students attending private schools?
4. How has the U.S. Supreme Court influenced the operation of public education?
5. How do the court decisions and the federal legislation discussed in this chapter affect the responsibilities and behavior of classroom teachers?
6. What is the difference between de jure and de facto segregation?
7. What has been the major factor in court decisions supporting metropolitan desegregation?
8. What myths about busing did Orfield identify in his research?
9. What were the essential elements in the decision of the U.S. Supreme Court in the Bakke case?
10. What are the primary aspects of affirmative action?

Supplemental Activities

1. Interview officials from private schools in your area to discuss what private education in America can do best.
2. Visit a racially integrated school and record your observations.
3. Procure and study the policy statements of a local

school district; look specifically for federal or state influence.

4. Interview a public school superintendent and inquire about the effects of federal legislation and court decisions on how a local school district operates.

5. Examine a negotiated contract between a school board and its respective teachers' association in regard to its policies for hiring and releasing employees, particularly as those policies relate to affirmative action.

Notes

1. Thomas J. Flygare, "State Aid to Parochial Schools: Diminished Alternative," *Phi Delta Kappan,* 57 (November 1975): 204.
2. William E. Collie, "*Schempp* Reconsidered: The Relationship between Religion and Public Education," *Phi Delta Kappan,* (September 1983): 59.
3. Gary Orfield, *Must We Bus? Segregated Schools and National Policy* (Washington, D.C.: Brookings Institute, 1978) as reported in *Education USA,* 1 (October 2, 1978): 35.
4. James S. Coleman, "Racial Segregation in the Schools: New Research with New Policy Implications," *Phi Delta Kappan,* 57 (October 1975): 76–77.

5. Ibid.
6. Robert L. Green, and Thomas F. Pettigrew, "Urban Desegregation and White Flight: A Response to Coleman," *Phi Delta Kappan,* 57 (February 1976): 401–402.
7. Robert G. Wegmann, "White Flight and School Resegregation: Some Hypotheses," *Phi Delta Kappan,* 58 (January 1977): 393.
8. Willis D. Hawley, "Achieving Quality Integrated Education—With or Without Federal Help," *Phi Delta Kappan,* 64 (January 1983): 335.

Bibliography

Flygare, Thomas J. "Schools and the Law." *Phi Delta Kappan.* (A regular feature in each issue of *Phi Delta Kappan* providing timely and pertinent information.)
———. "Supreme Court Confused by Reverse Discrimination." *Phi Delta Kappan,* 68 (September 1986): 77–78.
Hudgins, H. C., Jr., and Vacca, Richard S. *Law and Education: Contemporary Issues and Court Decisions.* Rev. ed. Charlottesville, Va.: Michie, 1985.
LaMorte, Michael W. *School Law: Cases and Concepts.* Englewood Cliffs, N.J.: Prentice-Hall, 1982.
McCarthy, Martha M. *A Delicate Balance. Church, State, and the Schools.* Bloomington, Ind.: *Phi Delta Kappan,* 1983.
Orfield, Gary. *Must We Bus? Segregated Schools and National Policy.* Washington, D.C.: Brookings Institute, 1978.
Reutter, Edmund, Jr. *The Supreme Court's Impact on Public Education.* Bloomington, Ind.: Phi Delta Kappan and National Organization on Legal Problems in Education, 1982.
Salome, Rosemary C. *Equal Education Under Law.* New York: St. Martin's Press, 1986.
Thomas, Stephen B., Cambron-McCabe, Nelda H., and McCarthy, Martha M. *Educators and the Law: Current Trends and Issues.* Jamaica, N.Y.: Institute for the Study of School Law and School Finance, 1983.
Wilkinson, J. Harvie, III. *From Brown to Bakke: The Supreme Court and School Integration, 1954–1978.* New York: Oxford University Press, 1979.

Organizing and Administering
Public Education

Focus Questions

- Why should you, as a future teacher, know or care about how schools are organized?
- How do you think changes could be brought about in the way schools operate at the local level?
- What benefits are there to you or the teaching profession by your belonging to a state and/or a national teacher association?
- Do you think teachers and parents should be active in influencing how schools are organized and operated? Why or why not?
- Should teachers be active in the political process? Why or why not?
- What benefits are there for teachers in knowing and understanding the roles, responsibilities, and duties of school administrators?

Key Terms and Concepts

Neighborhood schools
Federal involvement in education
State department of education
Chief state school officer
State board of education
Intermediate units
Local school district

Local board of education
Superintendent of schools
Local control
Teacher power
Public power
Lobbying

What Would You Do?

The members of the local teachers' association are debating whether or not they should publicly show their support of two candidates who are running for election to the local school board by personal signatures in an advertisement in the local newspaper. You are a beginning teacher without tenure. How do you decide where you stand on this issue?

You are a fifth-grade teacher and have one boy in your class who is constantly disruptive. He bothers and irritates other students when they are trying to study. He is not responsive to your efforts to discipline him. Where can you go for help to resolve this situation?

In discussing the legal foundations of education in Chapter 9, we examined the educational system primarily from a judicial and legislative standpoint. In this chapter we consider the organizational and administrative aspects of the educational system. Education in the United States is an immense enterprise. Currently, about 44.6 million students are enrolled in public and private elementary and secondary schools, and about 2.4 million teachers are employed to instruct these students. More than one out of every four persons in the nation directly participates in education as a student, teacher, or supervisor. Projections for 1993 indicate approximately 47.9 million students and 2.7 million teachers.[1] Approximately 15,500 local school districts function under 50 state governments. How is this huge enterprise organized and administered nationwide?

As we pointed out in Chapter 9, the U.S. Constitution does not specifically provide for public education. However, the Tenth Amendment has been interpreted as granting this power to the states. The states are the governmental units in the United States charged with the responsibility for education. Figure 10.1 shows a typical state organization for education.

Local school districts are the governmental units empowered by state law to administer and operate the school systems of local communities. Figure 10.1 portrays the relationship of the local school districts to the state.

Two other governmental agencies that are involved in public education are intermediate units and the federal government. Intermediate units may consist of one or more counties, with the executive officers referred to as county superintendents or regional superintendents. They typically have some direct responsibility to the state education agency, but intermediate units generally serve as a liaison between the state and the local school district. The intermediate unit is not included on Figure 10.1 because its *primary functions* in its relationships with public schools are not legislative or executive.

The federal government is also not listed on Figure 10.1. Its *primary functions* in its relationship to states or public school districts are not legislative or executive. As indicated in Chapter 9, one of its primary roles is to preserve the rights of citizens as guaranteed by the U.S. Constitution and federal laws.

This chapter provides information about the roles of the federal government, state government, intermediate units, and local school districts, in that order.

Federal Involvement

We mentioned in this book that under the Tenth Amendment to the U.S. Constitution, education is a function of the states. In effect, states have the primary responsibility for education, although the schools are operated by local governmental units commonly called school districts. The federal government is characterized as having a strong interest in education, particularly as it relates

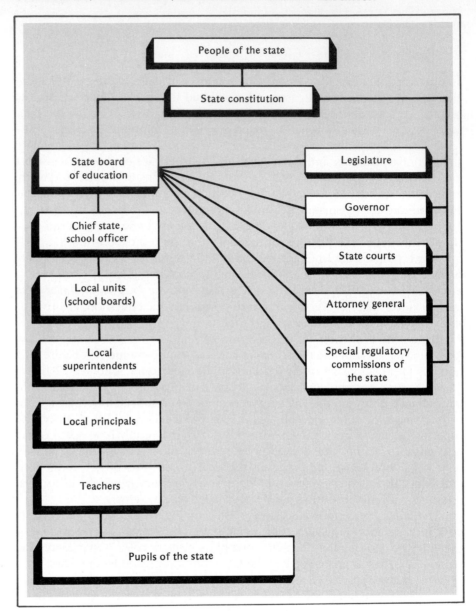

FIGURE 10.1   *Typical Structure of a State School System*

to the national security, national domestic problems, and the rights of citizens as guaranteed by the U.S. Constitution and federal laws.

National Security and Domestic Problems

Illustrations of federal actions in education with respect to national security include the National Defense Act of 1958, enacted after the Soviet Union launched the first satellite; this act provided federal money to enhance education in the sciences, mathematics, and foreign languages. Also, in 1984, in response to a lowering of student achievement scores, particularly in science and mathematics, Congress supported appropriations to improve science and mathematics education, primarily in secondary schools. The federal government has been involved in other areas as well. For example, Chapter 7 in this book provides illustrations of federal efforts to assist in solving domestic social issues such as poverty and non-English-speaking students. The federal role in guaranteeing the rights of individuals was explained in Chapter 9.

Leadership

The federal government has historically provided leadership in education in specific situations, usually in times of need or crises that could not be fully addressed by the leadership in states or local school districts. The time may be right for a more stable and consistent leadership role for the federal government, such as establishing national priorities in education similar to those issues addressed in *A Nation at Risk,* the report prepared by the National Commission on Excellence in Education, published in 1983.

$\boxed{31}$

That report was not a mandate, nor was funding recommended; but it did provide recommendations to be considered by states and local school districts. The identifying of national educational issues and the encouraging of forums on these issues at the state and local levels, along with soliciting responses, are appropriate. Such activities could be made regular rather than sporadic. Research on significant national educational issues should be continued. The dissemination of exemplary practices should be enhanced. Leaders of education in the states should meet to provide the impetus of a coalition to implement exemplary practices. The federal government should provide leadership; priority setting, research, and dissemination are appropriate leadership areas.

$\boxed{36}$

The federal government also includes a Department of Education, directly operates some educational programs, and provides some financial aid to states and local school districts. (Federal aid is discussed in Chapter 11.)

Department of Education

In October 1979 President Carter signed legislation creating a Department of Education. The Department of Education took on the functions of the U.S. Office of Education, which was created in 1953 as a unit within the Department of Health, Education, and Welfare. The first unit of education in the federal gov-

Consider teaching the children of military staff members who are assigned to bases throughout the world.
Consider employment in a state department of education.
Inquire about services that are offered by intermediate units.

**Professional
Perspectives**

ernment, established in 1867 through the diligent efforts of Henry Barnard, was also called the Department of Education. Later, it was called the Office of Education (1869), becoming a Bureau of Education in 1970 within the Department of the Interior. It was also called the Office of Education in 1929. In 1939 the "Office of Education" became a part of the Federal Security Agency, which in 1953 became the Department of Health, Education, and Welfare, wherein the U.S. Office of Education was assigned until the new department was created in 1979.

The Department of Education, in contrast with the first Department of Education (1867), has potential for becoming a powerful agency. The original 1867 Department had the following stated purpose:

> To collect such statistics and facts as shall show the condition and progress of education in the several States and Territories, and to diffuse such information respecting the organization and management of schools and school systems, and methods of teaching as shall aid the people of the United States in the establishment and maintenance of efficient school systems, and otherwise promote the cause of education throughout the country.

As a U.S. Office of Education from 1953 through 1979, it had its scope of activities increased, and the office gained power, expanding in data-gathering and dissemination activities. One of its primary functions during this period was the responsibility of awarding and administering federal grants. During this period grants increased dramatically both in numbers and in the amounts of money allocated. Many of the grants were for pilot experimental programs. The grant function, according to some authorities, permits the federal government to indirectly exercise control over education. There are also authorities who feel that such indirect control is not an appropriate function of the federal government. They prefer that the federal government forward money to the states to be used at the discretion of the states. They argue that the states know more about their problems and needs and therefore can use the funds more effectively without federal direction and control. There is no question that awarding grants is an effective way to influence the goals of education nationally. However, there are persons who believe that offices of the federal government should have a strong influence on education. They maintain that the socioeconomic forces of society are not contained within local school districts or state boundaries, and therefore direct federal intervention is needed. In fact, the states receive some funds from the federal government to use at their discretion, and they receive other funding from the federal government that is earmarked for specific purposes related to national priorities.

It is within this political educational context that the new Department of Education was created. Those who favored creating a new department felt that education was too important to be lost in the gigantic Department of Health, Education, and Welfare. Opponents took the position that a national Department of Education would result in more federal control and standardization.

|31|

Educational Programs Operated by the Federal Government

The federal government directly operates some school programs. The public school system of the District of Columbia depends on Congress for funds; for many years it was controlled by a board of education appointed by the justices of the U.S. District Court for Washington, D.C. Currently, school board members are chosen by popular election.

The Department of the Interior has the educational responsibility for children of national park employees, for Samoa (classified as an outlying possession), and for the trust territories of the Pacific, such as the Caroline Islands and the Marshall Islands. The schools on Indian reservations are financed and managed through the Bureau of Indian Affairs of the Department of the Interior.

The Department of Defense is responsible for the military academy at West Point, the naval academy at Annapolis, the coast guard academy at New London, and the air force academy at Colorado Springs. The Department of Education operates a school system for the children of the military staff wherever members are stationed. The education supplied in the vocational and technical-training programs of the military services has made a big contribution to the education of our nation. Many people transfer the technical and vocational skills acquired in military life to civilian occupations.

State Functions

The state is the governmental unit in the United States charged with the responsibility for education. State legislatures, within the limits expressed by the federal constitution and by state constitutions, are the chief policymakers for education. State legislatures grant powers to state boards of education, state departments of education, chief state school officers, and local boards of education. These groups have only the powers granted to them by the legislature, implied powers from the specific grant of power, and the necessary powers to carry out the statutory purposes. The responsibilities and duties of intermediate units are also prescribed by the state legislatures. Figure 10.1 shows a typical state organization for education.

State Boards of Education

State boards of education are both regulatory and advisory. Authorities generally agree that regulation by state school boards is important primarily so that local schools will operate consistently. Some regulatory functions are establishing standards for issuing and revoking teaching certificates, establishing standards for approving and accrediting schools, and developing and enforcing a uniform system for gathering and reporting educational data. The advisory function includes considering the educational needs of the state, both long- and short-range, and recommending to the governor and the legislature ways of meeting the needs. State school boards, in studying school problems and in suggesting and analyzing proposals, can be invaluable to the legislature, especially since the legislature is under pressure to decide so many issues. A state board can provide a continuity in an educational program that ordinary legislative procedures don't allow for. A state board can also coordinate, supplement, and even replace study commissions appointed by a legislature for advising on educational matters. These commissions frequently include groups studying textbooks, finance, certification, school district reorganization, school building standards, and teacher education.

The selection of state-adopted textbooks has become a controversial issue in recent years. Efforts have been made by individuals and groups to add creationism as a theory of human origin to the content of textbooks and to eliminate the theory of evolution. In other instances efforts have been made to eliminate topics such as sex education and single parenting. Publishers have been accused of modifying their books in order to ameliorate criticism and to continue or increase their sales. As a result of school reform, some states are insisting that publishers increase the rigor of the content in their textbooks. California, for example, rejected all science textbooks in 1986.

Members of state boards of education get their positions in various ways. Usually, they are appointed by the governor; they may also be elected by the people, the legislature, or local school board members in regional convention. The specific information about how members of state boards of education in each state get these positions is in Appendix B.

In 1947 nine states were without state boards of education; by 1983 only Wisconsin was without. Iowa, New York, and Washington have elective procedures unlike those of the other states. In Iowa, conventions of delegates from areas within the state send nominations to the governor, who makes the final appointment; in New York the Board of Regents is elected by the legislature; and in Washington the state board is elected by members of boards of directors of local school districts. The terms of members are usually staggered to avoid a complete changeover at any one time. Members usually serve without pay but are reimbursed for expenses. The policy of nonpayment, along with the staggered terms, is considered a safeguard against political patronage.

Chief State School Officers

Every state has a chief state school officer. Currently, nineteen of these officers are elected by the people, twenty-seven are appointed by state boards of education, and four are appointed by the governor. The specific information about how each chief state school officer gets the position is in Appendix C.

Arguments advanced for electing the chief state school officer hold that as an elected official, the person will be close to the people, responsible to them, and free from obligations to other state officials. As an elected person, he or she will also be independent of the state board of education. Opponents to the election method argue primarily that this method keeps the department of education in partisan politics, that an elected official is obligated to other members of the same political party, and that many excellent candidates prefer not to engage in political contests. Furthermore, they feel that as a matter of operating efficiency, the chief state school officer should not be chosen independently of the state board of education.

Those who advocate that the chief state school officer should be appointed by a state board of education claim that policymaking should be separated from policy execution, that educational leadership should not rest on the competence of one elected official, and that with this method recruiting and retaining qualified career workers in education would be enhanced.

Opponents of appointment by a state board of education claim mainly that the chief school officer would then not be responsible to the people. The principal objection to gubernatorial appointment is the inherent danger of the appointee's involvement in partisan politics. An elected state school officer is legally an "official" of the state, whereas an officer appointed by a state board of education is generally an "employee," not a legal official. When the chief school officer is elected, and hence is a legal official theoretically responsible to the people, the working relation between this official and the state board is not likely to be so clearly defined as when the official is appointed by the state board of education and hence is an employee of the board.

The chief state school officer can strongly influence educational ideas. This person tells the legislature, the governor, and the state board of education what he or she thinks education needs. The officer frequently reports to the legislature, perhaps suggesting legislation. Most often the chief state school officer is the executive head of the state department of education and as such, through a staff, supervises and regulates the schools. Specific duties of the office may include the following:

- To serve as secretary and executive officer of the state board of education.
- To serve as executive officer of any board or council that may be established to facilitate coordination of all aspects of the educational program.
- To select competent personnel for and serve as the administrative head and professional leader of the state department of education to the end that it will contribute maximally to the improvement of education.
- To arrange for studies and organize committees and task forces as deemed necessary to identify problems and to recommend plans and provisions for effecting improvements in education.
- To recommend to the state board of education needed policies, standards, and regulations relating to public education in the state.
- To recommend improvements in educational legislation and in provisions for financing the educational program.
- To explain and interpret the school laws of the state and the regulations of the state board of education.
- To decide impartially controversies and disputes involving the administration of the public school system.
- To submit frequent reports to the public and periodic reports to the state board, to the governor, and to the legislature giving information about the accomplishments, conditions, and needs of the schools.[2]

State Departments of Education

The state government carries on its activities in education through the state department of education, which is directed by the chief state school officer. These activities have been classified in five categories: operational, regulatory, service, developmental, and public support and cooperation activities.[3] Operational activities are those in which the state department directly administers schools and services, such as schools for the blind. Regulatory activities include overseeing that teacher certification standards are met, that school buses are safe, and that curricular requirements are fulfilled. Service activities include advising and consulting, disseminating research, and preparing materials (on state financial aid, for example). Developmental activities are directed to improving the department itself and include planning, staffing, and research into better performance for the operational, regulatory, and service functions. Public support and cooperation activities involve public relations, political activities with the legislature and governor, and relations with various other governmental and nongovernmental agencies.

Traditionally, state departments have not shown strong leadership. Their activities have mainly been operating and regulating. The Elementary and Secondary Education Act of 1965, under Title V, provided for funds to strengthen state departments of education. There is no question that departments have been strengthened, but the majority have not yet branched out into other activities. State departments of education, for example, have a role in the distribution of federal grants. However, their role has changed with the beginning of block grants, a concept implemented in 1981 through the Education Improvement Act by the federal government. Under the block-grant concept, within their own rules and regulations, states have greater freedom to make decisions on the level of funding they wish to apply to some federal programs. The block grant is a consolidation of former categorical aid. Categorical financial aid is that granted to be used for a specific purpose, such as compensatory education for the disadvantaged, bilingual education, education for the handicapped, and vocational education. Categorical aid is accompanied by strict rules and regulations to ensure that the aid is used for its intended purposes. Some specific categorical programs are continued as categorical programs with the usual restrictions on the use of the money. Since education is so closely related to the problems of society, the partners in education—federal, state, and local—must adjust their activities to meet complex needs.

Intermediate Units

The intermediate unit of school organization, which may consist of one or more counties, functions between the state department of education and the local school districts. The executive officer of an intermediate unit may be referred to as a county superintendent or a regional superintendent. As with chief state school officers, they may be elected or appointed. The arguments favoring the elected county or regional superintendent are very similar to those favoring the elected chief state school officer. Similarly, the arguments favoring the appointed county or regional superintendent are similar to those favoring the appointed chief state school officer.

Historically, the intermediate unit has served as liaison between the state department of education and the local school districts. In rural areas, where there is a preponderance of small schools, it has also had a direct educational function, such as providing counseling, special education, and psychological services.

A fundamental purpose of the intermediate unit today is to provide two or more local districts with educational services that they cannot efficiently or economically provide individually; cooperative provisions for special education and vocational-technical education have been very successful. Other services that intermediate units can provide include audiovisual libraries, centralized purchasing, in-service training for teachers and other school workers, health services, instructional materials, laboratories, legal services, and special consultant services. The in-service dimension of intermediate units has escalated in some states in the past few years, stimulated by educational reform.

According to an Educational Research Services study, there has been a trend toward legislature-mandated regional centers.[4] Eight states now require regional services, and four others have legislation that allows them. Many earlier intermediate units, except for county units, were voluntary consortiums. In Iowa the 15 area-education agencies have the same boundaries as community college and vocational districts. The Pennsylvania legislature dissolved county units, which served as intermediate units, and created 29 intermediate units.

Intermediate units or regional centers are developing closer ties with higher-education institutions and with other regional government subdivisions and social agencies, such as mental health agencies. The Educational Research Services study also raises some interesting questions about regional centers. Do they tend to bolster school districts that should be reorganized? How should they be financed? What kinds of governing boards should they have? Should they have the power to levy local taxes?

Local School Districts

A school district is a governmental unit empowered by state law to administer the school system of a local community. While school districts have similar purposes, they have widely different characteristics. School districts are governed by local boards of education composed of citizens living in the geographical area that makes up the district. Most boards of education cherish local control. Because many school districts are small, efforts have been made to reorganize and consolidate small districts to achieve a greater degree of effectiveness and efficiency. Quite often, school reorganization is viewed by citizens as a threat to local control. The chief executive officer of a school district is commonly referred to as a superintendent of schools. In large districts the superintendent generally has assistant or associate superintendents that also are involved in the administration of the district. Schools that serve a prescribed section of the school district are frequently alluded to as neighborhood schools or attendance centers.

School District Characteristics

School districts have similar purposes but widely different characteristics. Some districts provide only elementary education; others provide only high school education; still others provide both elementary and secondary education. Approximately 27 percent of the districts have fewer than 300 pupils, and their total enrollments make up about 1.4 percent of the total national enrollment. Only 1.0 percent of the districts have an enrollment in excess of 25,000 students, yet these districts enroll about 26 percent of the total. Thousands of school districts have only one attendance center; a few urban districts may have as many as 500.

Local districts provide one of the few opportunities for citizens to participate directly in public decision making. Board members are local citizens, and the majority of them serve on school boards in relatively small communities in districts that enroll fewer than 1,000 students. Only about 4.0 percent of board members serve in relatively large communities in districts that enroll over 10,000 students. Therefore in many school districts board members may know each other and many of their constituents by first names. The administration of local schools concerns people deeply, dealing directly as it does with their children. Local school districts also deal with local citizens' money in the form of taxation

Local school districts provide one of the few opportunities for citizens to participate directly in public decision-making. (*Source:* Owen Franken/Stock, Boston)

to provide funds to operate the schools. In many communities today the budget for schools is the highest of any local taxing agency. The local school district in many cases is the closest relationship citizens have with a governmental agency. Americans usually value this relation highly. Some look on the local district and its schools as a chance to determine their own destiny; others see the local district and local control as one of the few remaining opportunities to control public spending. The local district does have advantages over centralized governmental control. It permits citizens to have schools of better quality than the minimum prescribed by the state and gives them a chance to develop educational programs that meet local needs.

Local Control

Local control is an important and unique feature of American education; however, its value has been challenged recently. Some people argue that the mobility of our population and the interdependence of social elements have undermined the traditional concept that local people should have a strong role in determining education. Some also argue that our national survival requires policies and programs laid down under centralized control.

Local control, in a sense, is challenged each time a decision by a local board or a local school district is taken to the courts. Many court decisions dealing with the relationship between religion and the public school or with desegregation have been in response to local control. In some instances local control, combined with the traditional system of financing education, has resulted in inequality of educational opportunity rather than equality. The alternative to local control is centralization. We have come full circle; education in large cities is already centralized, and many of these large districts are trying to solve some of their problems by decentralization. Frequently, a centralized authority does not respond well to citizens' needs and demands. Ex officio boards and councils for local community or neighborhood schools, which advise officials on large city or county boards, represent efforts to keep some form of local control in the large centralized systems.

The operational control of education today is still primarily local, carried out under the powers delegated by the states. Federal and state involvement— both direct, through court decisions and mandates, and indirect, through federal and state aid—has been increasing. How the local, state, and federal governments are related in their control is complicated and must be resolved. New and intricate relations keep forming.

School Reorganization

Efforts have been made in the past to reorganize school districts for more effectiveness and more efficiency. The emphasis has been on reducing, by consolidation, the number of small rural districts. The number of school districts in the United States has decreased from approximately 100,000 in 1945 to approximately 15,500 today. California, Nebraska, and Texas have over 1,000 districts each. The progress made in consolidating districts has been slow but inevitable.

State legislatures have the power to reorganize school districts but have been reluctant to do so. Often the reorganization legislation is permissive; districts may consolidate with the blessing of the legislature, but little inducement is given. Financial incentives have been incorporated into some reorganization legislation, but still the reorganization is slow. In a few instances school district reorganization has been mandatory. The laws usually set time limits for reorganization, provide for local community committees to study and present proposals for state review, and offer financial incentives for reorganization. Some laws have stated that if there is a public impasse or if proposals are weak, the state can intercede and effect the reorganization. Local citizens tend to resist school district reorganization because of their sentimental feelings about their school, their desire to keep control local, their failure to recognize inferior schools, their need for the school as a social and recreational facility, and their fear of potential tax increases.

A 1976 study made under a contract from the National Institute of Education raises questions about how valuable it is to consolidate small rural schools.[5] The findings of the study are still appropriate today. The researchers, after reviewing the literature dealing with rural consolidation, made the following assertions:

- The purported economies to be gained are frequently offset by "diseconomies," such as increased transportation costs and the cost of administering and distributing products procured through bulk purchasing.
- Taxable wealth has not become equally spread among districts despite massive reorganization over four decades.
- Quality of education has not improved. (The researchers base this assertion primarily on the relationship of school size to pupil achievement.)

They make three recommendations:

1. More research on small schools should be done.
2. Alternatives to consolidation and reorganization, such as regionalization, should be seriously considered.
3. Research done to demonstrate the value of proposed reforms should be scrutinized carefully.

More research is needed to verify the proclaimed benefits of consolidation and reorganization. The number and kinds of variables that must be controlled—particularly if pupil achievement is to be the measure of effectiveness of reorganization—make such research very difficult. Furthermore, school reorganization in itself is probably one of the least powerful variables affecting pupil achievement, falling far behind variables such as native intellect, home environment, socioeconomic status, and motivation. Even after massive reorganization, approximately 27 percent of the school districts in the United States today still have fewer than 300 pupils, and about 55 percent have fewer than 1,000 students.

Urban districts also present reorganization problems. Rapid growth in urban areas, combined with unplanned and indiscriminate land use, has created immense problems. Wealthy districts with few pupils adjoin poor districts with many pupils. The desires and expectations of the residents for their schools vary tremendously from district to district. Communication between the citizens and the school authorities can become distant and distorted. New York City is one place where decentralizing the large school system has been tried. The teachers' strike there in 1968 focused on this issue and illustrated the complexities that may result from urban decentralization. Improving organization is an overwhelming and complicated task.

Local Boards of Education

Legal authority for operating local school systems is given to local boards of education through state statutes. The statutes prescribe specifically how school board members are to be chosen and what duties and responsibilities they have in office. The statutes also specify the terms of board members, procedures for selecting officers of the board, duties of the officers, procedures for filling any vacancies, and like matters. Local citizens serving as school board members are official agents of the state.

> 38

Ninety-five percent of the school boards in the United States are elected by popular vote; most members are elected in special, nonpartisan elections. About 5 percent are appointed. The percentage of appointed school boards is higher in school districts enrolling over 25,000 pupils; yet even in these large districts about three-fourths of the board members are elected. New York City and Chicago both have appointed school boards.

Citizens seeking election to school boards generally must petition for a place on the ballot. Candidates who meet the legal requirements to serve as school board members and follow proper petitioning procedures cannot be denied a place on the ballot. In some places an extralegal caucus committee approves a slate of candidates. This committee usually comprises representatives of community organizations. Members approved by a caucus committee must follow the same procedure as any other candidate placed on the ballot. The caucus process represents an attempt to nominate well-qualified candidates for board membership. This method, however, has been charged with recommending persons for board membership who would perpetuate alleged past inequities. A candidate on a partisan ticket is selected by the local party committee. School board members are usually elected from the district at large rather than from wards or precincts.

> 12

Appointments to boards of education (as opposed to election) are made by city councils, mayors, state legislatures, county boards, and other agencies. The most common procedure is appointment by a city council or mayor. Sometimes, an appointing official asks an extralegal committee of citizens to submit a list of persons to be considered for the vacancies. This procedure is an attempt to separate partisan politics and education and at the same time obtain highly qualified persons as board members.

Candidates for boards of education, elective or appointive, are frequently recruited from among citizens who have expressed an interest in the schools by serving on citizen advisory committees to boards of education. Local PTAs also serve as a source of potential candidates. Some persons desire and seek to become school board members. They may feel a public obligation to serve as a board member. Others may view being a board member as the beginning of a political career at the local level or, perhaps, at the state or national level. Some seek board membership to promote a specific cause, such as a higher emphasis on basic skills in instructional programs, or to represent a constituency that is totally disgruntled with the schools and wishes to gain a majority on the board to bring about their desires, for example, to improve efficiency and lower taxes.

The members of boards of education generally come from the proprietary and professional occupations. The number of farmers serving is steadily decreasing. Board members tend to have at least a high school education; many have college educations. Board members have a higher income than average citizens and generally represent middle class society.

A study conducted in 1977 by the National School Board Association investigated board membership in the nation's 51 largest school districts. It showed the following results:

- In comparison with 1967, five times as many professional educators serve on school boards—and only half as many attorneys.
- Minority representation has increased 3 percent from 1974 to 1977.
- Sixty-nine percent of the board members are male, of an average age of 49.

Quite likely, the percentage of male board members has decreased since this study was completed. The trend has been toward the election or appointment of more females and more members of minority groups to local school boards. (These trends may or may not prevail in small school districts.)

Teachers may not be board members in the districts where they teach; they may be board members, however, in districts where they live, while teaching in different districts. The trend in which more teachers are becoming board members most likely results from the stance that professional associations have taken to secure seats on school boards.

The powers and duties of school boards vary from state to state; the school codes of the respective states spell them out in detail. (The general powers and duties of local boards were discussed in Chapter 9.) Some duties are mandatory, others discretionary. Some duties cannot be delegated. If, for example, boards are given the power to employ teachers, the boards must be the ones to do this; the power may not be delegated even to a school superintendent. Boards can delegate much of the hiring process to administrators, however, and then act officially on administrative recommendations for employment. An illustration of a discretionary power left to the local board is a decision of whether or not to participate in a nonrequired school program—for example, a program of competitive athletics. Another illustration of discretionary power is a decision to employ only teachers who exceed minimum state certification standards.

Powers and duties granted to boards of education are granted to the boards as a whole, not to individual members. An individual member of a board has no more authority in school matters than any other citizen of the community unless the school board legally delegates a task through official action to a specific member; in those instances official board approval of final actions is necessary. A school board, as a corporate body, can act officially only in legally held and duly authorized board meetings, and these meetings usually must be open to the public. Executive or private sessions may be held but ordinarily only for specified purposes such as evaluating staff members or selecting a school site. Usually, any official action on matters discussed in private session must be taken in an open meeting.

$\boxed{14}$

Superintendent of Schools

One of the primary duties of the local board is to select its executive officer, the local superintendent of schools. In Illinois the school code is specific in granting this power and in delineating the superintendent's duties and the working relationship between the board and the superintendent. The Illinois law reads that a superintendent is to be employed

> who shall have charge of the administration of the schools under the direction of the board of education. In addition to the administrative duties, the superintendent shall make recommendations to the board concerning the budget, building plans, and locations of sites, the selection of teachers and other employees, the selection of textbooks, instructional material, and courses of study. The superintendent shall keep or cause to be kept the records and accounts as directed and required by the board, aid in making reports required of the board, and perform such other duties as the board may delegate to him.

Many states are not as specific as Illinois. While the Illinois statute is specific for a statute, it provides only guidelines for the local policies needed in establishing further board-superintendent working relations. The cooperative development of specific policies by the board and the superintendent helps establish the roles of both the board of education and the superintendent and therefore minimizes conflict in this crucial relationship. Generally, boards are policy-makers, and superintendents are executive officers; but it is often very difficult to make the distinction.

The quality of the educational program of a school district is influenced strongly by the leadership the board of education and the superintendent provide. Without high expectations being communicated and supported by boards and superintendents, high-quality education is not likely to be achieved. Curriculum programs over and above state-required minimums are discretionary. Local authorities, board members, and the superintendent frequently must convince communities that specified school programs are needed.

The superintendent of schools works with a staff to carry on the program of education. The size of the staff varies with the school district; and of course, some kind of organization is necessary. Many school systems use a line and staff organization like that shown in Figure 10.2. In this pattern, line officers hold the administrative power as it flows in a line from the local board of education down to the pupils. Superintendents, assistant superintendents, and principals are line officers vested with authority over the people below them on the chart. Each person is directly responsible to the official above and must work through that person in dealing with a higher official. This arrangement is frequently referred to as the "chain of command."

Administrative staff members are shown in Figure 10.2 as branching out from the direct flow of authority. Staff includes librarians, instructional super-

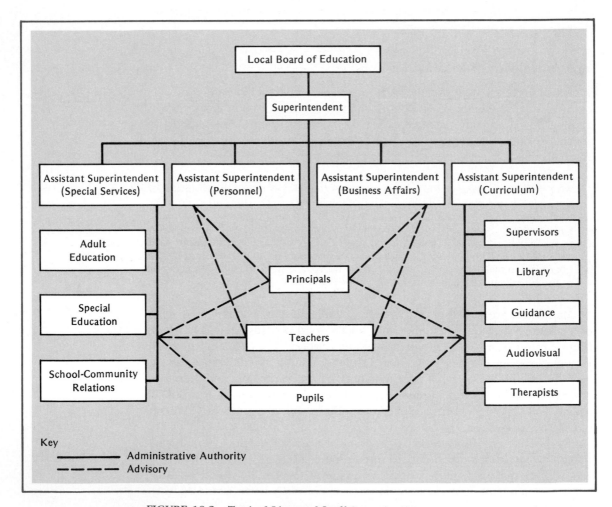

FIGURE 10.2 *Typical Line and Staff Organization*

231

visors, guidance officers, transportation officers, and others. They are responsible to their respective superiors, generally in an advisory capacity. Staff members usually have no authority and issue no orders. They assist and advise others from their special knowledge and abilities. Teachers are generally referred to as staff persons even though they are in the direct flow of authority. Their authority in this arrangement prevails only over pupils.

Administrator Roles and Decision Making

Every school district has an administrator or administrators. As mentioned earlier, the superintendent is the chief executive of a school district. In very small school districts the superintendent may be the only administrator. In larger school districts, in addition to the superintendent, there are likely to be other administrators referred to as assistant superintendents, associate superintendents, and perhaps directors that are subordinate to the assistant or associate superintendents. In other districts the term *director* may refer to a person who has the same responsibility and authority as an assistant superintendent in another district. In the following comments the term *assistant* is used. In reality, different terms may be used for persons with similar responsibilities. The focus in the comments that follow is on the decision-making aspects of the superintendent and subordinate administrators.

As the chief executive officer, the superintendent makes recommendations to the board about all aspects of the school district's operation for decisions by the board. For example, the superintendent may request decisions on his or her recommendations to the board about personnel, curriculum, budget, long-range planning, facilities, and policies. The superintendent also makes decisions based on recommendations from line staff members; in Figure 10.2 the line staff members are the four assistant superintendents and the principals. In general, the superintendent will meet regularly with the assistants and the principals where educational issues are discussed. For example, the assistant superintendent for personnel may express a concern about faculty development programs for teachers, or the assistant superintendent for business affairs may propose a new fiscal policy; and a principal may have a concern about discipline procedures. These matters will be discussed, and the superintendent may decide that the assistant superintendent for curriculum should assess the need for faculty development and provide that information to the assistant superintendents of personnel and business for their opinions and report back at a designated meeting in the future. A principal may be asked by the superintendent to meet with the assistant for personnel and establish procedures for reviewing and making recommendations with respect to discipline policies. In effect, the superintendent makes recommendations to the board for decisions, receives recommendations from assistant superintendents and principals, and makes decisions about their recommendations. Teachers may be represented on and involved in committees that make recommendations to principals, superintendents, and associate or assistant superintendents.

**Professional
Perspectives**

Be active in your local teachers' association.
Ask fellow teachers, an appropriate administrator, and/or other professional staff
when you need help.
Be aware of, and sensitive to, the characteristics and needs of the students in
your school.

The responsibilities of a specific assistant superintendent—for example, assistant superintendent for curriculum—may vary because of district size or organization. Nevertheless, the typical responsibilities of an assistant superintendent for curriculum include providing instructional services to students and teachers and coordinating staff planning efforts to develop educational specifications, curriculum development, and staff development. Thus the position requires organizing ways of selecting instructional materials and supplies, including textbooks, library books, computers and computer software, and other teaching aids necessary for effective teaching. In addition, the position involves responsibilities for preparing budgets for instructional materials and supplies. An assistant superintendent for curriculum, along with related staff members and teachers, develops and interprets the goals and objectives of the curriculum. Staff development includes providing teachers with the means to acquire and update their competencies, skills, and knowledge. An assistant superintendent for curriculum may also play a role in teacher selection. However, in many instances the principal makes the selection and an assistant superintendent for personnel takes over at that point. Assistant superintendents make decisions on the recommendations they will present to the superintendent. However, they have decision-making authority to operate their office and supervise their staff, as indicated in Figure 10.2, according to the policies, rules, and regulations of the school district.

The responsibilities of an assistant superintendent for personnel frequently include staff procurement and final formal appointment after recommendations from the superintendent or a principal; final assignment of staff and teachers after recommendations from the superintendent or a principal; administration of the office, including record keeping; administration of personnel rules and regulations; administration of substitute teacher services and employee relations; salary administration; administration of personnel provisions of negotiated contracts, along with principals; and development of personnel policies and procedures. Assistant superintendents make decisions about the recommendations they present to the superintendent, and they have the decision-making authority to operate their office and supervise their staff according to the policies, rules, and regulations of the school district.

Other assistant superintendents function with respect to their area of control in a manner similar to that of the two just described. The number of assistant superintendents is closely related to the size and wealth of the school district. As the number of assistant superintendents increases, the responsibilities for each generally become narrower in scope. As the number of assistants decrease, the responsibilities generally become broader in scope.

In very small school districts, say less than 1,000 students, of which there are approximately 1,800 in the United States, the superintendent is likely to be the only central office administrator in the district. As such, the superintendent not only is responsible for all aspects of educational administration but is expected to personally perform all the duties required. A school district with an organization like the one shown in Figure 10.2, with four assistant superintendents, is likely to have an enrollment of over 8,000 pupils.

A principal is the chief executive officer of an attendance center, generally reporting directly to a superintendent of schools or a designate, and is responsible for leadership and all aspects of the operation of the attendance center. The principal performs administrative tasks, similar to those of the superintendent, at the attendance center level and does so within the policies, rules, and regulations of the school district. The principal is typically responsible for instructional leadership, community relationships, staff personnel (including staff and teacher selection and evaluation), pupil personnel, facilities, finance, administration of personnel provisions of negotiable contracts, administration of the attendance center office, and business management.

Educational reform efforts in many states have focused on the responsibilities of principals, generally placing a much higher emphasis on teacher evaluation and instructional leadership for the attendance center. Without doubt, those two aspects of the principalship are the most important—so important that they should take at least 80 percent of a principal's time. Reform plans have called for updating or more training of principals in attendance center instructional leadership and teacher evaluation. In many instances principals may need additional assistance to cover the duties that they will not be able to do in addition to instructional leadership and teacher evaluation.

We indicated earlier that the principal has the authority to make decisions with respect to the attendance center for which he or she has responsibility as long as school district policies, rules, and regulations are followed. A principal must be able to decide when he or she should seek an opinion from the superintendent prior to making a decision. This situation may occur when a policy is not clear or when the issue is not covered by any policy, rule, or regulation. Principals make decisions about schedules, disciplinary action, and day-to-day operations. In small districts, they generally make recommendations to the superintendent; and in large districts they are likely to make recommendations to specific assistant superintendents about teacher assignment, in-service training, tenure, faculty remediation, textbooks, and supplies. Frequently, they are responsible for developing a budget and monitoring their expenses in terms of the budget.

Teachers who wish to express a concern should initially use the official administrative system. The first person to contact in most instances is the principal; sometimes, it may be a department head. If this method fails, a teacher may continue by contacting the principal's superior—the superintendent or an assistant superintendent. Another way is to file a grievance through procedures outlined in the negotiated contract given to teachers' organizations and the school district. In any instance it is wise for a beginning teacher or one new to the system to seek advice from experienced colleagues before taking action. In addition to knowing the system, one must know how the system works; colleagues can be helpful in that regard.

Attendance Centers—Neighborhood Schools

The school organization for pupils can be considered in two interrelated ways: grade-level grouping and attendance center grouping. Common grade-level groupings include K–8–4, a kindergarten through grade 8 school along with a four-year high school; K–6–3—3, a kindergarten through grade 6 school along with a grade 7–9 junior high school and a grade 10–12 high school; K–6–6, a kindergarten through grade 6 school and a grade 7–12 school. A newer type of grade grouping is K–4–4–4. The rationale for grade-level grouping is presumably based primarily on child growth and on developmental and curricular considerations. More often, grade-center grouping involves a need for complete space utilization. For example, a school district with growing enrollments may decide to build a new high school and convert the old high school to a grade 6–8 grouping, resulting in changing K–8 schools to K–5 schools. A district with declining enrollments may merge two K–8 schools into one K–8 school, and sell, lease, or demolish one of the K–8 schools. Attendance center grouping frequently is identical to grade-level grouping, although it need not be.

An attendance center is a school—within a district—to which pupils from a designated geographical area are assigned. Figure 10.3 illustrates the attendance center concept. In this illustration there are seven attendance centers: four K–6 centers, two 7–9 centers, and one 10–12 center. The attendance area for each of the K–6 centers is approximately one-fourth of the area of the school district. Their boundaries are represented by the exterior boundaries of the school district and the double dashed lines within the school district. Each 7–9 attendance center includes the area encompassed by two K–6 centers. The boundaries of the 10–12 center are the same as the district boundaries. In reality, school districts and attendance centers are not nearly so geometrically perfect. Most often, the boundaries are irregular and jagged. Occasionally, they even have long, peninsular projections extending deep into other districts. The number of attendance centers in a district may vary from one in a rural area to more than 500 in a heavily populated area.

School boards have the right to prescribe the boundaries for an attendance center. Establishing boundaries is difficult. Boards must be cautious in exercising this right, making certain that attendance areas are not determined by race, that the distances traveled by students either walking or being transported are not unreasonable, and that the safety of youngsters is not jeopardized.

The segregation issue has further complicated attendance area decisions. Segregation exists by race, creed, economic status, nationality, and many other characteristics. Neighborhood schools, frequently the most logical attendance centers, are under attack for perpetuating de facto segregation. No doubt the

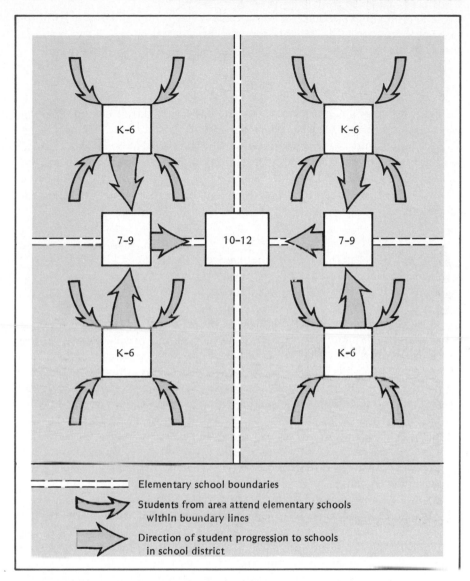

FIGURE 10.3 *School Attendance Centers Within a School District*

neighborhood school is often a segregated school, especially in cities. Attempts have been made to bus students from one neighborhood to another to integrate and balance the races. In other instances voluntary transfer plans, whereby students may elect to attend schools of their choice, have been tried. Neither plan has met with much success. Recent proposals suggest educational parks, built in carefully selected locations, that would foster racial integration and would permit drawing pupils from both the city and its suburbs. The middle school, composed of grades 5–8, 6–8, or 7–8, while conceived on a curricular rationale, also can sometimes accomplish racial balance by bringing together children who were in segregated neighborhood elementary schools. These many attempts, however, seem to be chiefly stopgap and short-term solutions.

Local Control: A Myth?

For many years local control was seen as the bulwark of the successful American education enterprise. To what extent does local control really exist? In recent decades local control has been termed a myth. Those said to be in actual control included professional administrators, teachers' organizations, and state and federal legislators and courts.

[31]

A 1977 report[6] notes four phases of control in the history of American education:

> *Phase 1*: Lay control (1835–ca. 1900)
> *Phase 2*: Control by local professionals (1900–ca. 1968)
> *Phase 3*: The nationalization of education (1954–1975)
> *Phase 4*: Education and the social goal (1975–present)

Phase 1 functioned with a mandate to educators to pursue limited educational goals that would enable citizens to survive and pursue livelihoods in their own small communities. Lay boards of education, representing the community, administered the schools. During this phase the nation had over a hundred thousand school districts; school board members represented relatively homogeneous and unambiguous constituencies. There was ample opportunity for the citizens to interact with their board members and to hold the board accountable for its actions.

Phase 2 was ushered in during a rapid growth in school population, particularly in urban areas. Board members found that they could no longer devote enough time to administrative tasks; consequently, the position of superintendent of schools was created. During this period the responsibilities for education were shifted from lay control to local professionals, mainly administrators. This change was partly inspired by the scientific management movement then taking place and by the desire of local citizens, including board members, to reduce political influence in education. Important changes were consolidation of school districts, centralization of administration, election of fewer board members at large and more from local wards, election of board members by nonpartisan ballots, and the separation of board elections from other municipal and state elections. Phase 2 had a larger mandate than phase 1; it called for the development of skills and values needed by a larger, homogeneous society. Phase 2 was characterized by stability, and schools were perceived as agents for transmitting knowledge, culture, and social norms.

Near the end of phase 2, the seeds for phase 3 were being planted. The decision in *Brown* v. *Board of Education* (1954) was an early step toward the school acting as an agent of social and economic change—the mandate of phase

3. Subsequent court decisions, federal and state legislation, and infusion of federal and state aid (with accompanying control of the funds) have all contributed to greater control by the federal government and other nonlocal units of government. The local administrative control of phase 2 was gradually eroded. Also contributing to the erosion was the influence gained by teachers' unions through collective bargaining.

The Ziegler study concludes that phase 3 governance cannot achieve the phase 3 mandate.[7] Ziegler bases this conclusion partly on (1) the research of James S. Coleman, which indicated that school quality and individual achievement are essentially unrelated; (2) the research of Christopher Jencks, who stated that school reform "cannot bring about significant social changes outside the schools"; and (3) the research of Raymond Bouden, who concluded that "educational growth as such has the effect of increasing rather than decreasing social and economic inequality, even in the case of an educational system that becomes more equalitarian."[8] In effect, the goal of phase 3, the nationalization of education, will not be attained in phase 4, identified with education and the social goal.

While the federal government clearly strongly encouraged, and in some instances mandated, social changes such as affirmative action, desegregation, and the rights of women and the handicapped from the early 1950s to the early 1980s, there is some evidence that economic considerations may play a more dominant role in the immediate future. Greater federal attention is likely to be given to the relationship of education both to domestic economics and to the role of the United States in worldwide economic competition.

Local control still exists but in a limited fashion. It has eroded considerably since the early 1900s. Court decisions and mandates by the state and federal governments, along with categorical financial aid, have contributed to its erosion. The strength of teachers' unions through collective bargaining has also been a factor in the weakening of local control. But erosion of local control is not necessarily a setback. For example, issues such as due process, free speech, and equality of opportunity would probably not have been addressed at the local level. Nor would actions have been taken at the local level to ensure that citizens would receive the rights granted to them by the U.S. Constitution, because they refer to life in general and to education.

Summary and Implications

Federal, state, and local governments all have a part in education. The federal government has an *interest* in education, which is a state *function* and a local *operation*. Each level of government has a purpose to be accomplished through education. The emphasis at each level has depended on the perspective at that level. Local school districts are concerned with immediate local educational needs; states with promoting the welfare of the state and ensuring children equal educational opportunities within the state; and the federal government with our national security, equality of opportunities, and solving national domestic problems. If local districts could and would completely meet all the needs of education—as the states and the federal government see them—then state and federal involvement would not be necessary. Federal and state involvement does seem necessary, however, so that each individual will have the right to an equal opportunity to pursue excellence in education and to achieve personal dignity. It seems likely that American public education will continue to be a local, state, and federal concern.

Knowing about the formal organization of schools and the political arena in which they operate is important to those who work in schools. From initial certification, throughout daily and yearly work, and finally during retirement, teachers are affected by state regulations. Teacher organizations (NEA, AFT) are very active politically; as members of these organizations, teachers are expected to participate.

Teachers have influenced American education at local, state, and national levels and will continue to do so. At the local level influence comes through teaching in classrooms and through interacting with the community and the board of education. The state and national teachers' organizations gain their strength at the local level. If teachers really know how education is organized at the local level, they have an invaluable tool in shaping and working toward the goals of American education. They can then also advance the goals of the teaching profession and its members.

A knowledge of the state and national organization of education is also essential. Through political action at these levels, legislation affecting education and the teaching profession at all levels is developed. Teachers' organizations are active at the state and national levels. Members of teacher organizations who are informed about educational politics can be effective participants in determining the future of American education and the teaching profession.

Discussion Questions

1. Why does the federal government become involved in elementary and secondary education?
2. What do you think an appropriate role for the federal government should be with respect to elementary and secondary education?
3. What are the functions of state legislature in public education in the United States?
4. What are the functions of state departments of education?
5. What are the advantages and disadvantages of choosing the chief state school officers by election? By a state board of education?
6. What are the functions of local boards of education?
7. How has the local control of education eroded? Why has it eroded?
8. How can teachers affect the operations of local school districts?
9. What are the advantages and disadvantages of school consolidation?
10. What are the major functions of intermediate units?

Supplemental Activities

1. Visit a meeting of a local board of education and write a critique of the meeting.
2. Examine and discuss educational bills considered by a recent session of a state legislature.

3. Examine policy manuals from local school districts in your area, looking particularly for policies that affect what you do as a classroom teacher and policies that deal specifically with student rights.
4. Interview one or more school administrators and ask them about the responsibilities and duties of their position.
5. Interview officers of local teachers' associations and ask them how they think they influence local educational policy.

Notes

1. Valena White Plisko and Joyce D. Stern, eds., *The Condition of Education 1985 Edition* (Washington, D.C.: National Center for Educational Statistics), pp. 3–7.
2. Edgar L. Morphet, Roe L. Johns, and Theordore L. Reller, *Educational Organization and Administration: Concepts, Practices and Issues,* 3rd ed. (Englewood Cliffs, N.J.: Prentice-Hall, 1974), p. 264.
3. Ronald F. Campbell, ed., Gerald E. Stroufe, and Donald H. Layton, *Strengthening State Departments of Education* (Chicago: University of Chicago Midwest Administration, 1967), p. 10.
4. Robert Stephens, *Regional Educational Service Agencies* (Arlington, Va.: Educational Research Services, 1975).
5. Jonathan P. Sher and Rachel B. Tompkins, *Economy, Efficiency and Equality: The Myths of Rural School and District Consolidation* (Washington, D.C.: National Institute of Education, U.S. Department of Health, Education, and Welfare, 1976), pp. 4–36, 40–41.
6. L. Harmon Ziegler, Harvey J. Tucker, and L. A. Wilson, "How School Control Was Wrested from the People," *Phi Delta Kappan,* 58 (March 1977): 534–539.
7. Ibid., 539.
8. Ibid.

Bibliography

Bakalis, Michael J. "Power and Purpose in American Education." *Phi Delta Kappan,* 65 (September 1983): 7–13.

Barnett, Bruce, and Young, Claudia. "Peer-Assisted Leadership: Principals Learning from Each Other." *Phi Delta Kappan,* 67 (May 1986): 672–675.

Glenn, Charles L. "Textbook Controversies: A Disaster for Public Schools?" *Phi Delta Kappan,* 68 (February 1987): 451–455.

Guthrie, James W. "School-Based Management: The Next Needed School Reform." *Phi Delta Kappan,* 68 (December 1986): 305–309.

Hoy, Wayne K., and Miskel, Cecil. *Educational Administration: Theory, Research, and Practice.* New York: Random House, 1985.

Keefe, James W., and Jenkins, John M. *Instructional Leadership Handbook.* Reston, Va.: National Association of Secondary School Principals, 1984.

Monahan, William G., and Hengst, Herbert R. *Contemporary Educational Administration.* New York: Macmillan, 1982.

Park, J. Charles. "Preachers, Politics, and Public Education: A Review of Right-Wing Pressures Against Public Schooling in America." *Phi Delta Kappan,* 61 (May 1980): 608–611.

Sergiovanni, Thomas J., Burlingame, Martin, Combs, Fred, and Thurston, Paul. *Educational Governance and Administration.* Englewood Cliffs, N.J.: Prentice-Hall, 1980.

Woodring, Paul. *The Persistent Problems of Education.* Bloomington, Ind.: *Phi Delta Kappan,* 1983.

=== 11 ===

Financing Public Education

Focus Questions

- Why should you as a future teacher know about how money is raised to support public schools?
- Why should it make any difference to you or the teaching profession if the expenditures per pupil differ widely from district to district and from state to state?
- Why should you be concerned about the effects of various kinds of taxes on taxpayers and the effectiveness of various kinds of taxes in producing money to operate schools?
- Do you know how states try to make certain that there is enough money provided for a basic education irrespective of the wealth of a particular school district?
- As a future teacher, do you think schools should be held fully accountable for student achievement? Why? Why not?
- Do you think students should be able to attend any school of their choice? Why? Why not?

Key Terms and Concepts

Property taxes
Planned-program budgeting
Regressive tax
State aid
Categorical aid
Foundation level
Fiscal equalization
Tax effort

Federal aid
Equality of opportunity
Equitable taxation
Accountability
Educational vouchers
Progressive tax
Proportionate tax

What Would You Do?

The school district by which you are employed is in critical financial condition. It needs a tax referendum in order to become financially solvent. The teachers employed by the district recently went on strike, admitting publicly that they realized the poor financial condition of the school district. You were a member of the striking group. The strike ended, but the teachers were not satisfied with the settlement. The school district has now announced that it plans a tax referendum. Some members of the community plan to work to defeat the referendum because "the school board will use the funds to pay the salary demands of the strikers." Your local professional association is trying to decide whether or not to work for the passage of the referendum. What would be your position on this matter? Why?

In the first few weeks of teaching second grade you feel that the instructional supplies that you have are not adequate for meeting the needs of your students. In conversations with other second grade teachers in your attendance center, you learn that they have substantially more supplies for their students than you have for your students. The number of students in their respective classes is essentially the same as you have in your class. How are you going to try to obtain adequate supplies?

A basic goal of public education is to provide an adequate education that is equally available to everyone—equality of opportunity. To achieve that goal, government must design a system of taxation that is equitable—fair to taxpayers. The United States has not yet met the goal nor achieved equitable taxation, although progress has been made toward the goal and toward equitable taxation.

Money to support education comes from a variety of taxes paid to local, state, and federal governments. These governments in turn distribute tax money to local school districts to operate the schools. The three principal kinds of taxes that provide revenue for schools are property taxes, sales or use taxes, and income taxes. The property tax is generally a local tax, and the sales tax a state tax; the income tax may be both a state tax and a federal one.

Table 11.1 portrays the percentages of revenue received nationwide from federal, state, and local sources over a period of years. Table 11.2 shows similar data for selected states. The trends are toward decreasing federal and local sources of revenue and toward increasing state revenue.

This chapter analyzes the different kinds of taxes in terms of equality of educational opportunity and taxpayer equity. It also addresses other issues directly related to funding for schools, including increasing enrollments, taxpayer revolt, financing educational reform, accountability, and educational vouchers.

Property Taxes—Local Revenue

The property tax is the primary source of local revenue for schools. It is based on the value of property, both real estate and personal. Real estate includes land holdings and buildings like homes, commercial buildings, and factories. Personal property consists of automobiles, machinery, furniture, livestock, and intangible property such as stocks and bonds. The property tax has both advantages and limitations. It does, however, on the average provide about 45 percent of local school revenues.

In addition to receiving revenues, school districts also spend money. A school district budget includes anticipated revenues and expenditures. A school district budget can be conceived as the educational program expressed in dollars and cents.

Property Taxes: Advantages and Limitations

The main advantage of the property tax is its stability. Although it lags behind other changes in market values, it provides a steady, regular income. Also, property is fixed; that is, it is not easily moved to escape taxation, as income might be.

The property tax has numerous limitations. It bears heavily on housing; it

TABLE 11.1 *Percentages of Revenue Received from Federal, State, and Local Sources for Public Elementary and Secondary Schools for Selected Years*

School Year	Percentage of Revenue		
	Federal	*State*	*Local*
1919–1920	0.3	16.5	83.2
1929–1930	0.4	16.9	82.7
1939–1940	1.8	30.3	68.0
1949–1950	2.9	39.8	57.3
1955–1956	4.6	39.5	55.9
1957–1958	4.0	39.4	56.6
1959–1960	4.4	39.1	56.5
1961–1962	4.3	38.7	56.9
1963–1964	4.4	39.3	56.3
1965–1966	7.9	39.1	53.0
1967–1968	8.8	38.5	52.7
1969–1970	8.0	39.9	52.1
1975–1976	8.9	41.6	46.5
1976–1977	8.8	43.4	47.8
1977–1978	9.4	43.0	47.6
1978–1979	9.8	45.6	44.6
1979–1980	9.8	46.8	43.4
1980–1981	9.2	47.4	43.4
1981–1982	7.4	47.6	45.0
1982–1983	7.1	48.3	44.6
1983–1984 (estimated)	7.1	48.5	44.4
1984–1985 (estimated)	7.0	48.7	44.3
1985–1986 (estimated)	6.9	48.8	44.3

Source: W. Vance Grant and Thomas D. Snyder, *Digest of Education Statistics, 1985–86* (Washington, D.C.: National Center for Education Statistics), p. 80.
Note: Years in which there were little or no changes are deleted, except in later years, 1975 to present.

tends to discourage rehabilitation and upkeep, since both of these would tend to raise the value of the property and therefore its taxes; it is often a deciding factor in locating a business or industry; and it is not likely to be applied equally on all properties.

A difficulty with the property tax lies in determining the value of property. In some areas assessors are local people, frequently elected, with no special training in evaluating property. Their duty involves inspecting their neighbors' properties and placing values upon them. In other areas sophisticated techniques involving expertly trained personnel are used for property appraisal. In any event, assessors are likely to be subject to political and informal pressures to keep values low. Appraisals generally take into account the location, area, and

TABLE 11.2 *Receipts of Public Elementary and Secondary Schools by Source and by State for Selected States, Including the District of Columbia*

State	Percent of Receipts		
	Local	*State*	*Federal*
District of Columbia	86.9	—	13.1
New Hampshire	86.5	8.6	4.9
Wyoming	68.1	28.8	3.1
Nebraska	66.6	27.1	6.2
Oregon	63.1	31.0	5.9
Colorado	55.2	40.3	4.5
Minnesota	50.0	45.2	4.8
United States (average)	44.6	48.3	7.1
Alabama	24.9	63.0	12.1
Mississippi	23.5	59.0	17.5
California	23.1	68.1	8.8
Washington	19.0	74.8	6.2
New Mexico	12.8	74.8	12.4
Alaska	14.3	78.0	7.7
Hawaii	0.1	87.9	11.9

Source: W. Vance Grant and Thomas D. Snyder, *Digest of Education Statistics, 1985–86* (Washington, D.C.: National Center for Education Statistics), p. 81.

use of the property. Homes are judged by the number of rooms, facilities, type of foundation, building materials, and landscaping. In some areas photographs of real estate are used for comparative purposes. Similar comparative scales are used to evaluate industrial and farm property. The value of real property is reviewed at regular intervals, frequently every four years, in an attempt to establish its current market value.

The assessed value of property is usually only a percentage of its market value. This percentage varies from county to county and from state to state. Attempts are made within states to equalize assessments or to make certain that the same percentage of full cash value is used in assessing property throughout the state. In recent years attempts have been made to institute full cash value for the assessed value. For the property tax to be a fair tax, equalized assessment is a necessity.

The property tax is most generally thought of as a proportionate tax—that is, one that taxes according to ability to pay. Since assessments may be unequal and since frequently the greatest wealth is no longer related to real estate, the property tax can be regressive. Regressive taxes, like sales and use taxes, are those that affect low-income groups disproportionately. There is some evidence to support the contention that persons in the lowest-income groups pay a much higher proportion of their income in property taxes than persons in the highest-income groups.

Inequities of the Property Tax

Significant support for schools across the nation is provided by the property tax. The total value of property within a school district when related to its number of pupils is an indicator of the wealth of a school district. A school district having an assessed valuation of $30 million, for example, and responsibility for educating 1,000 pupils would have $30,000 of assessed valuation per pupil. Usually, the number of pupils in average daily attendance is used as a divisor to determine assessed valuation per pupil. Since property tax rates are applied to assessed valuations, a district with a high assessed valuation per pupil is in a better position to provide quality education than one with a low assessed valuation per pupil.

Per-pupil expenditures can vary greatly, depending on a district's tax rate and its overall wealth. How can we ensure that *all* schools—not just those in wealthy communities—are adequately funded so that equal educational opportunities exist for all children? (*Source:* David S. Strickler/The Picture Cube)

If school district A has an assessed valuation of $90 million and 1,000 pupils, for example, and school district B has an assessed valuation of $30 million and 1,000 pupils, a tax rate of $2 per $100 of assessed valuation would produce $1.8 million for education in district A and only $600,000 in district B. School district A could therefore spend $1,800 per pupil, compared with $600 per pupil in school district B, with the same local tax effort.

Great differences exist in wealth per pupil from school district to school district. Concentrations of industrial developments increase valuation in one district, while a neighboring district may be almost completely residential with low valuation and many pupils.

Differences in wealth and concomitant differences in tax rates and per-pupil expenditures were most dramatically pointed out in the *Serrano* v. *Priest* (1971) decision of the Supreme Court of California.

In *Serrano* v. *Priest* the California Supreme Court was called upon to determine whether the California public school financing system, with its substantial dependence on local property taxes, violated the Fourteenth Amendment. In a six-to-one decision in August 1971 the court held that heavy reliance on unequal local property taxes "makes the quality of a child's education a function of the wealth of his parents and neighbors." Furthermore, the court declared: "Districts with small tax bases simply cannot levy taxes at a rate sufficient to produce the revenue that more affluent districts produce with a minimum effort."

At the time of the *Serrano* v. *Priest* decision the Baldwin Park school district, for example, spent $577 per pupil, whereas the Beverly Hills school district spent $1,232. Yet the tax rate in Baldwin Park of $5.48 was more than double the rate of $2.38 in Beverly Hills. The discrepancy was caused by the difference in wealth between the two districts. Beverly Hills had $50,885 of assessed valuation per child; Baldwin Park had only $3,706 valuation per child—a ratio of thirteen to one. The inequities resulting from the property tax are at least twofold: The tax is oftentimes inequitably applied to the taxpayer, and in poor districts the tax frequently results in unequal opportunities for education.

Officially, the California court ruled that the system of school financing in California was unconstitutional but did not forbid the use of property taxes. Within a year of *Serrano* v. *Priest* (1971) five other courts—in Minnesota, Texas, New Jersey, Wyoming, and Arizona—ruled similarly.

In 1973 the U.S. Supreme Court consented to hear an appeal of the *San Antonio* (Texas) *Independent School District* v. *Rodriguez* case. The elements in that case were like those of the *Serrano* v. *Priest* case. The U.S. Supreme Court, in a five-to-four decision, reversed the lower court in *San Antonio Independent School District* v. *Rodriguez* and thus reaffirmed the local property tax as a basis for school financing. Justice Potter Stewart, voting with the majority, admitted that "the method of financing public schools . . . can be fairly described as chaotic and unjust." He did not, though, find it unconstitutional. The majority opinion, written by Justice Lewis F. Powell, stated: "We cannot say that such disparities are the product of a system that is so irrational as to be invidiously discriminatory." The opinion also noted that the poor are not necessarily concentrated in the poorest districts, that states must initiate fundamental reform in taxation and education, and that the extent to which quality of education varies with expenditures is inconclusive. Justice Thurgood Marshall, in the dissenting opinion, charged that the ruling "is a retreat from our historic commitment to equality of educational opportunity."

Before the *San Antonio Independent School District* v. *Rodriguez* (1973) decision, but after *Serrano* v. *Priest* (1971), the National Legislative Conference Special Commission on School Finance recommended that "states should assume responsibility for seeing that elementary and secondary schools are funded properly, and that 'equal opportunity' responsibility enunciated in *Serrano* v. *Priest* (1971) be accepted, regardless of the courts, because the Serrano principle is right.[1] Since *Rodriguez,* eleven state supreme trial courts have struck down school finance systems. Those decisions were in the states of Arkansas, California, Colorado, Connecticut, Georgia, Idaho, Maryland, New York, Ohio, Washington, and West Virginia.[2] Within nine months of *Serrano* v. *Priest* 99 commissions or committees were organized to study the school finance systems of the 50 states.[3] Undoubtedly, changes are occurring in the state provisions for financial support for education. Equal expenditures per pupil may not, because of other factors, assure equal opportunity, but equal expenditures per pupil do, in fact, enhance the likelihood of equal opportunity.

The property tax is only one part of the comprehensive tax system. Local financial procedures and state and federal efforts in school finance also enter the picture.

Local Planning and Budgeting

The property tax rate of a school district is determined from the monetary needs of the district as expressed in its budget. A budget encompasses the financial plan of the school district. It can be conceived of as the educational program of the school district expressed in dollars and cents. Usually, budgets are prepared on an annual basis and project the income and educational costs for a year. States generally prescribe forms and procedures to be used in preparing, administering, and adopting the school budget.

The superintendent of schools, frequently helped by a staff, usually prepares the budget. In many districts the first step is for teachers to submit budgetary requests. Usually, the school board must act officially to approve the budget and finally to adopt it. In some states, school budgets must be approved by the state. In many states a public hearing is required before the school budget can be adopted.

The classification of budgetary expenditures has been standardized largely through the efforts of the former U.S. Office of Education. Educational expenditures are classified under three headings: capital outlay, debt service, and current expenses. Capital outlay includes expenditures for land, buildings, and equipment; debt service includes the repayment of borrowed money and the interest on the debt; and current expense includes the expenditures necessary for daily operation and maintenance. The largest category of current educational expense is instructional expenses, which include teachers' salaries and fringe benefits. This amount frequently exceeds 70 to 85 percent of the total budget. The budget, in its final form, expresses the amount of money needed for operating the school system; hence the budget determines the tax rate.

Planned-program budgeting seeks to classify expenditures by school program rather than by the traditional categories—salaries, instructional materials, and administration. A program budget, for example, would project expenditures for categories such as the elementary school reading program, the high school mathematics program, or the vocational educational program. School districts under program budgeting need to identify their programs and keep their records accordingly. An important advantage of program budgeting is accountability— the relationships between educational cost and educational accomplishment become clarified. In an accountability approach educational records of program accomplishment can be compared with the costs of the program. (Accountability is discussed more fully later in this chapter.)

The states usually grant by law a minimum property tax rate to cover current expenditures for local school districts. Frequently, increases in tax rate limits require voter approval. In some states there is no state limit on the school tax rate; with local approval the rate can be raised as high as desired. In other states the state establishes a maximum limit by law that cannot be exceeded, even with local approval. This maximum limit is often reached step by step with voter approval.

States usually limit how much capital outlay indebtedness a school district may incur. These limits are established in various ways. In some states the limit is an established percentage of assessed valuation; 5 to 10 percent is common. In other states no limits are set, but the legislature or the state office of public instruction must approve the indebtedness.

Limited tax rates for current expenses and limitations on indebtedness point out further the significance of assessed valuation as a factor in determining the quality of an educational program. A local school district can be making the maximum effort, taxing to the limit, and still not be able to offer a program comparable to what a wealthier neighboring district offers under a medium effort. The effort made by a local school district indicates the value that the citizens place on education; yet equal effort does not produce equal revenue, equal expenditures per pupil, or equal opportunity.

Expenditures per pupil vary widely, partly because the districts are not equally wealthy. States also differ in wealth and correspondingly in expenditures per pupil. The current average annual expenditure per pupil in the United States is $2,843. Alaska, Wyoming, and New Jersey, along with the Federal District of Columbia, all spend over $3,500 per pupil; Arkansas, Kentucky, Mississippi, South Carolina, Tennessee, and Utah all spend less than $2,000 per pupil.[4]

Property assessment practices differ from state to state; hence one cannot use assessed valuation per pupil as a measure in comparing the wealth of states. A more accurate index is personal income per capita. States with per capita personal income greater than $14,000 include Alaska, California, Connecticut,

Federal District of Columbia, New Jersey, Massachusetts, Maryland, and New York; Alabama, Arkansas, Mississippi, Utah, and West Virginia all have per capita personal incomes lower than $9,000.[5] In general, higher per capita personal income results in higher expenditures per pupil.

State Sources of Revenue

The main sources of tax revenue for states have been classified by the Department of Commerce in four groups: sales and gross receipts, income taxes, licenses, and miscellaneous. Sales and gross receipt taxes include taxes on general sales, motor fuels, alcohol, insurance, and amusements; income taxes include both individual and corporate; licenses include those on motor vehicles, corporations, occupations, vehicle operators, hunting, and fishing. The largest miscellaneous classification includes property taxes, severance or extraction of minerals taxes, and death and gift taxes. The two largest sources of state revenues are sales and income taxes.

On the average in the United States, the states provide about 48 percent of the fiscal resources for local schools. This money is referred to as state aid, and in most states all of the money or a portion of this money is used to help achieve equality of opportunity within a state.

Sales and Income Taxes

Sales and income taxes are lucrative sources of state revenue, and it is relatively easy to administer both. The sales tax is collected bit by bit, in a relatively painless way, by the vendor, who is responsible for keeping records. The state income tax can be withheld from wages; hence collection is eased. Some argue that this tax meets the criterion of a "good" tax because it is closely related to the ability to pay. Income taxes are referred to as progressive taxes, since they frequently are scaled to the ability of the taxpayer to pay. Sales taxes are "regressive," since they affect low-income groups disproportionately. All persons pay the sales tax at the same rate, so persons in low-income groups pay as much tax as persons in high-income groups. Part of the regression of the sales tax can be overcome by exempting food from taxation. Both sales taxes and income taxes are direct and certain; they fluctuate with the economy, and they can be regulated by the legislature that must raise the money.

State Aid

State aid to local school districts is paid out of tax revenue raised by the state; it is complicated and varies considerably among states. State aid for education exists largely for three reasons: The state has the primary responsibility for educating its citizens, the financial ability of local school districts to support education varies widely, and personal wealth is now less related to real property than it once was. We have already examined the first two reasons. The third reason relates to the property tax—the main source of local income for school districts. Since much individual wealth is not real property and since it seems reasonable that taxation should be based on ability to pay, then apparently the local property tax has serious limitations as a source of school funds. The progressive income tax seems more equitable; money so collected could be proportionately redistributed or shared by local school districts and also used to provide financial equalization for education.

State aid can be classified as having *general* or *categorical* use. General aid can be used by the recipient school district as it desires; categorical aid is earmarked for specific purposes. Categorical aid, for example, may include money for transportation, vocational education, driver education, and handicapped children. Frequently, categorical aid is given to encourage specified educational programs; in some states these aid programs are referred to as incentive programs. Categorical aid funds may be granted on a matching basis; thus for each dollar of local effort, the state contributes a specified amount. Categorical aid has undoubtedly encouraged needed educational programs.

Historically, general aid was based on the idea that each child, regardless of place of residence or wealth of the local district, should be entitled to receive a basic education. General state aid was established on the principle of equality of opportunity and is usually administered through a foundation program. A foundation program includes determining the dollar value of the basic educational opportunities desired in a state, referred to as the foundation level; determining a minimum standard of local effort; and determining an equitable way of distributing the money to school districts, considering their local wealth. The foundation concept implies equity for taxpayers as well as equality of opportunity for students.

Figure 11.1 represents graphically how a foundation program operates. The total length of each bar represents the foundation level of education required per pupil, expressed in dollars. Each school district must put forth the same minimum local effort to finance its schools; this effort could be a qualifying tax rate that produces the local share of the foundation level. This tax rate will produce more revenue in a wealthy district than it will in a poor district; therefore poor districts will receive more state aid than wealthy districts. Local school districts do not receive general state aid beyond that amount established as the foundation but are permitted in most instances to exceed foundation levels at their own expense.

The effectiveness of the use of various state foundation programs to achieve fiscal equalization has been limited. A major limitation is that the foundation established is frequently far below the actual expenditure or far below the level needed to provide adequate educational opportunity. For example, if a state established a per-pupil foundation level of $1,500 and the average per-pupil expenditure was $3,000, equalization would not have occurred.

A second limitation is that most general state aid programs do not provide for the different expenditure levels for different pupil needs. Special education and vocational education, for example, both require more money to operate than the usual per-pupil expenditure for the typical elementary or secondary

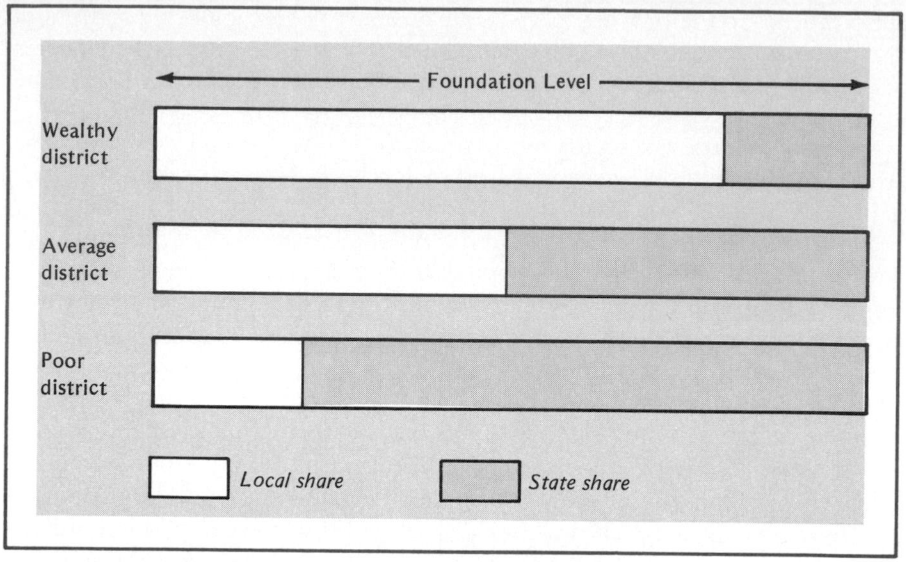

FIGURE 11.1 *Equalization and the Foundation Principle*

school pupil. These weaknesses and others—including the taxing inequities—have brought about strong and determined research efforts to find a more satisfactory and acceptable system for financing American education.

The method of distributing state aid differs from state to state. The percentage of current expenditures paid by state aid also differs from state to state, as does the ability of states to support schools.

In summary, the property tax is the largest local revenue source, and sales and income taxes are the largest state revenue sources. State taxes may be used to equalize opportunity resulting from unequal local tax bases. Raising local, state, and federal funds to support education by various kinds of taxation necessitates a tax system. We should look at each type of tax as a part of a system. Each individual kind of tax has its advantages and disadvantages, yet it is unlikely that any one of these taxes used by itself for education will be the answer. In evaluating a system of taxes, one should consider the varying ability of citizens to pay, economic effects of the taxes on the taxpayer, benefits that various taxpayers receive, total yield of the tax, economy of collection, degree of acceptance, convenience of paying, problems of tax evasion, stability of the tax, and the general adaptability of the system. It soon becomes apparent that systems of taxation are complicated—each is an intricately interdependent network.

Taxation exists to produce revenue. The allocation of revenue is complex; however, the educational theme applied to allocation is equality of educational opportunity. State equalization programs were designed to accomplish this objective, and although they have had some successes, these successes have been limited. Many people have suggested that the logical solution to the inequities that exist in the ability of states to support education is federal aid.

Become knowledgeable about educational fiscal affairs.
Use your knowledge of fiscal affairs to the benefit of education.
Work with colleagues toward equal opportunity in education.

Federal Aid

The United States has a history of federal aid to education, but it has been categorical and not general aid; it has been related to the needs of the nation at the time. Federal aid actually started with the Ordinance of 1785, before the U.S. Constitution was adopted, which provided land for public schools in "Western territories." Such federal aid has continued in a steady progression to the present. Almost 200 federal aid-to-education laws have been passed since the Northwest Ordinance. The Elementary and Secondary Education Act of 1965 has been discussed elsewhere in this book. Nevertheless, we note here one significant part of the act: It was categorical, yet it came as close to general aid to education as federal aid ever has and therefore established a precedent for ways that federal aid can be used.

Educational Improvement and Consolidation ACT (EICA)

Federal funding in recent years continued to be categorical until the passage of the Educational Improvement and Consolidation Act (EICA) in 1981. The act consolidated 28 separate federally sponsored educational programs into one block grant. Left out of the act were education for the handicapped; vocational, bilingual, and adult education; impact aid; ESEA Title IV civil rights programs; and the Women's Educational Equity program. ESEA Title I programs for the disadvantaged were kept as the first title of the new consolidation act. Title II of the act consolidated the aforementioned 28 programs, providing greater discretion for state and local educational agencies as to the use of the money. Block grants are viewed by many as a threat to tightly targeted categorical programs, historically designed to provide educational assistance related to the achievement of important national goals. The trend toward block grants is an early indication of possible transformation of the federal role in education.[6]

Federal Aid: The Controversy

Federal aid, while seemingly historically established, is still controversial. Advocates of federal aid point out that it is a logical answer to providing equality of educational opportunity for all children regardless of residence. They point out that federal aid to education helps the national defense and general welfare ultimately and that these national concerns cannot be adequately pursued at a local or state level. Proponents of federal aid to education hold also that this help does not necessarily mean federal controls, citing the land grant acts and the National Defense Education Act of 1958 as federal aid that was not accompanied by control. They feel that federal aid, through the income tax, is the most equitable way of paying for public education. Opponents of federal aid point out that education is a state and a local function. They argue that variations in fiscal ability to pay will always exist and that the distribution of federal funds will not guarantee that whatever differences now exist will be reduced appreciably. They point out that the nation is weakened by depending on the federal government for funds, that categorical aid is federal control, and that states can use the income tax as effectively as the federal government.

Despite these arguments the federal government will probably continue some financial support to American education. Interrelated domestic, social, and economic problems of national magnitude must be resolved; for financial and other reasons these problems have not been solved, and probably could not be, at local or state levels. The federal government has access to funds through the most equitable kind of tax—the progressive income tax, both personal and corporate. Personal and corporate income taxes now account for most of the national income; yet public schools in the main are still relatively heavily supported by local revenue generated by the property tax, which is less related to people's ability to pay. The inequality of the tax base among the states could be adjusted through federal aid; and certainly the quality of educational opportunity is related to how well states can support education. The principle of local support for education served well for many years; then, because of unequal tax bases, local communities needed the help of the state. Although average state support nationwide has increased to approximately 48 percent, further increases are likely to be difficult to secure. There is still a fiscal role for the federal government in education.

Clearly, the current system of school financing—with its relatively heavy reliance on local support gained from the local property tax—cannot realize equality of educational opportunity. Furthermore, the property tax itself in today's economy tends to be a regressive and unfair tax. State equalization programs have not been successful in securing equality of opportunity, although effective steps have recently been taken in some states. The federal effort has been feeble in terms of the total educational expenditure, contributing only abut 9.8 percent at its peak in 1979. The question that remains debatable is what the appropriate fiscal role of the federal government in education should be.

[40]

School Finance Issues: 1990s

The basic issue in school financing is not likely to be different in the 1990s from what it has been in the past. That issue is making an adequate education equally available to everyone, along with a system of taxation designed to be equitable— that is, a system in which taxpayers are all called upon to support education in proportion to their ability to pay, a progressive tax plan. Both equal opportunity and equitable taxation are difficult to achieve, as illustrated earlier in this chapter.

Some trends of the late 1980s may continue into the 1990s. Those trends include increasing enrollments, taxpayer revolt, inflation, and financing educational reform, which are likely to affect the adequacy of school funding and therefore further complicate the basic issue in school finance—providing an adequate education with equality of opportunity through an equitable system of taxation.

Increasing Enrollments

Enrollment in elementary and secondary schools grew rapidly during the 1950s and 1960s and reached its peak in 1971. From 1971 to 1983, total enrollment decreased rapidly, reflecting the decline in the school-age population over that period. Enrollment reached its low of 44.6 million in 1984. By 1993 total enrollment is predicted to be 47.9 million, an increase of 3.3 million, 7 percent over 1984.[7]

Increased enrollments have effects on the amount of money needed to adequately support education. During the decline teaching staffs were reduced and retiring personnel were not replaced in many school districts. Nevertheless, in general, expenditures were not reduced, primarily because of inflation. The new surge of students between 1985 and 1993, while it will be somewhat gradual, will undoubtedly increase expenditures. Increased revenue is very likely to be needed to maintain the current level of expenditures per pupil. Furthermore, according to one educator, "the rising public school enrollments will include larger numbers and percentages of minority, limited-English-proficient, poor and learning disabled students. All these special categories of students will require extra services to meet their needs."[8] Whether additional revenues will be available to provide educational services to the growing student population remains speculative.

Taxpayer Revolt

A most dramatic instance of taxpayer revolt occurred in California in June 1978 with the passage of Proposition 13, which limited by constitutional amendment the property tax as a source of revenue. Subsequent and similar propositions in other states in 1978 were not successful. Nevertheless, those efforts, along with a low rate of successful tax increase referenda nationally and the closing of school districts for periods of time because of insufficient funds to operate, indicated problems for the future funding of public schools.

Proposition 13 set a maximum tax of 1 percent on the fair market value of property, limited assessment growth to 2 percent per year, and required the state legislature to have at least a two-thirds vote to substitute new taxes for lost local revenues. Proposition2½, passed in Massachusetts in November 1980, proposed that no city or town be allowed to levy property taxes in excess of 2½ percent of the total evaluation. Furthermore, if a community taxed above this rate, Proposition 2½ called for a reduction in local property taxes by 15 percent each year until the tax floor was reached.[9] Proposition 2½ became effective on July 1, 1981. Other states have also placed constitutional or statutory limits on taxation or spending.

Proposition 2-1/2, passed by Massachusetts voters in 1980, severely limited property taxes, a major source of revenue for public schools. (*Source:* Sandra Johnson/The Picture Cube)

Property tax limitation amendments in California (Proposition 13, 1978), in Massachusetts (Proposition 2½, 1981), and in other states have had adverse effects on the services that local government agencies, including school boards, can provide. Community and educational services were cut, and alternative revenue sources, such as fees and other charges, were enacted. Some school districts filed for bankruptcy. The effect of the tax limitations was differential; that is, some localities and school districts were more adversely affected than others.[10] However, we note that during the years 1978–1983 the nation first experienced high inflation and then a recession, both of which had the effect of reducing fiscal resources for schools. Also, 30 states increased their taxes in 1983, primarily on the basis of a weakening economy.[11]

Taxpayer revolt continues to be an issue. In the fall 1986 elections twelve states had propositions dealing with school finance. There were five states with propositions which would establish state lotteries to raise funds for government agencies, which would be likely to include education. The voters in Florida, Idaho, Montana, and South Dakota approved the establishment of state lotteries. The voters of North Dakota did not approve a state lottery.[12]

States which had propositions that would limit taxation if approved were California, Colorado, Massachusetts, Oregon, and Montana. They were denied in Oregon, Colorado, and Montana. Montana had three propositions dealing with school finance. States which had propositions that would enhance funding were Arizona, California, Mississippi, and West Virginia. All were approved except the one in West Virginia.[13] In effect, in six propositions three resulted in raising taxes and three resulted in not placing limits on taxes. In four propositions one proposition to raise taxes was defeated and three limitations were passed. The trend in this small sample of twelve states is slightly toward approving more taxes and not approving limitations on taxation.

The Tax Reform Act of 1986 may have a negative effect on funding for schools. Effective in 1987 the act does not allow for the deduction of state and local sales taxes. Prior to the act individuals who itemized their deductions could recoup part of what they paid in state and local sales taxes. The sales tax in many states has been a popular way of increasing taxes. Governors and other state officials fear that taxpayers, because of the tax revision, will be more reluctant to support existing sales taxes or to approve increases in sales taxes. Thus taxpayer revolt may be stimulated by the Tax Reform Act of 1986.

Inflation

Inflation, which increased rapidly in the late 1970s and early 1980s, affected every person and every institution. In the case of public schools revenue simply did not keep up with expenses. The greatest effects of inflation on public schools were the dramatically increasing costs of energy and salaries. But taxpayers could not understand and accept the fact that the cost of education was increasing while enrollments were declining. Inflation was the culprit. In 1983 and 1984 the rate of inflation was reduced. Since then it has been relatively stable, ranging between about 2 percent and 4 percent annually. Nevertheless, whether inflation can be controlled is still not clear.

Financing Educational Reform

Estimates suggest that revenues would need to increase by at least 20 percent in order to pay for most of the proposed reforms. Yet from 1983 to 1985 expenditures per pupil, when adjusted for inflation, increased nationwide by only 7.2 percent. Federal funding over the same period dropped when adjusted for inflation; state and local funds, when adjusted for inflation, increased by 5.4 percent and 6.4 percent, respectively. Those increases, although encouraging, fall far short of the estimated 20 percent increase needed to fund educational reform.[14]

With enrollments increasing and with inflation, though modest, continuing to be a factor along with taxpayer revolt, strong increases in funding for educational reform in the late 1980s and the 1990s appear to be unlikely. On the positive side, if the economy gained in strength, more revenue from the increases might be possible. Some educators have also projected that the educational reform movement, if successful, has the potential to stimulate revenue increases:

> In my view, the crucial policy question for the next five years is whether the reform movement will maintain its momentum. If it does, then expenditures for education will outstrip inflation, and the underlying negative trends will remain in the background. However, if the public and key policymakers perceive that education reform has failed or has not been properly implemented, then a less favorable future is likely.[15]

The various components of educational reform need to be assessed and evaluated in terms of their effectiveness, particularly students' achievement. Assessment of educational reforms will be difficult because of the nature of reform and because of the many interacting variables. For example, is improved achievement the result of better teaching, more homework, or an improved curriculum? Many different types of assessment will have to be used. Nevertheless, the assessments and evaluations must be done and reported to the public. Accountability must prevail; in other words, the public needs to know which reform proposals didn't work and why they didn't, and which reform proposals are working and their cost-effectiveness. Cost-effectiveness, in general, is a measure of educational results and their respective costs. Assessments and evaluations, along with accountability, may fuel the momentum of reform and enhance the funding of reform.

Accountability and Educational Vouchers

Accountability and educational vouchers are topics that are directly related to financing education. Accountability was previously discussed as it related to educational reform. The point was made that the results of educational reform proposals must be assessed as to their educational effectiveness and those results be reported to the public along with their respective costs. The following discussion of accountability provides a somewhat different perspective, providing reinforcement of the concept, its history and application in schools, and its implications for classroom teachers.

The idea of using educational vouchers is not new, being first proposed in 1970. Essentially, vouchers provide funding, from taxes paid by the public, to the parents of public school students, elementary and secondary, to use to attend a school of their choice, public or private, secular or parochial. The concept of using educational vouchers is controversial, yet it appeared to be gaining support until 1986, when support declined by 5 percent since 1983.

Accountability

Schools in the 1990s will continue to be called upon to be accountable. Although there are many definitions of the term *accountability,* in education it means that schools must devise a way of relating the vast expenditure made for education to the educational results. For many years the quality of education was measured by the number of dollars spent or the processes of education used. In other words, a school system that had a relatively high cost per pupil or used educational techniques judged to be effective was considered an excellent school system. Seldom was the effectiveness of school systems judged by student outcomes—the educational achievements of their students. Now those achievements, and a clear record of the cost of them, must be accounted for.

Accountability has its roots in two fundamental modern problems. One is the continuous escalation of educational costs. Closely related is the loss of faith in educational results. The failure of the American educational system, particularly in the cities and in some remote rural areas, has been accurately documented. The expectations of citizens for their children have not been met. Although the American public schools historically have done the best job of any nation in the world in providing education for *all the children of all the people,* they still have failed for some of their constituents. Educational accountability is necessary. 39

When the Elementary and Secondary Education Act of 1965 went into effect, the federal government called for accountability; it asked to receive documented results of educational attainment. This was the first formal call for accountability.

How can school systems become accountable? First, they must specify goals. In other words, if one goal of an elementary school is "to have pupils learn to read," then this goal must be spelled out specifically for each grade or child, whichever makes better sense, and success in meeting the goal must be measured and reported. Only in this way can results be conveyed to the public. Some states are requiring a "school report card" to be submitted to the public annually. The report cards provide information about student achievement by subject, as measured by standardized tests, along with financial and other relevant data about the school district.

That many educational goals are not easily assessed should not prevent educators from dealing precisely with results that do lend themselves to objective measurement. When school systems can adequately report results with quantitative data, accountability will be possible.

Teachers should be aware that there are many factors over which they have little control that influence student achievement. Among them are the native intelligence of their students; the level of parental income, education, and interest in their children's education; home environment; type of family structure; and the amount of student mobility in the classroom. These factors and others must be allowed for in some fashion in order to be fair in judging teachers. Some school report cards provide the percentages of low-income and special education students, along with the percentage of student mobility. These factors represent aspects of fairness. We expect that the systems of measurement and reporting will improve, particularly in their fairness to students, teachers, and parents.

The second aspect, accounting for expenses related to educational results, is easier to achieve because of modern technology. Financial accounting systems that are designed specifically to record expenditures on each educational program can effectively reveal the costs of the educational results. When costs are known, one must measure them against what has been accomplished in performance. Advanced computer technology has increased the sophistication of accountability reporting systems; thus better-informed educational decisions are possible, and the way is cleared for regaining the public's confidence in the educational establishment.

Teachers play an important role in the quest for accountability. They are the primary contact with students. They are responsible for instruction and student achievement. Thus they are expected to do their utmost to cause students to learn and achieve. Accountability rests on data; therefore teachers need to keep accurate records in respect to achievement, particularly if standardized tests are not used to measure achievement.

Educational Vouchers

The underlying commitment of those advocating educational vouchers is to provide parents a choice of schools for their children to attend. Use of educational vouchers represents an attempt to reform education. Under a voucher system parents of all school-age children in a community are given vouchers roughly representing their children's share of the educational budget. A child then uses this voucher to attend any school he or she chooses, public or private, secular or parochial. Vouchers permit alternatives to the customary locked-in system of neighborhood education, wherein children proceed, usually without choice, from the neighborhood elementary school to junior and senior high schools, still in the same neighborhood. The rationale of the voucher system is that it causes schools to respond better to their constituencies in the face of competition. In a sense, public schools are monopolies; students cannot choose which school to attend.

Public schools do not function in a social milieu that inspires experimentation and responsiveness. They must, with rare exceptions, accept students assigned to them; the students in turn must attend these particular schools. In contrast, private schools select their students, and students, if they want and can afford private education, select their schools. The voucher plan tries to introduce the element of competition into public education; students choose the best school in the area, and the weaker schools, in theory, are forced to improve.

Voucher proposals that limit the use of the voucher to only public schools arouse less criticism than proposals that permit their use in both public or private schools. Proposals that limit the use of vouchers to within the school district that provides the vouchers are the most acceptable. The use of vouchers provided by public funds and used for private education provoke the greatest controversy. They are viewed by their critics as an inappropriate, if not illegal, diversion of public funds. Some see such a diversion as undermining public

Recognize the strong nationwide movement toward teacher accountability.
Do your utmost to cause your students to learn and achieve.
Keep accurate records of student achievement.

education. Others view the diversion of public money to private education as necessary to provide a choice and to promote competition among schools, using the assumption that the academically strong schools, public or private, will survive and the weak schools will either improve or be closed.

The idea of a voucher system has gained considerable support since it was first proposed in 1970. In 1970 a slightly higher percentage of those responding to the Gallup poll opposed the idea than favored it. By 1981 those in favor held a slight majority over those opposed. In 1983, when asked, "Would you like to see such an idea (voucher system) adopted in this country?" 51 percent favored the idea, and 38 percent were opposed. By 1986, 46 percent favored the idea, and 41 percent were opposed.[16]

Quite likely, the support for the voucher system and tuition tax credit is related to the public's dissatisfaction with the educational results of the public schools. Thus the improvement of this nation's public schools in the near future is vital.

Summary and Implications

Education is supported from a variety of taxes paid to local, state, and federal governments. The three principal kinds of taxes that provide revenue for the schools are property taxes, sales or use taxes, and income taxes. The property tax is generally a local tax, and the sales tax is a state tax; the income tax may be both a state tax and a federal tax. Historically, the property tax has provided the largest portion of local school income. State support has increased to the point that the nationwide average state share of support today is approximately 48 percent, with federal aid reaching a peak of 9.8 percent in 1979. The trend is toward increased state support and toward decreased local support along with a stable or decline in federal support.

State aid is based on the principle of equality of opportunity; that is, each child, regardless of place of residence or the wealth of the local school district, should be entitled to receive a basic education. There is wide variance in the financial capability of local school districts to support education. State aid is designed, in general, to equalize the amount of money available for education for each student in the state. Poor local school districts receive more money from the state than do wealthy ones.

The major challenge in financing schools is making an adequate education equally available to everyone and at the same time designing a system of taxation that is equitable—that is, a system in which taxpayers are all called upon to support education in proportion to their ability to pay. Accomplishing the goal of equality and equity is going to be increasingly difficult in the near future. Inflation, taxpayer revolt, increasing enrollments, and financing of educational reform are very likely to affect the adequacy of school funding. School districts may be expected to cut back expenditures and provide hard and convincing evidence that their students are receiving a sound basic education. Schools will continue to be expected to be accountable for student achievement and to be cost-effective. If educational vouchers are approved and implemented, some public money will be diverted to private schools.

With federal funding declining and likely to continue to do so, and with the difficulty of increasing local funding because of taxpayer revolt with or without state tax propositions, additional funding for education is more likely to come from the states. However, state services such as welfare, unemployment, and highway construction also need money and compete for the same, usually limited, funds. Furthermore, legislators and governors are concerned with maintaining a fiscal balance to keep their respective states solvent. Within this milieu those fund seekers with financial and political knowledge—and with power—are likely to be most successful.

Teacher organizations, as indicated earlier in this book, have become powerful and have been successful in shaping legislation throughout the country. Teacher organizations in the past have been politically active in seeking funding for education at the state and federal levels. They will need to continue and perhaps escalate their efforts to procure money for education in the future. Teacher organizations are known and respected for the size of their constituencies, their economic resources, their political activity, their research staffs, their legislative programs, and their lobbying efforts. Members of the profession should be familiar with the fundamentals of school finance so that they can understand the issues and be both effective and responsible in the political arena.

Discussion Questions

1. What are the main advantages and disadvantages of the property tax?
2. What are the advantages of the sales and income taxes?
3. What have been some of the noticeable effects of categorical aid—both state and federal—on the curricula of the local school districts in your area?
4. How is federal aid likely to change in the next decade?

5. What are the advantages and disadvantages of the increasing level of state support for education?
6. What other factors besides equalized expenditures affect equality of opportunity?
7. What are three trends that could seriously affect the adequacy of school funding? Why?
8. What are the primary reasons behind the call for accountability and for the call for educational vouchers?

Supplemental Activities

1. Study and evaluate the plan of state support of education in your state.
2. Interview members of local boards of education to determine their opinions on how schools should be financed.
3. Invite a tax assessor or supervisor of assessments to class to discuss assessing in your area.

4. Get a copy of a local school district budget and study it. Prepare questions about the budget, and invite a local school official to class to answer your questions and explain the budgeting.
5. Attending a local budget hearing and observe the interaction between school officials and citizens.

Notes

1. Robert J. Wynkoop, "Trends in School Finance Reform," *Phi Delta Kappan,* 56 (April 1975): 542.

2. David C. Long, "Rodriguez: The State Courts Respond," *Phi Delta Kappan* 64 (March 1983): 482.

3. Wynkoop, 543.

4. W. Vance Grant and Thomas D. Snyder, *Digest of Education Statistics, 1985–86* (Washington, D.C.: National Center for Education Statistics), p. 86.

5. *Ranking of the States, 1986* (Washington, D.C.: National Education Association, 1986), p. 26.

6. Joel S. Berke and Mary T. Moore, "A Developmental View of the Current Federal Government Role in Elementary and Secondary Education," *Phi Delta Kappan,* 63 (January 1982): 337.

7. Valena White Plesko and Joyce D. Stern, *The Condition of Education, 1985* (Washington, D.C.: National Center for Education Statistics), p. 3.

8. Allan Odden, "Sources of Funding for Education Reform," *Phi Delta Kappan,* 67 (January 1986): 340.

9. Richard A. Bumstead, "One Massachusetts School System Adapts to Proposition 2½," *Phi Delta Kappan,* 62 (June 1981): 722.

10. Lawrence Susskind, ed., *Proposition 2½: Its Impact on Massachusetts* (Cambridge, Mass.: Oelgeschlager, Gunn, and Hain, 1983), pp. 293–319. See also Chris Pipho, "Stateline," *Phi Delta Kappan,* January, May, and December 1983 issues.

11. Ibid.

12. William Montague, "Tax Proposals Receive Mixed Reception at Polls," *Education Week,* November 12, 1986, 14.

13. Ibid.

14. Odden, 336–337.

15. Michael Kirst, "Sustaining the Momentum of the State Education Reform: The Link Between Assessment and Financial Support," *Phi Delta Kappan,* 67 (January 1986): 342.

16. Alec M. Gallup, "The 18th Annual Gallup Poll of Public Attitudes Toward the Public Schools," *Phi Delta Kappan,* 68 (September 1986): 58.

Bibliography

Guthrie, James. "School Based Management: The Most Needed Education Reform." *Phi Delta Kappan,* 68 (December 1986): 305–309.

Harrison, Russell S. *Equality in Public School Finance.* Lexington, Mass.: Lexington Books, 1976.

Kirst, Michael. "Sustaining the Momentum of State Education Reform: The Link Between Assessment and Financial Support." *Phi Delta Kappan,* 67 (January 1986): 341–345.

———. *Who Controls Our Schools: American Values in Conflict.* Stanford, Calif.: Stanford Alumni Association, 1984.

Morgan, Edward P. "The Effects of Proposition 2½ in Massachusetts." *Phi Delta Kappan,* 64 (December 1982): 252–258.

Odden, Allan. "Financing Educational Excellence." *Phi Delta Kappan,* 65 (January 1984): 311–318.

———. "Sources of Funding for Educational Reform." *Phi Delta Kappan,* 67 (January 1986): 335–340.

Persell, Caroline H. *Education and Inequality.* New York: Free Press, 1977.

Prospects for Financing Elementary and Secondary Education in the States: Congressionally Mandated Study of School Finance. Final report, Vol. I. Report to Congress from the Secretary of Education. Preface by Donald J. Senese, Assistant Secretary, Office of Educational Research and Improvement. Washington, D.C.: December 1982.

Puckett, John L. "Education Vouchers: Rhetoric and Reality," *Educational Forum,* XLVII (Summer 1983): 467–492.

PART IV

Historical Foundations of Education

People have tried to educate their children in one way or another since the beginning of human life. In Part IV some of the important antecedents of American education are discussed. These antecedents have their beginning in ancient Greece where a serious attempt was made to systematically provide a rather general education, somewhat similar to what we know today, for large numbers of boys. Greek educators like Socrates, Plato, and Aristotle helped to develop educational ideas that molded education for centuries to come.

The church has greatly influenced education down through the ages. The Roman Catholic Church was a major force in government and had the resources and influence to largely determine who was educated and for what purposes. Quintilian, Charlemagne, and Alcuin are three of the many people who helped to develop education during this time, even though relatively little educational progress was made until A.D. 1000 when the revival of learning started in Europe. For the next several hundred years educators like Thomas Aquinas helped to harmonize the goals of the church with the goals of education. The Renaissance and Reformation periods thrust education into an even more important role. The contributions of Martin Luther, Ignatius of Loyola, Comenius, Rousseau, Pestalozzi, Herbart, and Froebel helped education grow in importance in Europe.

Many early educational practices in the American colonies were simply transplanted from Europe. Even today, many facets of our educational programs have their roots in other countries. In this part we also examine the highlights of educational development in the United States, from colonial times to the recent past.

The colonists did not take long to establish schools. In fact, some colonies even enacted laws encouraging parents to educate their children almost as soon as they landed in America. Dame schools, Latin grammar schools, and even a college (Harvard) were established very early in colonial America.

It was inevitable that a system for providing better education would become more important as our country developed and became more complex. An educated citizenry was essential to make our new democratic government function, and our nation characteristically went to work building a school system. Doing so required the dedicated work of countless educators. In this part we will briefly review the major contributions of just a few of these educators—Horace Mann, Samuel Hall, Benjamin Franklin, Noah Webster, Frederick Douglass, Emma Willard, Catherine Beecher, Mary McLeod Bethune, and Maria Montessori.

We will also examine more recent history-of-education developments—those that have taken place over the past 50 years. This recent period has been characterized by rapid growth of our educational systems—both in size and in complexity.

Present-day educators can learn much from past educational efforts. Through a careful study of the history of education, educators can avoid repeating past mistakes and can capitalize on past successes. ■

Antecedents of
American Education

Focus Questions

- Why do you think people created our first schools?
- How important has education been in the history of humankind?

- Is it important for teachers to understand the history of education? Why or why not?
- What lessons, if any, can we learn from Socrates?

Key Terms and Concepts

Ancient education
Greek education
Socrates, Plato, Aristotle
Scholasticism
Socratic method

Renaissance
Reformation
Age of Reason
Rousseau, Pestalozzi

What Would You Do?

You are conversing with colleagues in the teachers' lounge about schools of the past. One teacher expresses the opinion that Rousseau was wrong when he suggested in the 1760s that children are born "good" and only become "bad" in the hands of men. What do you say?

Most historians suggest that the lack of human progress during the Dark Ages was due primarily to the fact that people received virtually no education during that period. What are the implications of this apparent relationship between education and the human condition for the world today?

There is an old saying that states: "Nothing is new under the sun." This saying is especially appropriate when applied to the history of education, because all educational events have antecedents. In the history of American education, in particular, nearly all educational practices were adapted from other societies. This chapter briefly reviews some of the more important antecedents of American education.

The Beginnings of Education (to A.D. 476)

It is generally believed that human beings have been on earth for several million years. During 99 percent of this time there was very little progress toward civilization. Not until about ten thousand years ago did people start to raise food, domesticate animals, build canoes, and live in some semblance of community life. Not until approximately six thousand years ago was a written language developed.

Once there was a written language, humans felt the need for formal education. As societies became more complex and as the body of knowledge increased, people recognized a need for schools. What they had learned composed the subject matter; the written language allowed them to record this knowledge and pass it from generation to generation.

To determine the exact date that schools first came into existence is impossible. However, the discovery of cuneiform mathematics textbooks that have been dated to 2000 B.C. suggest that some form of school probably existed in Sumeria at that early date. There is also evidence to suggest that formal schools existed in China during the Hsia and Shang dynasties, perhaps as early as 2000 B.C. Not until about 500 B.C., however, was society sufficiently advanced to generate an organized concern for education. This event happened in Greece during the Age of Pericles.

Greek Education

Greece consisted of a number of city-states, one of which was Sparta. Sparta was a militaristic state whose educational system was geared to support military ambitions. Infants were exposed to the elements for a stated period; if they survived the ordeal, they were adjudged sufficiently strong for soldiering or, if female, to bear healthy children. From the ages of eight to eighteen boys were wards of the state. During this time they lived in barracks and received physical and moral training. Between eighteen and twenty, boys underwent rigorous war training; they then served in the army. All men were required to marry by the age of thirty so that they might raise healthy children to serve the state. The aims of Spartan education centered around developing such ideals as courage, patriotism, obedience, cunning, and physical strength. Plutarch (A.D. 46–120), a writer of later times, said that education of the Spartans "was calculated to make them subject to command, to endure labor, to fight, and to conquer." There was very little intellectual content in Spartan education.

In sharp contrast to Sparta was Athens, another Greek city-state, which developed an educational program that heavily stressed intellectual and aesthetic objectives. Between the ages of eight and sixteen, some Athenian boys attended a series of public schools. These schools included a grammatist school, which taught reading, writing, and counting; a gymnastics school, which taught sports and games; and a music school, which taught history, drama, poetry, speaking, and science as well as music. Because all city-states had to defend themselves against aggressors, Athenian boys received citizenship and military training between the ages of sixteen and twenty. Athenian girls were educated in the home. The aims of Athenian education stressed the development of the individual, aesthetics, and culture. $\boxed{43}$

The Western world's first great philosophers came from Athens. Of the many philosophers that Greece produced, three stand out—Socrates (470–399 B.C.), Plato (427–347 B.C.), and Aristotle (384–322 B.C.).

Socrates

Socrates left no writings, but we know much about him from the writings of Xenophon and Plato. Socrates developed a method of teaching that came to be known as the *Socratic method* in which the teacher would ask a series of questions that led the student to a certain conclusion.

Socrates traveled around Athens teaching the students who gathered about him. He was dedicated to the search for truth and at times was very critical of the existing government. Socrates was brought to trial for inciting the people against the government by his ceaseless questioning. He was found guilty and given a choice between ending his teaching or being put to death. Socrates chose death, thereby becoming a martyr for the cause of education. Socrates' fundamental principle, "Knowledge is virtue," has been adopted by countless educators and philosophers down through the ages.

Plato

Plato was a student and disciple of Socrates. In his *Republic* Plato set forth his recommendations for the ideal society. He suggested that society should contain three classes of people: artisans, to do the manual work; soldiers, to defend the society; and philosophers, to advance knowledge and to rule the society. Plato's educational aim was to discover and develop each individual's abilities. He believed that each man's abilities should be used to serve society. Plato wrote: "I call education the virtue which is shown by children when the feelings of joy or of sorrow, of love or of hate, which arise in their souls, are made conformable to order." Concerning the goals of education, Plato wrote: "A good education is that which gives to the body and to the soul all the beauty and all the perfection of which they are capable."

Aristotle

Like Plato, Aristotle also believed that a person's most important purpose was to serve and improve humankind. Aristotle's educational method, however, was scientific, practical, and objective, in contrast to the philosophical methods of Socrates and Plato. Aristotle believed that the quality of a society was determined by the quality of education found in that society. His writings, which include *Lyceum, Organon, Politics, Ethics,* and *Metaphysics,* were destined to exert greater influence on humankind through the Middle Ages than the writings of any other man.

Insight into some of Aristotle's views concerning education can be obtained from the following passage from *Politics:*

> That education should be regulated by law and should be an affair of state is not to be denied, but what should be the character of this public education, and how young persons should be educated, are questions which remain to be considered. For mankind are by no means agreed about the things to be taught, whether we look to virtue or the best life.
>
> Neither is it clear whether education is more concerned with intellectual or with moral virtue. The existing practice is perplexing; no one knows on what principle we should proceed—should the useful in life, or should virtue, or should the higher knowledge be the aim of our training; all three opinions have been entertained. Again, about the means there is no agreement; for different persons, starting with different ideas about the nature of virtue, naturally disagree about the practice of it.
>
> There can be no doubt that children should be taught those useful things which are really necessary, but not all things; for occupations are divided into liberal and illiberal; and to young children should be imparted only such kinds of knowledge as will be useful to them without vulgarizing them. And any occupation, art, or science, which makes the body or soul or mind of the freeman less fit for the practice or exercise of virtue, is vulgar; wherefore we call those arts vulgar which tend to deform the body, and likewise all paid employments, for they absorb and degrade the mind.[1]

The contributions that Greece made toward civilization and to education were truly outstanding.

Roman Education

In 146 B.C. the Romans conquered Greece, and Greek teachers and their educational system were quickly absorbed into the Roman Empire. Many of the educational and philosophical advances made by the Roman Empire after that time were actually inspired by enslaved Greeks.

Before 146 B.C. Roman children had been educated primarily in the home, though some children attended schools known as ludi, where the rudiments of reading and writing were taught. The Greek influence on Roman education became pronounced between 50 B.C. and A.D. 200. During this time an entire system of schools developed in Rome. Some children, after learning to read and write, attended a grammaticus school to study Latin, literature, history, mathematics, music, and dialectics. These Latin grammar schools were somewhat like twentieth-century secondary schools in function. Students who were pre-

> Remember that, for the most part, teachers have struggled through the ages with the same problems that teachers struggle with today.

paring for a career of political service received their training in a school of rhetoric. Rhetorical schools offered courses in grammar, rhetoric, dialectics, music, arithmetic, geometry, and astronomy.

The Roman Empire contained numerous institutions of higher learning that were continuations of former Greek institutions. For instance, a higher institution grew out of a library founded by Vespasian about A.D. 70. This institution, which later came to be known as the Athenaeum, eventually offered studies in law, medicine, architecture, mathematics, and mechanics.

Quintilian

Quintilian (A.D. 35–95) was the most influential of all Roman educators. In a set of twelve books, *The Institutes of Oratory,* he described current educational practices, recommended the type of educational system needed in Rome, and listed the great books in existence at that time.

Quintilian had considerable insight into educational psychology; concerning the punishment of students, he wrote:

> I am by no means in favor of whipping boys, though I know it to be a general practice. In the first place, whipping is unseemly, and if you suppose the boys to be somewhat grown up, it is an affront in the highest degree. In the next place, if a boy's ability is so poor as to be proof against reproach he will, like a worthless slave, become insensible to blows. Lastly, if a teacher is assiduous and careful, there is no need to use force. I shall observe further that while a boy is under the rod he experiences pain and fear. The shame of this experience dejects and discourages many pupils, makes them shun being seen, and may even weary them of their lives.[2]

Regarding the motivation of students, Quintilian stated:

> Let study be made a child's diversion; let him be soothed and caressed into it; and let him sometimes test himself upon his proficiency. Sometimes enter a contest of wits with him, and let him imagine that he comes off the conqueror. Let him even be encouraged by giving him such rewards that are most appropriate to his age.[3]

These comments apply as well today as they did when Quintilian wrote them nearly two thousand years ago. Quintilian's writings were rediscovered in the 1400s and became influential in the humanistic movement in education.

The Romans had a genius for organization and for getting a job done. They made lasting contributions to architecture; many of their roads, aqueducts, and buildings remain today. This genius for organization enabled Rome to unite much of the ancient world with a common language, a religion, and a political bond—a condition that favored the spread of education and knowledge throughout the ancient world.

Education in the Middle Ages (476–1300)

By A.D. 476 (the fall of the Roman Empire), the Roman Catholic Church was well on the way to becoming the greatest power in government and education. In fact, the rise of the church to a very powerful position is often cited as a main cause of the Western world's plunge into the Dark Ages. As the church stressed the importance of gaining entrance to heaven, life on earth became, in a sense, less important. Many people viewed earthly life as nothing more than a way to a life hereafter. We can see that a society in which this attitude prevailed would be unlikely to make intellectual advances, except perhaps in areas tangential to religion.

One can obtain insight into how much knowledge was lost during the Dark Ages by comparing writings from that period with earlier writings. During the seventh century a Spanish bishop, Isidore of Seville, wrote an encyclopedia that supposedly contained all the knowledge in the world at that time. A map of the world, as it was then known, was included in this encyclopedia. Comparing Isidore's extremely crude map with a surprisingly accurate one drawn in the second century by Ptolemy vividly illustrates the loss of knowledge over this 500-year period.

Fortunately, an interest in learning was slowly rekindled beginning about A.D. 1000. This renewed interest in knowledge, which gradually developed over the next several hundred years, is commonly called the Revival of Learning.

In this section we will briefly review the history of education in these two periods, the Dark Ages and the Revival of Learning. We begin our study by examining the achievements of two educators who lived during the Dark Ages: Charlemagne and Alcuin.

Charlemagne

During the Dark Ages one of the very few bright periods for education was the reign of Charlemagne (742–814). Charlemagne realized the value of education, and as ruler of a large part of Europe, he was in a position to establish schools and encourage scholarly activity. In 768 when Charlemagne came into power, educational activity was at an extremely low ebb. The little educating that was carried on was conducted by the church, mainly to induct people into the faith and to train religious leaders. The schools in which this religious teaching took place included catechumenal schools, which taught church doctrine to new converts; catechetical schools, which at first taught the catechism but later became schools for training church leaders; and cathedral (or monastic) schools, which trained clergy.

Alcuin

Charlemagne sought far and wide for a talented educator who could improve education in the kingdom, finally selecting Alcuin (735–804), who had been a teacher in England. While Alcuin served as Charlemagne's chief educational adviser, he became the most famous educator of his day. His main educational writings include *On Grammar, On Orthography, On Rhetoric,* and *On Dialectics.* Alcuin, in addition to trying to improve education generally in the kingdom, headed Charlemagne's Palace School in Frankland. Charlemagne himself often would sit in the Palace School with the children, trying to further his own meager education.

Roughly during Alcuin's time, the phrase *seven liberal arts* came into common usage to describe the curriculum that was then taught in many schools. The seven liberal arts consisted of the trivium (grammar, rhetoric, logic) and the quadrivium (arithmetic, geometry, music, astronomy). Each of these seven subjects was defined broadly, so that collectively they constituted a more comprehensive study than today's usage of the term suggests. The phrase *liberal arts* has survived time and is common now.

The Revival of Learning

Despite the efforts of a few men such as Charlemagne and Alcuin, very little educational progress was made during the Dark Ages. However, between 1000 and 1300—a period frequently referred to as the *Age of the Revival of Learning*—humankind slowly regained a thirst for education. This revival of interest in learning was helped by two events: first, the rediscovery of the writings of some of the ancient philosophers (mainly Aristotle) and renewed interest in them and, second, the reconciliation of religion and philosophy. Before this time the church had denounced the study of philosophy as contradictory to the teachings of the church.

Thomas Aquinas, more than any other person, helped to change the church's views on learning. This change in view led to the creation of new learning institutions, such as the medieval universities.

Thomas Aquinas

Harmonizing the doctrines of the church with the doctrines of philosophy and education was largely accomplished by Thomas Aquinas (1225–1274), himself a theologian. Aquinas formalized *scholasticism* (the logical and philosophical study of the beliefs of the church). His most important writing was *Summa Theologica,* which became the doctrinal authority of the Roman Catholic Church. The educational and philosophical views of Thomas Aquinas were made formal in the philosophy *Thomism*—a philosophy that has remained important in Roman Catholic parochial education.

Medieval Universities

The revival of learning brought about a general increase in educational activity and a growth of educational institutions, including the establishment of universities. These medieval universities, the true forerunners of our modern universities, included the University of Bologna (1158), which specialized in law;

the University of Paris (1180), which specialized in theology; Oxford University (1214); and the University of Salerno (1224). By 1500 approximately eighty universities had been established in Europe.

Although the Middle Ages produced few educational advances in the Western world, we must remember that much of the Eastern world did not experience the Dark Ages. Mohammed (569–632) led a group of Arabs through northern Africa and into southern Spain. The Eastern learning that the Arabs brought to Spain slowly, over the next few centuries, spread throughout Europe through the writings of such scholars as Avicenna (980–1037) and Averroes (1126–1198). These Eastern contributions to Western knowledge included significant advances in science and mathematics, particularly the Arabic numbering system.

Education in Transition (1300–1700)

Two very important movements took place during the transition period—the *Renaissance* and the *Reformation*. The Renaissance represented the protest of individuals against the dogmatic authority the church exerted over their social and intellectual life. The Renaissance started in Italy (around 1130), when humans reacquired the spirit of free inquiry that had prevailed in ancient Greece. The Renaissance slowly spread throughout Europe, resulting in a general revival of classical learning, called *humanism*. Erasmus (1466–1536) was one of the most famous humanist educators; two of his books, *The Right Method of Instruction* and *The Liberal Education of Boys,* formed a humanistic theory of education.

The second movement, the Reformation, represented a reaction against certain beliefs of the Roman Catholic Church, particularly those beliefs which discouraged learning and which, in consequence, kept lay persons in ignorance. We will examine both the Renaissance and the Reformation in this section.

The Renaissance: Erasmus

Erasmus had a good deal of educational insight. Concerning the aims of education, he wrote:

> The duty of instructing the young includes several elements, the first and also the chief of which is that the tender mind of the child should be instructed in piety; the second, that he love and learn the liberal arts; the third, that he be taught tact in the conduct of social life; and the fourth, that from his earliest age he accustom himself to good behavior, based on moral principles.[4]

His educational maxims indicated that Erasmus had much educational common sense:

> We learn with great willingness from those whom we love; Parents themselves cannot properly bring up their children if they make themselves only to be feared; There are children who would be killed sooner than made better by blows: by mildness and kind admonitions, one may make of them whatever he will; Children will learn to speak their native tongue without any weariness, by usage and practice; Drill in

reading and writing is a little bit tiresome, and the teacher will ingeniously palliate the tedium by the artifice of an attractive method; The ancients moulded toothsome dainties into the forms of the letters, and thus, as it were, made children swallow the alphabet; In the matter of grammatical rules, instruction should at the first be limited to the most simple; As the body in infant years is nourished by little portions distributed at intervals, so should the mind of the child be nurtured by items of knowledge adapted to its weakness, and distributed little by little.[5]

The Reformation

The Protestant Reformation had its formal beginning in 1517, when Martin Luther (1483–1546) published his 95 theses, which stated his disagreement with the Roman Catholic Church. One of these disagreements held great implications for the importance of formal education. The church had come to feel that it was not necessary for each person to read and interpret the Bible for himself or herself; rather, the church would pass on its interpretation to the laity. Luther felt not only that the church had itself misinterpreted the Bible but also that it was intended that people read and interpret the Bible for themselves. If one accepted the church's position on this matter, formal education remained unimportant. If one accepted Luther's position, however, education became necessary for all people so that they might read and interpret the Bible for themselves. In a sense, education became important as a way of obtaining salvation. It is understandable that Luther and his educational co-worker, Melanchthon (1497–1560), soon came to stress universal elementary education. Melanchthon's most important educational writing was *Visitation Articles* (1528), in which he set forth his recommendations for schools. Luther and Melanchthon felt that education should be provided for all, regardless of class, and should be compulsory for both sexes. They felt also that it should be state-controlled, state-supported, and centered around classical languages, grammar, mathematics, science, history, music, and physical education. Luther's argument for increased governmental support for education has a familiar twentieth-century ring:

> Each city is subjected to great expense every year for the construction of roads, for fortifying its ramparts, and for buying arms and equipping soldiers. Why should it not spend an equal sum for the support of one or two schoolmasters? The prosperity of a city does not depend solely on its natural riches, on the solidity of its walls, on the elegance of its mansions, and on the abundance of arms in its arsenals, but the safety and strength of a city reside above all in a good education, which furnishes it with instructed, reasonable, honorable, and well-trained citizens.[6]

Ignatius of Loyola

To combat the Reformation movement, Ignatius of Loyola (1491–1556) organized the Society of Jesus (Jesuits) in 1540. The Jesuits worked to establish schools in which to further the cause of the Roman Catholic Church, and they tried to stem the flow of converts to the Reformation cause. Although the Jesuits' main interest was religious, they soon grew into a great teaching order and were very successful in training their own teachers. The rules by which the Jesuits conducted their schools were stated in the *Ratio Studiorum;* a revised edition still guides the Jesuit schools today. The improvement of teacher training was the Jesuits' main contribution to education.

Another Catholic teaching order, the Brothers of the Christian Schools, was organized in 1684 by Jean Baptiste de la Salle (1651–1719). Unlike the Jesuits, who were primarily interested in secondary education, de la Salle and his order were interested in elementary schools and in preparing elementary school teachers. De la Salle was probably the first educator to use student teaching in the preparation of teachers.

Comenius

Many other outstanding educators existed during the transition period, one being Johann Amos Comenius (1592–1670). Comenius is perhaps best remembered for his many textbooks, which were among the first to contain illustrations. Concerning a school that he operated, Comenius wrote: "We pursue a general education, the teaching to all men of all the subjects of human concern."[7] Comenius advocated that an entire system of schools should be created to serve the youth. In this regard he wrote: "There should be a maternal school in each family; an elementary school in each district; a gymnasium in each city; an academy in each kingdom, or even in each considerable province."[8]

The invention and improvement of printing during the 1400s made it possible to produce books, such as those of Comenius, more rapidly and economically—a development that was essential to the growth of education. Much of the writing of Comenius reflected the increasing interest then developing in science.

Modern Period (1700–Present)

As shown thus far in this chapter, educational progress was slow and took place in only a few places up through the seventeenth century. In this section we will see why many of our current educational ideas can be traced to the early 1700s. We will look at two movements, commonly referred to as the Age of Reason and the Emergence of Common Man.

Age of Reason

The first of the two movements that took place during the early modern period and that influenced education was a revolt of the intellectuals against the superstition and ignorance that dominated people's lives at that time. This movement has been called the *Age of Reason,* and François Marie Arouet, who wrote under the name Voltaire, was one of the leaders. Those who joined this movement became known as rationalists because of the faith they placed in human rational power. The implication for education in the rationalist movement is obvious: If one places greater emphasis on human ability to reason, then education takes on new importance as the way by which humans develop this power.

Emergence of Common Man

The second movement of the early modern period that affected education was the *Emergence of Common Man*. Whereas the Age of Reason was a revolt of the learned for intellectual freedom, the Emergence of Common Man was a revolt of common people for a better life—politically, economically, socially, and educationally. One of the leaders in this movement was Jean Jacques Rousseau (1712–1778), whose *Social Contract* (1762) became an influential book in the French Revolution. Scholars have suggested that *Social Contract* was also the basal doctrine of the American Declaration of Independence.[9] Rousseau was a philosopher, not an educator, but he wrote a good deal on the subject of education. His most important educational work was *Émile* (1762), in which he states his views concerning the ideal education for youth. Rousseau felt that the aim of education should be to return man to his "natural state." His view on the subject is well summed up by the opening sentence of *Émile:* "Everything is good as it comes from the hand of the author of nature; but everything degenerates in the hands of man." Rousseau's educational views came to be known as *naturalism*. Concerning the best method of teaching, Rousseau wrote:

> Do not treat the child to discourses which he cannot understand. No descriptions, no eloquence, no figures of speech. Be content to present to him appropriate objects. Let us transform our sensations into ideas. But let us not jump at once from sensible objects to intellectual objects. Let us always proceed slowly from one sensible notion to another. In general, let us never substitute the sign for the thing, except when it is impossible for us to show the thing. . . . I have no love whatever for explanations and talk. Things! Things! I shall never tire of saying that we ascribe too much importance to words. With our babbling education we make only babblers.[10]

Rousseau's most important contributions to education were his belief that education must be a natural process, not an artificial one, and his compassionate, positive view of the child. Rousseau believed that children were inherently good—a belief that was in opposition to the prevailing religiously inspired belief that children were born full of sin. The contrasting implications for teaching methods suggested by these two views are self-evident, as is the educational desirability of Rousseau's view over that which prevailed at the time. Although Rousseau never taught a day of school in his life, he did more to improve education through his writing than any of his contemporaries.

Pestalozzi

Johann Heinrich Pestalozzi (1746–1827) was a Swiss educator who put Rousseau's theory into practice. Pestalozzi established two schools for boys, one at Burgdorf (1800–1804) and the other at Yverdun (1805–1825). Educators came from all over the world to view Pestalozzi's schools and to study his teaching methods. Pestalozzi enumerated his educational views in a book entitled *Leonard and Gertrude*. Unlike most educators of his time, Pestalozzi believed that a teacher should treat students with love and kindness:

> I was convinced that my heart would change the condition of my children just as promptly as the sun of spring would reanimate the earth benumbed by the winter. . . . It was necessary that my children should observe, from dawn to evening, at every moment of the day, upon my brow and on my lips, that my affections were fixed on them, that their happiness was my happiness, and that their pleasures were my pleasures . . .
>
> I was everything to my children. I was alone with them from morning till night. . . . Their hands were in my hands. Their eyes were fixed on my eyes.[11]

Key concepts in the Pestalozzian method included an expression of love, understanding, and patience for children; a compassion for the poor; and the use of objects and sense perception as the basis for acquiring knowledge.

Herbart

One of the educators who studied under Pestalozzi and was influenced by him was Johann Friedrich Herbart (1776–1841). While Pestalozzi had successfully put into practice and further developed Rousseau's educational ideas, it remained for Herbart to organize these educational views into a formal psychology of education. Herbart stressed apperception (learning by association). The Herbartian teaching method developed into five formal steps:

1. *Preparation:* Preparing the student to receive a new idea
2. *Presentation:* Presenting the student with the new idea
3. *Association:* Assimilating the new idea with the old ideas
4. *Generalization:* The general idea deriving from the combination of the old and new ideas
5. *Application:* Applying the new knowledge

Herbart's educational ideas are contained in his *Science of Education* (1806) and *Outlines of Educational Doctrine* (1835).

Froebel

Friedrich Froebel (1782–1852) was another European educator who was influenced by Rousseau and Pestalozzi and who made a sizable contribution to education. Froebel's contributions included the establishment of the first kindergarten (or Kleinkinderbeschäftigungsanstalt, as he called it in 1837), an emphasis on social development, a concern for the cultivation of creativity, and the concept of learning by doing. He originated the idea that women are best suited to teach young children. Froebel wrote his main educational book, *Education of Man,* in 1826.

Two developments in the late 1800s were the last important European

History has shown that the goals of education have varied considerably from place to place and from time to time. Teachers should be aware of how current educational goals differ from those of the past.

antecedents of American education: the maturing of the scientific movement, hastened by the publication of Charles Darwin's *On the Origin of Species* (1859), and the formulation of educational psychology near the end of the century.

The student of educational history must realize that even though many educational advances had been made by 1900, the average European received a pathetically small amount of formal education, even at that late date. Historically, education had been available only to the few who were fortunate enough to be born into the leisure class; the masses of people in the working class had received little or no education until that time. What little formal education the working person might have received was usually provided by the church for religious purposes.

Summary and Implications

This chapter has pointed out that the historical roots of our educational traditions can be traced to Europe. People who have helped to mold Western education include Socrates, Plato, Aristotle, Quintilian, Alcuin, Aquinas, Erasmus, Melanchthon, Rousseau, Pestalozzi, and Herbart. These and other educational pioneers labored against overwhelming odds to advance the cause of education, and many of the concepts and practices developed by them are still in use today. However, perhaps their greatest contribution was in helping humankind to discover and appreciate the potential value of education.

One important implication of this chapter for current teachers is that many of our contemporary educational beliefs are very old ideas. Today's teachers also have an obligation to study the history of education so that mistakes of the past will not be repeated.

Discussion Questions

1. What were the major factors that caused humans to first create schools?
2. What were the major differences between the Spartan and Athenian school systems? Why did these differences exist?
3. What factors contributed to the decline of education during the Dark Ages?

4. What were the strengths and weaknesses of Jean Jacques Rousseau's ideas about children and education?
5. Discuss the educational achievements of the Roman Empire.
6. What were the major educational advances made during the Reformation period?

Supplemental Activities

1. Read and discuss Quintilian's *Institutes of Oratory*.
2. Read and discuss Rousseau's *Émile*.
3. Read and discuss Pestalozzi's *How Gertrude Teaches Her Children*.

4. Make a chart showing the major contributions of the educators discussed in this chapter.
5. Do additional library research on one of the educators discussed in this chapter.

Notes

1. Paul Monroe, *Source Book of the History of Education* (New York: Macmillan, 1901), p. 282.
2. Quintilian, *The Institutes of Oratory*, trans. W. Guthrie (London: Dewick and Clark, 1905), p. 27.
3. Ibid., 13
4. Gabriel Compayre, *History of Pedagogy*, trans. W. H. Payne (Boston: Heath, 1888), pp. 88–89.
5. Ibid., 89.

6. Ibid., 115.
7. Ibid., 128.
8. Ibid.
9. Paul Monroe, *History of Education* (New York: Macmillan, 1905), p. 283.
10. Compayre, 299.
11. Ibid., 425.

Bibliography

Armytage, W. H. G. "William Byngham: A Medieval Protagonist of the Training of Teachers." *History of Education Journal,* 2 (1951): 107–110.

Bowen, J. "Towards an Assessment of Educational Theory: An Historical Perspective." *International Review of Education,* 25 (1979): 303–323.

Butts, R. Freeman. *A Cultural History of Western Education.* New York: McGraw-Hill, 1955.

Chambliss, J. J., ed. *Nobility, Tragedy and Naturalism: Education in Ancient Greece.* Minneapolis: Burgess, 1971.

Cole, Luella. *A History of Education: Socrates to Montessori.* New York: Holt, Rinehart and Winston, 1950.

Compayre, Gabriel. *History of Pedagogy.* Translated by W. H. Payne. Boston: Heath, 1888.

Cremin, Lawrence. *American Education: The National Experience, 1783–1876.* New York: Harper, 1980.

Hillesheim, James W., and Merrill, George D., eds. *Theory and Practice in the History of American Education: A Book of Readings.* Pacific Palisades, Calif.: Goodyear, 1971.

Kaestle, Carl, and Vinovskis, Maris. *Education and Social Change in Nineteenth Century Massachusetts.* Cambridge, England: Cambridge University Press, 1980.

Lucas, Christopher J. *Our Western Educational Heritage.* New York: Macmillan, 1972.

Meyer, Adolph E. *An Educational History of the Western World.* New York: McGraw-Hill, 1965.

———. *Grandmasters of Educational Thought.* New York: McGraw-Hill, 1975.

Painter, A. M. *A History of Education.* New York: Appleton, 1987.

Roper, D. "Coming Full Circle; Charity Schools in Public Education." *Social Studies,* 71 (March–April 1980): 90–94.

Early American Education

Focus Questions

- If you had been one of the early American colonists, how important would "education" have been to you? Why?
- What do you suppose life was like for the colonial schoolteacher?
- How much has education improved through the history of our country?
- How important has our federal government been in advancing education in America?

Key Terms and Concepts

Colonial education
Common schools
Horace Mann
Latin grammar schools
American Academy
Secondary education
Educational goals
Apprenticeship
Northwest Ordinance
Normal schools

The New England Primer
Blue-Backed Speller
Frederick Douglass
Emma Willard
Private education
Federal involvement in education
Monitorial school
Committee of Ten
Cardinal Principles of Secondary Education

What Would You Do?

Recently, a small school district decided to require their teachers to use the McGuffey *Eclectic Readers* (written in the mid 1800s) in each elementary grade. The board of education believes that these books will be more challenging and will help children learn to be honest, patriotic, kind, punctual, and persistent. What do you think?

If you could redo history, what major changes would you make in the role our federal government plays in American education?

The first permanent European settlements in North America included Jamestown (1607), Plymouth (1620), Massachusetts Bay (1630), Maryland (1632), Connecticut (1635), and Providence Plantations (1636). The motives that prompted most of these settlers to move to America were religious, economic, and political. Generally, these people were not dissatisfied with education in their homelands. Thus nearly all educational practices and educational materials in early colonial America were simply transplanted from the Old World.

The religious motive was very strong in colonial America, and it permeated colonial education. Colonists generally felt that a child should learn to read so that he or she could read the Bible and thus gain salvation. Beyond this desire, there was no demand for mass education. Since the clergy possessed the ability to read and write, and since the ultimate utility of education was to read the Bible, it was logical for the clergy to do much of the teaching.

Providing Education in the New World

The early settlement of the East Coast fell into three general groups of colonies: the Southern Colonies, centered in Virginia; the Middle Colonies, centered in New York; and the Northern Colonies, centered in New England.

41

The Southern Colonies soon came to be made up of large tobacco plantations. Owing to the size of the plantations, people lived far apart; few towns were established until later in the colonial period. There was an immediate need for cheap labor to work on the plantations, and in 1619, only twelve years after Jamestown was settled, the first boatload of slaves was imported from Africa. Other sources of cheap labor for the Southern Colonies included white Europeans from a variety of backgrounds who purchased passage to the New World by agreeing to serve a lengthy period of indentured servitude on arrival in the

45

colonies. There soon came to be two very distinct classes of people in the South—a few wealthy landowners and a large mass of laborers, most of whom were slaves. The educational provisions that evolved from this set of conditions were precisely what one would expect. No one was interested in providing education for the slaves, with the exception of a few missionary groups like the English Society for the Propagation of the Gospel in Foreign Parts. Such missionary groups tried to provide some education for slaves, primarily so that they could read the Bible. The wealthy landowners usually hired tutors to teach their children at home. Distances between homes and slow transportation precluded the establishment of centralized schools. When the upper class children grew old enough to attend college, they were usually sent to well-established schools in Europe.

The people who settled the Middle Colonies came from various national (Dutch, Swedes) and religious (Puritans, Mennonites, Catholics) backgrounds.

Boston Latin High School, established in 1635, was the first permanent educational institution in the United States. (*Source:* Jeff Dunn/The Picture Cube)

This situation explains why the Middle Colonies have often been called the "melting pot" of the nation. This diversity of backgrounds made it impossible for those in the Middle Colonies to agree on a common public school system. Consequently, the respective groups established their own parochial schools. Many children received their education through an apprenticeship while learning a trade from a "master" already in that line of work. Some people even learning the art of teaching school through an apprenticeship.

The Northern Colonies were settled mainly by the Puritans. In 1630 approximately one thousand Puritans settled near Boston. Unlike people in the Southern Colonies, people in New England lived close to one another. Towns sprang up and soon became centers of political and social life. Shipping ports were established, and an industrial economy developed that demanded numerous skilled and semiskilled workers—a condition that created a large middle class.

These conditions of common religious views, town life, and a large middle class made it possible for the people to agree on common public schools. This agreement led to very early educational activity in the Northern Colonies. In 1642 the General Court of Massachusetts enacted a law that stated:

> This Coʳ, [Court] taking into consideration the great neglect of many parents & masters in training up their children in learning . . . do hereupon order and decree, that in every towne y chosen men . . . take account from time to time of all parents and masters, and of their children, concerning their . . . ability to read & understand the principles of religion & the capitall lawes of this country. . . .

This law did nothing more than encourage citizens to look after the education of children. Five years later (1647), however, another law was enacted in Massachusetts that required towns to provide education for the youth. This law stated:

> It being one chiefe proiect of y ould deluder, Satan, to keepe men from the knowledge of y Scriptures. . . . It is therefore orded [ordered], ye evy [every] towneship in this iurisdiction, aft y Lord hath increased y number to 50 houshold, shall then forthw appoint one w [with] in their towne to teach all such children as shall resort to him to write & reade . . . & it is furth ordered y where any towne shall increase to y numb [number] of 100 families or househould, they shall set up a grammar schoole, y m [aim] thereof being able to instruct youth so farr as they shall be fited for y university [Harvard]. . . .

These Massachusetts school laws of of 1642 and 1647 served as models for similar laws soon created in other colonies.

Several different kinds of elementary schools sprang up in the colonies, such as the dame school, which was conducted by a housewife in her home; the writing school, which taught the child to write; a variety of parochial schools; and charity, or pauper, schools taught by missionary groups.

To go back a few years, in 1635 the Latin Grammar School was established in Boston—the first permanent school of this type in what is now the United States. This school was established when the people of Boston, which had been settled only five years before, voted "that our brother Philemon Pormont, shal be intreated to become scholemaster, for the teaching and nourtering of children with us." The grammar school was a secondary school, and its function was college preparatory. The grammar school idea spread quickly to other towns. Charlestown opened its first grammar school one year later, in 1636, by contracting William Witherell "to keep a school for a twelve month." Within sixteen years after the Massachusetts Bay Colony had been founded, seven or eight towns had Latin grammar schools in operation. These schools, transplanted from Europe where similar schools had existed for a long time, were traditional and designed to prepare children for college and "for the service of God, in church and commonwealth."

Harvard, the first colonial college, was established in 1636 for preparing ministers. Other early American colleges included William and Mary (1693), Yale (1701), Princeton (1746), King's College (1754), College of Philadelphia (1755), Brown (1764), Dartmouth (1769), and Queen's College (1770). The curriculum in these early colleges was traditional, with heavy emphasis on theology and the classics. An example of how far the religious motive dominated the colonial colleges can be found in one of the 1642 rules governing Harvard College, which stated: "Let every Student be plainly instructed, and earnestly pressed to consider well, the maine end of his life and studies is, to know God and Jesus Christ. . . ."

44

The Struggle for Universal Elementary Education

On the whole, colonial elementary schools were adaptations of schools that had existed in Europe for many years. When the colonists arrived in this country, they simply established schools like those they had known in Europe. The objectives of colonial elementary schools were purely religious. It was commonly believed that everyone needed to be able to read the Bible to receive salvation; therefore parents were eager to have their children receive some type of reading instruction.

A good idea about what a colonial elementary school was like can be gleaned from the following account of a school conducted in 1750 by Christopher Dock, a Mennonite schoolteacher in Pennsylvania:

> The children arrive as they do because some have a great distance to school, others a short distance, so that the children cannot assemble as punctually as they can in a city. Therefore, when a few children are present, those who can read their Testament sit together on one bench; but the boys and girls occupy separate benches. They are given a chapter which they read at sight consecutively. Meanwhile I write copies for them. Those who have read their passage of Scripture without error take their places at the table and write. Those who fail have to sit at the end of the bench, and each new arrival the same; as each one is thus released in order he takes up his slate. This process continues until they have all assembled. The last one left on the bench is a "lazy pupil."
>
> When all are together, and examined, whether they are washed and combed, they sing a psalm or morning hymn, and I sing and pray with them. As much as they can understand of the Lord's Prayer and the Ten Commandments (according to the gift God has given them), I exhort and admonish them accordingly. This much concerning the assembly of pupils. But regarding prayer I will add this additional explanation. Children say the prayers taught them at home half articulately, and too fast, especially the "Our Father" which the Lord Himself taught His disciples and which contains all that we need. I therefore make a practice of saying it for them kneeling, and they kneeling repeat it after me. After these devotional exercises those who can write resume their work. Those who cannot read the Testament have had time during the assemblage to study their lesson. These are heard recited immediately after prayer. Those who know their lesson receive an O on the hand, traced with crayon. This is a mark of excellence. Those who fail more than three times are sent back to study their lesson again. When all the little ones have recited, these are asked again, and any one having failed in more than three trials a second time, is called "Lazy" by the entire class and his name is written down. Whether

such a child fears the rod or not, I know from experience that this denunciation of the children hurts more than if I were constantly to wield and flourish the rod. If then such a child has friends in school who are able to instruct him and desire to do so, he will visit more frequently than before. For this reason: if the pupil's name has not been erased before dismissal the pupils are at liberty to write down the names of those who have been lazy, and take them along home. But if the child learns his lesson well in the future, his name is again presented to the other pupils, and they are told that he knew his lesson well and failed in no respect. Then all the pupils call "Diligent" to him. When this has taken place his name is erased from the slate of lazy pupils, and the former transgression is forgiven.[1]

Christopher Dock's comments show the extent to which religion dominated the curriculum of colonial elementary schools. This account also points out that the curriculum of these schools was limited to the rudiments of knowledge and that instructional materials were simple and meager.

In 1805 New York City established the first monitorial school in the United States. The monitorial school, which originated in England, represented an attempt to provide mass elementary education for large numbers of children. Typically, the teacher would teach hundreds of pupils, using the better students as helpers. By 1840 nearly all monitorial schools had been closed; the children had not learned enough to justify continuance of this type of school.

Between 1820 and 1860 an educational awakening took place in America. This movement was strongly influenced by Horace Mann (1796–1859). As secretary of the state board of education, Mann helped to establish common elementary schools in Massachusetts. Among his many impressive educational achievements was the publication of one of the very early professional journals in this country, *The Common School Journal*. Through this journal Mann kept educational issues before the public.

In 1852 Massachusetts passed a compulsory elementary school attendance law, the first of its kind in the country. It required all children to attend school. By 1900, thirty-two other states had passed similar compulsory school attendance laws.

Pestalozzianism and Herbartianism considerably affected elementary education when they were introduced to the United States in the late 1800s. Pestalozzianism emphasized teaching children with love, patience, and understanding. Furthermore, children should learn from objects and firsthand experiences, not from abstractions and words. Pestalozzian concepts soon spread throughout the country. Herbartianism was imported into the United States at the Bloomington Normal School in Illinois by three students who had learned about the ideas of Herbart while studying in Germany. Herbartianism represented an attempt to make a science out of teaching. The more formal system that Herbartianism brought to the often disorganized elementary teacher was badly needed at the

Professional Perspectives

Teachers in the past, just like teachers today, have had to be innovative and resourceful to serve their students well.

time. Unfortunately, Herbartianism eventually contributed to an extreme formalism and rigidity that characterized many American elementary schools in the early 1900s. An example of this formalization is the school administrator who bragged that at a given moment in the school day he knew exactly what was going on in all the classrooms. One can infer from this boast that teachers often had a very strict, rigid educational program imposed on them.

If we look back at the historical development of American elementary education, we can make the following generalizations:

- Until the late 1800s the motive, curriculum, and administration of elementary education were primarily religious. The point at which elementary education began to be more secular than religious was the point at which states began to pass compulsory school attendance laws.
- Discipline has traditionally been harsh and severe in elementary schools. The classical picture of a colonial schoolmaster equipped with a frown, dunce cap, stick, whip, and a variety of abusive phrases is a more accurate picture than one might expect. It is no wonder that children have historically viewed school as an unpleasant place. Pestalozzi had much to do with bringing about a gradual change in discipline when he advocated that love, not harsh punishment, should be used to motivate students.
- Elementary education has traditionally been formal and impersonal. The ideas of Rousseau, Pestalozzi, Herbart, and Froebel helped to change this condition gradually and make elementary education more student-centered; this began to show about 1900.
- Elementary schools have traditionally been taught by poorly prepared teachers.
- Although the aims and methodology have varied considerably from time to time, the basic content of elementary education has historically been reading, writing, and arithmetic.

The Need for Secondary Schools

The first form of secondary school in the colonies was the *Latin grammar school* mentioned previously, first established in Boston in 1635 only five years after colonists settled in the area. The Latin grammar school was largely concerned with teaching Latin and other classical subjects and was strictly college preparatory.

Harvard was the only university in existence in the colonies at that time. The entrance requirements to Harvard stated:

> When any Scholar is able to understand Tully, or such like classicall Latine Author extempore, and make and speake true Latine in Verse and Prose, suo ut aiunt marte; and decline perfectly the Paradigms of Nounes and Verbes in the Greek tongue; let him then, and not before, be capable of admission into the college.

European colleges and later colonial colleges also demanded that students know Latin and Greek before they could be admitted. For instance, in the mid-eighteenth century, the requirements for admission to Yale stated:

None may expect to be admitted into this College unless upon Examination of the President and Tutors, they shall be found able Extempore to Read, Construe, and Parce Tully, Vergil and the Greek Testament; and to write true Latin in Prose and to understand the Rules of Prosodia, and Common Arithmetic, and Shal bring Sufficient Testimony of his Blameless and inoffensive Life.

Since Latin grammar schools were designed to prepare students for college, it is little wonder that the curriculum in these schools was so classical and traditional. Needless to say, a very small percentage of children attended any Latin grammar school because very few could hope to attend college. Girls did not attend; colleges at that time did not admit women. As late as 1785 there were only two Latin grammar schools in Boston, and the combined enrollment in these two schools was only 64 boys.

By the middle of the eighteenth century there was a need for more and better-trained skilled workers. Benjamin Franklin, recognizing this need, proposed a new kind of secondary school in Pennsylvania. This proposal brought about the establishment in Philadelphia in 1751 of the first truly American educational institution, the American Academy. Franklin established this school because he thought the existing Latin grammar schools were not providing the practical secondary education needed by youth. The philosophy, curriculum, and methodology of Franklin's aacademy were all geared to prepare young people for employment. Similar academies were established throughout America, and these institutions eventually replaced the Latin grammar school as the predominant secondary education institution. They were usually private schools, and many of them admitted girls as well as boys. Later on, some academies even tried to train elementary school teachers.

In 1821 an English classical school (which three years later changed its name to English High School) was opened in Boston, and another distinctively American educational institution was launched. This first high school, under the direction of George B. Emerson, consisted of a three-year course in English, mathematics, science, and history. The school later added to its curriculum the philosophy of history, chemistry, intellectual philosophy, linear drawing, logic, trigonometry, French, and the United States Constitution. The school enrolled about one hundred boys during its first year.

The high school was established because of a belief that the existing grammar schools were inadequate for the day and because most people could not afford to send their children to the private academies. The American high school soon replaced both the Latin grammar school and the private academy and has been with us ever since.

About 1910 the first junior high schools were established in the United States. A survey in 1916 showed 54 junior high schools existing in 36 states. One year later a survey indicated that the number had increased to about 270. More recently, some school systems have abandoned the junior high school in favor of what is called the *middle school,* which usually consists of grades 6,7, and 8. The evolution of the American secondary school is presented schematically in Figure 13.1.

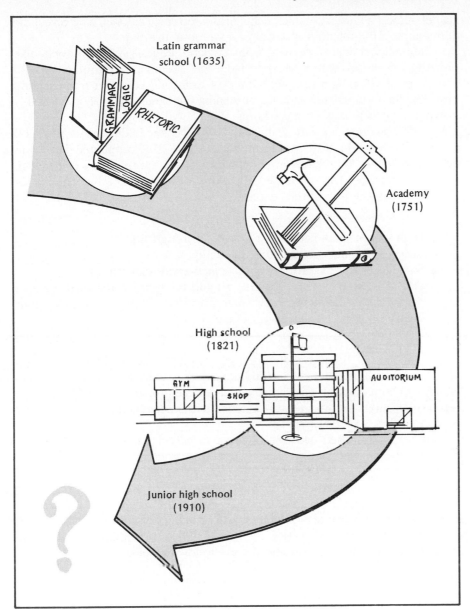

FIGURE 13.1   *Evolution of American Secondary Education*

Aims of American Public Education

The aims of American public education have gradually changed over the years. During colonial times the overriding aim of education at all levels was to enable students to read and understand the Bible, to gain salvation, and to spread the gospel. Almost all historical documents preserved since colonial days reveal the dominance of the religious motive in education at that time.

After independence was won from England, educational objectives—like providing Americans with a common language, attempting to instill a sense of patriotism, developing a national feeling of unity and common purpose, and providing the technical and agricultural training our developing nation needed—became important tasks for the schools.

In 1892 a committee was established by the National Education Association to study the function of the American high school. This committee, known as the *Committee of Ten,* made an effort to set down the purposes of the high school at that time. The committee made the following recommendations for high schools at the turn of the century:

- High school should consist of grades 7 through 12.
- Courses should be arranged sequentially.
- Students should be given very few electives in high school.
- One unit, called a Carnegie unit, should be awarded for each separate course that a student takes each year, provided that the course meets four or five times each week all year long.

The Committee of Ten also recommended trying to graduate high school students earlier to permit them to attend college sooner. At that time the recommendation implied that high schools had a college preparatory function. These recommendations became powerful influences in the shaping of secondary education.

Before 1900 teachers had relatively little direction in their work, since most educational goals were not precisely stated. This problem was partly overcome in 1918 when the Commission on Reorganization of Secondary Education published a report under the title *Cardinal Principles of Secondary Education;* these items are usually referred to as the *Seven Cardinal Principles.* In reality, they constitute only one section of the basic principles discussed in the original text, but it is the part that has become famous. These principles stated that the student should receive an education in the following fields:

1. Health
2. Command of fundamental processes
3. Worthy home membership
4. Vocation
5. Civic education
6. Worthy use of leisure
7. Ethical character

The following goals of education were listed by the Progressive Education Association in 1938; these "needs of youth" grew out of the Eight Year Study:

1. Physical and mental health
2. Self-assurance
3. Assurance of growth toward adult status
4. Philosophy of life
5. Wide range of personal interests
6. Esthetic appreciations
7. Intelligent self-direction
8. Progress toward maturity in social relations with age-mates and adults
9. Wise use of goods and services
10. Vocational orientation
11. Vocational competence

Also in 1938 another attempt was made to set down the goals of American education when the Educational Policies Commission of the National Education Association (NEA) set forth the "Purposes of Education in American Democracy." These objectives stated that students should receive an education in the four broad areas of self-realization, human relations, economic efficiency, and civic responsibility.

In 1944 this same commission of the NEA published another statement of educational objectives, entitled "Education for All American Youth":

Schools should be dedicated to the proposition that every youth in these United States—regardless of sex, economic status, geographic location, or race—should experience a broad and balanced education which will

1. equip him to enter an occupation suited to his abilities and offering reasonable opportunity for personal growth and social usefulness;
2. prepare him to assume full responsibilities of American citizenship;
3. give him a fair chance to exercise his right to the pursuit of happiness through the attainment and preservation of mental and physical health;
4. stimulate intellectual curiosity, engender satisfaction in intellectual achievement, and cultivate the ability to think rationally; and
5. help to develop an appreciation of the ethical values which should undergird all life in a democratic society.

In 1952 the Educational Policies Commission made yet another statement of educational objectives, entitled the "Imperative Needs of Youth":

1. All youth need to develop salable skills and those understandings and attitudes that make the worker an intelligent productive participant in economic life. To this end most youth need supervised work experience as well as education in the skills and knowledge of their occupations.
2. All youth need to develop and maintain good health and physical fitness.
3. All youth need to understand the rights and duties of the citizen of a democratic society, and to be diligent and competent in the performance of their obligations as members of the community and citizens of the state and nation.
4. All youth need to understand the significance of the family for the individual and society and the conditions conducive to successful family life.
5. All youth need to know how to purchase and use goods and services intelligently, understanding both the values received by the consumer and the economic consequences of their acts.

6. All youth need to understand the methods of science, the influence of science on human life, and the main scientific facts concerning the nature of the world and of man.

7. All youth need opportunities to develop their capacities to appreciate beauty in literature, art, music, and nature.

8. All youth need to be able to use their leisure time well and budget it wisely, balancing activities that yield satisfactions to the individual with those that are socially useful.

9. All youth need to develop respect for the other persons, to grow in their insight into ethical values and principles, and to be able to live and work cooperatively with others.

10. All youth need to grow in their ability to think rationally, to express their thoughts clearly, and to read and listen with understanding.

These various statements concerning education objectives, made over the last century, sum up fairly well the history of the aims of American public education.

History of Federal Involvement

The U.S. Constitution does not mention education; therefore by virtue of the Tenth Amendment—which states, "The powers not delegated to the United States by the Constitution, nor prohibited by it to the states, are reserved to the states respectively, or to the people"—education is a function of each state. There is some question whether the makers of the Constitution thoughtfully intended to leave education up to each state or whether they merely forgot to mention it. Some historians believe that our founding fathers wisely realized that local control of education would build a better America. Other historians believe that the framers of the Constitution were so preoccupied with what they believed were more important issues that they never thought to make national provision for education.

Even though the Constitution does not refer to education, the federal government has been active in educational affairs from the very beginning. In 1785 and 1787 the Continental Congress passed the Northwest Ordinance Acts. These acts provided for disposing of the Northwest Territory and encouraged the establishment of schools in the territory by stating: "Religion, morality and knowledge being necessary to good government and the happiness of mankind, schools and the means of education shall forever be encouraged." As the various states formed the Northwest Territory, they were required to set aside the sixteenth section of each township to be used for educational purposes.

In 1862 the federal government passed the Morrill Land Grant Act when it became apparent that existing colleges were not providing the vocational pro-

Professional Perspectives

A teacher who does not have clear goals in mind will teach by accident rather than design.

grams needed. The Hatch Act of 1887 established agricultural experimental stations across the country; the Smith-Lever Agricultural Extension Act of 1914 carried the services of land grant colleges to the people through extension services. These early federal acts did much to improve agriculture and industry at a time when our rapidly developing nation badly needed such improvement.

In 1917 the federal government passed the first act providing financial aid to public schools below the college level: the Smith-Hughes Act. This act provided for high school vocational programs in agriculture, trades and industry, and homemaking. High schools were academically oriented then, and the Smith-Hughes Act stimulated the development of badly needed vocational programs.

The 1930s were depresssion days, and the government was trying to solve national economic difficulties. Legislation was enacted during these years to encourage economic development, but this legislation indirectly provided financial aid to education. Five relief agencies related to education during this time included the Civilian Conservation Corps, National Youth Administration, Federal Emergency Relief Administration, Public Works Administration, and Federal Surplus Commodities Corporation.[2] These federal programs, although not sponsored primarily for education, benefited education and did so in response to the needs of the time.

The more recent involvements of the federal government, from 1940 to the present, are presented in the next chapter. Appendix D contains a chronology of the more important federal education acts.

Teachers and Their Tools

When we see the typical classroom of today, which is well equipped with a wealth of different types of learning materials, it is hard for us to realize that classrooms were once very sparsely equipped. Likewise, when we remember that our present-day teachers have at least four—and often five to eight—years of college training, it is difficult to believe that teachers have historically had little or no training. We will briefly look at these two topics in this section.

Preparation of Teachers

One of the first forms of teacher training grew out of the medieval guild system, in which a young man who wished to enter a certain field of work served a lengthy period of apprenticeship with a master in the field. Some young men became teachers by serving as apprentices, sometimes for as long as seven years, to master teachers.

The first teacher-training school we have any record of was mentioned in a request to the king of England, written by William Byngham in 1438, stating that "he may yeve withouten fyn or fee (the) mansion ycalled Goddeshous the which he hath made and edified in your towne of Cambridge for the free herbigage of poure scolers of Gramer. . . ."[3]

Byngham received permission and established Godshouse College on June 13, 1439. Students at this college gave demonstration lectures to fellow students as a rough way of practice teaching. Classes were conducted even during vacations so that country schoolmasters could attend. Byngham's college still exists as Christ's College of Cambridge University. At that early date of 1439 Byngham made provision for two features still considered very important in teacher education today—scheduling classes so that teachers in service may attend and providing some kind of student teaching experience. Many present-day educators would be surprised to find that these ideas are so old.

Teachers in colonial America were very poorly prepared; more often than not, they had received no special training at all. The single qualification of most of them was that they themselves had been students. Most colonial college teachers, private tutors, Latin grammar school teachers, and academy teachers had received some kind of college education, usually at one of the well-established colleges or universities in Europe. A few had received their education at a colonial American college.

Teachers in the various kinds of colonial elementary schools typically had only an elementary education, but a few had attended a Latin grammar school or a private academy. It was commonly believed that to be a teacher required only that the instructor know something about the subject matter to be taught; consequently, no teacher, regardless of the level taught, received training in the methodology of teaching.

Teaching was not considered a prestigious occupation, and the pay was poor. Consequently, many schoolteachers viewed their jobs as only temporary. For young ladies who taught elementary school, the "something better" was usually marriage. Men frequently left teaching for careers in the ministry or business. Not uncommonly, career teachers in the colonies were undesirable people. Records show that many teachers lost their jobs because they paid more attention to the tavern than to the school, or for stealing or swearing or other conduct unbecoming a person in such a position.

Since many colonial schools were conducted in connection with a church, the teacher was often considered an assistant to the minister. Besides teaching, other duties of some early New England teachers were "to act as court messenger, to serve summonses, to conduct certain ceremonial services of the church, to lead the Sunday choir, to ring the bell for public worship, to dig the graves, to perform other occasional duties."

Often the colonies used white indentured servants as teachers; many of the people who came to America bought passage by agreeing to work for some years as indentured servants. The ship's captain would then sell the indentured servant's services, more often than not by placing an ad in a newspaper. Such an ad appeared in a May 1786 edition of the *Maryland Gazette:*

Men and Women Servants
JUST ARRIVED

In the Ship *Paca,* Robert Caulfield, Master, in five Weeks from Belfast and Cork, a number of healthy Men and Women SERVANTS.

Among them are serveral valuable tradesmen, viz.

Carpenters, Shoemakers, Coopers, Blacksmiths, Staymakers, Bookbinders, Clothiers, Diers, Butchers, Schoolmasters, Millrights, and Labourers.

Their indentures are to be disposed of by the Subscribers,

> Brown, and Maris
> William Wilson

Some colonial teachers learned how to keep school by serving as apprentices to schoolmasters. Court records reveal numerous such indentures of apprenticeship; the following was recorded in New York City in 1772:

> This Indenture witnesseth that John Campbel Son of Robert Campbel of the City of New York with the Consent of his father and mother hath put himself and by these presents doth Voluntarily put and bind himself Apprentice to George Brownell of the Same City Schoolmaster to learn the Art Trade or Mastery—for and during the term of ten years. . . . And the said George Brownell Doth hereby Covenant and Promise to teach and instruct or Cause the said Apprentice to be taught and instructed in the Art Trade or Calling of a Schoolmaster by the best way or means he or his wife may or can.

One of Benjamin Franklin's justifications for proposing an academy in Philadelphia was that some of the graduates would make good teachers. Speculating on the need for such graduates, Franklin wrote:

> A number of the poorer sort [of academy graduates] will be hereby qualified to act as Schoolmasters in the Country, to teach children Reading, Writing, Arithmetic, and the Grammar of their Mother Tongue, and being of good morals and known character, may be recommended from the Academy to Country Schools for that purpose; the Country suffering at present very much for want of good Schoolmasters, and obliged frequently to employ in their Schools, vicious imported Servants, or concealed Papists, who by their bad Examples and Instructions often deprave the Morals and corrupt the Principles of the children under their Care.

The fact that Franklin said some of the "poorer" graduates would make suitable teachers reflects the low regard for teaching typical of the time. The academy that Franklin proposed was established in 1751 in Philadelphia, and many graduates of academies after that time did become teachers.

Many early educators recognized this country's need for better-qualified teachers; however, it was not until 1823 that the first teacher-training institution was established in the United States. This private school, called a *normal school* after its European counterpart, which had existed since the late seventeenth century, was established by the Rev. Mr. Samuel Hall in Concord, Vermont. Hall's school did not produce many teachers, but it did signal the beginning of formal teacher training in the United States.

The early normal school program usually consisted of a two-year course. Students typically entered the normal school right after finishing elementary school. Most normal schools did not require high school graduation for entrance until about 1900. The curriculum was much like the curriculum of the high schools of that time. Students reviewed subjects studied in elementary school, studied high school subjects, had a course in teaching (or "pedagogy" as it was then called), and did some student teaching in a model school usually operated in conjunction with the normal school. The subjects offered by a normal school in Albany, New York, in 1845 included English grammar, English composition, history, geography, reading, writing, orthography, arithmetic, algebra, geometry, trigonometry, human physiology, surveying, natural philosophy, chemistry, intellectual philosophy, moral philosophy, government, rhetoric, theory and practice of teaching, drawing, music, astronomy, and practice teaching.

Horace Mann was instrumental in establishing the first state-supported normal school, which opened in 1839 in Lexington, Massachusetts. Other public normal schools were established shortly afterwards. They typically offered a two-year teacher-training program. Some of the students came directly from elementary school; others had completed secondary school. Some states did not establish state-supported normal schools until the early 1900s.

During the early part of this century several factors caused a significant change in normal schools. For one thing, as the population of the United States increased, so did the enrollment in elementary schools, thereby creating an ever-increasing demand for elementary teachers. Likewise, as more and more people attended high school, more high school teachers were needed. To meet this demand, normal schools eventually expanded their curriculum to include secondary teacher education. The establishment of high schools also created a need for teachers highly specialized in particular academic subjects, and so normal schools established subject matter departments and developed more diversified programs. The length of the teacher education program was expanded to two, three, and finally four years, which helped to expand and diversify the normal school curriculum. The demand for teachers increased from about twenty thousand in 1900 to more than two hundred thousand in 1930.

Another factor contributed to the growth of the normal schools: The United States had advanced technologically to the point at which more college-educated citizens were needed. The normal schools assumed a responsibility to help meet this need by establishing many other academic programs in addition to teacher training. As normal schools extended their programs to four years and began granting baccalaureate degrees, they also began to call themselves *state teachers' colleges.* For most institutions the change in name took place during the 1930s.

Universities entered the teacher preparation business on a large scale about 1900. Before then, some graduates of universities had become high school teachers or college teachers, but not until 1900 did universities establish departments of education and add teacher education to the curriculum.

Just as the normal schools expanded in size, scope, and function to the point at which they became state teachers' colleges, so did the state teachers' colleges expand to become *state colleges.* This change in name and scope took place for most institutions about 1950. The elimination of the word *teacher* really explains the story behind this transition. The new state colleges gradually expanded their programs beyond teacher education and became multipurpose institutions. One of the main reasons for this transition was that more and more students coming to the colleges demanded a more varied education. The state teachers' colleges developed diversified programs to try to meet their demands.

Many of these same state colleges have now become state universities, offering doctoral degrees in a wide range of fields. Today, some of our largest and most highly regarded universities have evolved from normal schools. Figure 13.2 pictures the evolution of American teacher preparation institutions.

This completes our review of the history of teacher education. Obviously, establishing the teaching profession was a long and difficult task. Preparation of teachers has greatly improved since colonial times—when anyone could be a teacher—until the present, when the rigorous requirements for permanent teacher certification cannot be easily met by everyone.

Evolution of Teaching Materials

The first schools in colonial America were poorly equipped. In fact, the first elementary schools were usually conducted by housewives right in their homes. The only teaching materials likely to be found then were a Bible and perhaps one or two other religious books, a small amount of scarce paper, a few quill pens, and hornbooks. The *hornbook* was the most common teaching device in early colonial schools (see Figure 13.3). Hornbooks differed widely but typically consisted of a sheet of paper showing the alphabet, covered with a thin trans-

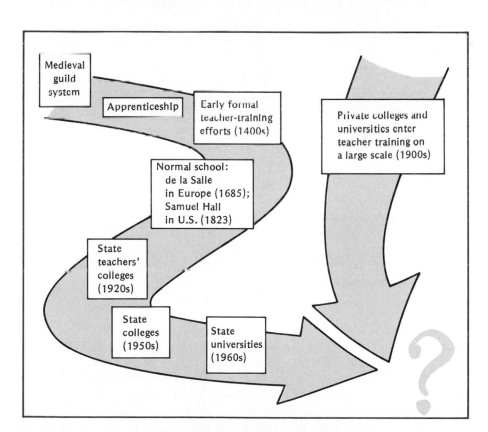

FIGURE 13.2 *Evolution of Teacher-Preparation Institutions*

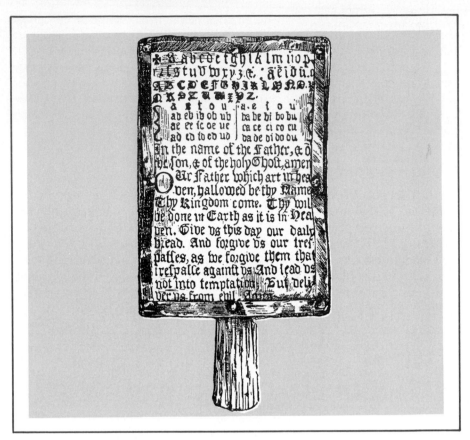

FIGURE 13.3   *A Hornbook*

parent sheet of cow's horn tacked to a paddle-shaped piece of wood. A leather cord was often looped through a hole in the paddle so that students could hang the hornbooks around their necks. Hornbooks provided students with their first reading instructions. Records indicate that hornbooks were used in Europe in the Middle Ages and were common there until about 1760.

As paper became more available, the hornbook evolved into a several-page "book" called a battledore. The battledore, printed on heavy paper, often resembled an envelope. Like the hornbook, it typically contained the alphabet and various religious prayers and/or admonitions.

The first real textbook to be used in colonial elementary schools was the *New England Primer*. Records show that the first copies of this book were printed in England in the 1600s. Copies of the *New England Primer* were also printed as early as 1690 in the American colonies. The book was advertised in the *News from the Stars Almanac,* published in 1690 in Boston (see Figure 13.4). The oldest extant copy of the *New England Primer* is a 1727 edition, now in the Lenox Collection of the New York Public Library.

Early American schools were often poorly equipped, with only the barest necessities. Compare this stark schoolroom with today's typical classroom. (*Source:* Meri Houtchens-Kitchens/The Picture Cube)

> ## ADVERTISEMENT.
> There is now in the Prefs, and will fuddenly be extant, a Second Impreffion of *The New-England Primer enlarged*, to which is added, more *Directions for Spelling*: the Prayer of K. *Edward* the 6th. and *Verfes made by Mr.* Rogers *the Martyr*, left as a Legacy to his Children.
> Sold by *Benjamin Harris*, at the *London Coffee-Houfe* in *Bofton*.

FIGURE 13.4 *Advertisement (1690) for the* New England Primer

The *New England Primer* was a small book, usually about 2½ by 4½ inches, with thin wooden covers covered by paper or leather. It contained 50 to 100 pages, depending on how many extra sections were added to each edition. The first pages contained the alphabet, vowels, and capital letters. Next came lists of words arranged from two to six syllables, followed by verses and tiny woodcut pictures for each letter in the alphabet. A reproduction of the verses and pictures is presented in Figure 13.5. The contents of the *New England Primer* reflect the heavily religious motive in colonial education.

The primer was virtually the only reading book used in colonial schools until about 1800, when Noah Webster published *The American Spelling Book.* This book eventually became known as the *Blue-Backed Speller* because of its blue cover. It eventually replaced the *New England Primer* as the most common elementary textbook. The speller reportedly sold over 24 million copies; its royalties supported Noah Webster and his family while he prepared his still famous dictionary. The speller was approximately 4 by 6½ inches; its cover was made of thin sheets of wood covered with light blue paper. The first part of the book contained rules and instructions for using the book; next came the alphabet, syllables, and consonants. The bulk of the book was taken up with lists of words arranged according to syllables and sounds. The book also contained rules for reading and speaking, moral advice, and stories of various sorts. Figure 13.6 shows a page from a *Blue-Backed Speller* printed about 1800.

FIGURE 13.5   New England Primer

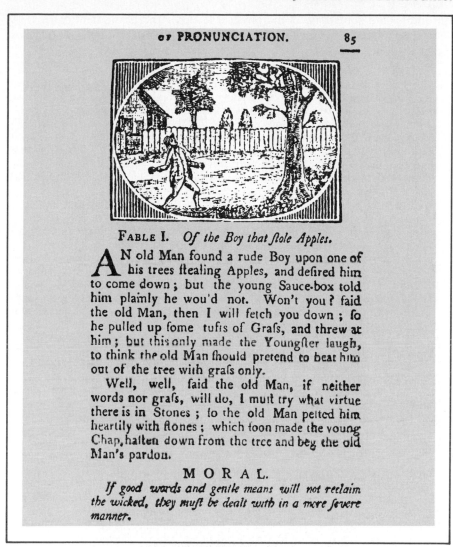

FIGURE 13.6 **The Blue-Backed Speller**

Very few textbooks were available for use in colonial Latin grammar schools, academies, and colleges, though various religious books, including the Bible, were often used. A few books dealing with history, geography, arithmetic, Latin, Greek, and certain classics were available for use in colonial secondary schools and colleges during the eighteenth century. Harvard College had a large library for its day, since John Harvard, its benefactor, had bequeathed his entire library of 400 volumes to the school.

By 1800, nearly two hundred years after the colonies had been established, school buildings and teaching materials were still very crude and meager. You can understand something of the physical features and equipment of an 1810 New England school by reading the following description written by a teacher of that school:

42

The size of the building was 22 × 20 feet. From the floor to the ceiling it was 7 feet. The chimney and entry took up about four feet at one end, leaving the school-room itself 18 × 20 feet. Around these sides of the room were connected desks, arranged so that when the pupils were sitting at them their faces were towards the instructor and their backs toward the wall. Attached to the sides of the desks nearest to the instructor were benches for small pupils. The instructor's desk and chair occupied the center. On this desk were stationed a rod, or ferule; sometimes both. These, with books, writings, inkstands, rules, and plummets, with a fire shovel, and a pair of tongs (often broken), were the princial furniture. . . .

The room was warmed by a large and deep fireplace. So large was it, and so efficacious in warming the room otherwise, that I have seen about one-eighth of a cord of good wood burning in it at a time. In severe weather it was estimated that the amount usually consumed was not far from a cord a week. . . .

The school was not infrequently broken up for a day or two for want of wood. The instructor or pupils were sometimes, however, compelled to cut or saw it to prevent the closing of the school. The wood was left in the road near the house, so that it often was buried in the snow, or wet with rain. At the best, it was usually burnt green. The fires were to be kindled about half an hour before the time of beginning the school. Often, the scholar, whose lot it was, neglected to build it. In consequence of this, the house was frequently cold and uncomfortable about half of the forenoon, when, the fire being very large, the excess of heat became equally distressing. Frequently, too, we were annoyed by smoke. The greatest amount of suffering, however, arose from excessive heat, particularly at the close of the day. The pupils being in a free perspiration when they left were very liable to take cold. . . .

The Instructors: The winter school usually opened about the first week of December, and continued twelve to sixteen weeks. The summer term commenced about the first of May. Formerly this was also continued about three to four months, but within ten years the term has been lengthened usually to twenty weeks. Males have been uniformly employed in winter, and females in summer.

The instructors have usually been changed every season, but sometimes they have been continued two successive summers or winters. A strong prejudice has always existed against employing the same instructor more than once or twice in the same district. This prejudice has yielded in one instance, so far that an instructor who had taught two successive winters, twenty-five years before, was employed another season. I have not been able to ascertain the number of instructors who have been engaged in the school during the last thirty years, but I can distinctly recollect thirty-seven. Many of them, both males and females, were from sixteen to eighteen years of age, and a few, over twenty-one.

Good moral character, and a thorough knowledge of the common branches, formerly were considered as indispensable qualifications in an instructor. The instructors were chiefly selected from the most respectable families in town. But for fifteen or twenty years, these things have not been so much regarded. They have indeed been deemed desirable; but the most common method now seems to be to ascertain, as near as possible, the dividend for that season from the public treasury, and then fix upon a teacher who will take charge of the school, three or four months, for this money. He must indeed be able to obtain a license from the Board of Visitors; but this has become nearly a matter of course, provided he can spell, read, and write. In general, the candidate is some favorite or relative of the District Committee. It gives me great pleasure, however, to say that the moral character of almost every instructor, so far as I know, has been unexceptional.

Instructors have usually boarded in the families of the pupils. Their compensation has varied from seven to eleven dollars a month for males; and from sixty-two and a half cents to one dollar a week for females. Within the past ten years, however, the price of instruction has rarely been less than nine dollars in the former case, and seventy-five cents in the latter. In the few instances in which instructors have furnished their own board the compensation has been about the same, it being assumed that they could work at some employment of their own enough to pay their board, especially the females.

The Instruction: Two of the Board of Visitors usually visit the winter schools twice during the term. In the summer, their visits are often omitted. These visits usually occupy from one hour to an hour and a half. They are spent merely in hearing a few hurried lessons, and in making some remarks, general in their character. Formerly, it was customary to examine the pupils in some approved Catechism, but this practice has been omitted for twenty years.

The parents seldom visit the school, except by special invitation. The greater number pay very little attention to it at all. There are, however, a few who are gradually awakening to the importance of good instruction; but there are also a few who oppose everything which is suggested as, at the least, useless; and are scarcely willing their children should be governed in the school.

The school books have been about the same for thirty years. Webster's Spelling Book, the American Preceptor, and the New Testament, have been the principal books used. Before the appearance of the American Preceptor, Dwight's Geography was used as a reading book. A few of the Introduction to the American Orator were introduced about twelve years since, and, more recently, Jack Halyard.

Until within a few years, no studies have been permitted in the day school but spelling, reading, and writing. Arithmetic was taught by a few instructors, one or two evenings in a week, but, in spite of the most determined opposition, arithmetic is now permitted in the day school, and a few pupils study geography.[4]

About 1820 a new instructional device was introduced into American schools—the slate. These school slates were thin flat pieces of slate stone framed with wood. The pencils used to write on the slate were also made of slate and produced a light but legible line. The wooden frames of some of the slates were covered with cloth so that noise would be minimized as students placed the slates on the desk. There were even double slates made by hinging two single slates together with cord or leather. Students wrote their assignments on the slates, just as today's students write on tablet paper. Later on, large pieces of slate made up the blackboards that were added to classrooms.

In the same way that Noah Webster's *Blue-Backed Speller* replaced the *New England Primer,* so did McGuffey's *Reader* eventually replace the *Blue-Backed Speller*. These readers were carefully geared to each grade and were meant to instill in children a respect for hard work, thrift, self-help, and honesty. McGuffey's *Reader* dominated the elementary school book market until approximately 1900, when it was gradually replaced by newer and improved readers written by David Tower, James Fassett, William Elson, and others. Figure 13.7 is a diagrammatic summary of the evolution of the textbook.

During the twentieth century teachers have gradually adapted a variety of tools to assist them in educating American youth. This variety has come about partly through the influence of Pestalozzi, John Dewey, and others, who demonstrated that children learn best by firsthand experiences. Likewise, school buildings have become larger, more elaborate, and better designed to encourage

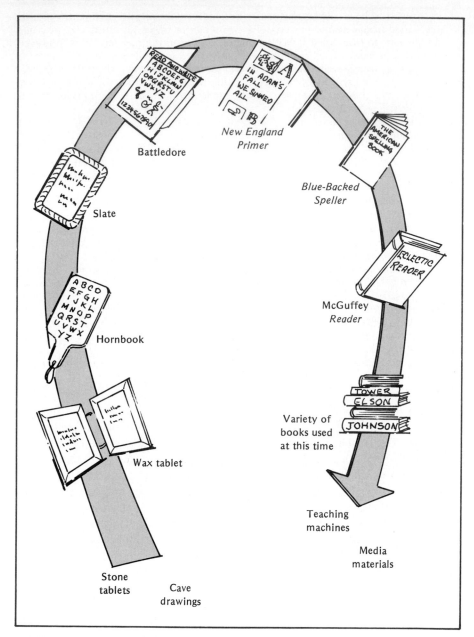

FIGURE 13.7 *Evolution of the Textbook*

learning. Today, many schools are equipped with an impressive array of books, laboratory equipment, movie projectors, filmstrip projectors, tape recorders, television devices, single-concept films, teaching machines, programmed materials, and learning devices of all kinds. Some of the modern school buildings are not only excellent from an educational standpoint but magnificent pieces of architecture as well. One cannot help but be awed by the contrast between American education today and its humble beginning years ago.

Education for Special Populations

In this section we will examine briefly the education of blacks and females as it has slowly developed through history in the United States. We will also review the extremely important role of private education in America.

Education of American Blacks

In 1619, only a dozen years after Jamestown was established, the first boatload of slaves arrived in the colonies. This event was recorded for history when, in that year, John Rolfe wrote in his *Journal* that the captain of a Dutch ship "sold us twenty Negroes." These slaves were imported as a source of cheap labor for the new colonies.

45

The number of imported slaves steadily increased; between 1700 and 1750 thousands of blacks were brought to the American colonies each year. By the Revolutionary War there were approximately 700,000 blacks in the colonies; by 1860 there were about 4.5 million.

Probably the first organized attempts to educate the blacks in colonial America were by French and Spanish missionaries.[5] These early missionary efforts set an example that influenced the education of black people throughout the colonies. The missionaries, in their endeavors to carry out their religious missions, provided instruction for blacks and also for the numerous offspring who were the result of mixed breeding. Educating slaves posed an interesting moral problem for the church. The English colonists had to find a way to overcome the idea that converting a slave to Christianity might logically lead to his or her freedom. The problem they faced was how to eliminate an unwritten law that a Christian should not be a slave. The church's governing bodies and the Bishop of London settled the matter by decreeing that conversion did not lead to formal emancipation.

40

The organized church nevertheless provided the setting in which black people were allowed to develop skills at reading, leadership, and educating their brethren. Often blacks and whites attended church together. Eventually, some preachers, former slaves, demonstrated exceptional skill in "spreading the gospel." The Baptists in particular, by encouraging a form of self-government, allowed blacks to become active in the church. This move fostered the growth of black congregations; because of it, the enslaved as well as the free black was given an opportunity for education and development not provided by many other denominations.

The efforts of the English to educate black slaves were largely carried out by the Society for the Propagation of the Gospel in Foreign Parts. The Society was created by the Established Church of London in 1701. In 1705 the Reverend

Samuel Thomas of Goose Creek Parish in South Carolina established a school fostered by the society, enrolling 60 black students. Nine years later the society opened a school in New York City where 200 black pupils were enrolled. Despite stringent opposition from many whites, who believed that educating slaves was a "dangerous business," the society went on to establish other schools for black people. The degree of success of these early efforts to educate blacks varied greatly. Initially, many people were not generally opposed to educating blacks. Education, however, seemed to make the slaves aware of their plight. In the South much of the unrest concerning slavery was attributed to the education of slaves. Insurrections, uprisings, and threats to overseers, masters, and their families produced fear among the whites. Consequently, some states even passed legislation that eliminated any form of education for the slaves.

The blacks' individual success in acquiring education, as well as their group efforts to establish schools, was greatly enhanced by sympathetic and humanitarian white friends. John Chavis, a free black born in 1763 in Oxford, North Carolina, was a black who was helped by whites. Chavis became a successful teacher of aristocractic whites. His white neighbors sent him to Princeton "to see if a Negro would take a college education." His rapid advancement under Dr. Witherspoon soon indicated that the adventure was a success. He returned to Virginia and later went to North Carolina, where he preached among his own people. The success of John Chavis, even under experimental conditions, represented a small step forward in the education of American blacks.

Benjamin Banneker, a distinguished black man, was born in Baltimore County, Maryland, in 1731. Baltimore maintained a liberal policy toward educating blacks, which permitted Banneker to learn to read, write, and do arithmetic at a relatively early age. He became extremely well educated. In 1770 one of his first accomplishments was to manufacture the first clock made in the United States. After attracting the attention of the scientific world generally, he turned his attention specifically to astronomy. Without any instruction but with the help of books borrowed from an encouraging white inventor, Banneker soon could calculate eclipses of the sun and moon. His accuracy far excelled that of any other American. The outstanding works of this inventor aroused the curiosity of Thomas Jefferson, who in 1803 invited Banneker to his home, Monticello. The acknowledgment of a black man's achievement by a noted American was still another milestone in the education of the blacks and in their elevation from subservience.

Frederick Douglass, born a slave in Maryland in 1817, ran away from slavery and began talking to abolitionist groups about his experiences as a slave. He attributed his fluent speech to listening to his master talk. Douglass firmly believed that if he devoted all his efforts to improving vocational education, he could greatly improve the blacks' plight. He thought that previous attempts by educators to combine liberal and vocational education had failed, so he emphasized vocational education solely.

One of the first northern schools regularly established for blacks appears to have been that of Elias Neau in New York City in 1704. Neau was an agent of the Society for the Propagation of the Gospel in Foreign Parts.

In 1807 free blacks, including George Bell, Nicholas Franklin, and Moses Liverpool, built the first schoolhouse for blacks in the District of Columbia. Not until 1824, however, was there a black teacher in that district—John Adams. In 1851 Washington citizens attempted to discourage Myrtilla Miner from establishing an academy for black girls. However, after much turmoil and harassment the white schoolmistress from New York founded her academy; it is still functioning today.

Prudence Crandall, a young Quaker, established an early boarding school at Canterbury, Connecticut. The trouble she ran into dramatizes some of the northern animosity to educating black people then. Trouble arose when Sarah Harris, a "colored girl," asked to be admitted to the institution. After much deliberation, Miss Crandall finally consented. White parents objected to the black girl's attending the school and withdrew their children. To keep the school open, Miss Crandall recruited black children. The pupils were threatened with violence, local stores would not trade with her, and the school building was vandalized. The citizens of Canterbury petitioned the state legislature to enact a law that would make it illegal to educate blacks from out of state. Miss Crandall was jailed and tried before the state supreme court in July 1834. The court never gave a final decision because defects were found in the information prepared by the attorney for the state, and the indictment was eventually dropped.

Finally, Boston, the seat of northern liberalism, established a separate school for black children in 1798. Elisha Sylvester, a white man, was in charge. The school was founded in the home of Primus Hall, a "Negro in good standing." Two years later 66 free blacks petitioned the school committee for a separate school and were refused. Undaunted, the patrons of Hall's house employed two instructors from Harvard; 35 years later, the school was allowed to move to a separate building. The city of Boston opened its first primary school for the education of black children in 1820—one more milestone in the history of black education.

Unfortunately, despite isolated efforts like these, blacks received pathetically little formal education until the Emancipation Proclamation issued by President Abraham Lincoln on January 1, 1863. At that time the literacy rate among blacks was estimated at 5 percent. Sunday school represented about the only opportunity most black people had to learn to read. In the late 1700s and early 1800s, some communities did set up separate schools for blacks; however, only a very small percentage of blacks ever attended the schools. A few colleges such as Oberlin, Bowdoin, Franklin, Rutland, and Harvard admitted black students; but again, very few blacks attended college then. There were even a few black colleges, such as Lincoln University in Pennsylvania (1854) and Wilberforce University in Ohio (1856); however, the efforts and opportunities for the education of American blacks were pathetically few in view of the size of the black population.

Although there was no great rush to educate black people, the abolishment of slavery in 1865 signaled the beginning of a slow but steady effort to improve their education. By 1890 literacy rose to 40 percent; by 1910 it was estimated that 70 percent of black Americans had learned to read and write. These statistics showing the rapid increase in black literacy are impressive; however, they are dampened by a report of the U.S. Commissioner of Education, which showed that by 1900 fewer than 70 out of 1,000 public high schools in the South were provided for blacks.

The most significant developments in the education of American blacks have been in the twentieth century, mostly since 1950. These developments are discussed more fully in the next chapter.

Education of Women

Historically, women have not been afforded equal educational opportunities in the United States. Furthermore, many authorities claim that our schools have traditionally been sexist institutions. Although there is much evidence to support both these assertions, it is also true that an impressive list of women have made significant contributions to our educational progress.

Colonial schools did not provide education for girls in any significant way. In some instances girls were taught to read, but they were not admitted to Latin grammar schools, academies, or colleges.

One of the first early efforts to provide better education for women was the Troy Female Seminary located in New York, which was opened in 1821. Troy was founded by Emma Willard, whose lifelong goal was to further the progress of women. Many of the graduates of Troy became prominent in various fields, including education. Many other female institutions were established and became prominent during the mid and late 1800s, including Mary Lyon's Mount Holyoke Female Seminary; Jane Ingersoll's Seminary in Cortland, New York; Julia and Elias Mark's Southern Carolina Collegiate Institute at Barhamville, to name just a few. Unfortunately, not until well into the twentieth century were women generally afforded access to higher education.

Even though women eventually could attend college, they were not given equal access to all fields of study. Considerable progress has been made in recent years, but remnants of this problem still exist today.

The fact that women have made significant contributions to our educational progress through the years has been well documented. In addition to the examples just mentioned and those discussed elsewhere in this book, we can add the following: Catherine Beecher (who founded the Hartford Female Seminary), Jane Addams (who proposed an expanded school as part of her new liberal social philosophy), Susan Anthony (who was a teacher in her early professional life), Mrs. Carl Schurz (who founded the first kindergarten in this country), and Mary McLeod Bethune (daughter of slave parents who became president of the American Teachers Association and founder of her own college).

Maria Montessori was still another important female educator. Born in 1870 in Italy, Montessori first became a successful physician and later a prominent educational philosopher. She developed her own theory and methods of educating young children. Her methods utilized child-size school furniture and specially designed learning materials. She emphasized independent work by children under the guidance of a trained directress. Private Montessori schools thrive in the United States today.

Private Education in America

Private education has been extremely important in the development of America. Private schools carried on most of the education in colonial America. The first colonial colleges—Harvard, William and Mary, Yale, and Princeton—were private schools. Many of the other early colonial schools were conducted by churches, missionary societies, or private individuals.

| 32 |

Not until after the Revolution, when there was a strong sense of nationalism, did certain educators advocate a strong public school system for the new nation. Such recommendations, however, were not acted on for many years.

In the meantime, some of the Protestant churches continued to expand their schools during the colonial period. For instance, the Congregational, Quaker, Episcopalian, Baptist, Methodist, Presbyterian, and Reform churches all, at various times and in varying degrees, established and operated schools for their youth. It was the Roman Catholics and Lutherans, however, who eventually developed elaborate parochial school systems.

As early as 1820 there were 240 Lutheran parochial schools in Pennsylvania. Although the number of Lutheran schools in that particular state eventually dwindled, Henry Muhlenburg and other Lutheran leaders continued to establish parochial schools until the public school system became well established. The Missouri Synod Lutheran Church has continued to maintain a well-developed parochial school system right down to the present. Currently, there are approximately 1,700 Lutheran elementary and secondary schools, which enroll about 200,000 pupils in the United States. Most of these schools are conducted by the Missouri Synod Lutheran Church.

| 44 |

The Roman Catholic parochial school system grew rapidly after its beginnings in the 1800s. This growth continued into the twentieth century; the Roman Catholic parochial school system is now the largest private school system in the world.

Summary and Implications

The history of American education is filled with many messages. Some of these messages tell of successes, some of failures, others of dedicated teachers, of humble beginnings, of the individual's thirst for knowledge—even of those who have been willing to die for the truth. A chronology of these highlights of the historical development of education in the United States is presented in Appendix E.

These historical events have implications for today's educator. Teachers can learn much from our educational history if they will listen carefully to these messages from the past. In particular, they will come to realize how very important education is to the preservation and progress of our society—perhaps even more important than any other human endeavor.

Discussion Questions

1. Discuss the evolution of elementary schools.
2. How did the development of public education differ in the northern, middle, and southern colonies?
3. What historical conditions led to that uniquely American institution, the comprehensive high school?
4. Discuss the role that private schools have played in American education.

5. How has the concept of the nature of humankind changed in the past 300 years? What effect has this change had on teacher education?
6. What are the highlights of the history of education of women in America?

Supplemental Activities

1. Invite an elderly retired teacher to your class to discuss his or her teaching experience.
2. Invite a professor from the history department to discuss the history of education from his or her viewpoint.
3. Create several artistic displays, charts, or exhibits, using various materials, depicting significant aspects of the history of education.

4. Make a hornbook, battledore, wax tablet, or quill pen.
5. Collect some old books and other educational artifacts. Study them, and then give them to your school so that future students may see and study them.
6. Devise a plan to solve one or two of the major problems that have plagued public education down through the ages.

Notes

1. Paul Monroe, *Source Book of the History of Education* (New York: Macmillian, 1901).
2. Roe L. Johns and Edgar L. Morphet, *Financing the Public Schools* (Englewood Cliffs, N.J.: Prentice-Hall, 1960), p. 378.
3. W. H. G. Armytage, "William Byngham: A Medieval Protagonist of the Training of Teachers," *History of Education Journal*, 2 (Summer 1951): 108.

4. Monroe, 282.
5. Much of the material dealing with the history of American blacks up to the signing of the Emancipation Proclamation (1863) was taken from the doctoral dissertation of Samuel David, "Education, Law, and the Negro" (Urbana: University of Illinois, 1970).

Bibliography

Buetow, Harold A. *Of Singular Benefit: The Story of U.S. Catholic Education*. New York: Macmillan, 1970.

Butts, R. Freeman. *Public Education in the United States: From Revolution to Reform*. New York: Holt, Rinehart and Winston, 1978.

Carpenter, Charles. *History of American Schoolbooks*. Philadelphia: University of Pennsylvania Press, 1963.

Church, Robert L., and Sedlak, Michael W. *Education in the United States: An Interpretive History*. New York: Macmillan, 1976.

Cohen, Sheldon S. *A History of Colonial Education 1607–1776*. New York: Wiley, 1974.

Cordasco, Francesco, and Cremin, Lawrence. *A History of Education in American Culture*. New York: Holt, Rinehart and Winston, 1953.

Cremin, Lawrence A. *The Transformation of the School: Progressivism in American Education, 1876–1957*. New York: Knopf, 1961.

Gartner, Lloyd P., ed. *Jewish Education in the United States: A Documentary History*. New York: Teachers College Press, 1970.

Griffin, Frances. *Less Time for Meddling: A History of Salem Academy and College, 1772–1866*. Winston-Salem, N.C.: Blair, 1979.

Gross, Carl H., and Chandler, Charles C. *The History of American Education Through Readings*. Boston: Heath, 1964.

Herbst, J. "Beyond the Debate over Revisionism: Three Educational Pasts in Written Language." *History of Education Quarterly,* 20 (Summer 1980): 131–145.

Klassen, Frank. "Persistence and Change in Eighteenth-Century Colonial Education." *History of Education Quarterly,* 2 (June 1962): 83-99.

Maxson, M. M., and Kraus, L. L. "Curriculum Censorship in the Public School." *Educational Forum,* 43 (May 1979): 392–407.

Perkinson, Henry J., ed. *Two Hundred Years of American Educational Thought.* New York: McKay, 1976.

Powell, Arthur G. *The Uncertain Profession: Harvard and the Search for Educational Authority.* Cambridge, Mass.: Harvard University Press, 1980.

Pulliam, John D. *History of Education in America.* Columbus, Ohio: Merrill, 1982.

Rippa, Alexander S. *Education in a Free Society: An American History.* 4th ed. New York: Longman, 1980.

Travers, P. H. "Historic View on School Discipline." *Educational Horizons,* 58 (Summer 1980): 184–187.

Tyack, David B. *The One Best System.* Cambridge, Mass.: Harvard University Press, 1974.

Warren, Donald R., ed. *History, Education and Public Policy: Recovering the American Educational Past.* Berkeley, Calif.: McCutchan, 1978.

Recent Developments
in Education, 1940–Present

Focus Questions

- What important changes have taken place in education during your lifetime?
- In what ways, if any, should the federal government be involved in education?
- How did the special education programs we have in our schools today come into being?

- What is meant by *equal educational opportunity*?
- What is the status of private schools in the United States today?
- What trends have been evident in our school system over the past 50 years?

Key Terms and Concepts

Educational growth
Educational critics
Federal role in education
Litigation's influence on education
Special education
Private education
Equal educational opportunity

Professional education
Analysis of teaching
Teacher characteristics
School district consolidation
Educational objectives
Teacher effectiveness

What Would You Do?

A friend of yours argues that little, if any, progress has been made over the past 50 years toward providing equal educational opportunity for all American youth. For instance, your friend points out that minorities have difficulty getting into college and that our schools are still sexist institutions. What would you say to your friend?

The superintendent of the school district in which you are teaching has asked your opinion about which of the recent trends in education seem to have the greatest value. Which trends would be on your "most promising education trends" list, and why would you select those trends?

You have been offered two new teaching positions—one in a public school and one in a private school. What information would you like about both of these teaching positions to help you decide which offer to accept?

There have been many changes in the American educational enterprise over the past half century. Space will not allow a detailed discussion of these relatively recent changes; however, we will briefly examine three general topics which seem to characterize these changes since about 1940: the rapid growth of our educational system, the increasing complexity of the educational enterprise, and the recent trends in our schools.

The Rapid Growth of the Educational Enterprise

Since World War II education has been characterized by a great deal of growth and change: growth in terms of school enrollment, educational budgets, complexity, and federal influence; complexity in terms of court decisions, proliferation of school laws, confusion about goals, school financial difficulties, struggle for control, and diversification of curricula. Perhaps the single most dramatic change that has occurred in education over the past half century is the growth of the educational enterprise. This growth took place in many ways.

Enrollment Growth

Table 14.1 shows that the total number of students in the United States approximately doubled from 1940 to 1980. While part of this rapid growth in school enrollment was due to overall population growth, a good part was due to the fact that greater percentages of people were going to school. Furthermore, people were staying in school much longer, as shown in the more than sixfold increased enrollment in higher education.

Need for More Teachers

Naturally, this dramatic increase in student enrollments required many more teachers. At times our colleges simply could not produce enough additional

TABLE 14.1   *U.S. Total Public and Private School Enrollment, 1940–1980*

Type of School	1940	1950	1960	1970	1980
Kindergarten	661,000	1,175,000	2,293,000	2,821,000	3,069,000
Grades 1–8	20,466,000	21,032,000	30,119,000	34,190,000	28,698,000
Grades 9–12	7,130,000	6,453,000	9,600,000	14,418,000	15,191,000
Higher education	1,494,000	2,659,000	3,216,000	7,136,000	11,570,000
Total	29,751,000	31,319,000	45,228,000	58,566,000	58,529,000

Source: Bureau of the Census, *Statistical Abstract of the United States 1982–83* (Washington, D.C.: U.S. Department of Commerce), p. 135.

TABLE 14.2   *U.S. Teachers, 1940–1980* (Public and Private, All Levels)

1940	1,098,000
1950	1,236,000
1960	1,831,000
1970	2,810,000
1980	3,331,000

Source: Bureau of the Census, *Digest of Education Statistics 1982* (Washington, D.C.: U.S. Department of Commerce), pp. 11–12.

teachers. In this situation teacher certification requirements were lowered, sometimes to the point at which no professional education training was required at all. Over time, however, the nation seemed to meet the demand for more teachers. This increase in teachers is shown in Table 14.2.

As one would expect, the increased numbers of students and teachers cost a great deal more money. More schools had to be built, more buses purchased, more books and other instructional materials obtained, more school personnel hired—more of everything required to provide education was needed.

School District Consolidation

The consolidation of school districts was one development that inadvertently led to increased busing costs. Table 14.3 shows that the number of separate school districts was reduced from 117,000 in 1940 to 16,000 in 1980. This table also shows the corresponding dramatic decline in the number of one-teacher schools over this same time period. These "one-room country schools" symbolized American education for millions of Americans. Although school consolidation undoubtedly had many educational advantages and even saved more school dollars in some ways, it did necessitate the busing of more students over greater distances.

TABLE 14.3   *Consolidation of Public School Districts, 1940–1980*

Year	School Districts	One-Teacher Schools
1940	117,000	114,000
1950	84,000	60,000
1960	41,000	20,000
1970	18,000	2,000
1980	16,000	1,000

Source: Bureau of the Census, *Digest of Education Statistics 1982* (Washington, D.C.: U.S. Department of Commerce), p. 61.

Growth of Busing

Table 14.4 shows the increase in school busing from 1940 to 1980. Both the number and percentage of students that were bused increased considerably over this period. Likewise, the total cost and per-pupil cost rose significantly.

Bigger School Budgets

The examples of educational growth just discussed are but a few of the factors that drove the nation's public education costs to record heights. This story of increasing public school budgets is vividly told by Table 14.5. Even if corrected for inflation, public education has become considerably more expensive. (The percentage of the gross national product spent on education rose from 3.5% in 1940 to 7% in 1980.[1])

Curricular Growth

The school curriculum also experienced considerable growth during the past 50 years. This curricular growth, like most change, was the result of an accumulation of many smaller events. One such event was the publication in 1942 of the *Eight Year Study* showing that students attending "progressive" schools achieved as well as students at traditional schools. This report helped create a climate for more experimentation with school curricula and teaching methodologies. The publication of a series of statements on the goals of American education (the 1938 "Purposes of Education in American Democracy," the 1944 "Education for All American Youth," and the 1952 "Imperative Needs of Youth") all helped to broaden our schools' curricular offerings.

Shortly after the Soviet Union launched *Sputnik*, the world's first artificial satellite, Congress passed the National Defense Education Act in 1958. This act provided massive infusions of federal dollars to improve our schools' science, mathematics, engineering, and foreign language programs. Eventually, innovative curricula such as SMSG mathematics, BSCS biology, and PSCS physics grew

TABLE 14.4   *Public School Student Busing, 1940–1980*

Year	Number of Students	Percent of Total Student Population	Total Cost Excluding Capital Outlay	Average Cost per Pupil per Year
1940	4 million	16	$83 million	$20
1950	7 million	28	$215 million	$31
1960	12 million	38	$486 million	$40
1970	18 million	43	$1218 million	$67
1980	21 million	57	$3833 million	$175

Source: Bureau of the Census, *Digest of Education Statistics 1982* (Washington, D.C.: U.S. Department of Commerce), p. 41.

TABLE 14.5 *Public School Budgets, 1940–1980*

Year	Approximate Total Budget	Percentage Source		
		Federal	*State*	*Local*
1940	$2 billion	2	30	68
1950	$5 billion	3	40	57
1960	$15 billion	4	39	56
1970	$40 billion	8	40	52
1980	$97 billion	10	47	43

Source: Bureau of the Census, *Digest of Education Statistics 1982* (Washington, D.C.: U.S. Department of Commerce), p. 75.

out of these programs. Other school programs, such as guidance, were later funded through this act. Note that in this case the federal government called upon our schools to help solve what was perceived to be a "national defense" problem. Regardless of the motive, the NDEA represented another milestone that contributed significantly to the growth of our nation's educational enterprise.

If one were to compare today's school curriculum in nearly any subject with the curriculum in our schools 50 years ago, one would find impressive changes. The 1940 curriculum was very narrow and designed primarily for classes of college-bound students, whereas today's curriculum is clearly broader and designed for students of all abilities. This 50-year growth in our school curriculum has come about through the dedicated work of many educators and represents one of the truly significant historical accomplishments in American education.

Growth of Special Education Programs

Perhaps curriculum growth is best illustrated in the area of special education. The public schools, historically, have not provided special education programs for handicapped children. Schools simply accommodated such children as best they could, usually by placing them in regular classrooms. Teachers had relatively little or no training to help them understand and assist the handicapped child. In fact, relatively little was known about common handicapping conditions.

Not until the federal government passed a series of laws during the mid–twentieth century—of which Public Law 94–142, Education for the Handicapped Children Act, was among the more widely publicized—did schools begin to develop well-designed programs for handicapped students. These new special education programs needed specially prepared teachers—teachers for visually handicapped students, for hearing-impaired students, for physically handicapped students, for various types of mentally handicapped students, for students with behavior disorders, and so forth. States and colleges then developed a wide variety of teacher-training programs for special educators. Table 14.6 lists some of the major federal laws that have helped develop special education programs in the United States.

TABLE 14.5   *Selected Federal Laws for Special Education*

Year Enacted	Law	Description
1948	P.L. 80–617	Prohibits discrimination in hiring physically handicapped persons in civil service jobs
1954	P.L. 83–531	Provides funds for research in mental retardation
1958	P.L. 85–926	Trains college instructors who will teach teachers for the mentally retarded
1963	P.L. 88–164	Provides funding for research and demonstration projects
1964	P.L. 89–10	Provides educational programs for the disadvantaged
1965	P.L. 89–313	Creates funds to support children in hospitals and institutions
1966	P.L. 89–750	Created the Bureau of Education for the Handicapped
1968	P.L. 90–480	Prohibits barriers for the physically handicapped
1968	P.L. 90–538	Establishes special education demonstration sites
1969	P.L. 91–230	Recognizes learning disabilities and gifted children
1972	P.L. 92–424	Mandates Head Start programs to serve handicapped children
1973	P.L. 93–112	The Vocational Rehabilitation Act Amendments of 1973
1973	P.L. 93–380	Requires actions by schools to remain eligible for federal funds
1975	P.L. 94–142	Calls for education for all handicapped children

Special education has developed very rapidly over a relatively short period of time in our recent history. It continues to evolve rapidly today and will likely continue to do so in the future.

The Increasing Complexity of the Educational Enterprise

Our current educational system is much more complex than the school systems of the past. This complexity is manifested in many different ways, some of which we will review in this section.

Increasing Federal Involvement

As we pointed out earlier, our federal government has played important roles in the development of national educational programs. This federal involvement in education has gradually increased over the years and reached a crescendo during the past half century.

The 1940s saw the nation threatened by war. The Vocational Education for National Defense Act was a crash program to prepare workers needed in industry to produce goods for national defense. The program operated through state educational agencies and trained over seven million workers. In 1941 the Lanham

Act provided for building, maintaining, and operating community facilities in areas where local communities had unusual burdens because of defense and war initiatives.

 The GI Bill of 1944 provided for the education of veterans of World War II. Later, similar bills assisted veterans of the Korean conflict. These bills afforded education to over 10 million veterans at a cost of almost $20 billion. Payments were made directly to veterans and to the colleges and schools the veterans attended. The federal government recognized a need to help young people whose careers had been interrupted by military service. In 1966 another GI Bill was passed for veterans of the war in Southeast Asia.

The National Science Foundation, established in 1950, emphasized the need for continued support of basic scientific research. It was created to "promote the progress of science; to advance the national health, prosperity, and welfare; to secure the national defense; and for other purposes." The Cooperative Research Program of 1954 authorized the U.S. commissioner of education to enter into contracts with universities, colleges, and state education agencies to carry on educational research.

Beginning in 1957 when the first Soviet space vehicle was launched, the federal government increased its participation in education even more. The National Defense Education Act of 1958, the Vocational Education Act of 1963, the Manpower Development and Training Act of 1963, the Elementary and Secondary Education Act of 1965, and the International Education Act of 1966 are examples of recent increased federal participation in educational affairs. Federally supported educational programs such as Project Head Start, National Teacher Corps, and Upward Bound are further indications of federal intervention in public education.

Appendix D lists some of the most important federal programs that have supported education. All these acts have involved categorical federal aid to education—that is, aid for a specific use. Some individuals believe that federal influence on education has recently been greater than either state or local influence. There can be no denying that through federal legislation, U.S. Supreme Court decisions, and federal administrative influence, the total federal effect on education is indeed great. Indications are that this effect will become even greater in the future. It will remain for future historians to determine whether or not this trend in American education is a wise one.

The Struggle for Equal Educational Opportunity

The past half century has also been characterized by an increasing struggle for equal educational opportunity for all children, regardless of race, creed, religion, or sex. This struggle was initiated by the black activism movement, given ad-

Professional Perspectives

Providing equal educational opportunity for each and every student is a major challenge for today's teacher.

Many teachers have developed techniques to individualize programs for each student. All teachers should strive to do so.

ditional momentum by the women's rights movement, and eventually joined by many other groups such as Spanish-speaking Americans, American Indians, and native Alaskans. The details of this relatively recent quest for equal educational opportunity are discussed in many other parts of this book. We mention it briefly at this point simply to emphasize that the struggle for equal educational opportunity represents an important but unrealized recent historical movement in education. Today, many observers are pointing out that with the accelerated growth of minority subcultures within our nation, our economic and political survival depends to a large degree on their educational opportunities and achievements.

The Professionalization of Education

As we pointed out earlier in this book, formal teacher training is a relatively recent phenomena. Teacher-training programs were developed during the first half of this century. By the midpoint of this century each state had established requirements for a teaching certificate. Since then, during the past 40 to 50 years, teacher training and certification have been characterized by a "refinement" or "professionalization" movement. Table 14.7 shows that teacher salaries also improved considerably over this period.

In addition to teacher education, this professionalization movement touched just about all facets of education—curriculum, teaching methodology, training of school service personnel (administrators, counselors, librarians, media and other specialists), in-service teacher training, teacher organizations, and even school building construction. To clearly understand this professionalization movement, one need only compare pictures of an old one-room country school with one of our new school buildings, or read both a 1940 and a 1985 publication of the AFT or NEA, or contrast a mid-twentieth-century high school curriculum to one from today, or compile a list of the teaching materials found in a 1940 school and a similar list for a typical contemporary school.

Revitalization of Private Schools

As indicated earlier in this part of the book, religion was the main purpose of education in colonial America. Children were taught to read primarily so they

TABLE 14.7 *Average Annual Teacher Salary, 1940–1980*

Year	Unadjusted	Adjusted to 1980–1981 Purchasing Power
1940	$1,441	$8,930
1950	$3,010	$11,008
1960	$5,174	$15,251
1970	$8,840	$20,271
1980	$16,780	$18,720

Source: Bureau of the Census, *Digest of Education Statistics 1982* (Washington, D.C.: U.S. Department of Commerce), p. 57.

could read the Bible and gain salvation. Most early colleges were established primarily to train ministers.

As the public school system developed, however, the religious nature of education gradually diminished to the point at which relatively few American children attended private schools. There have always been certain religious groups, however, that have struggled to create and maintain their own private schools so that religious instruction could permeate all areas of the curriculum. The most notable of these religious groups is the Roman Catholic Church. Over the past 25 years, though, enrollment in non-Catholic religious schools has grown dramatically while the Catholic school enrollment has declined. These changes in enrollment are reflected in Figure 14.1.

Recent Trends in Education[2]

Education experienced a major change following World War II when Dewey, Counts, Bagley, Charters, Terman, and other intellectuals who held sway during the first half of the twentieth century yielded to a somewhat less philosophically oriented breed of researchers represented by Harris, Maslow, Havighurst, Bloom, Guilford, Cronbach, Bruner, McLuhan, Chomsky, and Piaget. The Progressive Education Association closed its doors, and a series of White House conferences on children, youth, and education were inaugurated in an attempt to improve education.

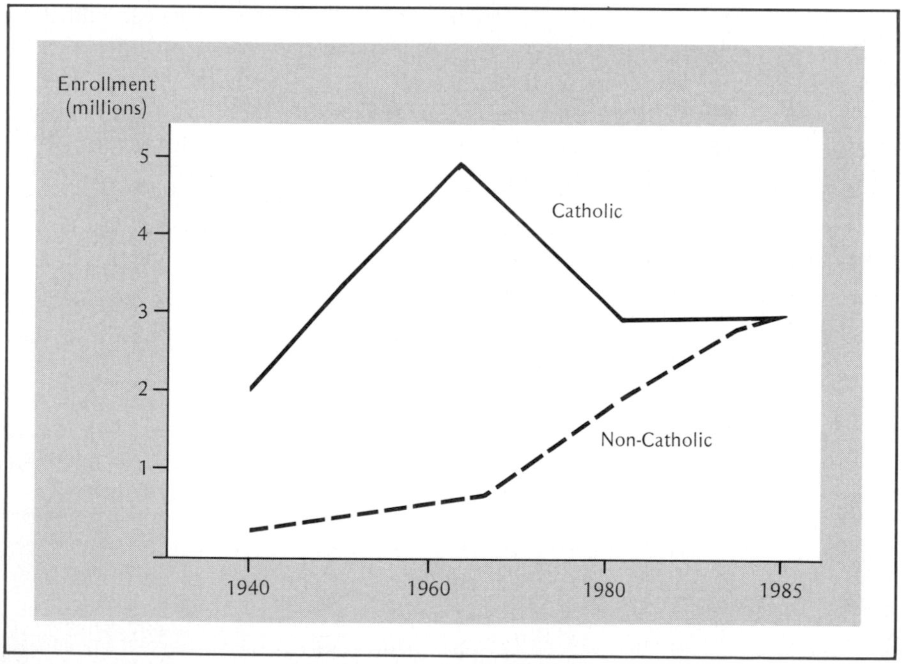

47

FIGURE 14.1 *Private School Enrollments Since 1940*

No school system on earth has been scrutinized, analyzed, and dissected as profoundly and as mercilessly as American education. During the late forties and middle fifties educational institutions at all levels were not only flooded with unprecedented numbers of students but also censored and flailed unmercifully by self-ordained critics (Rickover, Bestor, Mortimer Smith, and Flesch). In retrospect, this frantic rush to patronize and criticize an institution at one and the same time seems a curious contradiction. The public schools were characterized as "Godless, soft, undisciplined, uncultured, wasteful, and disorganized." Those who remembered the high failure rates among World War II draftees were determined to raise the levels of physical fitness and literacy; others who detected a weakening of moral and spiritual values were eager to initiate citizenship and character education programs. The enrollments in nonpublic schools doubled, correspondence schools of all kinds sprang into existence, and the popular press carried articles and programs designed to help parents augment the basic skills within the school program. In 1955 there were an estimated 450 correspondence schools serving 700,000 students throughout the country.

New Emphases in Education

Fortunately, though some people were highly critical of our schools, not everybody panicked. We had physical fitness programs, character education projects, and a general tightening of educational standards, and we had much more. Guilford, Torrence, Getzels, and others explored the boundaries of creativity; A. S. Barr and Ryans carried out exhaustive studies of teacher characteristics; and just about everybody experimented with new patterns of organization. There were primary block programs; interage groupings; Joplin, Stoddard, and Trump plans; core programs; and a host of other patterns or combinations of plans structured around subject areas, broad groupings of subjects, or pupil characteristics. There were programs for the gifted and the not-so-gifted, and there was a new concern for foreign language instruction as well as the functional use of English. We experienced a limited resurgence of Montessori and several one-of-a-kind schools such as Amidon and Summerhill. While all this was taking place within the schools, the school systems themselves were consolidating so that by 1965 there were only half as many school districts as had existed twenty years earlier.

[59]

We heard a great deal about automation during the fifties, but the tools that gave education its biggest boost were of a less pervasive nature. Social psychologists provided more advanced sociometric tools that offered us new insights into the functioning of groups; reading specialists and psychologists developed highly refined diagnostic instruments for use in studying learning disabilities; and some of our more imaginative statisticians devised new formulas and designs for controlling and analyzing data by using modern computers. New research tools such as regression formulas and factoral analysis yielded data we were unable to extract earlier. On a somewhat less sophisticated level we developed more interesting and more flexible teaching tools—audiovisual devices, learning games, more beautifully illustrated books, instructional television, and machines for programmed instruction. We also added additional personnel—teacher aides, counselors, social workers, and school psychologists.

Our efforts toward revamping and revitalizing American education were rather fragmented and uncoordinated until the late fifties and sixties, when several important developments converged to lend focus and direction to our endeavors. Studies of the structure of knowledge led researchers, notably Bruner, to the conclusion that priorities in both content and methodology could and should be developed. This observation resulted in a restructuring of mathematics, science, and language studies. NDEA institutes in science and mathematics emphasizing basic generalizations and techniques of inquiry were the mode of the day, and several taxonomies, notably *Bloom's Taxonomy of Educational Objectives,* provided frameworks within which content, methodologies, and objectives could be examined.

Another thrust was provided by the Conant report. Conant and his associates examined educational programs throughout the United States and offered guidelines for high schools in a wide range of educational areas, including school sizes and schedules, counseling practices, individualized and required academic programs, ability groupings, vocational training, reading programs, and specialized provisions for the academically talented. The recommendations were highly prescriptive and widely consulted. Commissions and councils vested with the responsibilities of making curricular decisions made frequent use of the Conant recommendations. Goodlad and Trump later added additional guidelines involving flexible scheduling and faculty differentiation.

Analysis of Teaching

Another emphasis found expression in the analysis of teaching. For half a century researchers had been attempting to identify the characteristics and teaching styles most closely associated with effective instruction. Hundreds of studies had been initiated, and correlations had been done among them. During the fifties the focus began changing from what ought to occur in teaching to what does occur. Flanders and other researchers developed observational scales for use in assessing verbal communications between and among teachers and students. The scales permitted observers to categorize and summarize specific actions on the part of teachers and students. These studies were followed by studies of nonverbal classroom behaviors.

Professional Perspectives

One mark of a professional is the urge to constantly search for better solutions to the problems one faces.
Teachers can monitor new educational research by reading professional journals, attending conferences, and enrolling in graduate courses.

Much recent educational research has focused on attempting to identify the characteristics and teaching styles most closely associated with effective instruction. (*Source:* Stuart Spates)

Another series of investigations involving the wider range of instructional protocols was patterned after the time-motion studies used earlier for industrial processes. Dwight Allen and several other educators then attempted to use some of these findings in delineating the components of effective teaching. Specific formats were used to introduce teacher candidates to the elements judged most important to good teaching. The change in focus from studies of teacher characteristics to analyses of what actually occurs in classrooms has provided us with some of our best insights into teaching and learning and given us usable instruments for further investigations of classroom behavior. We can now assess the logical, verbal, nonverbal, affective, and several attitudinal dimensions of instruction as well as the intricate aspects of cognition and concept development.

Recent research has focused even more closely on the instructional patterns of effective teachers. A recent review, *Teacher Effectiveness: An Annotated Bibliography,* by Powers and Beard catalogs over three thousand investigations into instructional competencies. Today's effective teachers are frequently viewed as having some important skills in common with the schoolteachers of 60 years ago. They are strong leaders who direct classroom activities, maximize the use of instructional time, and teach in a clear businesslike manner.

Structured, carefully delineated lessons are now employed. Larger topics are broken into smaller, more easily grasped components, and there is a focus on one thought, point, or direction at a time. Prerequisite skills are checked before new skills or concepts are introduced. Step-by-step presentations are accompanied by a large number of probing questions. Detailed explanations of difficult points are offered, and students are tested on one point before moving on to the next. Corrective feedback is provided where needed, and teachers are encouraged to stay with the topic under study until students comprehend the major points or issues. Effective teachers use prompts and cues to assist students through the initial stages of acquisition.

This new emphasis on demonstration, prompting, and practice is a far cry from the relatively unstructured classroom activities of just ten years ago. We now emphasize carefully created learning goals and lesson sequences. It will be interesting to see whether the educational pendulum swings back to a new focus on student concerns and intiatives ten years from now.

Sociological Studies

A major breakthrough in education has resulted from a series of sociological studies relating to social class, social perceptions, and academic achievement. Coleman and Deutch were among the first to demonstrate that it isn't the teaching equipment so much as children's social relationships that make the difference. Students' parents and peer groups at home and at school mold their perceptions and regulate their performances. These findings and those of Rosenthall and Jencks have given new direction to our efforts. Our concerns have changed, at least partially, from educational hardware to studies of pupil populations.

Study of the Learning Process

In relatively recent years a number of leading American and European researchers have sought to analyze and describe how children learn. All of these investigators have stressed the importance of successful early learning patterns and the problems associated with serious learning deficits. They also believe that important elements within the environment may be changed or modified to promote learning.

Maria Montessori, an Italian physician, believed that the child should be encouraged to teach himself through the use of manipulative materials. She developed a wide range of educational resources, many of which could be matched or sequenced according to specific attributes (size, color, pitch, etc.). Montessori did much to promote the concept of pupil discovery and the use of tactile learning materials.

Somewhat later, Jean Piaget, a Swiss biologist, studied children (mostly his own) to find out how they form concepts of space, time, velocity, force, and chance. His work contributed more to the field of cognitive development than any other investigator's. His emphasis on the four stages of development (sensorimotor, preoperational, concrete operational, and formal operational) caused major revisions in curricula and teaching strategies, particularly at the elementary school levels.

Robert Havighurst, a University of Chicago professor, has identified specific developmental tasks he believes children must master if they are to develop normally. He even suggests that there may be periods during which certain tasks must be mastered if they are to become an integral part of children's repertoire of responses. There may also be "teachable moments" (periods of peak efficiency for the acquisition of specific experiences) during which receptivity is particularly high. Havighurst, like Piaget, has caused us to look carefully at the motivations and needs of children.

A contemporary of Havighurst, Jerome Bruner of Harvard, has also postulated a series of developmental steps or stages which he believes children encounter as they mature. These involve action, imagery, and symbolism. Bruner's cognitive views have stressed student inquiry and the breaking down of larger tasks into components.

Benjamin Bloom, Distinguished Service Professor at the University of Chicago, has attempted to identify and weigh the factors which control learning. He believes that one can predict learning outcomes by assessing three factors: (1) the cognitive entry behaviors of a student (the extent to which the pupil has mastered prerequisite skills); (2) the affective entry characteristics (the student's interest in learning the material); and (3) the quality of instruction (the degree to which the instruction offered is appropriate for the learner). We can observe Bloom's research reflected in models of direct instruction, particularly mastery learning, in which teachers carefully explain, illustrate, and demonstrate skills and provide practice, reinforcement, corrective feedback, and remediation.

Helping Special Populations

The task of assisting the disadvantaged is clearly much larger than we first judged. The results of the programs Headstart, Upward Bound, Higher Horizons, Followthrough, Jobs Corps, and other types of enrichment or compensatory programs have been disappointing. Eighty percent of the Job Corps participants, for example, were found to have reverted to their previous nonproductive patterns five years after completing the program. If the basic potential of the disadvantaged is as limited as Jencks suggests, the job ahead may be a mammoth one. It may not simply be a task of teaching new language skills and thinking processes; it may very well involve the introduction of new life patterns. Jencks maintains that human differences exist and persist generationally despite education and that school integration and compensatory programs do not greatly affect these differences. The poor have, for example, not normally recognized the crucial role of delayed gratification in human endeavors, yet most major individual and group achievements appear to rest upon some type of prolonged effort. Training for professional levels of service takes time, effort, patience, and endurance.

Educational Critics

Another development in education was triggered by a phalanx of critics, including Edgar Friedenberg (*Coming of Age in America*), Charles Silberman (*Crisis in the Classroom*), Jonathan Kozol (*Death at an Early Age*), Ivan Illich (*Deschooling Society*), John Holt (*How Children Fail*), and a recent government report, *A Nation At Risk* (1983), which focused on low educational standards. Some, like Silberman, urge us to refurbish what we already have; others, including Illich, want to abandon the schools altogether. These critics have not gone unnoticed. Friedenberg's call for alternatives to traditional education, Silberman's endorsement of open education, and Kozol's plea for equal opportunity are all reflected to some degree in innovative programs from coast to coast.

In some instances alternative programs and open-concept schools were hastily established by educators who barely understood what they were about. In other situations the teachers who sought to initiate open classrooms failed to realize that this form of assocation requires more, not less, careful planning and attention to details. The free school movement fared far worse. Graubard's review of this radical concept of education (*Free the Children*) concludes with the explanation that these schools seldom enrolled more than 30 students or lasted more than two years. The point is that there is no real substitute for organized learning outside our formally constituted schools. Perhaps there should be, but we have not yet found reliable alternatives.

Litigation's Influence on Education

Finally, in the years since 1970 we have seen an astonishingly large segment of our school patrons and students resorting to courts of law in confrontations with school officials and teachers. Considerable space is devoted to discussing many of these law cases elsewhere in this book. Suits have been filed challenging pupil placements, grades, the failure of the school to teach properly, disciplinary actions, dress codes, and numerous other previously accepted educational practices. The Buckley Amendment, which gives students and their parents the right to view official school records, added immeasurably to the demands of those seeking redress of grievances. In addition, the rights of due process have been extended to include students at all levels in an effort to protect their constitutional rights. Due process requires that rules and regulations facilitate the educational goals of the school and be clearly publicized. There must also be provision for a fair hearing when someone violates regulations.

It is unfortunate that legal recourse has become a major modus operandi of recent years, for legal maneuvering is generally a substitute for good faith and mutual respect. But individual abuses have probably diminished in the wake of threatened legal sanctions.

Summary and Implications

In this chapter we saw that the past half century has been characterized by tremendous growth, increased federal involvement, a struggle for equal educational opportunity, professionalization, litigation, and criticism. Many of the specific educational events that have taken place during this time period are listed in Appendices D and E.

To draw meaningful implications from recent events that have not yet stood the test of time is difficult. Implications of recent educational events will eventually be found in the answers to questions such as these:

■ What should be the role of the federal government in education?
■ Is there equal educational opportunity in America?
■ How professionalized do we wish our school system to be?
■ To what degree should educational policy and practice be influenced by litigation?

Discussion Questions

1. Other than those mentioned in this chapter, what additional recent educational developments seem particularly important to you? Why are they important?
2. Has the increased federal involvement in education been good or bad for our schools?
3. In your opinion, how much progress have we really made in providing equal educational opportunity in the United States? Defend your answer.
4. In what respect, if any, has education become professionalized, in your opinion?
5. What is happening in education at this very moment that is likely to be written about in future history-of-education books?

Supplemental Activities

1. Interview a retired teacher about the educational changes that he or she witnessed over the past 50 years.
2. Scan several recently published history-of-education books, looking for significant recent changes in education.
3. Discuss with a fellow student who is a member of one of the minority groups mentioned in this chapter his or her views on equal educational opportunity.
4. Make a list of the ten most important federal educational acts enacted in the past 50 years.
5. Do a supplemental reading about an important educator in the past half century.

Notes

1. U.S. Department of Commerce, Bureau of the Census, *Digest of Education Statistics 1982* (Washington, D.C.: U.S. Government Printing Office, 1982), p. 23.

2. We thank Dr. Donald Barnes for many of the ideas presented in this section.

Bibliography

Avrich, Paul. *The Modern School Movement: Anarchism and Education in the United States.* Princeton, N.J.: Princeton University Press, 1980.

Best, John Hardin, and Sidewell, Robert T., eds. *The American Legacy of Learning: Readings in the History of Education.* Philadelphia: Lippincott, 1967.

Conant, James B. *The American High School Today.* New York: McGraw-Hill, 1959.

Cremin, Lawrence A. *The Transformation of the School: Progression in American Education, 1876–1957.* New York: Knopf, 1961.

Cuban, Larry. "Persistent Instruction: The High School Classroom 1900–1980." *Phi Delta Kappan,* 64 (2) (October 1982): 113–118.

French, William M. *American Educational Tradition: An Interpretive History.* Boston: Heath, 1964.

Krug, Edward. *The Shaping of the American High School.* New York: Harper and Row, 1964.

Lutz, J. P., Stone, Donald O., and Spillman, Carolyn U. "Looking Forward by Looking Backward." *Phi Delta Kappan,* 64 (6) (February 1983): 430–432.

Meyer, Adolphe E. *An Educational History of the American People.* New York: McGraw-Hill, 1967.

"The Negro and American Education." *Changing Education* (a Journal of the American Federation of Teachers), Fall 1966.

Ravitch, Diane. *The Troubled Crusade: American Education 1945–1980.* New York: Basic Books, 1983.

Recognizing Sex Bias. Chicago: Illinois State Board of Education (Urban and Ethnic Education Section, 188 West Randolph Street), 1979.

Sheenhan, Patrick M. "Growing Disillusionment with Public Education: An Historical Overview." *Action in Teacher Education,* Fall 1982, 1–5.

PART V

Philosophical Concepts, Educational Views, and Teaching Styles

Thinking is an ongoing process, and one of the most beneficial results of the study of educational philosophy is obtained if the student reaches the place where he or she is unable to think of educational practices in isolation from the basic questions of life and meaning that give those practices significance. We hope that the presentations of digests of classical philosophical concepts, educational views, and teaching styles relevant to the education profession will pique the interest of prospective teachers in the study of educational philosophy.

While you have been thinking about teaching as a career, you should have also been developing a philosophy of teaching to guide your actions in given teaching situations. Your experiences with and perceptions about working with students in the classroom, your notions about presentations, and your beliefs about subject matter, testing, discipline, and school policy all contribute to your teaching philosophy. We suggest that those teachers who are acquainted with both the classical schools of philosophy and modern educational views will have a strong foundation on which to build an effective philosophy of teaching. The purpose of Part V is to provide teachers with philosophical information that is relevant to several teaching situations.

Most of the current views on education have roots in the classical philosophies of the past. Chapter 15 presents selected classical philosophical concepts from which the six educational philosophies presented in Chapter 16 are drawn. Any attempt to outline the many aspects of even the most well-known philosophical concepts inherently risks oversimplification. Philosophy is an academic and comprehensive discipline. Students who want to develop a thorough knowledge of philosophy have to spend long hours studying the original works of many outstanding thinkers.

Each of the six educational philosophies (styles) considered in Chapter 16 conveys a distinct pattern of response based on selected indicators. Each educational philosophy stands on its own merits for given teaching situations when specific outcomes are desired. All of these teaching styles are used in today's schools. Essentialism, perennialism, and behaviorism are three styles that favor convergent thinking. Experimentalism, reconstructionism, and existentialism favor divergent thinking.

Finally, Chapter 17 provides prospective teachers with a useful analytical tool for analyzing teacher behaviors when dealing with students, subject matter, and learning objectives in a classroom setting. We believe that prospective teachers should be able to use this tool to assist them in formulating their preferred teaching styles, whether or not they have had any full courses in either classical or educational philosophy. Through the study and application of the analytical tool for analyzing teacher preferences, prospective teachers will at least have an enlightened feeling about various educational philosophies. Teaching style (philosophy) indicators from the four questions of the analytical tool reveal the nature of the learner to be passive or active, the nature of the subject matter to be amorphous or structured, the use of the subject matter to be cognitive or affective, and the behavior trends exhibited to be toward convergent thinking or divergent thinking.

The growth of the comprehensive American system of education parallels the growth of the American democratic way of life. Our democracy depends on an educated citizenry functioning under several systems of political thought. The comprehensive American system of education depends on an educated faculty functioning under several systems of educational thought. Most classroom teachers draw upon a given style as the learning needs of their students indicate. A healthy eclectic teacher is one who has knowledge about each philosophy and wisely chooses when to use a particular teaching strategy. Prospective teachers are urged to develop an awareness of the options available with several teaching styles (philosophies). ∎

Classical Philosophical Concepts

Focus Questions

- In your views about learners, do you perceive learners as all-capable and willing? Could your beliefs about students in school influence your teaching? How?
- Are you able to identify and order your own beliefs in light of theories about reality, knowledge, or values? What is real? How do you know? What is of value to you?
- Do you believe that real learning occurs only through life's experiences? How would you justify this belief?
- Do you believe that the universe came to exist through the working of a creator (God)? What other explanations are there for the existence of our universe?
- Why is it valuable for prospective teachers to study a classical philosophy?

Key Terms and Concepts

Metaphysics
Ontology
Naturalism
Epistemology
Skepticism
Empiricism
Rationalism
Axiology

Ethics
Aesthetics
Idealism
Realism
Neo-Thomism/scholasticism
Experimentalism/pragmatism
Existentialism

What Would You Do?

Most teachers teach in the ways they have been taught. However, you tell yourself that new beliefs are different from existing beliefs. So you become a teacher. Then what?

You begin to organize your teaching year by giving thought to what should be taught. While Greek philosophers suggest that "all men by nature desire to know," it does not specify "what" boys and girls in an American classroom desire or ought to know. How will you decide what should be taught in your class?

As illustrated in several chapters of this book and in the responses among the states to the several aspects of the educational reform efforts, our schools, public and private, and their respective teachers routinely adapt their curricular offerings and classroom strategies according to the societal demands and expectations of our schools. Ultimately, important questions about prescribed education courses need to be asked. For what purpose are prescribed courses taught, and why are they taught as they are? These larger questions may be viewed as the task of educational philosophy. Thus a major task of educational philosophy is to help educators think meaningfully about the total educational and life process so that they will be in a better position to develop a consistent and comprehensive program that will assist their students in arriving at the desired goal.[1]

Although it is very important for prospective teachers to have a good understanding of what their preferred teaching philosophy means with regard to the learner, to content, and to classroom management and discipline maintenance, there is another very important dimension of the task of educational philosophy. Educators (teachers, administrators, curriculum specialists, and all others) are challenged to consider the larger questions underlying the meaning and purpose of life and education. When considering these questions, one must engage in a philosophical study of such issues as the nature of reality, the meaning and source of knowledge, and the structure of values.

If we assume that the reader may not have had a course in philosophy, then the content of this chapter may be too philosophical in the classic sense, too abstract to have meaning for the prospective teacher. Yet without a brief examination of the classic philosophical concepts upon which our educational philosophies are founded, the entire discussion of the important philosophical aspect of teaching would be short-sighted. This chapter presents an overview of selected classical concepts of philosophy for the purpose of examining the root structures and historical antecedents underlying current educational views and preferences.

Meaning and Functions of Philosophy

In the most general sense, the word *philosophy* is often thought to be merely one's personal set of beliefs about a given point of discussion. But philosophy may be defined in various ways and also may be viewed in terms of selected functions, as we will see in this section.

Meaning

The literal meaning of philosophy is "love of wisdom." If one thinks of wisdom as "a high degree of knowledge," the extended literal meaning of philosophy becomes "love of a high degree of knowledge." On this point Aristotle made a statement that typifies Greek thought: "All men by nature desire to know." Aristotle's statement does not specify "what" men and women desire to know. What to know as the essence of wisdom is something about which individuals disagree. Wisdom as the basis of philosophy encompasses religion, science, and art; it engages one's thinking and deals with abstract concepts and theory. One who is seeking wisdom is concerned with observations, values, mental pictures, spiritual beings, knowledge, and nature.

Philosophy is speculative in that it attempts to construct patterns from life experiences that give meaning to reality in the universe. Philosophy is prescriptive in that it evaluates facts for the purpose of recommending what *ought* to be as well as what *is*. Questions examining good or bad, right or wrong, beautiful or ugly are questions of prescriptive philosophy. Philosophy extends scientific statements of fact by considering questions that lie beyond the scope of science.

There is general agreement that there are three fundamental questions that are important in describing philosophy:

1. What is real?
2. How do we know?
3. What is of value?

When you are able to determine your own answers to these questions, the answers will mean the most to you. Many individuals (teachers), however, borrow from existing systems of thought as they try to substantiate beliefs and discover wisdom. Classical philosophers tried to answer these basic questions; their speculations have proved of inexhaustible interest to all subsequent thinkers. Human life takes on meaning as the varied aspects of experience fall into some pattern. Philososphy tries to investigate the whole of reality by assessing experiences and then organizing those experiences in a way that is sensible to the individual. From this perspective philosophy can be considered to be an inquiry into the whole human and cultural enterprise.

Evaluation of Beliefs

One's philosophy functions as the analysis and criticism—that is, the evaluation—of one's beliefs. A system of beliefs can be analyzed solely to review and classify beliefs so that they have meaning. If one stops at analysis, the resulting ordered view of beliefs is no more than a presentation of the dogmatic convictions of the individual. Analysis must also apply principles or standards for judging beliefs. Most of us are willing to accept the part of analysis that calls for ordering our beliefs, but we are not so willing to accept the part that calls for judging our prized convictions. Perhaps we tend to be wary, fearful that judgment will show our convictions not to be valid over time. But convictions that withstand the stress of analysis and criticism will stand up over time far better than convictions based on sentiment. Finally, we should evaluate our beliefs in terms of current needs. Evaluation in this context has to do with ordering one's tested beliefs in reference to a given time. An underlying assumption is that analysis and criticism have shown the ordered beliefs to be worth keeping. Evaluation also obliges one to discard beliefs that cannot be substantiated through analysis and criticism.

Thought

Another function of philosophy is that it shows us how to think about new beliefs as they are different from existing beliefs and how they refute or support them. Each of the general questions of philosophy (What is real? How do we know? What is of value?) relates to a branch of philosophy. By considering just one of the three general questions, a person can order individual thought so that at least that single branch of philosophy is examined for what it means. For example, individual thought geared only to what is real may generate new beliefs about reality, or it may generate beliefs that refute or support existing beliefs about reality. Similar thoughtful examination of either the branch of philosophy dealing with knowledge or the branch of philosophy dealing with values may also generate new beliefs or refute existing beliefs about knowledge and values. Philosophy functioning in this way provides an introspective examination of one's system of beliefs.

Branches of Philosophy

Among philosophers, Plato, Aristotle, St. Thomas Aquinas, Hegel, and Dewey are identified with elaborate systems of philosophy. To expedite understanding, philosophers had to develop a language of philosophy. The resulting vocabulary has been mostly a straightforward development of words to identify activities or positions held within philosophy. Since most of the words have clear, straightforward meanings, confusion arises only when terms from our everyday forms of speech are loosely interpreted or carelessly used in solving philosophical problems. There are fully developed dictionaries of philosophy, but here we confine our interest to terminology identified with the three general questions of philosophy previously posed: What is real? How do we know? What is of value? *Metaphysics* (reality), *epistemology* (knowledge), and *axiology* (values) are important terms that describe these branches of philosophy.

Metaphysics

Metaphysics is the branch of philosophy that deals with various theories of reality. Metaphysics seeks to answer the first general question—What is real? Many persons have been reared according to the traditions of a Judeo-Christian culture such as that in the United States. *Ontology* is a branch of metaphysics dealing with the nature of being or reality. According to that influence, reality depends on an ultimate being in God. God made a perfect spiritual world, and humankind is a part of that world. Ultimate reality has been created from the Absolute Mind. Questions of reality also give rise to questions of physical existence. That is, does existence mean merely the occupation of time and space? Can we say that ultimate reality is vested in the physical world? Whether ultimate reality is believed to be spiritual or physical, the reasoning behind the belief may not be philosophically valid. Why must one subscribe to the belief that existence has an ultimate quality? Perhaps a more practical approach to reality would be to accept the position that existence constantly changes. If everything constantly changes, nothing can be considered as existing in any ultimate sense. *Naturalism* is the doctrine that all phenomena may be referred to as natural as distinguished from supernatural causes. Existence, then, is of the moment and defined by the circumstances and conditions of that moment. In the future, existence will not be the same as it is for our time; nor was existence the same in the past.

Teachers must carefully examine their own theories on the nature of knowledge to be effective in the classroom. What is knowledge? How is it acquired? (*Source:* Mike Penney)

Anthropologists believe that the nature of men and women is one important aspect of reality. Each of us needs to determine an acceptable belief relative to the nature of the self. In this view the self can be accepted as a spiritual, a physical, or a social phenomenon in a state of flux. Another way to deal with the nature of the self is to ask whether human beings are basically good, bad, or neutral. Many anthropological questions bear investigation so that beliefs about reality can be clarified. What is the relation of mind and body? Do mind and body interact? Consideration must also be given to the freedom of human beings. Are actions determined by forces greater than the person? Or do men and women have the power of choice through free will? Perhaps one is neither free nor determined.

Teachers are obligated to identify and order their own beliefs in light of these philosophical questions about reality since educational programs should be based on fact and reality. Obviously, all teachers will not have identical metaphysical beliefs and, therefore, will not believe in identical approaches to teaching. At minimum, all prospective teachers should understand the metaphysical dimension of their belief system.

Epistemology

Epistemology is the branch of philosophy that is concerned with theories of the nature of knowledge. Epistemology tries to answer the second general philosophical question—How do we know? If knowledge can be known, how can the truth of knowledge be known? A positive contention can be made that knowledge is based on experience and observation. On the other hand, some knowledge is self-evident. Certain truths have long been understood and do not require proof through observation and experimentation. Another view is that conclusive knowledge of ultimate reality is an impossibility. *Skepticism* holds a questioning attitude toward the possibility of gaining knowledge. *Agnosticism* is related to skepticism and particularly claims to not know about the existence or nonexistence of a Supreme Being.

Most of us feel that knowledge can be known and verified. What, then, are our sources of knowledge? *Empericism* holds that knowledge is gained through perceptual experience—through our senses. Through seeing and hearing, for example, knowledge grows. Knowledge also may be gained through reason coupled with our sensory experiences. *Rationalism* holds that one's mental power is capable of organizing experiences through the senses into meaningful expressions of knowledge.

In some instances knowledge is gained through intuition. This direct apprehension of knowledge is often said to be the result of a sudden flash of insight. Knowledge ascribed to this means should be verified against other means of knowing so one is not led to irrational generalizations. The antithesis of intuitive knowledge—which is personal, of the individual—is authoritative knowledge, which comes from experts—others. Textbooks and teachers, for example, are sources of authoritative knowledge. Although authoritative knowledge is easily gained, it is only as valid as its source. If the source is questionable, then the truth of authoritative knowledge is also questionable.

One of the functions of teachers is to assemble knowledge and transmit that knowledge to students. One of the functions of epistemology is to specify the means by which knowledge is acquired. The means of acquiring knowledge vary according to the beliefs of the several schools of philosophy. Future teachers need to be concerned with those theories about knowledge that they can accept as part of their personal philosophies. One of the primary forces relative to the development of classroom teacher practices is the careful attention to the epistemological domain, since schools deal in the communication of verifiable knowledge.

Axiology

Axiology is the branch of philosophy that specifies the nature of values, the kinds of values, and the values worth possessing. Axiology seeks to answer the third general philosophical question—What is of value? What we desire, we value. The interest theory of value suggests that values exist only as they are supported by the interest of the valuer. A value of interest to one person may not exist at all for a second person. An opposing theory holds that values exist independently of the valuer and his or her interest. In this context values are universal and exist for all.

Ethics is the realm of value that relates to good and bad. Ethics considers criteria of conduct in our lives and motivation of conduct. *Aesthetics* is the realm of value that searches for the principles governing the creation and appreciation of beautiful things. Other realms of value deal with religion, education, society, and utility.

In our pluralistic social world, frustration and anxiety may be induced when we behave according to the values of a group rather than as we would individually prefer to behave. By focusing on philosophical values, we can gain conscious awareness of our individually cherished values on which to base our personal behavior. Confusion about one's personal values leads to conforming behavior determined by group values for given situations. Behavior of this sort may be frustrating when the group behavior contradicts one's personally held— but not consciously identified—values.

Schools of Philosophy

Since philosophers have been unable to agree on the number of philosophies that exist, attempts to classify schools of philosophy are not very useful. The classical schools of philosophy we have chosen to examine most closely are idealism, realism, neo-scholasticism/neo-Thomism, pragmatism/experimental- ism, and existentialism. Each of the selected schools is identified and described in terms of the philosophical branches—metaphysics (reality), epistemology (knowledge), and axiology (values).

Idealism

If we are to include various philosophical tenets, perhaps the term *ideaism* should be substituted for the term *idealism*. Popular confusion exists, perhaps since idealism is related to both ideas and ideals. Historically, the term *idea* has been used to mean many things: form, semblance, universal, class concepts in the human mind, sense perception, faint image, and absolute. When we talk about ideas, we shall assume that activity of the mind is involved. Ideas are mental—of the mind.

Ideals are also mental—of the mind—and pertain to ideas. An ideal "something or other" is held to be perfect, judged by some standard. One can argue that such standards are external to the mind; but when one makes a judgment relating to standards, activity of the mind is involved.

Idealism embraces idea, mind, spirit, and thought. One's idealism is a function of one's mind. Idealism is often associated with the spiritual aspects of reality. This function of one's mind can be thought of as a conceptual process of the Ultimate Mind, in miniature, seeking reality, knowledge, and values. Idealism calls for the mind to perceive reality, knowledge, and values according to the ideal standards of perfection of the Ultimate Mind. Modern idealism strives to associate men and women with their spiritual existence.

How does idealism answer the question "What is real?"? What is the *metaphysics* of idealism? Reality is a world of mind; it is spiritual rather than physical. Material things are not regarded as reality. Reality can be identified essentially with subconscious spiritual principles. One of the timeworn topics of subconscious concepts of reality is the explanation of first events of nature. Any discussion almost always reaches the assertion that nature could not have brought itself into being. Consideration must then be given to what could have caused the first events of nature. Regression along a line of causes takes us back to the first cause as God. Certain theories of nature that include cause-and-effect relations suggest that the universe came to exist through the working of a creative cause. The pure idealist subscribes to the argument that the real objective existence of God is necessarily in the existence of the very idea of God and maintains that God created the universe.

Idealists hold, along with the premise of creationism, elemental conceptions about God. Although we can generally state that God and the universe have some relation, the way in which the relation is identified may be perplexing. Are God and the universe identical? Is God interested or not interested in the physical universe and in human beings? Pure idealism accepts the view of Christian theism that suggests that ultimate reality is a personal God who is more than the universe; the universe exists within and through God. The polytheistic doctrine that spiritual reality is plural (more than one god) could be contained within idealism. The distinguishing note is that idealism holds God or gods to be an ultimate reality that is more than the universe.

What about the nature of man or woman in relation to reality? A principle of idealism states that one has a self, which is one's soul. This soul is a spiritual being. Equating spiritual being with mind brings up how body and mind are related. Idealists usually solve this problem by purporting mind to be more fundamental than body—that is, body depends on mind. What does this mean? If one considers the mind as a miniature model of the Supreme Mind, idealism becomes deterministic. Since one's body depends on one's mind and since the mind is a working replica of the Supreme Mind, then actions are determined by forces greater than the individual. Such an analogy might be immediately countered with the suggestion that one's mind, whether or not it be considered a miniature of the Supreme Mind, works independently and interprets reality through the senses. The human mind can interpret reality. While these interpretations may be foreknown by God, this does not mean that actions of humans are necessarily determined by God. The deterministic quality of idealism is thus qualified.

What is the epistemology of idealism? What is knowledge? How do we know? Idealists have held various theories of knowledge at various times. Today's idealists generally believe that there are other instruments of knowledge besides the scientific method. Idealism also considers faith, authoritarianism, and intuition as instruments of knowledge. Faith is a way we come to know certain things. Faith suggests that people firmly accept their beliefs as knowledge, despite arguments against them. Idealists often accept knowledge on faith. Knowledge based on faith is more than a mere belief: One believes, for example, that God exists because faith as an instrument of knowledge has enabled one to know God. Whether it be called immaterialism, mysticism, spiritualism, or something else, such belief in the Supreme Mind is a significant aspect of the epistemology of idealism. Perhaps authoritarianism and faith in God become synonymous in relation to knowledge certified to us by authorities like the Bible and the church. If so, the indisputable authority of the Bible and the church may actually be a tool for formulating faith. In the absence of faith, however, important knowledge can be certified to us directly from the Bible and the church, or from any other authority, such as the state.

Intuition means to know in a direct fashion. Idealists believe that we can know some things directly without reasoning. Knowledge may come to us intuitively. One who takes an extended position on intuition as a source of knowledge would claim that all knowledge is based on intuition. Idealism includes intuition among the instruments of knowledge. Historically, in the realm of knowledge, idealists have conceived of truth as ideas. George Berkeley (1685–1753), an Anglican bishop and philosopher, was called an idealist because he believed that existence was mind-dependent. For anything to exist, it must be perceived by mind, but not necessarily the human mind. Berkeley argued that things exist even when a human mind is not perceiving them because the

49

Regardless of personal beliefs about the existence of God, teachers should, nonetheless, be able to mentally examine the notion that reality in the world may have been determined by a Supreme Being. Can you make such an examination?

Professional Perspectives

Ultimate Mind of God is perceiving all things. Idealism is not entirely Christian thought; but as a philosophy, it does concur with the philosophy of the deeply religious Berkeley in holding that ultimate existence and knowledge are perceived by the Supreme Mind.

What does idealism have to suggest about the most personal question of philosophy—What is of value? What is the *axiology* of idealism? Idealism has God as the standard of goodness. Moral persons seek God's principles. The inherent problem is for mortals to know the will of God. It follows that evil can be identified as action against the will of God. The assumption is that morality is based on the will of God as expressed in the Bible, in the teachings of Christ, and in the interpretations of the church. But what about the existence of evil? That has always been for idealists a most troublesome question. How can an omnipotent and benevolent God—a perfect God whose attributes of complete love, justice, and mercy cannot be expressed so as to be inconsistent with each other—allow evil to continue?

The continued existence of evil, however, can be linked to God's plan of free will for humans. If God gives free choice, there must be freedom not to choose His will and not to strive for moral perfection. The freedom not to strive for moral perfection produces evil. If God removed evil from the world, this action would be inconsistent with His gift of free will, because one could then choose only to follow Him. If, on the other hand, He removed all evil consequences from those seeking to follow His will and allowed evil consequences only for those who do not seek to follow Him, the freedom to choose would be meaningless. Under such conditions free will would not operate. It would be too obvious that choosing God's will is the only way to be rewarded and choosing not to follow God's will leads to immediate punishment. God would have to keep intervening in the universe to give special protection to His followers, even in the case of natural calamities. Then choice would have little meaning, and natural laws would also not be dependable. Imagine two skiers whizzing down a hillside. One skier has been seeking God's will in his life; the other has not. Both skiers crash into trees. For one skier the tree might suddenly become like soft plastic that would not injure anyone. For the other a tree would be the same predictably hard object we know, because God is not giving this skier special protection. As C. S. Lewis has explained in *The Problem of Pain,* perhaps this universe, with all its evils and imperfections, is the only possible universe, since God gives humans the freedom to choose and since His other attributes will not allow Him to contradict His perfect justice and love in permitting free choice.

In the Christian view, that evil be allowed to continue is also not inconsistent with God's demand for justice. Christ's sacrificial death is seen as the act by which He suffered a just punishment for all evils past, present, and future. In that sense any manifestation of evil has been judged, and the penalty for it has already been paid. All who believe this principle are seen as coming under its provisions and having the penalty for their evils paid by Christ's death. This principle hinges on the belief that Christ, as God in the flesh, had no inherent evil and could therefore die sacrificially for the evil choices of human beings.

Aesthetics in idealism logically grows out of the ethics in idealism. Beauty is described as the reflection of God. In other words, as people continually strive to become morally good by imitating God, they reflect God—the ideal— more and more. Such reflection of God becomes the aesthetics—the beauty— of idealism.

Realism

Realism, like naturalism, regards nature as all there is. Realism holds that objects of the external world are real in themselves. This attitude is antithetical to idealism. Realism is not the sole antithesis of idealism; materialism and natu-

Realism uses the inductive method of investigating nature in detecting general principles from observations. Nature contains truth, and that truth can be ascertained by investigating nature scientifically. (*Source:* Barry Stark/Northern Illinois University)

ralism are terms that have been used interchangeably to express the antithesis of idealism. Realism, as sketched in this presentation, essentially can be interchanged with materialism and naturalism. Realism denotes the physical world as the total of reality. There is no dependence on a mind—human or divine— to comprehend concepts. A realist rejects the existence of anything beyond nature. Everything comes from nature and is subject to scientific laws. Naturalism has been aligned with natural science; the physical world includes only what can be scientifically investigated. Objects that science can investigate are the physical or the material. Matter is a fundamental constituent of the universe. The theory of evolution accounts for the universe and its contents by the combination of separate and diffused atoms. Plato's dualism referred to an actual world of particulars and an ideal world of pure essences. Realism as naturalism suggests that human life—physical, mental, moral, and spiritual—is an ordinary natural event attributable in all respects to the ordinary operations of nature.

What is the *metaphysics* of realism? Realism specifies reality in things or objects. It holds that natural things have always existed, that the universe as a physical world evolved of itself naturally, as opposed to having been created by a supernatural force beyond nature. Realists consider causes of the events of nature but do not believe that the first cause is a God. A realist may hold that no ultimate reality exists behind the universe. Cause-and-effect relations are viewed as governed by natural law. A realist feels that if we cannot answer a question of cause, it is because we have not learned to understand all nature. When we know all about nature, we will have answers to all questions of causes.

A principle of naturalism views the self as essentially the same as the body. As far as the relation of body and mind is concerned, a realist believes mind to be something new and produced by nature in the evolutionary process, neither identical with body nor wholly dependent on it. Another realist concept suggests that mind is merely a function of the brain. In this context mind does not influence bodily activity but merely accompanies bodily activity. The stage for one's physical activity is and has been an orderly, purposeful universe. To exist in the universe is to occupy time and space as physical matter. Nature is identical with existence.

What are the instruments of *epistemology* in realism (naturalism)? What is knowledge? Realism affirms the possibility of knowledge. Truth is viewed as observable fact. Perceptual experience is the medium for gaining knowledge. Realists observe data obtained on the physical nature of the universe. From these observations general principles are formulated to make the universe intelligible. Realism uses the inductive method of investigating nature in detecting general principles from observations. Modern naturalism adheres to the scientific method for formulating general principles of knowledge. The essence of the epistemology of realism is that knowledge is based on experience and observation. Nature contains truth, and that truth can be ascertained by investigating nature scientifically.

Regarding the *axiology* of realism, values are also obtained from nature. From observing nature, one comes to know natural laws that provide the basis for ethical and aesthetical evaluations. Values will have a natural quality instead of a supernatural quality. Assuming that the universe is thus the standard of goodness, those who live in accordance with the general principles of nature are moral persons. This universe, as the standard of goodness for one's ethical structure, may also be considered the standard for determining evil; that is, evil becomes what violates one's ethical structure. Moral persons are responsible for selecting the laws of nature that denote good and then for conducting themselves by such laws. Nature provides the principles that govern appreciation of beauty; aesthetics is the reflection of nature.

Neo-Thomism

Translations of Aristotle's writings, which had been lost during the Middle Ages, appeared in the twelfth century in Western Europe. His ideas, while not always in agreement with accepted Christian thought, gave rise to the development of scholasticism. One of the leading scholars who attempted to rationalize faith and reason was Thomas Aquinas.

Neo means "new"; *Thomism* is the branch of Christian scholasticism associated with the work of St. Thomas Aquinas (1225–1274). Until the time of Aquinas the dualism of idealism and realism dominated philosophy. Divergence of thinking regarding supernatural and natural causes, mind and body, and physical objects and mental conceptions set the two philosophical camps apart, as shown in Figure 15.1. By the 1200s Christian philosophers wanted to inject Christian doctrine into their systems of thought. Christian discussions were concerned with such topics as the existence of God, the nature of humankind, and faith and reason. At this time the views of Aristotle were little known, and

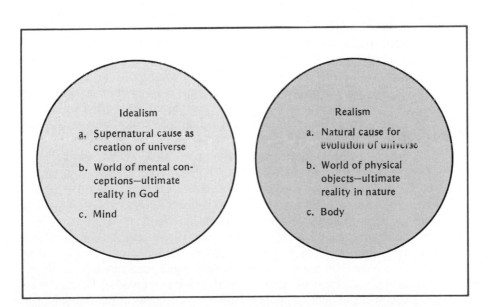

FIGURE 15.1 *Dualistic Position of Idealism and Realism Before the Middle Ages*

Thomas Aquinas was instrumental in getting Aristotle's works translated from Greek into Latin.

The works of Thomas Aquinas were a combination of Aristotle's thought and the thinking of church leaders at that time. Aquinas suggested that reason was the basis for universal organization; he contended that faith and reason do not conflict. St. Thomas, however, did assign preeminence to God, stating that since God cannot be at fault, any differences between conclusions based on reason and conclusions based on faith must come from faulty reasoning. In fact, scholasticism tended to emphasize deductive reasoning by beginning with principles revealed by God or the ancients and applying them to the specifics of living. This emphasis tended to minimize the chance of faulty reasoning. By contrast, realism and idealism emphasize inductive reasoning. That is, the realist looks at specific phenomena in nature and thinks of generalizations that might explain these phenomena. Such inductive reasoning is the core of the scientific method. Plato's idealism also relied on inductive reasoning about ideas through using a process of questioning (the dialectic) to reach general truths. A famous example is from the *Meno* dialogue. In this dialogue a slave boy is being asked by his teacher if he knows the Pythagorean theorem in mathematics. Although the slave boy insists that he has never heard of the Pythagorean theorem, his teacher's skillful questions about specific triangles leads the boy to derive the theorem. After these questions the boy comes up with the general principle that the square of the hypotenuse of a right triangle is equal to the sums of the squares of the other two sides of the triangle. He is then complimented by his teacher for having really "known" the Pythagorean theorem all along. He just had to use inductive reasoning to derive and understand a principle.

Although St. Thomas had little success in solving the idealism-realism duality, his views added new perspectives to the traditional Christian doctrines and consequently generated much interest in philosophical thought. The scholarship of the Christian philosophers is referred to as *scholasticism;* Thomism is but one facet of scholasticism. Scholasticism declined as a movement by the 1400s and rose again in the early 1600s, only to decline a second time before 1700. Pope Leo XIII (late 1800s) adopted Thomism as the official position of the Roman Catholic Church. The version of Thomism being revived today has come to be known as neo-Thomism. There are lay groups and ecclesiastical groups (Roman Catholic) of neo-Thomists.

The works of Thomas Aquinas and others have brought the philosophical positions of idealism and realism into contact with each other. Figure 15.2 shows the present relation between idealism and realism and also shows the related position of neo-Thomism. This schema also illustrates Aquinas's contention that faith from idealism and reason from realism do not conflict.

The nature of *metaphysics* in neo-Thomism is the harmony of faith and reason. Reality is proposed as a world of reason. Existence may be viewed as residing in the reasoning powers of the human mind. Ideas are real in themselves. Physical objects exist whether or not they are perceived by humans. The universe exists independent of people. However, Thomists argue, humankind, our ideas, our mind, and our spirit, as well as the physical objects in the world, have been created by God. Reality is dualistic to the Roman Catholic neo-

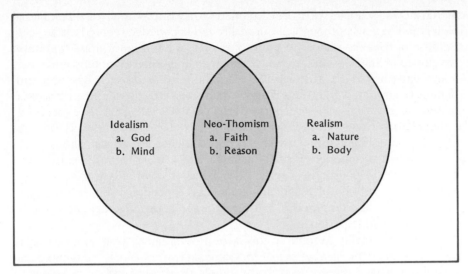

FIGURE 15.2 *Relationship of Idealism, Realism, and Neo-Thomism After the Middle Ages*

Thomists; God and physical matter do not have a purely antithetical relation, however, since they are not in equal balance. Although neo-Thomists consider both God and physical matter real, God as a perfect being is considered more important.

Neo-Thomists establish knowledge through both faith and reason. The ecclesiastical group added revelation to intuition as the basis of their *epistemology*. Faith, by which knowledge is affirmed, develops from history, the Bible, and God's word as taught by Jesus Christ. Knowledge also comes through reason and experience. Basic knowledge, in this context, is in the realm of human thought. Empiricism (discussed below) is an instrument of knowledge wherein experience becomes the medium for gaining knowledge. From knowledge gained, people reason toward truth. The fundamental truths arrived at by reason and faith are unchangeable and dependable.

What is the *axiology* to the lay and the ecclesiastical neo-Thomists? Like knowledge, values are permanent. Lay neo-Thomists value moral law discerned by reason. People should live by these rational moral standards. The rational acts of men and women, their moral conduct, and their relations with others constitute their ethics. The ecclesiastical neo-Thomists go beyond reasoning to insist that God has established moral law and has provided us with the power of reason for the purpose of finding God's moral law. Thus we are bound to conduct our lives according to God's moral laws because that is God's will.

Experimentalism

By the beginning of the 1600s, England was rapidly growing in power and territory; consequently, a more practical approach to reality and knowledge was needed. The vast amount of new information being brought to England by merchants and scholars had to be combined with existing knowledge. Traditional beliefs and systems of thought about reality and knowledge seemed inadequate. Because of these conditions, a philosophical movement known as *empiricism* developed in England. Empiricism postulated experience to be fundamental to reality and knowledge. Through the years the term *empiricism* has been ambiguously associated with numerous positions and practices. The term *experimentalism* describes the credence English empiricists gave to experience. Although early Greek philosophers first suggested that experience was the basis of reality, experimentalism grew largely out of English empiricism and is therefore classified as a modern view. Philosophical speculations in the early 1600s centered around questions of one's acquisition of knowledge (epistemology) rather than questions of reality (metaphysics). A general premise of experimentalism, and also empiricism, is that reality and knowledge depend on one's observations and experiences.

What does reality become in this system of thought? What about causality of the universe? The *metaphysics* of experimentalism appears to be flexible and capable of change compared with the rigidly fixed metaphysical positions of the traditional philosophical concepts already discussed. Each of us becomes a determiner of reality through individual conceptualizations. We may choose our beliefs regarding the origin and development of the universe. We may consider the universe as coming into existence as an act of God or by natural evolution. Experimentalists consider the self as an experience in consciousness rather than an existence in itself. Each of us exists as a social part of the universe. Our self then becomes directly observable as an appearance or action. Our mind exists as a function of the brain, so observations of activities can be pictured. From all the responses to such imaginings we draw out those responses that give direction and meaning to reality. Thus one's actions are not determined by forces greater than oneself, nor is one capable of genuine initiative, with free will or power of choice. Functioning in this manner, one becomes the determiner—or interpreter, if you prefer—of numerous considerations of reality. Experimentalists see purpose in the universe as the result of one's purposeful activity and not as inherent in existence or accidental. Reality is a changing quantity consisting of numerous activities, materials, and processes; everything is in a changing state. Nothing exists in the ultimate state—that is, immune from change.

In what way do we come to know truth? What is the *epistemology* of experimentalism? Is it possible to have ultimate knowledge when experimentalism does not allow for ultimate reality? What is the source of knowledge for the experimentalists? Questions about how we acquire knowledge are of primary

|49|

Professional Perspectives

Develop a rationale for illustrating that experience is the basis of reality. In your rationale, speak in support of or against the notion that the universe came into existence by natural evolution.

concern to experimentalism. Experimentalists believe truth to be what is functional. What is necessary to solve our problems becomes the essence of our knowledge. Knowledge, although based on observation and experience, is not concluded to be final by experimentalists. Rather, knowledge is considered to be functional insofar as it can be used to solve one's problems. Knowledge can be continually added to from the observations and experiences of the individual. Thus experimentalism does not accept reality as ultimate, nor does it accept knowledge as conclusive. A reasonable assumption is that rationalism is a part of the experimentalist system of acquiring knowledge. The epistemological view of experimentalism suggests that knowledge (truth) is what we know to solve our problems.

What of values? What is the *axiology* of this system of thought? Experimentalists' values are relative. From what we know of the epistemology of experimentalists, we can logically consider their ethics as tentative. What is good or evil today may not be so valued in the future. One's moral status is largely determined by how the public accepts one's conduct. Older persons often judge younger ones to be "going to pot," which implies that a less moral system of values exists for the younger members of society. Experimentalism points to such judgments as evidence that moral standards change from generation to generation. Judgments of older generations are made from a pattern of ethics that has changed to a different pattern for younger generations. Aesthetics are determined by the public taste. Democracy as a way of life becomes a necessary ingredient of experimentalism's values. Only in a democracy is it possible for good and evil and the creation and appreciation of beautiful things to be assessed from all points of view. Ethical and aesthetical values are in continuous process. Values exist in a state of flux and are relative.

Figure 15.3 shows experimentalism in relation to the schools of philosophy previously discussed. As indicated, experimentalism overlaps idealism, neo-Thomism, and realism.

Existentialism

Existentialism is a relatively recent philosophy spawned in Europe after World War I. Actually, Danish philosopher Sören Kierkegaard (1813–1855) laid the foundation for existentialism when he wrote and taught of our inner freedom to direct our own lives. Early in the 1900s scholars began to translate the works of Kierkegaard into German; English translations did not appear until the 1930s. As a consequence of both delayed translations of Kierkegaard and World War II, most of the development of existential philosophies has been recent. To some degree, existentialism emphasizes casting off traditional and modern philosophies. Emphasis is placed on one's responsibility for setting goals and making decisions free from group norms. The individualistic character of existentialism has often caused group-oriented societies to label existentialism as a faddish philosophy that is uninterested in morals. Such misinterpreted castigations of existentialism may be related to the popularity of the French playwright Jean-Paul Sartre. Before his death in 1980, Sartre was labeled the leader of the atheistic

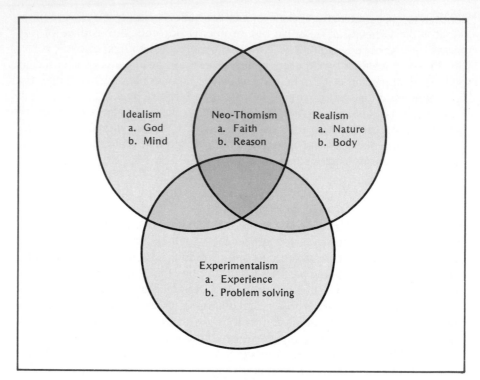

FIGURE 15.3   *Relationship of Realism, Idealism, Neo-Thomism, and Experimentalism*

camp within the existentialist movement. In practice, many existentialists are strongly theistic and hold that one's desires lead to knowledge of God. Of this group, Karl Jaspers, a German, and Gabriel Marcel, a Frenchman, who are both Roman Catholics, represent the theistic segment of existentialism. American George F. Kneller suggested that one of the obstacles in trying to understand the general nature of existentialism is that it cannot be studied objectively from without but requires that students identify themselves with its doctrines from within. Others say that existentialism is not a wholly new orientation of thought but an individualistic way of looking at other systems of thought.

With the emphasis on individual thought, existentialism has not been viewed as a systematic philosophy in the same sense as idealism, realism, neo-Thomism, and experimentalism. Rather, existentialism is sometimes considered as a label for several positons taken by various thinkers against traditional philosophy. Yet when compared with the branches of traditional philosophies, existentialism does speak from metaphysical, epistemological, and axiological terms.

With the inner freedom of human beings to determine existence, the *metaphysics* of existentialism becomes one's subjective existence. As one goes through life making choices and developing preferences and dislikes, one defines who he or she is as an individual:

Man is faced with the stark realities of life, death, and meaning, and he has the unutterable freedom of being responsible for his own essence. . . . The traditional philosophies surrender man's authenticity to a logical system, the Christian leans on God, the realist looks to nature for meaning, and the pragmatist relies on the community. All of these avenues are ways of removing man from the frightful reality of being responsible for his choices.[2]

What is the *epistemology* of existentialism? Existentialists hold that there is no difference between one's external and internal worlds. What is true is represented by personal choice. We know ourselves as actors on life's stage and act according to individual choice. Since it is the individual who gives meaning to such things as nature, meaning and truth could not be built into the universe. Knowing is based upon the authority of the individual, who makes the ultimate decision about what is true.

49

The realm of *axiology* is central to existentialism. Existential values consist of the morality of people choosing freely. The existentialist finds beauty in one's capacity to function apart from the public norms. Each individual makes and is responsible for his or her ethical decisions and aesthetic viewpoints—no one can make such judgments for other individuals. Each of us is free to determine the nature of good conduct. Similarly, beauty is in the "eye of the beholder" rather than in public standards. What is beautiful to me is beautiful; nevertheless, existentialism stresses responsibility. While personal choice is important, once the choice is exercised, the existentialist accepts the responsibility accompanying that choice.

Summary and Implications

Systems of philosophical thought consist of three distinct branches, which deal with the questions of reality (metaphysics), knowledge and truth (epistemology), and values (axiology). This chapter presented brief sketches of these three realms as related to the classical philosophies from which current educational theories are drawn. Prospective teachers may now identify the classical philosophical position that serves as the function of the six current views in American schools discussed in Chapter 16. Any one of the six educational theories may then be further examined with regard to the three dimensions. Such philosophical activity allows classroom teachers to become familiar with and knowledgeable about these facets of philosophical systems as related to any one educational theory. There is no implied best quality ascribed to one philosophical position over another. Rather, the most successful teachers are those who are dedicated to and thoroughly understand their preferred beliefs. Decisions about the nature of the subject matter emphasized in the curriculum are metaphysical commitments to reality—What is real? Questions related to what is true and how we know are epistemological. Classroom methods and practices aim to assist learners in acquiring knowledge and truth in the subject area. Classroom activities that deal with ethics (what is good or bad), beauty, and character are in the realm of axiology (values). The task of the teacher is to identify a preferred style, understand that style as deeply as possible, and utilize that style with a unique group of learners seeking to accomplish reasonable educational outcomes under the leadership of the teacher. The classical philosophical concepts discussed are broad categories within the vast academic realm of philosophy. Further in-depth study would reveal many specific schools of thought for each concept briefly highlighted.

 Educational implications with regard to curricular emphasis, preferred method, character education, and developing taste for each classical philosophical concept may be directly drawn. The metaphysical questions about reality in classical philosophy serve as the basis for the curricular emphases in current educational practices. Methodology in the classroom relates to the acquisition of knowledge, which is anchored in classic epistemological considerations. Character education (morals) and developing taste (aesthetics) are value determinants extended from the axiology branches of classical philosophies. Note that the relationships presented here are drawn from many elaborate schools and systems of philosophical thought, all of which provide the foundations for the six educational philosophies discussed in the following chapter.

Discussion Questions

1. Early Greek philosophers first suggested that experience was the basis of reality. Discuss the implications of that statement for classroom methodology.
2. What is your meaning of philosophy? Illustrate the extent to which individual beliefs are accounted for in your definition.
3. In your opinion, which is the most important aspect of a given philosophy (for the teacher)—the metaphysical view, the epistemological view, or the axiological view? State the rationale for your opinion.
4. One's philosophy functions as the analysis and criticism of one's beliefs. Illustrate the ways in which you analyze and/or criticize your beliefs about learners in the classroom setting.
5. Metaphysics seeks to answer the first general question—What is real? What is the reality of the expectations held for classroom teachers? Can teachers teach when all kinds of students are grouped in the same class?

Supplemental Activities

1. Request a philosopher from your school's department of philosophy to visit your class to discuss the importance of classical philosophy for prospective teachers. Invite his or her comments about educational philosophy courses.
2. Argue the cases for and against the inclusion of the following offerings in a high school curriculum: driver training, home economics, vocational agriculture, physical education, athletics, electronics, computer literacy, and typing and shorthand.
3. In idealism, character education may be enhanced through imitating exemplars—heroes in the historical record. Identify an exemplar educator from the 1800s, study that person, and explain the way in which you could teach character through this person's example.
4. Disciplining the mind, formal drill, and readying the spirit, are preferred methods in neo-Thomism. Arrange a panel discussion among your peers to explore the values of this methodology and the ways in which classroom teachers can stress its importance.
5. Classroom activities that deal with what is good or bad are in the realm of axiology (values). Prepare lists of several goods and bads regarding the professional life of a teacher. Present them to your class for elaboration of the good and bad lists.

Notes

1. George R. Knight, *Issues and Alternatives in Educational Philosophy* (Berrien Springs, Mich.: Andrews University Press, 1982), p. 3.
2. Ibid., 72.

Bibliography

Alder, Mortimer. "A Revolution in Education." *American Educator,* 6 (4) (Winter 1982): 20–24.

Bellanca, James. *Values and the Search for Self.* Washington, D.C.: National Education Association, 1975.

Coleman, James S. "International Comparisons of Cognitive Achievement." *Phi Delta Kappan,* February 1985, 403–406.

Dewey, John. *Democracy and Education.* New York: Macmillan, 1916.

Knight, George P. *Issues and Alternatives in Educational Philosophy.* Berrien Springs, Mich.: Andrews University Press, 1982.

Runes, Dagobert D. *Dictionary of Philosophy.* Totowa, N.J.: Littlefield, Adams, 1979.

Scheffler, Israel. *Conditions of Knowledge: An Introduction to Epistemology and Education.* Chicago: University of Chicago Press, 1978.

Soltis, Jonas F. *An Introduction to the Analysis of Educational Concepts.* 2nd rev. ed. Reading, Mass.: Addison-Wesley, 1978.

Taylor, A. E. *Elements of Metaphysics.* 12th ed. London: Methuen, 1946.

Wagoner, Jennings L., Jr. *Thomas Jefferson and the Education of a New Nation.* Bloomington, Ind.: Phi Delta Kappa Educational Foundation, 1976.

Educational Philosophies
in American Schools

Focus Questions

- How do you begin to formulate a philosophy of education if you have not had a formal course in educational philosophy? Do you agree with the notion that teachers teach the way they were taught? Explain.
- What do you consider to be an authoritarian view toward teaching? What does this view have to do with the way in which learners think?
- In what ways would the study of subject matter of a disciplinary nature helps discipline one's mind?

- Teaching practices which are nonauthoritarian regard the learners as active. How do these practices foster divergent thinking?
- What is meant by the reconstructionism emphasis which places more stress on the ends of education than on the means of education?
- Essentialism envisions subject matter as the core of education. How can this view be criticized as contributing to the slowness of educational change?

Key Terms and Concepts

Educational philosophy
Convergent thinking
Divergent thinking
Essentialism
Experimentalism (progressivism)

Reconstructionism
Existentialism
Authoritarianism/nonauthoritarianism
Behaviorism
Perennialism

What Would You Do?

At a recent parent/community meeting with your board of education, most participants strongly believed that all students should earn credit in advanced mathematics classes for high school graduation. Your assignment is with learning-disabled students who have difficulty with only very general mathematics concepts. How can students with such limited ability be given credit for advanced mathematics?

As a means of complying with state legal mandates, the usual recess period in your elementary school is labeled as a physical education period to satisfy the five-days-per-week physical education class requirement. You observe that the recess period continues to be poorly supervised with no recognizable physical education structure. Would you ask your principal about correcting the situation? What else would you do?

The five classical philosophies presented in the previous chapter provide the roots of the educational philosophies most commonly used in the American schools. Although the educational views in this chapter are discussed in terms of principles related to the nature of the learner, nature of subject matter, and behavior trends as learning outcomes, each of the views is anchored in the metaphysical (reality), epistemological (knowledge), and axiological (value) branches of classic philosophy. (See Appendix G.)

Many teachers hold to the view that the purpose of education is to train pupils' minds so that they can deal better with the intellectual concepts of life; they emphasize, in addition, the mastery of facts and information. The general notion that any child can learn any subject at any level if the subject matter is properly presented remains a strong challenge to teachers to arouse motivation for subject mastery among pupils. The concept of *mastery learning* suggests that, except for the few children who are mentally, emotionally, or physically impaired, every child can master the entire curriculum of the school when adequate time is given for the slower learners to master content. Continued attention to test scores, grade-level achievement, and other measures of subject matter competency reflect the importance still attached to the several views of education. School boards, parents, and the general public demand more and more often that teachers provide concrete evidence that their pupils have made progress in mastering subject matter. Those who identify with these views are considered to be more traditional regarding teaching strategies.

In contrast, many teachers uphold John Dewey's view that the mind is not just a muscle to be developed. They accept the notion that human beings are problem solvers who profit from experience. These educators also give credence to the existential position, which emphasizes the importance of the individual and of personal awareness. Since Dewey's philosophical views have prevailed in American teachers' colleges for the past half century, not surprisingly, American schools reflect this view more than do other schools throughout the world. When teaching techniques are focused on student interactions, teachers may find that some students appear to be aimless with regard to subject matter. In such instances the teacher is challenged to arouse student interest in inquiry leading to subject content, whereas the more traditional teacher is challenged to arouse student interest in subject matter directly.

Idealism, realism, and neo-Thomism tend toward authoritarian views which lean to convergent thinking. Experimentalism and existentialism tend toward nonauthoritarian views which lean toward divergent thinking. As will be discussed in this chapter, current educational theories are drawn from these classical philosophical systems. It follows, therefore, that certain educational theories would tend toward authoritarian-teaching views which would lean toward convergent-thinking outcomes in the classroom. Certain other educational theories would lean toward nonauthoritarian-teaching views which would lean toward divergent-thinking outcomes in the classroom. Table 16.1 lists various educational implications of authoritarian and nonauthoritarian views as related to the five classical philosophical concepts.

[51]

The six educational philosophies (styles) considered here are essentialism, perennialism, behaviorism, experimentalism, existentialism, and reconstructionism. To varying degrees, each of these views is drawn upon by classroom teachers. Figure 16.1 illustrates the relationship of these educational views to the classical philosophies discussed in Chapter 15.

[64]

Authoritarian Educational Views

Figure 16.2 identifies the six educational views as related to either authoritarian views tending toward convergent thinking or to nonauthoritarian views tending toward convergent thinking. Perennialism, essentialism, and behaviorism espouse an authoritarian approach to the subject matter and teacher which encourages convergent thinking. An illustrative class activity is provided as an introduction to the review of each of these three educational philosophies.

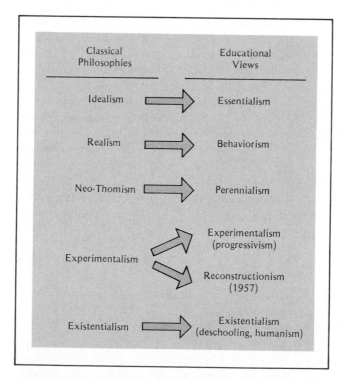

FIGURE 16.1 *Relationship of Educational Views to Classic Philosophies*

TABLE 16.1 *Educational Implications of Authoritarian and Nonauthoritarian Views*

Educational Aspect	Authoritarian Views (Convergent Thinking)			Nonauthoritarian Views (Divergent Thinking)	
	Idealism	*Realism*	*Neo-Thomism*	*Experimentalism*	*Existentialism*
Curricular emphasis	Subject matter of the mind: literature, intellectual history, philosophy, religion. Education should be the same for everyone. Three R's in elementary schools	Subject matter of the physical world: mathematics, science. Initiative in education with the teacher	Subject matter of intellect and spirit: mathematics, language, and doctrine	Subject matter of social experience. Creation of a new social order	Subject matter of personal choice
Preferred method	Teaching for the handling of ideas: lecture, discussion. Preparation for life	Teaching for mastery of factual information and basic skills: demonstration, recitation. Facts help individual adjustment to life	Disciplining the mind: formal drill (readying the spirit), catechism	Problem solving; project method. Scrupulous regard for democratic procedures	Individual as entity within a social context
Character education	Imitating exemplars, heroes. Greatest aspirations in the historical record	Training in rules of conduct	Disciplining behavior to reason	Making group decisions in light of consequences. Positive modification of society	Individual responsibility for decisions and preferences
Developing taste	Studying the masterworks. Values of the past heritage	Studying design in nature	Finding beauty in reason	Participating in art projects. Based on cross-cultural and even universal values	Personal view of the world. Self-initiated activities

Source: Adapted from Van Cleve Morris and Young Pai, *Philosophy and the American School*, p. 295. Copyright © 1976 Houghton Mifflin.

Perennialism

The basic educational view of *perennialism* is that the principles of knowledge are truly perennial. The foundation of the perennialist educational view is vested in the work of Thomas Aquinas, who stressed that the rational powers of humans, along with faith, are the instruments of knowledge. Thomism recognized the

---

Perennialist Class Activity

Ms. Rosemont's literature class had been studying the works of Henry David Thoreau. Today's session focused on "Reading" from *Walden,* and discussion was based on the following questions:

- Do the classics embody truth? Why or why not?

- Have all our emotions and problems been written about by great authors?

- Are none of our experiences unique?

- What makes a book great?

- Does popular literature ever serve a noble purpose? Why or why not?

- With whom can one talk about the best books?

- Can only great poets read the works of great poets? Why or why not?

- Does dealing with truth help us become immortal? Why or why not?

- How can we get the most benefits from our reading?

This lesson follows the Great Books procedure for questioning and could, therefore, be considered a perennialist investigation of human nature.[1]

In this perennialist class activity the nature of the learner is *active,* the nature of the subject matter is *structured,* the use of the subject matter is *cognitive,* and the behavior trend is toward *convergent thinking.*

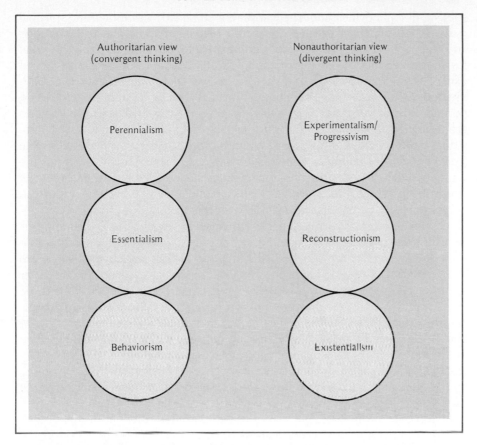

FIGURE 16 2 *Association of Educational Philosophies with Authoritarian and Nonauthoritarian Views*

importance of human daily life as well as the supernatural virtues not derived from experience; consequently, it has probably had as large a following as any Western philosophy. Nevertheless, when knowledge expanded, Thomism declined rapidly; it was difficult to fit the expanding knowledge into the confines of such a closed system of thought.

In the past few decades perennialist philosophy has been revived under the heading "neo-Thomism." A growing number of intellectuals adhere to the idea that the beliefs and knowledge of ancient cultures can be successfully applied to our lives today. Historically, Thomism has been associated with the Roman Catholic Church, but the revival of perennialism in America is associated mainly with lay educators. When judged by religious standards, the views of lay and ecclesiastical neo-Thomists show vast differences. Nevertheless, Roman Catholic educators have welcomed the revival of the scholasticism of Thomas Aquinas and share many educational views with lay perennialists.

The focus of learning in perennialism lies in activities designed to discipline the mind. Subject matter of a disciplinary and spiritual nature, like mathematics, languages, logic, great books, and doctrines, must be studied. Studying these subjects disciplines the mind. The learner is assumed to be a rational and spiritual person. Difficult mental calisthenics such as reading, writing, drill, rote memory, and computations are important in training the intellect. Perennialism holds that learning to reason is also very important—an ability attained by additional mental exercises in grammar, logic, and rhetoric, as well as through use of discussion methodologies. Reasoning about human matters and about moral principles that permeate the universe is the major focus of perennialism. Such learning activities are thought to contribute to the spiritual outreaching of idealism. As the individual mind develops, the learner becomes more like the Spiritual Being. The learner is closer to ultimate knowledge when he or she gradually assumes the mind qualities of God. Idealism also includes some of the recent findings that stress the psychology of learning; in this realm it is believed the mind can combine pieces of learning into whole concepts that have meaning.

As for the school curriculum, perennialists believe that early schooling is best directed toward preparing children for maturity and emphasize the three R's in the elementary schools. In this view, perennialism and essentialism share some thoughts. Some lay and ecclesiastical perennialists consider character training, enhanced through Bible study, to be equally as important as the three R's at the elementary level. A perennialist program for the secondary level is directed more toward educating the intellectually elite. Perennialism favors trade and skill training for students who are not engaged in the rigors of the general education program. Perennialists agree that the curriculum at the secondary level should provide a general education program for the intellectually gifted and vocational training for the less gifted. However, not all perennialists agree on a curriculum design for general education. Although the Great Books program associated with Robert M. Hutchins and Mortimer Adler has brought much attention to perennialism, other leaders in this movement do not support the program. Those who endorse the Great Books program maintain that studying the works of the leading scholars of history is the best way to a general education. Perennialists who do not agree maintain that more modern sources can be used to get knowledge. The ecclesiastical perennialists insist that all programs give first importance to the study of theology.

Essentialism

Essentialism, as a clearly defined educational philosophy, was formulated in 1938 by William C. Bagley.[3] It has dominated school practice worldwide, past and present. Although progressivism has been extremely popular in America, essentialism appears destined to continue as the dominant worldwide educational view. In the 1930s the Essentialist Committee for the Advancement of Education, led by Bagley, launched an attack on progressivism, which had gained considerable support in the 1920s. At present, educators still feel the strong influence of essentialism, even though the Essentialism Committee has been inactive since Bagley's death in 1946.

Essentialism holds that the essential elements of education should be selected from historical and modern thinking. The function of the schools is to

Essentialism advocates a return to the fundamentals of learning—the three Rs.
(*Source:* David S. Strickler/The Picture Cube)

Essentialist Class Activity

Ms. Wright's second graders had just learned to count money. She decided to let them play several games of "musical envelopes." Although there was one envelope per student, each contained a different amount of paper "nickels," "dimes," "quarters," and "pennies." When the music stopped, students had to count the money in their envelopes. The one with the most money for each game got a special prize.[2]

In this essentialist class activity the nature of the learner is *passive,* the nature of the subject matter is *structured,* the use of the subject matter is *cognitive,* and the behavior trend is toward *convergent thinking.*

Professional Perspectives

Classroom teachers should be able to illustrate the educational values which continue to uphold essentialism as our leading educational view.
Also, teachers should be able to explain the future of essentialism in the face of burgeoning new knowledge about our world.

teach the essentials of education. Essentialism primarily includes the tenets of idealism and, to a lesser degree, realism. From idealism comes the idea of viewing the mind as the central element of reality, which is significant in determining the essentials of essentialism. Realism contributes the basic view that reality is in physical things, leading to an emphasis on the quantitative aspects of education. Organization and factual mastery of content are imperative if one is to learn through observation and nature. Essentialism advocates a return to the fundamentals of learning—the three R's.

The essentialist curriculum, as developed from the idealist point of view, contains subject matter of symbol and content. Such subject matter includes literature, history, foreign languages, and religion. Methodology requires formal discipline through emphasis on required reading, lectures, memorization, repetition, and examinations. Realist philosophers of education differ in their views on curriculum, but they generally agree about including subject matter of the
[52] physical world. Mathematics and the natural sciences are examples of subjects that contribute to the learners' knowledge of natural law. Activities that require mastering facts and information on the physical world are significant aspects of realist methodology. With truth defined as observable fact, field trips, laboratories, audiovisual materials, and nature furnish methods. Habits of intellectual discipline are considered ends in themselves. Realism advocates studying the laws of nature and the accompanying universal truths of the physical world.

Essentialism envisions subject matter as the core of education. Severe criticism has been leveled at American education by those who advocate an emphasis on basic education. Essentialism assigns to the schools the task of conserving the heritage and transmitting knowledge of the physical world. In a sense, the school is a curator of knowledge.

With the burgeoning of new knowledge in contemporary society, essentialism may be contributing to the slowness of educational change. In this context, essentialism is criticized as obsolete in its authoritarian tendencies. Such criticism implies that essentialism does not satisfy the twentieth-century needs of our youth. Philosophers within the movement deny such criticism and claim to have incorporated modern influences in the system while maintaining academic standards.

Behaviorism

B. F. Skinner, the Harvard experimental psychologist and philosopher, is the
[53] recognized leader of the *behaviorist* movement. Skinner verified Pavlov's stimulus-response theory with animals and, from his research, suggested that human

---

Behaviorist Class Activity

Students in Mr. Drucker's civics class were given merit tokens for coming into the room quietly, sitting at their desks, preparing notebooks and pencils for the day's lesson, and being ready to begin answering comprehension questions in their workbooks. On Fridays, students were allowed to use their tokens at an auction to buy items that Mr. Drucker knew they wanted. Sometimes, however, students had to save tokens for more than two weeks to buy what they liked best.

In this behaviorist class activity the nature of the learner is *passive,* the nature of the subject matter is *amorphous,* the use of the subject matter is *cognitive* or *affective,* and the behavior trend is toward *convergent thinking.*

---

behavior could also be explained as responses to external stimuli. Other behaviorists' research expanded Skinner's work in illustrating the effect of the environment, particularly the interpersonal environment, in shaping individual behavior:

> These writers share a common belief that a student's misbehavior can be changed and reshaped in a socially acceptable manner by directly changing the student's environment. The Behaviorist accepts the premise that students are motivated by the factor that all people will attempt to avoid experiences and stimuli that are not pleasing and will seek experiences that are pleasing and rewarding.[4]

The concept of reinforcement is very influential upon the teacher practices of behaviorists. Positive reinforcers are used to reward approved behavior with something desired by the student (praise, special privileges, higher grades, etc.). Negative reinforcers are used to restrain behaviors that are not approved (reprimands, extra homework, lower grades, etc.). Behaviorists generally believe that negative reinforcement is ineffective. Furthermore, they believe that learning takes place when approved behavior is observed and then is positively reinforced. Charles H. Wolfgang and Carl D. Glickman developed a teacher behavior continuum as a construct in explaining particular teacher practices of the behaviorists (see Figure 16.3). They suggest that before using this construct

> the reader needs to reorient somewhat. Because the concept of reinforcement is so powerful and influential, all the other categories (visually looking on, nondirective statements, questions, and so on) are advocated as practices only when they are a form of reinforcement. In other words, the Behaviorists explain that all these practices emanate from the right hand side of our continuum.[5]

When visually looking on, a teacher may provide positive reinforcement (smiling, nodding approval, etc.) or negative reinforcement (frowning, shaking the head in disapproval, etc.). Similarly, nondirective statements, questions, and directive statements may be positive or negative. Both children and adults re-

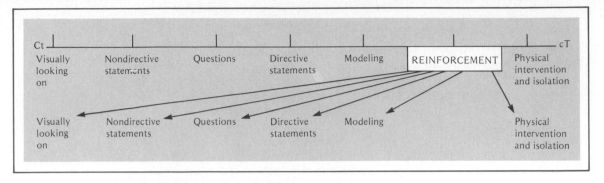

FIGURE 16.3   *Teacher Behavior Continuum* [*Source:* Charles H. Wolfgang and Carl D. Glickman, *Solving Discipline Problems: Strategies for Classroom Teachers* (Boston: Allyn and Bacon, 1980), p. 122. Reprinted by permission.]

spond to the models other people (peers, adults, heroes, etc.) represent to them by imitating the model behavior. Behaviorists contend that students tend to emulate behaviors that are rewarded. In the teacher behavior continuum (Figure 16.3), physical intervention and isolation refers to those times when a student, for whatever reason, does not exhibit some suitable behavior to recognize. In certain cases the teacher may physically intervene by removing the student from the classroom environment and isolating the student where reinforcement support is lacking.

The behaviorists have supplied a wealth of research that bears on the problems of attaining self-control, resisting temptation, and showing concern for others. Behaviorists do not attempt to learn about the causes of students' earlier problems. Rather, the teacher must ascertain what is happening in the classroom environment to perpetuate the child's behavior and what can be changed in the environment to "reverse the tide."[6]

Nonauthoritarian Educational Views

Experimentalism (progressivism), reconstructionism, and existentialism espouse a nonauthoritarian approach to the subject matter and teacher which encourages divergent thinking (see Figure 16.2). An illustrative class activity is provided as an introduction to the review of each of these three educational philosophies.

Experimentalism/Progressivism

With the rise of democracy in the late 1800s, the expansion of modern science and technology, and the need for people to be able to adjust to change, Americans had to have a new and different approach to getting knowledge to solve problems. An American philosopher, Charles S. Peirce (1839–1914), founded the

The Different Faces of Education

Education in the United States is as varied as the country itself. Today's children are learning in a number of different environments, each with inherent advantages and disadvantages.

Three distinct types of schools have been identified—urban, suburban, and rural. While many basic features are similar, each school has unique characteristics that are related to its particular sociological setting. What positive and negative features might you expect to find in each of the schools below?

The Picture Cube/J. Pennington

The Picture Cube/Sara Gold

The Picture Cube/John L. Barkan

Researchers found that determining the most effective learning environment was difficult, and their work in this area has been inconclusive. Clearly students can learn in environments with different strategies and objectives and that also vary in size. How do the following learning situations differ from each other? What kinds of skills does each promote? What are the potential advantages and disadvantages of each?

FPG International/David M. Doody

FPG International/M. Nelson

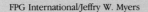

FPG International/Jeffry W. Myers

Every teacher has a distinct teaching style based on a personal set of beliefs about classroom learning. In certain situations some teaching styles are more effective than others, and experienced teachers are able to comfortably adapt their teaching styles to meet learners' needs. Think about your best teachers during the time you were in school. What kinds of teaching styles did they use? What kind of a teacher will you be?

FPG International/Jeffrey Sylvester

The Picture Cube/R.D. Brugger

FPG International/Jeffry W. Myers

The Future

What does the future hold for education? What will a typical classroom be like ten, twenty, or even one hundred years from now? Changes are occurring in society at a rapid pace, and many of those changes will have profound implications for education.

The family has become increasingly unstable as a result of divorce rates, single parent families, and working mothers. What implications do these changes have for education?

Rapidly changing technology has transformed the United States from an industrial-based society to an information-based society. How should education respond to this trend?

Every teacher has a distinct teaching style based on a personal set of beliefs about classroom learning. In certain situations some teaching styles are more effective than others, and experienced teachers are able to comfortably adapt their teaching styles to meet learners' needs. Think about your best teachers during the time you were in school. What kinds of teaching styles did they use? What kind of a teacher will you be?

The Picture Cube/R.D. Brugger

FPG International/Jeffrey Sylvester

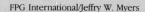

FPG International/Jeffry W. Myers

The Future

What does the future hold for education? What will a typical classroom be like ten, twenty, or even one hundred years from now? Changes are occurring in society at a rapid pace, and many of those changes will have profound implications for education.

The family has become increasingly unstable as a result of divorce rates, single parent families, and working mothers. What implications do these changes have for education?

The Picture Cube/Ellis Herwig

Rapidly changing technology has transformed the United States from an industrial-based society to an information-based society. How should education respond to this trend?

The Picture Cube/Richard Wood

Experimentalist Class Activity

Ms. Long's second graders read "Recipe for a Hippopotamus Sandwich" from *Where the Sidewalk Ends: Poems and Drawings of Shel Silverstein* (New York: Harper and Row, 1974). Each student was asked to draw a picture of the hippopotamus sandwich. For homework all class members were told to read the poem to someone, show the picture, and then tell about the person's reaction on the following day.[7]

In this experimentalist class activity the nature of the learner is *active,* the nature of the subject matter is *structured,* the use of the subject matter is *cognitive,* and the behavior trend is toward *divergent thinking.*

---

philosophical system called *pragmatism.* This philosophy held that the meaning and value of ideas could be found only in their practical results. Later, William James (1842–1910) extended Peirce's theory of meaning into a theory of truth. James went further and asserted that the satisfactory working of an idea constitutes its whole truth. Pragmatism was carried much further by John Dewey (1859–1952), who was a widely known and influential philosopher and educator. Dewey's philosophy was called *experimentalism* by some because he insisted that ideas must always be tested by experiment. His experimental beliefs carried over into his educational philosophy, which became the basis for what was usually described as *progressive* education.

Progressivism was a contemporary American educational philosophy. From its establishment in the mid 1920s through the mid 1950s, progressivism was the most influential educational view in America. Progressivists are basically opposed to authoritarianism and favor human experience as a basis for knowledge. Progressivism favors the scientific method of teaching and learning, allows for the beliefs of individuals, and stresses programs of student involvement that help students learn how to think. Progressivists believe that the school should actively prepare its students for change. Progressive schools emphasize learning *how* to think rather than *what* to think. Flexibility is important in the curriculum design, and emphasis is on *experimentation,* with no single body of content stressed more than any other. Since life experience determines curriculum content, all types of content must be permitted. Certain subjects regarded as traditional are recognized as desirable for study as well. Progressivist educators would organize scientific method-oriented learning activities around the traditional subjects. Such a curriculum is called experience-centered, or student-centered; the essentialism and perennialist curriculum is considered subject-centered. Experience-centered curricula stress the *process* of learning rather than the result.

Experimentalism as a contemporary teaching style has carried forth many of the tenets of progressivism since reconstructionism separated from the progressive education movement in 1957. Whereas reconstructionists place increased emphasis on the ends of education, experimentalists continue to emphasize the process of education in the classroom. Experimentalism is more

Progressivists favor human experiences as a basis for knowledge. These students are learning about democracy and the electoral process by participating in a statewide election to choose the official Illinois state fish. (*Source:* AP/Wide World Photos)

compatible with a core of problem areas across all academic disciplines than with a subject-centered approach to problem solving. It would be naive to suggest that memorization and rote practice are ruled out. However, they are not stressed as primary learning techniques. The assertion is that interest in an intellectual activity will generate all the practice needed for learning.

A tenet of experimentalism is that the school, to become an important social institution, be assigned the task of improving our way of life. To this end, experimentalism is deemed a working model of democracy. Freedom is explicit in a democracy, so it must be explicit in our schools. Certainly, freedom—rather than being a haphazard release of free will—must be organized to have meaning. Organized freedom permits each member of the school society to share in decisions, and experiences must be shared by all to ensure that the decisions are meaningful. Pupil-teacher planning is the key by which democracy in class-rooms is realized and is the process that gives some freedom to students, as well as teachers, in deciding what is studied. For example, the teacher might ask students to watch a film about an issue of interest and have them list questions about the issue that were not answered by the film but that they would like to investigate. Student questions can then be analyzed by students and the teacher and refined for research. Such questions can become the basis for an inquiry and problem-solving unit of study. However, even if pupil-teacher planning is not highlighted as a specific activity, any experimentalist lesson allows students to give some of their own input in ways that influence the direction of the lesson. In that sense experimentalist lessons always involve pupil-teacher planning. For instance, asking students to make statements about life in 1908, using reprint pages from 1908 catalogues as their information source, allows students to focus on any items from the catalogues *they* choose—not items determined by the teacher.

The learner is seen as an experiencing, thinking, exploring individual. Experimentalism exposes the learner to the subject matter of social experiences, social studies, projects, problems, and experiments that, when studied by the scientific method, will result in functional knowledge from all subjects. Books are regarded as tools to be used in learning rather than as sources of indisputable knowledge.

Many believe that the socialization aspect is the most valuable aspect of the movement. Experimentalism, in this way, represents the leading edge of our culture and teaches us how to manage change. However, experimentalism is criticized for placing so much stress on the processes of education that the ends are neglected. Its severest critics contend that it has little personal commitment to anything—producing many graduates who are also uncommitted and who are content to drift through life. Experimentalists counter by stating that their educational view is relatively young and, therefore, accepts criticism as an expected occurrence when trial-and-error methods are a part of the scientific method. The advent of progressivism as a counterview to the more traditional educational views provided exciting discussions which continue among thinkers in education.

Reconstructionism

Theodore Brameld, a leading American philosopher of education, is regarded as the father of reconstructionism. Although reconstructionism is sometimes considered to be part of progressivism, Brameld presents *reconstructionism* as a separate category having something in common with essentialism, perennialism, and progressivism. "Essentialism and Perennialism, especially, will be found to share a good deal of the same philosophic, educational, and cultural outlook, as do Reconstructionism and Progressivism share theirs."[9] Figure 16.4 illustrates the position of reconstructionism in relation to the other educational views. Thus experimentalism is related to reconstructionism because they both emphasize problem solving and divergent thinking. However, reconstructionism places more emphasis on the *ends* of education than does experimentalism, since reconstructionists use affective situations to persuade their students about the wisdom of specific social reform activities. However, students can accept or reject the reconstructionist's persuasive arguments. Therefore divergent thinking is honored. Reconstructionism is also related to experimentalism, essentialism, and perennialism in that factual realities about the world must be investigated

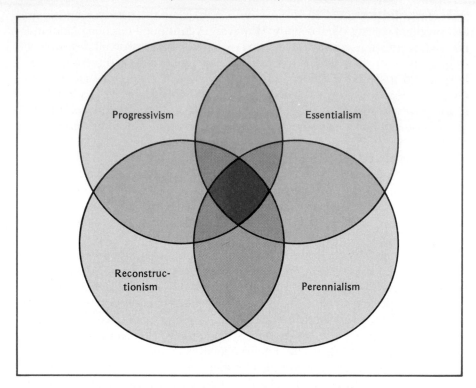

FIGURE 16.4 *Brameld's View of Reconstructionism as an Educational Philosophy*
[*Source:* Theodore Brameld, *Philosophies of Education in Cultural Perspective* (New York: Holt, Rinehart and Winston, 1955), p. 77. Reprinted by permission of the author.]

and learned, whatever the philosophy or teaching style. It is just that reconstructionism and experimentalism require students to engage in divergent thinking, whereas essentialism and perennialism are based on convergent thinking.

A persistent theme of reconstructionism is that public education should be the direct instrument of world reformation. As a logical extension of experimentalism, reconstructionism accepts the concept that the essence of learning is the actual experience of learning. Reconstructionism espouses a theory of social welfare that can effectively prepare learners to deal with the great crises of our time—war, inflation, rapid technological changes, depression. From the experiences of World War I, the Great Depression, and World War II, reconstructionist educators believe that the total educational effort must be seen within a social context.

As indicated earlier, John Dewey had an immense influence on progressivism. Dewey also made major contributions to reconstructionist philosophy with his efforts to define the individual as an entity within a social context. Reconstructionists go further in stressing that individuals as entities within a social context are urged to engage in specific reform activity. Classroom teachers tend to use affective emphases and moral dilemmas in directing attention toward social reform.

Reconstructionist Class Activity

Mr. Ragland asked his second graders to look at a cartoon that pictured a well-dressed man and woman in an automobile pulled by a team of two horses. The highway they were traveling along passed through rolling farmland with uncrowded meadows, trees, and clear skies in the background. He led a discussion based on the following questions:

1. What is happening in this picture?
2. Do you like what is happening in the picture? Why? Why not?
3. What does it say about the way you may be living when you grow up?
4. Are you happy or unhappy about what you've described for your life as an adult?
5. How can we get people to use less gasoline now?
6. What if we could keep companies from making and selling cars that could not travel at least 40 miles on one gallon of gasoline? How could we work to get a law passed to do this?[8]

In this reconstructionist class activity the nature of the learner is *active,* the nature of the subject matter is *structured,* the use of the subject matter is *affective,* and the behavior trend is toward *divergent thinking.*

Existentialism

Generally, the American system of education has depended on group processes and group norms. *Existentialism* does not function well as a philosophy of such a group-oriented system, since it concerns individual self-fulfillment. Currently, American educators are giving a lot of attention to problems and processes concerned with individual differences. Most of their efforts are aimed at minimizing individual differences by such tactics as forming homogeneous groups for particular subject matter instruction. The rationale is that group instruction proceeds more smoothly when individuals are adjusted to the group. But with regard to helping individuals adjust to the group, an existentialist would argue: "This we now know to be a lost cause, for studies in many fields lead us to the same conclusion, that the extent of these differences is far greater than we thought. Much injustice has been done in the process of ironing them out and many a personality violated."[11]

From the 1960s to the present, the influence of existentialism can be identified with various creative programs and written materials. A. S. Neill proposes a "radical approach to child rearing" in his book *Summerhill.* Charles E. Silberman, in his *Crisis in the Classroom,* calls for remaking American education to provide for greater consideration of the individual. Various textbooks discuss themes like the open-access curriculum, humanism in education, nongraded instruction, and multiage grouping, each of which attends to the uniqueness of the learner. Educators are now making various attempts in their school programs to individualize education. Modular scheduling permits flexibility for students to arrange classes of their choice. Free schools, storefront schools, schools

---

Existentialist Class Activity

Ms. Fenway wanted her ninth graders to think about the effectiveness of television and radio advertising. She asked students to write down any five slogans or "jingles" they could remember and the products advertised. Ms. Fenway selected from their items at random and tested the class. She read each slogan, and class members had to provide answers. The test was corrected in class by the students, who were very surprised that the grading scale was reversed. Those who had all correct answers received F's, and those who had only one correct answer received A's. When asked why she had reversed the grades, Ms. Fenway responded "Why do you think advertising is so effective?" She asked whether students resented some companies' selling tactics. Then she told students to help her make a list of questions to ask themselves in order to avoid spending money in ways they might later regret. She also asked for specific examples of spending money for items they later wished they had not bought.[10]

In this existentialist class activity the nature of the learner is *active,* the nature of the subject matter is *structured,* the use of the subject matter is *affective,* and the behavior trend is toward *divergent thinking.*

---

without walls, and area vocational centers provide alternatives to traditional schools. Educational programs that treat the needs of the individual are usually more costly per pupil than the traditional group-centered programs. Consequently, as taxpayer demands for accountability mount, individualized programs are often brought under unit-cost scrutiny. Nonetheless, increasing numbers of educators are willing to defend increased expenditures to meet the needs of the individual learner within the instructional programs of the schools.

Existentialism views all circumstances as they relate to the individual human being. This view does not imply that emphasis given to the development of the individual has no place in the public school merely because such activity would be contrary to the group orientation of the educational system. The classroom teacher would need to function from a conceptual base that rules out time-honored conventional notions. On the existentialist view of the individual as unique and its commensurate effects on the teacher's conception of education, George Kneller writes:

> To begin, it rules out three conventional notions: that education is primarily an agency of society, set up to perpetuate a cultural heritage; that it is a pipeline of perennial truths; and that it is a means for adjusting the young to life in a democratic community. In place of these, let education exist for the individual. Let it teach him to live as his own nature bids him, spontaneously and authentically.[12]

The phrase "as his own nature bids him" illustrates the emphasis given to the affective quality of existentialist teaching. Since the values and beliefs of learners are so wide ranging, existentialists would do their problem solving for divergent solutions among their learners.

Existentialist teachers honor divergent thinking so completely that they delay
giving their own personal opinions and do not attempt to persuade students to
particular points of view. Even though they emphasize the affective and thereby
may be supposed to make students feel a certain urgency about issues, it is
always left to the individual student to decide when to take a stand, what kind
of stand to take, whether a cause merits action, and, if so, what kind of action.

Summary and Implications

This chapter provided an overview of six leading educational views utilized in
part or entirely by teachers in the American schools. While one's ultimate teaching style may not be completely committed to essentialism, behaviorism, perennialism, experimentalism, reconstructionism, or existentialism, the basic
descriptions of those views should be helpful in identifying several preferences.
An individual's preferences are compatible with, if not formulated by, his or
her personality. The extent to which one's teaching practices fit one's personality,
and vice versa, is related to effective teaching.

Whether or not the teacher preparation program at your college or university contained formal coursework in classical or educational philosophy, we
encourage you to expand your study in this area so that you may extract from
the knowledge acquired meaningful beliefs to guide you in identifying preferences and methods for assisting your students.

Some classroom teachers continue to be skeptical about educational theory
and those who espouse theory as a basis for practice. Yet new theories about
educating children continue to proliferate, while the older beliefs remain strong
in today's schools. Chapter 15 presented digests of the structure and thoughts
associated with selected classical philosophies. This chapter illustrated the relationship of current educational views to the classical philosophies but described the educational views in terms of the learner, subject matter orientation,
and authoritarian/nonauthoritarian tendencies. The next chapter provides an
immediately useful tool for prospective teachers to determine a way to study
teaching behaviors for trends and preferences related to their personal style
(philosophy).

Remember that there are no perfect teaching styles or methodologies. There
are, however, suggested field experience guidelines designed to help one prepare to analyze teaching styles and clusters of techniques which complement
various teacher role models. There is also an analytical tool which can be used

with the field experience guidelines to ascertain the patterns of responses which illustrate how an observed teacher's style is associated with a particular educational philosophy. Chapter 17 provides those field experience guidelines and describes a procedure for studying and categorizing teaching behavior for trends and preferences.

Discussion Questions

1. What were the characteristics and behaviors of one of your favorite teachers who was authoritarian toward the students? Of a favorite teacher who was nonauthoritarian toward the students?
2. Experienced teachers often advise a beginning teacher to be firm with the students and let them know at the beginning how you intend to teach your classes. Is this advice good or bad? Discuss the pros and cons of such a procedure.
3. When might a teacher focus on personalized situations involving such things as death or injustice to stimulate student learning? How would such a strat-

egy relate to the back-to-basics expectations of our schools?

4. The concept of reinforcement is very influential upon the teacher practices of behaviorists. How would you use positive reinforcers and negative reinforcers while teaching your subject area concentration?
5. Existentialism rules out some of the conventional notions about educating youth. Emphasis is given to the development of the individual rather than to the structure of a curriculum. What are the implications of existentialism as related to the grouping of students in regular classes?

Supplemental Activities

1. Many application forms for teaching positions ask the candidate to state briefly a philosophy of education. Write your own philosophy of education, discussing classroom management, teaching methods, discipline, and evaluation of the learner as related to a specific lesson or technique. Avoid educational jargon and clichés in your statement of philosophy. Emphasize the relationship of your philosophy to the classroom environment as much as possible.
2. William C. Bagley was the leader of the Essentialist Committee for the Advancement of Education in the 1930s. Read about the work of the committee to determine how the work is still influencing teaching practices today.
3. Visit several elementary and secondary school classes

for the purpose of determining the prevalent philosophy of education. Report on the practices observed. What was the teaching style of the teacher? Why do you believe the teacher style was as you identified?

4. Invite a school superintendent to class to outline what is generally considered the educational philosophy of his or her school system and what is expected of beginning teachers.
5. Interview business leaders from two different companies in order to determine the importance of ethics in the operations of the businesses. Determine the extent to which the business leaders' values were influenced by teachers. List the recommendations for teachers made by the business leaders.

Notes

1. Lloyd Duck, *Instructor's Manual for Teaching with Charisma* (Boston: Allyn and Bacon, 1981), Item H, pp. 53–54. Used by permission.
2. Ibid., Item A, p. 40.
3. William C. Bagley, "An Essentialist's Platform for the Advancement of American Education," *Educational Administration and Supervision,* 24 (April 1938): 241–256.
4. Charles H. Wolfgang and Carl D. Glickman, *Solving Discipline Problems: Strategies for Classroom Teachers* (Boston: Allyn and Bacon, 1980), p. 121.
5. Ibid., 121–122.

6. Ibid., 121.

7. Duck, Item D, p. 41.

8. Ibid., Item N, pp. 47–48.

9. Theodore Brameld, *Patterns of Educational Philosophy* (New York: Holt, Rinehart and Winston, 1971), pp. 63–64.

10. Duck, Item C, pp. 50–51.

11. George F. Kneller, "Education, Knowledge, and the Problem of Existence," *Harvard Educational Review,* 31 (Fall 1961): 430.

12. Ibid., 428.

Bibliography

Ackerly, Robert L. *The Reasonable Exercise of Authority.* Washington, D.C.: National Association of Secondary School Principals, 1969.

Bagley, William C. "An Essentialist's Platform for the Advancement of American Education." *Educational Administration and Supervision,* 24 (April 1938): 241–256.

Brameld, Theodore. *Patterns of Educational Philosophy.* New York: Holt, Rinehart and Winston, 1971.

Lauderdale, William B. *Progressive Education: Lessons from Three Schools.* Phi Delta Kappa Fastback No. 166. Bloomington, Ind.: Phi Delta Kappa, 1981.

Morris, Van Cleve, and Pai, Young. *Philosophy and the American School.* 2nd ed. Boston: Houghton Mifflin, 1976.

Rich, John Martin. *Innovations in Education: Reformers and Their Critics.* Boston: Allyn and Bacon, 1985.

Rothman, Robert. "Standards Challenged in New Hampshire." *Education Week,* February 11, 1987, 11.

Skinner, B. F. "Programmed Instruction Revisited." *Phi Delta Kappan,* October 1986, 103–110.

Wolfgang, Charles H., and Glockman, Card D. *Solving Discipline Problems: Strategies for Classroom Teachers.* Boston: Allyn and Bacon, 1980.

Zahorik, John A. "Let's Be Realistic About Flexibility in Teaching." *Educational Leadership,* October 1986, 50–51.

Toward a Preferred Teaching Style

Focus Questions

- Assuming a special tool and accompanying guidelines were available to analyze teaching styles, how could you benefit from such analyses?
- How would observing another teacher's behavior permit you to understand the teacher's style? In what ways would prospective teachers benefit from observing other teachers?
- Why should a beginning teacher know about several classroom teaching styles? Wouldn't it be better to consistently follow one approach to teaching?

- Do you believe that students learn in similar ways, for the most part, or do learning styles vary among the students? Do you agree that teachers generally make too much of providing for individual differences? Explain.
- What are you prepared to say when you are asked to state your philosophy of education during a job interview?

Key Terms and Concepts

Analytical tool
Field experience guidelines
Teaching style/philosophy
Passive learners
Active learners
Amorphous subject matter
Structured subject matter
Cognitive domain

Affective domain
Divergent thinking
Convergent thinking
Classroom management
Discipline maintenance
Values education
Healthy eclectic

What Would You Do?

After observing the teacher to whom you have been assigned for your student teaching work, you are aware that you prefer to use a much different teaching style from your supervising teacher's. The students also let you know that they believe that your supervising teacher is one of the best teachers in the school. How would you discuss this concern with your supervising teacher?

You are assigned the task of observing three different teachers teaching the same lesson at the same grade level for the purpose of analyzing the three teaching styles. You are expected to detail the specifics of your analysis with observed teacher behaviors. How would these observations help you regarding your teaching style?

Extensive surveys of modern views of learning—as expressed in philosophy, psychology, and education journals and studies—reveal a seemingly endless and divergent range of views. Thus today's classroom teachers must identify their own beliefs about educating young people. Although labeling the classroom practice of any one teacher is risky, we recommend that you, as a prospective teacher, carefully identify a personal set of operational principles with regard to classroom techniques. Whether your operational principles are drawn from the brief descriptions of this text or elsewhere, you should strive for consistent teaching behavior within the framework of sound principles—that is, behavior based on your personal philosophy of education.

How you manage your classroom, and the content, the method, and the values you stress will be based on your personal belief system. All teachers should at least be aware of the options available when developing a preferred teaching style (philosophy). Instructional practices must fit the teacher's personality, and the teacher must believe in the effectiveness of the practices used. Since other teaching styles might be more effective in certain situations, experienced teachers sometimes draw from styles other than their preferred personal style. Perhaps the best goal for all teachers is to become *healthy eclectics* who can comfortably use a number of teaching styles in order to meet learners' needs more completely. As long as this eclectic strategy serves the instructional purpose well, and as long as the teacher has the ability to communicate to the students how they can succeed under various teaching styles, the use of various styles can be advantageous. However, if a teacher is merely trying technique after technique with no knowledge of how these techniques relate to teaching philosophies, the result is a state of *unhealthy eclecticism,* which should be avoided.

Condensed explanations of teaching styles/philosophies run the inherent risks of oversimplification and of being too judgmental, but prospective teachers do need a working framework to help them avoid the stereotypes associated with various educational philosophies. Effective teaching is not a matter of authoritarian versus nonauthoritarian methodologies, older versus newer theories, or controlled classrooms versus noncontrolled classrooms. Rather, responsible use of any teaching style/philosophy yields benefits for learners, whereas irresponsible use of any teaching style/philosophy yields no benefits for anyone.

How to Study Teaching Behavior for Trends and Preferences

Classroom teachers do borrow from classical philosophical concepts (see Chapter 15) and current educational views (see Chapter 16) primarily as a means to ensure variety in methods of instruction. However, a philosophical position is actually indicated by emphases and preferences that translate into teacher behavior. Thus it is the behavioral emphasis or preference that should be identified to reveal the underlying set of philosophical assumptions. Despite the tendency of many students when they have just completed an academic study of educational philosophy to rely on the term *eclectic,* most educators are not true eclectics. In fact, few, if any, teachers would apply all methodologies with equal degrees of enthusiasm and success.

An Analytical Tool

A useful analytical tool for studying teaching behaviors for trends and preferences was developed by Professor Lloyd Duck at George Mason University. In the following discussion of the four questions comprising the analytical tool, constructs from Duck's text *Teaching with Charisma*[1] are utilized to provide prospective teachers with a useful process for working toward a preferred teaching philosophy. If one is to identify a series of preferences, as opposed to a set of behaviors that belong to mutually exclusive categories, any beneficial analytical tool should have more than one indicator. Duck's analytical tool provides four indicators of teacher style by tabulating observed responses along a continuum associated with each of four questions. Figure 17.1 lists the four questions and the continuum for tabulating observed teacher behaviors and preferences.

Specific applications of the analytical tool will be detailed later in this chapter. In the following paragraphs each question and its respective continuum of response is discussed. You are encouraged to study this material carefully in order to have a better understanding of the use of the analytical tool at a later point.

In this procedure for studying teacher behavior for trends and preferences, an infinite variety of answers to the questions exist on continua for which extremes are delineated. The two extremes of the continuum for each question are illustrated as endpoints, as shown next.

1. What is the nature of the learner?

Passive   Active

Some teachers may feel that in particular subject areas the principal business of learners ought to be absorption of content. Remember that it is the extreme position regarding "absorption" of prescribed subject matter that is implied by the term *passive,* as we have used it here. The milder position of the teacher who wants youngsters to absorb knowledge about the subject matter but who finds classroom interaction pleasantly stimulating simply belongs further to the right on the continuum for this question about the nature of the learner.

Let us now look all the way to the right of the continuum to the extreme that has been labeled *active.* Imagine a teacher who has so much respect for what learners can contribute to the learning environment that he or she definitely

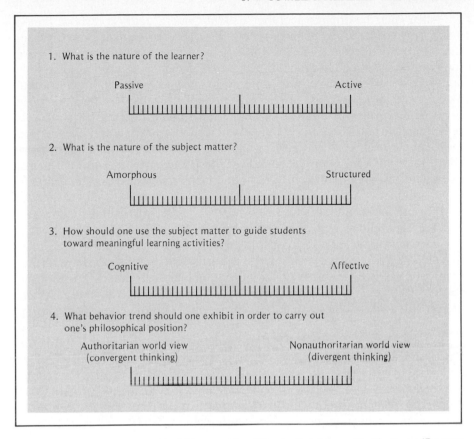

1. What is the nature of the learner?

       Passive   Active

2. What is the nature of the subject matter?

        Amorphous   Structured

3. How should one use the subject matter to guide students toward meaningful learning activities?

       Cognitive   Affective

4. What behavior trend should one exhibit in order to carry out one's philosophical position?

      Authoritarian world view   Nonauthoritarian world view
      (convergent thinking)   (divergent thinking)

FIGURE 17.1 *Analytical Tool* [*Source:* Lloyd Duck, *Teaching with Charisma* (Boston: Allyn and Bacon, 1981), p. 25. Reprinted by permission.]

does not want them to "absorb" prescribed subject matter, as the teacher sees that subject matter. Under such circumstances learners are viewed as very important in the classroom environment because they teach each other with their teacher through interaction, while inquiring about problems that are meaningful to them. Active students provide insights that are original to them at the time such insights are offered. For example, if students were asked to make their own statements about life in 1908 which they can justify only from the pages of a 1908 Sears catalogue, the students would need to be active learners. (Please note that students could be thoroughly involved with and enjoy a competitive drill in multiplication, but they would not be active learners by our definition because they would not be providing original insights.)

2. What is the nature of the subject matter?

    Amorphous   Structured

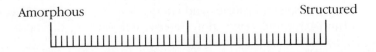

Allen Funt, the originator of the "Candid Camera" television show, filmed a skit in which he asked primary school youngsters to explain excerpts from the "Pledge of Allegiance" to the United States' flag. The children who were interviewed and filmed had memorized the "Pledge of Allegiance" very carefully and were delighted to have an opportunity to talk about what they had learned. The answers they gave could not have been more charming and ingenuous, but none of their remarks seemed to follow logic understandable to adults. As refreshing and humorous as the youngsters' responses were, it was obvious that they had not really understood what they had memorized, although they were very successful at imitating the sounds of the "Pledge of Allegiance." It is this extreme of the continuum which has been labeled *amorphous*. This extreme denotes the ability to repeat items and details without any corresponding capacity to demonstrate insights about relationships among separate items.

The "amorphous" label has been reserved for rote learning that emphasizes that each item to be learned is equal in importance to every other item that has to be learned; hence youngsters are not encouraged to find relationships among items, and no item is seen as being more important than others. It is as if the teacher who would teach history with this approach were to assume that facts of history are always inherently good, and one must improve oneself by learning as many of these bits and pieces of information as possible. Without considering the actual effects a certain subject area can achieve, some teachers give the impression that the more bits and pieces of the subject students learn, the more benefits they will derive. In truly extreme examples of this variety of learning, the teacher may feel so satisfied to hear students recite details verbatim that there is no attempt to check their actual comprehension. Use of the "amorphous" label implies that youngsteres do not comprehend what they are attempting to memorize.

If we look all the way along the continuum to the extreme labeled *structured,* we may expect to find a position represented by those who have quite a realistic view of what subject matter can never accomplish for youngsters, as well as a practical assessment of its benefits. The term *structured,* as used in this context, implies a view of subject matter expressed by Jerome Bruner, when he emphasized the "natural structure of a discipline." To be considered a discipline, any subject matter should be viewed as having a natural structure, which can help to explain relationships among its components and which can also be used to find out new information within that subject matter area.

Teachers can emphasize the structure of a discipline through problem solving or through lectures. Students who are given the problem of making statements about life in 1908 that they can justify from a catalogue are forced to explore relationships among components of the discipline they are using. In effect, they are asked to sort through the data from the catalogue, use facts relevant to the statements they have made, and ignore, at least for the time being, data not relevant to their statements. Another teacher might emphasize the structure of the discipline by lecturing about how mail-order businesses bridged the gap between factories and widely scattered markets. This teacher might explain facts about population density, efficiency of the postal system, and advertising techniques as they relate to the major generalization concerning factories and markets. Both teachers would be emphasizing the structure of the discipline.

The continuum we have just examined concerning the subject matter embraces a broad spectrum, ranging from the position that regards subject matter as a series of items to be known (approaching the amorphous extreme) to the position that views subject matter as a method for finding out new things (approaching the structured extreme).

3. How should one use the subject matter to guide students toward meaningful learning activities?

Cognitive   Affective

For this indicator's continuum the terms *cognitive* and *affective* are used as endpoints. The concepts deal not with mutually exclusive categories but, rather, with matters of emphasis and preference. If cognitive learning emphasizes intellectual skills devoid of emotion and affective learning emphasizes feelings and emotions, then both cognitive and affective learning can be, and usually are, closely linked. Thus the decision revolves around which of the two to emphasize. Since any responsible assumption of the teacher's role involves some degree of skill development and information giving among students, the question concerns the best way to develop skills and give information—either by emphasizing the cognitive or by stressing the affective domain. Selecting between these two approaches is each teacher's personal decision.

In order to illuminate factors involved in any teacher's decision to emphasize cognitive or affective learning activities, we consider the following addendum to our indicator for the question about the use of subject matter:

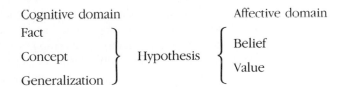

Practical definitions

fact a verifiable truth (e.g., A certain priest sold an indulgence as indicated by church records.)

concept a word or phrase containing at least one noun (e.g., indulgence, river, favorable balance of trade)

generalization a statement about facts or concepts, or both facts and concepts (e.g., Indulgences were sold in German principalities during the fifteenth century.)

belief a statement that is assumed to be true, often uncritically [e.g., I believe in God (when "meaningful" others believe in God and the speaker has not examined his position critically). I believe it is going to rain.]

value a belief about which someone cares deeply and which has been examined critically (e.g., I believe in God.)

hypothesis a statement that is assumed to be true for the purpose of critical examination [e.g., any one of the following statements in which one is uncertain about their validity and wishes to examine relevant evidence: (1) Indulgences were sold in German principalities during the fifteenth century. (2) I believe it is going to rain. (3) I believe in God.]

Let us assume that all subject matter disciplines are composed of three basic raw materials: facts, concepts, and generalizations. Let us also assume that youngsters bring to the classroom certain attitudes, which involve the emotions and which can be stated as beliefs and values. These beliefs and values are especially powerful in their capacities to influence the way youngsters perceive facts, concepts, and generalizations within any discipline. Some teachers see their roles as using the affective emphasis to stimulate student learning. Such teachers generally focus on personalized situations involving death, injustice, or passing time as it decreases one's power to make choices. Teachers who ask students to study inflation by having them examine the displacement of the poor as speculators renovate housing in the inner city or have students study science by asking them to measure and propose solutions for pollution in their neighborhoods are choosing to emphasize the affective. Other teachers avoid such controversial issues and emphasize understanding economics and the physical sciences through a cognitive approach. For example, inflation might be defined by such a teacher as "too much money chasing too few goods"—followed by explanations that do not highlight the social ills resulting from inflation.

Philosophical soul searching about the three questions we have just considered in our simple analytical tool has definite advantages. When students are convinced that a teacher is expert enough to decide what is beneficial about the subject matter he or she is selling, how he or she wants to sell it, and how he or she would like to use student contributions to the learning environment, the teacher will be perceived as being sincere in the desire to help students. More importantly, the teacher must feel secure enough to talk openly and directly with students about elements he or she considered in making decisions about these first three questions in the analytical tool.

4. What behavior trend should one exhibit in order to carry out one's philosophical position?

Authoritarian		Nonauthoritarian
(convergent thinking)		(divergent thinking)

The question about behavior is especially critical because an observer may hear in a teacher's voice one set of philosophical assumptions yet find that the teacher's behavior seems to support an entirely different set of philosophical assumptions. The terms *authoritarian* and *nonauthoritarian* have been chosen for extremes on this continuum. Although these two terms may seem to imply "strict" as opposed to "permissive" classroom management, the intention is to emphasize a more inclusive approach to classroom management than merely dealing with discipline problems. Thus it is an overall view in regard to the student and the subject matter that this indicator has been designed to examine.

Suppose some teachers encourage students to view subject matter only as experts in that field might view it; these teachers habitually accept for each major question under examination only one right answer, which all students are expected to adopt and understand. In terms of analyzing classroom behaviors, such teachers would be said to encourage convergent thinking. For the purpose of the analytical tool such a teacher exhibits an authoritarian behavior trend by rewarding convergent thinking.

Part of this tendency toward authoritarian behavior is indicated by the subject matter with which a teacher is dealing. For instance, a chemistry teacher might set up a laboratory "experiment" in which the students are asked to determine whether Boyle's law regarding the expansion of gases still holds. In such a situation all answers to the experiment should look alike, no matter which student or group of students derived them. No alternative answers would be accepted as true because all students are supposed to discover that, indeed, Boyle's law still holds. However, there are options to the use of convergent thinking even in introductory courses in physical sciences. Suppose, for instance, that the instructor wanted students to "measure" pollution within the local school district. Some youngsters will devise means to measure pollution in the atmosphere, others may examine water pollution, and some may look at impurities in foods. Several answers to this question about pollution are possible, and the teacher would probably be expected to encourage alternative plans of action to get rid of pollutants.

This second example in which students measure pollutants would involve what is called divergent thinking because more than one answer is encouraged for the question at hand. For the purposes of the analytical tool this behavior trend is nonauthoritarian. Although one might correctly expect the nonauthoritarian trend to be most frequently associated with the humanities and the social sciences, there is some evidence of its use with the physical sciences, as the previous example from a science class points out.

Answers to the first three questions have been in the process of formulation throughout a prospective teacher's entire educational preparation. What is it that causes some prospective teachers to want to deal primarily with the physical sciences and mathematics, while others are more comfortable in dealing with the social sciences and humanities? Is it that some are more adept with convergent thinking, while others are more adept with divergent thinking? If so, we would expect these feelings, or philosophical assumptions, which have been in the process of formulation for years, to manifest themselves quite clearly in a teacher's classroom behavior.

**Professional
Perspectives**

Carefully study Figures 17.1 and 17.2 together to gain an understanding for the continuums associated with each question. Follow your study with a review of Table 17.1 with Figure 17.1 to prepare for observations of other teachers.

There is only one other caveat indicated by classroom behavior trends. Do not assume that the terms *authoritarian* and *nonauthoritarian,* when applied to a behavior trend, connote "strictness" or "permissiveness" of classroom management. Everyone who assumes a teacher's role expects and must receive enough cooperation from students that learning can occur. This minimal amount of cooperation is necessary for every learning environment; hence a dichotomy between autocracy and chaos is definitely not the extent to which we envision the continuum for the last question in our analytical tool.

Educational Views and the Analytical Tool

The four questions in the analytical tool and the tendencies toward the continuum's extreme responses for each question are illustrated in Figure 17.2 as associated with each of the six teaching philosophies discussed in Chapter 16. Perennialist, essentialist, and behaviorist teachers encourage students to view the subject matter only as experts in that field view the subject matter. Such teacher behaviors exhibit an authoritarian curriculum trend encouraging convergent thinking. Experimentalists, reconstructionists, and existentialists encourage students to use the subject matter as a means of determining more than one answer to the question at hand. This behavior can be viewed as a nonauthoritarian curriculum trend encouraging divergent thinking.

Using Field Experience Guidelines

The following suggested field experience activities are designed to help one prepare to analyze teaching styles and clusters of techniques which complement various teacher role models. When using the field experience guidelines (Table 17.1) to study teaching preferences, remember that there are no perfect teaching styles or teaching methodologies. These guidelines should be used with the analytical tool (Figure 17.1). The observer should place check marks along each of the analytical tool question continuums from the observations of teacher behaviors and conversations with the teacher. From this procedure the question tallies will indicate tendencies along the question continuums. Such tendencies then can be associated with one of the educational views as illustrated in Figure 17.2. The guidelines may also be used with the analytical tool for personal assessment. If you use these guidelines for personal assessment, observe your own behaviors, answer the questions as indicated, and discuss with yourself the ways you prefer to teach. From this analysis you will have an idea of your preferred style (philosophy).

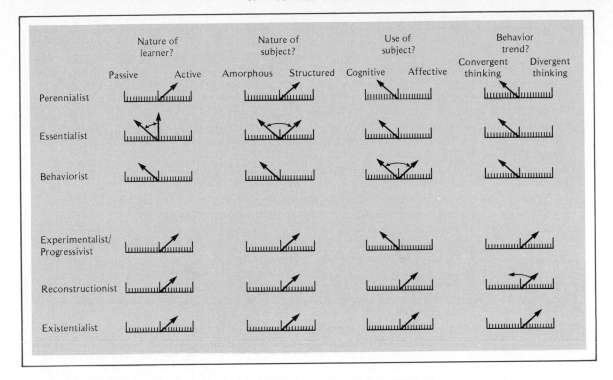

FIGURE 17.2 *Relationship of the Analytical Tool Questions to Educational Views*
[*Source:* Adapted from Lloyd Duck, *Teaching with Charisma* (Boston: Allyn and Bacon, 1981), pp. 226–227.]

Interpreting the Results

After identifying a preferred teaching philosophy by using the analytical tool with the guidelines, one must be careful to minimize the effects of natural weaknesses associated with each type of teaching styles. The three styles that emphasize convergent thinking tend to reward students for "reading the teacher's mind" by giving as an answer the exact phrase the teacher wants. Teachers using such methods must be very careful with their responses, or students may receive the message that they should not risk participating in discussion unless they are absolutely certain they have the exact answer. The divergent type of teaching styles may, on the other hand, require students to participate in interesting activities but not make them fully aware of why they are participating or what they are learning. If students are not required to justify the generalizations they make and are not made to see that they are learning many facts and skills, they may end up feeling that all answers are so relative that problem-solving processes are not worthwhile. Teachers who know enough about themselves and the teaching styles to show students how to succeed with both convergent thinking and divergent thinking are well on their way to reaching the ideal of being healthy eclectics.

TABLE 17.1 *Field Experience Guidelines*

1. Observe a discussion session for the kinds of student participation that occur. How often are students asked to participate in divergent thinking? How often are students asked to participate in convergent thinking? *(See the analytical tool for questions about behavior trend and the nature of the learner.)*

2. Observe teaching techniques to determine which ones involve students in convergent thinking and which ones involve students in divergent thinking activities. *(See the analytical tool for questions about behavior trend and the nature of the learner.)*

3. Observe a lesson and determine how many academic disciplines the teacher has decided to use in that lesson. How are these various disciplines integrated? *(See the analytical tool for the question about nature of the subject matter.)*

4. Observe a "discovery" lesson to determine the nature of the investigation and its outcome. *(See the analytical tool for questions about behavior trend and the nature of the learner.)*

5. Observe an "inquiry" lesson to determine the nature of the investigation and its outcomes. *(See the analytical tool for questions about behavior trend and the nature of the learner.)*

6. Observe a lesson in which individualization of instruction is a major focus. How does the instructor plan for helping students at different skill levels improve their expertise? *(See the analytical tool for questions about nature of the subject matter and use of the subject matter.)*

7. Talk with the cooperating teacher about the kinds of controversial issues which his or her students may be studying. Ask permission to observe a session in which a controversial issue is being examined in order to determine what the issue is and its resolution(s). *(See the analytical tool for the question about use of subject matter.)*

8. Talk with the cooperating teacher to find out which method(s) he or she prefers to use and why: "discovery," "inquiry," problem-solving discussions, simulations, lectures, directed reading of primary sources, directed reading of secondary sources, practice exercises, learning centers, individual research, and so forth. *(A summary activity for all questions in the analytical tool.)*

Source: Lloyd Duck, *Teaching with Charisma* (Boston: Allyn and Bacon, 1981), pp. 225, 228. Reprinted by permission.

When you are asked to explain your teaching style preference or philosophy, remember to follow the same order in formulating an answer that you would follow in using the field experience guidelines to study a teaching style preference. That is, always describe effective lessons first and then generalize as to |9| whether the preference is for essentialism, experimentalism, or any of the other educational philosophies. In this way you avoid sounding as if you are speaking in clichés. A similar procedure should be followed in studying teaching style preferences. Determine first whether convergent thinking or divergent thinking is the outcome of the lesson. Then make determinations about all questions in the analytical tool and apply the appropriate label. Both procedures begin with the specifics of a lesson and move to the application of the label. And remember that no one is *always* an advocate of the same teaching style for every lesson. Use of the label "experimentalism," for instance, indicates a preference for that style over others that may also be used occasionally. If no preference can be determined, then "eclectic" is the appropriate label to select.

Use of labels is not important in itself. However, knowing yourself and the options you have for teaching style choices is important. Acting on this knowledge and choosing wisely will help you to get increasingly closer to the ideal of being a *healthy eclectic*—that supremely effective educator who can change styles comfortably as the learning needs of the students might indicate.

A Day in the Life of a Teacher

In addition to the discussion of procedures to use when developing your teaching style preference or philosophy, let's pause to examine what teaching is really like. What does a teacher do between the time he or she enters the school in the morning and leaves at night? A teacher's day involves much more than simply standing in front of a classroom to teach a particular subject. Within the structured setting of a school day are many unstructured events that you may not have thought of.

Randy Steinheimer was chosen to be the 1985–86 Teacher of the Year in Illinois. He currently teaches fifth grade in the West Aurora School District in Aurora, Illinois, and has eight years of teaching experience. The following pages depict a typical school day for Randy and his student teacher, Denise Testin. How is their day similar to what you imagined teaching would be like? How is it different?

Before the Students Arrive

Filling the aquariums with pond water

Planning the school day with his teaching assistant, as they set up a science experiment which will be performed later in the day

Talking with students at their lockers before classes begin

At the school's learning center, teacher and class listen as a guest speaker describes her travels to Egypt

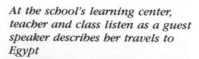

Math class using the computer

Helping students individually with their math problems

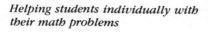

Working with students during lunch

Both teacher and class participate in a silent reading period following lunch

The School Day

Performing the science experiment, using hot air and balloons

Language arts class

Students prepare to leave for the day

Cleaning up the science experiment

Counting money collected for an up-coming field trip

End of the School Day

Calling parents to discuss students' progress

(Appendix F further illustrates two broad philosophical categories that are most easily recognizable by teaching styles and gives further differentiation of the six educational philosophies.)

Philosophy and the Classroom

Educational trends, identified by other terms such as the "back-to-basics movement," may also be related to certain philosophies of education. The back-to-basics movement centers on subject matter and is clearly in the realms of essentialism and perennialism, whereas "free schools" and "open education" concepts are experience-based and focus on student activity as identified in experimentalism and existentialism. Figure 16.2 illustrates the association of these primary educational philosophies with the authoritarian view honoring convergent thinking and the nonauthoritarian view honoring divergent thinking. Again, note that the terms *authoritarian* and *nonauthoritarian* are meant to provide an overall view in regard to the student and subject matter and not to imply strict or permissive classroom management. Since all of the educational philosophies discussed in this text are from the Western tradition, the classroom teacher has an active role in each of them.

Classroom Management

All teachers must be able to manage the classroom environment in such ways that the environment is conducive to teaching/learning. In fact, many school principals are quick to assert that the easiest way to predict the success of a beginning teacher is to determine his or her ability to manage the classroom. A common misconception is that good classroom management means maintaining a controlled atmosphere and refusing to allow any behavior that even looks like permissiveness. Actually, classroom management is a multifaceted aspect of teaching that requires similar analysis and selection as for the identification of a preferred teaching style/philosophy.

61

Classroom management strategies exist on a continuum, as do teaching styles. It is not a matter of only one approach being good or bad. It is rather a question of deciding what choice(s) may be acceptable because one's personality complements a certain classroom management strategy, just as is the case with teaching styles. Classroom management deals with such facets as lesson planning, utilization of furniture and materials, evaluation of students, and grading. These

Professional Perspectives

Whatever your preferred teaching style, manage your classroom in such a way as to establish firm, fair, and consistent discipline rules and procedures. Most elementary and secondary students respect their teachers' role in managing the learning environment.

facets of classroom management are important considerations for all teachers and most effectively contribute to student learning when each is consistent with the teaching style. Careful lesson planning is mandatory for effective teaching/ learning to follow. However, if the learners are considered to be passive, the lesson plan may emphasize absorbing the factual content of the subject matter. Adherents of teaching styles that consider the learners as active participants would tend to emphasize processes and skills to be mastered and view the factual content of the subject matter as important but variable. Similarly, the mere arrangement of classroom furniture and the use of classroom materials may be predicated upon the passive/active perception of the learners.

In evaluating student progress and assigning grades, most teachers utilize written examinations, term papers, project reports, group discussions, and various other tools. If the subject matter is treated as amorphous, for instance, teacher-made tests would tend to seek isolated facts and concepts as "right" answers, suggesting emphasis on convergent thinking; if the subject matter is treated as structured and applicable to problem solving so as to emphasize processes and skills to arrive at several "right" answers, teacher-made tests would tend to allow for divergent thinking.

Discipline Maintenance

The attention of the national media to disruptive behavior in the classroom has rekindled the conflicting views of adherents of opposing philosophies regarding discipline. Polls of parents and teachers alike list discipline among the top issues confronting the schools. The main source of dissatisfaction for nearly two-thirds of today's teachers is the inability to manage students effectively. Teachers also are concerned about the effect disruptive behavior has on learning. The discipline dilemma—stressing high teacher control in the classroom yet adhering to a more open philosophy advocating less teacher control—precludes the development of a school discipline policy that would satisfy both views. The divided views on classroom discipline have resulted in numerous books to assist teachers with discipline problems and many special courses and workshops developed to deal with classroom discipline strategies. Since beginning teachers are given little exposure to discipline strategies in teacher preparation programs, the vast range of alternatives makes it difficult to decide on strategies for those who have yet to develop their own style.

Classroom management as an aspect of teaching has been presented as an integration of the procedural, physical environment, and bookkeeping chores with a preferred teaching style. If classroom management is viewed as merely strategies to keep down the number of problems so that learning can occur, the management strategy need not be from the same philosophical base as the teaching style. In the latter case discipline maintenance would seem to be a more appropriate label.

Glickman and Wolfgang[2] have identified three schools of thought along a teacher-student control continuum (Figure 17.3). *Noninterventionists* represent the view that holds that teachers should not impose their own rules, since students are inherently capable of solving their own problems. *Interactionalists*

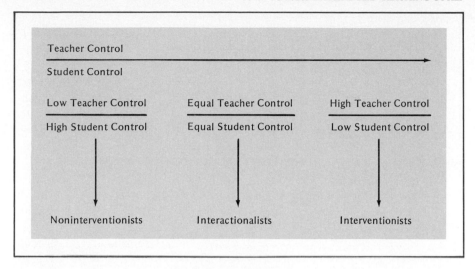

FIGURE 17.3 *Teacher-Student Control Continuum* [*Source:* Carl D. Glickman and Charles H. Wolfgang, "Conflict in the Classroom: An Eclectic Model of Teacher-Child Interaction," *Elementary School Guidance and Counseling,* 13 (December 1978). Copyright © 1978 American Association for Counseling and Development. Reprinted by permission.]

suggest that students must learn that the solution to misbehavior is a reciprocal relation between student and teacher. *Interventionists* believe that teachers must set classroom standards for conduct and give little attention to input from the students.

Beginning teachers are challenged to identify their own beliefs regarding discipline in the classroom in order to keep disruptive behavior at a minimum, thus enhancing the potential for learning as well as for job satisfaction. Where discipline maintenance is the primary concern, one might choose from among the entire range of possibilities along the Wolfgang-Glickman continuum (discussed in the section on behaviorism in Chapter 16), regardless of one's teaching style preference. Figure 17.4 illustrates how all the major theories of classroom management relate in terms of emphasis on selected references along the teacher-student control continuum given in Figure 17.3. Each of the six teaching styles/ philosophies addresses in some way all seven classroom teacher behaviors on the continuum. It is the professional responsibility of each classroom teacher to understand how each behavior may be utilized to support his or her preferred teaching style. A more detailed explanation of how each behavior is portrayed within those contexts is provided in the excellent Wolfgang and Glickman text *Solving Discipline Problems* (Allyn and Bacon, 1980).

Values Education

Increased attention is being directed toward the axiological (values) branch of philosophy, with particular emphasis on ethics and morals. With parents accused of yielding value development and character building to the schools, schools

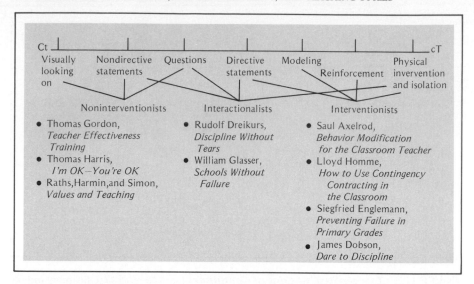

FIGURE 17.4 *Teacher Behavior Continuum (TBC)* [*Source:* Charles H. Wolfgang and Carl D. Glickman, *Solving Discipline Problems: Strategies for Classroom Teachers* (Boston: Allyn and Bacon, 1980), p. 18. Reprinted by permission.]

blamed for the misbehavior of youth, the political arena rocked by Watergate, Abscam, and other scandals, unethical business practices headlined, drugs and sex also highlighted as social issues, and racial problems spawning violence, it should not be surprising that the public is demanding that education be geared to strengthening the moral fiber of our youth.

American educators were concerned with the problem of providing moral and character education even before the days of John Dewey in the early 1900s. Some of the earlier approaches included textbooks such as the McGuffey *Reader* that sought to instill values through the content of stories. The "bag of virtues" approach sought to obtain a cultural consensus on values to be taught in the schools. Another approach emphasized the respect for authority, while the social adjustment approach focused on the mental health of students. During the past 50 years the continued research in psychoanalysis, behaviorism, and the humanistic and developmental schools of thought in American psychology has yielded information that educators and psychologists now consider when developing values education approaches in the schools. In the past decade and a half approaches related to values education have been identified with designations such as moral development, values clarification, cognitive developmental approach to moral judgment, behaviorism, ethics education, and self-identification.

Values have been taught in the schools on a hit-or-miss basis for years, but now some school districts are developing a specific values curriculum and requiring all teachers to set aside class time to build character. A school in Chicago's inner city teaches honesty, courage, helpfulness, and twelve other values in specific lessons at least twice a week, from kindergarten through sixth grade. A growing number of schools across the country are placing renewed emphasis on character formation or are planning to do so soon—including schools in Dallas, St. Louis, Baltimore County, Maryland, and Dade County, Florida. In New York State Governor Mario Cuomo is urging all public schools to begin teaching values.³

Earlier comments about teaching styles, classroom management and method, and discipline illustrated that these continua provide a far-ranging and, in some instances, confusing array of alternatives for the classroom teacher to identify with. Approaches to values education similarly range from the behavioral approach, which emphasizes the importance of modeling behavior to be adopted by the students, to values clarification, which has the teacher guiding students in clarifying their values.

Summary and Implications

While your preferred style may not be completely committed to perennialism, essentialism, behaviorism, experimentalism, reconstructionism, or existentialism, you should be able to use the analytical tool for studying teacher behavior to help you identify several preferences. Prospective teachers, whether or not they have had educational philosophy coursework in their preparation programs, should find the analytical tool an immediately useful way to study teaching behaviors for trends and preferences related to a teaching style/philosophy. Perennialist, essentialist, and behaviorist teachers encourage students to view the subject matter only as experts in that field view the subject matter. Such teacher behaviors exhibit an authoritarian curriculum trend encouraging convergent thinking. Experimentalists, reconstructionists, and existentialists encourage students to use the subject matter as a means of determining more than one answer to the question at hand. This behavior can be viewed as a nonauthoritarian curriculum trend encouraging divergent thinking.

When using the field experience guidelines (Table 17.1) to study teaching style preferences, remember that there are no perfect teaching styles or teaching methodologies. You simply need to know how to minimize the effects of the natural weaknesses associated with each type of teaching style. The three styles that emphasize convergent thinking tend to reward students for giving an answer that is the exact phrase the teacher wants. Teachers using such methods must be very careful with their responses, or students will not risk participating in discussion unless they are absolutely certain that they have the exact answer. The divergent type of teaching styles may, in contrast, require students to participate in interesting activities but not make them fully aware of why they are participating or what they are learning. If students are not required to justify the generalizations they make and are not made to see that they are learning many facts and skills, they may end up feeling that all answers are so relative that problem-solving processes are not worthwhile. Teachers who know enough about themselves and the teaching styles to show students how to succeed with both convergent thinking and divergent thinking are well on their way to reaching the ideal of being healthy eclectics.

In addition to choosing a preferred teaching style/philosophy, all teachers must be prepared to integrate the several facets of classroom management consistent with the teaching philosophy. Strategies for discipline maintenance, when necessary merely to keep down the number of problems so that learning can occur, are very important for teaching success. Discipline is maintained when there is balancing interaction between teacher control and student control. There are times, however, when a higher degree of student control is more effective.

The implications of this chapter are straightforward. Teachers who enter classrooms not understanding or knowing much about their preferred teaching styles, as well as not knowing which classroom management strategies best serve their philosophies, cannot be successful.

We hope that from the material presented in this chapter, you will be able to work out a personal philosophy based on reality, knowledge, and value. Also, you should be able to envision how philosophical concepts carry over into and influence educational views extant in our schools. These tasks are the theoretical, rational part of developing a personal philosophy of education.

 To perceive such a philosophy is one thing; to teach according to the philosophy is another. In teaching, one exhibits behavior that is compatible with a personal educational view. Most teachers find it advantageous to choose from various educational views. As long as this eclecticism serves the pedagogical purposes of the teacher and is a basis for consistent behavior by the teacher in the classroom, learning will take place. If, however, eclecticism causes the teacher to change behavior frequently and with no apparent purpose, thus distracting pupils from learning, the teacher should subscribe to one specific educational view.

Discussion Questions

1. Who was your favorite teacher? Why? Who was your best teacher? Why?
2. Teachers must be able to manage the classroom in such a way that the environment created is conducive to teaching and learning. How do you plan to manage your classroom to set up such an environment?
3. What is your version of democracy in the classroom? Should students be permitted to decide what they will study, when they will study, and how they will study?
4. What is the value of observing other teachers' classrooms? Is experience a valid criterion for effective teaching? How might a beginning teacher be one of the best teachers?
5. Approaches to values education range from the behavioral approach to values clarification. What procedures would you use to teach honesty and trust to your students?

Supplemental Activities

1. Conduct a class discussion about the use of the analytical tool (Figure 17.1) and the field experience guidelines (Table 17.1).
2. Visit an elementary school and a secondary school
to arrange interviews with students who were sent out of their classes for various reasons. Summarize and report your findings to your class for discussion.
3. Invite an experienced teacher to discuss effective

teaching styles with you or your class. Have the teacher also discuss teacher evaluation procedures used by the school administrative staff.

4. Invite a school principal to discuss effective teaching styles with you or your class. Have the principal also discuss teacher evaluation procedures used by the school administrative staff.

5. Read Chapter 7 of *Teaching with Charisma* by Lloyd Duck (Allyn and Bacon, 1981, pp. 224–271). Then write a summary view of your philosophy and individual preference of teaching.

Notes

1. Lloyd Duck, *Teaching with Charisma* (Boston: Allyn and Bacon, 1981), p. 2. A special note of thanks is extended to Lloyd Duck, not only for his permission to reprint excerpts of his work but also for his careful consultation, assistance, and additional writing in structuring the format of Chapter 17. For the most part, this chapter presents a digest of Chapter 1, "The Heart of the Matter: An Analytical Tool," from Duck's text.

2. C. Glickman and C. Wolfgang, "Conflict in the Classroom: An Eclectic Model of Teacher-Child Interaction," *Elementary School Guidance and Counseling* (13 December 1978): 82–87.

3. Casey Banas, "Lessons of Value," *Chicago Tribune,* October 5, 1986.

Bibliography

Bloom, Benjamin, ed. *Taxonomy of Educational Objectives: Cognitive Domain.* New York: McKay, 1956.

Cornett, Claudia E. *What You Should Know About Teaching and Learning Styles.* Phi Delta Kappa Fastback No. 191. Bloomington, Ind.: Phi Delta Kappa, 1983.

Duck, Lloyd. *Teaching with Charisma.* Boston: Allyn and Bacon, 1981.

Howe, Kenneth R. "A Conceptual Basis for Ethics in Teacher Education." *Journal of Teacher Education,* May–June 1986, 5–11.

Illich, Ivan. *Deschooling Society.* New York: Harper and Row, 1970.

Kierstead, Janet. "How Teachers Manage Individual and Small Group Work in Active Classrooms." *Educational Leadership,* October 1986, 22–25.

Kneller, George F. *Introduction to the Philosophy of Education.* 2nd ed. New York: Wiley, 1971.

Lazerson, Marvin, McLaughlin, Judith Block, McPherson, Bruce, and Bailey, Stephen K. *An Education of Value: The Purposes and Practices of Schools.* London/New York: Cambridge University Press, 1986.

Riley, Richard W. "Can We Reduce the Risk of Failure?" *Phi Delta Kappan,* November 1986, 214–219.

Silvernail, David L. *Teaching Styles as Related to Student Achievement.* Washington, D.C.: National Education Association, 1986.

PART VI

Program Design, Experiences, and Instructional Practices

Educational programs in the United States are complex, diverse images of the society they serve. In a very real sense schools reflect what the society values and what the society is willing to pay for. A nation that spends approximately 10 percent of its gross national product on formal education reflects the financial priority it has for schools. The local, state, and national expectations that have been verbalized by a multitude of national commission studies, national pollsters, and specially anointed educational critics predominately reflect significantly greater expectations than what the society pays for. Despite the many cited shortcomings of the public schools of the United States, schools do a very commendable job in meeting societal demands for mass education. That they could do better, however, is not refutable. The program purposes are sound, but the experiences and practices reflect an institutionalizing effect that tries to produce an educated citizenry without an expanding investment policy in people and programs. Thus schools reflect the real priorities of the society.

At the heart of all educational issues are the learners, who, as they are being educated, should have positive experiences that will prepare them for the future. Preparation of learners has become complicated, and scientific and technological advances have made predicting the future difficult. Because of the contradictions in our infinitely complex society, young learners question the importance of planning for the future. The contradictions abound. We can explore outer space, but we cannot keep our own environment free of pollution. Scientists are now capable of reproducing life on a microscopic scale, but cancer, heart disease, and other health problems continue to baffle them. Technology now gives us comforts and goods we never had before; yet we cannot safely handle the resulting pollution. Learning materials are now quicker and easier to get than ever before, but we have not found a way to handle leisure. And finally—what is critically important for young learners—we have not learned to live with one another despite all we have enjoyed in the closing decades of this century. Fear, tension, and competition continue to plague us in our quest for peace and harmony among people.

The main purpose of Part VI is to examine the design principles of the school's curriculum and recognize its patchwork structure. Differing philosophical viewpoints lead to differences in the implementation of contemporary and traditional programs. The teacher in training is expected to become familiar with the relevant issues and purposes that direct the host of programs school systems offer.

What can be observed, touched, experienced, and collected for examination becomes the practicing operation of the school program. This collage provides the operational picture of schooling and educational practices as they are perceived or experienced by learners, teachers, and other school specialists. Various kinds of administrative and space orientations promote different kinds of learning environments. The knowledge of how these different orientations affect school programs is important for new teachers to acquire. This knowledge is vital if new teachers wish to take part in creating quality learning environments for the pupils they encounter.

The key to the success of a well-designed curriculum is the way in which educational experiences are delivered to the learner. A good repertoire of instructional practices is a must for the successful teacher. Program design, experiences, and practice constitute the public's image of the school's program; where does the teacher fit in this picture? To help create and provide educational programs, teachers are charged, on the one hand, with preserving American traditions and, on the other hand, with initiating social changes required by society. What do these dual roles mean for the future of educational programs? Teachers, as the mainstay of the school's curriculum, must use all their professional skills to develop teaching materials, lesson plans, evaluation devices, and a humanistic learning environment so that students will react positively to the educational program. Today's school programs are preparing youth for the twenty-first century.■

18

Patterns of Curriculum Design

Focus Questions

- Why do beginning teachers need to be knowledgeable about issues that affect curriculum design?
- Why should daily lesson plans or unit plans reflect the goals and aims of a school district?
- What key questions should the teacher address before determining subject- or student-centered curricular offerings?

- Why should teachers continue to stress general education throughout the K–12 school program?
- Why should teachers be able to plan school programs that address differences among learners?

Key Terms and Concepts

Basics
Literacy
Survival skills
Competencies: testing and achievement
Accountability
Content and materials selection
Aims and goals
Reproduction
Readjustment
Reconstruction

Curriculum structure
Subject-centered curriculum
Fused curriculum
Student-centered curriculum
Core curriculum
Activity curriculum
General education
Exploratory education
Personal education
Carnegie unit

What Would You Do?

As a beginning teacher, you have been asked by your principal to join a curriculum development council that oversees the program for the school district. The council is currently engaged in the beginning efforts of a five-year, long-range plan. During your attendence at the first meeting, you are shocked to hear a growing consensus among council members that the district should abandon the current diversity in programs and institute a "no frills" attention to basics with increased emphasis on general education and a common set of requirements for all learners. You judge that there does not

seem to be a genuine concern for differences among learners. The chairperson of the council asks you to chair a subcommittee that will prepare a draft of a basic document to be used to guide all curricular decisions for the district. Your beliefs appear to be in conflict with those of your colleagues, but you feel obligated to accept the responsibility. Surely, this lack of concern for individual differences among learners cannot be the dominant attitude in your chosen profession. How do you prepare for the first meeting with your subcommittee?

There is no dominant design for the specific curriculum offerings in school districts across the nation. Although the 50 state departments of education have elements of commonality in what they require generically for inclusion in the curriculum, considerable variance is found in specific program offerings. This variance is due to the regional differences of the American society. Although all learners in American schools study literature, mathematics, and science, all learners do not read the same literature, study the same mathematics, or encounter the same social science programs. Thus an examination of the differences in curriculum design is necessary for preservice teachers if they are to appreciate why these differences exist.

[20]

Issues for the Curriculum

Beginning teachers are expected to be knowledgeable about the critical issues associated with curriculum change and program planning. The basic purpose here is to alert the new teacher to some of these issues and the need to address them when contemplating program changes. The list of issues is not exhaustive but is representative of the current issues that continue to be high priorities for numerous commissions, study groups, and polls by national groups.

Literacy and Survival Skills

The alarming rates of illiteracy, as discussed earlier in this text, are viewed as one of the national crises for schooling. Rather than focus on just the three R's, needed survival skills include literacy in reading, writing, speaking, computation, and computers. Other skills needed for survival are academic preparation for a career; ability to think independently, logically, and critically; respect for others; responsible self-behavior; assessment and evaluation of problems and alternatives; job placement and security; and good citizenship practice. This list of skills is by no means new but reaffirms the voluminous lists of needed learner skills that can be traced back to the *Seven Cardinal Principles*. What is different at this time is that the public has become more demanding in its expectations that these skills be developed by the schools. As elementary and secondary teachers prepare curriculum revisions and course materials, they must address the need to provide a school program that attends to all of the basic survival skills.

[59]

Achievement Performance

National scores on the Scholastic Aptitude Test (SAT) have dropped dramatically over the past twenty years. In 1983, for the first time since the decline began, scores began leveling off somewhat, but the criticism remained. Since that time

[59]

the scores have begun to rise but only modestly. During the period of decline virtually every graduating class appeared to be less able than the class before it. Some generally reported reasons for that decline include a relaxation of standards, watered-down secondary programs used to satisfy student unrest during the 1960s and 1970s, a more diverse body of students taking the tests, and poorly trained teachers with weak academic preparations. Some of these reasons probably contributed to the decline. Rather than continue the debate over the causes or search for scapegoats, however, the schools need to accept the reported data and take positive steps toward reversing the trend. A significant side effect to this decline has been the rise in private school enrollments. In addition, the continued decline in public secondary school enrollments—caused by lower birth rates (the slightly increasing rates are only being felt now in the elementary school)—and increased taxpayer pressure on the financing of public education have helped to create a monumental task for school program reform.

As achievement scores declined during the past two decades, grade performances in school improved. The grade inflation problem spread from the elementary school to the colleges and universities. Furthermore, many studies have indicated that the standardized achievement performance of U.S. students does not compare favorably with that of students in many foreign countries. Unfortunately, we may have "apple and orange" comparisons here because of the differences in students who take the tests, but the criticism remains. Clearly, as teachers revise their curricula, they need to reexamine their expectations of student performance for all kinds of students. A common expectation for all students will not address the vast differences found in any student body. These differences will always be present if the United States continues to foster mass education and equal opportunity for all. Whereas survival skills are needed by all students, higher levels of verbal and quantitative performance may be achieved only by a smaller segment of the school population. The implicaton for curriculum workers is that program and instruction need to become more individualized.

Competency Testing

Declining test scores, alarming rates of illiteracy among high school graduates, and demands for greater accountability for teachers all have spurred the competency-testing movement. A very significant curriculum issue exists for competency testing, however. That issue is: Should the tests dictate the curriculum, or should the curriculum dictate the tests? If the tests are to dictate the curriculum, then curriculum revision is focused, because the test content determines just what will be taught. In contrast, if the curriculum dictates the tests, then local, state, and national goals need to be more narrowly defined around a general set of expected learner competencies. In either case, competency testing is a delicate issue for those who design the curriculum. A related issue associated with competency testing is the establishment of minimal competencies. The minimal-competency-testing question suggests that if all learners are to be held accountable for some minimal-competency performance, that performance will have to be very minimal if all learners are to have any chance of meeting it.

The curriculum issue for competency testing seems clear. Goals, materials, and instruction must be common to all and endorsed uniformly by the teaching staff. Thus textbooks and other materials must be prepared for the tests, and [20] periodic assessments must be made to determine progress toward the expected graduation competency. How and to what degree the teacher works in curriculum development and revision becomes wholly dependent upon the competency-testing movement.

Discipline Management

The Gallup poll of 1987 continued to support the fifteen-year national concern over classroom discipline. Although chemical abuse problems have assumed number-one importance in 1986, classroom management problems remain a high-priority problem with the public.

But before examining this issue for effects on curriculum, we must consider the modern-day learner. Some of the current characteristics of youth have made it extremely difficult to return, as many would like, to the disciplinary methods used in the schools 40 or more years ago. For example, youth today have greater responsibilities and rights for making their own decisions. Learners do not experience the connection between today's school performance and tomorrow's [59] reward. The future is too uncertain. Modern families are not as close as they used to be; many parents are single; and young people look to their own culture rather than to the adult culture for norms. There is greater financial dependency [56] on parents among all youth today because of changes in our economy and technology. For increasing numbers of the young there is a cultural, political, and economic apathy. The society as they see it is not as they study it.

Teachers working in curriculum development need to explore the implications of whatever they revise or create in light of the learners who will encounter it. Classroom discipline or management cannot be improved qualitatively through fear of reprisal. The educational program must have utilitarian and effective meaning for all learners. It should not try to counter or thwart the culture of youth but find ways to utilize the youth culture meaningfully in the teaching-learning situation.

Materials and Content Selection

All previously mentioned issues affecting the curriculum influence materials selection. Material use can be broad or narrow, depending upon the definition of basic survival skills, expected level of student achievement performances, types of testing programs and their purposes, and expectations for student [59] personal performance and behavior in the classroom. Materials can be teacher-made or commercially prepared by companies. If materials are made or adapted by the teacher, the planned curriculum tends to direct material selection. If they are made by learning companies for exclusive use by the teachers, then the materials direct the curriculum. As we indicated earlier, the curriculum may be directed by textbooks or standardized tests for all to use. Teachers should

**Professional
Perspectives**

Remember that curriculum development requires an understanding of society's expectations for an educational program.
Plan to consider balance in all curriculum development efforts.
Develop a sound philosophical position for the type of curriculum structure you favor.

develop and select materials if they are to provide specifically for the needs of their students.

A key issue in curriculum design is how the curriculum is organized. Teachers need to understand the differences among the broad purposes and aims of education, subject- and student-centered emphases in curriculum, and program requirements. Why and how new experiences are incorporated into school programs are vital questions for teachers if they want to create learning opportunities for their students. All teachers need to be aware of curriculum development—to know how to recognize and discard the poor and to adopt the good so that learners may profit.

Purposes and Aims of Education: Curricular Roles

The traditional purpose of education, which can be traced to the ancient liberal arts, stresses a selected set of learning skills and a vast store of selected information for students. Traditionalists assume that students who acquire the necessary skills and facts are "educated" and thus will behave intelligently as adults. Students are not expected or directed to use their native intelligence creatively; they are to learn passively and store knowledge for future use. Learning is the same for all; knowledge that was relevant yesterday remains so today.

A contrasting purpose of education, stressing active student involvement in learning, evolved from the work of John Dewey and his associates after 1900. This position, referred to as progressivism, has not been universally accepted in practice. It is, however, still examined and studied as a school of thought; and as a theory, it has enjoyed considerable acceptance. Ideally, progressivism, expressed as learners living and practicing in the learning environment, calls for students to exercise their intelligence during learning. Students are encouraged to use their experience as a means to new learning. Intelligent adult behavior is not mystically granted at some accepted level of maturity but is acquired en route. This philosophy suggests that learning is relevant; learning is life; students learn best by participating in learning.

Curriculum planners, in formulating what the school has to do, frequently find that planning is easy but realization is not. National, regional, and state commissions have all expressed their thoughts about what education should be. The school may see its job as reproduction, readjustment, or reconstruction—or a combination. In Part II we related these tasks to the school as a social institution; we examine them here as they relate to the philosophical concepts that prescribe the school and curriculum.

Reproduction

If the school elects merely to reproduce, then its task is to transmit simply and unquestioningly our nation's cultural heritage to its youth. Subject matter selected should be what has survived through the ages. If the school is to fulfill only the reproductive function, the teacher must consider whether the subject matter has withstood the test of time and therefore should be included in the curriculum, or whether irrelevant material may have survived along with the relevant. The teacher must also decide whether the relevant subject matter of yesterday is enough for today's youth. The problems associated with making this decision are increased by the vast and continually growing amount of knowledge. In addition to the old knowledge that must be passed on, there is new knowledge that continues to press for its rightful place in the curriculum. How does a teacher cull the curriculum to make room for new knowledge when the school is committed to reproduction? Unfortunately, a curriculum designed solely to pass on the cultural heritage is fundamentally inadequate in an age when society is constantly confronted with social change.

Readjustment

Sole attention to readjustment calls for the school to gear its curriculum to social usefulness and efficiency. A curriculum for readjustment is concerned with preparing students for present-day adult life; it stresses civic training and social responsibility. Readjustment demands that the school retain parts of the past and also suggests that the school must do a certain amount of readjusting to meet current needs. Concentrating purely on this function may ignore some of the principles of child development and currently accepted psychology of learning. The child's need to understand and direct personal actions, the child's need to be able to adapt and organize in the light of prior experience, and the critical need for individual attention may be neglected when the social utility theme is forced on the school. Readjustment, if it is the sole role of the school, tends to prohibit personal behavior changes necessary for adult life.

Reconstruction

The school that adopts the educational role of reconstruction favors a curriculum that moves to the forefront of current thought and practice in society—and strives to change the status quo. The school then undertakes not only to prepare young people for the future but also to prepare the future for young people. A persistent advocate of the reconstruction role for American schools, George S. Counts, offered this challenge to education in 1932 when he introduced his controversial proposal: Dare the school build a new social order? To date, schools in the United States have not accepted this challenge. In designing the curriculum, the teacher must be aware of the pitfalls of this extreme approach and the hidden danger that past and current interests, traditions, and values may be sacrificed for the sake of change.

Combination of Roles

To overemphasize any one of the three roles for schooling—reproduction, readjustment, or reconstruction—would produce a top-heavy operational and philosophical concept inconsistent with the eclecticism needed today. So that students will have the best opportunity to become self-supporting, self-respecting, and self-directing participants in American and world society, the three functions must be constantly blended. We see blending as the following four tasks:

1. A systematic evaluation and reconstruction of the content of the discipline for instruction. The heritage to be preserved should be evaluated, and content considered necessary for existence in the future should be selected.
2. A reorganization of materials for instruction. This reorganization should produce not only knowledge of a variety of subjects but also a sense of direction in creating desirable attitudes and appreciations.
3. A plan for meeting the needs not only of the gifted and the slow learners but of all other learners as well. The average child and the mentally, emotionally, or physically handicapped learner are all too often neglected.
4. A plan for encouraging accelerated levels of personal aspiration. It is just as important to achieve excellence in the quality of personal and social life for all as it is to achieve excellence in space travel, computers, and gross national product.

Aims and Goals

Curriculum workers, in planning and stating aims and objectives of American education, must recognize at least five kinds of students who have to be accommodated:

1. *Terminal students:* Students who for various reasons drop out along the way and have to be absorbed by society. How a nation committed to mass education and with the necessary wealth can continue to have a national dropout rate between 25 and 30 percent is mystifying. In fact, that rate may approach 60 percent in many of the large cities of this country and among minority groups.

2. *College-bound students:* Students who are preparing for higher education. Nationally, approximately 50 percent of high school graduates pursue study beyond high school. This figure is misleading, however, because it does not account for those students who have dropped out before graduating from high school. The preparatory programs for the 50 percent must be varied because of the range of post–high school educational desires and opportunities. The number of students in college has been dropping during the 1980s because of the impact of population control. The number will be reduced even further because of declining secondary enrollments and young people finding an increasingly lower correlation between college education and job placement.

3. *Vocational students:* Students who are primarily preparing for jobs while in a comprehensive or vocational-technical high school. Some of these students, however, may further their education later on, formally or informally. Although the percentage of students who fall into this category varies by the criterion used, it appears to be on the increase. Data on job placement for college-trained students suggest a job shortage, whereas data for vocational-technical education suggest a healthy job market.

4. *Destination unknown:* The so-called late bloomers or latent students. These students have native ability but do not realize an expected level of achievement during high school.

5. *Special students:* Students who are identified as emotionally, mentally, or physically handicapped. Court decisions of the 1970s ordered that many special students be included as regular school students and accommodated by the regular curriculum. As explained earlier in the discussion of Public Law 94–142, this federal law now mandates a least restrictive environment for learning for exceptional children. Many of them are now being mainstreamed into the regular curriculum.

The best analysis of the current average school curriculum suggests that the needs of the college-bound students continue to receive primary attention. If priorities were otherwise, the national dropout rate—and especially the rate for urban areas—would probably not be so alarmingly high. Curriculum development should proceed from some special diagnostic attempts to identify the various kinds of students the curriculum is intended to serve.

As one tries to analyze aims and objectives, one must distinguish between the two as they relate to a total school program. Aims for curriculum devlopment are considered to be the broad goals for the system as a whole. They are usually formulated by national groups who try to cater to the needs of our pluralistic society. Objectives relate to the expected behaviors that the curriculum is intended to produce. The history of purposes and aims was presented in Part IV of this text.

Curriculum Structure

Any school system can choose its own pattern of curriculum organization. These patterns tend to range between the extremes of a subject-centered and a student-centered organization. Between the two extremes, a continuum of curricular organization exists, and schools use various elements from either extreme or both. In general, curricular organization that tends to be subject-centered is content-oriented; if it uses a student-centered pattern, it is learner-oriented.

By analyzing the curriculum continuum (see Figure 18.1), we can categorize

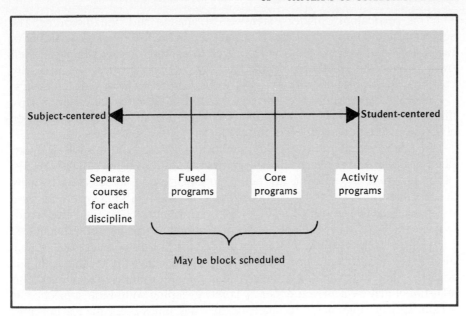

FIGURE 18.1   *A Curriculum Continuum*

those patterns that offer separate courses for the various academic disciplines and those that fuse the disciplines under the broad heading "subject centered patterns of curriculum organization." Correlated programs and activity programs are classified as student-centered patterns. You will recognize that often the patterns of curricular organizations used by various schools tend to be eclectic, borrowing from many sources. How a school district organizes its curriculum is related strongly to its philosophical position on the purpose of education.

Subject-Centered Curriculum

The subject-centered curriculum is the oldest form and still the most widely used in schools in the United States. Its history can be traced to the liberal arts of the ancient world. The ancient trivium was composed of grammar, rhetoric, and logic; the quadrivium included arithmetic, geometry, astronomy, and music. In time, the trivium came to include history and literature, and the quadrivium expanded to include algebra, trigonometry, geography, botany, zoology, physics, and chemistry.

    In the modern subject-centered curriculum all the subjects for instruction are separated. In the extreme use of this approach the disciplines of knowledge are taught in isolation and with no attempt at integration. The intent is to provide a discipline for students that alerts them to set classifications and to recognize arrangements of facts and ideas. An important criterion in selecting ideas for study is to choose those that have proved beneficial for solving problems of investigation in research. These facts and ideas are the ones that have lasted over time.

This curriculum calls for extensive explanation and oral discourse. The subject-centered curriculum uses a formal step-by-step study of ideas and facts; rarely are students expected or encouraged to explore or experiment on their own. The teaching methods include extensive verbal activities—lectures, discussions, questions, and answers—and written exercises such as term papers.

Often the curriculum is criticized for failure to develop critical or creative thinking. Those who decry this approach suggest that instruction is focused on absorption and memorization of the presented facts and ideas.

The subject-centered curriculum outlines in advance all the subjects everyone must take. The constant subjects (general education) usually make up most of the program, and students are not given much choice in selecting courses. Some authorities say that this curriculum alleviates the tracking system because it provides elective learning for students in various tracks. The rigid track tends to make the elective program required and constant. Within the subject-centered curriculum, however, there is some provision for individual interests and abilities. A few electives are provided for the students, and the teacher can also adjust for differences among students within the required core of subjects. This adjustment may be achieved either by ability grouping within the subject or by various special assignments designed for the many ability levels the teacher must accommodate.

The elementary teacher operating within a subject-centered curriculum may group students by subject within the self-contained classroom to provide for individual differences. A fair criticism of the subject-centered curriculum is that it tends to neglect individual differences and to establish common hurdles for all students.

One of the persistent problems with the subject-centered curriculum has been its failure to attend to recognizing and understanding current social problems. Educators tend to focus on the past rather than on the present and the future. For instance, students studying American history are not likely to study thoroughly anything beyond the Vietnam conflict, and yet most were born after that period. Also, they may be studying and memorizing facts that probably could be stored and retrieved by a computer. Although Alfred N. Whitehead made the following statement in 1929, his summation is appropriate today:

> There is only one subject-matter for education, and that is Life in all its manifestations. Instead of this single unity, we offer children—Algebra, from which nothing follows; Geometry, from which nothing follows; a couple of languages, never mastered, and lastly, most dreary of all, literature, represented by plays of Shakespeare, with philological notes and short analyses of plot and character in substance to be committed to memory. Can such a list be said to represent Life, as it is known in the midst of the living of it? The best that can be said of it is, that it is a rapid table of contents which a deity might run over in his mind while he was thinking of creating a world, and has not yet determined how to put it together.[1]

The world in which students now live and face the future is very different from the world of the past. In the teaching of literature in a subject-centered curriculum, modern writings are often neglected, as is the literature of cultures other than our own. Added to the problem is the fact that an increasing variety of moral majority pressure groups constantly challenge any materials generally thought to be secular. Principles of current economics and government also seem to escape this type of curriculum, and students are passed into the adult society with little or no knowledge or appreciation of these important fields.

Those who support and defend the subject-centered curriculum argue that subjects that have withstood the test of time are the most worthy. They also argue that just because some children do not learn well in such a curriculum does not imply any inherent weakness in the curriculum organizaton. This type of curriculum is supported by those who espouse an essentialistic philosophy of education. Advocates of the subject-centered curriculum point out that everything cannot be studied at once, nor can any study be all-inclusive. With the rapid increase in knowledge, there simply has to be an ordered, segmented approach if one is to study a subject effectively. The separated subjects therefore are a convenient way to clarify all this knowledge so that it can be comprehended by students.

The subject-centered approach to curriculum is not totally unworthy. Despite many attempts at curricular reform, the subject-centered curriculum has remained one of the most widely used curricular designs. Those who defend it point out, though, that the student-centered curriculum will not adequately prepare young people for the adult world they must live in.

Fused Curriculum

The fused curriculum has come about in an attempt to decrease the number of separate subjects gradually brought into the subject-centered curriculum. In place of separate and isolated classes in reading, writing, spelling, grammar, speech, and literature, for example, the fused curriculum combines these subjects under English or language arts. The subject-centered curriculum remains almost intact, but students are introduced to the field as a whole rather than to bits and pieces. Subject matter goals are left whole, but the fused approach provides teachers and students more latitude within a broad subject area. The fused social studies course, for instance, encompasses history, geography, economics, political science, sociology, and anthropology. Fused science programs combine botany, zoology, and geology. Mathematics fuses arithmetic, geometry, and algebra. Fusion can also take place in physical education, home economics, industrial arts, art, and music.

As an illustration of how fusion operates within the language arts, students may begin their study with a typical reading assignment. The teacher uses this basic assignment to explore principles of writing, discussion, vocabulary, and speech. The process may be reversed or arranged in any order, but the principle remains the same. Fusion tries to interrelate a core of subjects. This process is frequently called an integration of subject matter. The teacher of social studies may use an historical event to introduce principles of economics and civics. At the same time the teacher may focus attention on the geographical, sociological, and political implications of this particular historical event.

The fused, or broad-field, curriculum has enjoyed its greatest success at the elementary level. Separate subjects, once taught for short periods during the day, are now more apt to be taught in a fused fashion over longer periods. Common fused studies in the elementary school center around language arts, social studies, general science, mathematics, art, music, and physical education and health.

In the past, junior high schools developed several variations on the fused program. Some schools combined language arts and social studies with block scheduling, thus providing a longer period for teaching these two groups of subjects. However, in recent years the movement of subject matter to lower grades has caused junior high schools to adopt the predominately subject-centered pattern of the senior high school.

In the senior high school the fused curriculum has had relatively little success. Examples of the few high school courses that are so patterned are general science, problems of democracy in the social studies, and family living. The greatest effect the fused curriculum has had on the senior high school is probably the integration of unified areas into subject-centered courses. Many high school teachers of American history now try to interlace a certain amount of geography and political science into their history courses.

Those who favor the fused curriculum suggest that it has the following advantages:

- Subject matter may be integrated more readily.
- A logical and useful organization for presenting knowledge may be established.
- Students can learn with understanding and appreciation.
- Basic principles and generalizations necessary for critical thinking are emphasized more than isolated facts.

In reality, the fused curriculum has many of the advantages and disadvantages of the subject-centered curriculum. Some of the criticisms against the fused curriculum are that (1) compression of several courses into one does not guarantee integration; (2) fusion tends to result in a sketchy knowledge and a watering down of specific disciplines; and (3) with the emphasis on generalization rather than specifics, learning tends to be too abstract.

Student-Centered Curriculum

The concern for students' needs and interests has produced the student-centered curriculum. In the past, and also today to some extent, these needs have had both social and psychological interpretations. The needs of youth today generally are defined as what society expects of maturing young adults. Whereas, in an extreme interpretation, the subject-centered curriculum stresses that learning is most effective if it is rigorous and difficult, the student-centered curriculum emphasizes encouraging students' interest in learning and their appreciation for it. When the interests and needs of learners are incorporated in the curric-

60

The student-centered curriculum is based on the belief that learning is more
successful when it is built upon the learner's interests; motivation, therefore, tends
to become intrinsic, rather than extrinsic. (*Source:* George Tarbay/Northern Illinois
University)

ulum, motivation tends to become intrinsic rather than extrinsic. This description
does not imply that the student-centered curriculum is directed by the whims
of the learner. Rather, this curricular design is based on the premise that learning
is more successfully achieved if it is built upon the interests the learner has
developed before formal learning begins. As you read about core and activity
programs, compare and contrast the student-centered curriculum with the subject-centered curriculum.

Core Curriculum

The core curriculum grew out of a general dissatisfaction with the piecemeal
learning promoted by the subject-centered curriculum. Proponents of the core

curriculum, in trying to offer students a more enriching education, believe that subjects should be unified and new methods adopted. Since society has become increasingly fragmented, with more emphasis on science and technology, proponents feel that the only logical approach to developing social values and social vision is through a core organization. The core curriculum may have different degrees of organization and may cross broader subject lines; it places even greater stress than the fused curriculum does on the need to integrate subject matter.

The core curriculum stresses social values, and much time is given to studying the culture and its moral content. This curriculum propounds problems for solving as a learning method; within this approach, facts, descriptive principles, socioeconomic conditions, and moral rules of conduct and behavior are stressed. In its purest form the core is basically normative in its presentation to students. By *normative* we mean that concern centers around topics such as the social needs of today.

A typical application of the core curriculum is a study of the persistent themes of social living. The subject matter is not an isolated block of content; it is used to define and solve problems common to many or all students. However, student interest is not the sole criterion for selecting and organizing activities. Group processes and dynamics become the center of planned activity, and often the community becomes a resource for study.

Another special and distinguishing characteristic of the core program is the way in which students and teacher cooperate in planning learning activities. This joint planning is concerned with the "how" and the "what" of study. All students, regardless of their individual abilities, concentrate on the areas of learning that are essential to all members of society. All do not have to learn the same thing with the same degree of proficiency, but all are exposed to the common problems; and each is allowed to visualize himself or herself as accepting or rejecting a particular vocation within society.

There is maximum provision in the core program for special needs and interests as they arise. Since one feature of the core curriculum is a longer block of instructional time, the classroom program is flexible and includes remedial, developmental, and accelerated activities as they fit into the study. There is ample time for much-needed guidance and counseling, both individual and group. Skills are taught as needed to solve problems, and these problems are used to increase student motivation. Although it has declined in popular use, the core program still can be found, most often in the junior high school.

A core program demands many special considerations if it is to be reasonably successful. The foremost consideration is the teacher. Core teachers need, besides a broad preparation in the liberal arts, a keen understanding of social foundations, of child and adolescent psychology, of the structure and dynamics of group processes, of guidance, and of the problem approach to learning. The lack of adequately prepared teachers has hindered the growth and acceptance of the core curriculum. Other special needs involve classrooms and buildings, which must be large and flexible to provide for group activities. An abundance of supplementary teaching materials is essential. Schedules must include large, flexible time blocks. Also, flexible grouping of students by age and grade is necessary. Finally, an effective public relations program for parents and the community is vital if the core curriculum is to be understood and accepted.

Activity Curriculum

At the extreme right of a curriculum continuum is the activity curriculum (see Figure 18.1). In its purest form it operates with the child as the sole center of learning. Since education is life and life is ever-changing, the activity curriculum expects to change continually. Students' needs and interests are assessed, and the curriculum is built on that assessment. The psychology of learning in this approach is based on the emotional involvement of the learner. If a child develops an interest in something and becomes emotionally involved with it, learning is enhanced, according to the proponents of the activity curriculum. This curriculum, never fixed, crosses all subject matter lines. Completely flexible, the activity for the early learner may center on such topics as pets, toys, boats, letter carriers, or police officers. Emphasis is placed on observation, play, stories, and handiwork.

    The activity curriculum has not been as acceptable to the public as the subject-centered curriculum. When used, it has been most successful at the elementary level. Although it has never secured a foothold in the secondary school, the activity curriculum has had some influence on the high school program. The lack of full acceptance in the high school may be due partly to the subject orientation that secondary teachers and administrators have had. Also, the public seems to prefer the traditional organization and methodology of the subject-centered high school.

    The activity curriculum has several characteristics different from all other curricular patterns. First, the interests and purposes of children determine the educational program. Second, common learning (general education) comes about as a result of individual interest. Third, this curriculum is not planned in advance, but guidelines are established to help the students choose alternatives intelligently as they progress through the program. Activities are planned co-operatively by students and teachers, and what they plan and pursue may or may not have any deliberate social direction. In the pursuit of planned goals, solving problems becomes the principal teaching method. Little or no need for extracurricular activities develops because all interests are accommodated within the regular program.

    The teacher, in preparing to teach in the activity curriculum, needs all the prerequisites of the core teacher and more. Because the activity curriculum is flexible, the need for variety in space and scheduling arrangements is paramount. Schedules using large blocks of time are necessary to afford the program its maximum potential.

Curriculum Contrasts

The subject-centered curriculum and the student-centered curriculum represent the two extremes of a curriculum continuum. These two curricula can be contrasted in the following manner:

Subject-centered curriculum	Student-centered curriculum
Centered on subjects within the academic disciplines	Centered on learners and their diagnosed needs
Emphasis on subject matter to be learned	Emphasis on promoting all-around growth of learners
Subject matter selected and organized before it is taught	Subject matter selected and organized cooperatively by learners and teachers during the learning periods
Controlled by the teacher or someone representing authority external to the learning situation	Controlled and directed cooperatively by learners (pupils, teachers, parents, supervisors, principals, and others) in the learning situation
Emphasis on facts, information, knowledge for its own sake or for possible future use; generally, lower-order learning	Emphasis on meanings immediate to improved living and day-to-day problems
Emphasis on specific habits and skills as separate aspects of learning	Emphasis on habits and skills as integral parts of larger experiences
Emphasis on improving methods of teaching specific subject matter	Emphasis on understanding and improving through the process of learning
Emphasis on uniformity of exposure to learning and uniformity of learning results	Emphasis on variability in exposure to learning and in results expected
Education conforming to set patterns	Education aiding each child to build a socially creative individuality
Education considered schooling	Education considered a continuous, intelligent process of growth

50

Program Requirements

Embedded in the operating program of the school are three broad academic components that constitute the function of the educational program: general education, exploratory education, and personal education. Their placement and emphasis depend wholly on the learner's needs as they relate to growth and development, the psychology of learning, instructional strategies, and various administrative arrangements.

General Education

General education is the broad area of the school program that is primarily concerned with developing common learning. Its central purpose is helping students become participating citizens and well-adjusted individuals. Although general education is concentrated in the elementary school, some elements of it persist throughout the entire period of formal education. Although the other two broad areas of the school program, exploratory and personal education, contain general education outcomes, they are not organized primarily for that purpose.

The general education program concentrates on developing basic skills and introduces students to basic studies that include reading, composition, listening, speaking, and computing. Learners are expected to acquire creative and disciplined thinking skills that include different methods of inquiry and applying knowledge. General education also encompasses the humanities—an appreciation for literature, music, and the visual arts—and the social and natural sciences. Within a general education program learners are expected to acquire the essential, adult basic performance skills needed to function successfully in society. How this general education is accomplished varies among school districts. The identified components of common learning provide the core of general education in the elementary school and are improved and developed further throughout the total formal program of education. Figure 18.2 illustrates the general education emphasis for the formal N–12 structure.

One of the most perplexing problems facing general education planners is maintaining the placement sequence in the total scheme of education. As we have just seen, the number of years of schooling devoted to general education is determined by changing economic factors and by society's concern with efficiency and productivity. Those who demand accountability from today's schools have joined those who call for more general education. In the very recent past the need for specialization caused a slackening of interest in general education and an increased emphasis on specialized studies and the applied fields. In

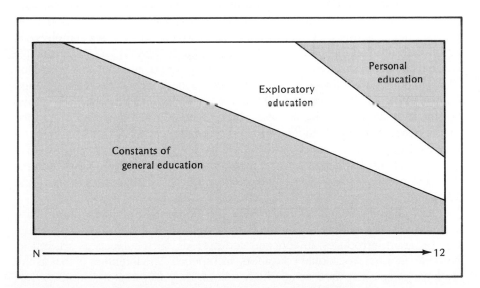

FIGURE 18.2 *Educational Emphases in the N–12 Program*

contrast, the decade of the 1980s will show more attention to the pressure for accountability in general education.

During the 1960s and 1970s increasing public pressure caused some subjects to be presented earlier in the curriculum. Advanced skills and some special training, previously reserved for the secondary school, were introduced into the elementary school. Thus today a regular practice is to introduce, at early levels, the formal teaching of foreign language, principles of economics, chemical and sex education, advanced principles of mathematics, and introductory programs of vocational career choices. Although there are justifiable reasons for this introduction, they do not change the nature and purpose of common learning in the elementary program. Because of this expanded common learning for younger students, educators must reassess the general education program. This reassessment may require a new definition of common learning. As preschool and early-childhood education receive increased philosophical and financial support, the general education program, identified as common learning for all, should be redistributed over a broader continuum, nursery school through grade 14.

Exploratory Education

The exploratory education program is designed primarily for an organization of education unique to America—the junior high school. Depending on school district organization, the junior high, intermediate, or middle school continues general education and introduces students, on a limited basis, to a variety of specialized subjects. There are five reasons why the junior high school exists:

1. Junior high school provides a transitional period, easing students' transfer from the elementary school to the high school. Junior high school is designed for students who are entering early adolescence, a trying period of growth and development. Since the transition period from childhood to adulthood is so critical, the junior high school is planned to accommodate the special physical, emotional, and social problems of this age group. In general, the students have come from an administrative unit that is child-centered, and they are preparing to enter one that is subject-centered. The junior high school has been planned to foster a gradual development of independence in learning and self-discipline. So that students have a "home base," block scheduling is sometimes used for the language arts–social studies programs, and the teacher for this block has a better chance to know and help the students. Junior high school students also take several courses taught by specialists; in this way they are gradually introduced to the departmentalized, subject-centered senior high school (see Table 18.1).

2. The junior high school allows for the exploration of interest, aptitudes, and abilities, thus aiding the students in vocational and educational planning. The program introduces, in concentrated periods, such subjects as art, music, home economics, vocational education, and speech. The intention is that as the students progress toward senior high school, they will explore subjects they

60

TABLE 18.1 *A Junior High School Exploratory Program*

7th Grade		8th Grade		9th Grade	
Subjects (Required)	*Periods per Week*	*Subjects (Required)*	*Periods per Week*	*Subjects (Required)*	*Periods per Week*
Language arts ⎱ Social studies (blocked) ⎰	10	Language arts ⎱ Social studies (blocked) ⎰	10	Language arts ⎱ Social studies (blocked) ⎰	10
Physical education	3	Physical education	3	Physical education	3
Science	5	Science	5	General science	5
Mathematics	5	Mathematics	5	Electives	17
Practical arts	5	Electives	12		
Band or chorus	5				
Art	2				

Electives		
Art	General business	Algebra
Creative writing	General mathematics	Industrial arts
Drama	Home economics	Mechanical drawing
Foreign language	Industrial arts	Music

may specialize in later. These exploratory programs may last nine weeks or one semester and are offered on a rotating basis.

3. Junior high school students are introduced to an elaborate program of guidance and counseling that continues through senior high school. This program is intended to help students plan intelligently for adult life. By using specially trained guidance personnel, the junior high school emphasizes the development of wholesome attitudes for mental, emotional, and social growth among the student body.

4. Providing for variety in junior high helps to lower the school dropout rate. Variable programming considers the differing special abilities of youth, and its rationale stresses the important effects of the students' socioeconomic background on their interests, aptitudes, needs, and personality development.

5. Articulation of the total twelve-year school program may be stimulated by the junior high school. This administrative unit has the advantage of examining the elementary program and planning for articulation with the senior high school. Articulation is successful when all the teachers within the school system work together to understand and appreciate the special tasks each must perform.

Like the elementary school, the junior high school has had to find ways to accommodate the continuing movement toward an earlier exposure to subjects. There is little doubt that the pressure of content requirements from the senior high school and the accompanying problems associated with Carnegie units of credits have caused the junior high school to become "a senior high school in short pants."

**Professional
Perspectives**

Be sure to attend to general education needs at whatever level or subject you teach.

Know the intended differences between the junior high school and the middle school.

Determine your role in providing basic skill development at the grade level you intend to teach.

To return to the initial philosophy that guided the junior high school: Many school districts have put the ninth grade back in the senior high school and created a new administrative organization of 5–8, 6–8, or 7–8, labeled the intermediate or middle school. The new middle school is intended to provide for the exploratory learning that the junior high school never quite achieved. Thus many of the early intentions of the junior high school continue for the middle school, with the exception of the ninth grade. Because of societal changes, improvements in health and nutrition, and more accelerated rates of physical and social maturation, ninth graders are much more like senior high school students today than they were when the original junior high school idea was conceived.

Personal Education

The senior high school assumes the special task of uniting the foundations of general education with the introductions to exploratory education, culminating in a rounded personal education. The senior high school will terminate formal education for many students; it will prepare others for more advanced and specialized education in college or for special post–high school training. Because a large number of high school graduates go on to college, school systems are tempted to overemphasize the college preparatory program. However, high school should offer programs designed to suit all students. Albert Oliver says that in secondary education attention should be given to individual choice in establishing various programs. By this recommendation he means a "program of study in each area of curriculum specialization—professional, business, industrial, and general."[2] Although students can register in certain programs, they may take subjects in another curriculum. Presumably, each designation refers to special interest education.

As the learner progresses through the educational system, the increased personalized education should encourage an individual's intellectual curiosity and passion for knowledge. It should also provide good habits for a particular kind of inquiry. Personalized education should develop high levels of learning within the cognitive domain.

The high school, in continuing the program for general education (see Figure 18.2), has an established core of general courses required for all students. These requirements have traditionally accounted for seven to nine of the sixteen to twenty Carnegie units required for graduation. The national concern with

High schools should offer educational programs designed to suit all students' needs.
(*Source:* Mike Penney)

the quality of education, as expressed in the many national commission reports, has led to an increase in the required number of general education requirements for graduation. However, the requirements vary from state to state. Increasing numbers of states are now requiring four units of English instead of three, two to three units of mathematics instead of one, and two to three units of science instead of one. The mathematics and science emphasis is particularly heavy and comes at a time when the nation's most critical teacher shortage is in those disciplines.

One Carnegie unit of credit is awarded for each class that meets for 200 minutes of formal education a week for 36 weeks in the school year. The remainder of the units required for graduation are satisfied by the elective programs for specialization and enrichment. The special programs vary in name, sequence, and scope, but the two most usual within the comprehensive senior high school are the tracking program and the constants-variable program (discussed in the next subsection). The main difficulty with the Carnegie unit system is that it does not take into account the research on student learning. All students do not learn at the same rate; nor do they maintain a constant learning rate. Yet the majority of American secondary schools continue to schedule students in established time modules consistent with the definition of a Carnegie unit given for time devoted to a particular experience. School systems simply do not apply sound reasoning supported by research when they conclude that all students need 200 minutes a week of varied instruction for 36 weeks to accomplish one Carnegie unit successfully. If learning objectives are clearly specified, some students meet them in less time than others. The criterion for success should not be time or attendance; rather, it should be the successful attainment of the clearly specified learning objectives and minimum requirements. When students meet the objectives, they should be awarded the credit determined for the objectives.

Constants-Variable Program

Professional educators have advocated the comprehensive high school for over 30 years but have not yet achieved it. Such a school would provide a secondary program for all learners, whether academic or vocational, and maintain a continuing emphasis on general education for all except the slow or gifted students. Unfortunately, the secondary school is still primarily a preparatory school for postsecondary work, usually emphasizing college preparation.

A *constants-variable* program affords more flexibility in career choices for the student and tends to soften the rigidity that usually accompanies tracking programs. It provides for various elective studies that students can pursue. With more freedom in selecting courses, students may work out individualized programs according to their needs and interests. Some form of flexible scheduling and differentiated staffing to challenge the Carnegie unit system will offer teachers and learners even greater program flexibility.

The basic high school course requirements, more commonly referred to as *constants,* are required for all students; and many electives, the *variable* program offerings, become required coursework for a particular avenue of learning. Within the constants, however, additional provisions are made to take into account the special needs, interests, and abilities of students; for example, a high school requiring three years of English may allow its students relative freedom in meeting this requirement. Other elective programs have, until recent years, provided this flexibility.

However, increased graduation requirements will now tend to restrict the elective flexibility of programs. If the program is too rigidly fixed within the time structure of the school day, then special elective courses may be eliminated. Students may no longer be able to select secondary programs that enhance vocational competence and enrichment.

Summary and Implications

Issues for the curriculum are constantly changing as society acquires new expectations. The teacher working in program development must be knowledgeable about current issues and how those issues bear on the purposes and aims of the school program. Applications of this knowledge assist the teacher in designing curriculum with student- or subject-centered emphases. Within this structure student needs must be addressed through general, exploratory, and personal education.

Faced with increasing demands on the education program, schools must still provide for the individual differences of learners. Increasing state requirements for general education places greater stress on the part of the student population that has had difficulty in meeting traditional academic standards. If increased requirements lead to increased standards of academic performance for all, the school may find it has an increase in dropout rates. How teachers meet this challenge depends wholly upon how well they accept special responsibility for curriculum development. Students may be expected to participate in more courses in general education—namely, mathematics, science, and English—but the reality and applicability of these subjects to the real world of the learner will have to be addressed.

Discussion Questions

1. How do the purposes of general and exploratory education differ?
2. How should the school curriculum be altered to address problems of basic literacy and development of survival skills?
3. Why should the general aims of education in the 1990s be different from those of the early 1900s?
4. Which type of curriculum, subject or student-centered, do you prefer? Why?
5. Is a student's passing of a competency test adequate evidence that the student is now educated? Explain.

Supplemental Activities

1. Examine the curriculum guide of a local school district and identify that part of the curriculum that meets the personal needs of the students.
2. Study your state's curriculum regulations to see how general, exploratory, and personal educational goals are to be met.
3. Compare and contrast the competency-testing program of several of the states near you.
4. Visit a vocational-technical school, and report on your observations of how the personal educational needs of students are being met by that curriculum.
5. Debate the question "When does the emphasis on competency testing become the determiner of the curriculum?"

Notes

1. Alfred N. Whitehead, *The Aims of Education* (New York: New American Library, 1957), pp. 18–19.
2. Albert I. Oliver, *Curriculum Improvement: A Guide to Problems, Principles, and Process,* 2nd ed. (New York: Harper and Row, 1977), p. 233.

Bibliography

Beane, James A., Toepler, Conrad E., Jr., and Alessi, Samuel J. *Curriculum Planning and Development.* Boston: Allyn and Bacon, 1986.

Brandt, Ronald S. "When Curriculum Should Be Locally Developed." *Educational Leadership,* 44 (4) (January 1987):3.

Doll, Ronald C. *Curriculum Improvement: Decision Making and Process.* 6th ed. Boston: Allyn and Bacon, 1986.

Eisner, Elliot W. "Creative Education in American Schools Today." *Educational Horizons,* 63 (special issue, 1985):10.

English, Fenwick, W., ed. *Fundamental Curriculum Decisions, 1983 Yearbook.* Alexandria, Va.: Association for Supervision and Curriculum Development, 1983.

Glasser, William. *Control Theory in the Classroom.* New York: Harper and Row, 1986.

Grant, Carl A. *Bringing Teaching to Life.* Boston: Allyn and Bacon, 1982.

Hunkins, Francis P. *Curriculum Development: Program Planning and Improvement.* Columbus, Ohio: Merrill, 1980.

Link, Frances R., ed. *Essays on the Intellect.* Alexandria, Va.: Association for Supervision and Curriculum Development, 1985.

Tanner, Daniel, and Tanner, Laurel. *Curriculum Development: Theory and Practice.* 2nd ed. New York: Macmillan, 1980.

School Practices

Focus Questions

- How are graded and nongraded schools different?
- What program advantages develop when teachers plan the curriculum together?
- What are some of the important practices that teachers should look for when visiting schools?
- What conclusions can be drawn about the grouping or nongrouping of students?
- What effect do school scheduling practices have on teacher performance and learner expectations?

Key Terms and Concepts

Graded school
Nongraded school
Articulation and continuity
Staffing practices
Scheduling
Space utilization
Grouping practices

Class size
Tracking
Testing
Grading
Nonacademic offerings
Early programs
Community education

What Would You Do?

You have been assigned to teach a group of junior high school learners who have been grouped homogeneously on the bases of IQ and the California Achievement Test. You have not seen the recorded performance of your students on these tests but have been told that two of the classes can be described as average, one as above average, and two as below average. The curriculum guide that you have been given for your teaching field is very general but does indicate minimum levels of expected competency for all learners before they can move on to a new educational experience the next year. Your students are reasonably astute about the grouping practices in your school; and when you attempt to discuss the year's activities with them, they respond in a manner that is consistent with the way the classes were described to you. A typical response from one of the classes is, "We know we're average and we'll do our usual average learning for you." You quickly conclude that you have an affective and cognitive learning problem with them. What are some steps you could take to plan for the differences in your learners?

When asked to describe an American school, one needs to create a picture that depicts the organization of space; the materials being used; the observed teacher, learner, and specialist behaviors; the grouping and teaching patterns of learners; the staffing arrangements of teachers; the pieces of written evidence that explain how things occur and what children learn; and so on. This brief list and many other pieces of observable, touchable, and experimental data constitute a patch-work portrait of the school. The interesting thing about this picture, however, is that it will be as different as the people asked to describe the school. This chapter examines some of the easily identifiable school practices and discusses their impact on the teachers and learners of the school.

Organizational Arrangements

School organizations vary from school district to school district, and various degrees of emphasis for some practices will be found in any description of the American school. There are, however, general categories of operation that are found in all schools. What is different is how these categories are emphasized. That difference can be attributed to the diversity of practices, size and wealth of the community, geographical location, and community expectations. Despite the fact that practices vary, there are some commonalities among all American schools, which we will discuss in this section.

Graded and Nongraded Schools

The graded school is a borrowed European concept for organizing pupils in some orderly fashion by chronological age. Historically, children in the United States have usually begun formal schooling at age five or six. In almost every state of the nation, that practice continues today. There are a few states that mandate age seven as the starting age for compulsory education, but most use age five or six. It became only natural that children starting their first year of formal schooling should be called "first graders." When they returned for a second year of schooling, they were called "second graders." Gradually, re-quirements and standards were established for each of the formal years of schooling, and the twelve-year graded school emerged. Because of the graded requirements, however, all students do not spend twelve years in graded schools. Those who fail to meet some of the graded requirements along the way must repeat a grade or several grades, and they may spend more than twelve years in school if they wish to receive a secondary school diploma. The diploma, however, indicates at least twelve years of successful formal education.

Most schools in the United States are graded schools. They provide organiza-tion of pupils by ages and have established standards for each grade. There are three weaknesses with this type of school organization:

1. Graded schools do not account for the differences in learners with regard to academic readiness and social, mental, and physical maturity. For example, it does not follow that thirteen-year-old girls and boys, who are vastly different physically, mentally, and emotionally, should be grouped together as seventh or eighth graders in an intermediate school. Girls are much more mature at this age than are boys, yet they are grouped with boys for learning. Additionally, all five- or six-year-olds are not similar in maturity. Since all children usually start school in September of the year and all have been born during different months of that year, there can be a spread of up to a year in the maturation rates of each new group starting school (though, in practice, the spread is usually ten months). Ten or twelve months does not seem like a great difference, but it does account for almost one-sixth of a child's life at that stage.

2

61

2. Graded schools do not account positively for what a learner has learned when the school decides that grade-level requirements have not been met and the child is forced to repeat the whole grade the following year. Early failure rates among young learners help to contribute to school dropout rates later in the graded school. Individual differences in learning rates and achievement are seldom attended to. Although many elementary schools attempt to address this problem, few secondary schools do anything about it.

3. Since most graded schools tend to use group rather than individual expectations for test performance, and since so few of the tests that are used meet accepted criteria for good test making, learners who do not meet standards for grade levels are penalized in terms of the assessment of their progress.

The nongraded school, as now defined, involves a school organization that allows each child to progress through the system at an individual rate of development. The lockstep grade-level concept, with its set curriculum for each grade, is abandoned in favor of an individual, flexible, and continuous educational program. Sometimes referred to as "continuous progress education," this plan introduces students to a series of stages of development geared to readiness for learning. Students are grouped flexibly according to age, ability, maturity, achievement, and other developmental factors. Within this grouping, students are encouraged to move ahead through each subject at their own speed; their grouping varies with the progress they make.

The nongraded curriculum makes the final move toward complete dissolution of the lockstep graded system. When an elementary school becomes nongraded, the kindergarten and early grades are often simply designated as the primary school. The upper elementary school, grades 5, 6, 7, and 8, becomes a new unit of organization labeled the intermediate or middle school, and the high school discards its strict traditional approach and graded pattern in favor of phases of learning and sequential development.

The nongraded school tries to minimize the shortcomings of the graded system, and the conventional grade designations of the typical American school are consequently discarded. With grade-level designations gone, able students can advance at a rate commensurate with ability. Whereas in the graded system it takes five years to teach the formal learning skills expected for grades K–4, children in nongraded schools can complete this learning in four or, in some cases, three years. In addition, in the nongraded school less able students do not have to experience psychological fear of failure or suffer the minimal learning associated with grade placement. They may take five or more years to master the necessary skills.

⟨2⟩ Most of the nongrading has appeared at the elementary level, although some high schools have attempted it. If nongrading were applied to all formal education, the curriculum could be divided into four parts: primary education, intermediate education, secondary education, and higher education. All these separate groups could be nongraded and could provide a continuous education organized around the individual progress of pupils.

Much of the adverse criticism of the nongraded school has come about because there is little or no empirical evidence showing its value over the graded school. If the nongraded school is to become popular, controlled studies must prove its worth. There are other problems with the nongraded school. One of these is associated with the growth and development of the learner. Some learners may be able to advance rapidly academically but need to be housed with learners of like social and physical development. One method of handling this problem is to establish transition-type learning environments in which the social, physical, and emotional development of more able learners can be addressed. Another problem is associated with the track-type programs of the high school. High school students tend to group themselves because of vocational direction, and learning experiences become rigidly sequenced within tracks. However, high schools could establish "schools-within-a-school" and thereby establish nongrading within tracks.

Critics of the nongraded school suggest that most of the desirable features of this type of program can be realized in the graded school. It seems fair to conclude that these critics would merely superimpose a nongraded organization onto the existing pattern. If the theory were then truly practiced, grade-level designations would tend to disappear.

Teachers examining the operations of school organization should look for evidences of articulation, or interrelation, of the educational program. The most common cause of poor articulation is a lack of cooperative planning among teachers of the various academic disciplines. Too often, teachers tend to teach their own subject without concern for what is taking place in other subjects in the same grade. Then teachers complain that there is little, if any, horizontal transfer of learning. However, a closer examination of this problem points to a lack of cooperation among teachers. For instance, ninth-grade social studies teachers may feel little obligation to correct a student's careless English in the social studies classroom. In class the social sciences are emphasized, and teachers can easily ignore correct English usage. The same lack of horizontal articulation occurs between the mathematics teacher and the science teacher. The science teacher focuses on scientific inquiry and tends to slight mathematical exactness.

Just as important as horizontal articulation among subjects is articulation within each subject. In many large schools where several teachers teach the same subject at the same level, they do not try to coordinate their presentations. Course guides and outlines, which theoretically could greatly improve the articulation within courses, do not even exist in many schools. Teachers tend to teach and emphasize what they want. With little or no supervision they go their own separate ways under the cloak of academic freedom. This lack of articulation also exists in large elementary schools among self-contained classrooms. Rarely do elementary teachers confer with one another to correlate the educational program. Probably any constructive move toward horizontal articulation should begin within the narrower confines of the subjects themselves before crossing subject lines for complete articulation.

Continuity within the school's curriculum refers to vertical articulation. In addition to considering horizontal articulation, the teacher must be concerned with the interrelatedness of all grade levels of the school program and how they provide students with continuous learning. Albert Oliver has suggested the following plan as a way to improve continuity in a school program:

> More comprehensive is the trend to plan continuity from kindergarten through grade 12. In some systems supervisors are given a K–12 responsibility rather than elementary or secondary. In such a plan the director of curriculum is an overseer of the total range. More effective for communication is the establishing of committees representing all levels. Certainly schools that are being consolidated need to look at their total offerings. Related to this is the development of guides, for example, those for social studies, on a K–12 sequence, with a statement of overall objectives and philosophy. A high school that is working on its philosophy and objectives for the school as a whole should bring in representatives from levels above and below in order to effect greater understanding and continuity.[1]

Figure 19.1 suggests one way of examining the vertical articulation of the total curriculum. It applies whether the school district uses grade levels or nongraded organization. Every discipline comprises established concepts that can be identified. Because some concepts are easier to grasp than others, some can be studied at an early stage of a learner's development, and others must be introduced at a later date. The teaching staff determines what concepts will be taught and to whom, at what stage they should be introduced, and their rate of study.

Although continuity demands the attention of all school personnel, the classroom teacher can do the most to improve vertical articulation. The teacher can improve continuity by planning lessons that take into account what a student has studied before and will study in the future. In planning for continuity, teachers must remember that learning proceeds best from the simple to the complex and from the concrete to the abstract. Teachers must also remember that students need to review a certain amount of what they learned before. Maintaining continuity is difficult and requires constant attention from educators.

Open and Fixed Space

Most school buildings have been constructed along conventional lines with large corridors and self-contained classrooms on both sides of the corridors. Library, physical education, and other resource rooms are conveniently located for easy

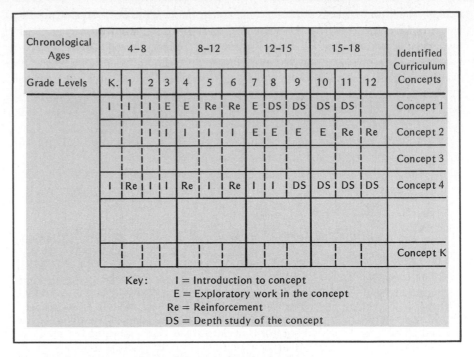

FIGURE 19.1 *Vertical Articulation in the Curriculum*

access to students. Use of space in this way usually supports a grade-level type of school organization. Flexible space for instruction is often lacking, and little or no cooperation among teachers for teaching is apparent.

Open-space facilities tend to be larger instructional areas with movable walls, flexible learning environments, and instructional organizations that are nongraded. This type of space, however, does not automatically guarantee an instructional program developed around the philosophy of open education. What an open-space facility does imply is the *capacity* for nongraded organization. Instead of having corridors faced by small classrooms—about 30 students per room—the school plant has large instructional spaces that can be kept completely open for all kinds of instruction or can be reduced to smaller areas by movable walls and furniture. A school like this tends to be more conducive to a variety of instructional and grouping patterns. Although its popularity has increased rapidly during the past fifteen years, the open-space facility is still found primarily at the elementary and middle school levels. One of the biggest problems associated with the intended use of open-space facilities is the lack of adequate preparation of teachers. When school districts contemplate the use of open-space facilities, they should plan for adequate in-service staff development. If teachers learn how to be comfortable in open space, they will use it as it was intended.

With the decline of school enrollments during the late seventies and early eighties has come a decline in the construction of new school buildings. If school districts are to provide open-space facilities while enrollment is declining, they must plan to renovate old buildings instead of constructing new ones. However, if elementary enrollments increase during the late 1980s, there may be renewed emphasis on building new open-space schools for students.

Staffing

Although many consider team teaching to be new, it is not entirely so. It has been practiced for some time in athletics; for example, groups of coaches— each a specialist—often work together but use the special talents of each. Team teaching has also been used successfully in the military services when, in a national crisis, it becomes necessary to train masses of soldiers in a short time. In the nation's schools, however, team teaching on a large scale is not used to any great degree.

The needs of students are more apt to be met when students are exposed to varied learning experiences. In team teaching, learning can be most successful when large-group instruction (100–150 students), small-group instruction (8–15 students), and independent study are combined. A teaching team, organized by subject or by a combination of subjects, can provide these three kinds of experiences. The distribution of time among the large groups, the small groups, and the independent study will vary according to the subject studied. Advocates of team teaching have suggested that, on the average, students should spend 40 percent of their time in large-group instruction, 30 percent in small-group discussion, and 30 percent in independent study.

Team teaching used in both elementary and secondary schools may take different forms; the size and composition of the team may vary; and the teams may teach one subject or may cross subject lines. Some of the specific advantages offered by team teaching include the following:

- The specialization of teaching, whereby the particular talents of a teacher are used to the fullest
- The improvement of supervisory arrangements, whereby team teachers criticize one another's teaching performance
- The use of nonprofessional aides for routine duties
- The expanded and multiple uses of many of the new mechanical teaching devices that aid the teacher

The teaching team can be organized in two general ways. The first, a formal approach, is referred to as hierarchical team organization. This approach is a line-staff organization wherein a team leader heads a team made up of regular teachers and teachers' aides. Usually, there is a pay differential, and the team leader receives a higher salary than the other teachers on the team. The aides may be noncertified personnel who handle routine administrative and clerical duties formerly handled by the classroom teacher. Aides may also, under the careful supervision of the teaching team, be assigned routine instructional tasks.

The second type of organization is referred to as a collegial, or equalitarian, team. There is no formal structure to this organization; leadership is shared or exchanged voluntarily, and all teachers receive the same pay and have equal responsibility and similar duties. Team organization is binding, however, in that teachers, although enjoying a more informal organization, must work together

2

at a common task. Note that the collegial team is different from the many kinds of cooperative or joint ventures that teachers may join voluntarily and from which they may withdraw whenever they wish.

Despite the many advantages of team teaching, there are several potential difficulties that may keep it from getting started or from being successful if it is already underway. First, preparation for team teaching is time-consuming, and in any planning, adequate preparation time must be allotted. Second, personality clashes are always possible and must be avoided by careful planning. If some teachers do not work well together, they should not be forced to be on a team. Third, there is the possibility that less attention will be given to individual students if the team teaching should degenerate into nothing more than large-group instruction with "turn teaching." Fourth, there may not be adequate physical facilities to enhance the success of team teaching. We do not mean to say that a team cannot teach well in many existing school facilities. However, if team teaching is contemplated and new or renovated facilities are needed, the building should accommodate this type of teaching. Fifth, team teaching cannot and should not be forced on teachers by the administration. Teachers must want to participate, since team teaching takes maximum cooperation and effort if it is to be successful.

Differentiated staffing has added a new dimension to the pattern for team teaching. It is, however, merely a refinement of hierarchical teaching. Specifically, it establishes a career ladder that links the paraprofessional job with the superintendent's office. Different levels of instructional personnel are created, and each level requires certain kinds of training and experience. The director of curriculum and instruction becomes the school district program team leader. Each instructional and research staff assignment carries special instructional charges. The essential elements for differentiated staffing consist of the following:

1. A minimum of three differentiated staff teaching levels are suggested: paraprofessional, staff teacher, and senior teacher.
2. Salary scales for the levels should be different, but each level should specify a minimum and a maximum salary.
3. Academic and professional preparation for each level should be different, with the senior teacher assuming the responsibility of staff leader.
4. All levels are responsible for delivering instruction, but only the staff and the senior teacher are responsible for curricular decisions.
5. All positions may be tenured, but the senior teacher should be on a yearly contract.

With differentiated staffing, as with hierarchical team arrangements, one of the main deterrents has been salary differences, usually confused with a merit

Look for variety in a school's organization when you look for a job.
Seek help from experienced teachers when planning instructional
arrangements.
Consider learner needs and interests when grouping for instruction.

pay system. Doubtless, some teachers are better than others at certain tasks. If
the profession is concerned about accountability and high-quality education,
then it seems obvious that teachers should be placed in jobs that match their
abilities. The profession desperately needs, in addition to special credentials
and advanced training, valid and reliable criteria for assigning special tasks to
the professional staff.

2

Scheduling

The two organizational terms *modular* and *flexible* refer to two different concepts in scheduling and should not be considered the same thing. Modular
scheduling has existed for some time in both elementary and secondary schools.
At the elementary level it has usually been associated with 30-minute time blocks
(modules); at the secondary level, with 40- to 60-minute time blocks. The secondary school time blocks are tied to the instructional time allocation of the
Carnegie unit. A modular schedule is just as rigid as the six- to eight-period
schedule used for so many years in the secondary schools. In contrast, a flexible
schedule uses smaller time blocks (mods), but the schedule changes regularly
during the school year as students' needs and teaching objectives are altered
for particular periods and types of instruction. Combining these two organizational concepts—modular and flexible scheduling—implies that the traditional
organization for instruction can be changed to meet changing needs and concepts of learning as students pass through the school.

The regime of the six- or eight-period day of the typical high school does
not allow enough flexibility for the best use of teacher and student resources
and abilities. Classes tend to be the same size for everything, and the concern
is one of maintaining an average teacher load. An increasing number of educators
question the advantage of devoting the same amount of time to each subject.
Some subjects can be taught best in shorter blocks of time for fewer periods a
week, but others can best be taught in longer blocks. Some classes may be
intentionally kept small; others may exceed the regular 30-pupil classrooms.
Size of class is better determined by intended objectives.

Modular and flexible schedules have unlimited possibilities regardless of
how the curriculum is organized—that is, regardless of whether it is a subject-
centered or a student-centered curriculum. However, as one introduces flexibility into the pattern for instruction, a theoretical shift begins to take place; the
philosophical rationale adopted for flexibility tends to direct programs toward
student-centered needs rather than subject-centered goals.

A potential deterrent to adopting modular and flexible scheduling at the secondary level has been the Carnegie unit. Despite this deterrent, some high schools have been effectively organized under the newer kinds of scheduling and have managed to fulfill the cumbersome Carnegie unit requirements by allowing independent study to be counted toward the time requirement. Since the Carnegie unit seems destined to be discarded, innovative scheduling should eventually be more widely accepted.

An example of a flexible schedule is one that calls for 20- to 30-minute modules for instruction. With this kind of time allotment a schedule has a better chance of being flexible. Also, modules can be combined in various ways, and such flexibility encourages the maximum use of teacher and student talents. Some schools have adopted both modular and flexible scheduling and also teaching teams for instruction, so that the special talents of the professionals can be utilized most effectively. At the same time, students may be introduced to more teachers who are specialists in their type of instruction.

Just as students have special needs and abilities, so do teachers. We have continually acknowledged the individual needs and talents of students but have ignored the individual needs of teachers. Teachers who are forced to fit into the traditional schedule must also come to grips with the frustrations experienced by their students. To operate effectively, teachers need three things:

1. *A good opportunity to use professional skills:* Typical classroom teachers spend, in addition to 25 or 30 hours of classroom contact with pupils, many other hours in planning, grading, keeping records, collecting money, sponsoring student activities, and multitudinous other duties. Such a heavy load makes it difficult for professional teachers to keep abreast of new developments in teaching, particularly in methods of instruction and evaluation. The average teacher spends up to two-thirds of the day doing nonprofessional, routine duties that could be done by others or by machines.
2. *A suitable place to perform professional work:* The schools of tomorrow need facilities where teachers can work together to develop instructional materials. The teacher needs an office and a conference room for individual work with students and parents.
3. *Appropriate salaries commensurate with the job:* As the school work schedule is rigid, so is the salary schedule. Regardless of performance, all teachers are paid equally. The superior teacher should be rewarded financially.

Teachers should not be bound to the rigid schedule of the typical K–12 school. Time should be provided during the regular school day for planning and conferring with students, other teachers, and parents. Students should still spend about thirty hours per week in planned school learning activities, but their time should be arranged so they derive the maximum benefit from scheduling.

Student Placement and Evaluation

During the past thirty or so years there has accumulated a vast collection of research that consistently suggests that all learners do not learn at the same rate or in the same way. However, schools have tended to ignore that research and to group children for learning in management-size clusters of 25 to 30 students to a teacher. The practice is based upon tradition.

Class Size

Determining the optimal class size for elementary or secondary schools continues to be an uncertain exercise. There is little doubt that if all classes could have a one-to-one ratio with teacher and student, learning and teaching conditions would approach an ideal setting. However, there are valid arguments that can be offered for learning environments that are something other than a

Research has shown that learning can occur in a variety of size environments. In group learning activities, students are expected and encouraged to interact with their peers. (*Source:* Mike Penney)

tutorial approach with a teacher. Significant numbers of studies on class size conducted over the past forty or so years have concluded little other than the notion that students can learn in a variety of class sizes. Valid arguments can be offered for group learning activities where the student is expected and encouraged to interact with his or her peers. Additionally, for some learning objectives the learner is expected to receive significant amounts of information, and this can best be delivered in large groups.

Some guidelines which educational theorists propose for class size tend to be related to the intended objectives of the teacher. For example, if the learning objective is to have the learner be a receiver of information, then class size may be any size that is manageable by space or attending personnel. But if the learning objective is to have students use information with other students in discussion, then the class size should be small enough so that all members can participate with equal time. Classes for this type of learning environment probably should not exceed ten or twelve students. This size not only allows each of the students to become an active participant but also allows the teacher to observe critically each student's degree of participation and assess the quality of that participation. One-to-one learning environments are necessary for individual learning activities that are designed to provide for individual needs. Modern technology is providing massive assistance in meeting the individual needs of learners, which can now be delivered by computer as the teacher directs.

Grouping

The special problems of ability grouping are closely related to any examination of a school's curriculum practices. Generally, ability grouping has been defended as a way in which the teacher can provide more adequately for individual differences. Whereas the elementary school tends to group pupils by subject area within the self-contained classroom, the secondary school tends to group students by subject, as learners develop and pursue special interests. The usual effects of grouping have caused special and separate classes to be established for the academically talented, the slow learners, and the average learners.

The position that school systems take on ability grouping largely depends on their conception of the individual child and of the general purpose of education. If the philosophical position of the school is focused on a predetermined curriculum, the school is more likely to support homogeneous ability grouping. In homogeneous grouping the school uses some set of criteria (e.g., intelligence scores, achievement tests) to group like students. If, in contrast, the school is concerned about the personal and social development of students and believes in diversity as a technique of stimulating education, it is more likely to favor heterogeneous grouping. With heterogeneous grouping the school intentionally puts students with a variety of abilities and interests together.

If ability grouping is practiced, students may be grouped through intelligence tests, achievement tests, reading levels, grades, teacher evaluation, or any combination of these measures. All too often, however, ability grouping has usually been established only from test results on intelligence and achievement. Because of the highly verbal nature of these tests, they tend not to be culture-free, placing undue restrictions and labels on minority group learners.

Despite the usual defense for ability grouping—that is, provision for individual differences—school programs still tend to be group-oriented, and individual differences are not given attention. Although ability grouping has been defended as a way to help increase learners' achievement levels, this defense is only weakly substantiated by research findings. Although many studies report positive achievement results for more able students, other studies report negative findings for less able students. One rather consistent type of research finding suggests more positive affective learning in heterogeneous grouping.

2

One of the chief difficulties in establishing truly homogeneous groups can be found in the lack of precision of the measurement instruments used to establish groups. Another constraint is the lack of flexible class and teaching assignments; it becomes almost impossible to select a completely homogeneous class when every class must have 30 students and when scheduling conflicts and student interests cause potentially valid diagnostic-testing data to be discarded. If the school population of a school district is a sample of the total population and if that sample is a mirror of some normal curve distribution, then all class sizes cannot be the same and still be classified as homogeneous for learning purposes.

The potential for problems generated by ability grouping far outweighs the scant benefits to be gained by rigid grouping. Some of the serious problems associated with rigid homogeneous grouping are the following:

- Teachers tend to favor teaching average or above-average groups rather than groups of low ability. Low-ability groups, however, are not always filled with low-ability students. These groups also become dumping grounds for discipline problem learners, some of whom are not of low ability.
- Students who are given labels of low ability usually perform poorly because of the teacher's low expectation of them.
- Problems associated with social class and minority group differences are usually increased with ability grouping.
- Ability grouping tends to reinforce unfavorable self-concepts among children placed in low-ability groups.
- Negative self-concepts are more severe among minority group learners when they are assigned to low-ability groups.
- For the learners, ability grouping does not enhance the value and acceptance of differences in society.
- Although academically talented students achieve better in high-ability groups, low-ability students tend to perform poorly in low-ability groups.

Despite the many negative aspects of ability grouping, the advantage of using some limited and flexible grouping pattern is that it can contribute to teaching effectiveness. There is little doubt that the task of instruction—and the general intent to provide individualized programs—is made easier if the range of abilities and interests is reduced through grouping. If grouping remains flexible and is based on abilities, needs, interests, and social practices and if students are not locked into fixed groups, the teacher can arrange instruction to achieve a set of appropriate objectives for a particular group.

The pressures for mainstreaming suggest that all grouping be heterogeneous; mainstreaming certainly requires the teacher to expect diversity in learners. As individualized programs (IEPs) are prepared for these learners, varied types of ability grouping will be used. When a classroom atmosphere of cooperation and helping is the intent, heterogeneous grouping will be warranted. But formal learning activities involving peer learning, cluster arrangements, or individual study will suggest flexible grouping.

The current federal mandates (P.L. 94–142) for special education require an individualized program for each exceptional child. Not surprisingly, since exceptional children get individualized programs, parents have begun to demand due process for their "nonexceptional" children. With the promise that mainstreaming legislation will be successful, individualized programs for all children should become the norm. Then ability grouping, as we have known it, will pass from the public school.

Tracking

Tracking provides rigid, specified programs built on a system of prerequisite courses. A student identified with a particular high school program (college prep, business) stays "on the track" to complete the program and does not benefit from the flexibility associated with a constants-variable program. Rigid grouping practices are added, and the track becomes more specific. Although tracking programs were thought to provide for individual differences, they have introduced a rigid program of constants, with little elective participation by the student. For instance, one of the common tracks, the college preparatory program, becomes a rigorous intellectual curriculum designed to prepare the student for more advanced learning. In so doing, it tends to limit the student's development in aesthetics and appreciation of art and music.

The typical college preparatory program demands the student to satisfy requirements of four units in English, three in social studies, three to four in science, three to four in mathematics, three in foreign language, and at least two units in physical education and health. These requirements total eighteen to twenty Carnegie units; therefore very little time is available for courses in art, music, drama, or practical skills like typing or driver education. These programs provide little other than instruction in the three R's. The broader aspects of the basic life-coping skills, aesthetic appreciations, an understanding of others, and a sense of necessity for economic productivity simply are ignored in these rigid tracking programs. As state and local curriculum requirements continue to reflect tighter college-type programs for all learners, the nonacademic survival and appreciation skills will be placed in serious jeopardy.

Testing in Schools

Teachers have a variety of techniques to appraise the curriculum. Using class-room tests, teachers can evaluate whether or not specific objectives set forth for a certain subject have been achieved. Although test results are used primarily for teaching and for determining grades, they also aid teachers in adjusting methodology and course content. Additionally, they may be used to diagnose learners' readiness before beginning instruction. Standardized tests give the school system perspective about its relation to the state, regional, or national picture. A few words of caution are offered, however, about standardized tests: They should not be considered an effective method of evaluating teachers, and they should not be assumed to be so important that they alone determine the curriculum. If tests were to determine the curriculum, the program would lose the richness it can enjoy with a creative teacher.

2

62

The teacher can conditionally evaluate progress toward educational objectives—associated with students' social development, educational and social interest, and values—by checklists, rating scales, inventories, and questionnaires. Teachers and guidance counselors can also assess certain kinds of curricular changes by observation, interview, anecdotal records, sociometrics, sociodrama, and student autobiographies. The school system can use opinion polls, can interview community employers, and can follow up on graduates to judge how effective the total school program is.

Norm-referenced (or normative) data—that is, data referred to local, state, or national norms—are easily obtained when teachers use standardized tests. In addition to the precautions mentioned earlier with regard to using standardized tests, an ever-present question is how effectively these tests measure a particular school program. These tests should be used with some degree of caution for student placement. Unless caution is exercised in identifying and interpreting student progress, these tests may be detrimental in evaluating the curriculum.

Criterion-referenced data are gathered from instruments specially designed to measure expected learning changes. These measuring instruments involve stated operational learning objectives. They do not yield test scores that indicate a percentage of achievement based on some class standards or norms; they do indicate how well a particular student has met the stated learning objectives of the teacher. If these tests are planned specifically to show minimum levels of learner competence, they can be valuable to the teacher, the student, and the parents. For instance, criterion-referenced tests not only yield total scores but also indicate how well each objective was reached. If certain objectives are not reached, the students repeat the learning activity for those objectives only and do not repeat the activities successfully completed. Instead of assigning grades for achievement, the teacher assesses pupil progress on a pass/fail basis. When these measuring instruments are used along with norm-referenced instruments, the evaluation of a curriculum, especially pupil progress, becomes much more accurate. Table 19.1 shows the difference between norm-referenced and criterion-referenced data.

TABLE 19.1   *Norm-Referenced and Criterion-Referenced Data Contrasts*

Norm-Referenced Data	Criterion-Referenced Data
Are gathered from instruments established from local, state, or national norms	Gathered from instruments established from local instructional objectives
Indicate how a learner or a group of learners has performed in comparison with peers	Indicate to what degree a learner has achieved a particular learning objective or set of objectives
Tend to be valid and reliable according to some national expectations or norms	Have a high degree of validity to a set of learner objectives; reliability of the data, by usual measurement standards, is questionable
Indicate a student's overall performance, aptitude, or attitude on some broad continuum or domain—usually used for ordering pupils	Indicate a specific level of competency or development as expected by previously stated objectives; usually used for individual diagnosis and prescription

Grading

Evaluating student learning is one of the most difficult tasks that teachers face. In a very real sense, the teacher is providing a label for the student when an evaluation takes place. One of the major difficulties of grading students involves the evidence that the teacher has gathered on the student's performance. This evidence is usually obtained from paper-and-pencil test performance or some planned program of teacher observation of student performance. Two questions that teachers must wrestle with as they prepare to evaluate their students are the following:

1. Are the measuring instruments that were used to assess student performance valid and reliable instruments? In other words, do the classroom tests that are used to determine grades accurately and consistently measure what has or has not been learned?
2. Has the teacher sampled enough of the learning behavior to determine that whatever has been observed or measured truly reflects a student's performance?

Grading is not an easy task, and many experienced teachers continue to have difficulty with it. How a teacher determines the grades for his or her students tends to be wholly related to their personal philosophy. A school district may determine what constitutes an A or B or C in a course, but the teacher learns how to adjust a predetermined grading program to his or her personal philosophy. Good teachers constantly search for fair and consistent approaches to grading.

Extended Programs

Schools may be directly or indirectly involved in one or several programs that extend beyond the regular K–12 program. These programs provide educational opportunities for very young children, older adolescents and adults seeking job opportunity–training programs, and outlets for avocational interests of community members who live in the school district. The extent of these programs depends upon the wealth and desires of the community.

Vocational Education

The narrowness of the typical track program in senior high schools has undoubtedly contributed to the continuing shortage of high school graduates who are well prepared in the vocational-technical fields. All too often, students drift into the vocational track because they can't meet the academic standards. Apparently, educators forget that this kind of training requires students who are capable of both academic and vocational-technical work. But the constants-variable program can include training for students that has meaning for new industry and the changing economy. Too often in the past, and even today, vocational-technical training has tended to be obsolescent. However, the constants-variable program can stress work experience and on-the-job training that relate to school experience.

63

A well-conceived vocational-technical program meets the following twelve criteria:

1. The program is directly related to employment opportunities, as determined by school officials in cooperation with occupational experts and other competent individuals and groups.
2. The course content is confirmed or changed by periodic analysis of the occupations.
3. The courses for a specific occupation are set up and maintained with advice and cooperation of the various occupational groups concerned.
4. The facilities and equipment used in instruction are comparable to what is found in the particular occupation.
5. The conditions for instruction duplicate as nearly as possible desirable conditions in the occupation itself and at the same time provide effective learning.
6. The length of teaching periods and total hours of instruction are determined by the requirements of the occupation and the needs of the students.
7. Training in a particular occupation develops marketable skills, abilities, attitudes, work habits, and appreciation to the point that the trainee can obtain and hold a job in that occupation.
8. Day and evening classes are scheduled at hours and during seasons convenient to potential students.

9. Instruction is offered only to persons who need and want it and who can profit from it occupationally.
10. The teachers are competent in the occupation and are professionally qualified for teaching.
11. Vocational guidance, including effective follow-up on all students who finish or drop out of a course, is an integral and continuing part of the program.
12. Continuous research is an integral part of the program.

The point here is not that vocational programs should be abandoned in the senior high school but, rather, that they should be reorganized. Federal funds in recent years have added new dimensions to the early vocational acts of 1917. For example, the Manpower Development and Training Act and the Vocational Acts of 1963 provided funding for a changing economy requiring new technologies, markets, materials, and occupations. These acts were strengthened by amendments in 1968 that afforded financial benefits to states that provided vocational education for the disadvantaged and physically handicapped. The whole vocational education movement now encompasses middle school and post–secondary school programs.

One of the big changes associated with vocational education during the 1970s was the development of a comprehensive vocational curriculum. In this curriculum learners are exposed to and trained in a program developed around a career cluster concept. This approach allows the younger learner to move horizontally and vertically within the career cluster as needs and future opportunities suggest. For example, a career cluster in agriculture would encompass not only courses in farm production but also courses in agribusiness, agricultural mechanics, food processing, horticulture, and landscaping. The young learner can prepare for a variety of careers within a cluster; these clusters are developed around specific job titles.

This type of vocational training has brought about significant changes in the comprehensive high school. Since it is extremely difficult and costly for a local school district to provide adequate vocational training in the regular high schools, area schools have developed for students from several participating school districts. The area vocational-technical school can provide a great variety of career clusters for vocational curricula. They also can provide a far more comprehensive program than a local high school can, attempting by itself to serve the needs of all of its students. Federal funding has assisted in this type of vocational training but not to the degree needed. As indicated in Chapter 8, the current administration has not been as supportive financially as were previous administrations.

Professional Perspectives

Remember to use criteria that are fair in evaluating students.
Be sure to identify and appreciate the special needs of vocational students who may be in your classes.
Be sure you understand the types of early-childhood programs that the children in your school have received.

Early-Childhood Programs

As increasing numbers of women have entered the job market, increasing numbers of single-parent families have developed. And as increasing numbers of research studies have emphasized the benefits of early learning for preschool learners, early-childhood educational programs have grown in number and kind. Originally, these programs were viewed primarily as child care programs for working families; but they now have assumed, in addition to providing for that continuing need, additional tasks in the formal education of young children. Although they are found in a variety of settings from sponsored day-care programs to private self-supporting schools, their aims tend to be similar in their offerings for young children.

    Current trends for early-childhood programs identify at least three types of programs for young children. The first can be labeled traditional in nature, and it promotes a program that is not uncommon for most kindergarten programs in the United States. Depending upon the age of the child, the program provides

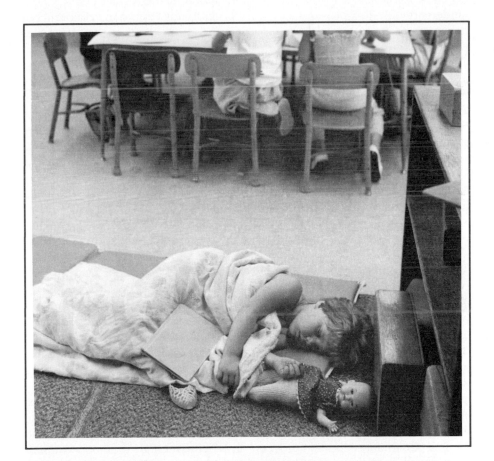

In addition to providing child care for working mothers or single parent families, many early childhood programs also prepare young children for their formal education. (*Source:* Mike Penney)

a readiness activity for the child as a preparatory stage for entering the public school structure. The philosophy of these programs is similiar to that practiced in the public schools and is basically essentialistic.

A second type of program is associated with the behavioristic philosophy of education and, generally, is a behavior modification program. This program also provides a day-care emphasis for very young children and a preschool program for older early learners who are about to enter the public school system. The major difference between this program and a traditional program is its emphasis on a reward system for expected institutional performance of the learners. Reinforcement tactics predominate, and the young learner is "schooled" in the expected readiness competencies for the kindergarten.

The third major type of early-childhood program is referred to as the child development approach. Some of the current early-childhood theorists refer to it as a play curriculum. Its roots are embedded in the activity curriculum, discussed in the previous chapter, and it uses the play concept to help children get ready for the more formal learning atmosphere of the regular public school kindergarten. It, too, provides a day-care program for very young children, but it introduces more formal learning activities, via play activities, for the older young child.

All of these programs remain outside the formal K–12 structure of the regular school, but increasingly, program efforts have been intended as part of the educational continuum for learners. The promise of these programs is that they do promote individual growth in learners, and undoubtedly, they have some important implications for the kindergarten and regular elementary program. That is, increasing numbers of young children are entering the formal school structure with varying degrees of readiness. These individual differences among young learners are creating increasing demands on the elementary school to accommodate a broader difference in readiness among learners beginning the kindergarten and first-grade programs.

Community Education

At the other end of the spectrum are adult learners who may or may not have completed their high school education. Increasing numbers of this group have also completed some form of post–high school education. As the United States population becomes older, the need for community education programs will grow. Pioneered by the Mott Foundation during the 1960s, community education programs have grown substantially since that time. Additionally, while the majority of early-education programs are not part of the regular school system's efforts, the community education programs are.

There are three types of adults that community education programs must accommodate. The first is the returning adult student who seeks to complete his or her high school diploma. Increasing numbers of these students are attending community education programs in order to increase their opportunities for worthwhile employment. The data that relate economic self-sufficiency with level of education are most compelling to those who have not completed a high school education. Many of these students seek the general education diploma

(GED) offered by the community program, but some students are also returning to the regular classroom.

The second type of adult that community education programs attempt to provide for is the adult who is contemplating a career or job change. These programs may be offered in the evening at the regular high school or at a nearby vocational school. The offerings may provide vocational training or a review of some of the basic skills needed to gain admission to some post–high school institution. The number of adult students returning to college and university campuses is on the increase, and colleges and universities are recruiting these students as the number of young applicants for admission declines.

The third type of adult to be accommodated by community education programs is the person seeking an avocational outlet for his or her leisure hours. As the adult population continues to increase, and as the percentage who complete high school and some form of occupational education increases, the need for community education programs that provide avocational offerings will also increase.

Thus we see that the expression "education from birth to death" will take on new meaning as we begin the last decade of this century. Community education programs will surely be on the increase.

Summary and Implications

In examining the program of the school, the teacher needs to consider several factors. Whether the school is graded or nongraded will affect the curriculum, the teacher, and the learner. Space, whether fixed or open, affects the type of operating school program. Scheduling practices affect both the teacher and the learner in the learning environment. Observed grouping and teaching practices provide yet another piece of data about the school. How teachers test, the types of tests they use, and the way in which they evaluate students all provide artifacts for the picture of schooling. The instructional organization of the teachers' day yields further information on the operating philosophy of the school program.

A teacher must have some knowledge of all of these areas in order to become an evaluator of school practices. Schools exist for learners; the learning atmosphere and the practices of the school depict the attention given to the practice of quality learning environments. Finally, although extended programs are generally found beyond the walls of the school, their existence and offerings have a pronounced effect upon the program of the school.

Discussion Questions

1. How can school scheduling practices provide for programs that address individual differences?
2. How do different teacher scheduling arrangements affect learning environments?
3. What are the pros and cons of ability grouping?
4. Should different grades be assigned to students on the basis of how they are grouped for instruction?
5. Should there be a career teaching ladder for classroom teachers?

Supplemental Activities

1. Invite a principal of a school to come to class and discuss how he or she builds a master schedule for a school.
2. Visit a school and observe how teachers work with students differently as a result of homogeneous grouping.
3. Visit several different early-childhood programs and prepare a report which discusses the different philosophies of education in operation.
4. Visit an elementary and a secondary school and write a paper contrasting the use of instructional space.
5. Invite a community education director to the class to explain the various programs that are offered for adults.

Note

1. Albert L. Oliver, *Curriculum Improvement: A Guide to Problems, Principles, and Process,* 2nd ed. (New York: Harper and Row, 1977), p. 229.

Bibliography

Abrams, Joan D. "Making Outcomes-Based Education Work." *Educational Leadership,* 43 (1) (September 1985): 30.

Armstrong, David G., Henson, Kenneth T., and Savage, Tom V. *Education.* New York: Macmillan, 1985.

Brubaker, Dale L. *Curriculum Planning: The Dynamics of Theory and Practice.* Glenview, Ill.: Scott Foresman, 1982.

Fullan, Michael. *The Meaning of Educational Change.* Toronto: OISE Press, 1982.

Keitz, Ruth. "Integrating Curriculum for Tomorrow's Students." *Educational Leadership,* 44 (4) (January 1987): 68.

McNeil, John D. *Curriculum: A Comprehensive Introduction.* 3rd ed. Boston: Little, Brown, 1985.

Palonsky, Stuart B. *900 Shows a Year: A Look at Teaching from a Teacher's Side of the Desk.* New York: Random House, 1986.

Patterson, Jerry L., Purkey, Stewart C., and Parker, Jackson V. *Productive School Systems for a Nonrational World.* Alexandria, Va.: Association for Supervision and Curriculum Development, 1986.

Roberts, Arthur D., and Cawelti, Gordon. "The Students." Chapter 4 in *Redefining General Education in the American High School.* Alexandria, Va.: Association for Supervision and Curriculum Development, 1985.

Squires, David A., Huitt, William G., and Segars, John K. *Effective Schools and Classrooms: A Research-Based Perspective.* Alexandria, Va.: Association for Supervision and Curriculum Development, 1983.

Delivering Instruction

Focus Questions

- How does writing objectives help the teacher do a better job of instructing?
- Are some methods of instruction more effective than others?
- Is there a relationship between the way an objective is written and the type of instructional practice that should be employed?
- What criteria does the teacher use when making decisions about what type of technology is best used with instruction?
- How can computers be used effectively by learners and teachers in enhancing learning?

Key Terms and Concepts

General objectives
Specific objectives
Taxonomies
Convergent learning
Divergent learning
Lessons and units
Lecture-recitation
Concept attainment
Inductive discovery
Group investigation
Guided discovery

Simulation/gaming
Inquiry
Mastery learning
Programmed instruction
Individualized learning
Staff development
Instructional television
Computer-assisted instruction
Computer-managed instruction
Microcomputers

What Would You Do?

As a beginning teacher, you are concerned about doing a fine job in instruction and relating well to your students. You are also keenly aware that your immediate supervisor will be observing and assessing your performance for tenure decisions. You have recently developed a new piece of software which you have been testing with your students. The students are not happy about using this software because of the "bugs" in it. As a result, they tend to get out of hand on occasion, and you have to apply some management practices. Your supervisor seems to be primarily interested in your maintaining a quiet and orderly classroom, and you have just learned that your supervisor is coming to visit your class. You are nearing the end of testing your software program, but you are also sensitive to the impending supervisory visit. How would you plan to prepare for the supervisory visit?

Instruction is the delivery system used to get the planned curriculum to the learners. This chapter is not intended to replace a well-planned methods or educational psychology course but is intended to show the important tie between the written curriculum and its practice in the classroom. Preservice teachers should grasp the intended notion that there are a multitude of ways that teachers can deliver instruction. The type of delivery should be based upon intended objectives. The chapter should also assist preservice teachers who are observing classrooms before beginning their formal student teaching experience.

Planning

The key to success for any planned curriculum is how the planned-for learning experiences are delivered to the learner. Instructional practice in the schools may vary considerably, depending upon expectations for student performance and the teacher's repertoire of instructional skills. The expectations for student performance should be based upon clusters of learning objectives by discipline, grade level, or combinations of disciplines in a nongraded school organization. Well-planned objectives assist the teacher in planning for instruction.

General Objectives

The broad aims that the many national committees and commissions have developed are valuable only if they have some relation to specific learning outcomes planned for the school. (These broad aims were presented in Part IV of the text.) Figure 20.1 offers a hierarchy of educational aims and objectives ranging from the general to the specific. Teachers preparing to plan the curriculum, teach the subjects therein, and evaluate the intended outcome should understand how planned-for objectives are reached. Educational goals change as the world adjusts to change; and so objectives are never final, the curriculum never finished. The curriculum/instruction activity is an active process.

During the 1970s a monumental effort was made to develop criteria by which instructional objectives could be stated operationally. One has only to examine the literature of this period to see how educators like Bloom, Mager, Popham, Glazer, Ebensen, Gagne, and many others have affected curriculum development. They tried to develop precise descriptions of how learner behavior is finally modified by instruction. They believed that if desired learner outcomes can be measured, then the goals (outcomes) of the curriculum can be measured and evaluated. These outcomes can be assessed on a pass/fail basis or on some percentage of success on cognitive tasks associated with specific goals. No preference has been reached, however, for criterion-referenced evaluation over norm-referenced evaluation. (Norm-referenced and criterion-referenced eval-

Teaching is most effective when it is guided by specific learning objectives. This teacher discusses nutrition with her class. (*Source:* Stuart Spates)

uations are discussed in Chapter 19.) Norm-referenced evaluation judges student performance against some group, while criterion-referenced evaluation judges student performance on an individual basis against some preestablished criterion.

Specific Learning Outcomes

Teachers often ask why the school has become so insistent about the use of specific learning outcomes. The usual defense for their use is that they assist in the teacher's organization of instruction. But there is an even greater need for specifying objectives. With the continuing growth of knowledge it is next to impossible to teach all that could be taught during the twelve years that a student

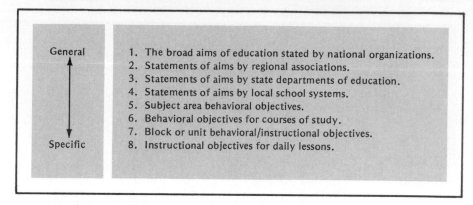

General

1. The broad aims of education stated by national organizations.
2. Statements of aims by regional associations.
3. Statements of aims by state departments of education.
4. Statements of aims by local school systems.
5. Subject area behavioral objectives.
6. Behavioral objectives for courses of study.
7. Block or unit behavioral/instructional objectives.

Specific

8. Instructional objectives for daily lessons.

FIGURE 20.1   *Hierarchy of Educational Aims and Objectives*

spends in school. The teacher needs continual assistance in making content decisions. Using objectives helps in making that decision, because the content emphasis is specified by the objective and all other content is set aside. Specific learning objectives consist of three explicit criteria:

1. The task confronting the learner
2. The expected observable behavior
3. The minimum level of expected performance

Table 20.1 shows how a given task can be judged by a specific outcome. This format for specific objectives has become accepted use for the development of individualized programs (IEPs; see Chapter 8) and most state requirements for planned courses of study.

More preservice and in-service teacher education programs are used to teach teachers to use effectively the criteria advocated by Mager, Ebensen, and others in preparing written operational objectives. Success in this effort is the first step in developing worthy curricula. Operationally stated objectives remain descriptive. Ideally, these operational goals are derived from a stated ideological mission of a school district, state program, or national purpose.

TABLE 20.1   *Criteria of a Behavioral Objective*

1. The task confronting the learner	Given the task of matching 15 chronological events of the Vietnam War with identified incidents of social stress on the American government
2. The expected observable behavior	The student will identify these common events
3. The minimum level of expected performance	With 80 percent accuracy

Taxonomies

There have been several attempts to clarify and develop educational objectives. One is the comprehensive approach of Bloom and others—the taxonomy of educational objectives. These educators classified the objectives in three groups according to the kind of learning to be produced. These groups, or domains, are described as cognitive, affective, and psychomotor:[1]

1. Cognitive objectives are concerned with remembering, recognizing knowledge, and developing intellectual abilities and skills.
2. Affective objectives are concerned with interests, attitudes, opinions, appreciations, values, and emotional sets.
3. Psychomotor objectives are concerned with the development of muscular and motor skills.

These three domains are outlined in Appendix II.

Convergent and Divergent Learning

Teachers work with learners to develop at least two types of learning practice and behavior: convergent and divergent. These behaviors are associated with the lower and higher levels of the taxonomies. Convergent learning has as its sole objective that the learner experience the discovery and manipulation of   new knowledge (for the learner) but then arrive at closure and acceptance of a single solution or generalization before moving on to new learning. This type of learning is planned for when the teacher's intent is to work with the learner   at the lower levels of the cognitive taxonomy.

Divergent learning encourages the learner to explore, develop hypotheses, gather information to test those hypotheses, and arrive at a defensible conclusion. The student does not have to search for the one "right" conclusion because there isn't one. This type of learning practice prepares students to search for and accept answers that are different from one another. Objectives that focus on divergent learning are derived from the higher levels of the cognitive taxonomy.

Strategies

There are many strategies for instruction. In fact, instructional theorists continue to examine and experiment with different instructional behaviors and systems as allied research in learning theory creates new knowledge about how people learn. The task for the beginning teacher is to examine some of the accepted strategies and understand their use with different specific objectives and the variety of learning models, experiences, and materials available for use with learners. Figure 20.2 shows the type of relationship that should exist for the planned curriculum of a school. The shaded central area of the circles depicts the interaction of the strategies, models, and objectives if there is to be a rationally planned school program.

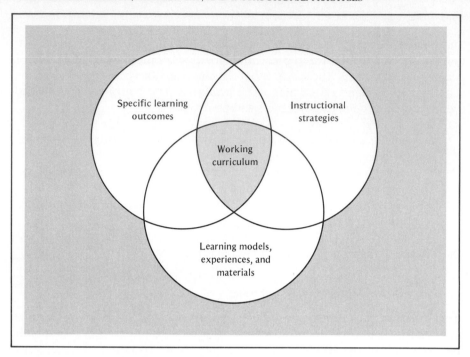

FIGURE 20.2 *The Working Curriculum*

There has been a deliberate attempt to define strategies as instructional delivery systems that are peculiar to the learning outcomes expected by teachers as they develop curriculum. Instruction is held to be directly related to the hierarchy of learning experiences between teacher and pupil. The cognitive domain of learning, developed by Bloom and his associates, ranks learning from a low order (knowledge) to a high order (evaluation). As instructional objectives are developed to enhance learning, particular teaching strategies should also be developed to give learners the best chance to meet the objectives. Thus objectives and instructional behavior are closely related. Figure 20.3 graphically presents the strategies to be examined.

Lecture-Recitation

The lecture or lecture-recitation instructional strategy is usually associated with a low order of expected learning (knowledge and comprehension). Learners are not thought of as active verbal participants in learning but are expected to digest specific knowledge for recall. Learners are viewed as receiving knowledge, and the strategy for instruction is viewed as the delivery system. This strategy requires teachers to do most of the talking. The lecture-recitation involves a live teacher lecture; linear or branched programmed instruction; or special technology like television, dial-access equipment, and computers. Convergence in learning is expected.

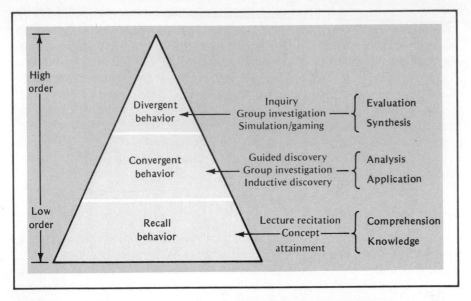

FIGURE 20.3   *Hierarchy of Learning Skills with Instructional Strategies*

Concept Attainment

The concept attainment teaching strategy attempts to develop the thinking process of students. Developed by Jerome Bruner and his associates, the strategy uses a categorizing process to develop thinking.[2] The teacher uses a sorting process of "yes" and "no" with objects, pictures, or statements to direct a learner toward some predetermined process. This strategy can be used with objectives at the comprehension or application levels. The strategy may be used with small groups of learners or regular classroom groups. If the intended learner objective is to involve all students actively in pursuing the concept, then the learner group should be kept small. Bruner suggests that all concepts have elements of (1) name, (2) positive or negative examples, (3) attributes, (4) values, and (5) rule. Attainment of the concept is reached when all elements are understood. Teachers using this strategy need to develop good questioning skills if they wish to keep learners actively thinking while they pursue the concept. Convergence in learning is expected with this strategy.

Inductive Discovery

The teaching strategy of inductive discovery also leads to convergent learning behavior. Specific objectives eliciting this type of learning outcome are prepared for the application and/or analysis levels of the cognitive hierarchy. Again, the teacher's skill in questioning techniques is crucial for this strategy. The strategy employs a deliberate set of processes to achieve concept formation, data interpretation, and application of principles. Initially, questions involve the identi-

fication of all data that may be relevant to the problem under study. Once identification has been accomplished, questioning is directed toward the sorting and explaining of data and some interpretation of relationships that may or may not exist among the data. Finally, the teacher's questioning behavior directs students to predict consequences and support those assertions with available data. This process is a three-stage teaching strategy; students may be introduced to logic chains, use of matrices, and the process of inductive thinking. The strategy may be used with large groups to teach the process and may be tried or tested with smaller groups to determine whether learners have acquired this inductive technique. Again, the intentions of specific learning outcomes should determine the use of this strategy.

Group Investigation

Group investigation can be used for either convergent or divergent learning behavior. In either case the role of the teacher is to structure the investigation. If convergent behavior is intended, the teacher should be an active member of the group, leading the group to some desired outcome. If divergent behavior is desired, the teacher's role is minimized, and the group functions without direct teacher guidance. The learners are expected to develop their own defensible solutions to problems. In either case students play an active role in discussing, researching, and formulating group responses to problems or issues. This strategy is best used with small groups.

Guided Discovery

The strategy of guided discovery is planned for application and analysis types of learning outcomes. As the teacher asks questions and students respond, the teacher's task is to use questioning techniques that are leading and thus to "guide" the students to desired responses. Rather than have the students give the "answers," as in a lecture-recitation strategy, the teacher, through a series of questions, guides the students through intermediary supportive knowledge to responses and ultimate correct answers. Convergent behavior is consistent with specific objectives deemed appropriate for this level with small groups. However, the teacher is the dominant figure and handles all questions. A crucial teacher behavior with the use of this strategy is the avoidance of supportive, praising, or agreement behaviors. If these behaviors are exhibited too early in the learning sequence, closure is reached too early and the guided part of this intended strategy is lost. In this situation the lesson becomes a question/answer technique. Praise and/or agreement should be used with this strategy only when the teacher has led the student(s) to closure.

Simulation/Gaming

Simulation and gaming techniques have received increased attention lately as appropriate instructional strategies if the objectives call for the personal in-

volvement of learners. These strategies are particularly well suited to the social studies curriculum but can be used in industrial arts, home economics, business, science, and communications in the elementary, junior high, and senior high schools. With these instructional strategies the teacher places the students in planned situations with a multitude of data available to all and some data available only to a certain few. The object of the strategy is to have the learners be part of lifelike situations that they must resolve to the satisfaction of all participants. Games can be varied so that they have one best solution (convergent learner behavior) or many possible solutions (divergent learner behavior). The special task of the teacher is to see that the students use all the available data in trying to solve the problem. This strategy is a kind of learner role playing; it meets a specific need for certain instructional objectives that are planned for analysis, synthesis, and evaluation. It may be used with large groups, with small groups, or with single individuals.

Inquiry

The goal of inquiry, as an instructional strategy, is to develop divergent thinking, which is considered the highest order of learning and is associated with synthesis and evaluation skills. There is less talk from the teacher and more from students. Through a series of questions and problems the teacher seeks assertions or hypotheses from the learners. If the teacher obtains two or more assertions from members of the group, it is the teacher's task to help the students develop support (based on logic or data) for their assertions. In this kind of teaching and learning the teacher must encourage and expect different "right" answers to student assertions or hypotheses. Thus learning behavior planned for divergent learner responses is associated with inquiry.

65

Figure 20.3 presents a summary of the strategies examined. If instructional objectives are planned to achieve the knowledge and comprehension levels of learning, then the lecture-recitation or concept attainment instructional strategy is appropriate. If analysis and application skills are sought for learners, then guided discovery, group investigation, or inductive discovery is appropriate for teacher and learner behaviors. As the learning behavior expected of the student moves from low order to high, the amount of teacher and student verbal output changes. At the low-order level the teacher talks most, and the students listen. As expected learner behavior moves toward higher-order learning (divergent behavior), the teacher has increasingly less to say and the pupils have more.

Professional Perspectives

Practice writing specific learning outcomes that are consistent with general objectives.
Remember the relationship between expected types of learning and instructional practice.
Look for the practice of different models of teaching when you visit schools.

Models of Learning

Students are different. They learn at different rates; they have differing abilities; some are more able and some are less able; some learn easier through some mediums of instruction, and others learn easier through other mediums of instruction. Teachers should consider using appropriate models of mastery learning, programmed learning, and individualized learning in order to meet the different needs of their students.

Mastery Learning Model

The mastery model of learning attempts to address problems of learning rate and differences in ability. Although students of differing abilities and learning rates may work with the same or similar objectives, they are all still expected to acquire mastery or satisfactory achievement of the objective. Some may be given more time than others, and some may be provided with opportunities of different levels of mastery in order to achieve the expectations. One of the keys to the success of a mastery learning model is the diagnostic and prescriptive work of the teacher. Teachers must be realistic in their expectations for learners and be reasonably confident that what they desire in learning outcomes is achievable by the students with whom they interact. If mastery learning is planned to be sequential, then the student success rate is very important. Students need to experience success in learning.

Mastery learning models are difficult to employ if the school curriculum is rigidly fixed by grade level and all students are expected to master certain objectives every year. It is used best in nongraded school programs where time (by the year) is not as crucial. These programs are more flexible, and differences in learning rates can be attended to with fewer problems. Specific objectives for learners are still used, however, and clusters of students or individual students work with those objectives.

Programmed Models

Programmed instruction can be traced to the early work of Sidney Pressy during the 1920s. Pressy was unable to promote his ideas very far during the 1930s, but B. F. Skinner presented them 30 years later. Since then, programmed instruction has gained significant acceptance. Although this model can be used, and has been, for application learning behaviors, it is perhaps best used for developing expected knowledge and comprehension.

Two approaches to programmed instruction are important for teaching. The first, linear programming, uses constructed-response frames for which the student must supply an answer. The student may receive immediate feedback to a single response or feedback only after a planned series of responses. In the second method, branch programming, the student proceeds to additional frames for learning only after correct responses are recorded; the learner is directed along an alternative route for remedial or reinforcement activities. This branching technique is designed to help the student correct and understand his or her errors before moving on to an advanced series of frames.

Programmed instruction is considered to have the following advantages:

- Students are free to learn at rates commensurate with their own abilities. Programmed instruction permits individual study.
- Fundamental subject matter can be presented through a program; thereby the teacher gains additional time to work with pupils on an individual basis.
- The confirmation-correction feature of the program provides reinforcement of learning and builds student interest.
- Programs can be designed to instruct in affective as well as cognitive areas of learning.
- Programming helps students understand a sequence of complex material and has the potential for doing so in less time than formal classroom instruction.

One of the primary considerations to be made in using programmed materials is the student's reading level. Since programmed learning relies on the printed word, there may be damaging effects on the poor reader. Another consideration is that although programs can be designed for learning appreciation as well as for skills, not very much has been done for learning appreciation so far.

Individualized Models

Audiotutorial and individually prescribed instruction (IPI) models provide for individual pacing of learning activities. Direct student-teacher contact is at a minimum except when the teacher provides remedial, developmental, or enrichment services to the learner as a result of some diagnosis. One of the chief characteristics of these strategies is test-teach-test. From predetermined instructional objectives curricular modules for individualized instruction are developed. For each module a diagnostic test is developed to measure, before instruction starts, how well the learner can reach the module objectives. After diagnosis the learner proceeds through the instructional package and is retested at completion. If learners reach the expected criterion for the learning package, they go ahead at their own rate. The learning packages become individual tutors for the students. The task of the teacher is to monitor learner progress through diagnostic activities and testing.

The term *audiotutorial* refers to audiotape recorders for the instructional delivery system, whereas IPI may use a whole host of instructional delivery systems ranging from paper materials to computers. Teachers using IPI generally follow these steps:

Step 1: Administer a diagnostic test for the learning module, and establish entering behavior.

Step 2: Have the learner experience the elements of the learning module indicated by an entry-level test.

Step 3: Test the learner as he or she completes the module.

Step 4: If the student attains the expected criterion for the module, move her or him to the next module and pretest.

Individually guided education (IGE) was developed by the Kettering Foundation's Institute for the Development of Educational Activities (IDEA) and the Sears Roebuck Foundation. The current activities of IGE are disseminated through two major national IGE groups. One is the IGE Teacher Education Project at the University of Wisconsin, and the other is the national IGE Project operating out of IDEA in Dayton, Ohio. Where IPI takes all learners through the same preplanned program with identical objectives, IGE promotes different specific objectives for individual learners and is heavily process-oriented. Objectives are planned by the teacher and student. IGE strongly emphasizes both individualized and group learning.

There are many types of instructional models that offer a variety of approaches to individualized learning. Cecil Trueblood[3] developed a model for categorizing these varieties (see Figure 20.4). The model illuminates the sources

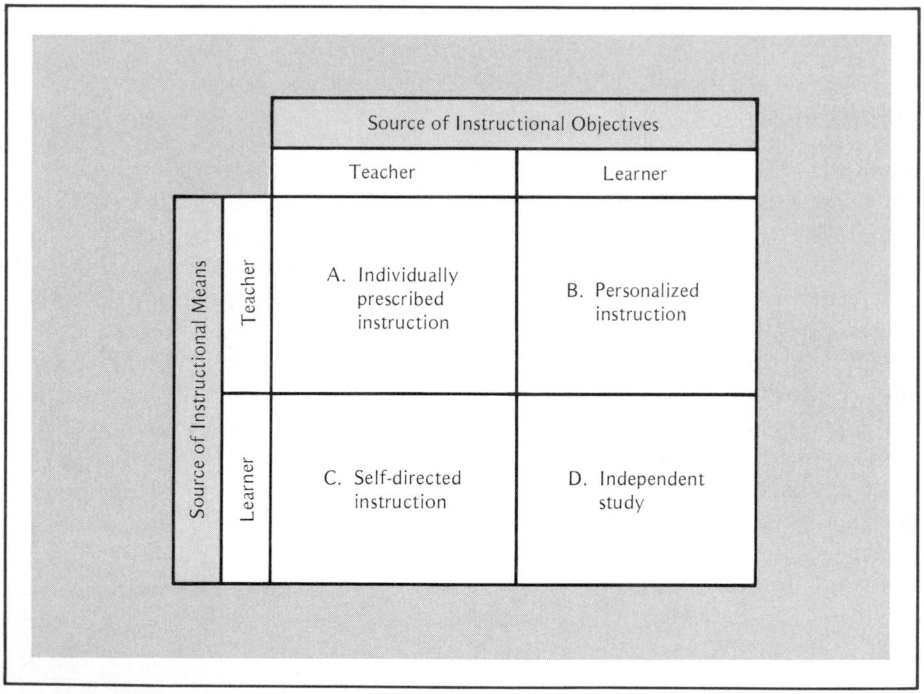

FIGURE 20.4 *Individualized Learning Matrix* (*Source:* Cecil R. Trueblood, "A Model for Using Diagnosis in Individualizing Mathematics Instruction in the Elementary Classroom," *Arithmetic Teacher,* November 1971, p. 507.)

of objectives and the sources of means of instruction as a classification matrix for individualized learning. Programs in which the teacher determines the objectives and means of instruction are described as category A. Programs in which the learner cooperates on either objectives or means of instruction are described as categories B and C, respectively. The most sophisticated type of individualized learning is one in which the learner determines his or her own objectives and means of instruction, category D.

Use of Technology

The past and current decades have witnessed an explosion in the creation of technological aids for teachers. This technology, however, has been slow in gaining regular use in the schools. Cost of equipment has certainly played a significant role in slowing the use of technology, but there are also other factors retarding the use of available technology. One factor is the lack of training on the part of teachers, and another is the dearth of educational materials available for use with the technology. These two factors are beginning to disappear; increasing amounts of new materials are now ready for use, and teachers are receiving additional training through staff development programs.

Learning Resource Centers

Learning resource centers are valuable for a variety of instructional strategies. This type of learning environment is not established to replace a school library but to enrich it. The typical verbal materials found in a library are supplemented with software and hardware instructional materials. With any teaching strategy the teacher uses, students may be assigned, or be free to use, a center to pursue learning on an individual basis or through small-group activities. The learning resource centers are equipped with books, programmed materials, closed-circuit television, and dial-access audiotape or videotape banks. A variety of other materials provide auditory, visual, and audiovisual learning.

Although learning centers were used initially at the elementary level, they are found increasingly in the junior and senior high school. As school districts use more varied organization and instruction, the need for learning centers becomes more apparent. The learning center has become more than an administratively planned area; it has become an adjunct classroom that the teacher can plan on for instruction. The only limitation to the learning center is the teacher's imagination as he or she develops objectives for learning experiences for children.

Teachers must be alert to keep informed about the new software and hardware media. The terms *software* and *hardware* acknowledge that this is an age of "systems" and "systems development," but in their capacity in education they refer to human resources and learning materials and their uses. Examples of software are books, filmstrips, audiotapes, and transparencies. Examples of hardware are projectors, television monitors, and computers.

Learning resource centers are valuable for a variety of instructional strategies, and can be used on an individual basis or through small-group activities. (*Source:* Frank Siteman/The Picture Cube)

Such products have greater significance today for learning than ever before. The amount of knowledge has continued to accelerate and has greatly affected the curriculum. The American educational system has to keep finding ways to incorporate systematically this new knowledge into the planned program. American inventive genius and advanced technology have produced a vast number of devices, programs, organizations for instruction, and materials to help the teacher to do a better job. While the lay person, the educator, and the academician have recognized and clarified the disciplines of knowledge, technological genius has produced mechanical aids ranging from very simple recording equipment to complex computers. Many of the new instructional media have become part of the vast educational team that will continue to produce more advanced hardware and software materials to improve learning.

Professional Perspectives

Seek assistance and learn how to load (boot) a microcomputer.
Take a planned lecture and put the information on a computer disk for student use.
Plan for the use of technology in your delivery of instruction.

Instructional Television (ITV)

Television can be used as an open- or closed-circuit medium as an aid to instruction. Closed-circuit units are usually used within a school building or within a district. Using closed-circuit television, school districts can create their own instructional materials as local needs dictate and provide all learners with access to the best teachers in the school system. Open-circuit units are usually those which receive television communication on a broader scale and not specific to a district. In both cases the television units use live or taped instructional packages for classroom use. The Communication Satellite System (COMSAT) has now opened new possibilities for mass education by television transmission anywhere in the United States. For formal class presentation television has the capacity for reaching extraordinarily large groups of students.

If instructional television is to be used successfully, it should fit into the general scheme of teaching. To allow it to become dominant in instruction is to misuse the medium. If the misuse is allowed, the instructional value of television becomes as questionable as the single-textbook approach or overuse of the motion picture. Continuous evaluation of television instruction is all-important, since as a medium of large-group instruction, its potential for misdirected learning or group indoctrination is ever present. Its primary emphasis should always be directed toward education—and not toward television for itself.

Another use of television is to help the teacher improve in instructional practices. Although the use of television is not an integral part of many of the *staff development programs,* those programs whose main objective is the improvement of instruction will find the use of videotape equipment very beneficial. An increasing number of teacher-training institutions have adopted television, or *microteaching,* techniques. If the initial endeavors of teacher training are to be successful, school districts should provide television equipment and help for teachers who are trying to improve teaching skills. Through videotapes teachers can watch their classroom performance and thus identify and modify or eliminate teaching weaknesses. Furthermore, television is a valuable tool for the in-service training of teachers. Through videotape many outside consultants can be brought to the school district, where in-service training is most effective.

Dial-access audio and video systems provide more ways of individualizing instruction. These systems can be used either as the sole method of instruction for some parts of the curriculum or as a supplement to regular classroom instruction. Dial-access equipment was first used, on an experimental basis, in 1961 at the University of Michigan. Since then, it has been used primarily for language study. Use seems to be divided evenly between teacher-mediated instruction (instruction that is part of the teacher's planned lessons) and enrichment instruction (instruction that is provided for students who complete all of the required work planned for all students). The dial-access carrels are conveniently placed in the school so that students can get direct help from a teacher if it is needed. The curriculum is built with instructional objectives, and students progress at individual rates based on diagnostic test batteries. This particular use of technology creates time for small-group learning activities with teachers; students can pursue the required common learning through individualized dial-access systems.

Another use of dial-access equipment is listening laboratories that accommodate small groups of students. These laboratories can be used with records or audiotapes. A more expanded use of existing language laboratories in many schools could provide similar instructional services.

Videodisks

Videodisks, which are almost look-alikes to the old 78 rpm records, offer another significant advance in technology. These disks carry prerecorded video material or can be used to tape specific television programs for instructional use. One of the distinct features of this technology is the capability for instant access to any part of a program and the high quality of still pictures from a program.

Videodisks, like videotapes, can be used for simulation programs and can help the teacher move a step closer to the individualization of instruction. These disks are currently being researched for combined use with microcomputers. The computer can be used to manage the individualizing of the instruction as the student proceeds through the videodisk frames.

Computer Technology

Computer-assisted instruction has opened a new vista for individualized learning. When a computer is used, individual learning is limited only by what the teacher can do. The established techniques of linear and branch programming can accommodate individual or small-group learning sessions in a variety of ways. The computer now acts as a tutor in the learning environment. Through computer-assisted instruction a teacher can serve a large number of pupils and still have instantaneous evaluation of pupil progress readily at hand. Thus the teacher as instructor takes on new dimensions. Instead of merely dispensing knowledge, the teacher can be, with increased precision, diagnostician, prescriber of learning materials, and devotee of increased teacher-learner interaction.

Computer-assisted instruction has also proved effective in gaming and simulation. Callahan and Clark report:

> In the multitude of cases where bona fide instructional practice is prohibitively expensive or excessively dangerous to life and limb, computer simulation of real life experiences has been found to be attractive as well as effective. One such example of simulation has been in medical schools where bodies have been fitted with sensors that feed signals to a computer program. The student's diagnosis and subsequent action upon the model result in the computer assessment of the success of such action, a rapid "recovery" or the untimely "death of the patient." Another example of long-standing use is the aircraft simulator, commencing with the Link Trainer of World War II fame and advancing to today's highly technical models that are capable of simulating nearly any eventuality that could befall an aircraft.[4]

Just as the computer can deliver instruction, it can also manage the whole instructional and record-keeping program of a school district. Records of student performance and accompanying reports, use of materials, management of scheduling, and records of learners' progress are but a few of the possibilities of computer-managed instruction. The computer management system operating in the Admiral Peary Vocational-Technical School in Ebensburg, Pennsylvania, for example, monitors learning progress for the teacher. As students complete prescribed tasks, modules, and units of learning, the students' progress is recorded and stored. Upon completion of a specified vocational program, the student is given, in addition to a regular high school transcript, a printout that shows the level of competency development for the whole program. This kind of information is more meaningful to prospective employers. With this technology now available for use, you might think that teaching has become greatly simplified. On the contrary, teachers now face curricular issues reserved in the past for administrators and supervisors.

Many of the early computer uses required an expensive mainframe computer with accompanying terminals for student use. As the technology continued to expand, schools that were using mainframe computers had to keep changing models with each new generation of mainframes—a costly exercise. So for a considerable period of time computer-assisted or computer-managed instruction was severely limited by cost. The introduction of microcomputers changed this situation.

Microcomputers

Microcomputers are now increasingly used in the schools, since their costs are much less than the costs of huge mainframe computers. The popular Apples, IBMs, Ataris, and the like, with their floppy and hard disks, are being used to answer the need for computer literacy and individualized instruction. The newer microcomputers use less sophisticated and more easily learned program languages for curriculum development. In addition, the computer corporations have developed a vast storehouse of academic programs for use with the computers.

There are three significant difficulties associated with the use of microcomputers for instruction. First, technology is expanding so rapidly that the market is increasingly flooded with new, more sophisticated models of computers. The question of which one to buy is tied not only to the original cost but also to the life cycle of the model. For instance, in the short span of five years the Apple computer has evolved through five models, each succeeding model more capable than its predecessor. The second problem is that the software for the various microcomputers available is not compatible. As the newer models emerge, there is greater compatibility of available software; but the problem still remains. Third, and perhaps most important, instructional staffs are not trained to program or use the microcomputers as they were intended to be used. Teachers cannot willy-nilly buy software and inflict it upon learners. Thus teachers need to be retrained to evaluate software in light of planned objectives for the curriculum and of learner models.

67

Microcomputers can be used for many of the same activities that were initially developed for mainframe computers. Teachers who have become computer literate and have microcomputers available to them can now manage instruction with them and maintain sophisticated records on students. As teachers develop test items for the programs they teach, these items can be easily programmed into a computer for random selection when testing students. Software houses have developed voluminous amounts of computer software to be used in the classroom in all of the content areas. So the special skill that the teacher now needs is the skill of software evaluation. Instructional programs and games are available for mathematics, science, social studies, foreign language, and the language arts. Microcomputers have become a popular delivery system for meeting the needs of special education learners. The special education teacher can prepare the required IEP with the computer and then provide programs for the learner to use. The common expression in the microcomputer field today is "user friendly," and the stress in development is to provide simple, uncomplicated hardware that encourages teacher and student use.

Computer literacy for the 1980s and beyond has become a new basic skill for all learners at all levels. As we entered George Orwell's 1984, we were no longer wondering about it; we were living in the age of the computer. Every daily encounter is somehow affected by computer technology. This textbook revision, for example, has been put together with the aid of computer technology. New word-processing programs now aid the authors in composing and editing text. The use of the typewriter has passed into oblivion. Thus the computer is more than just a tool for teachers to use in instruction. It is an instrument capable of mass communication and instantaneous decision making, and it could—if not harnessed, understood, and utilized by all the people—be used by some to gain advantage over many.

Summary and Implications

The delivery of instruction involves an orchestrated blending of specific objectives, appropriate teaching strategies, models of learning, and application of technologies. The teacher must become knowledgeable in all of these areas as they interact with learners. Without clearly stated objectives and specifically planned outcomes for learners, the school program wanders aimlessly. The curriculum issues cited in Chapter 18 will continue to plague school systems, and programs will have to change. So will instructional practices.

What this discussion implies is that as we move toward the twenty-first century, teachers must be more professionally prepared than ever before. That preparation is not terminal. Continual staff development must be encouraged by school districts if their staff is to remain up to date. With the increased use of technology the teacher must become even more sophisticated in his or her curriculum decision making.

Discussion Questions

1. From an educational philosophy point of view, why is it important to plan instruction with all three domains of learning?
2. Discuss how videotapes can be used to improve instructional practices.
3. Should there be a relationship between objectives and teaching strategies? Why?

4. What teaching disciplines lend themselves more easily to computer-assisted instruction?
5. How will increased use of technology alter what has generally been viewed as the traditional role of the teacher?

Supplemental Activities

1. After writing a specific learning objective for one of the three domains of learning, discuss the content selection and instructional strategy selection implied by the objective.
2. Visit a learning center and evaluate a program microcomputer disk that has been prepared for instructional use.

3. Prepare a concept attainment minilesson that can be used with your teaching field.
4. Obtain a videotape of a practicing teacher and critique the teaching strategy.
5. Visit a school and report on the type of teaching strategy you observed in use.

Notes

1. Benjamin S. Bloom, ed., *Taxonomy of Educational Objectives* (New York: Longmans, Green, 1956), pp. 6–8.
2. Jerome Bruner, Jacqueline J. Goodnow, and George A. Austin, *A Study of Thinking* (New York: Wiley, 1977).
3. Cecil R. Trueblood, "A Model for Using Diagnosis in Individualizing Mathematics Instruction in the Elementary Classroom," *Arithmetic Teacher,* November 1971, 507.
4. Joseph F. Callahan and Leonard H. Clark, *Innovations and Issues in Education: Planning for Competence* (New York: Macmillan, 1977), pp. 92–93.

Bibliography

English, Fenwick W., ed. *Fundamental Curriculum Decisions.* Alexandria, Va.: Association for Supervision and Curriculum Development, 1983.

Johnson, David W., Johnson, Roger T., Holubec, Edythe J., and Roy, Patricia. *Circles of Learning: Cooperation in the Classroom.* Alexandria, Va.: Association for Supervision and Curriculum Development, 1984.

Joyce, Bruce, and Weil, Marsha. *Models of Teaching.* 2nd ed. Englewood Cliffs, N.J.: Prentice-Hall, 1980.

Kepner, Henry S., Jr. *Computers in the Classroom.* Washington, D.C.: National Education Association, 1982.

Kibler, Robert J., Cegala, Donald J., Watson, Kittie W., Barker, Larry L., and Miles, David T. *Objectives for Instruction and Evaluation.* 2nd ed. Boston: Allyn and Bacon, 1981.

McNeil, John D. *Curriculum: A Comprehensive Introduction.* Boston: Little, Brown, 1985.

Marsh, David D., and Marsh, Maryalice Jordan. "Addressing Teachers' Personal Concerns About Innovation Through Staff Development." *Spectrum,* 4 (2) (Spring 1986): 41.

Pipho, Chris. "The Computer Literacy Dilemma in the Public Schools." *Educational Horizons,* 63 (3) (Spring 1985): 100.

Siegel, Martin A., and Davis, Dennis M. *Understanding Computer-Based Education.* New York: Random House, 1986.

Walker, Decker F., and Hess, Robert D. *Instructional Software.* Belmont, Calif.: Wadsworth, 1984.

PART VII

American Education
and the Future

American education has always been concerned with the past as well as the present. One of its important purposes has been to transmit knowledge and culture; another has been to respond to the needs of present-day society. Society today in the United States is knowledge-based and is referred to as the information phase, following the agricultural and industrial phases. Many of our businesses and industries gather, organize, and transmit information. Others manufacture the hardware and create the software to support the activities of the information age. Still others are engaged in research and development activities to further advance information technology. The information age is currently affecting the practice of education, and it will continue to do so. Educators of the future may spend more time facilitating the use of information by students than providing them with information.

The purpose of transmitting culture is also changing. The United States is multicultural, and the diversity of its population is changing rapidly toward increasing percentages of blacks, Hispanics, Asians, American Indians, and other minorities and a decreasing percentage of whites. The United States is pluralistic in nature and is seeking to define common cultural elements that will be acceptable to most cultures. The diversity of the population will also affect the practice of education.

Another purpose of education is to respond to the needs of society. Education does respond but only after a societal need has been firmly established. Education's response has been consistently retrospective, as opposed to looking toward planning, and creating a preferable society. Planning and creating a preferable society are futuristic, practiced by futurists in a relatively new discipline called futurism.

Futurism is one of the major topics in Part VII. Historically, all kinds of people in all walks of life have expressed concerns about the future. Futurism as an emerging academic discipline began to gain attention and strength in the past three decades. Concerns about the dramatic growth in population of the world, the capacity of the natural resources of the world to provide food and shelter for the population, the pollution of the environment, increasing urbanization, changing lifestyles, the development of technology, and other societal issues help foster the concept of futurism. The major goal of futurism is to bring about futures that are preferable to society. Contemporary authors who address the topic of futurism include Alvin Toffler, author of *Future Shock* (1970) and *The Third Wave* (1980); John Naisbitt, author of *Megatrends: Ten New Directions Transforming Our Lives* (1982); Harold Shane, author of *The Educational Significance of the Future* (1973); and Marvin Cetron with Barbara Soriano and Margaret Gayle, authors of *Schools of the Future* (1984). These authors, along with others, provide a sound background to the concept of futurism and its practical application. Students may enjoy and benefit from reading these books.

The second major topic in this part deals with the application of futuristic thinking to societal issues that have a direct relationship to education. Elementary and secondary education must address the effects of the changing American family on the students to be educated. The students of today come to school with different backgrounds from those of two or three decades ago, and they have somewhat different needs than their predecessors. The student population in the 1990s will be more diverse racially and ethnically than students in the past few years. Technology has changed dramatically in the recent years, and there has been an increasing emphasis on the relationship of education to economic development. These societal trends are presented in Part VII along with their implications for educational practices.■

21

Futurism and
Selected Societal Trends

Focus Questions

- Why should you as a teacher know about likely future changes in society?
- Do you think that trends in society such as the changing family and the diversity of the population affect the role of a classroom teacher? If so, how?
- Do you believe that classroom teachers should encourage and involve their students in thinking about,

planning for, and taking action toward creating a desirable future? Why or why not?
- How may the continuing growth and sophistication of technology affect the job of the teacher?
- How can the business community assist in the effort to improve elementary and secondary education?

Key Terms and Concepts

Futurism
Trend
Alternative futures
Intervention
Information society
Forecast

Changing family
Children in poverty
Diversity of population
School clinics
Technology
Business-education partnerships

What Would You Do?

Most young people are interested primarily in the present—the here and now. It is a challenge to motivate them to be concerned about societal issues with which future generations may have to cope and live. How can you as a teacher help young people to think futuristically and to decide to take what actions they can to create a desirable future both for themselves as they enter the future and for others who will follow them?

You were raised in a city that is part of a large metropolitan area and attended schools that were heterogeneous racially and ethnically. You received your college education at an institution in which the vast majority of students were white, yet they included students from

cities, suburbs, and rural areas. Your first teaching position is in a small and isolated rural school district where the students are white and of European ethnicity. You observe that your students are quite provincial in their attitudes from your perspective, and you are concerned that they will not be adequately prepared for life outside the school community, since many of them will be seeking employment outside the community. You mention your concerns to the principal and she agrees with you and asks you to raise the issue in the next teachers' meeting. You agree to do so. How are you going to convince your somewhat reluctant fellow teachers of the need to address your concerns?

This chapter has two major topics; futurism and the application of the techniques of futurism to societal trends. Thus the chapter provides a history and background of futurism and a discussion of its use as a planning strategy, noting how futures planning differs from traditional planning. Futures planning assumes that there will be a future and that it will be different from the past and the present. Can the future be determined? The first topic of this chapter, futurism, provides insight into the likelihood of people being able to bring about a future that they desire.

Futurism

The main goal of futurism is to bring about futures that are preferable for the welfare of our society. Futurists identify and study trends, interpret the trends and attempt to forecast their future effects on society, and generate alternative courses of action that may achieve the desired effects of the future. In some instances futurists may propose interventions—that is, planned actions to bring about a change in a trend that is viewed as undesirable, such as the steadily increasing percentages of children being raised in poverty in the world. Futures planning differs somewhat from conventional planning. For instance, it is directed by the planner's values, places a lower priority on linear projections of the past, and relies more heavily on anticipated developments perceived through observation and logic than does conventional planning.

The Setting

In *The Third Wave*[1] Alvin Toffler analyzed the forces that are creating a new civilization. In his conceptualization the first wave was an agricultural phase that took thousands of years, lasting approximately from 8000 B.C. to around A.D. 1650–1750. The second wave, an industrial phase, began during the latter years of the first wave and dominated until about 1950, a period of about three hundred years.[2] We are struggling out of the second wave and entering into the third. As Toffler states:

> A powerful tide is surging across much of the world today, creating a new, often bizarre, environment in which to work, play, marry, raise children, or retire. In this bewildering context, businessmen swim against highly erratic economic currents; politicians see their ratings bob wildly up and down; universities, hospitals, and other institutions battle desperately against inflation. Value systems splinter and crash, while the lifeboats of family, church, and state are hurled madly about.[3]
>
> A new civilization is emerging in our lives, and blind men everywhere are trying to suppress it. This new civilization brings with it new family styles; changed ways of working, loving, and living; a new economy; new political conflicts; and beyond all this an altered consciousness as well. Pieces of this new civilization exist today.

Millions are already attuning their lives to the rhythms of tomorrow. Others, terrified of the future, are engaged in a desperate futile flight into the past and are trying to restore the dying world that gave them birth.[4]

The preceding paragraphs deal with the relationships of the past, present, and future, with a direct perspective toward the future. Futurism is concerned with forecasts, trends, and ideas; the purpose of its study is to assist policymakers in choosing wisely among alternative courses of action available to them as they look to the future. In an earlier book, Toffler stated:

> Every society faces not merely a succession of *probable* futures, but an array of *possible* futures, and a conflict over *preferable* futures. The management of change is the effort to convert certain possibles into probables, in pursuit of agreed-on preferables. Determining the probable calls for a science of futurism. Delineating the possible calls for an art of futurism. Defining the preferable calls for a politics of futurism.[5]

Futuristic research therefore includes not only studying and considering the knowledge of the past and present but also conjuring up alternative futures. It further involves using values in choosing a desired alternative and then planning and acting to create the preferred alternative.

Our ability to forecast the future is limited, like our ability to generate possible alternative futures. Furthermore, choosing preferred alternatives from possible alternatives is likely to be more than difficult; and finally, creating or bringing about the desired state of the future may be impossible. Yet a basic assumption is that there *will* be a future that will be different from the past and the present. Can it be determined? Can the present human inhabitants of the world, with their finite wisdom and frailties, determine desirable living conditions for future inhabitants?

After extensive interviews with futurists, Harold Shane concluded that futuristic research differed from conventional planning in the following ways:

1. Futures planning is deliberately directed by the planner's examined values and is action-oriented. It emphasizes alternative avenues rather than linear projections and concentrates on relationships among probabilities, their cross-impact upon one another, and the possible implications of such influences.
2. Futures planning is designed to point to more alternative courses of action than does conventional planning; to keep good ideas from being overlooked.
3. Traditional planning has tended to be utopian, to see tomorrow merely as an improved model of the present. Futures research recognizes the need to anticipate and to plan genuinely different concepts of the future.
4. It relies more heavily on the rational study of anticipated developments and their consequences and gives less heed to statistical analysis or projection *per se*.
5. In futures planning, the focus is not on the reform of the past. Rather, it concentrates on the creation of a "probabilistic environment" in which alternative consequences and possibilities are given careful study before choices are made.[6]

Shane holds that futures planning therefore focuses on imagining and creating a better human and physical environment, first considering alternatives and their consequences before translating them into action.

Change

One certainty of the future is change. From second to second, change occurs. It occurs both imperceptibly and dramatically and slowly and rapidly. It is expected and unexpected. It is, however, inevitable.

Change has been described as a roaring current, "a current so powerful today that it overturns institutions, shifts our values, and shrivels our roots."[7] Toffler coined the term *future shock* in 1965 to describe the "dizzying disorientation brought on by the premature arrival of the future."[8] Change has at least two dimensions: direction and rate. Note that the rate of change has implications different from, and sometimes more important than, the direction of change.

An illustration of the rate of change deals with "the 800th lifetime." This concept divides the past 50,000 years of human existence into lifetimes of approximately 62 years each. Of the approximately 800 lifetimes, 650 were spent in caves. According to Toffler:

> Only during the last seventy lifetimes has it been possible to communicate effectively from one lifetime to another—as writing made it possible to do. Only during the last six lifetimes did masses of men ever see a printed word. Only during the last four has it been possible to measure time with any precision. Only in the last two has anyone anywhere used an electric motor. And the overwhelming majority of all the material goods we use in daily life today have been developed with the present, the 800th, lifetime.[9]

Although change is inevitable, its direction and rate can be somewhat under human control; futurist researchers try to forecast the direction and rate of change. They also try to decide what types of change should occur and the direction and rate at which such changes might or should occur.

Futurists' opinions on the desirability of planned intervention vary. Whether planned or not, however, intervention occurs. Present actions soon become history—but meanwhile, they do alter the future. Why do we suffer from pollution? Why is world famine a crisis? Why are we searching for new sources of energy? Daniel Bell clearly illustrates how present actions (interventions) influence the future:

> Time, said St. Augustine, is a three-fold present: the present as we experience it, the past as a present memory, and the future as a present expectation. By that criterion, the world of the year 2000 has already arrived, for in the decisions we make now, in the way we design our environment and thus sketch the lines of constraints, the future is committed. Just as the gridiron pattern of city streets in the nineteenth century shaped the linear growth of cities in the twentieth, so the new networks of radial highways, the locations of new towns, the reordering of graduate-school curricula, the decision to create or not create a computer utility as a single system, and the like will frame the tectonics of the twenty-first century. The future is not an overarching leap into the distance; it begins in the present.[10]

In summary, change is inevitable. It has two main interacting components: content (or direction) and rate. Certainly, there is little question about the

Encourage students to think toward the future.
Prepare students to be effective participants in society.
Explain to students how education helps bring about changes in society.

desirability or need for intervention to control change in order to avert disaster. However, there is much debate about how sound any existing data would be when applied to the future, and there is no firm consensus on the kind of future environment we should create. Yet as Daniel Bell points out, the relationship between present decisions and future events is clearly important.

One goal of futures research is to generate possible alternative futures. There are *probable futures*—future events that are likely if there is no intervention in present trends; *possible futures*—future events that could occur with intervention; and *preferable futures*—future events that are valued and that could occur with intervention. Many forecasts of probable futures are dismal and bleak. Others—based on intervention and the premise that humans can, after a fashion, determine their own destiny—are brighter and more palatable.

Some present trends may decidely affect the future of society and, at the same time, the future of education. In the next section we have selected a few societal trends with implications for education for you to consider.

Selected Societal Trends: Implications for Education

The trends to be examined in this section are those that have implications for elementary and secondary education. Topics to be addressed include the changing family, children in poverty, school clinics, diversity of the student population, technology, and business-education relationships. A summary of the trend or trends and their relationships to and implications for education, proposed interventions, and forecasts for their success or failure are presented. With the exceptions of topics of technology and business-education relationships, most of the data supporting the summary of the trends are presented in Chapter 7. You may wish to review Chapter 7 and refer to it as you read about the topics presented here. All topics are presented separately, except for the changing family and children in poverty, since those two topics are closely intertwined.

Changing Family—Children in Poverty

The general trend of the changing family is toward greater instability. Contributing to this general trend are increasingly higher divorce rates, increasingly more single-parent families, usually with the mother as the head of the household, and a high rate of remarriages. As a result, the backgrounds of the children in school today and those just entering school are dramatically different from those of a generation ago, which implies that schools need to change in order

As more and more mothers enter the workforce, the enrollment of children in daycare will continue to increase. What positive or negative implications might this have for schools? (*Source:* Martha Stewart/The Picture Cube)

to effectively educate the current and future students. The trend toward family instability is likely to continue into the next decade and may become the common pattern for future years. Therefore for the benefit of children, planned interventions for education in the schools seem to be necessary.

A second more specific trend that is related to the changing family is the increasingly higher percentages of women in the work force, including 45 percent of all mothers with children under age two. Approximately 70 percent of women with children are in the work force. This trend is likely to continue.

Working parents need child care of some sort while they are at work. The enrollment of children in public and private preschool has increased dramatically. The U.S. Census Bureau has reported that 3.5 million three- and four-year-olds were enrolled in nursery schools nationwide in 1985, a 25 percent increase from 1980 and a 400 percent increase over 1965. Currently about six hundred

United States companies offer some type of child care programs. Many private entrepreneurs also operate private child care facilities. At least five states—Connecticut, Michigan, Missouri, New York, and South Carolina—are working toward or considering proposals for early-childhood programs for four-year-olds. The National Governors' Association has taken a strong position on the need for helping at-risk preschool children become ready for school. The trend for providing educational services for preschool children is likely to continue and grow. The implication of this trend is that public schools are likely to be expected to provide more services and education for preschool children.

Related to the need for providing services and education for preschool children is the need to provide services for school-age children, many of whom have parents that are working and are not home at the end of the school day. These children are referred to as "latchkey" children. They now number about 5.2 million elementary school children. To accommodate these children, some public schools have arranged to provide after-school care for them. The trend for providing such services is just emerging. The implication of this trend is that public schools are likely to be strongly urged to provide some type of care for these children.

The percentage of children living in poverty has rapidly increased in the past few decades. Approximately 24 million children in the United States live in poverty. In fact, the majority of poor people today are children. Children bear most of the burden of poverty today. Emily Feistritzer has reported the following specific data:

1. Nearly one in four children under 6 years of age live below the poverty line, as do one-fifth of all the nation's children of school age 5 to 17 years old.
2. One in 3 female householders subsisted at below the poverty level. More than half of the children living with them are likewise poor.
3. The poverty percentage for all children under 6 years of age is not less than 23.3 percent, and for those under 6 years living with a female householder, it is 67 percent.
4. Children—that is, all those under 18—slipped from 14.2 percent below the poverty level in 1973 to 21.3 percent in 1983. For Black children, the increase was from 40.6 percent to 46.3 percent; for Hispanics from 27.8 percent to 37.8 percent, and for white children, 9.7 percent to 16.9 percent.
5. Poverty rates inside inner cities are much higher than for other parts of metropolitan areas and non-metropolitan areas. Nearly one in five residents in inner cities is classified as poor (19.9 percent), whereas for others outside the central city in metropolitan areas the percentage is 9.3 percent. Overall the poverty rate for metropolitan areas is 13.7 percent, and for non-metropolitan areas, 17.8 percent.[11]

The trend toward increased levels of children living in poverty is likely to continue. The increased levels of children in poverty is related to the relatively low income of the relatively high percentage of female householders.

Poverty is frequently related to the instability of families; therefore the characteristics of children raised in poverty are similar to those raised in families lacking stability. There will, of course, be exceptions to that generalization. Increasing numbers of children in poverty implies that schools may need to provide more nonacademic services such as adequate nutrition and health care. More compensatory educational enrichment programs may also be expected of the public schools, which has implications for the state and federal governments.

The impact of the backgrounds of children from unstable families implies that schools are likely to have increased behavioral problems and lower academic achievements for these children than for children raised in stable families with income above the poverty level. There is some evidence to indicate that the implication is accurate. One study has revealed that "only 4 percent of the children living with both biological parents had seen a psychologist or psychiatrist for treatment of behavioral problems. For children living with a mother or father only, the figure is 11 percent. It's 12 percent for those in mother-stepfather families, 15 percent in father-stepmother units, and 16 percent for children living with neither biological parent."[12]

Note that not all children raised in family instability or poverty will have behavioral problems or low academic achievement. Some children will not have behavior problems or academic problems; however, they are very likely to be the exceptions.

Research by Feistritzer provides insight into the relationships between family incomes, family structure, and education of parents and student achievement. She concluded:

> Students who live with both parents, come from high-income families, the top socio-economic status quartile (SES), have relatively highly educated parents, with both parents in the home—these students score highest on achievement test scores, according to unpublished data from the most recent "High School and Beyond" tabulations compiled by the National Center for Education Statistics.
>
> Students who are poor, in the bottom SES quartile, live with one parent or have some other arrangement, and whose parents have little or no education—these score lowest on achievement test scores.[13]

The background of children raised in poverty and in families that lack stability is related to their lack of success in school, both socially and academically. Their chances to be successful in society are also limited. Many of them are likely to end up on welfare. The cycle of poor backgrounds, behavioral problems and low academic achievement, and welfare dependency is related to the perpetuation of a permanent underclass—persons who cannot seem to escape and to become self-sustaining and productive members of society. The cycle must be broken for the benefit of individuals and society. Effective interventions are necessary, and education must play an important role in the solving of this social problem.

An intervention that could have an immediate effect is to modify and/or redesign teacher preparation programs to provide prospective teachers with the skills necessary to cope with and effectively educate the students of today and the future. Directly related to that intervention, and likely to result in more immediate effects, is to provide in-service training to experienced teachers designed to update and improve their instructional skills for the students of today and the future. Administrators, counselors, social workers, and other professionals who have direct contact with students and parents may also need initial, appropriate academic preparation or an updating of their skills. Initially, the major efforts to implement those interventions should be targeted where the predominant needs exist—that is, in inner cities and in nonmetropolitan or rural areas. Another intervention is to reduce pupil-teacher ratios to enable more intensive and individualized instruction, along with reducing case loads for counselors, social workers, and other professionals having direct contact with students and parents.

While these interventions seem appropriate and necessary, some educators forecast that they are unlikely to be widely implemented in the next few years. The reason for this forecast is that there appears to be considerable skepticism about the likely success of such interventions, which results in a lower priority for this proposal than for other proposals, which, in turn, means lower funding at both the state and federal levels.

All interventions, if implemented, must be monitored and evaluated for their educational- and cost-effectiveness. Only with those conditions will they stand a chance to be implemented. Furthermore, only with those conditions will we learn what practices are effective and worthy of continuing use.

Another intervention deals with the need for child care, particularly for at-risk children, which is well documented and implies that public and private elementary schools should take steps to provide such care. Such care as it exists today ranges from very basic custodial care to formal instruction for preschool programs. There is, however, some evidence that good preschool educational programs can increase the IQs of children and reduce delinquency and teenage pregnancies.[14] "Quality in early childhood programs calls for parental involve-ment, programmatic leadership by supervisors and directors, competent and genuinely enthusiastic teachers, an articulated curriculum of proven effective-ness, a sound inservice training program, and the feedback provided by program evaluation."[15] Programs must be designed for preschool children, recognizing their stages of development. They should not be kindergarten programs simply pushed downward. They also require a delicate balance of informal and formal instruction. The National Association for the Education of Young Children has prepared high-quality standards for early-childhood education.

With the likelihood that the need and demand for child care will continue and escalate, that there is promise in quality early-childhood education, and that money is currently being spent for child care that may or may not be effective, an intervention is proposed that high-quality, early-childhood programs be im-plemented by both the public and private sector and that such programs be monitored and evaluated for their educational- and cost-effectiveness. Newly created programs should meet high-quality guidelines, and existing programs should be modified to meet the guidelines. Such programs are likely to provide the highest benefits to children and eventually to society. This intervention is clearly long range; at least one generation will pass before its effects will be realized. However, its eventual effects, if adequately and continuously funded, has promise for reducing the number of people in the underclass.

The forecast for the implementation of high-quality, early-childhood programs is that they will be implemented, particularly for at-risk children, by the public sector funded by federal, state, and local governments; and by the private sector, primarily by corporations, as a benefit to their employees and the corporations as they continue to recognize the need for well-educated people for future employment. Private entrepreneurs will also implement such programs. Implementation will begin slowly but will grow steadily, and many high-quality programs will be operative in the next decade. The reasons for this forecast are the strong demand for child care, the positive attitude toward the need for early-childhood education, the acceptance of preschool education programs by at least one-half of the states, and a strong endorsement by the National Governors' Association in 1986.

Closely related to the need for child care for preschool children is the need for care for elementary school children popularly referred to as latchkey children. The trend toward providing such care started later than the trend for preschool care. It is, however, emerging and gaining support. However, it has less public support and is not as clearly defined as preschool programs. Many questions about caring for latchkey children are still unanswered. Should the programs be simply custodial? If so, is it appropriate for public schools to expend funds for services that are only marginal in their relationship to instruction? Should they be instructional? Who should be eligible to participate? How will the programs be funded? Should participants pay fees? What provisions will be made for fees for poor families? What are the long-range benefits to the individuals and society? An appropriate intervention at this stage of development of the emerging trend may be to have the respective states determine what role, if any, the public schools should have in providing child care services before and/or after regular school hours; and if it is determined that there is a role for public schools, this role should be clearly defined.

The forecast for this intervention is that very few states will take action on the proposed intervention. It is more likely that the private sector, charitable organizations or entrepreneurs, will provide child care for latchkey children. The reasons for the forecast are that the latchkey issue is not yet perceived as an urgent one, the role of the public schools has not been clearly defined, and there is skepticism about whether the public funding, if provided, would be likely to provide positive benefits to children and society.

School-Based Clinics

Societal trends that have influenced the establishment of school-based clinics include the increasing use and misuse of illicit drugs, alcohol, and tobacco by youth; increasing youth suicide rates; and the sexual revolution resulting in increasing teenage pregnancies, abortions, sexually transmitted diseases, and other sex-related psychological problems. Those trends are not desirable for society and have had an undermining effect on the social behavior and academic success of students.

School-based clinics have emerged as a planned intervention to reverse those undesirable trends. School clinics are highly controversial because in addition to providing the traditional health services, such as physical examinations, immunizations, and first aid, they provide birth control counseling and, in some instances, contraceptives. They also provide prenatal care for pregnant teenagers and counseling for drug abuse, alcohol abuse, and depression. Persons opposed to the clinics believe that the sexually related areas the clinics deal with should not be their concern since such areas are the prerogative of parents; that clinics, by providing birth control information and contraceptives, are encouraging sexual promiscuity rather than sexual restraints; that they encourage abortions; and that many clinics are located in schools with large minority student populations and therefore are using those students in social engineering. Proponents of clinics, however, cite studies that claim that distribution of free contraceptives to students has dramatically reduced teenage pregnancy rates without promoting sexual activity and that parental guidance has not been effective in reducing the teenage pregnancy rate. The National Research Council, a research arm of the National Academy of Sciences, has recommended that contraceptives be distributed widely and inexpensively to male and female teenagers to combat a serious problem of unwanted pregnancies. The American Medical Association has recognized the health problems of adolescents and has pledged to address the broad range of adolescent health problems. [72]

The establishment of school-based clinics is a strong and growing trend. The first clinic was established in Dallas in 1970. By 1983 there were 23 clinics, and today there are about 70 clinics, with others in the planning stages. Clinics are funded both publicly and privately and are not intended to replace community clinics and private doctors. Students are not forced to use the clinics. Yet many students who do use the clinics have no other medical care.

The need for adequate medical care for teenagers, particularly for the poor, and the general acceptance of the broad medical services that school-based clinics can provide supports a forecast that they will continue to grow in number and become increasingly more effective in providing medical services. Furthermore, the controversial birth control and contraceptive issues will be resolved, perhaps by requiring parental consent for these two services.

Diversity of Population

The U.S. population projections for the next few years indicate growth to 265 million people by the year 2020. Also projected is that the ethnicity of the population will change dramatically over the same period. The trend is toward a decreasing percentage of whites and increasing percentages of blacks, Hispanics, and Asians in the total population of the United States. The fertility rates of whites are lower than those of nonwhites. Immigration, both legal and illegal, also raises the numbers of Hispanics and Asians. The nonwhite student population is increasing at a significantly greater rate than the white student population nationwide. The distribution of nonwhite student population will not be even throughout the United States. In other words, some states and local school districts will be more affected by the trend than others. Other school districts and some schools will remain relatively homogeneous—that is, predominantly white, black, Hispanic, or other, such as American Indian. The implication of the trend is that many schools will have to change their education practices. Students of different cultures, including different languages and limited English, if any, currently are and will continue to provide social and instructional challenges to the school. Such challenges must be met for the benefits of students and society.

[70]

The following intervention is proposed for those schools that are experiencing an influx of students with different cultural backgrounds among them and different from the cultural backgrounds of the current student body: to modify and/or redesign teacher preparation programs to provide prospective teachers with the skills necessary to cope with a mix of students of different cultural backgrounds in order to effectively educate the students. Similarly, experienced teachers should have in-service training designed to update and improve their instruction skills to effectively educate all their students. Furthermore, administrators, counselors, social workers, and other professionals who have direct contact with students may also need training to deal effectively with cultural diverse student populations.

A second intervention is related to the personnel of those schools that have student populations that are totally, or almost totally, racially and ethnically homogeneous. The personnel and students of such schools also need knowledge of and experience with persons whose culture is different from their own. The intervention is to provide such knowledge and experience to the personnel for their enrichment so that they can provide such knowledge and experience to their students to enable them to function effectively in the larger society.

Both of these interventions are currently being implemented but not widely. While they receive intellectual acceptance, the concepts and their value to society have not been widely internalized.

The forecast for these two interventions is that throughout the next decade or two they will be more strongly accepted and internalized by society. A major factor in the acceptance of the intervention will be the pressure of the increasing stresses on society as the impact of the population changes in the next decade occur.

A third intervention deals with the issues associated with the instructional approaches to enable non-English and limited-English persons to become proficient in English. It is a cultural as well as a language issue. The three most debatable instructional approaches are maintenance, transition, and English as a second language (ESL).

The maintenance approach is characterized by its emphasis on providing instruction for an extended length of time in both English and the native language. From a cultural perspective it preserves the native culture through maintaining the language. The transition approach also advocates providing instruction in both English and the native language until the student is proficient enough in English to learn and understand the content of the subject being taught. The ESL approach can be referred to as English immersion. The students receive intensive instruction in English with little or no instruction in the native language. Instruction of culture related to the native languages, in both the transitional and ESL approaches, is viewed to be essentially a function of the families and other similar cultural groups not affiliated with the schools. Research on the three approaches at this point has not been sufficient to strongly support any one of the approaches. All three approaches, however, have one commonality: that if people are going to live and work in the United States, it is essential that they learn English to be successful individually and to be productive contributors to society. Another thought is that to be literate in one or more languages in what is rapidly becoming a global society is clearly an advantage.

The proposed intervention is that current pilot projects in bilingual education be carefully monitored and evaluated for their effectiveness and that more pilot projects be started with sound research designs including an evaluation of their effectiveness. The forecast is that the debate will continue and more research will be done in the next few years, the need for bilingual instruction will increase, and within a decade bilingual instruction will primarily be hybrid, based on research and also on subjective judgmental opinion. The forecast is based primarily on the need for effective bilingual instruction.

Closely related to the need for effective bilingual instruction for limited English-speaking students is the need for English instruction for the many limited English-speaking adults. Adult illiteracy has been estimated at 13 percent of the adult population of the United States. Adults are not likely to be enrolled as regular full-time students in elementary and secondary schools. They need instruction at times convenient to them, and their major desire is to become literate in English as quickly as possible. Many of these adults are immigrants; others are people who, for whatever reason, never did learn to read or write in English even though they attended schools and, sometimes, graduated. The intervention for adult literacy is essentially the same as that for limited English-speaking elementary and secondary school full-time students. Another intervention, however, seems appropriate. To know for certain the complete extent of adult illiteracy is difficult, because many limited English speaking adults, because of their illiteracy, are not aware of how they can receive help. Others who have previously had instruction and have failed may not wish to admit their illiteracy for fear of it being revealed and resulting, for example, in their losing their jobs. A proposed intervention is that greater and more creative efforts be made by educators and others, including the media, to notify them that help is available, and without reprisal whenever possible. The forecast is that instructional programs for adult illiterates will increase in number as greater attention is given to the issue, and that the percentage of illiterates will increase for the next few years and then decline slowly as the results of the intervention take effect. The reason for the forecast is that illiterates, in general, cannot be as productive citizens and employees as people who are literate can be; therefore society and employers are likely to support the intervention. The jobs of the

70

future require highly skilled employees, and literacy is a prerequisite. It has been said that the question of the future is not how many jobs are available but, rather, how many people there are who are qualified to fill the jobs.

Changing Technology

There is little question that the use of technology in society has advanced dramatically in the past three decades. The shift from an industrial-based society to an information society both created and enhanced the development of technology. Computers and robots, in one way or another, affect the ways that people live today. Technology has also had an impact on schools, both in the management of the schools and in the education of students. In many school districts computer education starts in the first few years of elementary education. Parents have home computers, as do many children. The societal trend is toward more and more use of technology by more and more people in their homes and their employment. A similar trend has developed in the schools; however, the trend in elementary and secondary schools has lagged behind the overall societal trend.

The implication of the societal and educational trends is that schools should use more technology and use it to the best advantage for students, teachers, and administrators—in other words, in learning, teaching, and management. From a management perspective the costs of education have escalated in the past decade and the productivity—that is, the achievement of students—has declined or, at best, remained about the same. In other words, schools have not been cost-effective. Better use of technology in management could reduce costs and also increase learning. The use of computers in school management, particularly for fiscal affairs and record keeping, has been generally accepted and implemented and has improved cost-effectiveness to some extent. Learning has not become more cost-effective, partly perhaps because of management.

A Johns Hopkins study revealed that the number of computers in the schools increased from 250,000 to 1 million between 1983 and 1985. In contrast, a youngster in a typical computer-using elementary school spent only 20 minutes a week at a terminal in 1983 and two years later spent only 35 minutes a week. In the same period the time high school students spent with the machines went from 45 to 90 minutes per week.[16] Computers have little academic impact, perhaps because of the ways they have been used in computerized instruction. One recent study reported that although 96 percent of U.S. school districts were using various kinds of technology to improve instruction, only 14 percent had developed policies about how they planned to use the technology.[17] Clearly, training is desperately needed if technology is to achieve its potential in its use in the schools. Training must emphasize an understanding of how technology can make teachers more productive in improving student achievement; otherwise, the training efforts are likely to be wasted.

While the evidence seems to indicate that computers are not being used as effectively as they could be used, the facts are that schools have computers and they are using them. There are other technologies, however, that are also avail-

Schools must learn to incorporate technology into their educational programs as much as possible, and use it to the best advantage for students, teachers, and administrators. (*Source:* Stuart Spates)

able, such as satellite-delivered instructional programming, laser disks, and videocassettes along with closed-circuit television. These technologies are probably underused and could be used more effectively in student learning. Teachers tend to stick with print materials, and certainly they should do so, because print material is of major importance in communication. Nevertheless, it is also important that technology be used in instruction in ways to enhance student learning and reduce costs. Interventions are needed to improve the use and effectiveness of technology in teaching, which may change the role of the teacher but may also enhance teacher effectiveness and student achievement.

    Three interventions are proposed. One is that research and development be expanded with a specific focus on the usefulness of technology for teachers and students. Technology has been introduced into schools, but its effectiveness as a tool for instructional purposes for teachers and students has not yet been sufficiently substantiated to encourage its use by teachers and students. The forecast is that this intervention, which has begun, will continue and will grow in the next decade. Reasons for the forecast are that technology is strongly believed to have promise for its uses in education and that schools will tend to grasp the technology. Yet its uses for teachers and students have not been clearly defined or widely accepted.

A second intervention is that extensive teacher training be provided, particularly in the use of technology where there is strong promise that it can be effective along with some evidence of its success, as in the use of computers in instruction. The forecast is that such training, which is now occurring, will grow rapidly in the next few years. The reasons for the forecast are that there is a strong need for such training and that many state officials now recognize the need and also recognize that without training the use of technology for instruction is not likely to grow.

The third intervention is that an effort be made to encourage the use of other technology currently available and concurrently research its effectiveness. The forecast is that while the intervention seems appropriate, it is not as likely to be implemented as the previous two interventions. The reason for the forecast is that few of the other technologies, with the exception of perhaps satellite television, have the popular appeal and the promise that computers have.

Business-Education Relationships

Business-education partnerships have grown considerably in the past few years, inspired by what many business executives perceived as the deteriorating quality of education in the elementary and secondary schools of the United States. The many national reform reports about education helped to confirm their perceptions. Businesses also have experienced trouble hiring job applicants who can read, write, and solve problems. Businesses need a well-educated work force, and they rely on the schools to provide that work force. Furthermore, the relationship between a well-educated population and a healthy economy has been well documented. There were very few, if any, business-education partnerships in 1980. Today there are at least fifteen hundred such partnerships.

Businesses, both large and small, are involved in a number of different ways to help schools. They provide their employees the opportunity to enrich classes by sharing their skills and knowledge with students; they contribute hardware and software and allow access to selected data; they volunteer mentors to work individually with students, people who may also serve as models for the student; they supply scholarships; they serve on curriculum advisory councils at the local school district level; they sponsor and work in dropout programs; they provide child care for employees; and they support schools in many other ways, including the Adopt-A-School Program that may involve many of the aforementioned activities. Some of the large corporations that are involved include the New England Mutual Life Insurance Company, Metropolitan Life Foundation, Digital Equipment Corporation, and the Hewlett-Packard Company; there are undoubtedly many more. Small businesses are also involved. As reported in *Toward Excel-*

lence: Private Sector Initiatives in Education, a publication of the U.S. Department of Education (1985), small businesses make up the largest proportion, 37 percent, of the private alliances with schools.

Some notable business-education projects that have received considerable publicity include those initiated by the New England Life Insurance Company and Metropolitan Life Foundation. A coalition, the Stanford Mid-Peninsula Urban Coalition, has also been active, as well as a business-education, bridge-building organization, Cities in Schools, based in Washington, D.C.[18]

The New England Life Insurance Company spearheaded an effort that resulted in Boston companies pledging $5 million for an endowment fund to expand business-education cooperative programs in Boston. In the initial program the businesses of Boston promised to hire all graduates of the city's public high schools. The schools were to certify that the graduates received certain skills and that those skill levels increase each year. The new program guarantees support to go to college. Graduates of Boston public high schools are now guaranteed a job or college or both. With the leadership of the New England Life Insurance Company, and their contribution of the first million dollars for endowment, 104 companies have made contributions and more than 350 companies have pledged jobs.[19]

The Metropolitan Life Foundation has committed more than $1 million to sponsor education programs, most of which focus on the needs and concerns of teachers. These programs include scholarships for prospective teachers, state forums for debating issues of teacher education, and research studies on the profession. The Education Commission of the States will receive $110,000 for a series of five forums that will involve policymakers and educators in the debate over teacher education reform. The Rand Corporation will be given $100,000 to establish the Rand Center for the Teaching Profession.[20]

The Stanford Mid-Peninsula Urban Coalition has a program with the Sequoia Union High School District to meet three program objectives: reduce the high dropout rate of the minorities, reduce youth and minority unemployment, and reduce the number of unfilled entry-level jobs in the region. The Stanford Mid-Peninsula Urban Coalition acts as a link between schools and the Hewlett-Packard Company and other area businesses. The Coalition has formed a partnership to improve both the educational and employment opportunities of minorities.[21] A similar partnership with a similar goal, concentrating on reducing the dropout rate, is the Cooperative Federation for Education Experiences (COFFEE) located in Oxford, Massachusetts, and working with the Digital Equipment Corporation.[22]

The Cities in Schools program existed for many years prior to the recent efforts for business-education cooperation. Their projects over the years have included such corporations as Union Carbide, McGraw-Hill, American Airlines, IBM, and First City National Bank. Recently, Atlantic Richfield joined in the funding and development of Cities in Schools, a national partnership with programs now in operation in fourteen United States cities. Along with fifty other companies, foundations, and financial institutions, Atlantic Richfield is working with urban schools to organize and coordinate the services and resources of communities to help at-risk students.[23]

Professional
Perspectives

Demonstrate to students how education responds to societal trends.
Explain to students how educational practices are affected by societal trends.
Remember that as a teacher, you are a major factor in creating and
implementing educational practices.

There is clearly a strong and growing trend toward business-education
relationships emerging as partnerships and alliances to address a variety of
educational problems. The efforts of the partnerships and alliances are, in fact,
interventions. Interventions are based on businesses' perceptions of the schools'
relative ineffectiveness in producing well-qualified persons for employment,
who are essential for the success of businesses in the information age and for
the economic growth in the United States. Businesses also recognize the plight
of minorities and the loss of potential productive employees resulting in part
from that plight.

There is data to indicate that the interventions have been successful, and
there is little reason to suspect that they will not be successful in the future.
Therefore the forecast is that more business-education partnerships and alliances
will be formed in the next few years. Two major factors that could affect the
growth of business-education relationships are an economic recession, which
may affect the funding provided by the private sector, and a lack of success of
programs, making their funding a poor investment. Nevertheless, the concept
has been accepted, as indicated by the trend; and it is likely to continue to be
accepted in spite of a few problems along the way.

Summary and Implications

This chapter had two major topics: futurism and the application of futurism
procedures to selected societal trends. Each societal trend was discussed in
terms of its direction and strength, its implications for the practices of education
in elementary and secondary education, proposed interventions if appropriate,
and forecasts for the future if the interventions were implemented.

Futurism deals with making forecasts on the basis of past and current trends.
Trends may emerge from the analysis of statistical data, from the observation
of events, or from ideas or imagination. Futurists identify and study trends,
interpret the trends and attempt to forecast their future effects on society, and
generate alternative courses of action that may achieve the desirable effects of
the future. Selected courses of action are often referred to as interventions
designed to bring about a change or changes. The major goal of futurism is to
bring about futures that are preferable for the welfare of our society. It involves
not only developing alternative courses of action but also making value judgments in choosing a desired alternative and then planning and acting to create
the future.

The selected societal trends presented in this chapter included the changing family, children in poverty, school clinics, diversity of student population, technology, and business-education relationships. The general directions of the trends were toward increasing instability in families; more children living in poverty; the establishment of school clinics to deal with sexually related issues and trends in addition to conventional services; increasing diversity of the population; increasing use of technology; and the growing number of business-education cooperative relationships. Implications for education were drawn from these trends, interventions were proposed, and forecasts made for each intervention.

The teachers of today and those of the future are, and will be, working with a student population dramatically different from the student population of two generations ago. More students today, as contrasted with the past, are likely to be raised in a single-parent household and with a mother who is a member of the work force. Also, the number of children raised in poverty has increased dramatically in the past few years. Finally, family instability and poverty are strongly related to increasing numbers of student behavior problems and decreasing student achievement. Teachers need to be able to cope with such students and educate them effectively. The percentages of minority populations are increasing, as are the percentages of limited English-speaking students. Those changes also require modified teacher preparation programs, in-service training, and additional compensatory services. Adolescents of today, confused and disturbed about sexuality and frequently having low perceptions of themselves and low levels of self-confidence, also require more attention from the schools than adolescents of two generations ago. Teachers of today and those of the future must be well prepared for the challenges they face and have improved working conditions and adequate professional support personnel to enable them to function effectively for the benefit of their students and society.

Technology, primarily computers, has already had effects on teachers and teaching. The use of technology in schools is likely to increase, and its applications to instructional practices are likely to improve. The role of the teacher may change in the future as a result of technology's increased use and instructional applications. The role of the teacher may change from information giver to information facilitator. These changes also require changes in teacher preparation and the updating of experienced teachers.

Cooperative efforts by business and education hold promise for the improvement of education. In general, those efforts have included businesses providing their employees to meet with classes or to share their skills and knowledge with students, volunteering mentors, contributing hardware and software, providing scholarships, sponsoring and working in dropout programs, and providing child care for employees. The business-education partnerships have demonstrated interest in at-risk and gifted students as well as regular students. They also have provided scholarships for prospective teachers and sponsored in-service training for experienced teachers. Education in general, including students and teachers, is likely to benefit from business-education partnerships in the future.

Discussion Questions

1. How does futurism differ from conventional planning?
2. How can educators today begin to determine the future?
3. What societal trends other than those proposed in this chapter do you think will have decided effects on educational practices?
4. Are the educational interventions proposed in this chapter likely to be effective in changing the related societal trends?
5. How do you think the educational practices in the year 2000 will differ from today's practices?

Supplemental Activities

1. Read a book or an article about futurism.
2. Choose a societal trend from those presented in this chapter, analyze the trend from your perspective, propose interventions, and make a forecast.
3. Make a list of forecasts about the characteristics of schools of the future, and state the assumptions on which you based each forecast.
4. Interview teachers about how they think the role of the teacher will change in the next decade.
5. Interview retired teachers about the changes that occurred in teaching during their teaching careers.

Notes

1. Alvin Toffler, *The Third Wave* (New York: Morrow, 1980. Reprinted by Bantam, 1981.)
2. Ibid., 30.
3. Ibid., 17.
4. Ibid., 25.
5. Alvin Toffler, *Future Shock* (New York: Bantam, 1971), p. 460.
6. Harold G. Shane, *The Educational Significance of the Future* (Bloomington, Ind.: Phi Delta Kappa, 1973), p. 2.
7. Toffler, *Future Shock,* 1.
8. Alvin Toffler, "The Future as a Way of Life," *Horizons,* Summer 1965, 109.
9. Toffler, *Future Shock,* 14.
10. Daniel Bell, "The Year 2000—The Trajectory of an Idea," in *Toward the Year 2000: Work in Progress,* ed. Daniel Bell (Boston: Houghton Mifflin, 1968), p. 1.
11. C. Emily Feistritzer, *Cheating Our Children: Why We Need School Reform* (Washington, D.C.: National Center for Education Information, 1985), pp. 31, 32, 35.
12. Ronald Kotulak, "Youngsters Lose Way in Maze of Family Stability," *Chicago Tribune,* December 14, 1986.
13. Feistritzer, 1–2.
14. Lawrence J. Schweinhart and David P. Weikart, "Evidence That Good Early Childhood Programs Work," *Phi Delta Kappan,* 66 (April 1985): 545–55l.
15. Lawrence J. Schweinhart, John R. Berrueta-Clement, W. Steven Barnett, Ann S. Epstein, and David Weikart, "The Promise of Early Childhood Education," *Phi Delta Kappan,* 66 (April 1985): 553.
16. Reported in "Computers in School Fall Short," *Chicago Tribune,* December 21, 1986.
17. John H. Sumunu, "Will Technologies Make Learning and Teaching Easier?" *Phi Delta Kappan,* 68 (4) (November 1986): 220.
18. Manuel Justiz and Marilyn Kameen, "Business Offers a Hand to Education," *Phi Delta Kappan,* 68 (5) (January 1987): 379–383.
19. *John Naisbett's Trend Letter,* 5 (18) (September 18, l986): 1.
20. *Teacher Education Reports,* Feistritzer Publications, 8 (16) (August 28, 1986): 7.
21. Justiz and Kameen, 382.
22. Ibid., 381.
23. Ibid., 383.

Bibliography

Cetron, Marvin, Soriano, Barbara, and Gayle, Margaret E. *Schools of the Future: How American Business and Education Can Cooperate to Save Our Schools.* New York: McGraw-Hill, 1985.

Counts, George S. *Dare the School Build a New Social Order?* New York: John Day, 1932. Reprinted by Southern Illinois University Press, 1978.

The Futurist. Washington, D.C.: World Future Society. (A bimonthly journal of forecasts, trends, and ideas for the future.)

Gollnick, Donna M., and Chinn, Philip C. *Multicultural Education in a Pluralistic Society.* Columbus, Ohio: Merrill, 1986.

Goodlad, John I. *A Place Called School: Prospects for the Future.* New York: McGraw-Hill, 1983.

Jennings, Lane, and Cornish, Sally, eds. *Education and the Future.* Washington, D.C.: World Future Society, 1980.

Naisbitt, John. *Megatrends: Ten New Directions Transforming Our Lives.* New York: Warner Books, 1982.

Toffler, Alvin. *Future Shock.* New York: Random House, 1970. Reprinted by Bantam, 1971.

———. *The Third Wave.* New York: Morrow, 1980. Reprinted by Bantam, 1981.

APPENDIXES

A

A Bill of Rights
for High School Students

B

Methods of Selecting
State School Board Members

C

Methods of Selecting
Chief State School Officers

D

Selected Federal Education Acts

E

Important Dates in the
History of Education

F

Philosophical Categories
Recognizable by Teaching Styles:
Differentiation of Philosophies

G

Schematic Summary of Education Views

H

Domains of Learning

I

Selected National Education Reports 1982–1987

A Bill of Rights
for High School Students

Neither students nor teachers shed their constitutional rights to freedom of speech or expression at the schoolhouse gate. That has been the unmistakable holding of the Supreme Court for almost fifty years. (*Tinker* v. *Des Moines,* 1969)

The following statement of students' rights is intended as a guide to students, parents, teachers, and administrators who are interested in developing proper safeguards for student liberties. IT IS NOT A SUMMARY OF THE LAW, BUT SETS FORTH IN A GENERAL WAY WHAT THE ACLU THINKS *SHOULD* BE ADOPTED. . . .

Article I.   Expression

A. Students shall be free to express themselves and disseminate their views without prior restraints through speech, essays, publications, pictures, armbands, badges, and all other media of communication. Student expression may be subject to disciplinary action only in the event that such expression creates a significant physical disruption of school activities.

14 B. No reporter for a student publication may be required to reveal a source of information.

C. Students shall have the right to hear speakers and presentations representing a wide range of views and subjects in classes, clubs, and assemblies. Outside speakers and presentations may be limited only by considerations of time, space, and expense.

D. Students shall be free to assemble, demonstrate, and picket peacefully, to petition and to organize on school grounds or in school buildings subject only to reasonable limitations on time, place, and manner designed to avoid significant physical obstruction of traffic or significant physical disruption of school activities.

E. Students shall be free to determine their dress and grooming as they see fit, subject only to reasonable limitations designed to protect student safety or prevent significant ongoing disruption of school activities.

F. No student shall be required to participate in any way in patriotic exercises or be penalized for refusing to participate.

Article II.   Religion

A. Students shall be free to practice their own religion or no religion.

B. There shall be no school-sanctioned religious exercises or events.

C. Religious history, ideas, institutions, and literature may be studied in the same fashion as any other academic subject.

Source: American Civil Liberties Union of Maryland, Baltimore, Md. Reprinted by permission. (See also Alan H. Levine and Eve Cary, *The Rights of Students,* Avon Books, 224 West 57th Street, New York, NY 10019.)

Article III.   Privacy

A. Students should be free from undercover surveillance through the use of mechanical, electronic, or other secret methods, including undercover agents, without issuance of a warrant.

B. Students should be free from warrantless searches and seizures by school officials in their personal effects, lockers, or any other facilities assigned to their personal use. General housekeeping inspections of lockers and desks shall not occur without reasonable notice.

C. Student record files

1. A student's permanent record file shall include only information about academic competence and notation of the fact of participation in school clubs, sports, and other such school extracurricular activities. This file shall not be disclosed to any person or agency outside the school, except to the student's parents or guardian, without the student's permission.

2. Any other records (e.g., medical or psychological evaluations) shall be available only to the student, the student's parents or guardian, and the school staff. Such other records shall be governed by strict safeguards for confidentiality and shall not be available to others in or outside of the school even upon consent of the student.

3. A record shall be kept, and shall be available to the student, of any consultation of the student's files, noting the date and purpose of the consultation and the name of the person who consulted the files.

4. All records shall be open to challenge and correction by the student.

5. A student's opinions shall not be disclosed to any outside person or agency.

Article IV.   Equality

A. No organization that officially represents the school in any capacity and no curricular or extracurricular activity organized by school authorities may deny or segregate participation or award or withhold privileges on the basis of race, color, national origin, sex, religion, creed, or opinions.

Article V.   Government

A. All students may hold office and may vote in student elections. These rights shall not be denied for any reason.

B. Student government organizations and their operation, scope, and amendment procedures shall be established in a written constitution formulated with full and effective student participation.

Article VI.   Due process

A. Regulations concerning student behavior shall be formulated with full and effective student participation. Such regulations shall be published and made available to all students. Regulations shall be fully, clearly, and precisely written.

B. No student shall be held accountable by school authorities for any behavior occurring outside the organized school day or off school property (except during school-sponsored events) unless such behavior presents a clear, present, and substantial ongoing danger to persons and property in the school.

C. There shall be no cruel, unusual, demeaning, or excessive punishments. There shall be no corporal punishment.

D. No student shall be compelled by school officials to undergo psychological therapy or use medication without that student's consent. No student may be required to participate in any psychological or personality testing, research project, or experiment without that student's written, informed, and willing consent. The nature, purposes, and possible adverse consequences of the testing, project, or experiment shall be fully explained to the student.

E. A student shall have the right to due process in disciplinary and investigative proceedings. In cases that may involve serious penalties, such as suspension for more than three days, expulsion, transfer to another school, a notation on the student's record, or long-term loss of privileges:

1. A student shall be guaranteed a formal hearing before an impartial board. That student shall have the right to appeal hearing results.
2. Rules for hearings and appeals shall be written and published, and there shall be full and effective student participation in their formulation.
3. The student shall be advised in writing of any charges brought against that student.
4. The student shall have the right to present evidence and witnesses and to cross-examine adverse witnesses. The student shall have the right to have an advisor of his or her own choosing present.
5. The hearing shall be open or private as the student chooses.
6. The student shall have a reasonable time to prepare a defense.
7. A student may not be compelled to incriminate himself or herself.
8. The burden of proof, beyond a reasonable doubt, shall be upon the school.
9. A written record of all hearings and appeals shall be made available to the student, at the school's expense.
10. A student shall be free from double jeopardy.

Methods of Selecting
State School Board Members

State	1947			1981		
	Elected by People or Representatives	Appointed by Governor	Other	Elected by People or Representatives	Appointed by Governor	Other
Alabama		X		X		
Alaska		X			X	
Arizona			X		X	
Arkansas		X			X	
California		X			X	
Colorado			X	X		
Connecticut		X			X	
Delaware		X			X	
Florida			X			
Georgia		X			X	X
Hawaii		X		X		
Idaho		X			X	
Illinois		(No state board)			X	
Indiana		X			X	
Iowa		(No state board)		X		
Kansas		X		X		
Kentucky		X			X	
Louisiana	X			X		
Maine		(No state board)			X	
Maryland		X			X	
Massachusetts		X			X	
Michigan	X			X		
Minnesota		X			X	
Mississippi			X			
Missouri		X			X	
Montana		X			X	X
Nebraska		(No state board)		X		
Nevada	X			X		
New Hampshire		X			X	
New Jersey		X			X	
New Mexico		X		X		
New York			X	X		
North Carolina		X			X	

Source: Adapted from David E. Elder and Milburn P. Akers, "A State Board of Education," *Illinois Education,* 27 (January 1965):214; R. F. Will, *State Education Structure and Organizations,* U.S. Office of Education, OE–23038, Misc., No. 46 (Washington, D.C.: U.S. Government Printing Office, 1964); and data made available by the Council of Chief State School Officers.

State	1947			1981		
	Elected by People or Representatives	*Appointed by Governor*	*Other*	*Elected by People or Representatives*	*Appointed by Governor*	*Other*
North Dakota		(No state board)			X	
Ohio		(No state board)		X		
Oklahoma		X			X	
Oregon		X			X	
Pennsylvania		X			X	
Rhode Island		(No state board)			X	
South Carolina		X		X		
South Dakota		(No state board)			X	
Tennessee		X			X	
Texas		X		X		
Utah			X	X		
Vermont		X			X	
Virginia		X			X	
Washington			X	X		
West Virginia		X			X	
Wisconsin		(No state board)			(No state board)	
Wyoming			X		X	
Total	3	30	8	16	31	2

Methods of Selecting
Chief State School Officers

State	1947 Appt. by State Board	Appt. by Governor	Elected by People	1981 Appt. by State Board	Appt. by Governor	Elected by People
Alabama			X	X		
Alaska	X			X		
Arizona			X			X
Arkansas	X			X		
California			X			X
Colorado			X	X		
Connecticut	X			X		
Delaware	X			X		
Florida			X			X
Georgia			X			X
Hawaii		X		X		
Idaho			X			X
Illinois			X	X		
Indiana			X			X
Iowa			X	X		
Kansas			X	X		
Kentucky			X			X
Louisiana			X			X
Maine		X		X		
Maryland	X			X		
Massachusetts	X			X		
Michigan			X	X		
Minnesota	X			X		
Mississippi			X			X
Missouri	X			X		
Montana			X			X
Nebraska			X	X		
Nevada			X	X		
New Hampshire	X			X		
New Jersey		X			X	
New Mexico			X	X		
New York	X			X		
North Carolina			X			X

Source: Adapted from David E. Elder and Milburn P. Akers, "A State Board of Education," *Illinois Education,* 27 (January 1965):216; R. F. Will, *State Education Structure and Organizations,* U.S. Office of Education, OE–23038, Misc., No. 46 (Washington, D.C.: U.S. Government Printing Office, 1964); and data made available by the Council of Chief State School Officers.

State	1947			1981		
	Appt. by State Board	*Appt. by Governor*	*Elected by People*	*Appt. by State Board*	*Appt. by Governor*	*Elected by People*
North Dakota			X			X
Ohio		X		X		
Oklahoma			X			X
Oregon			X			X
Pennsylvania		X			X	
Rhode Island		X		X		
South Carolina			X			X
South Dakota			X			X
Tennessee		X			X	
Texas			X	X		
Utah			X	X		
Vermont	X			X		
Virginia		X			X	
Washington			X			X
West Virginia			X	X		
Wisconsin			X			X
Wyoming			X			X
Total	11	8	31	27	4	19

Selected Federal Education Acts

1787	Northwest Ordinance	47
1862	First Morrill Land Grant Act	36
1867	Department of Education Act	
1887	Hatch Act	
1890	Second Morrill Land Grant Act	
1911	The State Marine School Act	
1914	Smith-Lever Agriculture Extension Act	
1917	Smith-Hughes Vocational Act	
1918	Vocational Rehabilitation Act	
1919	An act to provide for further educational facilities	
1920	Smith-Bankhead Act	
1935	Bankhead-Jones Act	
1935	Agricultural Adjustment Act	
1940	Vocational Education for National Defense Act	
1941	Lanham Act	
1943	Vocational Rehabilitation Act	
1944	GI Bill of Rights	
1944	Surplus Property Act	
1946	National School Lunch Act	
1946	George-Barden Act	
1948	United States Information and Educational Exchange Act	
1949	Federal Property and Administrative Services Act	
1950	National Science Foundation	
1950	Financial assistance for local educational agencies affected by federal activities	
1950	Housing Act	
1954	Cooperative Research Act	
1954	National Advisory Committee on Education Act	
1954	School Milk Program Act	
1956	Library Services Act	
1958	National Defense Education Act	
1958	Education of Mentally Retarded Children Act	
1958	Captioned Films for the Deaf Act	
1961	Area Redevelopment Act	
1962	Manpower Development and Training Act	
1962	Migration and Refugee Assistance Act	

1963	Vocational Education Act
1963	Manpower Development and Training Act
1963	Higher Education Facilities Act
1964	Civil Rights Act
1964	Economic Opportunity Act
1965	Elementary and Secondary Education Act
1965	Higher Education Act
1965	Health Professions Educational Assistance Amendments
1965	National Foundation on the Arts and the Humanities Act
1965	National Technical Institute for the Deaf Act
1965	National Vocational Student Loan Insurance Act
1966	International Education Act
1966	Adult Education Act
1966	Model Secondary School for the Deaf Act
1966	Elementary and Secondary Education Amendments
1967	Education Professions Development Act
1968	Elementary and Secondary Education Amendments
1968	Handicapped Childrens' Early Education Assistance Act
1968	Vocational Education Amendments
1968	Higher Education Amendments
1970	Elementary and Secondary Education Assistance Programs
1970	National Commission on Libraries and Information Science Act
1970	Office of Education Appropriation Act
1970	Environmental Education Act
1970	Drug Abuse Education Act
1971	Comprehensive Health Manpower Training Act
1972	Title IX Education Amendment
1972	Drug Abuse Office and Treatment Act
1972	Education Amendments
1972	Indian Education Act
1973	Older Americans Comprehensive Services Amendment
1973	Comprehensive Employment and Training Act
1974	Educational Amendments
1974	Juvenile Justice and Delinquency Prevention Act
1974	White House Conference on Library and Information Services Act
1975	Education for the Handicapped Act
1975	Indian Self-Determination and Education Assistance Act
1975	Indochina Migration and Refugee Assistance Act
1976	Education Amendments
1977	Youth Employment and Demonstration Projects Act
1978	Career Education Incentive Act
1978	Tribally Controlled Community College Assistance Act
1978	Education Amendments
1978	Middle Income Student Assistance Act
1979	Department of Education Organization Act
1980	Asbestos School Hazard Protection and Control Act

1980	Amendments to the Higher Education Act of 1965
1981	Education Consolidation and Improvement Act
1983	Release of "Nation at Risk" Report by Presidential Commission
1984	Education for Economic Security Act
1984	Perkins Vocational Education Act
1984	Talented Teachers Fellowship Program enacted

Important Dates in the History of Education

	ca. 4000 B.C.	Written language developed
	2000	First schools
42	1200	Trojan War
	479–338	Period of Greek brilliance
	445–431	Greek Age of Pericles
	404	Fall of Athens
	336–323	Ascendancy of Alexander the Great
68	303	A few private Greek teachers set up schools in Rome
	167	First Greek library in Rome
	146	Fall of Corinth: Greece falls to Rome
	0	Christ born
	A.D.31–476	Empire of Rome
	70	Destruction of Jerusalem
	476	Fall of Rome in the West
	800	Charlemagne crowned Emperor
	1100–1300	Crusades
	ca. 1150	Universities of Paris and Bologna
	1209	Cambridge founded
	1295	Voyage of Marco Polo
	1384	Order of Brethren of the Common Life founded
	ca. 1400	Thirty-eight universities; 108 by 1600
	1423	Printing invented
	1456	First book printed
	1487	Vasco de Gama discovered African route to India
	1492	Columbus lands in America
	ca. 1492	Colonists begin exploiting Native Americans
	ca. 1500	250 Latin grammar schools in England
	1517	Luther nails theses to cathedral door; beginning of Reformation
	1519–1521	Magellan first circumnavigates the globe
	1534	Founding of Jesuits
	1536	Sturm established his Gymnasium in Germany, the first classical secondary school
	1568	Indian school established in Cuba by the Society of Jesus

1601	English Poor Law, established principle of tax-supported schools
1618	Holland had compulsory school law
1620	Plymouth Colony, Massachusetts, settled
1635	Boston Latin Grammar School founded
1636	Harvard founded
1642	Massachusetts law of 1642 encouraged education
1647	Massachusetts law of 1647 compelled establishment of schools
1662	First newspaper in England
1672	First teacher-training class, Father Demia, France
1684	Brothers of the Christian Schools founded
1685	First normal school, de la Salle, Rheims, France
1697	First teacher training in Germany, Francke's Seminary, Halle
1723	Indian student house opened by William and Mary College
1751	Franklin established first academy in the United States
1762	Rousseau's *Émile* published
1775–1783	Revolution, United States
1789	Adoption of Constitution, United States
1798	Lancaster developed monitorial plan of education
1799–1815	Ascendancy of Napoleon, Waterloo
1804	Pestalozzi's Institute at Yverdon established
1806	First Lancastrian School in New York
1819	Dartmouth College Decision
1821	First American high school
1821	Troy Seminary for Women, Emma Willard, first higher education for women, United States
1823	First private normal school in the United States, Concord, Vermont, by Rev. Hall
1825	Labor unions come on the scene
1826	Froebel's *The Education of Man* published
1827	Massachusetts law compelled high schools
1837	Massachusetts had first state board, Horace Mann first secretary
1839	First public normal school, United States, Lexington, Massachusetts
1855	First kindergarten in United States—after German model, Mrs. Schurz
1861–1865	Civil War
1861	Oswego (New York) Normal School (Edward Sheldon)
1862	Morrill Land Grant Act: college of engineering, military science, agriculture in each state
1868	Herbartian Society founded

	1872	Kalamazoo Decision, made high schools legal
	1888	Teachers College, Columbia University, founded
	1892	Committee of Ten established
47	1909–1910	The first junior high schools established at Berkeley, California, and Columbus, Ohio
	ca. 1910	The first junior colleges established at Fresno, California, and Joliet, Illinois
	1917	The Smith-Hughes Act, encouraged agriculture, industry, and home economics education in the United States
	1932–1940	The Eight Year Study of 30 high schools completed by the Progressive Education Association; reported favorably on the modern school
	1941	Japanese bomb Pearl Harbor
	1941	Lanham Act
	1942	The Progressive Education Association published the findings of the Eight Year Study
	1944–1946	Legislation by 78th Congress provided subsistence allowance, tuition fees, and supplies for the education of veterans of World War II
	1945	The United Nations Educational, Scientific, and Cultural Organization (UNESCO) initiated efforts to improve educational standards throughout the world
	1946–1947	National "baby boom" eventually causing huge increase in school enrollments
	1948	*McCollum* v. *Board of Education;* court ruled it illegal to release children for religious classes in public school buildings
	1950	The National Science Foundation founded
	1952	The GI Bill's educational benefits extended to Korean veterans
	1954	U.S. Supreme Court decision required eventual racial integration of public schools
	1954	Cooperative Research Program
	1956	The Russians launched Sputnik
	1958	Federal Congress passed the National Defense Education Act
	1959	James B. Conant wrote *The American High School Today*
	1961	Federal court ruled de facto racial segregation illegal
	1961	Peace Corps established
	1961	Approximately four million college students in United States
	1962	In *Engle* v. *Vitale,* court ruled compulsory prayer in public school illegal

1963	Vocational Education Act
1963	Manpower Development and Training Act
1964	The Economic Opportunity Act provided federal funds for such programs as Head Start
1964	Civil Rights Act
1965	The Elementary and Secondary Education Act allowed more federal funds for public schools
1965	Higher Education Act
1966	The GI Bill's educational benefits extended to Southeast Asia war veterans
1966	One million Americans travel abroad
1948–1966	Fulbright programs in 136 nations involving 82,500 scholars
1966	U.S. International Education Act
1966	The Coleman Report suggested that racially balanced schools did not necessarily provide a better education
1967	Education Professions Development Act
1972	Indian Education Act passed, designed to help Native Americans help themselves
1972	Title IX Education Amendment outlawing discrimination on the basic of sex
1973	In *Rodriguez* v. *San Antonio Independent School,* the Supreme Court ruled that a state's system for financing schools did not violate the Constitution although there were large disparities in per-pupil expenditure
1975	Indochina Migration and Refugee Assistance Act (Public Law 94–23)
1975	Public Law 94–142, requiring local districts to provide education for special and handicapped children
1979	Department of Education Act
1980	The U.S. Secretary of Education became a cabinet post
1983	*High School: A Report on Secondary Education in America* by the Carnegie Foundation
1983	*A Nation at Risk: The Imperative for Educational Reform,* report by the National Commission on Excellence in Education
1983	Task Force on Education for Economic Growth, Action for Excellence, Education Commission of the States Report
1983	Task Force on Federal Elementary and Secondary Education Policy, Making the Grade, the Twentieth Century Fund Report
1980–1984	Moral majority fundamental religious movement advocating prayer in the schools and teaching of biblical creation story

1984	Public Law 98–377 added new science and mathematics programs, magnet schools, and equal access to public schools
1984	Perkins Vocational Education Act to upgrade vocational programs in schools
1984	Public Law 98–558 created new teacher education scholarships and continues Head Start and Follow Through programs
1985	NCATE Redesign Standards published
1986	Holmes Group report published
1986	Carnegie Report of the Task Force on Teaching as a Profession

Philosophical Categories Recognizable by Teaching Styles: Differentiation of Philosophies

Two Broad Philosophical Categories That Are
Most Easily Recognizable by Teaching Styles

Perennialist/essentialist	S-R associationist theories of learning
	Behavioral objectives
	Assumption of one right answer per problem
Experimentalist/existentialist	Gestalt theories of learning
	Cognitive-affective objectives
	Assumption of alternative appropriate answers for each problem

Further Differentiation of Philosophies

- *Perennialism*—emphasis on humanities as presented in great books; assumption that there are absolute truths and standards more real than the physical world
- *Essentialism*—emphasis on physical sciences as used by authorities; assumption that there are no absolute truths and that success is based on absorption of knowledge about the physical world
- *Experimentalism*—emphasis on social sciences as a framework for problem solving; assumption that physical world is constantly changing
- *Existentialism*—emphasis on problem solving about highly controversial and emotional issues in any subject matter area; assumption that learners define themselves and their relationships to the environment by their choices
- *Reconstructionism*—implies one has decided what the perfect form of society is and seeks to reach that society through teaching techniques associated with experimentalism/existentialism
- *Behaviorism*—implies that one has decided what the perfect form of society is and seeks to reach that society through teaching techniques associated with essentialism

Source: Lloyd Duck, *Teaching with Charisma* (Boston: Allyn and Bacon, Inc., 1981), p. 26.

Schematic Summary
of Education Views

Comparative Philosophies

	Definition		Idealism	Realism	Neo-Thomism	Experi-mentalism	Existen-tialism
Metaphysics	The study of reality: What is real?		A world of mind	A world of things	A world of Reason and Being/God	A world of experience	A world of existing
Epistemology	The study of knowing and knowledge: What is true?		Seeing with the "mind's eye"—con-sistency of ideas	Spectator Theory: sensation and corre-spondence	Intuition, logical rea-soning, and revelation	Testing to see what works	Subjective choice, personal appropria-tion
Axiology	The study of valuing and values: What is good?	**Ethics**	The imitation of the Absolute Self	The law of nature	The rational act	The public test	The anguish of freedom
	What is beautiful?	**Aesthetics**	Reflection of the Ideal	Reflection of nature	Creative intuition	The public taste	Revolt from the public norm

Source: Adapted from Van Cleve Morris and Young Pai, *Philosophy and the American School,* 2nd ed. (Boston: Houghton Mifflin, 1976), pp. 294–295. Reprinted by permission.

Educational Implications

	Essentialism	Behaviorism	Perennialism	Reconstruction	Existentialism
Curricular Emphasis	Subject matter of the mind: literature, intellectual history, philosophy, religion	Subject matter of the physical world: mathematics and science	Subject matter of intellect and spirit; disciplinary subjects: mathematics and language and doctrine	Subject matter of social experience: the social studies	Subject matter of choice: art, ethics, moral philosophy, religion
Preferred Method	Teaching for the handling of ideas: lecture, discussion	Teaching for mastery of factual information and basic skills: demonstration, recitation	Disciplining the mind: formal drill—readying the spirit: catechism	Problem solving: project method	Arousing personal response: Socratic questioning
Character Education	Imitating exemplars, heroes	Training in rules of conduct	Disciplining behavior to reason	Making group decisions in light of consequences	Awakening the self to responsibility
Developing Taste	Studying the masterworks	Studying design in nature	Finding beauty in reason	Participating in art projects	Composing a personal art work

51

Domains of Learning

The levels of cognitive learning are numerically ordered from the most superficial to the most advanced to establish a hierarchical arrangement for evaluating depth of learning.

1.00 Knowledge
    1.10 Knowledge of specifics
    1.20 Knowledge of ways and means of dealing with specifics
    1.30 Knowledge of the universals and abstractions in a field

2.00 Comprehension
    2.10 Translation
    2.20 Interpretation
    2.30 Extrapolation

3.00 Application

4.00 Analysis
    4.10 Analysis of elements
    4.20 Analysis of relationships
    4.30 Analysis of organizational principles

5.00 Synthesis
    5.10 Production of a unique communication
    5.20 Production of a plan or proposed set of operations
    5.30 Derivation of a set of abstract relations

6.00 Evaluation
    6.10 Judgments in terms of internal evidence
    6.20 Judgments in terms of external criteria

Source: Benjamin S. Bloom, ed., *Taxonomy of Educational Objectives* (New York: Longmans, Green, 1956), pp. 6–8.

The taxonomy also presents the following scheme for classifying different levels of affective learning:

1.00 Receiving (attending)
    1.10 Awareness
    1.20 Willingness to receive
    1.30 Controlled or selected attention

2.00 Responding
    2.10 Acquiescence in responding
    2.20 Willingness to respond
    2.30 Satisfaction in response

3.00 Valuing
    3.10 Acceptance of a value
    3.20 Preference for a value
    3.30 Commitment

4.00 Organization
    4.10 Conceptualization of a value
    4.20 Organization of a value system
5.00 Characterization by a value or value complex
    5.10 Generalized set
    5.20 Characterization

Source: David R. Krathwohl, Benjamin S. Bloom, and Bertram B. Masia, *Taxonomy of Educational Objectives* (New York: McKay, 1964), pp. 176–193.

The taxonomy for the psychomotor domain was presented by Anita J. Harrow in 1972. Her levels of learning for this taxonomy are as follows:

1.00 Reflex movements
    1.10 Segmental reflexes
    1.20 Intersegmental reflexes
    1.30 Suprasegmental reflexes
2.00 Basic-fundamental movements
    2.10 Locomotor movements
    2.20 Nonlocomotor movements
    2.30 Manipulative movements
3.00 Perceptual abilities
    3.10 Kinesthetic discrimination
    3.20 Visual discrimination
    3.30 Auditory discrimination
    3.40 Tactile discrimination
    3.50 Coordinated abilities
4.00 Physical abilities
    4.10 Endurance
    4.20 Strength
    4.30 Flexibility
    4.40 Agility
5.00 Skilled movements
    5.10 Simple adaptive skills
    5.20 Compound adaptive skills
    5.30 Complex adaptive skills
6.00 Nondiscursive communication
    6.10 Expressive movement
    6.20 Interpretive movement

Source: Anita J. Harrow, *A Taxonomy of the Psychomotor Domain* (New York: McKay, 1972), pp. 1–2.

Selected National
Education Reports
1982–1987

1982–1984

Adler, Mortimer H. *The Paideia Proposal.* New York: Macmillan, 1982.

American Association of Colleges for Teacher Education. *Educating a Profession: Profiles for a Beginning Teacher.* Washington, D.C.: American Association for Colleges for Teacher Education, 1983.

Boyer, Ernest. *High School: A Report on Secondary Education in America.* New York: Harper and Row, 1983.

College Board, Project Equality. *Academic Preparation for College: What Students Need to Know and Be Able to Do.* New York: College Board, 1983.

Education Commission of the States. *Action for Excellence: A Comprehensive Plan to Improve Our Nation's Schools.* Denver, Colo.: Education Commission of the States, 1983.

Goodlad, John I. *A Place Called School: Prospects for the Future.* New York: McGraw-Hill, 1983.

National Commission on Excellence in Education. *A Nation at Risk: The Imperative for Educational Reform.* Washington, D.C.: U.S. Government Printing Office, 1983.

National Education Association. *Excellence in Our Schools, Teacher Education: An Action Plan.* Washington, D.C.: National Education Association, 1982.

National Science Board Commission on Precollege Education in Mathematics, Science and Technology. *Educating Americans for the 21st Century: A Report to the American People and the National Science Board.* Washington, D.C.: National Science Board, National Science Foundation, 1983.

Sizer, Theodore. *Horace's Compromise.* Boston: Houghton Mifflin, 1984.

Southern Regional Education Board. *The Need for Quality.* Atlanta, Ga.: Southern Regional Education Board, 1983.

Twentieth Century Fund Task Force on Federal Elementary and Secondary Education Policy. *Making the Grade.* New York: Twentieth Century Fund, 1983.

1985–1987

American Association of Colleges for Teacher Education. *Teacher Education Policy in the States: A 50-State Survey.* Washington, D.C.: American Association of Colleges of Teacher Education, 1987.

Association of Teacher Educators. *Visions of Reform: Implications for the Education Profession.* Reston, Va.: Association of Teacher Educators, 1986.

Bennett, William J. *First Lessons: A Report on Elementary Education in America.* Washington, D.C.: U.S. Office of Education, 1986.

Carnegie Forum on Education and the Economy's Task Force on Teaching as a Profession. *A Nation Prepared: Teachers for the 21st Century.* Hyattsville, Md.: Carnegie Forum on Education and the Economy, 1986.

Education Commission of the States. *The Next Wave: A Synopsis of Recent Education Reform Reports.* Denver, Colo.: Education Commission of the States, 1987.

Goertz, Margaret. *State Educational Standards: A 50-State Survey.* Princeton, N.J.: Educational Testing Service, 1986.

Heritage Foundation. *A New Agenda for Education.* Washington, D.C.: The Heritage Foundation, 1985.

Holmes Group. *Tomorrow's Teacher's: A Report of the Holmes Group.* East Lansing, Mich.: Holmes Group, 1986.

National Commission on Excellence in Teacher Education. *A Call for Change in Teacher Education.* Washington, D.C.: American Association of Colleges for Teacher Education, 1985.

National Governors' Association. *Time for Results: The*

Governors' 1991 Report on Education. Washington, D.C.: National Governors' Association, 1986.

Roueche, John E., and Baker, George A., III. *Profiling Excellence in American Schools.* Arlington, Va.: American Association of School Administrators, 1986.

Southern Regional Educational Board. *Major Reports on Teacher Education: What Do They Mean for States?* Atlanta, Ga.: Southern Regional Educational Board, 1986.

Glossary

Ability grouping assigning pupils to homogeneous groups according to intellectual ability, for instruction.

Academic freedom the opportunity for a teacher to teach without coercion, censorship, or other restrictive interference.

Academic program a program of studies designed primarily to prepare students for college.

Academic support expenditures for the support services that are an integral part of an educational institution's primary mission.

Academic year the period of time, generally extending from September to June, that a school is open.

Academy an early American secondary school that stressed practical subjects.

Accelerated program the more rapid advancement of superior students through school.

Accountability holding schools responsible for what students learn.

Accreditation recognition given to an educational institution that has met accepted standards applied to it by an outside agency.

Achievement test an examination that measures the extent to which a person has acquired certain information or mastered certain skills, usually as a result of specific instruction.

Activity curriculum a curriculum design in which the interests of and learning purposes for children determine the educational program; teacher and pupils together select and plan activities.

Admission test scores standardized admissions tests or special admissions tests, used to make decisions about admitting students to a school or program.

Adult education courses and other organized educational activities taken by persons seventeen years of age and over, excluding courses taken by full-time students in programs leading toward a high school diploma or an academic degree and occupational programs of six months or more duration. It includes all courses taken for credit by part-time students. Providers of instruction include not only public and private educational institutions but also business and industry, governmental agencies, private community organizations, and tutors.

Advanced placement programs provided by high schools, in cooperation with community colleges or universities, in which qualifying students take college-level courses.

Aesthetics referring to the nature of beauty and judgments about it.

Affective domain attitudinal and emotional areas of learning, such as values and feelings.

Affective learning the acquisition of feelings, tastes, emotions, will, and other aspects of social and psychological development gained through feeling rather than through intellectualization.

Affirmative action a plan by which personnel policies and hiring practices do not discriminate against women and members of minority groups.

AIDS (acquired immune deficiency syndrome) disease which attacks the body's defense system, gradually rendering it incapable of fighting diseases.

Alternative education unconventional educational experiences for students inadequately taught in regular classes; alternatives include schools without walls, street academies, free schools, and second-chance schools.

Alternative school a school—private or public, innovative or fundamental—that provides options or alternatives to the regular public school.

American Federation of Teachers (AFT) a national teachers' union primarily concerned with improving educational conditions and protecting teachers' rights.

511

A Nation at Risk a highly publicized report on the condition of schools in America.

Aptitude the ability to profit from training or instruction of a specific kind.

Area vocational center a shared-time facility that provides instruction only in vocational education to students from throughout a school system or region. Students attending an area vocational center receive the academic portion of their education program in regular secondary schools or other institutions.

Articulation the relationship between the different elements of the educational program.

Associate degrees degrees and awards based on less than four years of work beyond high school.

Attendance center an administrative unit consisting of the territory from which children may legally attend a given school building.

Audiovisual material any device to encourage and facilitate the learning process through sound or sight or both.

Authoritarian encouraging and upholding authority against individual freedom; power that commands influence, respect, or confidence.

Axiology the study of values and of value judgments.

Bachelor's or first-level degree lowest degree conferred by a college, university, or professional school requiring four or more years of academic work.

Back to basics a broad, largely grass roots movement evolving out of a concern for declining test scores and student incompetence in math and reading.

Behavioral objective precise statement of what the learner must do to demonstrate mastery at the end of a prescribed learning task.

Bilingual education educational program in which both English-speaking and non-English-speaking students participate in a bicultural curriculum using both languages.

Board of education agencies, constituted at the state and local levels, responsible for formulating educational policy; with members sometimes appointed but more frequently elected at the local level.

Busing a method for remedying segregation by transporting students to schools that have been racially or ethnically unbalanced, either voluntary or mandatory.

Capital outlay expenditures for land or existing buildings, improvement of grounds, construction of buildings, additions to buildings, and initial or additional equipment. Includes replacement and rehabilitation, and installment or lease payments (excluding interest) that have a terminal date and result in the acquisition of property.

Career education educational experience through which one learns about occupational opportunities and about work.

Carnegie unit a unit awarded to a student for successfully completing a high school course that meets for a minimum of 120 clock hours.

Categorical aid financial aid to local school districts from state or federal agencies for specific, limited purposes only.

Certification the act by a state department of education of officially authorizing a person to accept employment in keeping with the provisions of the credential.

Chief state school officer the executive head of a state department of education.

Child advocacy movement a movement dedicated to defining, protecting, and ensuring the rights of children.

Child-centered instruction instruction designed for the interests, abilities, and needs of individual students.

Classroom environment the physical structure, emotional climate, aesthetic characteristics, and learning resources of a classroom.

Classroom teacher a staff member assigned the professional activities of instructing students, in classroom situations, for which daily student attendance figures for the school system are kept.

Clinical experiences on-the-job learning experiences built into teacher-training programs.

Code of ethics formal statement of appropriate professional behaviors.

Cognitive domain the area of learning that involves the acquisition and utilization of knowledge.

Cognitive learning the learner's acquisition of facts, concepts, and principles through intellectualization.

Coleman Report (1981) a study comparing the effectiveness of public school and private school education.

Collective bargaining a procedure, usually specified by written agreement, for resolving disagreements on salaries, hours, and conditions of employment between employers and employees through negotiation.

Collective bargaining agent an organization such as the National Education Association, American Federation of Teachers, etc., recognized by the institution, either voluntarily or through agent elections, as representing the interests of faculty in collective bargaining.

College a post–secondary school that offers general or liberal arts education, usually leading to a first degree. Junior colleges and community colleges are included under this terminology.

College work-study program designed to stimulate and promote the part-time employment of students with demonstrated financial need.

Committee of Fifteen historic NEA committee that reversed the findings of the Committee of Ten (1895).

Committee of Ten historic NEA committee that studied secondary education (1893).

Common school a school open to the public and providing similar education for all social classes.

Community school a school intimately connected with the life of the community that tries to provide for the educational needs of all in the locality.

Compensatory education enriched or extended educational experiences or services made available to children of low-income families.

Competency the demonstrated ability to perform specific acts at a particular level of skill or accuracy.

Competency-based certification the general process by which the state (or agency or organization authorized by the state) provides a credential to an individual. Processes may require individuals to demonstrate a mastery of minimum essential generic and specialization competencies and other related criteria adopted by the board through a comprehensive written examination and through other procedures that may be prescribed by the board of educational examiners.

Competency-based education learning based on highly specialized concepts, skills, and attitudes related directly to some endeavor.

Comprehensive secondary school a general secondary school offering programs in both vocational and general academic subjects, but in which the majority of the students are not enrolled in programs of vocational education.

Compulsory education school attendance required by law on the theory that it is for the benefit of the state or commonwealth to educate all the people.

Computer-assisted instruction (CAI) direct, two-way, teaching-learning communication between a stu-

dent and programmed instructional material stored in a computer.

Computer-managed instruction (CMI) a record-keeping procedure for tracking student performance by using a computer.

Computer software programs, procedures, and associated documentation that instruct the computer to perform certain tasks.

Consolidation the act of forming an enlarged school by uniting smaller schools.

Contact hour a unit of measure that represents an hour of scheduled instruction to students.

Content subject matter.

Continuing education extended opportunity for study and training following completion of or withdrawal from full-time school and college programs.

Convergent thinking to tend toward one point of view; coming together by gradual approach (teaching).

Core curriculum curriculum design in which one subject or group of subjects becomes a center or core to which all other subjects are correlated.

Corporal punishment infliction of physical punishment on the body of a student by a school employee for disciplinary reasons.

Cost-effectiveness analysis a means of analyzing the extent to which an undertaking accomplishes its objectives in relation to its cost.

Counseling service activities designed to assist students in making plans and decisions related to their education, career, or personal development.

Credit recognition of attendance and/or performance in an instructional activity (course or program) that can be applied by a recipient to requirements for a degree, diploma, certificate, or other formal award.

Credit course if successfully completed, can be applied toward the number of courses required for achieving a degree, diploma, certificate, or other formal award.

Credit hour a unit of measure that represents an hour of instruction that can be applied to the total number of hours needed for completing the requirements of a degree, diploma, certificate, or other formal award.

Cultural bias accepting one's own cultural values as valid for all.

Cultural pluralism a way of describing a society made up of many different cultural groups coming together to form a unified whole.

Curriculum all educational experiences under supervision of the school.

Custodial student a student who is so limited in mental, social, physical, or emotional development that institutional care or constant supervision at home is required.

Dame school a low-level primary school in the colonial and other early periods, usually conducted by an untrained woman in her own home.

Day-care center a place or institution charged with caring for children.

Decentralization a process whereby a higher central source of responsibility and authority assigns certain responsibility and authority to a subordinate position.

Deductive reasoning a system of logic that begins with first principles or generalizations and arrives at secondary principles or specifics.

De facto segregation the segregation of students resulting from circumstances such as housing patterns rather than from school policy or law.

Degree an award conferred by a college, university, or other postsecondary educational institution as official recognition for successful completion of a program of studies.

Degree-seeking students students enrolled in courses for credit who are recognized by the institution as seeking a degree or formal award. At the undergraduate level they include students enrolled in vocational or occupational programs.

De jure segregation the segregation of students on the basis of law, school policy, or a practice designed to accomplish such separation.

Desegregation the process of correcting past practices of racial or any other form of illegal segregation.

Detention keeping a student after school or in a classroom during time usually devoted to a recreation.

Developmental task a task that arises at or about a certain time in an individual's life; its successful achievement leads to the individual's happiness and success with later tasks.

Differentiated staffing educational personnel, selected, educated, and deployed so that optimum use is made of their abilities, interests, preparation, and commitments.

Diploma a formal document certifying the successful completion of a prescribed program of studies.

Divergent thinking to extend in different directions from one point of view; to differ in approach (teaching).

Doctor's degree highest academic degree conferred by a university, including Ph.D. in any field, doctor of education, doctor of juridical science, and doctor of public health (preceded by professional degree in medicine or sanitary engineering).

Dropouts persons not enrolled in school and not high school graduates.

Due process the procedural requirements that must be followed to safeguard individuals from arbitrary, capricious, or unreasonable policies, practices, or actions.

Early-childhood education education for a child before the normal period of schooling begins.

Eclecticism drawing elements from several educational philosophies.

Educational park a large campuslike school plant containing several units with a variety of facilities, often including many grade levels and varied programs and often surrounded by a variety of cultural resources.

Educational television (ETV) educational programs that are telecast usually by stations outside the school system and received on standard television sets by the public.

Education major a student whose program of studies gives primary emphasis to subject matter in the area of education and who, according to his or her institutional requirements, concentrates a minimum number of courses or semester hours of college credit in the specialty of education.

Elementary school grades 1–6 inclusive; grades 1–8 inclusive in some school systems.

Emergency certificate a substandard certificate for teachers who have not met all the requirements for certification.

Endowment the portion of an institution's income derived from donations.

Endowment funds received from a donor with the restriction that the principal is not expendable.

English as a second language (ESL) a component of virtually all bilingual education programs in the United States designed to help instruct students whose primary language is not English.

Enrollment the total number of entering students in a given school unit.

Environmental education the study and analysis of the conditions and causes of pollution, overpopulation, and waste of natural resources and of the ways to preserve our planet's intricate environmental balance.

Epistemology the branch of philosophy that examines the nature of knowledge and learning.

Equal educational opportunity giving every student the educational opportunity to develop fully whatever talents, interests, and abilities she or he may have without regard to race, color, national origin, sex, handicap, or economic status.

Essentialism emphasis on physical sciences as used by authorities; assumption that there are no absolute truths and that success is based on absorption of knowledge about the physical world.

Ethics the branch of philosophy that examines values and their relation to human actions.

Evaluation testing and measurement to determine the effectiveness, quality, and progress of learning and instruction.

Exceptional learner one whose growth and development deviates from the normal so markedly that he or she cannot receive maximum benefit without modification of the regular school program.

Existentialism emphasis on problem solving about highly controversial and emotional issues in any subject matter area; assumption that learners "define" themselves and their relationships to the environment by their choices.

Expenditures per pupil charges incurred for a particular period of time divided by a student unit of measure, e.g., average daily attendance or average daily membership.

Experimentalism emphasis on social sciences as a framework for problem solving; assumption that the physical world is constantly changing.

Experimental schools schools in which new methods or materials are tried under controlled conditions.

Expulsion the action, taken by school authorities, compelling a student to withdraw from school for reasons such as extreme misbehavior, incorrigibility, or unsatisfactory achievement or progress in school work.

Fellowships grants in aid and trainee stipends to graduate students. Usually excludes funds for which services to the institution must be rendered, such as payments for teaching, or student loans.

First professional certificate an award that requires completion of an organized program of study designed for persons who have completed the first professional degree.

Flexible scheduling a technique for organizing time more effectively to meet the needs of instruction by dividing the school day into uniform time modules that can be combined to fit a task.

Fringe benefits cash contributions in the form of supplementary or deferred compensation other than salary.

Full-time staff persons on the payroll of the institution and classified by the institution as full-time.

Futurism focuses not only on predicting future developments but also on formulating techniques and procedures needed for preparing for such developments.

Future shock term coined by Alvin Toffler that refers to the accelerated pace of change and to the disorientation of those unable to adapt to altered norms, institutions, and values.

General education learning that should be the common possession of all educated people.

General educational development (GED) program academic instruction to prepare persons to take the high school equivalency examination.

Gifted learner term most frequently applied to those with exceptional intellectual ability; it may also refer to learners with outstanding ability in athletics, leadership, music, creativity, and so forth.

Graded school system a division of schools into groups of students according to the curriculum or the ages of pupils, as in the six elementary grades.

Graduate student holds a bachelor's or first professional degree, or equivalent, and is taking courses at the postbaccalaureate level.

Handicapped a "handicapped" person is one who has one or more of the exceptionalities defined below, whether or not he or she requires special education.

Educable mentally retarded a condition of mental retardation that includes students who are educable in the academic, social, and occupational areas even though moderate supervision may be necessary.

Trainable mentally retarded a condition of mental retardation that includes students who are capable of only very limited meaningful achievement in the traditional basic academic skills but who are capable of profiting from programs of training in self-care and simple job or vocational skills.

Hard of hearing a hearing impairment, whether permanent or fluctuating, that adversely affects a student's educational performance but that is not included under the definition of "deaf" in this section.

Deaf a hearing impairment that is so severe that the student is impaired in processing linguistic information through hearing, with or without amplification, with adverse effects on educational performance.

Speech-impaired a communication disorder, such as stuttering, impaired articulation, a language impairment, or a voice impairment, that adversely affects a student's educational performance.

Visually handicapped a visual impairment that, even with correction, adversely affects a student's educational performance. The term includes both partially seeing and blind children.

Seriously emotionally disturbed a condition exhibiting one or more of the following characteristics over a long period of time and to a marked degree, that adversely affects educational performance: an inability to learn that cannot be explained by intellectual, sensory, or health factors; an inability to build or maintain satisfactory interpersonal relationships with peers and teachers; inappropriate types of behavior or feelings under normal circumstances; a general pervasive mood of unhappiness or depression; or a tendency to develop physical symptoms or fears associated with personal or school problems. The term includes children who are schizophrenic or autistic.

Orthopedically impaired a severe orthopedic impairment that adversely affects a student's educational performance. The term includes impairments caused by congenital anomaly or disease as well as those from other causes.

Other health-impaired limited strength, vitality, or alertness due to chronic or acute health problems such as a heart condition, tuberculosis, rheumatic fever, nephritis, asthma, sickle cell anemia, hemophilia, epilepsy, lead poisoning, leukemia, or diabetes, that adversely affects a student's educational performance.

Specific learning-disabled a disorder in one or more of the basic psychological processes involved in understanding or using language, spoken or written, which may manifest itself in an imperfect ability to listen, think, speak, read, write, spell, or do mathematical calculations. The term includes such conditions as perceptual handicaps, brain injury, minimal brain dysfunction, dyslexia, and developmental aphasia. The term does not include children who have learning problems that are primarily the result of visual, hearing, or motor handicaps, of mental retardation, or of environmental, cultural, or economic disadvantage.

Deaf-blind concomitant hearing and visual impairments, the combination of which causes such severe communication and other developmental and educational problems that they cannot be accommodated in special education programs solely for deaf or blind students.

Multihandicapped concomitant impairments (such as mentally retarded–blind, mentally retarded–orthopedically impaired, etc.), the combination of which causes such severe educational problems that they cannot be accommodated in special education programs solely for one of the impairments. The term does not include deaf-blind students. This category includes those students who are severely or profoundly mentally retarded.

Head Start program federally funded program at the preelementary school level designed to provide learning opportunities for those children who have not had access to environments and experiences conducive to academic achievement.

Herbartian method formal system of presenting subject matter to students by using the five formal steps of preparation, association, presentation, generalization, and application.

Heterogeneous grouping a group or class of students who show normal variation in ability or performance.

High school diploma (or recognized equivalent) a document certifying the successful completion of a prescribed secondary school program of studies or the attainment of satisfactory scores on the tests of general educational development (SED) or another state-specified examination.

Home study a method of instruction designed for students who live at a distance from the teaching institution. Instructional materials are provided to the student through various media, with structured units of information, assigned exercises for practice, and examinations to measure achievement, which in turn are submitted to the teaching institution for evaluation.

Homogeneous grouping the classification of pupils for the purpose of forming an instructional group with a relatively high degree of similarity in regard to certain factors that affect learning.

Hornbook a single printed page containing the alphabet, syllables, a prayer, and other simple words, used in colonial times as the beginner's first book or pre-primer. Hornbooks were attached to wooden paddles for ease in carrying, each covered with a thin sheet of transparent horn.

Humanistic teacher education an approach to teacher education concerned not only with teacher candidates' cognitive development but with their emotional and attitudinal development as well.

Idealism a doctrine holding that all knowledge is derived from ideas and emphasizing moral and spiritual reality as a preeminent source of explanation.

Independent school a nonpublic school unaffiliated with any church or other agency.

Individualized education program (IEP) the mechanism through which a handicapped child's special needs are identified; goals, objectives, and services are outlined; and methods for evaluating progress are delineated.

Individualized instruction instruction that is particularized to the interests, needs, and achievements of individual learners.

Individually guided education (IGE) an individualized instructional program in which teachers and students plan together the learner objectives.

Individually prescribed instruction (IPI) individualized instruction in a systematic, step-by-step program based on a carefully selected sequence and a detailed listing of behaviorally stated instructional objectives.

Induction programs programs designed to help teachers during their first few years on the job.

In loco parentis term used to describe implied power of schools to function in place of a parent.

In-service education continuing education for teachers who are actually teaching or are in service.

In-state student a legal resident of the state in which he or she attends school.

Institutions of higher education postsecondary institutions that are legally authorized to offer at least a one-year program of college-level studies leading toward a degree.

Instructional faculty staff employed full-time as defined by the institution and whose major regular assignment is instruction.

Instructional materials center (IMC) an area where students can use books, newspapers, pamphlets, magazines, sound tapes, slides, and films; spaces are usually provided for students to use these materials (see learning resource center).

Instructional technology the application of scientific method and knowledge to teaching and learning, either with or without machines but commonly responsive to the learning needs of individual students.

Instructional television (ITV) lessons telecast specifically for educational institutions, usually received only by special arrangement and on special equipment.

Instruction expenditures money spent to support the instructional efforts of an educational institution.

Integration the process of mixing students of different races in schools to overcome segregation.

Interest centers centers usually associated with an open classroom that provide for independent student activities related to a specific subject.

Intermediate school a synonym for middle school.

Intermediate unit (1) a division of elementary school comprising grades 4, 5, and 6; (2) a level of school organization between the state and the local district, often but not necessarily coterminous with the county.

International education the study of educational, social, political, and economic forces in international relations with special emphasis on the role and potentialities of educational forces; also includes programs to further the development of nations.

Intervention a proposal to change the direction of a trend.

Kindergarten term coined by Froebel, who started the first schools for children aged four, five, and six.

Labeling categorizing or classifying students for the purpose of educational placement.

Laboratory school a school under the control of, or closely associated with, a teacher preparation institution whose facilities may be used for demonstration, experimentation, and student teaching.

Land grant college a college maintained to carry out the purposes of the first Morrill Act of 1862 and the supplementary legislation granting public lands to states for the establishment of colleges and to provide practical education such as agriculture and mechanical arts.

Latin grammar school a classical secondary school with a curriculum consisting largely of Latin and Greek; its purpose was preparation for college.

Learning a change of behavior as a result of experience.

Learning disability an educationally significant discrepancy between a child's apparent capacity for language behavior and his or her actual level of language functioning.

Learning resource center a specially designed space containing a wide range of supplies and equipment for the use of individual students and small groups pursuing independent study (see instructional materials center).

Least restrictive environment the program best suited to meet a handicapped child's special needs while remaining as close as possible to the regular educational program.

Liability condition of being responsible for a loss or penalty for damages.

Librarian an individual doing work that requires professional training and skill in the theoretical or scientific aspect of library work, or both, as distinct from its mechanical or clerical aspect.

Library an organized collection of printed, microform, and audiovisual materials which is administered as one or more units, is located in one or more designated places, and makes printed, microform, and audiovisual materials, as well as necessary equipment and services of a staff accessible to students and to faculty.

Life-adjustment education experiences through which the unique and total resources of each individual are discovered and developed.

Limited-English proficient (LEP) students who have limited ability to understand, speak, or read English and who have a primary or home language other than English.

Local education agency (LEA) a public board of education or other public authority legally constituted within a state for administrative control of, direction of,

or to perform service functions for public elementary or secondary schools.

Magnet schools specialized schools open to all students in a district, sometimes on a lottery basis.

Mainstreaming a plan by which exceptional children receive special education in the regular classroom as much of the time as possible.

Maintenance or developmental bilingual education an attempt to preserve and develop the students' first language while they are adding a second.

Master's degree an academic degree higher than a bachelor's but lower than a doctor's.

Mastery learning an educational practice in which an individual masters one task before moving on to the next.

Mean test score the score obtained by dividing the total sum of scores of all individuals in a group by the number of individuals in that group.

Mentally handicapped student a student whose mental powers lack maturity or are so deficient that they hinder normal achievement.

Mental retardation below-average intellectual functioning.

Metaphysics the division of philosophy that examines the nature of reality.

Methodology procedure used to teach the content or discipline.

Microteaching a clinical approach to teacher training in which the teacher candidate teaches a small group of students for a brief time while concentrating on a specific teaching skill.

Middle school a type of two- to four-year school organization containing various combinations of the middle grades, commonly grades 5–8, and serving as an intermediate unit between the elementary school and the high school.

Migration movement of students into or out of state to attend college. Net migration equals the number of students who come into a state minus the number of students who leave the home state to attend college.

Minicourse a short, self-contained instructional sequence.

Minimum competency testing exit-level tests designed to ascertain whether or not students have achieved basic levels of performance in areas like reading, writing, and computation.

Modular scheduling arrangement of class periods in units of fifteen, twenty, thirty, or forty minutes to permit greater flexibility; sometimes called flexible scheduling.

Monitorial schools schools developed by Joseph Lancaster and Andrew Bell in which one teacher taught a number of bright students or monitors who, in turn, taught other groups of children.

Motivation impetus causing one to act.

Multipurpose high school features comprehensive, diversified offerings to meet the needs of all students regardless of their special interests, aptitudes, and capacities.

National assessment a massive national testing program that helps ascertain the effectiveness of American education and how well students have learned.

National Council for the Accreditation of Teacher Education (NCATE) an organization that evaluates teacher education programs in many colleges and universities.

National Education Association (NEA) the largest organization of educators; the NEA is concerned with the overall improvement of education and of the conditions of educators.

Nongraded school a type of school organization in which grade lines are eliminated for a sequence of two or more years.

Normal school historically, the first American institution devoted exclusively to teacher training.

Norm-referenced data data based on local, state, or national norms.

Nursery school a school that offers supervised educational experiences for prekindergarten children.

Objective purpose or goal.

Objective test a test yielding results that can be evaluated or scored by different persons with like outcomes.

Observation techniques structured methods for observing various aspects of the entire school or specific classroom environment.

Open classroom a modern educational innovation in which self-contained classrooms are replaced by an open plan with individualized instruction and freedom for the child to move about the school.

Open enrollment the practice of permitting students to attend the school of their choice within their school system.

Open-space school a school building without interior walls.

Overachievement performing above the level normally expected on the basis of ability measures.

Paraprofessional one who serves as an aide, assisting the teacher in the classroom (see teacher aide).

Parochial school an institution operated and controlled by a religious denomination.

Pedagogy the science of teaching.

Perennialism emphasis on humanities as presented in great books; assumption that there are absolute truths and standards more real than the physical world.

Performance-based education learning designed to produce actual accomplishment as distinguished from knowing.

Performance contract an agreement between schools and commercial educational agencies or teachers that guarantees to produce specified educational results.

Permanent certificate certificate issued after a candidate has completed all the requirements for full recognition as a teacher.

Philosophy of education principles that guide professional educators in decision making.

Planned programming-budgeting system (PPBS) an application of systems analysis to the allocation of resources to various competing educational purposes and needs through systematic planning, programming, budgeting, and evaluation.

Political action committees committees associated with various organizations which engage in political activities in support of the organizations' purposes or causes.

Pragmatism a philosophy that maintains that the value and truth of ideas are tested by their practical consequences.

Primary school a separately organized and administered elementary school for students in the lower elementary grades, usually including grades 1–3 or the equivalent and sometimes including preprimary years.

Print materials consist primarily of words and usually produced by making an impression with ink on paper. Included in this category are materials that do not require magnification: books, government documents, braille materials, ephemeral print materials, and the like.

Private school a school that is controlled by an individual or by an agency other than a state, a subdivision of a state, or the federal government, usually supported primarily by other than public funds, and the operation of whose program rests with other than publicly elected or appointed officials.

Program a combination of courses and related activities organized for the attainment of broad educational objectives described by the institution.

Programmed learning any learning device that may be used by a student in such a way that a reaction to the student's activities is immediately supplied.

Progressive education an educational philosophy emphasizing democracy, the importance of creative and meaningful activity, the real needs of students, and the relationship between school and community.

Progressive tax a tax frequently scaled to the ability of the taxpayer to pay; the income tax is a progressive tax.

Progressivism educational philosophy in which learning focuses on the experiences of the child while he or she is acquiring the content of the curriculum.

Property tax a tax based on the value of property, both real estate and personal.

Proprietary school an educational institution that is under private control and whose profits derived from revenues are subject to taxation.

Psychomotor domain motor skill area of learning.

Psychomotor learning the acquisition of muscular development directly related to mental processes.

PTA Parent Teacher Association; officially, the National Congress of Parents and Teachers.

Public school a school operated by publicly elected or appointed school officials in which the program and activities are under the control of these officials and which is supported primarily by public funds.

Racial bias the degree to which an individual's beliefs and behavior are prejudiced on the basis of race.

Racial discrimination any action that limits or denies a person or group of persons opportunities, privileges, roles, or rewards on the basis of race.

Racial/ethnic group classification indicating general racial or ethnic heritage based on self-identification as in data collected by the Bureau of the Census or on observer identification as in data collected by the Office for Civil Rights. These categories are in accordance with

the Office of Management and Budget standard classification scheme presented below:

White a person having origins in any of the original peoples of Europe, North Africa, or the Middle East.

Black a person having origins in any of the black racial groups of Africa.

Hispanic a person of Mexican, Puerto Rican, Cuban, Central or South American, or other Spanish culture or origin, regardless of race.

Asian or Pacific Islander a person having origins in any of the original peoples of the Far East, Southeast Asia, the Indian subcontinent, or the Pacific Islands. This area includes, for example, China, India, Japan, Korea, the Philippine Islands, and Samoa.

American Indian or Alaskan native a person having origins in any of the original peoples of North America and maintaining cultural identification through tribal affiliation or community recognition.

Racism the collection of attitudes, beliefs, and behavior that results from the assumption that one race is superior to other races.

Realism a philosophy holding that knowledge is derived from perceptual experience; it emphasizes the natural sciences in its attitude that the physical world assists a person's search for true knowledge.

Reconstructionism implies that one has decided what the "perfect" form of society is and seeks to reach that society through teaching techniques associated with experimentalism/existentialism.

Regressive tax a tax that affects low-income groups disproportionately; the sales tax is a regressive tax.

Religiously affiliated school a private school over which, in most cases, a parent church group exercises some control or to which it provides some form of subsidy. Catholic schools include those affiliated with the Roman Catholic Church, including the "private" Catholic schools operated by religious orders. Other affiliation includes schools associated with other religious denominations. An unaffiliated school is usually privately operated or under control of a board of trustees or directors.

Remedial courses planned diagnostic and remedial activities for individual students or groups of students, designed to correct and prevent further learning difficulties that interfere with the student's expected progress in developing skills, understandings, and appreciations in any of several required courses.

Reorganization the act of legally changing the designation of a school district, changing the geographical area of a school district or incorporating a part or all of a school district with an adjoining district.

Resegregation a situation following integration wherein segregation returns.

Resumé a written statement of qualifications prepared by an applicant for employment.

Revenues all funds received from external sources, net of refunds, and correcting transactions. Noncash transactions such as receipt of services, commodities, or other receipts "in kind" are excluded, as are funds received from the issuance of debt, liquidation of investments, and nonroutine sale of property.

Revenue sharing distribution of federal money to state and local governments to use as they wish.

Reverse discrimination a situation in which a majority or an individual of a majority has not been accorded certain rights because of different or preferential treatment provided to a minority or an individual of a minority.

Sabbatical a leave usually granted with pay after a teacher has taught for a specified period of time.

Salary the total amount regularly paid or stipulated to be paid to an individual, before deductions, for personal services rendered while on the payroll of a business or organization.

Scholarships grants in aid, trainee stipends, tuition and fee waivers, and prizes to undergraduate students.

School a division of the school system consisting of students comprising one or more grade groups or other identifiable groups, organized as one unit with one or more teachers to give instruction of a defined type, and housed in a school plant of one or more buildings.

School bonds a typical method for financing a substantial, one-time educational expenditure such as a new school building.

School district an educational agency at the local level that exists primarily to operate public schools or to contract for public school services. This term is used synonymously with the terms *local basic administrative unit* and *local education agency*.

School finance the ways in which monies are raised, allocated to, and handled in the schools.

School superintendent the chief administrator of a school system.

Schools without walls a type of alternative education program that stresses involving the total community as a learning resource.

Secondary school a school comprising any span of grades beginning with the next grade following an elementary or middle school and ending with or below grade 12.

Self-contained classroom a form of classroom organization in which the same teacher conducts all or nearly all the instruction in all or most subjects in the same classroom for all or most of the school day.

Self-instructional device a term used to include instructional materials that can be used by the student.

Senior high school a secondary school offering the final years of high school work necessary for graduation and invariably preceded by a junior high school.

Separate but equal a doctrine that holds that equality of treatment is accorded when the races are provided substantially equal facilities, even though the facilities are separate.

Sexism a belief that one sex is superior to the other.

Special education direct instructional activities or special learning experiences designed primarily for students identified as having exceptionalities in one or more aspects of the cognitive process and/or as being underachievers in relation to the general level or mode of their overall abilities. Such services usually are directed at students with the following exceptionalities: (1) physically handicapped; (2) emotionally handicapped; (3) culturally different, including compensatory education; (4) mentally retarded; (5) having learning disabilities. Programs for the mentally gifted and talented are also included in some special education programs.

Standardized test an instrument presenting a uniform task or series of tasks to be performed according to specified directions and under uniform conditions so that individual performances may be compared with one another and with a reference or normative group.

State aid funding provided to local school districts out of tax revenue raised by the state. Frequently used in an effort to provide equality of opportunity within a state.

State educational agency operations activities performed for the purpose of executing the responsibilities of the state educational agency, an organization established by laws for the primary purpose of carrying out at least a part of the educational responsibilities of a state.

Student an individual for whom instruction is provided in an educational program under the jurisdiction of a school, school system, or other educational institution. No distinction is made between the terms *student* and *pupil;* the term *student* is used to include individuals at all instructional levels.

Student services expenditures funds expended for admissions, registrar activities, and activities whose primary purpose is to contribute to students' emotional and physical well-being and to their intellectual, cultural, and social development outside the context of the formal instructional program.

Subject-centered school or curriculum a curriculum organization in which learning activities and content are planned around subject fields of knowledge, such as history and science.

Suspension temporary dismissal of a student from school by duly authorized school personnel in accordance with established regulations.

Subjective test a test that will not necessarily have the same outcome when scored by different persons.

Systems analysis a rational and systematic approach to education that analyzes objectives, then decides which resources and methods will achieve those objectives most efficiently; each step is carefully measured, tested, and controlled to make sure it moves toward the next objective.

Teacher aide a lay person who assists teachers with clerical work, library duties, housekeeping duties, noninstructional supervision, and other nonprofessional tasks (see paraprofessional).

Teacher certification establishes requirements in each state for a teacher to be licensed or granted the privilege to teach in the respective state.

Teacher contracts fix terms of employment and compensation for teachers; boards of education have the statutory authority to employ teachers by issuing such contracts.

Teacher Corps a federally funded program that gives teachers and student teachers opportunities to work with disadvantaged children in their homes and communities while attending courses and seminars on the special problems they encounter.

Teacher effectiveness a movement to study and understand those conditions associated with successful teaching and learning.

Teacher preparation programs departments, schools, and institutions of higher education that confer degrees in education.

Teaching center combination library, workshop, and laboratory with rich resources to help teachers solve problems and grow professionally.

Team teaching a plan by which several teachers, organized into a team with a leader, provide the instruction for a larger group of children than would usually be found in a self-contained classroom.

Tenure a system of school employment in which educators, having served a probationary period, retain their positions indefinitely unless dismissed for legally specified reasons through clearly established procedures.

Tracking the method of placing students according to their ability level in homogeneous classes or learning experiences where they all follow the same curriculum, i.e., college preparatory or vocational.

Two-way bilingual education an integrated model in which speakers of two languages are placed together in a bilingual classroom to learn each other's language and work academically in both languages.

Unemployed civilians who, during a survey period, had no employment but were available for work and (1) had engaged in any specific job-seeking activity within the past four weeks or (2) were waiting to be called back to a job from which they had been laid off or (3) were waiting to report to a new wage or salary job within 30 days.

Unemployment rate the number of unemployed persons seeking employment as a percent of the civilian labor force.

Ungraded school a synonym for nongraded school.

Unit of learning a series of organized ideas and activities planned to provide worthwhile experiences for an individual or group and expected to result in a desired outcome.

Values principles that guide an individual in personal decision making.

Values clarification a model, comprised of various strategies, that encourages students to express and clarify their values on different topics.

Video materials materials on which both pictures and sound are recorded. Electronic playback reproduces both pictures and sounds by using a television receiver or monitor.

Vocational education training that is intended to prepare the student for a particular job or to give a basic skill needed in several vocations.

Voucher plan a means of financing schooling whereby funds are allocated to students' parents who then purchase education for their children in any public or private school.

Work-study program program that combines part-time classroom study with gainful employment in industry or in the community.

Name Index

Subject Index